# A Man Called Shoeless

Howard Burman

MASTER ARTS PUBLISHING

**Also by Howard Burman**

*A Story Told by Two Liars*

*An O. Henry Christmas*

*Surrounded*

*Paradise by Paradise*

*Gentlemen at the Bat*

*Season of Ghosts*

*To Hate Like This is to Love Forever*

*Here Be Dragons*

*Willie, Mickey & The Duke*

*You Can't Win (with Barbara Zajak)*

*You Shoot Me Now*

*Duckrabbit*

Format and Layout by Red Raven
www.redravenbookdesign.com
Cover by Diogo Lando
www.diogolando.com

A Man Called Shoeless/ Howard Burman
Master Arts Publishing
ISBN 978-0-692-55787-7

www.howardburman.com

Shoeless Joe Jackson

"Hey, bigmouth, how do you spell triple?"
--Joe Jackson to a heckler.

# A Man Called Shoeless

## CONTENTS

# A Man Called Shoeless

*For* Karen

# A Man Called Shoeless

# ACKNOWLEDGEMENTS

A special thanks to Tim Wiles Director of Research at the National Baseball Hall of Fame for his help in locating material on some of the lesser known characters who appear in this book, to Josh Lindblom for his tireless hours in front of microfilm viewers, and to Ronald Allan-Lindblom for his continued support.

# A Man Called Shoeless

# 1

# THE GOD'S HONEST TRUTH

**JOE JACKSON** I don't deserve this thing that's happened to me. That's the God's honest truth.

I've become almost like some made up character in a book or something. Every time I hear somebody telling a story about me they always say two things and they're always the same two things—Joe was stupid and Joe was a crook. Well, saying things a lot of times don't make them true, so let me tell you this right at the start. Them things just ain't true. Now, if you've heard all the stories and don't want to believe anything else you might as well stop right here. No sense wasting your time. But if you're willing to listen to the truth then you can keep on going, because that's what you're gonna get, at least as best as I know it. I know I kept quiet about these things most of my life because that's what I was taught was right, but now I think maybe it's time to speak up, so that's just what I aim to do.

I don't care what anybody says, I ain't dumb. I know what dumb is. I seen plenty of dumb players in my time. I seen players that can't remember signs for half an inning. That's dumb. I seen players that can't remember what the pitcher threw them the last time up or maybe even two pitches before. That's really dumb. I hit .356 in the Bigs. You can't be dumb and do that. You just can't, that's all.

I never learned to read and I never learned to write. If you want to know the truth, where I growed up in South Carolina, any boy that learned to read or write was looked at like some freak. Except I could of learned if I growed up someplace else, or in another time, maybe. Once, my manager, Mr. Mack, said he'd pay for some young guy to teach me. He said he'd even follow me on road games and all, but how would that've looked to the other guys? I told him I got that far without reading, so I guess I could get along just fine without knowing. He got kind of mad about that, but I wasn't gonna let him think he could push me around. Maybe people wouldn't of said all them things about me if they thought I could read and write. I had my chances, I know, but sometimes you don't always take advantage of all the chances life gives you, and sometimes you take advantage of some you shouldn't of. Besides, reading and writing ain't a matter of how smart you are. It's a matter of how much learning you have—two very different things.

I suppose you expect me to feel sorry for myself for all the unfair things that have happened to me, but I don't. I won't say I'm not angry at all, but I'm not sorry. So many people have said, "Poor Joe, he was just too stupid to know what was happening to him." Well, I'm here to tell you that ain't so. I've always known what I was doing. So what if I couldn't write about it? People don't understand that very good. That's what I get mad about. Going to Harvard don't make you smart, it only means you know more about some things, and a lot of that stuff don't matter anyway. I always knew a lot about things you could use.

Let me give you an example. Once, when I was still playing on the mill team, the team we was playing had this jerky left fielder named Stuffy McGuire. Now, ol' Stuffy was a little guy with this red-like hair. I never liked Stuffy much because he always thought he was this great player on account of his being as good as he was and so little and all. But he wasn't that great. A lot of left fielders was better than ol' Stuffy. I could name a whole bunch if I wanted to, but that don't have nothing to do with this game I want to tell you about.

We was playing on a Saturday afternoon, and Stuffy managed to get a scratch single through the infield in the ninth inning when his team was already down by 12 runs. Now, in case you don't know too much about baseball, I can tell you that the stupidest thing you can do when you're down by 12 runs in the ninth inning is to try to steal second base. Anybody that knows anything about baseball knows that. You just can't take the chance of being thrown out when you need so many runs. But I'm in the outfield and I see this dummy slowly inching away from the base while our pitcher is throwing a lot of balls to the batter that is fouling them all off. Our pitcher, Slim Mitchell, isn't paying much attention to the runner, because, like I said, nobody would be stupid enough to try to steal second, down 12 in the ninth.

But I keep watching ol' Stuffy and I can see the way he is inching his way off the bag and the way his arms is dangling loose by his sides, that he is gonna go. Want to know how I knowed that? Because I seen Stuffy on first before, and I watched him real careful and seen how he did some things different when he was gonna try to steal than when he wasn't. That's what a smart player notices. So when I see that he is getting ready to steal, I motion to our shortstop, Hugh Glynn, by taking off my cap and running my hands through my hair. That was a signal that everybody on our team was supposed to remember. Then Hugh signals Billy McFarland, our catcher, and he calls for a pitchout, which is what you're supposed to do to stop someone from stealing.

Well, the next pitch is a pitchout, and sure enough ol' Stuff takes off for second. The throw beats him by five feet, so Stuffy barrels into Billy Ricketts, our second baseman, trying to get him to drop the ball. There is a big crash and Stuffy breaks his collarbone, because he was a lot smaller than Billy, who wasn't so big himself, but almost everybody was bigger than Stuffy. So not only was Stuffy out, but that was the end of his season, and since it was only April, it was a pretty stupid thing to do. Ol' Stuffy never got the collarbone fixed right and, as far as I know, never was as good a player again. So you tell me. Who was smarter, Stuffy or me? It don't take a genius to figure that one out.

I could tell you a lot more stories like that one. I really could. But I hope you get the picture. I ain't afraid to tell the world that it don't take school learning to help a fellow play ball.

**CONNIE MACK** I never thought Joe was stupid, but that was the easy way to excuse what happened to him. "Joe didn't know any better. What could you expect from such an illiterate country bumpkin?" Somehow, this was supposed to explain all his problems.

The biggest mistake I made was not pressing him to learn to read and write. It would have made things a lot easier on him and I might have been able to keep him on the team. That way he never would have gotten mixed up with that bad element in Chicago.

**BILL STEEN** I roomed with Joe for several years in Cleveland. I liked him. He was a good roomie, clean, quiet, but it wasn't always that easy. I had to do a lot of little things for him—look up telephone numbers when he wanted to call someone, read menus to him, that sort of thing. Joe wasn't too bright, but oh, how he could play, and, all in all, he was a pretty good guy.

**STEVE O'NEILL** I know it's become real popular of late to say that Joe was really a bright guy and that he was some kind of victim of his youth. Well, let me tell you that I played with Joe for several years. I dressed next to him in the locker room, I ate many a meal with him, I traveled and sat around more hotel lobbies with him than I care to remember, and I can say without any hesitation that Joe was not a bright guy. It wasn't his fault, of course, but he would never recognize the fact that God gave him brilliant physical talents far beyond most mortals, but not the brains to know how to handle himself when problems came up.

**HARRY DAVIS** Joe was the most gullible, naive player in the history of baseball.

**TOPSY HARTSEL** Dumb? Let me put it to you this way: when he said hello Joe told you everything he knew.

**KENESAW MOUNTAIN LANDIS** Joe Jackson was a crook and a cheat.

**JOE JACKSON** The other thing is, I ain't a crook and I didn't cheat. You'll see this as I tell my story.

# 2

# WE WAS LUCKY

**SCOOP LATIMER** No player in baseball history ever had to overcome such abject poverty as did young Joseph Jackson. It has oft been reported that he frequently went to bed hungry, his entire large family forced to sleep in one room with no electricity, water or sanitary facilities. So poor were they, that Joseph didn't even own a pair of shoes until he was 15. That's the popular story anyway.

**JOE JACKSON** Where we come from was Pickens County, which was in South Carolina, in case you didn't know. The best as I can tell, I was born there either in 1888 or 1889. Now, you may think you got to be pretty dumb not to know when you was born, but back then nobody in them parts had what you would call real birth certificates. Instead the names and birth dates of all the family members was in the family Bible. The preacher would write all that in for us, and my mother would put it in a chest in her bedroom for safekeeping until the next baby was born. It was the only book we had, but it was an important one. I guess the Jackson family Bible had the right date in it for my birthday, but when a fire went clean through the house, it got burned up, so I don't know the right date for sure. We don't know my brothers', Davey and Luther's, exactly either, but it don't really matter that much.

I can't say as how I remember a lot of Pickens County except that we lived on a small piece of land that Father cropped on shares. We had a horse and a pig and some chickens. Father went to work in a nearby sawmill when there was work to be had there, but that wasn't all that often.

We had lots of family around though, because Father's three brothers and their families lived nearby.

**DAVID JACKSON** I was too little when we left the plantation to really remember a whole lot about it, but Mother told us often of this old fire-eater who owned it and who was always carrying on and fighting with the tenants. Mother never said it in so many words, but I think Father got into a big fight with him one day and that's why we left.

**LUTHER JACKSON** The fellow that owned the plantation was plain nuts. That's what everybody said. You couldn't blame Father for leaving and moving to Brandon Mill.

**J. C. HATCH** I saw lots of families come into the mill in my 21 years as mill secretary, and the Jacksons were like most—poor as the dirt on their farms but happy enough to have a real house and jobs for everybody in the family. At one time or other, Joe, his father, five brothers, and two sisters all worked in the mill. That's the way it was for most of the poor families from the area.

**JOE JACKSON** Everybody that lived in Brandon Mill had something to do with the mill. We landed there when I was about six or seven, just the age to start working in the mill.

When we was getting ready to make the move, Father told us the story of Colonel Thomas Brandon, who was supposed to have been given thousands of acres of land instead of money for his help to General Sumter during the war between the states. Most of the city of Greenville once belonged to him. Since the people in them parts was so poor, the mills was looked on as a miracle way to save all the poor people.

People all over was getting up petitions to ask a local banker, or somebody like that, to start a mill. So Colonel Brandon started the one that we moved to.

**COOPER ANDERSON** Brandon Mill is outside Greenville. Although we know that it was established in 1874, no one knows for sure exactly how Greenville came by its name. Some say it was named in honor of General Nathanael Greene of Revolutionary War fame, others recall Isaac Green, an early settler. I prefer the assertion that it got its name because of the rich, verdant setting. In fact, the green beauty of the city is quite remarkable for a manufacturing center. The many parks and shady residential streets on which are situated handsome homes set back from the street on green spreading lawns surrounded by opulent gardens make Greenville feel like one lush park. Add to that the Reedy River, with two falls of over 30 feet, which traverses the town, and you have a city of considerable beauty and charm.

I spent a fair amount of time with Joe when we were young and working together in the mill, so it's not difficult for me to see the lure which the city always held for him.

**JOE JACKSON** Some people think Greenville was nothing but a hick town, but it was a lot more than that. We had a big brick courthouse, a whole bunch of hotels and three livery stables, an opera hall, lots of churches, two colleges and a military institute. That ain't nothing.

**T. M. YOUNG** In 1902 I came from England to the United States to do a study of the American cotton industry for the *Manchester Guardian*. Among my visits to the mills of the American South was one to Brandon Mill.

Greenville was a clean little city of some 15 thousand people, which had relatively recently been visited by the specter of northern industrialism. All around the outskirts of the city red brick buildings had quickly sprung up to answer the North's pressing need for cotton products. Such was quickly becoming the heritage of the South. I counted 11 such factories in the Greenville area alone employing about 20 thousand persons.

Brandon Mill was typical of the mills in that area. It seems that they primarily employed illiterate whites. One of the supervisors at Brandon Mill assured me authoritatively that, "the mountain whites in the area were almost fully employed, but that the Negro would never become an efficient machine-minder."

It appeared to me that the whites in the southern mills were more slaves than the Negroes; they were not so well cared for, and they gained by their slavery just what the Negroes used to gain—food, clothing, shelter—but nothing more. They were paid infrequently, thus being forced to obtain the necessities of life at a store owned by the mill. The prices were extortionate, the goods of inferior quality, and if any balance remained to their credit when the store bill had been paid, then, and then only, they received it in cash.

**JOE JACKSON** Maybe we didn't have much money, but we had good jobs and they wasn't easy to come by in them days. We was lucky, and we knew it.

**T. M. YOUNG** I remember looking out of the window of the train on the way to Greenville and seeing the red, red Piedmont soil—soil that looked as if it still bore the stains of the blood so freely spilled upon it in the Civil War. I saw miles of pine, live oak and white honeysuckle. And I could see Negro women in sunbonnets hoeing in the fields, and ragged children, both Negro and white, untroubled by any school inspector, playing in the sunshine. The white children were not always to be seen with their Negro brothers, for if there was a cotton mill within reach, the little white would be at work, and the little Negro would be playing alone.

**DAVID JACKSON** I know Joe was called a racist by them northern writers, but that ain't right. We didn't have nothing to do with the Negroes, so I don't see how you can be a racist if you don't treat them bad or nothing.

**T. M. YOUNG** The farms in the environs of Greenville were dotted with little wooden cabins, most knowing neither paint nor whitewash, although some were redeemed by blazing roses. It was in homes and amid surroundings such as these that the population had been bred from which the newer southern mills were drawing their labor, people who had that fine physique which one found in Irishmen bred even in the poorest country cabins. But one could not see the stunted children in the mills without thinking of the physical degeneration in store for this fine race. Here and there a dark-brick cotton mill one or two stories high, surrounded by a huddle of row houses stood for the new order to which the old was giving place.

At night the rows of brightly-lighted windows in these mills told a tale of ceaseless activity strangely in contrast with the easygoing ways of the Old South.

**JOE JACKSON** Now I don't want you to think that this place was heaven on earth or nothing, but it wasn't as bad as some people made it out neither, especially northern sportswriters.

We lived near the end of one of the long rows of houses that made up the mill village. All of these little square houses had a pointed roof on top and was the same color—sort of a dirty whitewash. But all the families made some little changes to mark theirs. Our door had the biggest pine cone you ever seen on it. My brother Davey found it one day down by the creek and Father nailed it to the door. Others had little wreathes or crosses or some other marker. When I was little and looked up and down the street at all the same-looking houses I could always find ours by that pine cone.

There was no grass, trees or shrubs anywhere except, of course, by the bosses' houses, but they was some way away from us. None of the roads in the village was paved and when it rained hard, you could hardly get up the street at all. In the summer, the sun would beat down something awful on the baked earth, and it would cake up and crack into little pieces that was pretty good for throwing.

Most of the backyards, and sometimes the fronts too, was cluttered with tin cans, papers, old rags and things like that. When I think back on it now, it was pretty messy, to tell you the truth, but we didn't think too much about things like that because we was just so glad to have the mill jobs. Besides, some of the things you could find in the yards was pretty good to play with when you was little, except, of course, we didn't have a whole lot of time to do that.

There was little porches in the front of each house, and on some of them you could find a broken down chair or two. You'd be surprised at how many things you could make a chair into if you had a good imagination. A chair could be a fort or a boat, or it could be a throne or even a covered wagon going through Indian Territory.

The steps up to our porch was rotten and a couple of times had to be fixed when someone like Mr. Basker who lived next door broke through. Father would swear at the steps, but to be honest though, me and my brothers always thought it was pretty funny when somebody fell through.

Because of the size of our family, we was lucky to have a house with four rooms. The front room we called "the company room." That's where my sisters, Gertrude and Lula, slept. The second room was for Mother and Father, and when they was little, for the twins, Earl and Ernest, too. When they got bigger, the twins moved into the back room with me and Davey and Jerry and Luther. We each had our own bed but we all shared a big shiny yellow oak dresser—one drawer each. The little room on the side we used as both a kitchen and a dining room.

Mother and Father's room, even though it had a big bed in it, was used as the living room. It had a fireplace with a small coal grate and a mantel holding up Mother's big old windup clock, which she got from her mother who told her it was from someplace in Europe. The trundle sewing machine sat in the corner next to a little table.

Despite what a lot of them northern writers said about me later, we did have electricity. How did they suppose we ran the mill—donkey power?

Since we was near the end of the row, we was pretty close to the village cold drink stand. This was good because the lint in the air made for a lot of thirsty people, and the dope and lime there was the best I ever had.

Down at the other end of our row was three small churches—Baptist, Methodist and Presbyterian. A lot of the families went to church most every Sunday, especially the Baptists, and when a revival come to town, well that was a special event.

We was Baptists more or less, but none of us went to church very much except for weddings and christenings, and things like that. This meant more free time on Sundays, which was a good thing. About the only thing that we'd do that was sort of religious was that we never cooked on Sunday. Mother said that if it was God's day off, it was hers too.

Across from the churches was the small store where we bought all our groceries. The store was run by old Hamie. Nobody really liked him very much because he wasn't from a cotton mill family himself. He thought he was maybe a little better than the mill families, but he wasn't.

Old Hamie was the skinniest person I ever seen, with his veins sticking out all over the place. His company store was where we bought almost everything we had because it was the only place in the village to buy anything, except of course the cold drink stand, but you could only buy drinks there.

Hamie's store was one big square room with lots of open wooden shelves. It was here that all us eight-hundred mill workers bought what we needed—our food, clothes, and just about everything we had. If you needed something Hamie didn't have, like a special colored dress or something, you just told Hamie and in a few days he'd have it. Once one of the workers ordered a cow and old Hamie got that for him, and another time he got a real organ for Mrs. Watts who started playing it in the Methodist church on Sundays.

Everybody that worked in the mill got paid with a company check, except of course us kids. Our money was paid to our father as part of his check. These checks was then given to Hamie, who then gave our family credit for how much the check was. This was what was called the trade check system. The problem came when you wanted to go into Greenville and maybe buy something in one of the big stores there. This didn't happen a lot, but every once in a while, Mother or Father would get the itch. About the only thing they could do was take their check into Greenville. But off the mill, it wasn't worth very much, so we pretty much couldn't do that.

Some of the families complained a little about this, but most of it was kept pretty quiet because everybody was afraid that if they talked too loud, they might get the company angry, and nobody wanted to see the mill go someplace else because the workers wasn't happy.

For us kids, though, it wasn't always that simple. We was working 12 hours a day during the week and six hours on Saturday, and we seldom seen any money. To make matters worse, we couldn't use the credit in Hamie's. Only our parents could.

Once in a blue moon if we was lucky we'd have a penny or two that Father got in Greenville, to buy a piece of rock candy that looked like a big chunk of almost clear glass and was about the best thing any young fellow could buy. To this day I can still taste the sweet syrupy flavor of them rocks. That's a taste you just couldn't find in Philadelphia, Cleveland or Chicago no matter how hard you tried.

It was just this love for rock candy that got me into my first bit of trouble. One Saturday afternoon after the mill was shut for the weekend, me and my little brother Davey was in Hamie's just kind of looking around at what new treats Hamie might have put on the shelves, all the time wishing with all our might that we had a penny to buy a rock. But we didn't, and Hamie knew we didn't so he kept watching us, and I guess he was wondering what we was up to. It didn't happen often, but once in every once in a while, somebody would come in the store who had an extra penny or two and they would buy a piece of candy for a couple of young boys that looked like they could use it. So this particular day we got lucky. Old Mrs. Watts came in. She was the one I told you about with the organ. Well, she bought some jam, and I guess had some money left over, so she looked at me and Davey and asked if we would like a piece of candy. That's exactly what she said, "Would you boys like a piece of candy?" We both said at the same time, "Yes, ma'am," and faster than a Walter Johnson fast ball, we each grabbed a piece and hightailed it out the front door, across the mill yard, and down to the creek where we sucked on those candies until they became little specs in our mouths and then disappeared. The reason we didn't go home right away was that one of our other sisters or brothers would've wanted us to break off a piece for them, and we counted this as our good luck and not to be shared with anybody.

Just about time it was getting dark, we headed home for dinner, mighty pleased with ourselves and filled with the good taste of Hamie's best. When we came around the corner of the last house in the row we could see skinny old Hamie and our father talking on the front porch. Now old Hamie didn't come to your house unless there was a problem with credit or a bill or something, so we quickly ducked down behind the Ferguson porch to try to hear what was going on.

"Took two and only paid for one," old Hamie said.

"I didn't think they had a penny between them," our father answered.

"Mrs. Watts gave 'em a penny. But they took two, and everybody knows they is a penny each, not two for a penny."

"They don't steal. My boys don't steal."

"I'm gonna dun your credit for the extra penny, but I mostly want you to know what they is up to, stealing and all."

"There's got to be some explanation. Joey and Davey don't steal, that's all there is to it," we heard our father say defending us like a good father should.

"Did this time. Ask Mrs. Watts if you want."

"I'll ask my boys."

"Don't expect them to fess up, do you?"

"I do."

Later that night after dinner, Father asked us if we stole candy from Hamie's. We said we didn't, that we thought she meant one piece each and that's what we took. That ended the matter at home, but not in the village. Hamie told everybody that we stole from him. Maybe some people believed him, maybe some didn't, but for a long time, there was always that suspicion. Hamie was an adult. Hamie ran the village store. We was just boys.

**HAMIE** Of course Joe stole from the store. All the boys did. It was part of being accepted by the others. It was sort of like belonging to a club that all the boys had to join. You couldn't be a full-fledged member until you swiped something of value from the store. Everybody knew it, but the company didn't like it one bit, so when I caught one of them I had to tell the family... and the company.

**JOE JACKSON** I should've learned right then, it don't always matter what you do—it's what people think you do that counts. Them two things ain't always the same.

# 3

# I LEARNED ABOUT HARD WORK

**JOE JACKSON** Father was a slight man but all muscle. The one thing that everybody always remembers about him—he had the longest arms you ever seen. Father didn't say a lot, but when he did say something people usually listened on account of that being so unusual. A number of times, sportswriters asked me what I learned from him, what kind of advice he gave me, but I can't honestly think of anything like that. He was always there, when I was growing up, but he pretty much left the taking care of things and the giving of advice to Mother. I guess, if anything, I learned about hard work from him, because that's what he did just about every day of his life. I can't think of one day that he called in sick, or didn't go to work, or even complained about having to go to work. He growed up as a backwoodsman who learned to get along without a lot of the things life had to offer, but if that bothered him, he never let on to us.

He liked to pass his free time with the other men of the village, hunting or fishing, or sometimes drinking. He didn't show his emotions easily, or smile a whole lot, but on the few times that he got angry, he got really angry, and we learned real quick to keep our distance.

**DAVID JACKSON** Father had enough of a temper that we never wanted to cross him. Mostly what we did was stay out of his way as much as we could which that wasn't all that difficult, because he never played with us or anything like that. Actually, I don't think he was comfortable with kids at all, that's why he spent so much of his time with his buddies.

**J. C. HATCH** Joe's father was an odd sort of duck. Loved to hunt, worked hard, all that sort of stuff, but I don't remember him taking a whole lot of interest in the kids. At least not that you would notice in public anyway. He pretty much let them go their own way, and as long as they were all working in the mill, and staying out of trouble, he didn't seem to pay them a whole lot of heed.

He was a pretty quiet guy most of the time. I wouldn't exactly say moody. Maybe taciturn. But when he did speak up, at a town meeting or some occasion such as that, people kind of paid attention to him a little. If you were going to make a film about him, I guess you would have to cast Gary Cooper.

**JOE JACKSON** When Davey broke his arm for about the fourth time in a mill accident, Father was still working in the mill and had one of his big angry spells. The belt stopped and everybody went running to where Davey was lying and crying out in pain. Somebody went and got Davey a shot of whiskey from the bosses' office, which is what you always got if you was hurt serious. Father looked down, and without saying a word to Davey, went right to the foreman and began telling him in this real loud way that they needed to have a safety guard on the belt where Davey got caught up. The foreman didn't like being talked to that way and told Father that he'd better stop that kind of talk in front of the men, or else.

"Or else what?" Father asked.

Everybody heard that and stopped to watch the argument, because you just didn't do that in the mill—talk back to a foreman.

"Or else you'll be out of a job," the foreman said, getting real angry now because everybody was watching to see what would happen to a worker who shouted at a boss.

"It ain't right, it just ain't right," Father kept saying.

"The company decides what's right, Mr. Jackson, not you."

"The kid's hurt again. That ain't right."

"He should be more careful, that's all," said the foreman with great certainty.

"Not again in the same place."

Davey's arm would be in a cast for many weeks, and during that time he wouldn't be able to work, and when you didn't work, you didn't get paid.

Father wouldn't let go of the argument and so what always happens when you fight with a boss happened to Father. At the end of the week, when he went to pick up his pay, he got the pink slip in the envelope with his money. None of the bosses talked to him about it. They didn't have to. He knew what the slip meant, and why he got it, and he knew that if he made a fuss about it, the rest of the family might get the slip too, so he said nothing. He just walked out of the mill and never returned. A guard was never put on the belt where Davey was hurt even though people kept getting hurt at the same spot.

Sometimes, even when you've been done wrong, it don't pay to complain because you might make the situation worse.

**J. C. HATCH** Joe's father worked in the mill most of these years, but finally got into some disagreement with the management and decided to go into business for himself as a butcher, supplying meat for the mill operatives. The business was a small one, but Joe occasionally helped him in the business when work in the mill was slack.

I remember the elder Jackson as a man with abnormally long arms. I don't think he was particularly athletic—simply one of the wiry type of South Carolina back woodsmen.

Joe's mother, Martha, was a rather large woman with long black hair which she generally wore pulled up tight into a knot at the back of her head. She was known around the village as a pretty fair cook and a conscientious housekeeper, wife and mother. Martha Jackson stayed home and took care of the house which was the wont of the older women in the village. Like the rest of the Jacksons, she wasn't one to talk a whole lot, but when she did have something to say she usually said it quietly but with conviction. When she referred to Joe, it was always "my Joe."

**LUTHER JACKSON** Of all us kids, Joe was probably the closest to Mother.

**MARTHA JACKSON** My Joe was a good boy. He was a hard worker and he was always honest. That's a fact.

# 4

# THE AIR WAS ALWAYS BAD

**COOPER ANDERSON** Up before daybreak to the whine of the whistle and out of the mill to the whine of the whistle. We were obedient to that shrill whistle blast as though we were so many living machines.

**JOE JACKSON** Excepting Sundays, most of our days at Brandon Mill was pretty much the same.

The first whistle blew at 5 o'clock. It woke everybody up, but that was all right because everybody worked in the mill anyway, or, like old Hamie, had something to do with working in the mill.

Mother was the first one out of bed because she had to get dressed really fast so that she could kindle the fire and then make breakfast. Every day was a long day in the mill, so we needed a good breakfast, and Mother was good at making breakfast.

While we was eating breakfast the second whistle would blow telling us that we had 25 minutes to get to the mill. Then in a little while, three short blasts of the whistle meant that we had to be on our way.

Everybody going in the same direction. All the men in overalls, and all the women and girls in gingham dresses.

Every day, me, my father (until he left), my two sisters, and my five brothers headed for the mill and to the spinning or spooling department, or to the weave shop, or wherever we worked.

**COOPER ANDERSON** During the winter it was still dark as we followed the whistle into the mill, stumbling along briskly, for lateness was not tolerated without some very good excuse.

**JOE JACKSON** The mill was this long, narrow, five-story-high, red brick building that had one tall smokestack sticking up. Right in the middle was a big door that we all went into. Just inside was a row of clocks where we punched in.

At exactly 5:55 the fourth and last blast of the whistle sounded. The machinery started and the day's work began.

You could hear the hum and buzz of the machinery most every place in the village. You could set your watch by it if you had one. The machines whirred up to speed at the same time every morning, six days a week, month after month, year after year.

**DAVID JACKSON** There was only four holidays a year when the mill was shut: Fast Day which came sometime in March or April, the Fourth of July, Thanksgiving and Christmas. Once in a while the mill shut down for repairs to the machinery.

**JOE JACKSON** In all the years I worked in that mill, there was very few unusual events that made one day different from any other. I suppose I can remember the mill being down once for two days because they was putting in some new equipment, and I can remember the time Charlie Haese dropped dead of a heart attack right on top of his machine, and what happened to old Evelyn McTear, and, of course, I can remember all Davey's accidents, especially the time he got caught up in the belt and got carried all the way to the ceiling and then thrown back to the floor. He was hurt pretty bad, but as soon as he was able, he was right back at his station. If you didn't work, you didn't get paid. Life was real simple in the mill.

All in all, though, that isn't a lot of memories for more than nine years working in the same place.

All the machines was driven by these flying black leather belts that came down from a long overhead shaft way up near the ceiling. The sound was something awful. The machines was loud enough to begin with, but the brick walls and cement floors kept bouncing the noise back and forth. Each part of the mill had its own sound—the spinning room with a loud hum, and the loom rooms with their nonstop clatter. Usually visitors who came into the mill couldn't stand the noise and would have to leave, but when you work with the noise every day you get used to it and forget it's there. When the machines shut down at night you didn't even notice the silence.

**COOPER ANDERSON** With so many moving belts and wheels and the whirling and twisting and thumping of machine parts, the very floor itself trembled. We learned to read lips because nothing could be heard above the constant and deafening thunder of the machines—and for so many hours of our day.

**JOE JACKSON** During all my years in the mill, I guess I did most of the jobs you could do there without being a boss, and workers didn't become bosses. Bosses came in from someplace else. They was bosses. We was workers. I started out like most of the kids, by sweeping floors. Later I also tended the loom where the yarn was woven into cloth, and I worked in the slasher room where the warps was slashed and dried on these big steam-filled copper drums.

The thing that I did for the longest time though, was to work as a doffer boy. I sat beside the spinning frame on a bobbin or a waste box and waited for the bobbins to fill with yarn. Then I passed them down the side of the frame, grabbing the full bobbins from their spindles and replacing them with empty quills. I got so good and fast at doing this that somebody watching me could hardly follow my movements, my hands was flying so fast. There is no doubt in my mind that all the years of doing this same thing for hours at a time is what made me such a good hitter of baseballs. It took good eyes and fast hands moving together to go as quick as I did. Mr. Hatch, the mill secretary, told people that nobody had quicker movements on a bobbin than I did.

**COOPER ANDERSON** The mill was extremely efficient, because each stage in the making of cloth was given to one section of the mill. Few workers viewed what they did as part of the whole. Generally, when you mastered one aspect of the process, you remained there your entire working life.

By the time Joe was 13 and had already been working in the mill for seven years he became a full time doffer. He was so coordinated and quick with his hands that he may have been the best doffer of all.

**JOE JACKSON** To try to prove how stupid I was, one of them northern sportswriters once asked me, "Joe, since you spent so many years in a mill, can you tell us a little about how cotton cloth is made?"

"No," I said, "can you?"

See, we didn't pay no attention to how anything worked. We did our job and, when the whistle blew, we went home.

**COOPER ANDERSON** Although Greenville and Brandon Mill lay adjacent to each other, there remained in some ways a yawning abyss between them.

**JOE JACKSON** Lots of times you could still see the cotton lint sticking in people's hair. Sometimes when we went into Greenville and forgot to comb the lint out, people would laugh at us and call us lintheads.

Once when we was walking along the sidewalk in Greenville, somebody called my little brother, Luther, a linthead. Luther wasn't all that big at the time, but he lit into the fellow who did the name calling and gave him a pretty good licking. Me and my brothers didn't do nothing to stop him and he probably would have hurt the name caller real bad except some townspeople stopped the fight. Father came along and drug us all back to the village. He didn't say a word. He didn't have to. That was the day Luther growed up, and we all knowed it.

It seems there's a lot of people in the world that think they can prove they're better than you by the names they call you. I never have cared much for them people. "Linthead" may have been the first name I was ever called, but it sure wasn't the last.

**COOPER ANDERSON** One absolute of working in a mill was that it was extremely regimented. Everything was organized to a set schedule so the workers always knew what was coming next. It was a strictly controlled environment.

Like all of us, Joe was governed by a never-changing timetable. There was a certain contentment in that. There were no choices that had to be made, no decisions to be arrived at. It was only after Joe had left and had to make choices on his own that trouble set in.

**JOE JACKSON** For six hours, we pretty much stayed doing whatever job we was assigned to, waiting always for the 12: 00 o'clock whistle which meant that the machinery stopped for a 55-minute dinner break. We hurried back home the fastest way we could, crossing everybody's yards to take the straightest way. I always thought it must have looked pretty strange to a bird looking down. First the whole village looked empty, then this loud noise and hundreds of people come pouring out of the big building, hurrying in crisscrossing patterns all over the place, and then just as sudden as they started, they all disappear into little buildings and it's quiet again.

By the time we got home, Mother had dinner on the table. We washed our hands then dug into the food as fast as we could. Even though Mother always told us to slow down, and we said we would, we never did.

At 12:30, the whistle blew again, and we was on our way back to work. Sometimes I'd stop at the soft drink stand for a lemonade or a dope and lime and drink it in about two swallows before going into the mill. Another blast of the whistle at 12:55 meant it was time to begin again. We worked to 6:00 in the evening (except Saturdays when we stopped at noon), then went back home for supper which was also on the table when we got there. It was usually leftovers from the noon meal, but we was mighty glad to have them, and we never didn't have enough food, like lots of people in the South who didn't have the chance to work in a mill.

After I became famous I heard it said so many times that I was so poor when I was growing up that I went to bed hungry every night. Like so much else that was written about me, that just wasn't true. I guess a lot of these writers thought they could sell more papers or magazines by making up these exaggerated stories, or maybe some of it they thought was true and just didn't bother to find out the facts or to ask me about the truth. That bothered me for a long time before I came to understand that if you're a famous person in America a lot's gonna be said and written about you that's wrong and there's not much that you can do about it.

I could of stayed there with all my family and all my friends, working every day. Sure, the work was hard, but it was easy, too. You didn't have to face the reporters every day, you didn't have to have people poking into all the little corners of your life, and you didn't have to make a lot of decisions that maybe wasn't right. All you had to do was go to the mill every day, which is what I done. And I didn't create no problems either.

**T. M. YOUNG** At Brandon Mill I was told, quite candidly, that the management had found great difficulty in obtaining good help, and from what I saw in the spinning room especially, I could believe that. Some of the machinery stood idle for want of efficient labor, and some of the equipment that did run only spoiled cotton. Children seemed to be doing three-fourths of the work, and many of them were very young. I spoke to one boy who said he was just 10, to another who gave his age as nine, and to a third little chap who said that he was eight and that there were plenty of boys in the mill younger than himself—as young as five. The mill superintendent assured me that he would rather not employ young children, but that he was forced to take them in order to get the older and more useful family members.

At any rate, the superintendent insisted they did not employ any children under the age of 12. When I assured him I spoke with numerous children who both appeared to be, and said they were, under that age, he asserted they were only there to help their older sisters.

Massachusetts law, as I understand it, meets this evasion by forbidding young children to work in the mill for anybody. The southern mill owners, however, were not evading the law, for there was no law for them to evade.

**JOE JACKSON** The thing that bothered me most in the mill was that the air was always so bad. This was because they had to have a lot of wetness in the air to keep the threads from snapping, so they was always spraying steam all over. Even when it was boiling in the summer, the bosses usually kept the windows nailed shut to keep the wet air in. In the winter it was even worse though because of the hundreds of lamps which made the heat and smoke real bad.

**T. M. YOUNG** The mill superintendent told me they were offering, "a dollar a day for good ring-spinners—that is 20 cents more than any other mill in the area." One possible reason for this suggested itself to me when I learned that each spinner was expected to mind a whole alley of spindles running on medium counts—eight sides of 2,120 spindles—for a dollar a day. Even in England I never heard that any spinner, however dexterous, was given more than 1,456 ring spindles. The superintendent, however, contended that one good spinner could run the lot and sit down.

**LUTHER JACKSON** We could always run more spindles than we let the bosses know we could. After all, if they knowed we could run more, they would expect us to and then lower the pay if we didn't do it.

**T. M. YOUNG** The wage paid for picking was 75 cents per day, and the laborers were all Negroes. No Negroes were employed for any other indoor work at Brandon Mill. The Negro grows the cotton, harvests it, gins it, bales it, and brings it to the mill door in a mule wagon, and sometimes he may open the bales and put the cotton into the hopper of the first machine which treats the fiber. After that he gives way to white labor. Why?

Not because of race feelings, as is commonly supposed in England, and even in the northern states, for in all sorts of other occupations one finds the Negro and the white working side by side on good terms. And not because the Negro is driven out by the competition of the whites. I am satisfied that if the Negro does not work in the cotton mills it is simply because he does not choose to. He has a child's impatience of any monotonous occupation that demands constant vigilance. He dislikes to breathe the mill air, laden with moisture and fine particles of lint cotton. He loves the sunshine and the open sky, and he is loath to forsake them for indoor work unless that work ministers a little to his vanity and sense of dignity. That is why, I think, you will find George—all southern Negroes are assumed by the whites to be called George, and are invariably addressed by that illustrious name—wearing the evening dress of a waiter or the livery of a porter in a hotel, or serving as a conductor or assistant conductor on a Pullman car, and why you will not find him standing for 11 hours a day in front of a slubbing frame or a group of frames.

No doubt the Negro's natural antipathy to such work would make him a poor workman if he were driven to seek employment in a cotton mill. But he seems to feel the game is not worth the candle so long as he can live happily by working three or four days a week in the fields.

**JOE JACKSON** Most of the best jobs in the mill went to us boys because the work needed quick hands, agility and good eyesight. There wasn't any Negroes doing this because they just wasn't very good at it. I guess they wasn't born that way.

The best pay, too, went to the men under 30, and when you got older than that, you began getting less pay. Sometimes someone in his forties or fifties would come into the village looking for work, but it was always hard for them because most of the openings, when there was any at all, went to younger workers.

The company, though usually took pretty good care of someone who worked for them for a long time. Mr. Elliot, who lived two doors down from us, had worked for the mill since it opened, but by the time I was in my teens, he was pretty old and began dropping things and was having trouble with his machines. I could see that his hands was shaky sometimes, too. By that time, all three of his sons had left the village. They wasn't such good workers anyway and nobody was sorry to see them leave, except, of course, Mr. and Mrs. Elliot.

One night in the dead of winter, old Mr. Elliot came over to our house and started crying. I hated that because it made me embarrassed for him. Here he was this big, tall man and he was crying. Father never cried, and I always thought that times like that should be private anyway. But, Mr. Elliot was afraid that he was gonna lose his job on account of his not being able to do it very good anymore.

It wasn't hard to see why Mr. Elliot was so upset because none of the mill families got to save very much—if any—money, and there was no such thing as a company retirement plan, so Father calmed him down and told him that he'd talk to the foreman in the morning. It wasn't two days later that Mr. Elliot had a job as a sweeper which was a lot easier than handling the machinery with shaky hands. Later on he became a watchman and stayed with the company until he died, and Mrs. Elliot came to live with us. He's buried in the little cemetery behind the Presbyterian Church. Like so many others, he was born a share cropper but spent most of his time and died as a mill worker.

Mr. Elliot was a good example of what happened if you didn't have a big family, or if your family moved away and left you. Not everybody was as lucky as he was, though. Some of the older men was turned loose to find whatever jobs they could, but there wasn't many available. Sometimes they went back to the farms where they came from. Mr. Callahan, when he couldn't work in the mill any longer, cared for workers' gardens. Another man bought a mule to cultivate a small patch of land behind one of the rows of houses which the company gave him to raise some fresh vegetables to sell to the workers' wives. Some of the older men and women kept an eye on the grandchildren so that the young mothers could go to the mill.

Family was always important in a mill village, and when I moved away I always helped take care of my family. I did this even when the writers was attacking me for it, but I tell you, I'd do it again today. In the mill you learn the value of family and you don't forget it.

**J.C. HATCH** The Jackson family stuck pretty close together. If one of them didn't report to work, the others always had their stories "straight." If one of the boys got into a scuffle, you could bet his brothers would be there to back him up. These backwoods families was all pretty much like that.

**JOE JACKSON** At one time or other, my sisters, Gertrude and Lula, worked in the mill, but I don't think that in all her years Mother ever once stepped foot inside.

Mostly the women worked the spinning frames, spending all them hours every day looking sharp up and down the long machines for tufts of white on the waste rollers which told them that a thread was broken.

When the machines were running up to speed, the women sometimes sat in the window to rest and talk to the other women as best they could over the noise. Sometimes you could see some of the older women dipping snuff from a tin snuff box with a little black gum wood brush.

**LULA JACKSON ELLIS** When I first went into the weaving room, there was so many bands turning, wheels spinning, and springs in constant motion that it was confusing and frightening. I stood inside the room and began shaking because I was absolutely sure I could never learn to weave. The harness and the reed confused me, and then, to make matters worse, before anybody could even tell me what to do, the shuttle flew out and hit me on the side of the head, raising a considerable bump. The first time I tried to spring the lathe, I broke out a quarter of the threads. By the time the last whistle sounded, my head throbbed in dull pain, my ankles hurt, every bone in my body was aching and there was in my ears, a strange noise that sounded like crickets, frogs and Jew's Harps all mixed together.

That night, Joe, acting like a big brother, told me not to worry, that in time I would get used to it. He was right about that. Eventually the machines became less terrifying and the pain eased off, both to be replaced by something far worse—monotony.

**GERTRUDE JACKSON TRAMELL** Like Joe, I started as a doffer changing the bobbins on the spinning frames every three-quarters of an hour or so. It wasn't really very hard, but it wasn't very interesting either. While we was waiting to change the next bobbin, us bobbin girls would run around the mill teasing and talking to the older girls. Sometimes on long winter days we'd sit in a corner and all sing some old song. Sometimes, if we was not too busy they would let us go home in the middle of the day to help Mother with the housework or the cooking.

**J. C. HATCH** Most girls, in time, attained a reasonable degree of skill because they were paid by the piece.

**COOPER ANDERSON** If one girl earned, by extra exertion, $4 per week, it was blazed abroad from Maine to Mexico that girls in that mill earn from $1 to $4 per week. The fact of the matter was, the average wage never fell much below nor rose much above $2 a week, because in order to keep wages constant, it was necessary for the company to reduce rates every time the pace of the work increased. Whenever this was done, there was a temporary decrease in each girl's pay until she adjusted to the speed-up.

**HAMIE** Sometimes when the girls speeded up a bit and before the company adjusted the pay rates down, they would find themselves with a few extra dollars to spend. I had a sign I would put in the window especially on those occasions. "Ladies Superior Work Boxes, Needle Books, Macassar Oil, Cologne Water, Rowland's Kalydor for beautifying and preserving the complexion, Battledores, Dominoes, Fancy and Ring Top Inks and Sands."

Most of the girls like the Jackson sisters couldn't read the sign, of course, but I could always count on there being somebody around to read it to them. I have to admit it wasn't real difficult to separate the girls from any extra money they made.

**JOE JACKSON** Usually the mill girls married mill boys, and they married real young. There wasn't much of a chance for the girls to meet boys from anyplace else and we liked it just fine that way anyhow. This is how I met Katie.

If a girl wasn't married by the time she was about 25 she was in real trouble, because not many ever got married after that, and without a big family it was just about impossible to get along in a mill town.

Evelyn McTear, who was about 25, was a short, plump girl with bad skin. She was nice enough and all, but she was so shy she was always afraid to talk to the boys, and none of the boys really wanted to be seen talking to her because that would mean that they couldn't do any better. So Evelyn mostly stayed to herself. Then one day, when she didn't come home after work, her daddy came looking for her. By late that night, after he had asked everybody if they seen her, and nobody had, he went to bed, thinking that maybe she had run off. He didn't go to any of the bosses because he didn't want them to think he was causing a problem that might cost him his job.

In the morning, when we all got to the mill, there she was, hanging by the neck from one of the overhead shafts, her eyes bulging out, and her face turning blue. It was the first dead body I ever seen, and it was a picture I will never forget.

I guess she did it like that so that everybody could see her. I think it was her way of getting even with the village. The strange thing is though, I didn't feel all that sorry for her. I figure she knew what the future held in store for her and felt that this was better. If she'd been killed in an accident in the mill or something like that, then I would of felt real sorry, but this way it was her choice, and I think when someone makes a choice, then whatever happens because of that choice, they really can't complain about it. I know a lot of the bad things that have happened to me was because of the wrong choices I made, but I can't go back and unmake them, so I'm just going to have to live with them as best I can.

# 5

# MY FAVORITE PLACE

**JOE JACKSON** My favorite place near Brandon Mill was always the creek that ran across the edge of the village then out into the low hills away from Greenville. You could walk for about 20 minutes and come to this pool of the clearest water you ever seen.

Out there you could get away from the noise of the mill machinery and the whistles that cut up your day into neat little pieces.

We hunted along this creek in the early fall mornings when the leaves was all red and yellow and golden. We swam in this pool on the hot and sticky summer weekend afternoons. We picked blackberries on the banks when the farmer wasn't looking, and we spent many a Sunday just being lazy, laying on the sloping bank doing nothing.

Hunting and fishing was mostly what we did when we wasn't in the mill. I especially liked to hunt all kinds of birds that made the South Carolina fields their home. We had wild turkeys all over the place, partridges, which if we was lucky, we could eat in October or November, and doves which was lots easier to find in winter than in summer. Sometimes we could shoot plovers which would stop in Carolina for a few weeks every April on their way north. We would always look for them in the high open pastures where the cattle grazed because I guess the cattle somehow provided them with their food. They was a skittery bird, so you had to be real quiet when sneaking up on them. They didn't taste all that good, but the hunt sure was fun. Sometimes we could find woodcocks and snipes when it got so cold up north that they was driven down to us, and sometimes we could find wild geese and wild ducks, too, and when we shot them we would find their craws loaded with rice.

We got pretty good at hunting, and once in a while we could even sell a bird to one of the women in the village and get real money, not credit at Hamie's, in case we ever wanted to buy something in Greenville.

**J.C. HATCH** The practice of fire hunting was forbidden by law but that didn't stop a lot of the back woodsmen from doing it. Joe's father, who was himself a backwoodsman before he came to the mill, could easily have taught his boys all the tricks of illegal hunting. I don't think he ever had much respect for the law anyway. Most of his kind didn't.

**JOE JACKSON** Hunting is what got me into big trouble once. I tell this story so you won't think I'm trying to show I was some kind of saint or something. I was no more a saint than I was a cheat.

One fall evening when I was about 16, Davey and me decided to go out fire hunting for a buck out in a nearby pea field.

I told Davey to go to the pine barrel and get some pine nuts while I slipped into the house and got Mother's biggest pan. I'd for sure have it back before she noticed it was missing.

Father never showed us how to be fire hunters, but we had hidden in the bush before and seen him do it, so we figured we could do it just as good. Lots of the men did it and never got caught, so why not us?

As soon as it was dark, we real quiet-like made our way around the field moving wide to avoid the farmer's house. We carried our equipment—gun, tinder box, lightwood and frying pan. The night was clear and the dew was heavy on the leaves and grass.

"The moon is down," said Davey. "In a half-hour or so, he should begin to feed."

Davey always paid attention to things like this. He was a pretty smart kid.

We checked for the wind, but there wasn't much of any.

"That's bad," I said. "If he noses us he'll be off in a wink."

"Let's strike the fire and get started," Davey said, real anxious for the adventure.

We lighted the chips of lightwood and waited until they was blazing, then put them in the frying pan. Davey waved the pan slowly back and forth, lighting up everything near and far except the space kept in shadow by his head. We knew it was in this shadowy space, that the eyes of the buck would become visible to the fire hunter, and stunned by the light, he would freeze.

According to what I heard Father and the other men say, you could figure the distance by the size of the eyes. I knew you couldn't sneak up till you seen their horns, because no buck that growed up to be as big as this one was stupid enough to let you get that close.

We crept closer to the spot we was looking for. "Follow me close so that I can keep in the shade made by your body. Make sure you throw the shadow right on me."

We got to the pea field and didn't go more than a few yards before we came upon about the best antlered buck you ever seen feeding on the little vines. But he must've seen us as well as the fire, because he stomped his feet, sniffed the air and was off so quick that I didn't even have a chance to get off a shot.

"Damn it all," I muttered.

"There's more," Davey said. "Don't worry."

We continued to move through the field, trying to be even quieter. I stayed in front, Davey behind with the flaming pan, staying so close to me, that we threw only one shadow.

It took a while, but we eventually caught glimpses of a deer's eyes that looked like balls of green flame.

We moved very slowly forward until the deer suddenly lifted his head and stared directly at our fire. I stopped instantly, drew the gun to my shoulder, and fired. The sound of the shot in the still and quiet night came echoing back from the woods that surrounded the field like a wall.

"He's done for," said Davey, after a moment's pause.

We moved to the spot where we found the big buck lying in a pool of blood. We quickly turned him over on his back and dragged him by the horns to the fence at the side of the field.

We felt proud because we was now as hunters, equal to our elders. We cleaned and divided him. We had some trouble with the hind quarter but we got it done. We was still struggling with that when Davey heard a noise.

"I hear another one," he said. "It's the light he's seen."

I picked up my gun in one hand and the fire pan in the other.

"Wait here, till I fire," I said.

Oh, how I wished I hadn't been so greedy that night. Wasn't one big buck enough?

Stepping on tiptoe, I moved forward in the direction Davey pointed the sound come from. The ground on the edge of this field was not so open as we was in before. Some bushes kept getting in the way of my view, but soon I caught sight of a green eye glaring from the middle of a group of bushes. I quickly fired the barrel which I had in reserve.

Davey came running up to find me standing over the body of a fine black and shiny colt.

"The devil!" I cursed loudly. "If that was clear ground I never would've done that. Davey. See where he's shot."

"What's the use, Joey, he's dead as a door nail," said Davey.

"What are we going to do now?" I said beginning to get scared.

"Let's get out of here, fast," Davey answered.

If the farmer found out it was us, or anybody in the mill, we was gonna get into big trouble. None of the farmers really trusted the mill hands, and they would just as soon see us out of the way, so something like this would be good for them. Besides, if we had to go before a judge in Greenville he would always take the side of the farmers over us.

"Wait a minute," I said. "Here, help me."

We took off the top rail from the fence, and I drove the sharp point of it into the side of the colt, right where I shot him.

"It's gonna take a pretty smart farmer to figure out you ain't died of a snag," I said to the dead animal.

"What do you think, Davey?"

"I think you're about the smartest guy around, that's what I think," he answered.

Still, I had this knot in the pit of my stomach for a couple of reasons. I wasn't sure we could get away with it, and I was kind of sick about shooting the colt in the first place.

We buried the buck because we figured that if we showed up with it, everybody would think that we might've been in the field where the colt died.

For a couple of days nobody said nothing about it and we was beginning to think that the rail hole did the trick, but then the farmer who owned the colt showed up in the village and wanted to know which one of the village "low lifes" was responsible for killing his colt. He was real mad but since he said he had no evidence, some of the men in the village got just as mad because the farmer just assumed it was one of us in the village and not one of the townspeople from Greenville. A lot of times we took the blame for things that we didn't do, and this got some of the men all riled up.

Well, the farmer raised a big fuss in the village for a few days and demanded that somebody pay for the colt. Me and Davey felt real bad about what happened but we didn't have no money so we just didn't say nothing.

**J.C. HATCH** The time that farmer made such a ruckus about his colt, word went round the village that it was the Jackson boys that did it, but none of them was going to say anything against any of the other villagers. That's the way it was in the village. They protected their own.

**JOE JACKSON** We didn't sleep for a lot of nights after that, and I suspicioned Father knew we done it. Others probably did, too, but nobody would tell on another member of the village. Loyalty was important to us, and it has been to me ever since. You don't snitch on your friends.

**JOE JACKSON** We had this policeman in the village named Murray. I don't know if he was a real policeman or not, but he was paid by the company to keep the peace and break up fights—things like that. Most of the time he didn't have a whole lot to do, mostly because we was in the mill so many hours of the week that we didn't have a lot of time to get into trouble. Oh, once in a while, somebody would have too much to drink, or some fellow would get into a bit of a squabble with his wife, and Murray would have to act like a real policeman, but most of the time he just walked around the village acting like he was tough, but we all knew better.

Murray was a big round Humpty-Dumpty man with a large drooping black mustache and sad watery eyes. Everybody thought he was the brother of one of the bosses, but he always said he wasn't and told us how his name was different to prove it.

Anyway, after that bad time fire hunting, Murray came around and started asking questions about if we knew about the dead colt, but everybody said they didn't know nothing. After that, every time I seen Murray I thought he really knowed the truth. But, like I said, he was a pretty good guy so he didn't squeal, and that's something I've always tried to do, too, even if it got me into trouble.

So many times I been asked to tell what really happened in Chicago, but I didn't want to be no squealer. I guess it would've been easier on me if I would've, but that's not how I learned to treat people.

# 6

# THE LAST TIME WE TALKED ABOUT SCHOOL LEARNING

**COOPER ANDERSON** In some respects, the mill was like a prison. Once acculturated into its ways, few ever escaped. The mill was a life sentence for most. Joe and I were two of the few who managed to tunnel our way to freedom—Joe because he was physically gifted, I because I harbored an insatiable desire to learn to read.

Some of the corporations which ran the mills in the South actually encouraged educating the children, others like the one which ran Brandon Mill, believed that education would only create a workforce for occupations other than mill work. To educate the children, they believed, would be to diminish the pool of available labor.

Nevertheless, by persistent badgering, I convinced my parents to let me go to a school in Greenville. The income they thus lost by my not working was a considerable burden on them, but I was not to be denied.

The reading habit, once learned, would, for me, never go away. Eventually I graduated from Furman with a degree in Philosophy and, as that was of limited use in a mill, I have found myself committed to the life of an academic.

You have to wonder if there were great minds in the mills which never had the opportunity to be exercised. Was Joe one of these? Probably not. But still, had he gone with me to the school in Greenville, how different his life might have been.

**J.C. HATCH** From time to time some social reformer would come down from up north to try to get the company to start a school for the children. At Brandon, management took the position that the government had no right interfering in what they took to be the business of the employer and the employees, and since the employees didn't seem to be pressing for a school, there was no reason to start one. It was the old situation of not wanting to fix what wasn't broken.

**JOE JACKSON** A big fuss was created one night when a fat man, whose name I can't remember, came into the village. He went around the mill telling everybody that he was an official from the state of South Carolina and that he was calling a meeting that night for all the families in the village.

"Be back at eight o'clock," he told everybody. "I want at least one member of every family. All of you, if possible."

He sure looked like he was important all right, with his black suit and bowler hat and big stomach, but nobody in the village cared much for government people. We didn't ask a lot from the government, and expected even less, so all during the day, people was asking each other if they should go to the meeting or not. By the end of the day it was pretty much decided we'd go, but our guard was up. We wasn't gonna let any fat politician from Columbia tell us what to do or how to do it. We was independent enough in the village and we wanted to keep it that way. We didn't want to lose jobs because of the government sticking their nose into our business. Besides, none of us voted anyway, so we could hardly expect them to be looking out for us. We decided to show up, but not until 8:30. That way, the fat guy with the hat would know that he couldn't push us around any old way he wanted.

The meeting was in one of the old storerooms of the mill. We sat on boxes and spools while he stood up in front on a couple of pallets. I guess that was so he'd look taller and more important.

**COOPER ANDERSON** After the official spent a lot of time telling us how he represented the state of South Carolina, and that he had come to Brandon Mill to look after our interests, he finally got to the point.

"There is a lot of interest in this state in raising the legal age of the workers," he said, "and I'm here to get your support."

It usually took a lot to get these workers riled up about anything, but the mere mention of raising the working age lit a spark quicker than lightning in a dry forest.

"That what you come all the way down here for, mister?" said someone in the back. "Shoulda saved yourself the trip."

"Ain't nobody in Columbia can tell us when and how and where we can work," somebody else said. "We'll damn well work as we see fit."

"We can't have little kids in the mill working long days for short wages," the official said. "That's exploitation of our youth, and it's neither in the best interests of our children nor of our society in general."

"The hell it ain't," said another worker. "Our kids don't work, we don't eat. Think you fat slobs in Columbia can understand that?"

"Then we'll fight for higher wages for you so your kids don't have to work," the official said.

"We ain't that stupid, mister," said the man in the back again. "Wages go much higher the mills close down."

"In a free market economy that may happen, yes, but after a leveling off period ..."

"Stuff your fancy words, you big fat slob," said another worker. "We got jobs now, all of us, because of the mill, and we got houses of our own because of the mill, and we got food because of the mill, and we ain't gonna do nothin' that shuts this mill down. If our kids gotta work, let 'em. What the hell else they gonna do anyway, become president?"

A lot of "that's right," and "better know it" was shouted from the group, almost like a revival meeting.

"We know what it's like to be dirt poor, do you?" someone else said. "We been share croppers, most of us, and that ain't a fittin' way to live. We've gone to bed plenty of nights without enough to eat, and we ain't doin' it again, mister. Not because some politician in a fancy suit comes marchin' in without bein' invited and tells us what he thinks we should do. We know what we should do and we're doin' it."

"Some of us have lived in more places than we can count, but now we got good jobs and we ain't movin' again, so why don't you just leave us be."

The heavyset official took off his hat and began wiping his brow. I don't know how many of these meetings he'd been to before, but this sure looked like his first one. He was getting real nervous. People began popping up all over the room shouting at him, sometimes all at the same time.

"The state ain't tellin' us what our kids are gonna do, mister. We're tellin' our kids what they're gonna do."

"Go back to your rich friends and do anything you want with your own kids, but leave ours alone."

"We all work here, mister, and it don't hurt nobody."

"Besides, work is good for kids. Teaches them things."

This went on for some time, before everybody had their say. The official listened to it all, wiping his forehead and shaking his head "no." When it quieted down enough for him to talk again, he said in a quiet, but firm way, "The children need to be in school, not in the mill."

"Why?" asked one of the workers.

"So they can learn to read and write," he says.

"Why?" asked the same worker again.

"Don't you want them to have a better life?"

"They ain't gonna have a better life, mister. They is gonna work in the mill, just like us."

"But they don't have to."

"We've made good without reading, haven't we? Don't see any reason our kids can't do the same thing."

"If they learn to read and write, they can improve their social and economic status in life."

"Don't need to do that if all they is gonna do is work in a mill."

"Let's let the kids answer that," said the official. "Maybe they don't want to work in the mill all their lives. Maybe they've got dreams of a better life that you're keeping them from."

He turned and looked out over all the people in the big room and then, for some reason, looked right at Joe.

"What about you, son?" he asked. Don't you want to learn to read and write and have a better life?"

**JOE JACKSON** I wanted to disappear right through the floor. Why did he have to look at me when there was lots of us kids there? We didn't speak at these meetings, the grownups did. I didn't know what to say anyway. I never even thought about leaving the mill. The best I could hope for was maybe a better job in the mill.

"Well, don't be afraid, son, speak up," he said.

He was embarrassing me in front of all my family and friends and I didn't like it one bit.

"Don't you really want to learn to read and write?"

I sat there and began to shake.

Finally my father came to my rescue. "Leave the kid alone. He don't need no schooling."

"I'll bet if you ask him he'll tell you he'd really like to read."

"Read what?" my father asked.

"How about the Bible for starts."

"If he wants to know what's in the Bible, the preacher will read it."

"Besides, education don't pay," somebody else added.

"Yeah, and it makes people mean."

"Our kids are mill workers, mister, and they'll be mill workers next year and the year after that and for many a year to come. Schoolin's just a waste of time, and any time away from the mill is money that ain't made."

The fat man looked at me again.

"Is that right, son? You going to be a mill worker all your life?"

I shrugged my shoulders as if to say 'I don't know.'

That was the last time we ever talked about school learning.

# 7

# STORIES FROM ANOTHER WORLD

**COOPER ANDERSON** By the time Joe was about nine or 10, he and his brothers began listening to stories—romantic tales of heroes and villains, of miraculous accomplishments on baseball diamonds far away. To boys imprisoned in the mill, these stories opened up whole new worlds never before even imagined. Remember, they had never read books. They had never even had stories read to them by teachers or parents. They had no radio to bring in distant places. Their world did not go past the outer reaches of the Greenville area, that is, not until Charlie Lebeau took an interest in them.

**JOE JACKSON** Almost all of what we knowed of major league baseball, and it wasn't all that much, came from Mr. Lebeau. He was some kind of salesman with the mill and spent most of his time traveling by railroad to the big cities in the North selling the stuff we made in the mill. At one time or other, he made stops at all the cities that had big league teams, and while he was there he usually went to see a game. He knowed all the teams, and he saw all the players, and for a long time, what he told us was all we knowed about big-time baseball.

I think he loved to tell them stories and looked forward to it as much as we did. Lots of summer evenings after dinner was spent sitting under a tree out by the creek listening to his tales of games and players. He'd take his time, drawing out each story as long as he could, keeping us guessing about how it would end. I don't think there ever was a baseball announcer that painted a better picture of what a game was like than Mr. Lebeau. There was something almost like magic in the way he would describe the game with his accent that he said was French. He had a smile as big as the mill and a voice that sounded more like he was singing than talking.

Everything we knowed about the big leagues came from him. If he told us a particular player was the best hitter in the game, then he was. We had no reason to believe anything else.

He told us the best strikeout pitcher was Rube Wadell, but the hardest thrower was Walter Johnson. So, to us, these things was so. We imagined what it would be like to stand up to the plate and face Johnson. Because Mr. Lebeau told us he threw so fast you could hardly see the ball, we imagined an invisible ball whistling as it flew by.

He told about Wildfire Schulte who he said could throw the ball farther and harder than any outfielder in the game. Oh, how we loved that name—Wildfire. He described how Schulte, with his back against the outfield wall, could take one step forward and throw a strike to home plate. It was because of these stories that later on I began going behind the outfield fence to throw home. I knew I had a specially strong throwing arm, but nobody could throw better than Schulte because Lebeau told us so.

He told us about little Johnny Evers, the smallest player in the majors, who he said wasn't over 120 pounds. That gave us confidence since some of us kids was already bigger than that at 12 or 13. He told us that Kid Elberfield, The Tabasco Kid, was the best base runner; Cy Young the best control pitcher; and The Flying Dutchman, Honus Wagner, the best hitter.

We became them players in our games. The thing was, though, you had to become a player who played the game like you did, even if they played it much better. If you could hit the ball a long way, you could become somebody like "Wahoo Sam" Crawford; if you could pitch fast, maybe Johnson. Once you staked claim to a player, he was pretty much yours until you either got too old to be somebody else, or you stopped playing because you had a family, or maybe you just wasn't good enough to play anymore.

I was Wildfire Schulte; Davey, The Flying Dutchman; Luther, Harry Davis. For a while Jerry was Rube Wadell, but then when he found out how crazy Wadell was, he changed and became Christy Mathewson. Lots of kids wanted to be Christy Mathewson, because he was not only one of the best pitchers, but he was also the best looking, so Jerry had to fight off some of the others to get him. Earl and Ernest was both pretty small so they argued a lot about which one was Wee Willie Keeler. Finally, Mr. Lebeau had to come up with another good little player for one of them, and Ernest became Topsy Hartsel who was good, but not as good as Keeler. Sometimes they switched and Ernie took his turn as Keeler, but he always had to give him back later.

Mr. Lebeau told us a lot about Wagner who he loved and Hal Chase who he hated. Naturally, none of us was ever Hal Chase. Chase was a cheater, said Mr. Lebeau, and none of us was cheaters. Chase would steal other players' cigars and cheat at cards. He would start fights on the field and once even smashed another player's bats because he wouldn't loan him one. There was rumors about him throwing games for profit. Chase was our villain and always played on the opposition's team.

The best and longest stories, though, Mr. Lebeau saved for when he could talk about his most favorite player of all, Napoleon Lajoie.

**CHARLIE LEBEAU** I tried to teach those kids about the good players who were also good men, players like Larry Lajoie.

**DAVID JACKSON** More than anybody, Mr. Lebeau loved the big Frenchman, Napoleon Lajoie. He would sometimes tell us stories about him for what seemed like hours. So, because we knowed most about him, we always liked him even when we was pretending to be somebody else.

What we liked most was that he grew up poor like we did, yet he got the chance to play major league baseball, and he became a great player who all the fans loved.

I'm not sure about Joe, but I know I wanted the chance Larry had (that's what Mr. Lebeau called Lajoie—Larry), and I was sure if I got it I could become a professional ball player.

**CHARLIE LEBEAU** I know I talked a lot about Larry Lajoie, about how poor his French Canadian parents were when he was growing up on Rhode Island.

I told the boys that things got really desperate when Larry's father died when Larry was only 5 years old. Along with his brothers and sisters, he had to go to work as soon as anyone would give him a job. He quit school after the eighth grade to take a job in a lumber yard.

Larry loved baseball, though, and every time he had a chance, he'd skip away from the yard to play ball. It wasn't long before people all over the area started talking about the French kid with the funny name.

One day a man came up to him after a game and asked him if he'd like to play for his Fall River team in the New England League. The man offered him $100 a month. Larry couldn't believe he was being offered more than three times his regular salary to do nothing more than play ball. Of course, he took the money and eventually he was making a lot more than that.

I know the situation wasn't exactly the same as these boys faced, but I was hoping the message wouldn't be lost on them—poverty couldn't hold you back if you had the talent and the desire.

**DAVID JACKSON** When I heard what Napoleon Lajoie was paid to be a ballplayer, it didn't sound real. I didn't know anybody that made more than $15 a week in the mill, except probably the owners of the mill, and I wasn't even sure about that.

Still, if Mr. Lebeau was telling the truth, then that was something I aimed to be part of, because I knew if I could do anything, I could play baseball real good.

**CHARLIE LEBEAU** Did Joe take notice of any of these stories? I don't know for sure, because I never heard him talk about his ambitions. But he did listen.

**JOE JACKSON** Lebeau told us about a lot of really good players but I never thought I would ever meet any of them let alone play with them. They was stories from another world, a world I didn't know nothing about. Besides, if anyone in our village had a chance to play ball outside of there it was Davey, not me.

# 8

# THAT'S ABOUT WHERE OUR DREAMS ENDED

**CHARLIE LEBEAU** As popular as baseball was in the South, not many people thought southern boys would get a chance to play major league ball. After all, major league baseball was a northern industry and, let's face it, the memory of the Civil War was still real in the minds of many. The big league rosters were made up of hundreds of players from the Northeast and Midwest, even some from Canada and Europe, but almost none from the South. This, despite the fact that the Southern Association had been operating as a minor league since 1885. Of course, it didn't operate as a farm system as we have come to know it, yet there were more than a few pretty fair players on its teams.

So it was natural that good southern players like Joe never dreamed of playing in the big leagues. It just wasn't being done much. Of course, this changed after Ty Cobb came out of Georgia and was so successful, but for Joe and his brothers, big league baseball wasn't even a thought, much less a dream. They played the game because they enjoyed it, and because it gave them favored status in the workforce.

**JOE JACKSON** We really didn't think about the future when we was working in the mill because we figured that 20 or 30 years down the road we'd still be there. And why not? It gave us food for the table every day, and it was a whole lot better than cropping shares.

When we had a break, us boys sometimes went outside and laid under the shade of a tree in front of the mill and smoked cigarettes, all the while telling jokes or whistling at girls. But never, in all them years, can I remember us talking about a future away from the mill. Our world was pretty much between Brandon Mill and Greenville, and that's about where our dreams ended, too.

**J.C. HATCH** Joe worked fulltime in the mill for about 12 years, always more of a counter puncher than an attacker, going along with whatever came next. This, of course, would explain, at least to a considerable degree, the trouble he got himself into later in life. I'm sure if you asked many of his co-workers about his problems, you'd find that there weren't a lot of surprise unless it was that he made it as far as he did before the roof caved in.

**DAVID JACKSON** Tell you the truth, I don't know how Joe stood it, working in the mill every day for all them years and not complaining much. Me, I hated it and let everybody know that any time I had the chance. Joe, though, kept pretty quiet about it. Most of the time he didn't say nothing about work, but I know he didn't like it no better than me. Some people bellyache a lot, and some don't. Joe didn't.

**SCOOP LATIMER** He didn't dream of a better world. He didn't long for a life free of the mill, because he didn't know of any. The work was long and hard and seemingly without end. It was what he knew and it was all that he knew. What he wished and waited and prayed for instead was a better job in the mill—a job where the work was easier, or the lint was less. This was the better life.

**COOPER ANDERSON** The romantic image of the disadvantaged youth from the deep South who stoically, but with considerable determination, pursues his lifelong dreams to play in the major leagues and who, in the process, overcomes defeat after defeat only in the end to realize the dream is a paradigm which just doesn't fit Joe. He had no lifelong plans. Joe did whatever came next. He played baseball because he could, and others persuaded him to go in that direction because it was in their best interest, not necessarily Joe's.

# 9

# I ALWAYS PLAYED

**JOE JACKSON** I don't remember when I first played baseball. As far as I know, I always played it. I guess I started sometime, but I must've been pretty little, because I have no memory of a time when I didn't play. I guess you could say I was born a baseball player.

**J.C. HATCH** Soon after villages like Brandon Mill were completed, the mill owners sent recruiters into the mountains and rural areas of South Carolina in search of cheap labor. Times were rough in the South and the owners figured they would have an endless source of labor by just enticing the poor whites in the area to come down from the mountains or to leave the farms in favor of the new mill villages.

Once the owners got them into the villages, a bigger problem arose—keeping them there. Most of these rural folk were totally unprepared for life in the industrial world, and the seventy-hour workweek inside the noisy, lint-filled, crowded factories was more than many of them could tolerate. Some of the workers quit and returned to their farms or mountain shacks, but most were irrevocably trapped by a system they neither understood nor relished. The result, for some families, was a life of perpetual wandering from one mill village to another in search of ... something better. But there wasn't anything better, as one mill was pretty much like another, and the wages varied little, if at all.

Since the turnover of workers was a serious problem, many a plan was hatched to entice the workers to remain in the village and thereby create a reasonably stable, permanent workforce.

One of the plans was to build a baseball field on the mill grounds and organize teams of workers. This proved to be a big success. The mill hands took to the game, which was new to many of them, like ducks to water. Quickly, loyalty to the team, and thus the mill, spread from the players to their fans, to the mill families.

With little else to do in the villages outside of work, baseball became one of the most important aspects of mill life. It seems almost everybody in the villages played, or followed the game. If cotton wasn't the king, as some people were suggesting, baseball certainly was.

**LUTHER JACKSON** We played lots of ball whenever we got the chance—all us Jackson boys. We played "one o' cat," and "three o' cat," and when we didn't have enough for a game, we just played catch. Joey and Davey were the best players and everybody always wanted to beat whatever team they was on. Sometimes the games would get a little rough and some of the guys would start fights and things like that, but the Jacksons always stood together.

**DAVID JACKSON** Maybe we didn't have the best equipment, but that didn't stop us from playing every chance we got. The Jackson brothers could've made a pretty good team, too. We sure played a lot! Sometimes Mother would have to call us a lot of times to come in for Saturday dinner, because when you're in the middle of a game, you can't always just stop like that and go and eat. So after a while, Mother stopped calling more than once, and when we didn't come in pretty soon, she just put the food away. Father said it meant that much more food for him, so he didn't care if we came in or not.

Many times we went to bed hungry but that was OK with us.

**J.C. HATCH** Joe looked like a good athlete from the start but we thought his brother, Davey, was also going to be a pretty fair player, but he had so many accidents in the mill that he never had a chance. He broke his right arm five or six times and that ended any real hope he had for a career. The arm was left slightly bent and stiff and as a result he couldn't catch the ball real well all the time.

**LUTHER JACKSON** I seen a lot of good ballplayers in my time. Most worked hard to get where they was, because for most of us the game takes a lot of practice. But Joe and Davey was different. It's not that they didn't play a lot, but for them, the game always came easy and they could always do what they had to on the field. They wasn't good because they worked hard at it, they was good because they was good!

**JOE JACKSON** Of course the field we played ball on at Brandon Mill wasn't much compared to the ones I played on later, but it was all we knew.

The field was out back between the mill itself and the village dump. The infield was dirt that we trampled down. It wasn't real smooth but that actually helped us some because if you learned to field good there you could probably do it good anywhere. The outfield was grass and weeds and bumpy, but that taught us to never take your eyes off the ball or it might jump right up and take out a tooth or two which it did to Luther once.

On the third base side of the field was the railroad tracks that brought the trains into the mill.

Sometimes when the sun got low behind the mill, the building made a long shadow come across the field and that made it tough to catch the ball.

It wasn't the easiest thing, playing ball on this field, but it sure made good players out of you if you stuck with it.

**J.C. HATCH** When the mill decided to start its own team, the owners asked me to become the manager, which I did.

The Brandon Mill team was similar to most mill teams in the area. We usually had about 12 men on the team—all workers from the mill. We played the other mill teams in what came to be called the Textile Mill League.

Our team was pretty good and we won our share of games over the years, but for a long time we had our eyes on Joe. It was pretty obvious, even when he was young, that he was better than all the other kids. I'd watch him and his brothers play pickup games on the field when the team wasn't using it, and we all could see he had natural talent. What impressed me most was that arm of his. Oh, how he could throw! That was probably because it was longer than any I had ever seen, except of course, his father's.

When he turned 13, I went to some of the men on the team and asked them what they thought about asking Mrs. Jackson if we could use Joe. Some of them didn't like the idea at all. They didn't want to be playing with a 13-year-old, so what they said was that they were afraid that he might get hurt. Joe was probably less likely to get hurt than some older players who didn't have Joe's quick reflexes or natural instincts.

So, for a while we let it go, but I kept watching Joe. After a couple of tough losses I decided to go see Mrs. Jackson regardless.

**MARTHA JACKSON** Mr. Hatch from the mill came to the house to ask if my Joe could play on the mill team. He knew right then he was the best player around so he wanted him to be the team's catcher. They said they'd even pay him something.

I said he could join the team if he wanted to. Of course, I knew he would.

That night Joe asked me what I thought. I told him it was up to him. I just didn't want to see him get hurt, but Joe has a scar on his forehead that he got in those early days. He was catching behind the plate and this big mill hand was pitching to him. He threw one so hard that it forced Joe's hands back pushing the mask into his forehead, leaving a deep cut.

**SUMNER HOCKETT** At first we weren't too crazy to have Joe on the team. The rest of us were in our twenties or thirties and Joe was only a kid, but it didn't take long to see that he could throw just about as good as anybody we had, so Hatch, our manager, put him in as catcher, which wasn't a great idea. Joe didn't know nothing about running a game which a catcher has to do, and he was too young anyway to tell anybody else on the team where to position themselves which our catcher usually did. Besides that, he got hurt a couple of times. I think his mother told Hatch that he couldn't catch anymore, because after he got smashed in the face one time, he never caught again. That was another problem with his being so young—you had to ask his mother everything.

Then Hatch put him on third. I'm not sure, but he probably asked Joe's mother if that was OK. That wasn't the best position for him either, because things happened pretty fast around third and he wasn't always sure what he was supposed to do. So some players yelled at him a few times and he got pretty upset.

I played first, and I remember once when Monoghan Mill had the bases loaded against us with only one out and the batter hit a ground ball to Joe at third, but he wasn't sure whether to come to first, or go home, or try for the double play, so with everybody yelling at him he held the ball too long. By the time he threw it to me at first, everybody was safe, the run scored and we lost the game.

Maybe he should've asked his mother.

**J.C. HATCH** I know the team didn't exactly accept Joe at first, but that all changed one Saturday afternoon.

We were playing Victor Mill, always one of the strongest teams in the league. It was late in the game. I don't remember exactly which inning, but what Joe did I will remember for the rest of my life. The game was tied 2-2 and Biff McGuire was up for Victor with a runner on second and one out. Biff was one of the strongest guys I've ever seen, so it wasn't exactly a surprise when he unleashed a wicked line drive directly over Joe's head who was by then playing right field. The runner on second took off for home, secure in his belief that the ball was up against the fence for at least a double. Nobody could catch up to that ball, I thought, and immediately conceded the run in my mind. I just hoped Joe could track the ball down in time to stop McGuire at second. Well, what happened then you had to be there to see. No description I can give you will do it justice. Joe got a jump on the ball, seemingly just as it was coming off the bat, turned and raced toward the foul pole in the right field corner, reached up with that long arm of his, caught the ball, then whirled and threw in one fluid motion, delivering a perfect strike to second base. The ball never touched the ground, and the runner was doubled off by plenty.

I'm telling you, I've never seen a better play in my life, and I doubt that there are many players in the entire history of the game who could have even caught the ball, let alone made that throw.

From that play on, Joe was a full-fledged member of the team. Nobody could deny him that.

**JOE JACKSON** I pitched for a little while after I stopped catching, but I didn't like that much. What I really liked was playing the outfield because there all you had to do was go after the ball and do the things that came naturally. Besides, I don't think the guys on the team liked me pitching because I threw fast but I didn't always have the best control.

It was hard because I was so much younger than anybody else on the team. Nobody ever said nothing to me about it, but I know they didn't want me on the team at first. But when I started to hit real good and help win games, then they kind of liked me a little.

None of my friends or brothers was on the team, and the older guys didn't talk to me much, so when I wasn't working I was playing and all my friends was together without me. But that was OK, I guess, because I was doing something they couldn't and they probably would've done the same thing if they could've.

**J. C. HATCH** Joe was a terrific natural hitter from the first. Of course, he wasn't a finished ball player by any means. Those of us who knew him never even considered the possibility that he could succeed away from the mill team.

**CHARLIE LEBEAU** That the Jacksons stayed in Brandon Village all those years was a testimony to the power of baseball. All the boys played at seemingly every opportunity. Eventually Davey joined Joe on the team and both became stars who were given better jobs in the mill in deference to their ball-playing skills.

**RICHARD COLZIE** I worked in the mill all them years with Joe and his brothers, and I worked there a lot longer too, because I wasn't no good at baseball. Most of us who stayed in the mill didn't like that the players got treated better than we did. Besides, most players didn't do very good on the job. Joe, for instance, he wasn't a good worker at all. Oh, he did his job when he had to, but that's all he ever done. If he could get away without working at something, then he would. I remember lots of times the foreman got mad at him for not working hard enough, but me, I always worked hard so it don't seem right that Joe and the others got the breaks because of what they could do outside the mill. Once he became the big shot of the baseball team, he hardly did anything in the mill except punch in and punch out. That just didn't seem fair.

**COOPER ANDERSON** The Textile League was a big deal back around the time Joe was playing in it. The mills were connected by a railroad line known as the Belt Line which enabled the teams and their fans to spend their Saturday afternoons at the games.

The games were so popular it wasn't unusual to see most of a village watching. The spirit that was engendered by these contests was something akin to that of a college football game in the twenties.

When Joe became the unquestioned star of the team, he became the biggest thing in the Jackson family's world. What the Tigers and the Athletics were up to was in another world. To the populations of the southern mill towns, the Textile League was the most important sporting endeavor on earth.

**BUDDY DONAHUE** Whenever I could get away from my butcher shop in Greenville I went to the games. The boys played good baseball, tough, aggressive baseball, and Joe was the best of them all.

The first time I saw him was in a game against Victor Mill. He made every play look like it was easy. He was like a big cat, he was so graceful and natural. You could pick him out in a crowd from a half mile away just by the way he ran. He had these long, easy strides that ate up the ground as he glided across the outfield. For a kid as big as he was, he was incredibly graceful.

In that game, he hit a home run over the center field wall that I don't think was ever more than 6 feet off the ground. His home runs, which everybody began calling "Saturday Specials" because so many of them came on Saturdays, always looked more like they were going to go through the outfield wall rather than over it. He never hit that high towering type like Ruth and some of the others did, but his were hit about as hard as anybody's I ever saw.

He got a couple of more hits that day, but it was what he did after the game that really impressed me.

After the last out, Joe stayed in center field while the manager, J.C. Hatch, picked up a ball and fungo bat and standing near second base swung as hard as he could and sent a ball into deep center field. Joe turned, tracked the ball down in the middle of the dump which was beyond the edge of the field, then, almost without setting himself, unleashed a throw toward home plate that sailed over the backstop. The ball had to travel well over four hundred feet on the fly. The crowd let out the biggest cheer of the day.

These "show-outs" as they became known, soon were a regular part of the Saturday afternoon games. Nobody left a game early because everybody wanted to see Joe throw. People started coming from all over to see these "show-outs," and the legend of Joe Jackson was born.

**COOPER ANDERSON** It did not take Joe long to prove that he was the pre-eminent player in the mill circuit, but a position of such status did not come without its own form of pressure. After a while Joe was expected to perform at a level above all the others. That he did so much of the time was a tribute to his undeniably superb innate talent. On the occasions, however, when he did not deliver all that was expected of him, his mood could quickly turn dark. He was wont to become even more taciturn than usual, and for days at a time he acted positively morose.

Was this pressure he was placing on himself? Or was it imposed on him by others? I suppose these are questions that could be asked of any highly successful person.

Despite these moody turns, however, much of the time Joe seemed to enjoy the adulation. He became as respected a mill hand as there was in all the South.

**LUTHER JACKSON** While Joe was playing for the mill we made money because of him. Every time he hit one of them homers, me, Davey, Jerry, and the twins would go through the stands with an old hat in our hands and the people would throw money into it. One time we collected more than 25 dollars for one of his "Saturday Specials." After the game we went home and split the money up, so when Joe had a good game we all had money to go to Morrison's Drugstore in Greenville or to save up and spend on something special.

**JOE JACKSON** Mother could make biscuits and apple jelly about as good as anybody. I used to love to sit in the kitchen when she was making them and smell the jelly while I told her about my games. She heard about every at bat—at least when I was still in Brandon Mill. Father didn't talk to me about the game, but I think he always checked to see how I was doing.

**J.C. HATCH** Joe got lots of gifts from admiring fans. This was an expected part of playing in the Textile League. Without doubt, though, the best gift anybody ever gave him was Black Betsy. It became as much a legend as Joe himself.

**CHARLIE FERGUSON** I was known in the area to be a pretty good bat maker, and since I seen most of the games I knew Joe Jackson was a damn good country hitter. So one day I decided to make a bat especially for him and to give it to him as a present. It was a present for two reasons: first, he didn't figure to be able to pay for it anyway, and second, I kind of hoped he would become a famous player someday and that if he used one of my bats then I would be able to advertise that and sell more bats.

I hunted around till I found this especially good four-by-four length of hickory. It was seasoned and strong and just waiting to be made into a bat for somebody as powerful as Joe. I took my time with it and made it really good. When it was finally done, I spent the better part of a week rubbing coats of tobacco juice into it till it shined deep and black and beautiful. Everybody knew Joe loved black bats, and this was about as beautiful a black bat as I or anybody else ever seen.

Joe didn't know nothing about it, until one cold January night I went over to the Jackson's house and gave it to him. Well, I tell you, his eyes lit up like a little kid's on Christmas morning. I bet Joe slept with that bat, he loved it so much.

From that night on, Joe became famous for that bat, and I did, too. Of course, he went on and done a lot of famous things, while I only done that one, but I'm still pretty proud about it.

**JOE JACKSON** Charlie Ferguson gave me a homemade bat one day and I right away began calling it "Black Betsy." It was a beauty and it worked real good, so I decided to take special care of it. After every game I rubbed sweet oil into it and wrapped it in cotton cloth and put it away real careful. Black Betsy was always good to me and I was always good to her.

**COOPER ANDERSON** I don't know who was better known in the area, Joe or Betsy. As Joe became gradually more famous, so did she. When Joe had a successful game, he shared the praise with her and when he had a poor game, she came in for as much blame as he. Everybody who knew Joe also knew Betsy. She took on a personality of her own.

**J.C. HATCH** Joe became real possessive of Betsy. He wouldn't let anybody else use it, or if he could help it, even touch it. Joe, like a lot of the backwoods guys, wasn't always the most self-confident guy in the world, and deep down in his heart, I think he really believed that some of his success came from that bat. Betsy was more than just his bat. She was his talisman, his friend, his confidant.

**DAVID JACKSON** Don't get me wrong about this, because I was glad to see Joe doing so good in the mill games, but I was always a little jealous about it, too, because I was as good a player as Joe, but I was unlucky. If I wouldn't've hurt myself so many times in the mill, maybe I could've done what he done. But then, maybe I was really the lucky one, because if I was a big league ballplayer like Joe, maybe I would've got into a lot of trouble like he did, and maybe I would've had all the problems he did. I guess I'll never know.

# 10

## MAYBE I SHOULD OF STAYED

**J.C. HATCH** One day just before we were to play a doubleheader, Joe came to me and said that he had been approached by the manager of the Victor Mill team and offered more money to play for them.

My first reaction was anger. Although it happened a lot, I didn't like this idea of recruiting and raiding players. All that meant was that the mills which were making the most money would eventually get the best players, and that didn't seem right. I guess we could have paid Joe more and kept him, but I wasn't about to be blackmailed by this kid who was still a teenager.

I told Joe we couldn't pay him more and that if he left the team he would be a traitor to everybody in Brandon. Joe said he'd have to think about it and give me his answer the next day.

After I calmed down some, I reasoned that there was no way I was going to be able to keep Joe anyway. He was just too good to stay where he was. Sooner or later he would move on.

**JOE JACKSON** I didn't exactly like the idea of playing for Victor Mill, but they offered me $4 a game, and that was a lot better than I was making for Brandon. Besides, they had a real good team.

I talked to Mother about it, and she told me to do what I thought was right. I didn't know for sure what that was, but I kept thinking that what if I got hurt or something, and couldn't play anymore, like Davey? A player should get as much money as he can because he don't know when he wouldn't be able to get any more.Some of the people in Brandon didn't like it a whole lot when I started playing for Victor, but I'll bet they would've done the same thing if they had the chance. A player's got to make money when he gets the chance.

**SUMNER HOCKETT** When Joe took the money and ran to Victor leaving his home team without even thinking of loyalty or his friends, it was just an example of how he was going to act later.

He never cared about anybody except himself. He was just plain greedy, and that's what got him into so much trouble.

To tell you the truth, that's pretty much the way he played the game, too. He cared more about his record than he did about the team's. Sometimes he'd swing for a home run when he should've been concerned about just getting a runner to second, or he'd make a long throw to home, just to show off, when he should've thrown to second.

**COOPER ANDERSON** Let there be no doubt about it, Joe was good for Brandon Mill. He gave the workers there something to be proud of, and they were thrilled to call him one of their own. When Joe signed with Victor, some villagers felt betrayed.

**JOE JACKSON** I played good for the Victor Mill team. I don't mean to sound conceited or nothing, but like everybody says, it ain't conceited if you can do it. Well, I did it. I hit over .400 for the team all season, had a bunch of home runs, and played pretty good outfield.

I got to admit I did get a little spoiled once in a while. Mostly though it was on account of my throwing, because every now and then I'd kind of play a ball sort of slow so that the runner would think he could make the next base, and ... wham! I'd nail him easy. I know that ain't always right, but I never done it if the game was real close.

We played on Saturdays mostly, and the rest of the time I was still working in the mill, only some of the bosses was a little mad that I wasn't playing for Brandon no more, so sometimes I got bad jobs in the mill.

The people at Victor Mill treated me real good all season. I even got a raise to $4.25 a game and they let me keep the Saturday Special money.

In about the middle of the season, some of the fans began sticking dollar bills into the holes in the outfield fence every time I come to bat. If I hit a home run, I got to keep the money. "Fence money" they called it.

So I was doing pretty good at Victor Mill. Maybe I should of stayed there forever, but things just didn't work out that way.

# 11

# I ALWAYS LIKED KATIE

**LOLLIE GRAY** There never was as much connection between the lintheads and the citizens of Greenville as you might think. Those of us who lived in the town had our own social circles and little or no connection with mill families. Oh, sure, we'd see them come into town once in a while to do some shopping for something that they couldn't buy at their company store, or to go to Harrison's Drugstore, things like that. But there were two distinct groups—the lintheads and the Greenville citizens.

I probably saw Joe and his brothers in town from time to time, but if I did, I paid no attention to them. It wasn't until I saw Joe playing for Victor Mills, down in Greer, that I took any notice whatsoever.

In those days I was obsessed with the game of baseball, with watching it, with playing it, with organizing it. I was a pretty good athlete at Clemson College where I played baseball and football. When my college days were behind me, I still longed to play the game. With the help of my father, General J. W. Gray, who was then an official for Greenville County, I organized a semi-professional baseball team and began scouting for the best ballplayers in the Greenville area. Since we didn't have a formal arrangement with any professional league, I called the team the Near Leaguers. This was in 1906.

Right away I collared some good area talent—Scotty Gray (no relation) from over in Easley and Jimmy Piccard from Spartanburg signed up immediately. They, like most of the boys on the team, were college chums. We had a pretty good team but were short a good left-handed power hitter. For some time I'd heard stories about this mill kid, Joe Jackson, who was supposed to be able to throw like a pro with his right hand and hit like a pro left-handed. Still, I was hesitant to go see him play. After all, he was an illiterate kid. How the hell was he going to fit in with the college guys? Besides, the stories from the Textile League were all exaggerated. If you listened to all those stories, you would have thought every other guy on the team was a Honus Wagner or a Nap Lajoie.

The biggest problem, though, was that nobody on the team wanted to play with Negroes or with lintheads. Baseball in our circles was considered a gentleman's game played by decent and honest men. There was no place in the game for the likes of a Joe Jackson.

The team got off to a bit of a rough start and I was feeling the pressure to produce a winning team. Since we weren't affiliated, we needed to be successful if we were going to survive. The more we lost, the more the name Joe Jackson kept popping up. I kept hearing that Joe Jackson, the stupid linthead, could play the game as well as anyone in the area. So, one day after a particularly bitter loss, I took the short train ride over to Greer to see for myself.

Joe was playing center field. By the fourth inning he had already thrown a runner out at the plate, hit one line drive over the fence in right, and one up against it, and snared every ball hit his way. I didn't need to see any more. Between innings I introduced myself to him and asked him to join the team. He asked me how much we were paying and I told him $5 a game. Apparently that was all he wanted to hear, because he said yes. I told him I'd be back the next day with a contract for him to sign.

"I don't need no contract," he said. "Your word's good enough for me."

I didn't think at the time, of course, he didn't want a contract because he could neither read it nor sign it. But, I'll say this, with me he always lived up to his word.

I knew some of the guys weren't going to be real happy about Joe joining us, but I also saw that he could play and I figured that would eventually make a difference to our boys.

Joe was, I think, about 19 that day when I saw him play, and what I remember most, what has stuck with me all these years, was the sound his bat, Black Betsy, made when she hit the ball. I tell you, nothing in the game has ever sounded like that. I don't know what it was, whether it was the particular kind of wood that the bat was made of, or something in his swing, but anybody who ever heard it, and who loves the game, remembers it as something truly special.

**JOE JACKSON** When Mr. Gray asked me to play for the Near Leaguers, it was good because it meant that I could play for his team and for the Victor Mills team, too, seeing as how they played games at different times. Anyway, all the best players played for more than one team.

From then on, I began to work less and less in the mill, and finally not at all. Father, by this time, had a portable sawmill, so when I wasn't playing or working in the mill, I helped him. So did my brothers. Mostly, though, I was almost a full-time player. I really thought that I was playing about as much as I ever would, or about as good for that matter.

With the Near Leaguers I went back to doing some catching, but I also played third base and the outfield. Wherever Mr. Gray wanted me to play was all right, so I didn't complain or nothing, because I knowed most of the players on the team was college players, and I didn't want to give them any reason to get mad at me.

**SCOTTY GRAY** Not that it was all their fault or anything, but those boys from the mill were always trouble. They weren't educated and they just didn't understand how to get along in civilized society. I know that I never left any money or anything of value lying around the locker room when Joe was near. Most of the time, he wasn't around though, because he pretty much didn't have anything to do with the guys on the team. I mean, he didn't eat with us or anything. How could he? He couldn't even read the damn menu!

**LUTHER JACKSON** Joe was the best player on the Near Leaguers just as he was on the Brandon team and the Victor team, only some people didn't want to say that. Some people didn't want Joe to be the best player on the Near Leaguers because he come from the mill.

**SCOTTY GRAY** Some guys—not just me—gave Joe a hard time. I mean, if he couldn't take it, what the hell was he doing on the team in the first place?

**JOE JACKSON** It was about the time I started playing for the Near Leaguers that I begun seeing a lot of Katie. She came to most of the games and usually we went back to Brandon together and talked about a lot of things, but mostly baseball. She begun learning all about the game, and I liked that because I didn't really have no friends on the team.

**KATIE WYNN JACKSON** You know how it is when you know somebody so long you can't remember not knowing them? Well, that's how it is with Joey and me. As far as I can remember, I've always known him. We were kids together, we grew up together and did all the things people do when they've known each other so long.

At first I didn't pay much attention to him. He was just one of the boys in the village, and us girls didn't have much to do with them. They were working most of the time, anyway. But later, as I grew up and began to fancy the company of boys, it was always Joey.

We didn't do a lot of very exciting things I'd have to say. Sometimes we'd go for walks out along the stream, or into Harrison's for a dope and lime, or we'd just sit on the steps in front of my house and talk. Of course, I did most of the talking, I guess, because Joey wasn't exactly what you'd call a real good conversationalist. But he was a pretty good listener. Mostly we were just good friends.

**JOE JACKSON** I always liked Katie because she had gone to school and could write and read but she never acted like she was smarter than me or nothing. She never talked about what she could read, and she would never read when I was around unless it was something like a sign or a menu. Even then, she never made a fuss about it. She would just read something then act like a normal person.

# 12

# MAYBE SOMEDAY I COULD PLAY IN THE MAJORS

**CHARLIE LEBEAU** It's difficult to overemphasize just how popular baseball was in the years immediately following the turn of the century. Nearly every town, village and city had a team. The population was going baseball mad. And it wasn't just the men. Women, too, were becoming fans in increasing numbers, and even the Negro population was flocking to the ball fields.

Newspaper coverage was expanding. Presidents were throwing out first balls, Teletype re-creations of games were beginning, and fans were attending games in record numbers. Baseball was firmly cementing its hold on the public consciousness and laying unchallenged claim to the title of "The National Pastime."

At the center of this passion were the professional major leagues. Although limited geographically to the northeast quadrant of the country, they nevertheless dominated what was happening in baseball around the rest of the country. How much did Joe and his brothers know about the major leagues? Well, I told them lots of stories about some of the great players and they heard some of the re-creations over at the Grand Hotel in Greenville.

**COOPER ANDERSON** Throughout the latter years of the 19th century and the earliest years of the 20th, baseball leagues, organizations, and teams came and went about as quickly and often as the change of seasons. One thing was certain, though—the country was falling in love with the game, even if it was unclear as to what shape and form the organization of the game would eventually take.

At first the National League held unchallenged claim to the title of "the major league." Then, in 1903, Ban Johnson's American League arose primarily out of the Midwest as a viable second league. In between there were numerous other pretenders to the throne but none survived their infancy.

The minors, too, were becoming increasingly popular, but they were being formed and dismantled at a furious pace.

Let me give you just one example—the International League which grew out of the Eastern League. It began as a 10-team league in 1884, dropped four teams at the end of that season, and changed its name to the New York League. Two years later it merged with a handful of Canadian teams, became an eight-team league and changed its name to the International League. The following year it became a 10-team league again when it picked up two teams from the recently-folded New Eastern League. The following year it dropped two teams, then the next year it exchanged two of its teams for new ones. Instability reigned even as the popularity increased. No region of the country remained untouched by organized baseball.

In 1901, the minors, concerned about stability in the face of the expanding major leagues, organized the National Association of Professional Baseball Leagues. One of their first acts was to create a hierarchy of leagues, albeit something of an arbitrary one. In 1903 they recognized the National and American as major leagues and divided the remainder of the leagues into rankings known as Class A, B, C and D.

**BUDDY DONAHUE** Greenville was baseball hungry in those days. Oh, we had the Textile League and it was doing extremely well, but its primary appeal was to the mill workers and their families, and we had Lollie Gray's Near Leaguers who played good ball and attracted big crowds, but many of us longed for a fully professional team—a team in organized ball's minor leagues.

In 1907 and 1908 the South Carolina League operated as a Class D league with teams in Chester, Florence, Orangeburg, Rock Hill, Spartanburg and Sumter. A number of us businessmen in Greenville got together for a series of meetings to discuss putting up the money for a local franchise. We reasoned that baseball was good for business and that Greenville could be good for baseball. Like a lot of business ventures this took its sweet time coming together.

Then in the winter of 1908, a new league was formed—The Carolina Baseball Association. Greenville was to be one of its charter members along with Anderson and Spartanburg from South Carolina, and Charlotte, Greensboro and Winston-Salem from North Carolina.

There was, right from the start, a lot of excitement about the team. The paper wrote story after story about the upcoming season, the mayor made speech after speech, and considerable energy was poured into arguing about a suitable name. Finally the "Spinners" was chosen over the "Weavers."

I was one of the representatives on a committee to find a manager. We wanted someone who was familiar with both the area and professional baseball. After interviewing a number of candidates, we settled on Tommy Stouch.

**CHARLIE LEBEAU** Tommy was a tall and lanky one-time infielder for the old Louisville Sluggers of the National League. Mostly, though, he spent his career as a player-manager in just about every league in the South and at a few southern colleges to boot. He was a pleasant man with a warm smile and an easygoing manner.

**TOMMY STOUCH** I was playing second base in a game against the Near Leaguers when a tall, thin fellow stepped to the plate. He didn't appear to have it in him, but he drove the ball on a line like a bullet toward the very spot where I was standing. Now, I had a lot of baseball experience and though getting a little old for active service, I still prided myself that I knew how a ball ought to be fielded. But that pellet caromed off my shins before I had time to make any effort to field it, and it hurt. I thought to myself, if this rube hits them like that every time, he must be some whale.

In that game, he made three hits, two of them for extra bases, and they were all ringing smashes that left a trail of blue flame behind them as they shot through the air.

I said to my pitcher, "Bill, you watch this young fellow and see if you can discover his weakness."

We played five games in all at the burg, and every day Jackson walloped the ball. The last day he drove one straight at Bill's head. Bill looked at it for about a thousandth of a second, and then ducked as if he were dodging a shell from a Krupp mortar.

"Did you discover his weakness?" I asked Bill after the game was over.

"No," replied Bill, "but he certainly discovered mine."

After the series I hunted up Jackson. "I am going to manage Greenville next year," I told him, "and I would like to have you play with me, if we can agree upon terms."

"All right," said Joe right off. "I would like to play with Greenville."

"How much are you getting now?" I asked.

"Thirty-five dollars a month in the mill," replied Joe.

"Very well," I said, "how much do you want to play for me?"

"Well," said Joe, "you see, I am getting along pretty well. I get $35 a month from the mill, and I get $5 a game on Saturdays for playing ball so that gives me $55 a month in all. I wouldn't want to give up my job unless I could see something in sight. I think I ought to be worth $65 a month to you."

"Joe," I said, "if you will promise to let corn whiskey alone and stick to your business, I will pay you $75 a month."

"I will work my head off for $75," said Joe, and that was our bargain.

**SUMNER HOCKETT** I come over to the Spinners just like Joe right when the team was being started.

It was a real exciting time for all of us. The city was buzzing over the team and it seemed that just about everybody was catching baseball fever. I got to admit that Joe was part of the reason. People seen him play for the Near Leaguers, so they knew he was darn good, but we had some other good players, too. The problem was, he got most of the attention so that didn't make him any more popular with us. The fact was, he wasn't any too popular anyway, him being from the mill.

**TOMMY STOUCH** When spring training began, I knew right off that Joe had a spot on the team all but locked up, so rather than pretend that he was competing for a position, I announced to the *Greenville News* that he would be the opening day center fielder. The news was greeted with great enthusiasm by the Brandon faithful, who by all appearances, were still eager to claim him as their own despite his defection to Victor Mill.

The rest of the team wasn't as obvious to me, but in time I put together a squad of some local boys mixed with a few from other southern states and even a couple from as far north as Illinois and Pennsylvania. Several of them I had known from my college ball days, and most of the others had come recommended by former teammates.

As would be his fate for the next decade or so, Joe stood alone on the team. He was an illiterate mill hand in the midst of players with at least some education. Now I don't want to characterize the Spinners, or any of the other teams he played on for that matter, as a group of geniuses. How many of them ever read anything more challenging than the morning sports page is questionable. If any of them could have told you more about *Moby Dick* other than he was a whale, I would be surprised. But by not being able to read at all, Joe was in a whole other world—almost as if he were a blind man in the world of the sighted.

As far as I know, he never had any real friends on the team. Some boys teased him mercilessly, but he seemed to tolerate it reasonably well. At the very least, he could get away from the ribbing by going home to Brandon every night where he fit in perfectly.

There was never any doubt in my mind that eventually Joe would move on to play ball at a higher level, but always in the back of my mind was the obvious question: could he adjust to life outside the mill? I had my doubts.

**JOE JACKSON** Ol' Tommy Stouch was a good manager. I got along with him from the start because I knowed he had a lot he could teach me about baseball. I mean, Mr. Hatch knowed something about the game, too, but he never played in the majors like Tommy, and I don't think he ever went to college like Tommy either. Anyway Tommy made me the center fielder on the Spinners and that was all right with me because he said my future as a player was in the outfield, and I believed him. The thing was, he talked like there would be a future in the game for me, and for the first time in my life I began thinking about that—about the future.

Maybe someday I could play in the majors like Tommy said. I began talking to Katie about this and she said Tommy probably knew what he was talking about seeing as how he played there.

I found out that he only played in four games for the Louisville team, but that was still more than anybody else I ever knowed.

I decided to listen close to what he had to tell me and then see what happened from there.

**BILLY PRESSLY** When I first seen Joe, he was standing next to the bench looking kind of lost, like he was waiting for somebody to tell him what to do. He'd probably still be standing there if Tommy hadn't told him to go out to center field. I pointed to center just to make sure and then trotted out next to him to play left. I talked to him a little bit about calling loud for the ball so we wouldn't run into each other. He seemed to get the picture.

He was a good-looking athlete, I got to say that. He didn't look like he had any fat and he had that kind of easy walk that only the great players have. His jet black hair was carefully flattened down and parted right dead in the middle. He had sharp features, steady eyes and a downright pleasant smile.

I found out as the season went on that he could talk about baseball easy enough, but he always seemed to be on guard like he was afraid the conversation might turn to something that would embarrass him. Mostly though, he stayed out of long conversations.

**BUDDY DONAHUE** We played our first home game against the Anderson team. They called themselves the Electricians. The Spinners against the Electricians, not very exciting names to be sure, but certainly they suggested the nature of the towns they came from.

**G. HEYWOOD MAHON** I was proud to be the mayor of Greenville when Joe was playing for us. In fact, I threw out the first ball at the first game in the first season for the Spinners. It was a proud moment in Greenville's proud history.

A lot of people don't remember that Greenville residents opposed secession in 1860, making our city a true island of Unionist sentiment deep in the heart of the South. So we had always been an independent lot and proud of it. Then with the coming of the Spinners we had a team we could rally behind, and with mighty Joe leading the way, we showed the spirit that made us famous.

**LUTHER JACKSON** What I remember most about that first Spinners game, other than what Joe done, of course, was the stupid mayor throwing out the first ball which sailed over the catcher's head and into the backstop. The crowd went wild for the longest time.

**COOPER ANDERSON** The crowd for opening day was something! Greenville hadn't seen anything quite like it since they announced the War Between the States was over.

The town band played outside the ball grounds as just about everybody in town headed for the game. Those who came from elsewhere used the new line put in by the Greenville Traction Company just to facilitate the team's fans. The stands were decked out in red, white and blue bunting, and every politician within a hundred miles was in a front row seat.

Every seat was taken and every inch of standing room was contested for. If you were lucky enough to get a ticket, a good one could be had for a quarter, a better one for 40 cents. If you had a car or a buggy, you could, for 50 cents, park it along the left field foul line.

The whites were in the best seats, the blacks in their special section, and young boys who couldn't get in, hung around outside with high hopes of being lucky enough to run down a foul ball, or if the gods were really smiling, maybe even one of Joe's Saturday Specials.

Long before the first pitch, Joe was carrying the hopes of the city.

**JOE JACKSON** If truth be told, when I woke up that morning of the first Spinners game and seen that it was all drizzly and overcast, I was really hoping that the game would be called off because I was kind of nervous. I didn't want to look bad in front of all them fans and with a wet field you never know what might happen.

Once the game started, my jumpy stomach mostly went away.

**"SPECS" McLAUGHLIN** I umpired that opening game for the Spinners and distinctly remember Joe out in center field. It was the first time I had seen the young man, but not the first time I had heard of him. Word was he was something special. I guess he was.

The first time he came to bat I could see a look of panic in his eyes. This was one scared young man, make no doubt about it. I wanted to say something to him about how this was only a game, and that he should relax, or maybe crack a joke or something to loosen him up, but as umpire that wasn't really my place and I was afraid someone would take it the wrong way.

I actually felt a little sorry for the kid. He was under a lot of pressure, and he sure didn't give the impression he was up to the task at all. Then the most amazing thing happened. On the first pitch, he unleashed the most fluid but viciously hard swing I had ever seen, sending the ball to the center field wall on a line. He may have been nervous but he knew what to do with a bat. When he saw the pitch that he liked, his natural instincts took over, and what instincts they were.

Joe got two doubles, a triple, and a line out that almost took the first baseman's head off. But it was his fielding that I remember most. Late in the game he raced full speed into right center and caught the ball, leaping and timing the catch perfectly. What was so impressive was that the ball squirted out of his glove while he was still going full speed, and without hesitating Joe reached out and speared it with his bare hand and then turned and made a perfect throw to the second baseman. The locals went so wild that I had to hold up the game for several minutes.

Now let me tell you, I pitched in the majors for a few years but never saw anybody with better natural reflexes. Joe was born to be a ballplayer. My baseball career was certainly nothing special, but I did umpire the first professional game that Joe Jackson played. That's something I will always remember.

**G. HEYWOOD MAHON** We won that first game 14 to 1 and forever after were known as the city that brought Joseph Jefferson Wofford Jackson to the American public. He was a fine young man then. I don't know and don't care what happened to him later, but when he was playing for us he was a gentleman, a great athlete and a tribute to Greenville, South Carolina. I, for one, am proud to have known him.

**COOPER ANDERSON** The conditions under which teams like the Spinners played were varied, to say the least. Schedules were inconsistent and sometimes changed with little or no warning; press coverage was, at times, thorough beyond belief, at other times, virtually nonexistent. Papers didn't always publish on holidays so some games went unreported on altogether. Box scores sometimes listed the same player with different first names in successive games. If something exceptionally newsworthy demanded more paper space than usual, they didn't publish them at all.

More than a few games were decided by rocks and gopher holes. Some of the infields were stone hard, others soft sand; a few slanted up hill. At least one was built partially over the water, another was built on rollers, and then stored in a barn when the game was over.

A history of some minor league franchises would read more like a history of the fire departments, as wooden grandstands often went up in flames, but concrete and steel were out of the price range of most teams. The clubhouses themselves were often lacking in such basic amenities as locker rooms for the players.

Despite these irregularities, however, many a great player came up out of the minors during these years—Joe, and Tris Speaker, Nap Rucker and Ty Cobb just to mention a few.

Of course, some of the players became "legends" in the minors without that translating to major league fame. Most of the fans in the Greenville area knew of Glenn Liebhardt, for example. Liebhardt played for Memphis in the Southern Association in 1906 when he completed 45 of his 46 starts, winning 35 games including nine of 10 in the five doubleheaders he started. Percival Wheritt Werden of the Western League once hit 45 home runs and batted .428 in a season before those kinds of power figures were even dreamed of.

**KATIE WYNN JACKSON** One day near the beginning of the Spinners season, me and Joe were walking out by the creek when I turned to Joe and said we ought to set a date to get married now that he had a professional career. I wasn't exactly serious because we had never really talked about this in a real way, but without even looking up he said, "OK."

That was pretty much it, no big romantic scene or anything, just, "OK."

"When do you think?" I asked.

Joe thought for a minute. "Well, July 19 is an off day. I guess that'll be as good as any."

"I guess it will," I said.

So that was that. We told our parents that night and they said they thought it was all right, too.

I was real happy as me and Joe were best friends and it sure looked like he was going to do well playing baseball. I didn't want to stay in Brandon all my life, and although I wasn't sure Joe shared that dream, I was pretty certain even then that he was fated for something better.

**MARTHA JACKSON** I always liked Katie. She was a nice young girl who was schooled in Greenville and could read and write. I figured she would be good for Joe. If Joe was going to play baseball for a living then somebody would have to take care of his business things like contracts. For certain I didn't know nothing about professional baseball, but I was sure the people who ran it would take advantage of people like Joe if nobody watched out for him.

Of course, I wasn't thinking about him playing away from the South. That was something that none of us expected.

**DAVEY JACKSON** I wasn't surprised when Joe told us he was getting hitched to Katie—nobody was. In the village everybody seen them together for such a long time that it was just expected that they would get married when the right time come. I guess Joe thought this was the right time.

**COOPER ANDERSON** Joe had known Katie since they were little kids running around the village, so it seemed natural that they would eventually get married. In fact, I can't ever remember Joe spending time with any other young girl. He was 19 and she 15. In the South, marrying at such a tender age wasn't unusual. Since they had few opportunities to meet anyone else, the mill boys generally married girls from their mill village.

**LUTHER JACKSON** Just like when he was playing for Brandon and Victor, Joe was the best player on the Spinners team right from the get-go. People came from all over the South just to see him play. Pretty soon every place I went people was calling me "Joe's little brother," which was a pretty good thing to be called. Sometimes people would buy me a free dope and lime or even lunch just because of Joe.

Being Joe would've been the best, but being his brother wasn't bad.

**COOPER ANDERSON** It continues to amaze me how a simple game like baseball can unite people in such common purpose. The Spinners were Greenville's claim to fame, and Joe was quickly becoming the most famous of them all. By mid-May, he was hitting over .350 and leading the league in home runs. His Saturday Specials were bringing the good folks of Greenville to their feet.

**SCOOP LATIMER** Covering Joe as I did from the very start of his professional career—I was the sports beat writer for the *Greenville News*—I saw him gradually ascend a pedestal, the height of which he never knew until he fell from its lofty elevation.

**COOPER ANDERSON** The team got off to a flying start which made Buddy Donahue and the partners in the business venture extremely happy. However, in early July the team went into a protracted slump, losing 11 of 13 games, and dropped into second place. Even Joe, although still hitting over .300 wasn't hitting with the power he had demonstrated earlier in the season.

Some of the players began bickering and some of the fans were calling for a shake-up of the lineup. Like the other teams in the league, however, we only carried 12 players, so there weren't a whole lot of changes we could make without getting new players, and since all the good players were already signed, we were pretty much locked into what we had.

For a while some of the fans started getting a little nasty, but never with Joe. He was a hero from day one, and slump or no, he was their champion. Some players though were the targets of angry fans. One of them, Scott, our big first baseman, even went into the stands one afternoon after one of the hecklers.

It's so difficult for me to believe all those things people said about Joe later. He always played hard simply because he knew that if you play hard people will like you.

Joe wanted to be liked. I could see that in the way he treated children. He didn't talk down to them because he didn't have to. After almost every game they would cluster around him and he would take the time to talk to them, equal to equal. Joe always seemed to be more comfortable with the kids than with his teammates. Perhaps he cherished the time with them precisely because it was time he didn't have to spend with teammates.

I don't think he was ever as comfortable with the adult fans as he was with the kids. Oh, he liked their adulation all right but from a certain distance—say from the stands. And sportswriters were even more difficult. They asked challenging questions that he didn't understand; they probed depths better left undisturbed.

**BILLY ESKEW** I was the luckiest kid in Greenville in 1908, because Mr. Donahue, who was a good friend of my father's, let me be the official mascot for the Spinners. I got to wear the uniform with the big green "G" on it. At 9 years old I was a part of the greatest thing ever to happen to Greenville.

I traveled with the team to faraway places like Charlotte and Anderson; I sat on the bench with the team; I knew the players. I was the envy of every kid in town.

To me, the players on the team were giants, figuratively and literally. They were the heroes of my youth, plain and simple, and they will never be replaced no matter how long I live, for heroes are of a particular time and place.

These 9-year-old eyes saw some great players on that team, and although I've seen thousands since then, my memory tells me I've never seen better. There was Hyder Barr who seemingly scored in every game and who not only hit .299 for the season, but started 12 games as a pitcher, and Scott, our big first baseman, who scooped up every ball that came his way, and Brumfield who could defy the laws of nature with acrobatic moves at shortstop which must have been taught to him by the very devil in exchange for his soul. Pressley, our tall right fielder, could cover more ground in the outfield with every stride than any man or animal alive. McFarlin, our primary pitcher, could throw so hard that sometimes the ball traveled faster than the speed of light and would disappear on its way to the plate. Tommy Stouch, our second baseman and manager, must have been present when God invented the great game because he knew everything there was to know about baseball. By "everything" I mean everything. He was the world's foremost authority and nobody argued with him about anything related to the game. When he made a pronouncement it was if the clouds parted and heavenly authority spoke from on high.

Each of these players was, you see, at least 8 feet tall and in the heat of competition shot fire from their eyes. Or so it seemed to this 9-year-old.

Yet above these deities stood another—the god of the gods, a man whose skills were so great that the world stood still every time he stepped to the plate or unleashed a throw from the artillery that was his left arm. Joe Jackson was simply not mortal, and any kid who doubted the truth of this and had the gall to say so in public was likely to be pummeled by me and the other cognoscenti to the very edge of his existence or until we were pulled off the villain by someone bigger than us. Joe was the kids' champion. He talked to us, and who would have expected a god to converse with any mortal, especially a kid? He let us hold "Black Betsy," and where else could you actually touch the sacred hammer of the gods?

Joe Jackson was and is my hero. If he today stands blemished I cannot see the stains. I see only a giant talking to a kid on his knees at the altar of greatness.

**LUTHER JACKSON** When Joey was in that slump with the Spinners, I knew exactly what was wrong with him. Them papers didn't get it right. They said he was tired. He wasn't tired, he was nervous.

What with the wedding and everything in front of him he couldn't think enough about baseball.

The reason I know I was right about that is, look at what happened after the wedding. He started hitting like the old Joe and the team started winning again.

**SCOOP LATIMER** Joe Jackson made the greatest home run of his career in Greenville. The home run was made on Cupid's diamond and the victory was a fair young lady named Katie.

**BUDDY DONAHUE** As soon as Joe got the wedding out of the way, he began concentrating on baseball again and as a result, the team took off in the standings. It was becoming readily apparent to everyone that as Joe went, so did the Spinners. The only problem for us in the lower minor leagues was that if a player shone too brightly, he was likely to move up the ladder. It was a real dilemma for me and the other owners. Promote Joe in the press and we sold more tickets; promote him too much and he would be gone.

So what we tried to do was strike a healthy balance. Maybe we'd pull Joe from a game in which we had a big lead so that he wouldn't run up his numbers; maybe we'd push Scoop to go easy on the superlatives once in a while.

But deep down we knew the inevitable—Joe was too good for us.

Before the season was over, a few scouts from the major leagues began sniffing around. When we spotted one, we did what we could to throw him off the scent. One time, I remember, some guy came down from Boston saying he was a bird dog for their team. Well, we gave him a great seat right behind the plate, but we made sure he was surrounded by a couple of the locals who were clued in. In the third inning Joe made an especially good running catch in center.

"I'll be dammed," said one of our guys loud enough for anybody within five rows to hear. "That's the first time all month he's made a decent catch."

"How many balls did he drop last week alone?" asked the guy sitting on the other side of the scout. "Four, wasn't it?"

"Five I thought it was. At least five."

"Problem is he don't care."

"Ah, that's the way he acts most of the time."

"I don't think he really wants to play ball."

"Way I hear it, he'll never leave the South."

"Ain't good enough anyway, so I don't see as it really matters much."

And so it would go through the course of a game. A man's got to protect his investment. That's the American way.

**JOE CANTILLON** While I was managing the Washington club, on a tip from a writer, I went down to South Carolina to check Jackson out. The trip turned out to be a bloody bore and the same went for Jackson. As far as I could tell, he was nothing more than a bush-league flash in the pan.

Well, was I right?

**SUMNER HOCKETT** Harrison's Drugstore developed into something of an agora—a public meeting place where the locals rehashed the daily doings of the Spinners in particular and baseball in general. Often Charlie Lebeau held court as the resident expert on baseball in the North, or one of the local "bugs," as the avid fans were sometimes called, expounded on some theory as to what was wrong with Tommy Stouch's batting order or why Hyder Barr couldn't hit the curve ball. Such is the nature of the game that even a casual observer can determine culpability. The game is simple enough, and most males, having played it on some level, feel completely confident in expressing opinions delivered as expertise.

About Joe, everyone, it seems, had an opinion. Take your pick: he's lazy, irresponsible, stupid; he's talented, unsullied, natural; he's taciturn, uncommunicative, immature.

When Latimer referred to him as illiterate in a long piece that was essentially supportive the "Joe is stupid" refrain caught on. When he misjudged a fly ball he was deemed to be "lacking in the concentration of an educated man."

Joe, for all of his brilliance on the field, didn't handle the criticism well. His psyche just wasn't strong enough to deflect the barbs. Usually, when attacks got to him, he retreated to Katie or his mother or brothers. Sometimes he would spend time with the little kids who loved him unconditionally. As time when on he made fewer and fewer visits to Harrison's. It was his wont to avoid anything which might hurt.

**RICHARD COLZIE** As soon as Joe became the big shot on the local team, his head got even bigger. He thought he was better than the rest of us in the mill but he wasn't. He didn't want no part of us, but he was the same as us. He couldn't read no better than us which wasn't at all and he couldn't work no better than us. He could hit a baseball farther than us, but that didn't make him better, just stronger.

I ain't afraid to admit it: I didn't have no use for Joe when he worked with us in the mill and I sure as hell didn't have no use for him when he became this famous baseball player with a big head.

**CHARLIE LEBEAU** Because he was so good, Joe was the subject of considerable controversy. This naturally happens with good players. When you're on a pedestal, you may be higher up, but you're also a better target.

Not even Lajoie was above the name calling, and he was unquestionably the greatest second baseman who ever lived. One scout from Boston even said Larry would never amount to much as a hitter. So much for expert opinion!

The difference was that Joe let it get to him, Larry never did. Maybe ultimately that's why Larry is in the Hall of Fame and Joe isn't.

**SCOOP LATIMER** It was about this time that Joe picked up the moniker, "Shoeless Joe," placed on him appropriately enough by yours truly.

What precipitated the name-giving was an event in a game the Spinners played in Anderson. Jackson was hailed in from the outfield to pitch. The following day he was dispatched to the outfield with an extremely sore foot resulting from pushing off the rubber. When he came to bat, he slipped off his shoe and proceeded to unleash Black Betsy, the result of which was a vicious home run over the center field wall. As he rounded third base, an Anderson fan called out within earshot of this reporter, "You shoeless son of a bitch!"

I printed that the next day, and the name has stuck ever since. It has, in fact, perpetuated and ensured his everlasting fame.

**HAMIE** The story I heard, and which has been repeated a million times in the village, is that he often played the outfield without shoes, despite all the junk which was out there.

"I'm quitting," he tells the manager.

"Why's that? The rocks and glass cutting your feet?" the manager asked him.

"Naw. But they're fuzzin' up the ball and I can't throw it," he answered.

I'll tell you this, Joe was dumb enough to have done just that.

**JOE JACKSON** I don't know how many times I got to set the record straight about my "Shoeless Joe" name, but here it is again:

One day I played the field with new shoes which Tommy give me and they rubbed blisters something awful. The next day we had a couple of men down with injuries so Tommy told me I would have to play, otherwise we would be forced to give up the game.

At first I tried to play with the shoes on but my feet started bleeding and hurting real bad. I told Tommy I would have to come out, but he said I was going to play if my feet hurt or not. So I done the only thing I could think of—I took my bloody shoes off and went to the outfield in my stocking feet.

I didn't have to do much in the field, but along about the seventh inning I hit a long triple and legged it to third. That was in Anderson and the bleachers was in real close to the bag. As I hit the base, some big guy stood up and hollered:

"You shoeless sonofagun you!"

Everybody thought that was pretty funny, so they began calling me that all-around the league.

The thing is, I never played the outfield in my bare feet, and that was the only time I ever played in my stocking feet. Some papers said I played with bare feet. I never did but the truth don't always seem to matter to a lot of people.

"Shoeless Joe" sounded pretty good and it has stuck with me all my life, so I'm not going to complain about it, but like a lot of things they wrote about me, it just ain't true that I played like that all the time.

**SUMNER HOCKETT** Would Joe have had the notoriety without the catchy name? Perhaps not. Joe became so associated with the "Shoeless Joe" label that he is virtually unknown without it. Joe became the name and the name became him, and they became legend—a part of the very fabric of American culture.

**FRED WESTERVELT** I was umpiring in the Carolina Baseball Association when Joe was playing there. It was he who provided the play which prompted the most difficult call I ever had to make.

The Spinners were playing the final series of the season against the Greensboro Patriots, a series which would decide the league championship. Owing to a rain out earlier in the season, this was a four-game series with Greenville needing to take three for the championship.

Thousands of people showed up for each game. The Patriots led off with their ace pitching the first game. He blanked the Spinners 1 to 0.

The next day was a doubleheader and the place was crammed to overflowing with locals and hundreds of Greenville's most ardent fans who took the train down for the day. Greenville took the first game 5 to 2 but their bats went suddenly silent in the second game and they found themselves losing 6 to 0 when they came to bat in the ninth. The Spinners were down to three outs for the season unless they could pull a miraculous rally out of their hats. With the help of some timely hitting and a lucky bounce or two, they scored five runs and loaded the bases with only one out. The fleet Joe Jackson was on third when the batter hit a crisp grounder to the second baseman who scooped it up cleanly and fired to the catcher in an attempt to get Joe before he could tally the tying run. Joe, who was no dummy when it came to playing baseball, realized that he was going to be out from here to Sunday, so he did what his instincts told him to do. He lowered his shoulder and, in full stride, barreled into the poor catcher.

The catcher dropped the ball, and the force of the impact caused Joe to turn a complete somersault in the air, landing hard on his back. Joe didn't get to the plate which the catcher had completely blocked. Both of them lay on the ground partially stunned and then, almost in unison, they both realized what had happened. The catcher reached for the ball laying next to him, and Joe dove for the plate stretching out his long left hand to touch the corner of it just as the catcher and the ball arrived.

It was one of those calls which could have gone either way, and no matter what the call is, you know there is going to be a beef. But an umpire has only two choices: "out" or "safe." I took a long look, trying to postpone the inevitable as long as possible then hollered and signaled "out."

The ruckus I expected materialized instantly. Me and Tommy Stouch got into it pretty good, but Joe didn't say anything. He didn't argue with umpires much anyway, but I don't think Tommy would have let Joe be tossed anyway because he was so essential to their success.

It took me a while, and even though the fans were pretty riled up, I eventually got the game restarted. The next batter struck out and thus ended the season with the Patriots winning the pennant.

**BUDDY DONAHUE** That damn Westervelt's call on Joe irked us all mightily. We had the momentum going our way, the bases loaded then ... it was gone in one bad call. The catcher dropped the ball, plain and simple, then Joe beat him back to the plate, plain and simple. So we protested loud and long. Me and a couple of the guys from Greenville went up to Winston-Salem to the Association offices. We argued to the league officials that the makeup game itself was illegal since the Association rules clearly stated that the makeup game was not played within the specified time limit.

If the makeup game didn't count then we would have won the pennant on the basis of our winning two of the three legal games. If the game counted, then the Patriots won.

While we waited for the results of our protest, the issue got hotter and hotter. At Harrison's that's about all you heard. It was the first pennant for the Association and nobody knew who really won.

**JOE JACKSON** Yeah, I was out on that play at the plate but I wasn't about to say nothing. Everybody was so frazzled by that game that I didn't dare open my mouth. It's real hard to please everybody when you're playing baseball, so sometimes the best thing to do is shut up. That's exactly what I done.

**SCOOP LATIMER** For the season, Joe, as was his destiny, led the league in hitting. He ended the season with a .346 average beating out the despised Jule Watson from Spartanburg by five points.

**BUDDY DONAHUE** A couple of days later at the directors' meeting of the Carolina Association, I withdrew the protest. A lot of people are still angry with me about that, but I know it was the right thing to do. You see, the Association's first year was a great success. Lots of people came to the games and the league fielded some pretty respectable players, headed of course, by Joe. But minor leagues were awfully fragile and so many of them came and went in the blink of an eye. Before the meeting, one of the directors asked me to withdraw the protest in the interest of keeping the league's reputation intact.

"We just don't need a lot of controversy right now," he told me, "not in our first year of operation anyway. Let's think of the future of the league first."

I didn't like it, but I knew he was right.

"Besides," he added, "we're going to rule against the Spinners."

**TOMMY STOUCH** Some of the fans got upset at the team for not sticking to the protest and wanted to stage a demonstration to express their anger, but they were diverted by the biggest baseball news ever to hit the area. One of their own was going to play in the majors.

# 13

# I WASN'T TOO CRAZY ABOUT THE IDEA

**CHARLIE LEBEAU** While Joe was wowing them with the Spinners, Major League baseball up north was engaged in two of the closest and most exciting pennant races ever.

In the American League, four teams duked it out most of the way with Detroit barely edging out Cleveland. Both teams won 90 games but Detroit lost 63 and Cleveland 64. So Detroit took the flag only because they never made up a rained-out game. Who said life is fair?

Young Mr. Cobb won his second consecutive batting crown, a feat that was beginning to become a habit with him. Actually, he led the league in just about everything except making friends. Come to think of it, that was also becoming a habit.

Not to be outdone by the new kids on the block, the National League race ended in a dead tie between the Cubs and the Giants. A record 35,000 fans showed up for the tie breaker at the Polo Grounds in New York, but most went home dejected as Chicago's Three Finger Brown came on in relief and bested the great Christy Mathewson 4-2.

Despite the tight races, the season will forever be remembered for a play which occurred in a September 23rd game between those two teams, a play which I was fortunate enough to have seen while I was on a trip for the mill. Freddie Merkle was the culprit, his culpability easily out-living anything else he ever accomplished in his long major league career. It's funny, isn't it, that some players will forever be remembered for their career accomplishments while others for one game or one at bat or one play. It's kind of too bad in Freddie's case as he was a decent player. He came to bat maybe six thousand times in the majors but he's remembered for only one, and that one, a huge blunder. But whose fault was it really?

Here's what happened: Merkle, then a 19-year-old kid found himself standing on first with two outs in the bottom of the ninth in a 1-1 tie. Moose McCormick was on third. The Giant's batter, Al Bridwell, lines a single to center, at which point the crowd begins pouring out on to the field and Merkle, thinking the game won, heads for the New York clubhouse without bothering with the formality of touching second base. But Chicago second baseman Johnny Evers sees this and touches the base with the ball all the while screaming for the umpire's attention. The umpire sees him and calls Merkle out thereby nullifying the potential winning run.

Well after this, all holy hell broke loose and all sorts of protests and protests to the protests and hearings and appeals were unloosed on the National League office. When the smoke cleared, the National League president ruled that the game would be replayed if it proved to be necessary to sort out the league championship. That resulted in the Three Finger Brown win I told you about.

"Merkle's Boner Costs Giants the Pennant" ran headlines all over the country. But I'm not quite so sure. First of all, it seems to me that all the Giants, and that includes the manager, John McGraw, should have been yelling at him to touch the base. But nobody did, and secondly, I don't think Evers used the game ball. I was watching pretty closely, and despite all the confusion and the rowdy crowd, I could swear I saw him get a practice ball from the first baseman.

But none of that mattered. For all the world, Freddie Merkle was the dumbest player in baseball—until Joe arrived.

**BILLY PRESSLEY** Those bird dog scouts come sniffing around long before the season was half over. Of course, we was all hoping that they'd be looking at us, but the fact is, mostly they wanted to see Joe, which we didn't like but understood, and sometimes Scotty Barr, which we didn't understand but liked better.

We always knew when a bird dog was in the stands, and sometimes that made us play a little harder, but to each other we said we didn't care because southern ball was just naturally better than northern and we had no intention of going up there.

That was just one of the lies we shared. There isn't one of us who wouldn't have jumped at the opportunity. That is except Joe. He got the opportunity but he didn't exactly jump.

**TOMMY STOUCH** What Joe did at Greenville is history now. He led the league in hitting, as in fact, he has led every league he ever played in. And he developed so fast that before the season, I knew we couldn't keep him so I decided to sell him to the majors.

I was an intimate friend of Connie Mack, so naturally my first thought was of Mack and the Philadelphia Athletics.

Mack was as good a manager as there was in baseball and a strong individual. Joe, I knew, would need both if he was going to survive in the majors.

**CONNIE MACK** Tommy Stouch, who was then managing a team in South Carolina, kept sending me telegrams about a kid on his team named Joseph Jefferson Wofford Jackson. I was more interested in looking at the college kids in the Northeast, so at first I paid him no heed, but Tommy, himself once one of the best-known coaches in the South, was a pretty fair judge of talent. After several persuasive messages from him my interest was finally piqued.

I sent a telegram to Tommy asking if young Mr. Jackson was an individual of character. Tommy replied that he was extremely shy, but yes, he felt he possessed sufficient character to play for the Athletics.

**TOMMY STOUCH** At first Mr. Mack was a mite suspicious. Why didn't I set Joe up at my college if he was that good? Why was I offering him to the Athletics? I didn't exactly answer that question honestly. Joe could have used the seasoning that a collegiate season or two would have provided, but the admissions officer would have had me put away in a little padded room had I even suggested it.

Jackson was, in many respects, a queer fish. When I told him I was going to take him to the big leagues, he didn't show the enthusiasm I expected.

"I hardly know how I would like it in them big northern cities," he told me.

"Oh, you will like it fine there," I said, not believing for a moment that he was buying it.

**CONNIE MACK** Since he was injured and not playing much, I asked Socks Seybold, one of our veteran players, to take a ride down to South Carolina to look at Joe and one of his teammates, Scotty Barr, who Tommy Stouch was also promoting.

**TOMMY STOUCH** I knew convincing Joe to go north wasn't going to be an easy task. He liked playing ball all right, but I don't think he ever had what you would call a driving ambition to succeed. The idea of playing in the majors was probably more frightening than enticing.

Aware of this problem, and after communicating with Mr. Mack about it, we decided there were a couple of things we could do. One was to sign not only Joe, but also Hyder Barr, who we all called Scotty. Scotty wasn't anywhere near as good as Joe, but he was about Joe's age, from Tennessee, and eager to make it to the majors. Another player Joe knew going with him seemed like a good bet. The other was to send Socks Seybold to bring Joe and Scotty back. We felt Socks was a good choice because he was truly one of the nicest, most affable players in the game. Everybody liked and trusted Socks. Surely Joe would, too.

Socks was a big bear of a man with a barrel chest and limbs like oaken mill posts. The writers sometimes called him the "human box car." He was a terrific hitter and a more agile base runner than you would think, but his love for second helpings at the dinner table was beginning to get in the way of his career.

Mr. Mack may have also been sending Socks a message: He was becoming more valuable as a messenger than as a player.

**TOPSY HARTSEL** Mr. Mack knew what he was doing sending Socks down to fetch Joe and Scotty. As the Athletics were struggling on the field anyway, what did we have to lose?

Because of his size, Socks could be real dangerous running the bases, but I never once saw him spike anybody or even trip or bump them. He was one of those guys who wanted to be known as a "clean" player and took more pride in that than in his batting. Once I even saw him caught off first by a perfect throw because he didn't want to hurt the first baseman by landing on him.

Yes, sir, he was a real chesterfield all right. I doubt if Ty Cobb ever invited him to dinner.

**HARRY DAVIS** As I was the captain of the Athletics, Mr. Mack told me about wanting to send somebody down south to pick up this hick playing for some D League team. It didn't add up. Send him a ticket and a map to the ballpark. That's about all the rest of us ever got. But he insisted that he was going to send either Socks or Chief Bender down after the kid. I argued that the Chief was too important to the team. Socks was hurt and near the end of his career. Besides, the big guy loved trains.

**SOCKS SEYBOLD** When I got down to Greenville Tommy introduced me to Joe right away. I could see he wasn't at all sure about me, so I decided to take a day or so just to talk to him friendly like without trying to put pressure on him.

Since I couldn't exactly talk about working in the mill, I talked to him a lot about the farm I grew up on in Ohio. I told him how I used to ask my father for a half holiday to get a treat—a chance to walk to the neighboring town and wait to see the express go through at a 60-mile-an-hour clip, snatching the mail pouch off the platform tree as it flew past, and then the mail clerk throwing out the day's mail pouch for the little town.

These were happy days, I told him, but even then, I had the idea that someday I would have enough money to travel where I wanted on a fast railway train.

"Since getting to the major leagues," I said, "I've put in enough miles to make me a 33rd degree traveler. But now I have another bug that needs to be worked out—getting a mercantile house of my own. Bender and myself might be wholesale or retail jewelers someday, who knows?"

Joe listened politely, but didn't say a lot. He was a hard guy to get to say much. I didn't talk about the Athletics or even baseball for a whole day, but rather tried to find out what his dreams were. He said he didn't have any. More precisely, he said, "I don't got any."

**FRED LAKE** I was scouting for the Red Sox in '08 when our playboy owner, John Taylor, was tipped off about some kid in the South who was said to be a better hitter than Cobb. "Better than" stories were a dime a dozen in baseball, but Taylor insisted I go down and check the kid out.

By the time I got there after an unbearably hot train ride from Boston, I found Socks Seybold and Joe were already talking like they were hillbilly kin. I was from Nova Scotia, Canada. What could I possibly have had in common with this stupid mill kid? Anyway, it didn't take a genius to see that Socks had him sewed up. I took the next train back from mosquito junction without ever seeing him play.

Later Taylor took a lot of heat for not signing Joe.

**HYDER BARR** When two scouts showed up for our game in Charlotte, I thought at first that they was there just to see Joe, but Socks Seybold said they was there to see me, too. That was probably the second most exciting day of my life. (The first was the day I started playing for Mr. Mack's Athletics.) But, old Joe, he didn't act excited at all. At first I didn't care about that, but then Socks told me that we either both went north or neither of us went.

That's when I began talking strong to Joe about being nice to Socks and paying attention to what he said, but I don't think he was listening a lot. I started to get worried that he might be squelching the deal for us both.

**JOE JACKSON** Oh my, how Socks could talk up a blue streak. The thing is, though, I liked him. He told me why he was there, so I kept expecting him to talk to me about how great Philadelphia was, and what a great man Mr. Mack was, and things like that, but he didn't. We talked about hunting and fishing, and farming and about me.

**SOCKS SEYBOLD** After chewing the fat with Joe for a day, I finally got a chance to see him in a game against the Charlotte Hornets. All he did was damn near hit for the cycle, getting a double, triple, and home run in four at bats. Even though his four-bagger was called back when he missed touching first base, I could see what all the fuss was about. He was a graceful, beautiful athlete, with unlimited potential.

That night I sent a telegram to Mr. Mack from Charlotte. "Sign Joe now.

Ask questions later." He immediately wired back asking about Hyder Barr. "Take the whole team if you have to, but get Joe," I responded without hesitation.

Despite my unbridled enthusiasm, I had some qualms. I didn't doubt that I was doing the right thing for Mr. Mack, the Athletics and baseball, but I wasn't sure I was doing the right thing by Joe. A major league locker room is a far cry from a southern mill village.

**TOMMY STOUCH** As soon as he got the word, Scotty caught the next train to Philadelphia. Knowing Scotty, he was probably annoyed that it took so long to pack. He couldn't get to the Athletics fast enough. He'd played for the Davidson College team and knew his way around. He was a perfect choice for Connie Mack who preferred college players. The only thing was, he wasn't nearly the player Joe was. Mack called him up more as a baby sitter for Joe than anything else.

As soon as he got to Philadelphia I got a telegram from Mack wanting to know when Joe was coming, and although he didn't say so, I imagine he was trying to figure out what to do with Scotty without Joe.

In the meantime, Joe stayed around playing in an exhibition game against his old Victor Mill team. He hit what was undoubtedly the longest home run ever hit on the Greer field. It must have made everybody that much more anxious about Joe. The major league season still had a few weeks left to go, and although the Athletics were out of the race, Joe's presence certainly would have boosted the attendance and left a feeling of promise for things to come.

But Joe was never the most decisive guy in the world and I figured too much pressure would only confuse him more. I kept talking to him, trying to nudge but not push.

**JOE JACKSON** Everybody I knew in the whole world lived in Brandon village, or nearby. I didn't even know anybody except Mr. Lebeau that had ever been in Philadelphia. I didn't know a lot about a city like that except that I knew the people there wasn't like us. They was northerners and northerners was different kinds of people, though at the time I didn't know exactly how different.

I wanted to tell Tommy, "No, I wouldn't go," but he kept telling me everything would be all right. I didn't know what to say to that. I got sick to my stomach but he kept telling me not to worry. That didn't help much, though.

I went home and talked to Mother and Father. What I really wanted was for them to tell me not to go, or at least give me a real good excuse not to go, but they didn't. All Father said was, "It's up to you," and all Mother said was, "Do what you think is right." I didn't know what was right, but I knowed what I wanted—I wanted to stay in Brandon village. I just wanted somebody else to make that decision for me.

Davey kept saying I should go, that I would be famous. I was already famous enough for me. I never said I wanted more than that.

Mr. Lebeau said I should go, that I could be a great ballplayer. I thought I was already about as good as I could get.

Mr. Hatch said I should go, that I would be a real "inspiration" to other boys in the mill. I didn't see how I could ever be that.

Katie said I should do what I wanted, but if I wanted to be a big baseball player I would have to go north sooner or later and maybe I wouldn't get this kind of chance again. Besides, Mr. Mack was offering me $900 and practically nobody in Brandon ever seen that much money at one time before.

Nobody seemed to be on my side. I couldn't sleep. This was the toughest decision I ever had to make.

In the morning, when I went in for breakfast, Tommy was waiting for me. Mother had a little valise that she had bought at Hamie's with some of my clothes in it. I don't think that I ever said "Yes," I would go. It was just kind of expected that I would go. So I did.

**J.C. HATCH** I was surprised he got on that train at all. Mill boys didn't leave the mills much, and if they did, it was for some other place in the South. Some of them went back to the mountains or farms that they came from. A few of them went into the cities like Greenville, but not many headed for the North. Face it. Southern mill boys were ill-equipped for life in the industrial North.

To help keep Joe calm, Tommy Stouch sat next to Joe on the train.

**JOE JACKSON** The big wooden Pullman car was the most beautiful thing I ever seen. The wood inside was painted this deep red and it had a high curved ceiling and electric lights and electric fans at each end of the car. The green seats was real comfortable and they had what I think was supposed to be tulips all over them.

The only trouble was that my stomach got more and more jumpy with every mile closer to Philadelphia.

**TOMMY STOUCH** All during the train ride toward Philadelphia, Joe sat holding on to his suitcase staring out of the window as mile by mile the southern pines gave way to trees the likes of which he had never seen.

**JOE JACKSON** I started thinking about Katie and my family and about how good they was to me. The more I thought about them the more I got this dull, sick feeling.

**TOMMY STOUCH** We were on the train for a few hours when a Negro porter came over and very politely asked if there was anything he could do for us. He wasn't at all uppity like some of them.

I thought I would order something to drink for me and Joe. Maybe that would relax him some.

"We'd like a dope and lime and a lemonade, George," I said.

Joe turned to me with this startled look on his face and asked me how I knew this Negro. I said I didn't know him at all, but that all porters were called George, probably after George M. Pullman.

I could see that Joe was becoming more agitated by the minute so I tried to engage him in a bit of conversation to take his mind off the trip. I told him about the man in Iowa who founded an organization called the SPCSCPG which was the "Society For The Prevention Of Calling Sleeping Car Porters 'George.'" This guy spent most of his adult lifetime and a small fortune on the project. Even the King of England was a card-carrying member of the Society.

I was still telling him this story (which I thought would amuse him) when he grabbed his suitcase, got up, walked over to the porter and said, "George, when is the next stop?"

"Never mind that, Joe," I told him and got him settled down again.

We talked for a while about some of the guys on the Spinners and he seemed to relax a little.

I guess I nodded off for a short time. When I woke, Joe was gone. I looked all over the train—no Joe. Finally the porter came up and said Joe had gotten off at Charlotte.

One hundred and 50 miles from Greenville and Joe had quit on a dream thousands of players in the South would have given almost anything for.

There wasn't much to do other than continue on to Philadelphia and break the news to Mr. Mack personally.

He didn't take the news well.

# 14

# I WANTED TO DISAPPEAR

**HAMIE** Joe didn't exactly have a lot of what you might call giddyap in his gait.

**CONNIE MACK** What kind of a kid making peanuts on a D league team in the South Carolina sticks would walk away from a chance to play for the Athletics? Not one with character. What was he afraid of? Was he a coward? These and other like questions came to mind as I waited word that he had reconsidered. The biggest question though was, was he worth it? If he was frightened of a train ride, how would he fare against a Walter Johnson fastball? A hard tag by Nap Lajoie?

I was beginning to doubt whether he had the intestinal fortitude to stand up for himself even if he did come. Maybe illiterate mill kids weren't cut out for big league life.

**RICHARD COLZIE** I wasn't surprised to see Joe back—not for a second. Joe didn't want to leave in the first place, but he didn't have the guts to not leave. But then, that was the story of his whole career, wasn't it? Joe could be pushed around by just about anybody who had a stronger will than he had, and that was almost everyone.

**JOE JACKSON** I really thought that I was going to pass out if I stayed on that train, but I didn't feel a lot better when I got home. I didn't want to go and I didn't want to stay. I know that don't sound right, but that's how I felt. Mostly I wanted to disappear, but everybody in Brandon wanted to know what happened. Nobody would leave me alone.

Right then I didn't want to be a big league baseball player. What was so wrong with playing for Greenville anyway?

What I wanted was to go out hunting with Davey. What I wanted was for people to say it was all right not to go to Philadelphia.

But, excepting Katie, they didn't say that. Everybody thought I was stupid for not going, but they didn't understand.

I mean it was fine for Luther and Davey and everybody to say go, but they didn't have to get on that train and go someplace they never been, and have to talk to people they didn't know, and everybody expecting them to be this great player and all.

**LUTHER JACKSON** I told Joe he was just plain stupid getting off that train. He had a chance to get out of the mill forever.

He got mad when I told him that, but I didn't care, because sometimes you just got to tell people the truth even if it hurts them.

Joe told me I didn't know what I was talking about and we got into a fight, which is something Joe didn't do a lot, but I could tell he was real upset about this.

**COOPER ANDERSON** That Joe was frightened shouldn't have come as a surprise to anyone. He was being asked to leave the only world he had ever known for one he neither knew nor had the resources to learn about.

I am sure that behind his fear lay the issue of his illiteracy. To the illiterate, life becomes a steeplechase, and he is surrounded by complex assumptions that reduce rather than increase his capacity to make choices aimed at altering the situation. The fear generated by the illiterate's continual vulnerability as he moves through a world where others understand and act on the written word while he cannot, can be overwhelming and paralyzing.

**JOE JACKSON** It's a frightening feeling not being able to read something, like maybe on a street sign. You never know what's going on unless someone tells you. Nobody understood how hard it was.

Sometimes I had to do something even if I didn't know exactly what was going on because I couldn't read what everybody else could. Sometimes when I did things it was like opening a bottle, putting a stick of dynamite in it, and hoping it don't go off.

**COOPER ANDERSON** Lots of young men and women growing up in the South around the turn of the century could neither read nor write—maybe as much as 10 percent of the white population and certainly more than half of the black population.

I asked Joe once if he ever regretted not learning. He said no, he was about as good a ballplayer as he could be anyway, and that reading wouldn't make him any better, but it might make him worse. He reasoned that if he read too much about himself he might try to make adjustments in his game that he didn't need to.

"I just want to go up to the plate and swing at a ball I think I can hit," he said, "and I don't have to read the label on the ball to do that."

I didn't believe him when he said that, and I still don't. I believe Joe resented not being able to read, but he didn't dare admit it.

**CHARLIE LEBEAU** Joe not only put the Athletics in a bind, he created possible problems for himself as well. If Joe didn't turn around and hightail it to Philadelphia he was liable to be blacklisted which would mean the end of his career in organized ball. Mr. Mack had that power and anybody who ever knew him knew damn well that he would exercise that power if pushed far enough. Mr. Mack was a man of inestimable principle and Joe was violating an important principle of baseball, a principle upon which the very foundation of baseball rested.

Ever since the 19th century, the owners recognized the fact that they had to have a way of tying a player to a club once they had contracted with that player. Failing this, the wealthiest owners would be free to entice a player to switch clubs at the end of every contract period. So, to protect their own interests, they made every contract include a reserve clause. This clause locked in each player to an owner for the life of the player's professional career, or until the owner traded the player to another club at which time the player would have to sign another contract with another reserve clause.

This provision was probably the single most important element in keeping professional baseball from completely disintegrating in the latter years of the 19th century and the early years of the 20th.

The thing is, Joe had a contract with Mr. Mack. The fact that Katie probably signed it for him is beside the point. He had a contract, and he had the $900, but Mr. Mack didn't have a ballplayer.

In adopting the reserve clause, the owners also agreed not to tamper with a player on another team, not to play against a team which utilized a player who violated the reserve clause, and not even to let a team in violation of the clause use its field.

Mr. Mack held all the power in the relationship, and it was unlikely he would wait forever. If Joe didn't rethink his defection, his career would be over before it started.

**TOPSY HARTSEL** For days all we heard in Philadelphia was "Joe this," and "Joe that" as if he was some kind of messiah. Well, I'm here to tell you we already had some pretty good players on our team, and although the season wasn't exactly going too good, we wasn't sitting around and waiting for some dumb kid from South Carolina.

Then the papers started writing about him every day. Some of them even said he was the next coming of Ty Cobb and would single-handedly fix what was wrong with the Athletics. Of course even if he was with us, he wouldn't have known that because he couldn't have read the damn papers anyway.

**HARRY DAVIS** Of course the fans always like the promise of the up-and-coming young player—until he goes 0 for 4 in a big game or drops a routine fly ball. Hope springs eternal and the new kid on the block brings the hope.

Joe was getting so much build up in the press and the fans were so eager to see him that it began to take its toll on the team. When the fans began to chant "We want Joe" every time we made a mistake it only helped to create a less-than-enthusiastic team.

Some players resented Joe even before they met him.

**HYDER BARR** "The fences around Columbia Park will have some dents in them when Joe Jackson gets into action," I told one reporter.

That was the longest quote from me that was ever printed.

**CONNIE MACK** I was willing to wait for the kid, but not forever. Yet the longer he stayed in Greenville, the more the press built him up, and the more the press built him up, the more we needed him. With expectations building by the day, I didn't dare not deliver him.

Finally I sent Seybold back down to fetch him. Socks seemed to have gotten on with him when he was there, and besides, Socks would love another train ride.

**SOCKS SEYBOLD** Mr. Mack told me to go get Joe, "and if need be, bring his whole damn family if that's what it takes."

When I got back to Greenville, I found Joe playing hide-and-seek. When I finally cornered him at his house, I found a pretty confused kid. He wanted to play baseball on the major league level, but he wanted to play it in Greenville.

I sat down with him and Tommy Stauch and Katie and did my best to put him at ease. I talked about all the nice guys on the team, Harry Davis and Eddie Plank and some of the others, too. I could see that mostly what he wanted was to not have to make any decision at all.

**KATIE WYNN JACKSON** I think when Joe first saw Mr. Seybold coming down the street he was afraid that he was going to get mad at him for getting off the train. If he was, he certainly didn't let on about it. Joe never did like people getting angry at him. Well, I guess nobody does, but Joe always took it kind of hard that way.

After a while me and Mr. Seybold walked outside without Joe and he told me that Mr. Mack was being considerate in not blackballing Joe, but that if Joe didn't go to Philadelphia soon he wouldn't have any choice but to do it, and then Joe would be in a lot of trouble.

I didn't know what the right thing was to do any more than he did. Remember, I was only 15 at the time and I'd never been to any place as big as Philadelphia either. I guess I wasn't as afraid of it as he was, but then I could read and write.

After talking again to Mr. Seybold, Joe looked tired and still confused.

"I guess I'll go back," he said sadly.

# 15

# THE BUSIEST PLACE I EVER SEEN

**CHARLIE LEBEAU** About the time Joe came up to the major leagues, baseball was going through a period in which rough play and violent activity were particularly rampant. Some of this was precipitated by the emergence of Ty Cobb as a dominant player. Cobb, like Joe, was from the South but unlike Joe he was extremely aggressive. Maybe he was more suited to the times than Joe. Certainly he took better advantage of it.

But Cobb wasn't the only aggressor in those days. I remember "Turkey Mike" Donlin, who split his time almost equally between playing hard and drinking hard. "Turkey Mike" once terrorized a train load of passengers with a gun. Frank Chance threw a bottle into the stands once in Chicago injuring a child and setting off a small riot. Billy Evans, a young umpire, was hit in the head by a bottle thrown from the stands and spent time in the hospital with a fractured skull. On the field there were countless fights and acts of hostility.

It's not that Joe wasn't tough but he was quiet and reserved and withdrawn at a time when the game was aggressive and rambunctious. Ty fit perfectly; Joe didn't.

**COOPER ANDERSON** I can well imagine the shock Joe must have felt when he finally got off that train in Philadelphia. It was a world of electric trolleys and gas buggies where horses should have been. It was a world just beginning to fall in love with motion pictures and wireless radio, with disk-type records and Teletype machines.

There wasn't a stream to fish or a field to hunt in sight.

**JOE JACKSON** Me and Socks Seybold walked from the train station through narrow streets with buildings so tall they blocked out the sun. I knowed right there that those people who say the mill is a loud place ain't never been to Philadelphia at 5 o'clock on a Wednesday afternoon. People was everywhere, pushing and shoving, going God knows where in such a almighty hurry that not one of them even slowed down so much as to say howdy. If I ever had any doubt that the big cities of the North was different from Greenville, it was gone by the time we was 5 feet outside that station.

We walked straight to the Hotel Walton. It was bigger by far than the Brandon Mill, and bigger than anything in Greenville. It sat on the corner of two busy streets and had steps leading up to entrances on both of them. The building was made of dark red bricks and stone and was maybe 10 or 11 stories high with steep pointed round towers on each corner that rose up even higher. And then on top of the towers there was tall flagpoles with big round gold balls on top of them. It looked something like what I imagined an old-time castle would look like except without the water and crocodiles around it.

Inside there was, I don't know how many rooms, but hundreds at least, off these long, long dark halls with red carpets. In all the time I stayed there, it always took me some time to find my room, because all them floors and all them rooms was alike.

My room had round walls because it was in one of them towers in the back corner. To this day I don't know why someone would want to go to the bother of building a room with round walls, but I had one anyway.

The hotel was big, noisy and confusing. Boys dressed in what looked like red soldiers' uniforms was all over the place. When I first got there, one of them grabbed my suitcase away from me and carried it a few feet to where we had to get the key to the room. Socks had to pay him for that! I didn't understand why I could carry the bag all the way from Greenville to Philadelphia, but I had to have help carrying it a few feet across a hotel lobby. To this day, after tipping hundreds of bellboys in every big city, I still don't understand it!

The Walton Hotel was uncomfortable from the start. I didn't know how much to pay the boys for doing anything, so mostly I tried to avoid them. Whenever I saw one coming toward me I turned the other way because I was afraid they was going to make me do something I didn't want to do then I was going to have to pay them, and I didn't know how much.

Mostly, when I wasn't at the ballpark, I stayed in my room.

The first day Socks walked up to my room with me.

"You gonna be OK, Joe?" he asked.

"Sure I will," I said.

"Here's your key, don't lose it," he said handing me this big key. "And make sure to lock your room."

At home I don't think any house was ever locked. I'm not even sure the mill was. I don't even know why I had to lock the room in the hotel. I didn't have a whole lot anybody would want to steal unless they wanted my shirt and pants, but that didn't seem likely because everybody I saw in Philadelphia had better clothes anyway.

As soon as Socks said that about the key, I began to worry about it. What if I did lose it? What would I do then? Maybe the boys in red would have to break down the door and then I would have to pay for that. How much would that cost? I hardly had any money. Maybe the people who owned the hotel would make me leave, and then where would I go? Maybe everybody in the hotel would be laughing at me thinking I was just some stupid southern mill boy. And if I did lose the key, who would I tell about it? And what would Mr. Mack think?

From that moment on, I thought about the key almost all the time. I never left the room without checking to see if it was in my pocket. Even sometimes when I was playing, I would think about the key in the pocket of my pants hanging in my locker and hoping that nobody would take it. A couple of times I even woke up in the middle of the night thinking that the key was gone, but when I got up and looked, it wasn't.

You was even supposed to lock your door on the inside while you was in your room. Let me tell you this, locking yourself in a little room with round walls high up in a big castle building was not a comfortable feeling for a boy from a little mill village.

I didn't sleep too good, worrying about the key and because of the noise. I was used to going to bed early and getting up early, but I guess big-city people weren't, because I could hear them in the halls all hours of the night. People didn't walk around much in the middle of the night in the South.

**SOCKS SEYBOLD** I tried to get Joe to relax, but I remember thinking at the time that if he was this tight walking into a hotel, how the hell was he going to play ball in front of thousands of people? I was beginning to think that Mr. Mack was in for a bigger challenge than he imagined.

**JOE JACKSON** "Here's a couple of bucks Mr. Mack asked me to give you," Socks said. "I guess he'll tell you about pay day and all when you meet with him tomorrow."

Socks handed me five one-dollar bills. "Restaurant's downstairs on the first floor. Mr. Mack says charge anything you want."

I wasn't exactly sure what he meant by charging anything, but I guessed he meant it was like Hammie's.

"I'll come by 'bout 10:00 to pick you up and take you to see Mr. Mack. Be downstairs in the lobby, OK?"

"Yeah, sure, OK," I said.

"A lot of people are looking forward to seeing you play," he said.

Why was they looking forward to seeing me play? I never met anybody from Philadelphia in my life before.

"Need anything else before I go?" he asked.

"No, I don't think so, thanks," I said.

"You're gonna love playing ball in Philadelphia, just give it a little time. See you in the morning," he said as he disappeared down the hall that was about as long as the whole Brandon Mill floor.

I was mighty hungry, since I didn't have nothing to eat since early on the train, but I wasn't sure about this restaurant thing. So I decided to just go to bed hungry and worry about breakfast in the morning.

It was pretty warm in the room so I laid on top of the bed sheets and stared up at the ceiling fan for the longest time. I tried to stop thinking, but I couldn't. I kept thinking about meeting Mr. Mack and the ballplayers and, of course, the key. Would I look foolish trying to play ball with the other players? Would Mr. Mack be angry at me? What would the bugs think about me? Would there be other boys from the South on the team? Is there anybody else in Philadelphia who ever worked in a mill? I couldn't turn them and lots of other questions off. They came roaring through one by one like the box cars on the Friday freight train through Greenville.

Another thing I was worried about was how I was going to find my way around Philadelphia without being able to read the signs. I decided as soon as I left the hotel in the morning with Socks, I was going to make a point of marking every turn by a building on the corner, or some particular looking sign, or something else unusual that I could remember. But how many could I remember at one time? How far was the ball field from the hotel, and how many turns would that be to remember?

For a long while I listened to Murray argue with Florence in the hall. I couldn't tell for sure what they was arguing about, but I could imagine. At one point I thought I heard him hit her, but I wasn't sure. I thought about getting up and looking but I decided that wasn't such a good idea.

It seemed like I didn't sleep at all that night, but I must have for a little while because I woke up wondering if Florence was OK.

I could tell by the light that it was still early, but I knowed I needed breakfast. There was a couple of problems with the restaurant. First of all, I wasn't sure how to charge anything. At Hamie's the most we ever said was "charge it," but mostly we didn't say nothing because old Hamie charged almost everything anyway. Second, I wasn't sure how I was going to order anything unless it was on the counter like Harrison's Drugstore where I could just point at it. Besides what kind of food did they eat in the north for breakfast anyway? Maybe I wouldn't recognize any of it. What about the other players? Were they staying at the hotel too? Would they be eating at the restaurant? What if one of the players came over to sit by me? What would we talk about? More than anything, I didn't want to act like some fool.

Now this might not seem like such a big deal to you, but to someone who never done this before, it was pretty scary. I was starting to get real nervous trying to figure things out when there was a knock at the door. I jumped out of bed instantly and stood in the middle of the room.

"Chamber maid." It was a young-sounding girl's voice from the other side of the door.

"Hello," I said quickly, not knowing what else to say.

"Do you want me to make up your room now?" she asked.

Do I? Is she supposed to do that now? What am I supposed to say?

The only thing I could think to do was to get back to the train station and get a train to Greenville if I could figure out exactly how to do that.

"Sweetheart, it's not that tough of a question," she said after a long pause while I was trying to think what to answer. "Sweetheart?" She didn't even know me and I never heard anybody call somebody they didn't know that.

"Yeah ... OK ... I guess so," I said finally because it didn't look like she was going to go away until I said something.

She rattled the doorknob a few times then asked, "Well, are you going to unlock the door or am I supposed to come through the keyhole?"

"No, don't come through the keyhole, I'll open it. Just a minute," I said as I reached in my pocket for the key.

I opened the door and let her in. She was a young, cute little red-haired girl carrying a basket with some cleaning things in it.

"Thanks, honey, I won't be a few minutes," she said as she headed right to the bathroom and started cleaning.

I wasn't at all sure about someone calling me "sweetheart" and "honey." In the South, we didn't say those sorts of things to people we didn't know. It wasn't proper to have a girl in your room like this anyway, so without even thinking, I said, "I'm just going to get some breakfast," and I walked out into the hall.

I stopped quickly, returned to the room and handed her a quarter, not sure whether this was too little or too much.

"Well now, a real gentleman," she said with a big smile. "Thank you, sir."

I didn't think I was old enough to be called "sir" but I didn't say nothing. I just went down to the restaurant.

The restaurant was big and it was crowded. Tables was all over, and waitresses ran between them every which way. I was hoping I'd see Hyder, but there was so many people I'm not sure I would've seen him even if he was there. I saw an empty table and started walking over to it when this man in a black suit came up to me. "Excuse me, sir, would you like a table for one?"

"Yeah," I answered.

"If you wouldn't mind waiting over here for a moment, while we set one up for you," he said, pointing at a place for me to stand.

I felt like a kid being scolded by his father. I realized right away that I made a big mistake coming to the restaurant. I wanted to leave, but just as soon as I started to go, the man came back.

"Your table is ready, sir, won't you please follow me."

I followed him to a table. Guess what? It was the exact same table I tried to sit at a few moments before. I didn't say nothing; I just gave him a quarter and he handed me a menu and left like maybe wasn't enough.

I quick looked around for Scotty, but didn't see him, so I opened the menu and held it up in front of me like I was reading it but all the time I was looking to the side to see what the people at the next table was eating. It looked like some kind of eggs but the waitress came by before I could get a good look at it.

"Can I take your order?" she asked?

"I'll have eggs," I said, hoping they had eggs.

"Just put your order on that slip," she said pointing to some pieces of paper sitting next to the sugar.

"Just eggs," I repeated.

"You're supposed to write your order down on them slips," she said, "then give them to me, and I'll give it to the cook and he'll make what you want then I'll bring it to you. That's how it works. Anything you don't understand about that?"

"I understand."

"Because it ain't that difficult, you know."

"I'd just like two eggs, fried if you can."

"Look, I got a lot of customers here, can't you see that? They all fill out their slips like good little boys and girls. Why don't you do the same? There's the slips; there's the pencil

If you make up your mind fill it out. If you don't, it don't matter to me. I got a lot of customers, anyway. I'll be back."

She walked away. I picked up the slips and the pencil. Two eggs. That's all I wanted, two eggs. I didn't have no idea how to make a "2" much less "eggs."

Now you might think that was a pretty simple thing, but if you didn't know how to do it, it wasn't that simple at all. Whether something is hard or not depends on if you can do it easy or not. For example, you might think hitting a fast ball is a hard thing to do because you can't do it too good. But to me it's pretty easy on account of I can do it. Well, at least some of the time I can. Since I couldn't write "eggs," that was hard for me. So it just depends if something is hard or not.

I was starting to feel a lot less hungry. Where was Scotty, anyways?

She came back awfully fast for somebody who was supposed to be so busy.

"You ready now, sport?" she asked.

"Here," I said as I put down two ones on the slip. "Eggs please."

She looked at what I wrote. "OK, let's do this the hard way. How do you want your eggs?"

How do I want my eggs? What did she mean by that? Eggs are eggs, ain't they? Maybe they have different kinds of eggs up here. Maybe they ain't chicken eggs. Maybe they come from some different kind of animal. But what kind?

There was a long, stupid pause. I was sure everybody in the restaurant was watching me. That was the worst part of it.

"Sunny side up? Over easy? Over hard? Broken yolks or no?" she said after what seemed like a long time of people watching me look stupid.

"Sunny side up" I said happy to have choices but not knowing exactly what she meant.

"Anything to drink, sport?"

"No," I said, thinking that was by far the safest answer.

As she walked away, I saw everybody around me looking. I think some of them was even laughing. They could probably tell by the way I was dressed that I wasn't from the city.

When the waitress brought the eggs, I was glad to see that they looked like they was from a chicken. The only problem was, there was a whole lot of them—a really big pile in fact.

"Here you are sport," said the waitress plopping the plate down right in front of me, "11 eggs sunny side up, just as you ordered, no coffee. Enjoy." She walked away before I could even pay her.

I was so nervous about everything that was happening that I didn't enjoy the breakfast at all. I did however, learn what sunny side up meant, and that two ones got you more eggs than you could want. I ate them, though, every one of them.

It seems to me that life don't have to be as complicated as most people make it

When I was done eating all 11 eggs, the waitress came back.

"Would you like some more, sport?" she asked kind of smiling.

"No thank you," I said.

She handed me the bill. "You can pay me, if you'd like.

"Charge it," I said, trying to sound as confident as I could.

"Room number?" she asked.

Now all of a sudden, as bad as things was, they just got a lot worse. I know this will sound idiotic, but it was very true at the time. I never thought about rooms being numbered because I never saw a room with a number on it before.

I guess I could've told her you walk up the three flights of steps over by the entrance to the restaurant, turn right, then right again and then, as soon as you pass this big plant in a pink pot, you turn left down the hall between pictures of mountains, one in a gold frame, and one in black. Count four doors past the mountains on the right, and there you are. But on account of I didn't know the number, all I could say was, "I don't know."

"Check you room key, sport," she said, "it's on the key."

As I reached in my pocket, panic hit me. It wasn't there. The key was in the back of the door in my room. I used it to let the cleaning lady in.

I could feel sweat coming out on my forehead and my heart pounding. I hadn't been in Philadelphia a full day yet and already I had made all them mistakes. Maybe I just wasn't cut out to be living in a big northern city. Maybe I was supposed to work in a cotton mill all my life. Maybe there are certain things that are just right and certain things that are wrong, and maybe you can't change that, no matter how hard you try.

"I guess I left it in my room, I'm sorry," I said

"Are you staying in this hotel?" she asked, now acting like she was getting real annoyed.

"Yes, in a round room, three flights of stairs up."

"Well, you either have to give me cash or a room number, sport. I got to have something to show for all them eggs, what with you being such a big eater and all."

"Oh, I didn't know I could pay cash."

"You didn't know you could pay cash?"

"I didn't know," I repeated.

"You can pay cash."

"OK, I'll pay cash."

"I mean, what country did you think this was anyway?"

"Philadelphia," I said.

"Well in the country of Philadelphia we take cash, sport. You can use your wampum someplace else."

I reached in my pocket and asked, "How much is it, please?"

She was starting to get angry I could see, because one of the bosses in the mill looked just like she did when he was mad at you for something.

"Just what it says," she answered, picking up the bill and handing it back to me.

I was about to hand her all the money I had, when Scotty walked up.

"Don't pay for that, Joe," he said, "charge it to your room and let Mr. Mack pay for it. He can afford it a whole lot better than we can, believe you me."

I can't tell you how glad I was to see somebody I knowed.

"Room 377 is his, miss," he said.

The waitress picked up the bill, wrote the number on it, and handed it back to me. "Just sign, please," she said with a smile that said by then she knew damn well I couldn't do that.

Scotty come to my rescue for the first, but definitely not the last time.

"I'll tell you what," he said, "why don't you just charge it to my room. Mr. Mack is going to pay for it all anyways. This way it will be easier on him." He took the bill from me, scratched out my room number, added his and signed.

"Let's go play baseball," he said, then looked right at the waitress. "We play for Mr. Mack's Athletics. Maybe you've heard of them?"

I knew right then and there that it was not going to be easy to live in Philadelphia, but I had no idea how hard.

**TOPSY HARTSEL** When I found out that Joe hated living in the hotel, I made sure to tell him about Nat Hicks, the old ballplayer who had just recently choked to death on gas in his hotel room. Joe didn't like that story a lot.

**HYDER BARR** Me and Joe was both scared but for very different reasons. I was afraid I couldn't cut it as a player. I don't think Joe worried much about that. Why should he? Every place he ever played he was the star, the best player in the league.

I knew that Mr. Mack wanted somebody to stick with Joe and see that he could get along OK. Who better than an old friend from back home?

So I helped Joe every chance I got.

**EDDIE PLANK** Maybe Philadelphia wasn't the easiest place to live in for a kid from the Deep South. The village where he came from, I gather, was made up mostly of his own kind. But here in Philadelphia, he was truly faced with a cosmopolitan melting pot. Italians, Poles, Russians, Germans, Irish, as well as Negroes made up a big part of the population. Everywhere he looked, he saw people different from himself. Many were foreign born, speaking with accents he had never heard and couldn't understand. Almost all were educated, and most practiced urban occupations.

Joe knew little of this world and he was completely ill-equipped to make the personal changes necessary to adapt to it.

**TOPSY HARTSEL** I think Joe had a constant stiff neck from rubbering at all the tall buildings in the city.

**JOE JACKSON** Philadelphia was the busiest place I ever seen. Streets was plenty wide, with sidewalks on both sides and buildings taking up every inch of the way. It was hard to find a tree or even an empty space. The buildings was all brick and stone with signs and awnings going every which way. The streets paved with stone had trolley tracks running right down the middle and all sorts of trolley wires and electric wires crisscrossing on most of the corners. Policemen on horseback, trolley cars, horse-drawn wagons and carriages, and people crowding the sidewalks was everywhere. There was even some motor cars making lots of noise, and there was bridges going across some of the streets for people walking, just so they didn't have to fight their way past the trolleys and horses.

It wasn't easy finding breathing space.

**TOPSY HARTSEL** To give you some idea how raw Joe was when he came to Philadelphia, he says it was the first time he ever seen a row of houses with numbers on them. So what does he do? He goes to a hardware store and buys some big brass numbers to send to his mother to put on their house.

Now I ask you this? If nobody else in that mill village had numbers on them, how did he decide what number his house was supposed to be?

He had to have been a real genius to figure that one out.

**DANNY MURPHY** Among all the things that Joe didn't know, he didn't know about anybody who was important. I mean, in the clubhouse we'd talk about things when we were getting dressed and after the game. Joe never had any idea what we were talking about. He didn't know who Barney Oldfield was, or even Jim Jeffries. He didn't know the names Thomas Lipton, or Jack Johnson or Willie Anderson, and all these guys were professional athletes! When we talked about the Harvard-Yale football game he acted like we were talking about something taking place on Mars. If the names Enrico Caruso, Sarah Bernhardt, John Philip Sousa, Admiral Peary or even Buffalo Bill Cody came up, we might have been talking in a foreign language for all the reaction we got from Joe. If somebody even mentioned the Boxer Rebellion, the Boer War or the Russo-Japanese conflict, the conversation floated so far over Joe's head that he didn't even bother to look up.

Now, I don't want to characterize the clubhouse as a hotbed of intellectual curiosity, because clearly it wasn't that, but many of the guys on the Athletics had a college background and some of us even occasionally used words of two syllables or more. We just didn't speak the same language as Joe, either figuratively or literally.

**HYDER BARR** Seeing as how I got to Philadelphia before Joe, I was able to figure a few things out to help him a little.

The first thing is that the crowds were a lot bigger, and they dressed up a lot more, too, what with the men usually wearing suits and derby hats and the ladies decked out in their "Sunday best." The newfangled automobiles were everywhere and the owners were even finding places for them beyond the outfield fences as fans were beginning to drive them to the games.

Inside the clubhouses, there were shower baths where we could clean up after games. This was only for the home team, though, because when you were on the road you had to suit up in the hotel and ride a trolley to the game.

Compared to where we come from, it was pretty expensive to see a game. The prices could be as much as a dollar if the grandstands were covered, but sometimes only 25 cents for the bleachers in the outfield.

Our field was called Columbia Avenue Park and was surrounded by buildings where fans could get a free view of the game.

This was big-time baseball, and for the sake of my own career, I knew I had better help Joe with it.

**CAPPY GOLD** 1907, the old *Philadelphia North American* gave this young cartoonist a chance to try out his drawing skills by letting me do a series of cartoons sketches of each day's baseball doings. Lo and behold, the public took to them, and my cartoons became a fixture for a number of years. What I'd do was draw a collage-type cartoon that showed caricatures of each of the important players for a given game.

Well, I got to tell you, Joe Jackson quickly became one of my favorite subjects, and one of the public's, too. Boy, was he ever easy to do. He was tall and skinny and goofy-looking ... at least in my drawings. I made him look like what I think everybody thought of when they imagined a dumb, backwoods, country bumpkin—cap pulled down low over his eyes, with this aquiline nose poking out from the shadow of his bill, and usually with his mouth hanging open a little bit, kind of dopey like.

Joe told me a couple of times he didn't like it, but I didn't figure he was going to be reading the paper much anyway. Besides, that was my job—to develop a readily-identifiable character for each of the players, and this image of Joe seemed consistent with what I knew about him, his complaints notwithstanding.

Since we weren't using photographs much yet, these caricatures were all that thousands of fans knew about the looks of Joe. Oh yes, I should mention too, that I drew him without shoes as befitting his reputation.

# 16

# THANK YOU, MR. MACK

**HARRY DAVIS** According to the story often recounted by Mr. Mack, early on when he was struggling to get the Athletics going, John McGraw, who was then the manager of the Baltimore club, scoffed at Mr. Mack's efforts by declaring, "The Athletics are going to be the white elephants of the American League." So in spite, Mr. Mack adopted the white elephant as the logo for the team, and we've used it ever since.

The problem for Joe, though, was that in some respects, he was the living embodiment of that logo.

**CONNIE MACK** We were mighty eager to see what young Mr. Jackson could produce for the Athletics. When he joined us, we were in the midst of our first losing season ever! We knew he was young and raw, but if he were an individual of character, I knew he could help us. I was determined to find out.

You see, the Athletics were getting used to winning and anything less was unacceptable to me, and to our fans. In 1901, when Ban Johnson created four eastern clubs for his new American League, he asked me to manage a club he intended to start in Philadelphia. I was a bit skeptical at first, but the offer of part ownership in the club was more of an inducement than I could resist.

The first year we finished fourth, but the next year with a strong effort down the stretch we won our first pennant. We had six players hit over .300 and with Rube Wadell's strong pitching we were pretty tough to beat. The next two years we again began strong, but faded a bit, late in the season. In 1905, after a long struggle with the Chisox, we clinched our second flag. In our first World Series, though we ran into a buzz saw named Christy Mathewson who blanked us three times as the Giants took the Series 4 to 1. I never saw such a pitching performance before or since. He was just about unhittable. My boys batted a mere .161 for the entire Series. Only little Topsy Hartsel could figure out how to hit him, and that just wasn't near enough.

In 1906 a big slump in August did us in. The next year, though, after struggling in fifth place for much of the early season, we rallied to take a 2 1/2 game lead in September, but unable to make up a rain out and a tie, we came up a game and a half short of the Tigers.

So you can see, we were a club which was pretty much used to being a factor in the American League—until 1908. Most of the year we struggled around sixth place. Detroit with the young Cobb and "Wahoo Sam" Crawford tearing up the league, and Cleveland with Nap Lajoie having another great season, were making it pretty tough on the rest of us. Jimmy Dygert was chalking up a lot of strikeouts for us, and Rube Vickers threw something like six shutouts, but with the exception of Topsy Hartsel leading the league in walks, we didn't produce a whole lot offensively.

That's why I was so eager to see Mr. Jackson. They told me he swung a good stick, and that was something we surely were in need of.

**JOE JACKSON** I don't mind telling you, I was more than a mite nervous the first time I met Mr. Mack, and anybody who don't think he could make you that way either don't know what they're talking about or is a complete fool.

He looked exactly like what I thought the undertaker should look like—tall and skinny with pointy features.

When I walked into his office, he was standing next to a big brown desk that looked like it covered half the office. The room was dark with lots of brown wood and some baseball pictures on the wall, only I didn't see what the pictures were on account of being so nervous. A small lamp with a green glass shade was about all the light there was. Mr. Mack wore a black suit like the one you've probably seen in all them pictures of him standing on the steps of the dugout looking real serious.

He shook my hand right away with a real firm shake. That means something to me. Men who do that usually do what they say and stand by their word.

He told me to sit so I did, in this hard straight chair in front of his desk while he went around behind and sat in his own chair. He sat up real stiff and straight and looked right at me with eyes that looked like they could stare right through.

"Glad you're finally here, Joseph," he said. Nobody hardly ever called me "Joseph" so I knew right away he was going to be formal. In the South we're a little more friendlier.

"Thank you, Mr. Mack," I said, because that's what I always heard him called—Mr. Mack." Even much later when he was an old man and nobody in baseball used "mister" very much, he was always "Mr. Mack." One of his players told me once that his parents didn't even give him a first name because they figured he didn't need it. Can you imagine a little baby crawling around on all fours and being called "Mr. Mack?" I didn't really believe that story, but that's what they said. I found out later that his name was "Connie," and sometimes when he wasn't around, we called him that. "Old Connie this," and "old Connie that," but when he looked at you with them hard eyes of his, you can bet he was "Mr. Mack." Anyways, Mr. Mack did just fine for about a hundred years in baseball without a first name.

"Joseph," he said with a twinkle coming into his eyes, "I understand you've spent a little time in a cotton mill?"

"Yes, sir, I surely have," I answered.

"Well, I guess that makes us about equals then."

"You know about mills, Mr. Mack?"

"I guess I do. Now I can't rightly say it was in the South, because at the time I was born, my father was fighting against the South with the Massachusetts Regiment, but I trust you're not going to hold that against me."

"No, sir."

"I started working in the mill when I was about nine. What about you?"

"When I was six or seven."

"Well, you got me there."

I could see right away what he was trying to do, trying to make me feel comfortable. That was perfectly all right with me, because I was still feeling all jingly-jangly.

"It was at the East Brookfield Cotton Mill. Ever hear of it?" he asked.

"No, sir, not that I can think of."

"Ever been in Massachusetts?"

"No, sir, I never been in the North before yesterday."

"It isn't much different" he said. "People are people everywhere you go. Treat them right and they'll treat you right. Treat the game of baseball right and it will take real good care of you. Like it has me."

"Yes, sir."

"I'll bet you spent some time as a doffer boy."

I couldn't believe my ears. Here was this famous baseball man, who everybody in the country knew, and he was talking to me about doffing. Well, we must have spent an hour talking about mill work—about spinning frames and bobbins, about quills and sticking belts. For the longest time we never said nothing about baseball. He didn't even get up from behind his desk, and even though I was getting pretty antsy sitting that long, I didn't dare get up unless he did.

Finally, after a lot of mill talk, he got around to baseball,

"I was given an hour for lunch," he told me, but I seldom used more than 15 minutes of it to eat. I preferred to spend the rest of my lunch time playing any kind of a game involving a bat and a ball—one o'cat, four o'cat, roundball, baseball."

"Me too," I said. "That's exactly how I begun. Then on Saturday afternoons, and sometimes, when my mother didn't know, even on Sundays."

"Well, I'll be darned. You and me seem to be cut from the same cloth. Or at least we cut the same cloth." He laughed a little at that.

"You're going to do just fine up here, Joseph, just fine."

Well, I didn't know about that, but I could see right away why he was supposed to be such a great man.

"By the time I was 16," he said, "I had grown to over 6 feet tall and felt pretty silly sitting in that little desk they gave me at school, so I quit right there. It didn't seem right to spend a lot of time on schooling when I knew I was going to be a baseball player anyway. My parents weren't quite as certain as I was, but I bet you can understand that."

"Yes, sir, I surely can."

"Doesn't take a lot of learning to be a baseball player, I've always said. What it takes is a lot of talent and a lot of will. Think you have those things?"

"Well, I think so."

"Because you've got to have both. Now I know about the skill. What about the will?"

I didn't know exactly how to answer that, but it didn't matter much, because before I could think of something to say, he kept right on going.

"Always been an outfielder? he asked.

"Mostly, but I pitched a little bit and caught some, too."

"You know, I was a catcher. I'll bet you we're the only two mill hand catchers in Philadelphia."

I didn't even know he was a player at all. I thought he was always a manager.

"But I'll tell you this. It was a very different game when I started playing, very different. Would you like something to drink?"

I said I would but I wasn't sure what kind of drink he had in mind. My first thought was that maybe he meant hard liquor and I didn't want him to think that if all the players up here drank that at their meetings, that I couldn't be like that, but I was glad when the lady brought in two glasses of lemonade.

I kept waiting for him to get around to the part where he was going to tell me what I was supposed to do, and when I was supposed to be at the ballpark and things like that, but instead, he just kept going on about his time as a catcher.

"The darndest thing happened one day in Waterbury, Connecticut. I was in my catching position, which in those days was about 15 feet behind home plate. We caught the pitches on a bounce with a little glove without any fingers in it. You should have seen those gloves, not like the ones you fellows play with today with those long fingers. Anyway, I had been thinking for some time that there must be a better way to pitch than the way we were doing it. See, what the pitcher was doing, was hopping and skipping, and running through this little pitching box, and delivering the ball underhanded to the batter in such a way as to allow the batter to strike at the ball. Usually, the batter told the pitcher what height he wanted the ball, and the pitcher was obliged to do his best to do just that. And on top of that, the batter got seven balls and four strikes."

"I never knowed that."

"Well, on this particular day, the batter was one of those annoying fellows who kept complaining that the pitches weren't to his liking and I was feeling kind of ornery for some reason. I called time and went out to talk to the pitcher. I'd been thinking about this for some time anyway, so I figured this was as good a time as any to try out my new idea. Standing in front of the pitcher, I drew a line in the dirt with my toe. 'Try throwing the ball overhand from this line,' I told him. Well, I'm telling you he looked at me like I had lost all my marbles, but I was firm with him. He was used to paying attention to the catcher anyway, so he put his foot on the line and gave it a try. Well, the batter, who was surprised by the speed of the pitch, swung and missed it by a mile. After a couple of more throws like that, the Waterbury fans got the idea in their head that their side was being cruelly had, and they started getting rambunctious and made as if they were going to come out on the field after the pitcher. I ran out to him and told him, 'Don't listen to these fellows. Just pitch like I told you.' He did, and that's the God's-honest-gospel-truth about how pitching came to be like we know it today."

The more he talked, the more I wasn't quite sure what he wanted me to say about all these things, so mostly I didn't say nothing. I just sat and sipped my lemonade, which was pretty good, but not nearly as good as you could get from the cold drink stand in Brandon village.

"I always had a little bit of the devil in me," he said, "and we could get away with a lot of shenanigans back in those days because we only had one umpire and you couldn't expect him to see everything that was happening on the field. The only time I ever really got caught doing something tricky was once by an old ballplayer named Weaver. I think I was with Washington at the time. Anyway, this Weaver fellow, he got angry with me after I tipped his bat a few times, and he said he was going to get even with me. Did he ever. By gosh, the next time he had two strikes on him he just stepped back from the plate and instead of swinging at the ball he brought his bat down across my wrists. I dropped like a shot. Let me tell you it hurt like the dickens. But I right away figured out a way to get back at him. I bided my time until the final game of the year against Weaver's team. On Weaver's last time at bat he had two strikes on him, so I tipped his bat again, just to show him I could still do it."

For the longest time Mr. Mack told me stories like this. I supposed that he was trying to tell me that it was pretty tricky up in the bigs and that I better be ready for anything. Well, I wasn't really worried about that, because I figured I could handle myself pretty good on the playing field, but I was wanting him to tell me about what I was supposed to do. Besides, the chair was getting more uncomfortable the more he talked.

"I'd have played a lot longer except that I fractured an ankle when I was with Pittsburgh in a meaningless game against Boston, so I guess the Pittsburgh owners decided that rather than wasting the rest of my salary they might as well make me the manager. And that's what I've been doing ever since, and probably will till the day I drop. That's because there's so much to learn in this great game, and I'm learning all the time. I tell you, I make so many mistakes, that I might as well keep at it until I make them all. Then maybe I'll be a real smart manager. We all make mistakes in this game, Joseph, and I suspect you're not likely to be an exception to that. The question is, can we learn from our mistakes? I don't want you to feel you can't make mistakes out there on the field, but I would like you to learn from them. Work to get better all the time. Do your best on the field at all times. You owe that to baseball, you owe that to the Athletics, and you owe that to yourself. Will you guarantee me that? Will you promise me that? Because if you always give your best, you and I will get along just fine, and you will be rewarded by baseball in ways you can't even imagine."

"I will always give my best, Mr. Mack," I said. "I don't know no other way."

And let me tell you right now, I have done just that. I have always played every inning of every game as good as I can.

"As a matter of fact, I made a big mistake last season," he continued. "We were running nip and tuck with Detroit. We've got a pitcher named Jimmy Dygert, who you'll meet tomorrow. Now Jimmy can beat anyone for seven innings, but then he's finished. I could have pitched him seven innings any day of the week. If I'd been smart enough to realize this in time, I could have won that pennant. Instead, I didn't realize it until after the season, so we finished second and Detroit won the league. But I learned from that, and I won't make that mistake again, I'll guarantee you that."

I figured right then and there that if I could play baseball for anybody in the big leagues, I could play for Mr. Mack.

**EDDIE PLANK** I think Joe took an instant liking to Mr. Mack, but like all of us, he was a little afraid of him, too. Mr. Mack could give you a tongue-lashing the likes of which I never heard before. The thing is, though, he always did it privately behind closed doors. I know Joe disappeared into his office a few times and I can only imagine the scene. Mr. Mack was always very proper and preached sobriety and decorum and the avoidance of profanity. He was indeed, an awesome and dominating figure. I doubt if Joe, or any other player for that matter, had ever encountered such an imposing individual before.

**CONNIE MACK** I always liked boys who knew their Greek and Latin, and their algebra and geometry, and who put intelligence and scholarship into the game. They were the players around whom I built the Athletics. But, once in a while, a talent so prodigious came along that you couldn't ignore him whether or not he could read Keats.

**EDDIE PLANK** Now, I can't tell you I know how he felt, but I can sympathize a bit with Joe's problems when he first came up. Mr. Mack liked what he called, high-caliber athletes. To him that meant one thing—a college graduate. He wasn't one himself, but he sure liked to be associated with them. I doubt if ever before in baseball history had so many college men been recruited to one team as we had on the Athletics. Most ballplayers, if they were good enough, signed a professional contract when they were young and so, didn't have the chance to go to college. A few of us did, and it seems that Mr. Mack went and collected as many of us as he could. In '08, when Joe came up, we had Eddie Collins of Columbia College, 'Colby Jack' Coombs of Colby College, Chief Bender of the Carlisle Indian School, Jack Barry of Holy Cross, and me from Gettysburg College. Then, along came Joe.

**TOPSY HARTSEL** You would've thought we was running some kind of literary society with all the college men we had. The rest of us could at least read a goddamn menu without moving our lips.

**JOHN McGRAW** I had no use for collegers on my teams. What you need to win games are good players, not big thinkers. Most of the college boys I knew couldn't play worth a damn, but guys like Jackson ... well let's just say he knew enough to play about as well as anybody.

**HUGHIE JENNINGS** Despite the fact that I myself hold a law degree from Cornell University, I am of the firm belief that in the main, as ballplayers go, sandlotters are far preferable to collegians.

Maybe Joe never had a real chance given Mr. Mack's prejudice for the highly educated.

**HARRY DAVIS** If anything, Mr. Mack showed more patience with Joe than Joe deserved, but patience was a quality in which the manager specialized.

Once when one of our guys was thrown out at third base after hitting what should have been a cinch triple, Mr. Mack called him over to where he was standing on the dugout step.

"If you hit another triple, son," Mr. Mack said to him very calmly, "please stop at second base."

**TY COBB** Joe couldn't have done better than Mr. Mack for his first major league manager. I only played for him for two years, and those were the last of my playing career, but I wish I could have played all of them for him.

He was one hell of a smart baseball man, not like most of the morons who became managers. Let me give you one little example.

I was out there in the outfield just after joining the A's, and a player came to bat that I had played against for several years. I looked toward the dugout and Mr. Mack was cutting the air with that score card. He wanted me to move to the right. Now, I ought to know more about this than Connie Mack does. I thought he was wrong, but I moved to my right anyway. He kept on waving and I moved another dozen feet to the right. By this time Mr. Mack was halfway out of the dugout, signaling frantically. He didn't stop waving until I was 20 more feet to the right.

You know what happened? The batter hit the ball right into my hands. I didn't move one step. I decided then and there that Mr. Mack was the best outfielder in baseball.

He could have taught Joe a lot. It's a shame he didn't get the chance.

**EDDIE PLANK** Whether Mr. Mack was the best or the worst choice to be Joe's first manager is a matter of some debate.

On the one hand his fascination with the college educated ballplayer certainly did not bode well for Joe. On the other hand, Mr. Mack was something of a con man who could coax good performances from players where others might fail. He could talk a whippoorwill out of its song. Some of us even thought he could talk Joe into being happy in Philadelphia. Never a man of violence or of strong language, he was as glib and as shrewd as they came. It was said that as a catcher he talked many a hitter into striking out and countless players into fits of anger that interfered with their effectiveness. He seemed always to know exactly what topic would distract each batter, and better yet, when to introduce it. But his *piece de resistance* as a catcher was a cute little trick he perfected early on in his career. He developed a method of slapping his hands together in a close approximation of the sound of a ball skinning a bat. Many an umpire was tricked into thinking it was a tipped ball, which if caught was, of course, an out.

When the umpires caught on to that one, he developed the art of unobtrusively tipping the end of the bat on the batter's back swing. That worked until one day a wary batter smashed his hand, ignoring the ball altogether.

On several occasions I saw him keep the game balls on ice which he determined would diminish the distance they could travel, and more than once he ordered the groundskeeper to mix soap in with the dirt around the pitcher's mound to lessen the footing for enemy batters.

Mr. Mack was as guileful and resourceful as they came. I hoped he could apply some of his cunning to the problems coming his way with Joe's arrival.

**JOE JACKSON** Mr. Mack wasn't around much, other than the game and practice and times like that. The only time I ever seen him outside the ballpark was on the train and in the hotel dining room, and even then he didn't talk much to us. He was the manager and the owner and we was the players. I think he wanted to make sure we knowed that.

# 17

# I HATED PHILADELPHIA

**HARRY DAVIS** That 1908 season was a difficult one for all of us, so Joe didn't exactly come into an ideal situation. But, disaster or not, we were a team, and the guys felt pretty strong about that. Any interloper into our group was going to face problems. We were a team that didn't make a lot of changes during the season. Socks Seybold was set to be our right fielder, but when he broke his leg on a spring training trip, Jack Coombs took over in right. He started out strong, but when his average dipped in the middle of the season, Mr. Mack moved Danny Murphy from second to the outfield and replaced him at second with Eddie Collins. Rube Oldring and Topsy Hartsel manned the other two outfield spots. I was at first, Simon Nicholls handled shortstop, although he struggled all season to keep his average above .200, and Jimmy Collins played third with the same problem. By the time Joe got to us, Doc Powers was doing most of the catching.

We were a team that got along reasonably well. Anyone coming in would have to prove himself. Joe didn't, or couldn't do that.

**JOE JACKSON** The first time I was in the locker room I seen this little half-dressed man sitting on a stool.

"Call me Topsy, everybody else does," he said.

At first, I didn't even think he was a ballplayer, because he was so small. I thought all the players for Philadelphia would be big guys, probably even bigger than me. But here, looking like a little rabbit, was about the smallest guy I ever seen and he had white hair and eyebrows and gray eyes.

"I'm Joe," I said.

"Yeah, we've been hearing about you for some time now. Where the hell you been?"

"In the hotel."

"Must have been a helluvah hooker," Topsy said choking back a smile.

I didn't get a chance to say anything about that, because right away he asked me what position I played.

"Outfield," I said.

"Funny thing about that, Joe. We got five already on the team."

"I didn't know that."

"I play left, what about you?"

"Don't really matter."

"I like playing left," said Topsy slamming the locker door hard, but still smiling.

"I'd rather play right, or someplace like that," I said.

"Good, cause I got a wife to support. And wives cost a lot of money, know what I mean?"

"Yeah, I know."

"Just as long as we understand each other."

"Oh, yeah, I understand."

"Besides," he said putting his face real close to mine, "most of the little guys play the infield and leave the outfield to big guys like me."

I believe he was joshing me, because there just couldn't be a lot of players smaller than him, not even if they wasn't ballplayers.

"I bat leadoff," he said. "You're not a leadoff hitter are you?"

"Nah, I never batted leadoff."

"Good, cause I like batting there, and Mr. Mack likes me to swipe a base or two before the little guys come up. Know what I mean?"

"I guess so."

"And I been doing it for him for eight years. You don't swipe bases, do you?"

"Well, once in a while I do."

"That's OK in the bushes, but I wouldn't do that here if I was you. Mr. Mack don't want nobody doing the pilfering here but me. Know what I mean?"

"Don't pay attention to Topsy," said the big man that come walking in the door. "We're just hoping that someday, when he grows up, he'll be big enough to have a brain."

"Harry's the Cap, Joe," said Topsy, "but that don't mean you have to pay any attention to him. Hell, nobody else does."

"Hi, I'm Harry Davis," said the big man holding out his hand in an official way. "Anyway, what do you expect from a grown-up man named Topsy?"

"Character, integrity and talent," said Topsy.

"Know how he came by that handle, Joe?" Harry asked.

"Well, I never seen nobody named that before," I said.

"He got that handle because he's the exact opposite of that character in *Uncle Tom's Cabin*. That ought to tell you just about everything you need to know about him."

"Oh, yeah," I said, "I know what you mean."

It seems like everybody in the clubhouse went by some special nickname. Sometimes they called Harry, "Jasper," which Topsy said was the name in some minstrel song, but most of the time, everybody just called him "Cap" or "Captain."

"Listen," the captain said, "I've got a few rules here you might want to give the once over." He took out of his pocket a piece of paper with a lot of writing on it and handed it to me. "Not a big deal really, but there are a few rules that we all live by."

I looked closely at the paper.

"Don't play first, do you?"

"Sometimes I do, but not most of the time."

"Doesn't really matter though," he said. "You always play your best, and produce, you'll get your playing time; don't and you won't."

Harry Davis looked to me to be too old to still be playing baseball, but as I found out, he was the one Mr. Mack most trusted and when Mr. Mack had to be gone from the team for some reason, Harry took over for him.

He had led the league in home runs the last four years and everybody said he was about the smartest player around.

He must have been smart because, as I learned later, his father died when he was only little and he was sent to an orphanage in Philadelphia. I guess he done pretty good there, though, because he became such an important person with the Pennsylvania Railroad Company that he didn't even want to play ball, but Mr. Mack kept asking him to play for the Athletics because he needed a first baseman. He kept saying he was going to keep working for the railroad, but then one day he said OK to Mr. Mack who almost always got his way. He's been real good friends with Mr. Mack ever since.

I think he was practicing to become a manager someday. He sure knowed a lot about baseball so I always listened to what he had to say.

"You got any questions about the rules" he said pointing to the paper in my hand, "you be sure to ask."

"All right, I will," I said.

"As soon as you get dressed, come right out on the field. My son will warm you up, then you can hit a few."

I thought he was old, but I didn't think he was old enough to have a son on the team.

"Cap's kid's sort of a mascot," said Topsy probably noticing the confused look on my face. "Warms the guys up, and stuff like that."

I began putting on the Philadelphia Athletics uniform for the first time. The white elephant on the front was a famous picture, and the Mack Men, as the players were called, were about as well-known baseball players as there was. Heck, they had already been champions a couple of times.

But the truth is I didn't know any of this that first day I got there. This was a major league team in a big city far from Brandon Mill. That's about all I knew.

"Topsy, which of these rules you think is the most important?" I asked after a couple of minutes of looking at the paper.

"The one that says rookies always carry the luggage of the leadoff hitter. You can start by bringing my bat and glove when you come out, will ya," he said as he walked towards the door.

So I picked up Topsy's bat and glove and followed him to the field.

**JACK COOMBS** Seeing Joe in the locker room for the first time, he appeared to be exactly what I expected—a big, strong, farm boy type. But, boy, was he ever jittery. His eyes, they darted around the room like an enemy soldier waiting to be ambushed at any moment. He was an ingenuous, raw hick who was an easy target for our locker room shenanigans. Anybody who thinks that was wrong doesn't understand how a baseball locker room works. Here was a place where only one type of person could be found—male athletes.

As athletes we were always under pressure to perform at a high level. Don't do that and you are no longer part of the group; you are no longer admitted to the clubhouse. Outlets to this pressure took several forms not the least of which was hazing rookies. In that respect, Joe was no different from any other rookie.

**TOPSY HARTSEL** To hear Joe talk, you would think he was the only rookie on the team. Well, he wasn't. Hal Krause, Frank Baker, Jack Barry, and Biff Schlitzer was all in their first year when Joe come up, and they was all about his age, too.

Look, they all took a lot of ribbing as rookies. That was part of baseball then, and it still is. The only one that didn't take it so good was Joe.

**RUBE OLDRING** We got on all the rookies. Anything that we could find to make fun of, we did. That's how we let off steam and that's how you become tough in the world of the baseball player—you took the heat and never let on that it bothered you. Joe never learned that. It seemed everything bothered him, and the more we got on him, the more he responded, and the more he responded, the more we got on him. That's the way it was. It wasn't personal.

Yeah, that first short season of Joe's we got on him a lot, but not any more than we did to Krause who looked like he was 12 years old, but was recommended to Mr. Mack by some undertaker in San Francisco. There was no way we were going to let those kind of things go without a hell of a lot of ribbing.

**HENRY KRAUSE** Earlier in the year that Joe and I and a few others joined the Athletics, I pitched for the St. Mary's College team out by Frisco. One day Mr. Mack himself showed up at a game. He either liked what he saw or he was impressed by my 26 straight wins. At any rate, he offered me a lot of money to ignore the Pacific Coast Leagues and head straight to Philly. I just about dropped dead on the spot, but recovered in time to catch the next train east.

By the time I got to Philly, the papers were already calling me the "boy wonder," mostly because I looked so damn young. When the older guys on the team saw that, they never let me forget it. "Hey little boy, does your mamma know you're out this late?" "Isn't it past your bedtime, sonny?" I heard cracks like that and a hundred more.

The only thing I could do was ignore them and go out and pitch the best I could. I only got in four games that first season. The next year when I won 18, most of the wisecracks stopped.

A couple of times I told Joe to try to ignore the ribbing, but I guess he couldn't. Anyway, nobody was apt to take a lot of advice from somebody who looked as young as I did.

**FRANK BAKER** When I come up to the Athletics in September 1908, Joe was already there. I could see how unhappy he was, being a kid from the South, but damnation, so was I. The difference was that I made the most of it instead of whining about it all the time like Joe. Hell, I was born on a farm in Trappe, Maryland, to a family that could date its ancestors back to sometime before the Revolutionary War, and it was the only place I ever knew before I left to play baseball.

I only come to bat 31 times that first year, but at least I didn't run back to the farm as soon as things got tough. See, Joe wasn't strong that way. I mean he had lots of muscles, but he didn't have strong character.

**HARRY DAVIS** Although Joe and Frank Baker were both rural southern boys, you never saw two guys with less in common. Joe was quiet but played the game with grace and ease, Frank was not a very graceful third baseman but he played like a tiger. Although he wasn't real big, he was probably the only guy on the team who wasn't afraid to take on Ty Cobb. Once Ty slid into him spikes-high, but Frank never backed down. Mr. Mack got angry about that and told everybody that Cobb was the dirtiest player the game ever knew.

Anyway, if Joe could've had some of Frank's moxie he might have been a lot better off, and if Frank could've had some of Joe's grace he might not have gotten spiked so badly.

**EDDIE PLANK** Joe was given a locker next to Jack Coombs. Other than maybe hunting and fishing which they both loved, I can't imagine what they could have possibly talked about while dressing for games. Get this: Jack was from Maine, Joe from the deep South; Jack graduated from Colby College with honors, Joe couldn't even read his name; Jack had a quick biting wit, Joe was, well ... let's say, not quick; Jack was personable with a big engaging smile, Joe was withdrawn, and at least when he first came up, downright shy and sullen.

Colby Jack, as the press often referred to him, was my best friend on the team, and easily the brightest guy I've ever known.

If anything typified the problems Joe faced when he joined us it was exactly this dichotomy—Joe and Jack trying to coexist as teammates. Why Mr. Mack thought Joe could fit into this group I couldn't begin to guess. I blame Mr. Mack in part for the problems that arose.

It's not that Jack gave Joe a particularly bad time, it's that they couldn't possibly have understood each other. Everything that Jack did, he did well and I mean everything. He was the best damn hunter I ever saw, one of the best pitchers in the game, an outstanding outfielder, a terrific hitter and as I said, a real bright guy. Hell, the year Joe came up, Jack pitched in something like 26 games and played the outfield in maybe another 50. He was a true phenom!

**CONNIE MACK** My brother, Tom McGillicuddy, who ran a hotel in Worcester, Mass, found Coombs for me. He saw him with the Barre-Montpelier team during the one summer he spent in the Northern League.

I didn't have him long when it became readily apparent that I had someone who, as great as he was at pitching, could do more than that. At college he played every position at one time or another, even filling in as catcher when needed and to top that off, batted from either side of the plate. He was a great sprinter in college, played football, and apparently was brilliant in the classroom.

I had Joe put next to him in the locker room, hoping he would know how to help Joe adjust.

**JACK COOMBS** Joe was a good enough guy but he was like a duck out of water. He was quiet, didn't talk much to the guys. Anyway, what could you talk to him about? I doubt if he could have even told you who the president was. I did spend enough time around him, though, to realize that behind his somewhat stoic demeanor was a man of considerable imagination. I truly believe that, had he had the opportunities to acquire a reasonable education, he could have become a good writer—such were his gifts for invention and fancy. His was not a dull mind, but a mind lacking the tools of expression. There is a difference.

We took a lot of long train rides, some of which, like the one between Philadelphia and Chicago, seemed to last forever. Mostly we horsed around a little, slept when we could, and read a lot. Joe usually sat by himself and stared out the window. A couple of times I wanted to go over and talk to him, but other than that day's game, we didn't have a lot that we could talk about and sometimes you just didn't want to talk about the game. I think Joe was lonely right from the get go. Looking back on it, I probably could have, and should have made more of an effort on Joe's behalf, but it wasn't the best of times for me, and I have to admit, my attention was mostly elsewhere—on myself.

**EDDIE PLANK** In '06, Jack had startled the baseball world by pitching the A's to a 24-inning, complete-game victory over Boston, the longest game in Major League history. He was remarkable, and everybody predicted he would become the next great pitcher in baseball.

The following season, he started out like that was exactly what would happen, but it wasn't too far into the season that his arm fell limp at his side. The papers said he snapped a tendon in his arm, but lots of people around the league figured the problem was a result of pitching that long game. "Arms aren't made to withstand 24 innings of hard throwing" went the reasoning. Jack took some time off to rest then came back throwing again, but not with the same power. Anyway, we lost the pennant that year in a close race with the Tigers, and Jack took a lot of gaff for not pitching like people expected him to do.

So, in '08, Mr. Mack, figuring his arm wouldn't be much help in the twirling department made him one of the outer gardeners. Then when Joe came along, Jack was struggling to get back his form as a pitcher, as well as playing the outfield. Now, Jack was very much a gentleman, but I'm sure he couldn't have been too eager to help Joe develop his outfield skills without knowing for sure whether his future was there or back on the mound.

It was a tough situation for both of them.

**DOC POWERS** I tried to help Joe a little—you know, tell him about where to play some of the hitters, that sort of thing. I had to do something. I sure as hell wasn't hitting much that season. In fact, we used four catchers in all. Ossee Schreckengost hit something like .220 before Mr. Mack sent him packing. Syd Smith managed to bat barely .200 before he was also sent packing. Jack Lapp spent a little time behind the plate too, but he didn't even hit .150, so I was getting most of the playing time when Joe came up. As I said, I wasn't hitting much either, but Mr. Mack liked the way I handled the pitchers, and I wasn't too bad with the leather. So, anyway, I spent what time I could talking to Joe about positioning, but I'm not so sure he listened. He was the kind of player who mostly went on instinct. He didn't like to analyze anything too much. I think it confused him, and he may have been right anyway. With his God-given talent he didn't have to think much in the outfield. He could run down just about anything and he could throw better than anyone I ever saw.

**TOPSY HARTSEL** Mr. Mack gave Joe his lecture on what he called "pride and self-respect." It embarrassed the hell out of Joe, and the next day he got Socks to go out with him and buy a suit. It was the stupidest looking suit I ever seen.

**SOCKS SEYBOLD** Mr. Mack asked me to take Joe downtown and help him find a decent suit—one that he could wear on road trips. He said to take him to Gimbel Brothers on Market Street, charge it to the team, and that he'd take it out of Joe's first paycheck.

Gimbels' was right next to Leary's Book Store, so I stopped for a minute to look for something my sister-in-law asked me to get. Joe stood next to me for a minute then picked up a book and began looking at it like he was reading it. This is something Joe got pretty good at after a while, and I doubt if most people knew the truth.

In Gimbels', Joe went for the worst looking suit you could imagine. I didn't say anything, but I got a kick out of seeing the look on Mr. Mack's face when Joe walked in wearing it the next day.

**DANNY MURPHY** I remember Topsy once told a story about a catcher from some one-horse town in Georgia—a kid named Billy Morgan. It was a true story, too. I remember it being in the papers. It seems this kid was in Chattanooga, Tennessee, for a game when he up and dies of blood poisoning he got from the coloring in his uniform—and he was only 23.

Now Topsy made sure Joe was in earshot of the story—even though he was acting like he wasn't telling it to him, he really was.

"See, the reason this kid died," says Topsy kind of loud, "is because he couldn't read the damn washing instruction on the label. Can you believe that? He died of stupidity. I'll tell you, this is a real dangerous game if you can't read the instructions."

**TOPSY HARTSEL** If we didn't take him with us once in a while to a restaurant, he would have starved to death. He'd hold up the menu in front of him like he was reading it. I don't know who he thought he was fooling. I guess the waiter or somebody.

He'd wait for somebody to order then he'd order the same thing. We all knew that so sometimes we'd order something really strange so Joe would do the same, then we'd change it leaving Joe with the first order. I can't tell you how many times he had things like sardines and ice cream for breakfast.

**JOE JACKSON** When I first walked out onto the Columbia Park field where the team played its games, I was a little surprised. It was big, all right, but not nearly as grand as I thought it would be. It had a one-story high covered stand that went down each foul line as far as the bases, then open bleachers going the rest of the way down the lines in the outfield. The grandstand was very plain, nothing like the Walton Hotel. Poles holding up the roof came down right in the front. Behind the plate on top of the roof was this little box where all the writers sat. Why they was so far from the field, I'll never know, but Mr. Mack once told me it cost $7,500 to build the park, which was a lot of money, so I guess they could put the writers anyplace they wanted.

The stadium was made of wood and painted dark green. Still, it was a good field to play on. It had a lot less rocks and holes in the outfield than any field I ever seen. The outfield was big, with lots of room to run down long fly balls.

When I walked out on the field for the first time on that hot and sticky August afternoon, I looked first up into the stands.

"Don't let it bother you, kid," said Harry Davis. "There's only about 6,000 people here today."

That didn't bother me. Heck, I'd played in front of that many before, only they was all from the South.

**JIMMY DYGERT** When Joe came out onto the field that first time, Mr. Mack asked me to throw him a little batting practice.

He looked as nervous as a pot of boiling coffee but once he got to the plate and began swinging, boy, oh boy, did he ever look pretty. I pitched to a lot of young batsmen in my time, but he had as natural a swing as I ever seen. I don't think I ever seen anybody with a faster bat in my life.

I began by throwing easy, but when he kept knocking ropes into the outfield, I started picking up the pace. When he hit them, too, I tried mixing in a few curves, and then a spitter or two. He didn't get hold of all of them, but he hit enough that the other guys stopped what they were doing and began watching. Now, I was in my fourth season in the majors and I wasn't about to be showed up by no rookie, so after he hit one off the wall in center, I sent him a message pitch right under his chin. He spun away so quickly I couldn't believe it. He had about the quickest reactions I ever saw, but he was making me look bad in front of the guys, and that I couldn't let continue.

They may have called me "Sunny Jim" because I was usually upbeat, but that season I was putting up a losing record after winning 20 games the year before, so I was feeling a little ornery. On the next pitch I threw the ball as hard as I could right into the kid's ribs. Nobody was quick enough to get away from that. He winced, grabbed his side and dropped to one knee, then right away bounced back up into his batting stance.

I don't know which made a bigger impression, his courage or his stupidity. On the next pitch I hit him again and would have continued to do it until he stopped getting up, but the captain came over and took the ball from me.

**RUBE OLDRING** When little Jimmy Dygert plugged Joe not once, but twice in a row the first time he come to bat, we all practically choked laughing so hard. See, Jimmy couldn't have weighed more than 135 pounds and was about as big as a good-sized bag of peanuts. He got by on the skill of his spitter, certainly not his fastball, so despite what he always said about that incident, he didn't hurt Joe none at all. But what he did do by making Joe a target for his slippery one, was to set up Joe as a kind of target for the rest of us.

**TOPSY HARTSEL** Everybody knew that the Cap was the home run king of Columbia Park. In fact, he hit over 40 there. Socks, too, hit a lot and I hit my share, but the way the papers told it, Joe was going to be the big fence-buster on the team.

Well, when Jimmy hit Joe he sent a real clear message. Not everybody on the squad was happy with what the papers were writing. Joe would have to prove himself, and that was going to be no easy task. Hit more dingers than the cap? Not likely.

**JOE JACKSON** Heck, all I was there to do was help win games and I thought that's what teammates was for, but I guess they didn't all think that way.

They played tricks on me and things like that because I was different than they was. Most of the time I pretended like it didn't make no difference, but in it wasn't no fun.

I never cried but there were times when I felt like it.

Like one time when we went to eat at a restaurant with Topsy and Danny and a few of the guys, and the waiter come and asked me what I wanted. I said I was still deciding. Then Danny ordered meatloaf and potatoes, so I told the waiter I'd have the same thing. Well, while the waiter was going to get the food I noticed this little bowl of water on the table.

"That's special water for drinking," Topsy says.

"They do that at good restaurants a lot," says Danny, "especially in Philadelphia. In fact, it's kind of a Philadelphia tradition. Go ahead and taste it. You'll like it."

Well, I never seen water served in a little bowl like that before, but all the guys seemed to know about it so I picked it up and drank it down in one gulp. Everybody broke out laughing. I hated it in Philadelphia.

# 18

# I PLAYED PRETTY GOOD

**HAMIE** That Joe succeeded as well as he did is a perfect example of how far a man may go in this world without any brains whatsoever.

**ART GRIGGS** Seeing as how I was one of the few who played with both Joe and Ty Cobb, I have been asked over and over to compare the two. Now, I like to think that I know a little about playing the game since at one time or other I played for 15 clubs and that includes every position on the field except shortstop, and I probably could've played that too if anybody would've asked me. I also played football for the University of Kansas where I was an All-American halfback, and a couple of years at Pittsburgh. So, I guess you could say I had the background to compare a couple of pretty good athletes.

Now the first thing you got to realize is that Joe had a build very much like Ty's. They were both around six foot, and 175 or 180 pounds. In fact, they were so similar that the line used to be that you couldn't tell them apart—from the neck down.

Let's face it, Ty Cobb dominated the game, and except maybe for a few old-timers, is generally considered to be the greatest player ever. But how did he compare to Joe? Well, there's no arguing with Ty's record, or with the fact that he was a brilliant hitter, but I'll tell you this: Joe Jackson was a better natural hitter by a country mile. The fact that Ty got better and better as a major leaguer is a testament to his brain, which probably worked faster than his feet. But Joe's record shows that he was a brilliant hitter from the first.

Ty studied the game like a master chess player, Joe responded like an instinctual animal. Ty was crafty and quick-witted, Joe was impulsive and simple.

Ty worked every angle in hitting. He out-guessed and out-psyched the pitchers. He beat out hits with his dazzling speed. He tricked fielders into mistakes and used every con and ruse the game has ever known. Joe stood silently at the plate and when he saw a pitch he thought he could hit he swung with natural ease and grace. He didn't try to outguess anyone. He just swung the bat and let nature take over.

As a fielder, Joe was a keen judge of distance, possessed great natural speed, and had a throwing arm maybe as good as anyone who ever played the game. On more than one occasion I saw him throw out runners at first from right field on sharply hit balls, and many a time I saw him reach over the outfield fence to take sure home runs away from frustrated hitters. If Ty was a better outfielder it was only because he was mentally more alert, but his arm certainly couldn't come close to Joe's.

On the base paths, Ty's records remain unsurpassed, but he was no faster than Joe. A couple of times guys tried to set up a race between the two, but Ty would have none of it. That means only one thing: Ty didn't think he could win. Otherwise you can bet he would have leapt at the challenge. But, there's no denying, overall Ty was the better base runner. He worked at it. He studied the moves of every pitcher in the league, he faked and tested them every time he got on base, and of course, he intimidated scores of fielders with his aggressive running.

Joe Jackson, combined in one body all the natural talents needed to be a great ball player. On the mental side of the game Ty outshone everybody.

Ty was the greatest, but Joe should have been.

**JOE BIRMINGHAM** I played with Joe for a few years and even managed him for a time, and I'll tell you flat out. I wouldn't have traded Joe Jackson even up for Ty Cobb. Of the two, I considered Joe the greater asset to a club. Everybody knows Ty could play the game, but so could Joe. Don't let all the other stuff get in the way of believing that. Ty was trouble in the clubhouse, Joe wasn't. I'd take Joe any day of the week.

**WALTER JOHNSON** I consider Joe the greatest natural player I ever saw.

**EDDIE PLANK** From the minute Joe first stepped onto the field he had to live up to his own press. And did he ever! He threw right handed like he was armed with a rifle, whistled line drive after line drive left handed, and ran like a gazelle.

**VINCENT ALEXANDER** I consider it one of the greatest thrills of my life that I was at Columbia Park the day Joe Jackson made his initial appearance. I guess it was kind of fate, because it was the first time that I had been to a professional game. It was my ninth birthday, August, 25, 1908. My father took me to the game as a birthday present. It was then, and has remained ever since, the best present I ever received.

My father owned and ran a small restaurant on the south side of Philadelphia—a lunch counter really. Since my mother died after suffering a terrible illness when I was seven, and I had no brothers or sisters, my father took care of me every day even though he had to go to the restaurant. After school and in the summers, what I would do was go to the restaurant and sit up against the wall on the last stool at the counter. Mostly I read, or sometimes I drew pictures until Father was ready to go home. What I usually read was any part of the paper left by a customer. That generally meant the sports page. In time I became a grade school expert at reading box scores.

Box scores are incredible things if you think about it. Each one is an entire game in microcosm. Each one, if you apply enough imagination to it, has all the color and the drama of a real game. I came to love and devour them daily. Blessed with something of a photographic mind, I committed to memory scores and statistics by the page full. Ask me today how many strikeouts Jimmy Dygert had in 1908 and I will tell you 164 without batting an eyelash. Ask me who among the Athletics regulars that year had the highest batting average and I will tell you it was the second baseman, Danny Murphy, who hit .265. You can look it up.

I didn't have the time or the ability to make a lot of friends when I was growing up because until I got older, I had to spend all my spare time in the restaurant. So even though I had never seen or met them, in a way the players on the Athletics became my closest friends.

Then, on my ninth birthday, about noon, my father, without saying a word to me, hangs a big sign in the window of the restaurant. "Gone To A Baseball Game With My Son. Will Reopen Tomorrow At 6:00"—this from a man who never, and I mean never, closed the restaurant except on Christmas and Easter. It's hard to explain how excited I was. Even now, so many years later, I get misty-eyed just thinking about it.

It was a cool drizzly day, but I didn't care. For weeks the papers had been full of stories about the arrival of a baseball savior—Joe Jackson. According to Hyder Barr who was widely quoted in the papers about Joe's prowess, "The people of Philadelphia have never seen anybody like Joe. He's going to put Philadelphia back on the baseball map."

We got to the park early, bought two tickets, and took our places in the stands behind first base just in time to watch the Athletics take batting practice.

Now I've been to hundreds of games since, but there is nothing like the first time you walk into a real baseball stadium and see the perfect green grass, the perfect white lines, the neatness of it all. Going from my black and white box score world to the Technicolor symmetry of Columbia Park was the most magical moment of my young life. It is an immutable memory, now as much a part of me as my right hand, only far more cherished.

Adding to the special character of this event was the fortuitous convergence of three elements in my life: it was my first trip to a professional baseball game; it was Joe Jackson's first game in the majors; and it was the only game I ever saw with my father. He died suddenly about a year after this and I went to live with my aunt—his sister—on the other side of town. She had no interest whatsoever in the game, but my love for the sport continues to this day as does the memory of that first game.

Before the game started we found out that Joe would be playing center field and batting fourth. How incredible! A rookie in his first game batting cleanup! It looked like Hyder knew what he was talking about. Harry Davis usually batted in that position, so I wondered what he must have thought about moving down the order for this new kid.

The Athletics were playing The Cleveland Naps, a team named after their manager and greatest player, Napoleon Lajoie. From the box scores, I had learned about everything there was that a kid could learn about the little second baseman. I knew that at that point, at the peak of his career, he had a lifetime .350 average and had already won three American League batting crowns.

Now, for the first time, I was seeing him in person, a real honest-to-goodness god of the game. There on the field in front of me was Larry Lajoie and George Stovall, and Harry Davis and Jack Coombs—box scores come to life. And of course, there was Joe Jackson ready to write his name into a major league box score for the first time.

My father was positively beaming with pride as he pointed out player after player on the field. It was an act of genuine love and giving the likes of which I seldom recall seeing from my otherwise stoical father.

Cleveland was battling with Detroit and Chicago for the league title, so this game was extremely important. Philadelphia was pretty much out of the race, but the interest in seeing Joe was so strong that the park was filled to capacity and an atmosphere of tremendous anticipation was everywhere.

Heinie Berger was the starting pitcher for the Naps. He was having a good season, his second in the majors, and was being counted on by Cleveland to supply some key wins down the stretch.

When the game finally started, I was so captivated, I could hardly contain my enthusiasm, which, mirroring that of most in the large crowd, peaked when Joe came to bat for the first time in the bottom of the first inning. There were two outs with Danny Murphy on second. The crowd gave Joe a tremendous ovation which he acknowledged with a little smile. If he was nervous, he sure didn't look like it to these eager 9-year-old eyes. Berger threw a mean spitball most of the time, and on this dark, misty day, it must have been particularly difficult to pick up. On his first pitch to Joe, the big righty came inside and Joe smoothly stepped into it whipping Black Betsy around, pulling the ball foul down the right field line. The fans cheered Joe's aggressive attempt. On the next pitch, Joe waited a split second longer, timed the pitch perfectly, and sent a screeching line drive into left field, easily scoring Murphy from second. The crowd went wild. The mighty Joe Jackson had finally arrived.

As the game continued the sky got darker and darker, but Joe continued to light up the park. Twice he hit screaming line drives directly at Bill Bradley, the Nap's third baseman who managed to catch them in acrobatic acts of self-preservation, and once to the fence in right where Billy Hinchman stretched his six-foot frame to its limit to haul it in.

In the second inning, Berger hit a looping fly over Joe's head in center. Everyone in the park, including me, was sure it would drop in for at least a double. Everyone, that is except Joe, who turned tail to home plate, and racing at full speed caught the ball over his left shoulder just a few feet shy of the flagpole in dead center. Again the crowd went wild.

It was his throwing, though, that really set people off. A single off the bat of Joe Birmingham skipped close to the wall in left center. Joe scooped it up and fired a perfect one-bounce strike to Jimmy Collins at third. Then later in the game, just to show that it was no fluke, he unleashed a perfect throw to the plate from deep right center which the pitcher cut off and fired to Davis at first to nab Birmingham who had rounded the bag. Birmingham just stared out to center in utter disbelief. Joe's cannon-like right arm was on display for everyone to see.

All Philadelphia was thrilled with his debut. Even though the Athletics lost the game, salvation seemed at hand, and Joe's debut was the talk of the town.

I floated home after the game with my father. We were never closer than we were that afternoon.

From that day on, I collected every box score of every game Joe ever played in the majors. Somehow in my mind we were inextricably linked. His debut coincided with the most memorable day of my youth. How could I ever ignore that!

**WILL McGEORGE** We sportswriters began searching through our memory archives to find a parallel to Joe's style of playing. With his brilliant arm, graceful speed, and uncanny timing on fly balls, we came up mostly with a few players from the 90's—guys like Georgie Treadway who could throw as hard as anyone I ever saw. Someone else suggested Curt Welch, who some of us remembered from the days when he patrolled center field for the Philadelphia team in the old American Association. Curt, who could go get 'em as well as anybody, played with a rugged swashbuckling style seldom seen in the players of '08. But Joe, he kind of reminded us of those players from an older age. He was a throwback, and we were looking forward to the opportunity of writing about his kind again. Based on that first game alone, we all assumed he would be around for a long time to come.

**CONNIE MACK** I was concerned that the press, the players, and fans give Joe time to learn and develop without expecting too much out of him. Remember, he was only a boy, and fresh out of the Deep South at that.

**JOE JACKSON** I was nervous in that first game. Sure I was. I played pretty good but I would've liked to have had a couple more hits. The fans though was real good to me, but the players, they was a different story.

**RUBE OLDRING** Hell, if anybody had a right to be a trifle upset, it was me. I play most of the games in the outfield, mostly center, right? Then they bring the two kids up. First they put Scotty Barr in center and then when the prima donna finally shows, they put him in center. Jackson gets one hit. Big deal, right? The fans go nuts. The kid's a savior they say. Savior my ass. He was so scared I thought he was going to wet his pants and run home to mommy.

Well, one out of two ain't bad.

**TOPSY HARTSEL** Joe got one hit for crying out loud, but the way the press played it up, you would've thought he was the second coming of The Flying Dutchman. Well, he wasn't. Not by a long shot.

# 19

# I HEARD THE RUMORS

**CHARLES "RED" DOOIN** The Major League baseball world that Joe joined in 1908 wasn't as pure as some people think. I can attest to that. That was the same year that I was approached to throw the last seven games of the pennant race. I was the catcher on the Philadelphia team in the National League and we were having a pretty good season, but in mid-September we were still trailing New York, Chicago and Pittsburgh. Our last series of the season was with McGraw's Giants and they were out for the sweep they needed to take the pennant.

What happened was this. Just before the Series started, me and three of the pitchers on our team were sitting at a secluded table at a downtown Philadelphia cafe when two big guys came in and in broad daylight threw this black satchel right on top of the table. We knew what was coming next so none of us said anything. Well, one of the big guys opened up the satchel—must have had $150,000 in it.

"Help yourself, boys, don't be shy," he said.

Look, we weren't stupid. We knew exactly what they were about.

"It's real easy," said the big guy who was obviously in charge. "Stub your toes a couple of time in the Giants Series, and you can make more money in a few days than you'll make for the rest of your careers. Who's gonna know? Nobody's gonna know, that's who."

Nobody said anything. We just sat there with all that money sitting right in front of us. The big guy was right about one thing. It would've been easy.

"What do you guys care anyway," he said. "You're out of it, right? You can't win anything, so what do you have to lose? I'll tell you what, you don't have nothing to lose, but a whole lot to gain. Besides, nobody's gonna get hurt but we can all make a little money. What's wrong with that? I'll tell ya. Nothing's wrong with that. It's smart, that's all. Just plain smart."

Now, I've often wondered what would've happened if they had approached just one person at a time. Would any of the guys have gone for it? I don't know. I know I wouldn't because I don't do things like that.

Everybody said no, that we weren't interested, and that isn't the easiest thing in the world to do. It's not just the money, it's these two big guys standing in front of you who look like they might be able to get real dangerous real fast if you get them angry. But, they didn't do anything. They just packed up the satchel and walked quickly out the door.

But that wasn't then end of it. Right after the first game of the series, I was sitting alone in front of my locker putting my stuff away when a little guy with a suit that was too big for him comes in and stands right in front of me. How he got in, I have no idea, but I can imagine. Anyway, I wasn't surprised to see him, only I didn't think he'd be so brash as to do it right there in the clubhouse. He pulls a big wad out of his pocket and sticks it right under my nose.

"Here's $8,000 in cash," he says. "Count it if you want, but I'm an honest kind a guy."

"Yeah, you look like it," I says, the sarcasm going right over his head.

"There's $40,000 more if you sit out the rest of the games in the series."

"You want to pay me not to play?"

"Yeah, what a deal, huh?"

"What a deal," I repeat.

Just then, our first baseman, Kitty Bransfield comes into the room. His locker's next to mine, and believe me, despite being called "Kitty," he was one tough guy.

"This schlemiel," I says to Kitty, "wants me to throw the rest of the series. What do you think about that?"

"Yeah?" says Kitty. "Is that what he wants? Well let me show you what I want. I want your sorry ass out of here."

With that he grabs the guy around the neck in a choke hold, drags him down the hall, and shoves him down a flight of stairs. See, we didn't want gamblers around our team. We were going to play the game straight. That's all there was to it.

The next night, while I was walking outside the hotel I was jumped and hit over the head with a blackjack. When I came to I was in an empty room with no windows and a locked door. I knew right away that whoever done this to me expected to hold me there until the series was over, but catchers are tough. I took one heck of a run at the door barreling into it with my left shoulder. The reason I used my left shoulder is that I throw right and I didn't want to hurt my throwing arm because I had every intention of playing the rest of the games. Well, I'll tell you, that door came down like it was a cardboard box, and I just kept on running, and I never did look back.

I played the rest of the series and we even won a couple of the games which meant that the Giants and the Cubs tied for first place. In our last game, the Giant's first baseman, Fred Merkle, failed to touch first base and that became one of the most famous plays in all baseball history. We finished 15 games back.

I'll tell you something else, though. This wasn't the only time I seen gamblers trying to get players to cheat. It happened plenty.

Myself, I saved organized baseball four times by fingering the crumbs who approached players that I knew. They couldn't handle me and that is probably the reason I was forced out of the game when I was. There are too many stool pigeons. They want birds they can handle.

**BILL KLEM** Someone asked me once how rampant cheating was in baseball when Joe was playing. It was all over. Even as an umpire I could see it.

Just before the playoff game in 1908 between the Giants and the Phillies, which I was umpiring, I was approached by Giants team physician, Joe Creamer.

"Bill, you'll be set for life if the Giants win," he said to me like he was talking about some real estate deal. "Tammany Hall has assured me of that."

I told him I wasn't interested, but he kept following me and even pressed a stack of bills into my hand at one point.

Can you imagine what would happen to the game of baseball if umpires were on the take?

I got away from Creamer by walking out onto the field. He didn't dare follow me in front of the fans.

A year later he was barred for life from entering any stadium in organized ball, but as far as I know nobody ever found out who was behind his activities. I can tell you this, though, it wasn't McGraw. He'd do almost anything to beat you, but not pay for opponents to take a dive. He'd rather beat your brains out fair and square.

**JOHN McGRAW** Of all the World Series that I took part in, the one in 1905 really stands out.

Everybody was looking forward to a showdown between Christy Mathewson and Philly's Rube Wadell. But Wadell said he hurt his shoulder wrestling with a teammate. The rumor circulated among the fans that Rube had been bribed by gamblers to fake the injury. Even the papers published stories of a big conspiracy by gamblers. Although the rumors were never proved, the gossip that the World Series had been fixed lasted for years.

I never believed that story. To this day I think Rube was afraid of Matty. After all, he had good reason.

**CONNIE MACK** Rube was hurt. Forget about that supposed gambling story. The Philadelphia Athletics were not cheaters.

**JOE JACKSON** When I joined the Athletics, I didn't know nothing about the Series in '05. It didn't take long, though, before I heard the rumors. I never believed them. It's easy to start some rumor that this or that player cheated, and once it gets into the papers, just about everybody takes it to be true.

Rube Wadell was gone from the team by the time I got there, but I met him a couple of times later and he sure didn't look like no cheater to me, and if you listen to them sportswriters, I'm a guy who ought to know something about cheating.

**CONNIE MACK** I know it's become popular to say that baseball in the early years of this century was crooked, but that's just not accurate. Oh sure, we had some rotten apples, but what business didn't? The game itself though was pure—always has been, always will be. Baseball is America, and America isn't crooked even if a few of its citizens might be.

# 20

## IT DIDN'T SEEM RIGHT

**CONNIE MACK** In retrospect I suppose I should have seen the trouble coming, but I didn't.

After Joe's coming-out party against the Naps, we were scheduled to play a crucial four-game series against the Tigers—crucial for the Tigers, that is, because they were four games out front in a hotly contested pennant chase. The Tigers were a team of stars, the brightest of which was certainly the Georgia Peach, Ty Cobb.

Cobb was in his fourth major league season and had already established himself as a serious rival to the game's greatest player, the Flying Dutchman, Honus Wagner. The year before, Cobb won his first of what would eventually be 12 batting titles. He was as good as they came, and as tough as they came.

The papers were already playing up the confrontation between Joe and Ty, and we were selling out the park on the anticipated rivalry. The reigning king versus the pretender. It looked like a perfect match-up, except for one factor: it began raining cats and dogs. First one game, then another was rained out.

What is clear to me now is that Joe needed to play. He was reasonably at home on the field, but with the rain outs he was forced to do what waiting ballplayers do. He spent hours sitting around the hotel lobby, hours during which he was at the mercy of the other players, many of whom resented the attention being lavished on this gullible and insecure kid.

**WILL McGEORGE** With no games to report on, we had to find or create stories to keep our readers' interest. With Cobb in town, even the rawest of scriveners could find some conflict on which to base a story.

Readers always go for a David and Goliath story and this one practically wrote itself. Shoeless Joe takes on the Peach. Two southern boys duke it out. Brains versus brawn. Take your pick.

**TOPSY HARTSEL** Maybe Joe couldn't read all them stories coming out about him during that rain delay in the Detroit series, but we sure as hell could read them to him. Why not? The rest of us had to read stuff about us all the time. Why should his idiocy shield him from what the rest of us had to put up with?

**RUBE OLDRING** If there was a story about Ty Cobb that any of us knew, it was paraded front and center for Joe's benefit. Ty was depicted as the most arrogant, hostile, aggressive player in the game, one who ate rookies for breakfast, which by the way, was the God's honest gospel.

We assured Joe that baseball wasn't a game to Cobb, it was war, and he couldn't wait to get at the enemy—us! Nobody could demoralize the opposition the way he did. He was a blooming nightmare on the base paths, always taking extra bases, always stretching the single into a double, always doing what you didn't expect him to do. The result was that the fielders were forced into panicking, into throwing to the wrong base, fumbling the ball, things like that. And the infielders, they were afraid of being spiked or knocked senseless by his aggressive slides.

"You could get killed out there with him, Joe and that's no joke."

"And he hates anybody else from the South."

"Did they name that team after him, or what?

"His father's a teacher, did you know that? Taught Ty to read and write like a college prof. He's real smart, that Ty. Of course he can't stand anybody who isn't smart like him. Those are the guys he particularly goes after."

"Killed a greenhorn once just because he was stupid. That's what I heard."

"They say he's killed a bunch of guys."

"Welcome to the big leagues, Joe."

**HARRY DAVIS** I remember all of us sitting around the hotel lobby waiting for a decision as to whether we were going to play that day or not, and we started talking about the game the year before against the Tigers that ended in such a huge ruckus.

We were percentage points ahead of the Tigers in late September when they came to town for a three-game series that would decide the pennant. They took the first game, but then it started raining. I guess that was the story of the Athletics-Tigers rivalry. So we had to play a double header on Monday on account of the law about playing on Sunday.

We are up by two runs when the Tigers come to bat in the ninth. With Crawford on first, Cobb hits one out of the park to tie the game and Mr. Mack brings in Eddie Plank to take over on the mound.

Well, we go into extra innings, and each team scores one in the 11th. Then in the bottom of the 14th, I hit a line drive into the overflow crowd in the outfield. A ground rule double, right? That's what everybody thought, except Cobb goes after the umpire and screams bloody murder that a cop who was trying to hold the crowd back, interfered with Sam Crawford, their center fielder as he tried to make the play.

That's when all holy hell broke loose. Both teams emptied onto the field, and everybody started swinging at everybody else. Cobb was a madman. First he started pounding Jimmy Dygert, then Eddie Plank. I guess he was looking first for the pitchers. Me and Germany Schaefer got into it pretty good, and so did Rube and Claude Rossman, their first baseman. The crowd was going nuts and before long the fight turned into a complete free-for-all with players sprawled on the ground everywhere. I don't think anybody got hurt real bad, but it was one hell of a fight. I've never seen one like it since. When everybody got tired, the fight wound down, and order was eventually restored. Ty would probably still be out there if a couple of guys from his team hadn't pulled him off Topsy.

Silk O'Laughlin was the chief umpire that day and after checking with the other umps, decided I was out. How he came to that conclusion, I'll never know, because it was dead wrong. But what can you do? Cobb got his way and the game ended on account of darkness in the 17th inning with the game still tied, 9-9. Since the Tigers had to leave town the next day for another series, the second game was never played.

So the Tigers beat us out for the pennant by percentage points, all on account of that lousy call and the fight started by Cobb. We should have been the champs in '07, no doubt about that. Needless to say, we weren't real happy with Cobb, but then again, who was?

**CONNIE MACK** Silk O'Laughlin had it in for us, plain and simple. Either that, or like a lot of other folks, he was afraid of Cobb. Cobb could play a little, but oh was he a bully!

I was hoping Joe would be our Cobb, albeit with a completely different personality.

**HYDER BARR** Man, oh, man alive, did Joe ever come in for a verbal lathering while we was waiting for the Detroit series to continue! I mean some of the guys was absolutely merciless. I guess I was lucky, because they rode him so hard, they pretty much forgot about me. One really good target I suppose was better than two mediocre ones.

See by now they all knew that he couldn't read or write and that translated into him being "moronic," "dim-witted," "idiotic," "feeble-minded," "simple-minded," or just plain old "dumb."

They used these terms to each other, but sometimes within earshot of Joe. I know he heard them, and I know he was bothered by them, too.

There must have been a million "dumb Joe lines."

"The closest thing Joe will ever come to a brainstorm is a light drizzle."

"Joe's actually brighter than he looks. But then he'd have to be."

"He's living proof of reincarnation. He must be. Nobody could get that dumb in one lifetime."

"It takes real talent to be as dumb as Joe."

The guys baited him with endless strings of questions.

"Hey Joe, do you suppose if you stand in front of a mirror with your eyes closed you can see what you look like when you're asleep?"

Joe said that was stupid.

"Is it true, Joe, that in South Carolina if you want to raise a litter of puppies, all you need to do is plant a piece of dogwood?

Joe said he didn't think so.

Not all the guys did this all the time, of course, but it was pretty hard to resist. Joe was real gullible, and the more gullible you was, the more you became a target. That's the way it was in the clubhouses and in the hotel lobbies. It didn't start with Joe, and it didn't end there, but it was rough in his case.

Looking back on it I suppose I could have been more of a help to him, but I was as new as he was, and I didn't want to become any more of a target than I already was. Helping Joe was good, but siding too much with him when the players were around just didn't seem like a good idea

**TY COBB** I didn't have anything against Joe, really I didn't. In fact, I kind of liked him. He was a good old southern boy like myself and a good player. Up north we had to stick together a little as there was always prejudice against us by some of those northern snobs—especially in cities, like Boston and Philadelphia.

The thing is though, baseball isn't tidily winks. You have got to be tough to play it and you have to use every advantage you can find. I liked Joe, but I wasn't about to give him an inch on the field. That's not the way you play the game, and I think Joe understood that. See, with Joe, you could use psychology. You could psych him out a little and sometimes a little is all you need to get the edge.

**JOE JACKSON** When I went down to the lobby to see if the game was canceled on account of rain, there was a lot of the Tigers players standing around because they wanted to know the same thing.

I didn't know none of them, but as soon as I got to the bottom of the stairs one of the Tigers came right up to me and put out his hand friendly like.

"Hi, I'm Ty Cobb," he said pumping my hand real hard, "and I take it you're Joe Jackson?"

"Yeah, I am," I said.

"Well, it's good to finally meet you," he said. "We southern boys have to stick together."

"Yeah, I know what you mean," I said.

"I've heard a lot about you," he said, looking me over hard.

"Really? Me too," I said. "I've heard a lot about you, too."

"Way I hear it, you've got a pretty good stick."

"Yeah, I guess so."

"But that you're having a tough time against major league pitching."

"I don't know, really. I've only just played one game so far."

"Well, don't worry if they send you back down," he said real firm like, "in a couple of years if things go your way you can always work your way back. Yes, sir, I've seen a lot of players like you who can't hit big time pitching first time they come up. So I wouldn't worry about it very much if I were you."

He winked and went back to the other players.

Man, I thought to myself, I just met the greatest player in the game, and he even talked to me.

**EDDIE PLANK** There was a story going around that McGraw hired a private detective to dig up dirt on opposing players, so he would know how to needle them. Nobody had to do that with Joe. He looked and spoke so much like the country bumpkin that the onslaught began from the moment he arrived.

The best thing to do if you're being jockeyed, is to keep your mouth shut, which is essentially what Joe did.

The only difference in Joe's case is that usually you do it to guys on the other team, not your own. But Joe was just such a perfect foil—naive and innocent—that it was hard to resist.

**RUBE OLDERING** I remember once when one of the fellows—I won't say which—loaded Joe's suitcase with bricks. It brought the place down when he tried to pick it up.

**TOPSY HARTSEL** I sent him out for a can of striped paint once, and the moron took me seriously.

He was part of our entertainment and the release we needed from the pressure of a pennant chase.

**JOE JACKSON** I knowed the players was making fun of me and it made me sick. I was shaking all the time and I couldn't eat nothing. Sometimes it was even hard to breathe. I tried my best to stay by myself as much as I could, but sometimes you just had to be with the team.

All I wanted to do was to play baseball. It didn't seem right.

I hated Philadelphia, I hated the players, and I hated myself for letting them do that to me, but I didn't know what else to do.

I wanted to go home. I wanted to see Katie. I wanted to stop feeling sick.

**HYDER BARR** I went up to Joe's hotel room after he had been through a particularly rough time with a couple of the players. I thought maybe he could use a down-home friend. I knocked, but he didn't answer. I knocked again. Still no answer.

I found out the next morning he had caught a train back to Greenville.

One game in the majors and it looked like his career was over. There was no doubt Mr. Mack would blackball him now. What a shame, I thought. He could have been one of the best. Now he would just be remembered as a quitter.

# 21

# THIS TIME FOR GOOD

**DAVID JACKSON** Word got back from Philadelphia on the telegraph machine that Joe had a good first game, so we didn't expect him home so early.

So, boy, oh, boy, was we surprised when Joe got off that train. Lollie Gray seen him right away, and before Joe even got to the house, everybody in the village knowed that he was back.

**MARTHA JACKSON** Of course I was glad to see Joe, but I didn't like to see him feeling so bad. He talked to me about what happened in Philadelphia, and I can't say as how I exactly blamed him. Joe was welcome home any time he wanted. He didn't have to have no excuse neither.

**CONNIE MACK** The day after Joe disappeared, I received a telegram from his mother.

"Joe is game, and he has always been game. He left Philadelphia because I sent for him. His wife was very sick and his uncle is not expected to live."

I had Tommy Stouch check on it. He telegraphed back that someone in the family was in fact ill, but his wife was fine. It was clear that his mother was covering up for her son.

Once again doubts began to arise that Joe possessed character sufficient enough to allow him to be a successful player in the major leagues. There was a reason why I preferred college players—when you brought them to the team, they stayed there!

**HAMIE** Anybody who said they was surprised when Joe ran home after one game didn't know Joe.

**JACK COOMBS** Stories began circulating on the heels of Joe's defection that he was afraid of the impending confrontation with Ty Cobb. More likely he was afraid of the confrontation with his own teammates.

**VINCENT ALEXANDER** The papers said nothing initially about Joe's departure, so thousands of fans jammed the park the next day. When word finally got around, there was considerable disappointment.

I know it was fashionable at the time to subscribe to the theory that Joe was a coward, that he was afraid of Cobb, and that's why he left.

There is something else to consider, however. How about Cobb? In the series he went 1 for 14. Maybe he was afraid that Joe would show up at any minute.

**COOPER ANDERSON** Fear can take lots of forms. What's one man's tiger is another's pussy cat. Some people are petrified to speak in public; some relish the opportunity.

But fear, whatever the source, can be completely debilitating. Never mind that the source may seem to be irrational or inconsequential to an outsider, if a person truly fears something strongly enough, paralysis or flight will often follow, and rationality be damned.

What frightened Joe so much that he was willing to risk the future that he so dearly longed for?

Ostracism from the other players? That can be as crippling a fear as any.

**TOMMY STOUCH** I was beginning to think that maybe I'd have Joe back on the Spinners after all, but I was worried he would be blackballed. I had seen it happen before.

Then I received a wire from Mr. Mack telling me to bring Joe back to Philadelphia immediately. If I could get him there soon enough, it appeared that we could avoid the blacklist.

There was one person I knew could persuade him quickly, if she wanted to—his mother. I decided to pay her a visit.

**MARTHA JACKSON** Anybody who thought Joe ran away from Philadelphia because he was scared just doesn't know my Joe. Joe is game, and he has always been game. He left Philadelphia because I sent for him. His wife was very sick and his uncle was not expected to live. That was all there was to the story.

**TOMMY STOUCH** Mrs. Jackson was adamant.

I told her about the blacklist which would certainly spell the end to Joe's professional baseball dreams, but she said family came first.

I asked to speak to Joe.

"Well you can't" she said. "He's tending to family sickness business."

The fact was, Joe was hiding, and as he would do on a number of occasions, he was refusing to defend or explain himself.

**DAVID JACKSON** While everybody was getting all riled up about Joe, we was mostly out hunting. Joe didn't say much except that he didn't want to go back ever.

He said that there was lots of baseball in the South that was every bit as good as any played in them northern cities and that he could be perfectly happy playing down here for the rest of his life.

**SUMNER HOCKETT** I can't swear to the truth of it, but there was a story going around when Joe come back that a lot of people talked about for a long time.

It seems that he was out hunting with his brother Davey when they come across this old back woodsman everybody called Rabbit who gives Joey a lucky rabbit's foot, because he thought it would bring him good luck when he was playing.

Joe tells him he "wasn't playing no more and didn't need no lucky charm," so he throws it in the stream and it disappears down between the rocks.

Ol' Rabbit took it kind of personal that Joe wouldn't take his good luck charm, so after that he told everybody that he put a curse on Joe.

Joe said he didn't care about things like that, but I think he really did.

**HAMIE** One thing is for damn sure, a deserter is looked on with about the same regard in big league baseball as in the army.

**KATIE WYNN JACKSON** A few days after Joe came home we received a telegram from Mr. Mack. "Report at once" is all it said.

I read it to Joe. He didn't say a word. Just picked up his gun and went out into the woods.

I thought it would be best for Joe if he went back, but I knew that pushing him wouldn't accomplish anything except to get him more upset and he was already upset enough.

A little time was all he needed, but I wasn't sure Mr. Mack was going to give it to him.

**JOE JACKSON** After being home maybe 10 days, Mother talked to me about going back. She said I could learn to live in Philadelphia because it wasn't going to be for all time. She figured that I have to live there less than half the year, and a lot of that time we would be at the ballpark. I would have all winter to spend in South Carolina, and after all, that was the best time of the year there anyways.

The next morning I got on the train to Philadelphia and Katie wired Mr. Mack that I was on my way.

It seemed like a longer ride this time especially because I was by myself. I was a little worried, too, about what Mr. Mack would say.

**CONNIE MACK** I realized when Joe returned, that if he was going to be successful in the major leagues we would have to treat him differently. He needed special attention, but the question was, would the results be worth it?

Special attention to one player always created problems with other players, but as our team wasn't going anyplace anyway, I reasoned that the effort was warranted.

I offered to get him a tutor to teach him to read and write. He said he didn't think he wanted to do that. To be more precise he said, "It don't take no school stuff to help a fella play ball."

Well as it turns out, maybe it did.

**TOPSY HARTSEL** When he came back, I think Joe thought things would somehow be different. They weren't.

Joe stayed pretty much to himself again. He went from the ballpark to his hotel room, period. I mean he didn't even come out of his room to eat in the hotel restaurant. What he was living on, I have no idea, but it sure as hell wasn't food!

**VINCENT ALEXANDER** The Philadelphia faithful had largely abandoned the park by the ninth inning in Joe's return engagement, as the outlook seemed settled by then. The A's were down by two in the ninth when Hartsel popped out to Conroy at third for the first out. Mack sends Eddie Collins in to hit for Oldring. He gets two strikes on him and then singles up the middle. Coombs goes in to run for him. Barry draws a walk, setting the stage for Joe. It was a perfect situation for him. Come through and he's a hero. Come through and maybe some of the criticism slackens. Joe takes a pitch, and then on the second offering he digs in and drives the ball to deepest center field. The ball doesn't miss going out by much, but Charlie "Eagle Eye" Hempill gets a good jump and runs it down, catching it against the fence.

I have long wondered how it might have been different had Joe gotten another 3 feet on that ball. The fans longed for a hero in what was settling into a disappointing season for them. They might have embraced Joe as some kind of savior. Instead they turned on him for his faults. Who said baseball is a game of inches?

Harry Davis, always up for a challenge, sends the next pitch over the fence by way of Twenty-ninth Street. He is the hero of the moment but he is 35 and his best years are behind him. The crowd wants to see the possibilities of the future, and Joe is the future.

Such are the pressures of expectation.

The next afternoon, the Athletics play the New York Highlanders again, this time facing Happy Jack Chesbro, a tough little righty with a pretty good record. The A's fall behind early, largely due to two errant throws by Doc Powers. Joe got one harmless single and caught one ball in center.

The crowd started getting on him some. Joe came packaged as a great hitter and great hitters need to hit.

**JACK COOMBS** The day after the two New York games, we had a travel day and took the train down to Washington for a doubleheader the next day. Washington didn't have the best club in the world, but they did have two of the better pitchers in the game—Long Tom Hughes and Walter Johnson. As luck would have it, we had to face both that day.

I talked to Joe a little on the train about Johnson.

"You can't hit what you don't see," I told him, "and you sure as hell can't see the Big Train's ball, so just listen for the sound of it coming toward the plate, close your eyes and swing easy. Sometimes you get lucky."

He asked me with a straight face if he should really close his eyes.

**CHIEF BENDER** While we were talking on the train I found out that Joe was a trap shooter, and a good one at that. I invited him to join some of us over the winter for a shoot. I thought it might be good to get him involved with some of the guys. Keeps the eyes sharp. Lots of the guys did it—Speaker and Cobb were particularly good at it. Heck, I got 25 straight one time, and 22 was easy most of the time. It's sort of like baseball with one big difference. In trapshooting you got to hit it where it is, and in baseball where they ain't.

Joe wouldn't do it. He just didn't seem to want to have a whole heck of a lot to do with the other guys. A number of years later though, he did. Could he ever shoot! That sonovagun had an eye like an eagle.

**DANNY MURPHY** I guess Joe finally got hungry enough that he had to go down to our hotel restaurant in Washington. Me and Topsy sat down next to Joe and Topsy told him he really looked hungry. He said he was.

Joe buried his head in the menu. God only knows why. I mean everybody on the whole damn team knew he couldn't read a lick, so I don't know why he thought he had to carry on with the charade.

Anyway, he was pretending to read the menu when the waitress came by and asked us for our orders.

"Go ahead, Joe," I said, "I'm still deciding."

"Me too," Topsy said.

"Me too," Joe said, "I'm still deciding, too."

"You know," Topsy said to the waitress, "I think I'll just have a small glass of milk."

Topsy gave me that "go along with me" look of his, so I said, "Make it two."

Now Joe really did look like he was starving, but all he could muster was a weak, "Yeah, that sounds good to me, too."

"I thought you was hungry," Topsy said.

"Not too hungry, really."

We drank our milks—small glasses each—and I went to my room with Topsy and ordered two room service steaks with baked potatoes. We were starved.

**JACK COOMBS** One of the guys—I won't say who—heard a story about Gabby Street, the Washington catcher. As part of a bet, it seems Gabby caught a ball dropped from the top of the Washington monument. He told Joe it was something all rookies had to do when they came to Washington. He said Joe should go with him out to the monument and wait at the bottom while he climbed up to the top to throw out the ball.

Joe said he thought he could do that.

Lord knows how long Joe waited, but his fellow player, of course, went immediately back to the hotel. When Joe finally realized he had been had, he left, but never said a word about the incident

**JOE CANTILLON** First time I saw Jackson I didn't figure he could ever make it in the big leagues. Fact is, no man can who can't read or write. That's pretty much proven to be the case, hasn't it?

I was managing a dismal Washington squad in '08 when Joe and the Athletics came to town for a doubleheader. I made sure Johnson pitched one of the games. I really wanted to see how Joe would fare against the best.

**VINCENT ALEXANDER** On September 12th, The Athletics played a doubleheader in Washington against the Nationals. Joe started and played all of both games.

The great Walter Johnson pitched the first game, and although he wasn't in top form, he managed to win the game 2 to 1, besting Eddie Plank. Joe was blanked in four at bats, but he was hardly the first batter to come away empty-handed against the Big Train.

In the second game, Jack Coombs completely shut down the Nationals while the Athletics had a field day against the tired arm of Tom Hughes banging out 15 hits on their way to a 7-0 win. Rube Oldring collected five hits himself including a home run. Danny Murphy added four more hits as just about everybody got into the act. Everyone that is, except Joe. He went 0 for 5.

**WALTER JOHNSON** I almost took pity on Joe that day, and probably would have had he not been the opposition. I could see right away that he was pressing too hard and I knew I could take advantage of that, which is exactly what I did. Baseball is a mighty hard game to play well when you're not relaxed.

I thought I was about the greenest rookie that ever was. I didn't even know there was a bus to carry the players downtown, and after my first game I walked down Pennsylvania Avenue in my uniform, with a curious crowd following me. That night I was standing on the street, looking at a big electric sign on a building that said, "JOHNSON HOTEL." A stranger came up to me and said, "Kid, you're famous already. See, they've named a hotel after you." And you know, I actually believed him.

I've got to admit, though, Joe may have been my equal or better in the greenness field.

**JOE JACKSON** Walter Johnson was about the toughest pitcher I ever seen. We had plenty of boys down on the mill teams that could throw hard, but none of them was like Johnson. The thing is, he not only throwed so hard, but he never put the ball in the middle of the plate where you could get a good swing at it.

The first time I seen him, Rube Oldring and Danny Murphy got a couple of hits off him, and Doc Powers got a scratch double but I don't see how. I didn't even get close.

In the second game, Mr. Mack dropped me down to sixth in the order. The pitcher was Long Tom Hughes, a big right hander. I remember Rube Oldring hit a long home run to left off him, but I didn't do nothing.

The feeling in the locker room was real tense. Some of them acted like I wanted to not get a hit all day. Well, let me tell you, it made me almost sick to my stomach. I was trying so hard. One thing was for sure, they wasn't just funning me.

After the game we went back to this big hotel, only I didn't go to my room. When nobody was looking, I walked out and went directly to the train station. I bought a one-way ticket for Greenville.

Yes, I was going home again, only this time it was for good.

**VINCENT ALEXANDER** A lot of the things written about Joe over the years just aren't accurate. One small example: all the records show that Joe played in five games for the Athletics in 1908, came to bat 23 times and got three hits for a .130 batting average. The fact is, he got only two hits for a .086 average.

I've collected every box score for games in which Joe played, and I've checked these carefully.

Don't believe everything you've read or heard about Joe. Some of it just isn't so.

**KATIE WYNN JACKSON** Mr. Mack kept sending telegrams, first pleading, then telling Joe to return to Philadelphia. Joe didn't answer any of them. He just kept saying, "I'm not a baseball player anymore, so why doesn't he save his money and stop sending me all them telegrams?"

Joe was in pain and he was angry.

"What are you going to do, Joe?" I asked him.

"I'm gonna go back to the mill where they leave a man alone."

Finally, a last telegram came from Mr. Mack. It read: JOE JACKSON HEREBY SUSPENDED FROM BASEBALL FOR LIFE. WILL NEVER PLAY ORGANIZED BALL AGAIN.

# 22

# I COULD ALWAYS COME HOME

**J.C. HATCH** Joe's father, always an independent cuss, had set up a small butcher shop and was operating it full time by the time Joe returned. As I recall, he worked with his father all that winter, wielding a meat cleaver with the same sweet skill as he had swung a bat.

During the winter, opinions about Joe's baseball future were flying hot and heavy. Harrison's was awash in speculation. It seems that everyone but Joe had a comment to make about his future. He said nothing, at least publicly. Nevertheless he had become Brandon's one and only celebrity. Joe had played in the major leagues, and even if he never returned he had a taste of glory the likes of which the rest of us would never experience.

He wasn't seen around the village much, and he didn't go to Harrison's anymore. He spent his time hacking meat and with Katie and his family.

The more distant he became, the more the rumors flew. Joe would never play league ball again; Joe would play in the southern leagues for the rest of his career; Joe had a deal with Mr. Mack to trade him to the National League; Joe would come back the next year with the Athletics as a pitcher; Joe had agreed that he would only play in Greenville; Joe was hurt, that's why he left the team.

The guessing games helped pass what was a particularly wet and gray winter.

**RICHARD COLZIE** The big question was, would Joe come back to the mill, or was he too much of a big shot? Some of us put together a betting pool and guessed when we thought he would be back. The first time he put his foot on the mill floor was what counted, and whoever guessed the nearest date would win. We had close to a hundred guys that was sure enough he would be back to put money in.

Every once in a while, he would pass by the mill and somebody would shout, "Joe's coming!"

**JOE JACKSON** Working in the butcher shop was a whole lot better than working in the mill. For one, there was no lint, and two, there was no clock to punch. Davey, Luther, the twins, all of us spent some time in the shop that winter, but it wasn't big enough for all of us to work there at the same time. In fact, it was a pretty small place, but it was nice to see Father a lot happier.

Don't get me wrong about the work. It was still pretty hard, but I figured that carrying heavy sides of beef and doing all the other heavy work would help keep me fit in case I went back to playing ball. Not that I was sure I was going to, but just in case.

**LUTHER JACKSON** Father's shop was really a tiny little room in what used to be a storage building.

Some of the villagers would come by in the morning on their way to work and place an order, then while they was at work Father would get their order ready so they could pick it up on their way home.

Joe worked with him sometimes because I think it was easier than having to go to the mill every day and explain why he wasn't still with the Athletics.

**MARTHA JACKSON** The way I figure it, anybody has got a right to decide what they want to do with their life without somebody else making them do something they don't want to do. That's what I told Joe.

**CONNIE MACK** It was time Joe came to grips with his own destiny, so throughout that offseason, I let it be. I didn't send any more telegrams, and I didn't send any retrievers down after him.

If he decided to play, he knew where to find me.

He was blackballed, of course, but those kind of things didn't have to be written in granite.

It wasn't me who was stopping Joe from playing ball. It was Joe.

Maybe because most players had to work so hard at it, they appreciated what they achieved, while with Joe it came so naturally that he never treasured what he had until it was taken away from him.

**CHARLIE LEBEAU** I stopped by the butcher shop a few times ostensibly to order some steaks for dinner but really to see if I could talk to Joe.

"I'm kind of busy working here, Mr. Lebeau," he would say, "and my father wouldn't like it much if I was talking and not working."

"You can do both, Joe," I responded. "You can work and talk at the same time."

"You got to really concentrate to cut the meat right, Mr. Lebeau; it ain't as easy as it looks."

This went on for several visits. Then one rainy afternoon in December I stopped by with an old friend.

"Joe, this is Jim Egan," I said. "He wanted to come by and meet you."

Egan was maybe 60, but his weathered features made him look all of that and more. As Joe continued to chop away at hunks of raw beef feigning only passing interest, Egan told him how years ago he had faced a golden opportunity. He was only a youngster when he and his best friend, Cap Anson, had their contracts sold to Chicago of the National League. After years of struggling in the bushes, it was his big chance to play major league ball. Anson went on, but Egan had serious reservations.

Eventually he turned down the offer so that he could work for $1.78 a day as a brakeman on the Missouri Pacific Railroad. A life in baseball was so uncertain those days, he said, that it took more courage than he could muster to commit his life to it. You could be out of a job by the time you were 30, and he had a wife and two small children to consider.

"The decision to stay worked out pretty good," he said. "The railroad's been good to me. Always gave me fair pay for honest work, and that's about all a fellow can ask out of life. I'm retired now and I got a lifetime railroad pass to go anyplace I want.

"What about your friend? What happened to him?" I prompted.

"Oh, Cap? Let's see, he had a pretty fair career with Chicago, but he don't have no lifetime railroad pass, I can tell you that."

Joe had to know about Cap Anson, one of the greatest players in the history of the game, but he didn't respond at all. He kept chopping and slicing and getting bloody.

**JOE JACKSON** The more I forgot about Philadelphia, the better I felt.

By February everybody was saying I should try to go back. If I didn't, I might not get the chance again. Katie went into Greenville one warm Sunday and sent a wire to Mr. Mack asking him if I could report to spring training. Since he said I couldn't play no more, we weren't sure. I was still half hoping he'd say no.

He wired back saying I should report right away to their camp in Atlanta.

"At least it's the South," she said, "and you can always come home if you don't like it."

We bought a ticket to Atlanta, and as soon as we did, I started feeling nervous again. That night I didn't sleep at all.

At least everybody would get off my back about playing, and like Katie said, I could always come home if things got real bad again.

So with Black Betsy at my side I headed to Atlanta to see Mr. Mack.

# 23

# I TRIED TO GET ALONG

**CONNIE MACK** Between the end of the disastrous 1908 season and the beginning of 1909 spring training, we made a number of personnel changes. We were committed to returning to the top echelons of the American League.

During the offseason Jimmy Collins retired. He hung them up with a career .294 batting average and headed back to his home in Buffalo. Socks Seybold also announced his retirement after eight productive years on the team. His leg injury obviously wasn't getting better, and although he also wasn't in my long-range plans for the team, I had some misgivings about seeing him go. I knew that if Joe did come back, Socks could prove to be a good babysitter, a role that was now open on the club. Ossee Schreckengost was also gone, having been traded to Chicago just before the end of the last season.

New to the team were two catchers--Ira Thomas, who we picked up from the Tigers and Paddy Livingston, who had last played for Cincinnati in 1906, and an 18-year-old infielder, Stuffy McInnis. If nothing else, we would have someone even younger than Joe, assuming he stuck around.

I knew Joe could help if, and only if, he was committed to playing. I had to be careful, though. Yes, I wanted Joe to give it another go, but I also knew that I had to maintain control of the team, and I had banned Joe. I told Harry Davis that I was going to let Joe back because it was in the best interests of the team, but that I would monitor the situation closely, and that if he continued to create problems in the ranks, I would release him immediately. I couldn't be seen to be wavering in my authority, but I also couldn't pass up the opportunity to see if Joe could contribute. I was counting on the other players to understand this. At least I was gambling they would.

Having Joe with us in spring training in Atlanta I thought would help. Atlanta was a southern city with charm and warmth. It was a long way from Philadelphia both in terms of geography and culture. Surely Joe would be more comfortable. Surely he would have the time to adjust to his teammates without the pressure of a league race.

It was up to Joe.

**HARRY DAVIS** Joe showed up in Atlanta looking just like the scared kid who had already twice deserted the team. If he wanted a better reception from the guys he sure didn't go out of his way to show it. He practiced with us on the field, but off, he was still very much a loner and he still remained the butt of every locker room joke.

**J.C. HATCH** About the time Joe got his first taste of the majors, most of the teams were made up primarily of young men from the lower-middle-class echelons of the bigger cities or from middle-class villages, and while almost all saw the game as a way of improving their lot in life, very few came from the lowest most rungs on the economic ladder as did Joe. When he looked around the clubhouse, he didn't see anybody who looked like him. That might be a difficult and troubling situation for most, but for someone without the ability to read even the simplest signs like "Men's Room," it must have been terrifying.

The urban populations of big cities such as Philadelphia were expanding rapidly, and with that expansion came an increased interest in baseball. What was drawing so many people to the cities and away from the rural areas was the promise of work—most often in the factories of an increasingly industrialized society. However, much of the work in the factories was highly repetitive and often extremely boring. Baseball became one of the most popular means of escaping the drudgery of the factory. Ironically, of course, this is exactly the pattern which drew Joe from the mill in the first place. Baseball was a drug, a means of escape, a boredom-killing elixir. With this increase in interest in the game came the longing for a Siegfried—an American hero, a working-class model for a working-class audience.

Joe had all the qualities needed. He had talent. He was a working-class stiff. He had brooding good looks and the quiet demeanor so often associated with our rugged heroes. So what if he had flaws? So long as he displayed promise they would be conveniently ignored.

Concomitant with his illiteracy was the widespread and loudly-trumpeted belief that he was stupid, moronic, simple-minded or even retarded. I would be more inclined to support this position had Joe seriously attempted to learn to read and write and failed. I don't think he even so much as sat down to learn the letters of the alphabet. The fact that he couldn't read is not proof of the inability to do so. As a society we are quick to jump on the "intelligence bandwagon." We have continually and consistently made fun of individuals considered to be dumb. Our cartoons are full of them, our literature rife with them, and our films peopled by them.

One sub-sets of "fools" are the country bumpkins, who though ridiculed, are loved for their simple-minded, but affable ways. It didn't take long for Joe to be cast in this role, and it's one which stayed with him for much of his career, only to be replaced later by a more sinister one.

In literature, many of these "country bumpkin" figures enjoy, even revel in their notoriety. They laugh "with" their attackers, they share in the joke. Joe Palooka went along with the jokes, Joe Jackson didn't. He simply wasn't comfortable playing the fool. Perhaps he didn't have the self-confidence to accept the challenge, or perhaps he couldn't see any advantage for him in it. His way of coping was to flee.

**DR. WILLIAM GILES** Since the 1870s baseball has been an important part of the Atlanta sports scene. Back then, the young men of the town made up their own nines, sometimes bringing in professional pitchers and catchers to fill out their squads. Regular schedules were unheard of, with most games being arranged on the basis of one team challenging another. Then in 1884 Atlanta played Augusta in the first professional game. The following year Atlanta won the pennant in the Southern League's first year of operation. Atlanta has been a good baseball town ever since.

Every spring we looked forward to the coming of the Athletics for their spring training. I remember as a kid waiting patiently through the winter months for the arrival of Harry Davis, Rube Waddell, Danny Murphy, Chief Bender and the others. But none engendered the excitement that Joe Jackson did that spring of 1909.

My friends and I ditched school to watch practices because we had heard so much about the kid from South Carolina—a good old southern boy who could play the game like he was born to it. And how he lived up to our expectations! He glided across the outfield like a gazelle, sent screaming line drives off or over the fences with regularity, and unleashed head-high throws from deep in the field.

From what we saw, he was already the best player on the team. Besides, he talked to us. We would wait for him out by the fence in right, and he would always stop—unless there was an adult with us then he would just keep going and say, "See you tomorrow, boys."

Say what you want about him, but he took time with us kids when nobody else did, and I'll never forget that.

**CHARLIE LEBEAU** That February of 1909 saw me pack up and head to Atlanta to participate in the rites of spring known as spring training. It was a pilgrimage on which I gladly embarked, for it marked the end of the winter freeze and the beginning of longer, more hospitable days. Spring training was always a time of warm sun, and hope and endless possibilities. It was a time of teaching and learning and unbridled optimism. It was a chance to get close to the game and the players in ways that didn't exist during the regular season.

I knew that Joe was going to be there, and as I had probably seen him more than anyone else, it made me feel like an insider. I firmly believed that he was ready to make his mark on the league and that he would prove it that spring. I wanted to think that in some small way I had helped him land on this threshold of opportunity. I had a connection with Joe on a very spiritual level, and it was a connection I would always cherish.

Joe certainly didn't let me down. He hit, fielded and threw brilliantly. He and Amos and Stuffy made it look like the Athletics would have a bright future.

**JOE JACKSON** That spring things went pretty good. I hit good most of the time, and even once made a one-handed catch in the field that brought applause from the crowd. You've got to remember that in them days we had these little gloves that wasn't much bigger than ones farmers used when they was working a hoe, so one-handed catches you didn't see very much.

On the way north, we played a couple of games in Louisville, and in one of them I got hold of a pitch perfect and hit one over the right field fence. That made me feel good for a couple of days.

Off the field, though, things wasn't no different than they was before. I tried to get along, but some of the other players just didn't seem to want to, so they made the trips and the nights in the hotels awful bad.

**EDDIE PLANK** As we played ourselves north those train rides could be tough. Sometimes we wouldn't get into a town till the early hours of the morning, then we'd have to go out and play two.

More than once we had to get on a train with wet, sweaty uniforms. What we did was hang them out the train window to let them dry in the air. It must have looked pretty silly to a farmer watching this laundry train speed through his fields.

Joe liked to stay to himself on the train, but guys were always getting on him about something.

One time, Joe took a quick hit of some corn liquor he had with him, thinking nobody saw him, but ole' Topsy did, and, of course, he couldn't let that go by.

"Remember Eddie Delahanty?" Topsy asked of nobody in particular. "Eddie was a heck of a Philadelphia outfielder a few years back. Could've been one of the best, except that he had a hankering for whiskey something awful. Heck, I think he batted something like .350 for his career, but think of what he could've done if he stayed off the juice. Anyway, one day he's on the train after a game and he's sneaking corn whiskey mile after mile, and eventually this conductor sees him and has him thrown off the train somewhere near Niagara Falls. But Eddie, who never was the brightest guy, knows he's got a game the next day, so he starts walking along the tracks in the direction of the train. Now Eddie wasn't exactly too steady and he falls through a drawbridge and goes over the falls. No one ever seen him again. I tell you, drinking and riding trains is real dangerous."

Of course drinking was done on trains all the time, but I can't ever remember Joe doing it after that. Maybe he just got better at sneaking it.

Another time I remember Joe was on the train wearing a straw hat his mother had bought for him so he would look good with the other players. Joe put it on the railing over his head. When he woke up from his nap and reached for his hat, he found it had a large bite taken out of the brim.

**TOPSY HARTSEL** Joe didn't play poker. He didn't play checkers. Didn't tell jokes. Didn't read. Didn't laugh with the guys. Never sang songs. Seldom smiled.

**EDDIE PLANK** What I remember about that spring training with Joe was the way that Danny Murphy went about trying to befriend him. Danny was a stocky Irishman with a twinkle in his eyes that only those descendants of the Emerald Isle seem to possess. Danny was a charmer, and with the possible exception of Sam Crawford, there wasn't another right fielder in the business who was his equal.

I think the thing that got Danny so interested in helping Joe was that Danny was born in Philadelphia and took it personally that Joe was expressing such disdain for the city.

Danny's specialty was stealing signs. Often Mr. Mack would let him coach first or third where he would tip off batters on the pitches about to be thrown. Danny had keen eyes and a quick mind. I know he tried to teach Joe this, but Joe didn't have those kind of instincts.

Wherever you saw Joe, Danny could be found close by. Danny didn't have to make the club. His position was secure, so he could afford to help Joe. Whether Joe appreciated it or not, I don't know, but he didn't act like he did.

**DANNY MURPHY** I thought Joe could use a friend that spring, and since I didn't see any other takers for the job, I decided I'd appoint myself.

Joe was a tough nut to crack. He didn't exactly endear himself to the other players with his reticent attitude. Some guys thought he was aloof and arrogant. He wasn't. He was anxious. I'm afraid the more I tried to get to know him, the more he withdrew. The pity of it all is, I could have helped him.

**FRANK BAKER** Mr. Mack got this bright idea to split the squad into two teams during that spring. He wanted to play two exhibition games a day and get twice the gate. One team he called the Regulars. They had Harry Davis, Topsy Hartsel, Danny Murphy, Rube Oldring and the rest of the older veterans. The other team he called the Yannigans, but don't ask me why. Me and Eddie Collins, and Stuffy McInnis, and Amos Strunk and the other younger players like Joe were on that team.

It was pretty obvious that we were damn good and would be the future of the Athletics.

**RUBE OLDRING** After a while, all spring trainings became horrible experiences. I mean, once you've got the club made, nobody needed all that long to get ready for the season, but that's not the way the system worked. In those days we all went to some southern city like Atlanta usually in late February. Interestingly enough, nobody back then was going to Florida. Usually before I reported I spent a couple of days in Hot Springs, Arkansas boiling out. Then I reported to camp where we limbered up, took fielding and batting practice for a few days and generally ran around the park a lot. Oh, yes, and we had massages which were the best part of training.

After a couple of weeks of this we headed north on a long barnstorming tour homeward. Along the way we played in every jerkwater stadium they could find—sometimes more than one game a day. The fans down in the South, since they didn't have any major league teams, liked it and there was money to be made for the club, but we found it a real pain in the you-know-what.

Rookies, they were another thing. They were there for other reasons—like learning how to play the game the right way, which on our club meant Mr. Mack's way. Whatever else is certain about the rites of baseball spring training, this is a law I think was passed down from Moses: veterans shalt not help rookies. Bushers were on their own and woe be the veteran who violated this law! But it went even further. It was considered a mortal sin to teach any greenhorn the finer points of the game, violation of this law bringing immediate expulsion from the baseball veterans' fraternity. Furthermore, it was every veteran's duty to hinder the progress of the rookies by any means legal, moral or undetectable by the manager, press or spectators.

Help Joe? Hell no. We didn't help any busher.

**JACK COOMBS** I remember the time in spring training when Joe got his bed short-sheeted. That's where someone takes the top sheet off the bed and doubles over the bottom sheet, making it look like there are two sheets. When the unsuspecting player gets into bed he puts his feet right through the doubled sheet, ripping it to shreds. Now, this has happened to countless rookies, but when it happened to Joe, his response was quite unlike any I had ever seen. Joe jumped into bed, his feet ripping the doubled sheet, just like it was planned. But he was so embarrassed that he just turned over and stayed like that all night.

**CONNIE MACK** In those days we headed north slowly, playing games at every rinky-dink ballpark along the way. It was pretty obvious to everybody that the further north we got, the edgier Joe became.

We stopped at Reading, Pennsylvania for one of our final games before reaching home. The whole team was standing on the train platform, waiting for our ride to the hotel. Maybe Joe could smell Philadelphia from there, because you could just see him begin to stiffen up. Across from the platform stood a whole row of large milk cans, each with a big red label, on which was written the name of its destination. You could read them from where we were standing—"Allentown," "Baltimore," "Knoxville," and maybe 50 more.

I could see Joe just staring at those cans as if he were in a trance. Then he turned to me. "I wish that you'd put a red tag on me and ship me down South along with the milk cans."

"Do you really mean that, Joe?" I asked.

"Yeah, I do."

"Where would you like to go?"

"Savannah."

I've often felt Joe was one of those people who went through life in any direction he might be facing, so the thought of him picking a city based on a milk can isn't that farfetched.

Now, I wanted Joe on my team, let there be no question about that, but I knew that if his heart really wasn't in it, he would be of little value to us. I didn't see that passion in Joe. Talent will only take you so far. The rest of the road to baseball greatness is paved with desire.

On March 28, 1909, I optioned Joe to Savannah in the South Atlantic League.

# 24

# IT WASN'T LIKE PHILADELPHIA

**CHARLES LONGSTREET** In those days, Savannah was an elegant, tree-lined city, with a remarkably cultured and refined population. This was a city of true southern belles and genteel southern gentlemen for whom the War of Secession was a holy cause and still part of the public consciousness.

To some like my father, Colonel Longstreet, baseball was still suspect as a game for gentlemen. Its increasing popularity notwithstanding, we were urged to place our sporting interests elsewhere.

My father's proclivity was for horse racing. He was secretary of the Savannah Jockey Club and raced his own horses there. I remember him riding through our streets on his famous horse White Cloud, both horse and rider presenting a majestic appearance.

Much to my father's chagrin, as a youngster I developed an interest in baseball, an interest which for the most part remained relatively clandestine.

I would slip out of the house on warm summer afternoons, and run the length of Habersham Street all the way out to the ball field. There, among the young players was Joe Jackson, a true southern boy, albeit a little short in the upbringing department. He was exactly the kind of person, Father insisted, who made up the ranks of professional ballplayers. He was uneducated, uncouth and uncivil. At least that's what the Colonel said. "He is simply not a gentleman," was the oft-repeated phrase that signaled the end of any conversation on the subject.

Gentleman or not (and I certainly couldn't argue the point) his pure brilliance in the field made him a very attractive figure to watch.

The memory of the very first time I saw him, however, still evokes a certain charming irony. In those days, the most notable hotel in the city was the Pulaski House, a hostelry which for years had hosted many of the city's most distinguished guests. Tom Thumb was said to have arrived there in his own little carriage, and I remember my Father talking about the visit of the renowned Seminole Indian chief, Billy Bowlegs. Even before that, the famous English actor, William Macready, stayed there briefly. He offered negative remarks about dueling in Savannah which were apparently occasioned by a duel fought that day between two members of the Savannah bar. At any rate, Joe and some of the players were apparently on their way to the hotel one morning, riding, as was the custom, in the hotel's omnibus. As they passed in front of me I saw Joe sitting on the front seat next to the driver, several other players sitting in the back. The irony of the situation comes from the fact that he was sitting next to the man known to all of us kids as "Shakespeare." He was a tall, good-looking man with a long neatly-trimmed black beard. How he came by that name, none of us ever found out, but without doubt he handled those horses more gracefully and skillfully than any man I have ever seen.

Joe and Shakespeare riding together! I wonder what their conversation was like.

**JOE JACKSON** I got down to Savannah about as fast as I could. I loved the city from the first time I seen it. It had lots of green grass, and pretty trees, and room to move around without always bumping into somebody. It had southern cooking and southern teammates. Best of all, though, it had Bobby Gilks.

**BOBBY GILKS** As manager of the Savannah team, I was putting the players through their paces in late March of 1909 when I got a wire from Connie Mack telling me that Joe Jackson was being sent down to our team, hopefully for the full season. I was thrilled. We didn't often get players as good as Joe, but I knew he was only with us because he was having trouble adjusting emotionally to major league ball, not because he lacked the ability.

I vowed right from the get go that I would try to deal with Joe on a very personal level. See, the way I had it reasoned, one of my jobs as a manager was to get the best I could out of every player, and that meant finding out what motivated each man. It just didn't make sense to me that you should treat each player the same, because they weren't the same. Some you needed to shout at. Some you needed to sweet talk. Some responded best when you paid a lot of attention to them, and others when you left them alone. Criticizing a player was always a tricky thing, but generally I had better luck when I did it in private.

Of course, I had heard about Joe's defections from the Athletics, so I knew I had to treat him carefully. I told myself that I would suspend any judgment about past behavior and spend as much time as I needed with Joe until I got to know him, until I got to know what he liked and didn't like, and what made him tick. Then I would use that knowledge to find ways to motivate him. If I had to be a stern task master, then I would be that. If I had to be a surrogate mother, I could be that, too.

I had a few things against me from the start: I was a big-city boy from the North—Cincinnati actually—and I played for a big-city team from the North—Cleveland. But I had spent my share of time in major league clubhouses, and on team trains, and in hotel lobbies with major league players, so I thought I knew a little of what it was like, and how cruel and difficult it could be on some young men.

If what ailed Joe was something wrong between the ears, then I figured I could find it and maybe make it right. Well, at least I could try.

**CHARLIE LEBEAU** Bobby Gilks was one of the great characters of baseball. He was all of 5' 8" with a craggy face, a big smile, and a shock of unkempt hair sticking out from under his cap. He was one of the best of the old short-fielders and had long been considered by many baseball people one of the cleverest handlers and best judges of players in the world. Bobby was a pure baseball man, plain and simple.

**W.R. JOYNER** I was president of the South Atlantic League in 1909. We were a Class C league then, but we had some pretty fair ballplayers. Most were good southern boys, a number of whom eventually made it to the majors. But there was nobody in the league quite like Joe Jackson. He had already been to the majors for a cup of coffee and we all figured he'd be back, but in the meantime, I had a calculated intent to exploit his every hit and fielding gem for all it was worth. We had a couple of shaky franchises so any promotional edge we could find was going to be used to our advantage.

Joe didn't disappoint. Of course he couldn't sign autographs worth a tinker's damn, but wherever he went he drew fans like a flower draws bees. He was good for the league in a lot of ways. He was polite with the press and engaged in any number of promotional activities. I can't rightly say he was much of a public speaker, but he posed for pictures almost any time he was asked.

I liked Joe and I think he liked the time he spent with us.

I don't think it's a stretch at all to say that baseball in Dixie was as popular then as it was in any area of the country. Heck, I read someplace that North Carolina alone once had professional teams in 70 cities. I didn't even know North Carolina had 70 cities!

What we had then, were fans who knew the game, and they knew who Joe was from the minute he stepped onto the Savannah field.

**BOBBY GILKS** We had a few players who either had played or would play in the majors. Simmy Murch, our big second baseman, had already spent a little time with St. Louis and Brooklyn. Frankie Manush, our third sacker, got in a handful of games with the Athletics when Joe was up there the year before. Al Demaree, a right handed pitcher, went on to pitch for a few years for several different clubs. Our big star, though, was unquestionably Joe. Even if he had yet to produce on the big stage, his reputation from what he had already accomplished was solid. So like most of the minor league franchises, ours was populated by a handful of players on the way up, a handful on the way down, and the rest going no place fast.

It didn't take too long to figure out how to best handle Joe—put on kid gloves! Joe didn't take too kindly to criticism. I don't think his confidence level was ever all that high to begin with, so knocking it down another notch didn't make sense. I went to the other extreme. I praised everything he did well and told him not to worry about the mistakes. I think the other players caught on real fast, but nobody said much. The more I told Joe he was great, the better he got. The better he got, the more I told him so.

**FRANKIE MANUSH** Just like Joe I was a southern boy, and like Joe I was sent to Savannah by the Athletics. The only difference between us was, he was a whole lot better, and I knew it. During the season I began thinking that my chances of getting back to the Mackmen might be better as a babysitter than as a player. I seen what Scotty Barr did for Joe, and I reckoned that I could do the same. Joe needs a southern pal. Hell, I could do that! I couldn't hit like Joe, but I could read a menu and sign a hotel bill.

I stuck by Joe like a stamp to a letter. I did his reading and writing for him, and I talked to him about hunting in the offseason even though I had never held a gun in my life. I helped him keep track of his spending money, and I filled out his laundry list. Joe might have been dumb, but I wasn't.

**BOBBY GILKS** When the season began we had teams in Chattanooga, Columbus, Augusta, Charleston, Jacksonville, Macon, Columbia, and, of course, Savannah. We opened the season down in Jacksonville, where the mayor declared the day a city holiday. Led by a big band and thousands of cheering fans we all marched through the center of that old town. There was much speech-giving and hoopla and a pretty good game followed.

As the season moved on, Joe proved to be as good as advertised. By the time he had a hundred at bats, he had his average well over .400. Everyplace we went in the league, huge crowds showed up, and they weren't there to see me manage.

Simmy Murch, Dobard, Wagnon, Pelky—none of them were hitting a lick, our infield booted more balls than a South American soccer team, and our pitchers ... well, let's just say they were about as consistent as a jackrabbit crossing an open field.

Before the season was 25 games old we were in last place, and guess whose scalp the fans began calling for? You got it—the manager's. Now, I didn't tell our shortstop to throw one out of every three balls over the first baseman's head, but listening to the fans you would have thought I was responsible for every mistake short of the Civil War.

**JOE JACKSON** It wasn't fair, the way everybody got on Bobby so much because we was losing so many games. It wasn't his fault. He was a really good manager—one of the best I ever seen in any league. He taught me a lot of little things that you might not think of on your own. Things like where to play certain players which you could tell by how they was standing in the box, and how to shade your eyes good with your glove when looking up into a bright sky. Things like that.

**SIMMY MURCH** I liked Bobby all right. He was a standup guy, but I think he was so much in love with Jackson that he forgot about the rest of the team. If he hadn't, maybe we would have won a few more games. Maybe he thought that when Joe went back up to the majors he would go too as a coach or something.

**FRANKIE MANUSH** The team started going to hell in a hand basket right out of the chute, and everybody started pointing fingers, a lot of them in the direction of Bobby Gilks. I've got to admit, that like a lot of the players, I started worrying more about myself than the team. So anything that padded the stats was good and anything that didn't I wanted no part of. Can you blame a guy? Bobby was taking care of Joe, so I didn't see that I had much of a choice but to look out for myself.

**BOBBY GILKS** I went to the owners of the team and told them that if they wanted to win they were going to have to find me some infielders who could throw the ball to first base on a fly, and some pitchers who could find home plate without a map. They said they'd think it over and talk to me after the doubleheader that Saturday against Chattanooga. We lost both games on bonehead plays and I lost my job. I guess they decided it would be easier to find a better manager than better players.

The fact that the team continued to lose after I was gone might be taken as vindication by a lesser man, but far be it from me to suggest that.

**JOE JACKSON** When the rumor started going around that there was going to be a shake-up of the team on account of us not winning, we all thought that meant that some of us was going to be gone and some new players was going to come in.

I wasn't too worried because I was hitting pretty good. Then one day Bobby come over to the rooming house where I was staying.

"Well they shook-up the team all right," he said, setting down in a big old leather chair we had in the sitting room.

"But I'm still on the team, though, right?" I asked.

"Oh, you're on the team, Joe," he said. "You'll be on the team until you move up or you get too old to play, whichever comes first."

"Huber?" I asked, thinking about our shortstop who had already made about a hundred errors.

"No. The guy they let go hasn't made an error all season," he said, kind of teasing me.

I couldn't think who that could be unless it was one of our pitchers. "Nobody. You mean they didn't let nobody go?"

"Yeah, they let me go, Joe."

I couldn't believe it. At first I thought he was just funning me, but then I seen he was serious, and I started to get mad. I told him I was going to quit. If he wasn't the manager no more then I wasn't the center fielder no more.

Don't do that, Joe" he said. "Quitting would be the dumb thing to do.

I guessed he was right, but I didn't like it one bit. One of the things I learned in my life in baseball is it's a great game but it ain't always fair. If anybody should know that, it's me.

After he was gone, I guess I worried about it some because my batting average fell about 100 points, but I was still leading the league even though we was still losing most of our games.

**W.R. JOYNER** Joe was still our biggest gate attraction even though his team wasn't doing much. But problems were developing in the league. The Chattanooga Lookouts, led by Scotty Alcock, were running away from the rest of the league, and without a tight race to keep up fan interest, attendance was waning. On top of that, the Charleston club was finding it difficult to make its payroll. On July 1 it surrendered its franchise. I met with the league directors and it was decided that we would transfer both the Charleston franchise and the team to Knoxville, Tennessee.

To make matters worse, the press started writing that the Lookouts were lying down because they were so far out in front that they virtually had the pennant won by July. This in turn led to all sorts of speculation about gambling on the games. The papers carried all manner of stories. *The Savannah Press* even ran a photograph of a handful of dandies sitting in some unidentified bleachers over a caption reading: "Betting at American League Games."

I knew I had to do something, and do something fast. I knew fans bet on ballgames, but there was no way in hell I was going to admit that in public. Baseball was at a critical stage in its development. The popularity of the game was increasing rapidly, but we all knew that if the public thought gamblers controlled the outcome of games for their own financial gains, then it could spell the very death of the sport. Baseball had to decide: either become a part of the mainstream American cultural scene, or slide into the shadows of the underworld.

I began an aggressive counter attack through a series of speeches I gave in every city in our league, and through interviews in every major paper. "The gambling must stop," I shouted loud enough for everyone to hear. I also visited the clubs with my impassioned anti-gambling speech. I talked about how gambling could destroy the game we loved, how it could undermine the values on which this country was built, how any player caught gambling, throwing games, or even consorting with known gamblers, would be barred from organized baseball for life. I did a hell-fire and damnation act in my most convincing manner. Whether it did any good or not, I have no way of determining, but I do know they heard it—every player in the league, including Joe Jackson.

In a further attempt to eliminate any possibilities of throwing games that didn't matter because of the Lookouts big lead, we closed the season on July 3 and started a new campaign on July 5. Chattanooga was crowned the first half winner and if they won the second half would be the league champion. If another team won the second half, there would be a playoff. We were, of course, hoping for the latter, so we put a salary limit on teams, hoping it would help balance out the league.

**SIMMY MURCH** We all heard old man Joyner's speech about gambling, but mostly we laughed at it, because he acted like he was talking to a room full of little children. I was never involved with any kind of gambling on baseball, but I can guarantee you this: if I was, his silly little speech wouldn't have stopped me. I thought he made a fool of himself ranting and raving like that in front of the players. Look, it's as simple as this: you can't stop a gambler by telling him to stop gambling any more than you can stop an alcoholic by telling him to stop drinking.

**FRANKIE MANUSH** Everybody knew that Chattanooga was paying their players more than the league allowed. Not that we wouldn't have liked to have gotten more too, but the league had a salary limit for teams. If they was paying more than that, then they was cheating.

**W.R. JOYNER** Of course the players didn't like the salary limits but it was the only way to keep the league solvent and to insure a reasonable balance between the poor and the rich clubs.

**JOE JACKSON** All I knew was that I was leading the league in hitting all season, and should have gotten more money than guys hitting 100 points lower than me. I didn't say nothing, though, because I was happy to be there.

**W.R. JOYNER** In the second half of the season, the race was considerably tighter. Throughout all of this, though, Joe remained the brightest star in our galaxy. People wanted to be able to say, "I saw him play when he was only a kid in the minors." So we capitalized on a promotional campaign which said, "See Joe Jackson now, before it's too late." The "too late" referred to the inevitable recall by the Athletics.

**JOE JACKSON** Everybody kept saying that I was going back to Philadelphia soon. I tried not to think about that much because I would just as soon have stayed in Savannah, but in the back of my mind I guess I knew that I would have to face that possibility again someday.

**LUTHER JACKSON** That summer I asked Mr. Hatch if I could take a little time off from the mill to go see Joe play in Savannah. He said I could so I took a train down there to see him play some games against Knoxville. It was the first time I ever been that far from Greenville.

I stayed with Joe in his rooming house and met a lot of the players because everybody ate together in the dining room.

I guess Joe's batting average dropped a little after Bobby Gilks was fired, but by the time I got there, it was back up again. Joe looked better than I ever seen him. He was hitting good and fielding great and had gotten a lot better at stealing bases. In fact several people there told me he was the best base runner in the league. He even pitched a few times. He probably could've been a real good pitcher if he wanted to.

While I was down there, the league had their voting for the league all-star team, and Joe was everybody's choice for center field.

The team wasn't all that good, though, and they was only in fourth place. Boy, could they have used a few more Jacksons!

**SIMMY MURCH** Everybody knew that Joe couldn't read or nothing, and that he couldn't get along with anybody in Philadelphia, but when you can hit close to .400 nobody is going to say much. Still, most of the guys thought Joe was a little strange.

**JOE JACKSON** I was sitting on the porch of the rooming house on an off day, talking to Luther who was about to head back to Greenville. We was drinking lemonade and talking about nothing in particular when this boy runs up to us with a telegram.

"You're Mr. Jackson, ain't you?" he asked, handing me the message.

When I told him I was, he said he seen me play, and that I was his favorite player. I opened the telegram and looked at it so he wouldn't think I wasn't interested.

"Is there any reply, sir?" he asked.

I looked at Luther who just stared at me. "No, not right now. Thank you." I said, handing him a dime for a tip.

I put the telegram in my pocket and went in and asked Mrs. Murchison, who ran the house to read it to me.

"Report at once to Philadelphia to complete the season with the Athletics. Connie Mack."

Even though I wasn't too crazy about the idea, I knew I needed to do exactly what Mr. Mack said.

The next morning I was on the train with Luther.

**W.R. JOYNER** By the time Joe left, he had played in 118 games and ended up leading the league in hitting with a .358 average. Joe never gave me one iota of trouble and to this day remains probably the most famous player to ever have played in our league. I just wish the reasons for some of the fame were different.

# 25

## People Wasn't Very Nice

**JOE JACKSON** I stopped home on the way back to Philadelphia to see Katie and my family. When I was getting set to take the train to Philadelphia, Katie said she wanted to go along, that she had never been to a big city like that, and that she wanted to see me play in a big league game. I told her that Philadelphia was busy, and crowded and noisy and smelly, and that the people wasn't very nice to southerners, but she said that didn't matter none, because she wanted to be with me, so I said OK. Actually, I was kind of happy about it, because at least I would have one friend there, and she could do the reading when I needed it. Only, I wasn't sure Mr. Mack was going to like this it.

**KATIE WYNN JACKSON** I never told Joe this, but what actually happened was, that before Joe came home from Savannah, I received a telegram from Mr. Mack telling me that he called Joe back to the Athletics, and that he wanted me to come along. He even said he would pay for my expenses. I guess he thought I could help keep Joe from feeling so lonely.

So we went on the train together to Philadelphia and checked into the hotel. Although Joe didn't say anything about it, I knew him well enough to know that he was doing what he thought he had to, but his heart wasn't in it. I did my best to try to keep the conversation on everything but baseball, but he wasn't eager to talk about much of anything. So I let him be.

**HARRY DAVIS** The team that Joe rejoined was not the same one that he left the year before. We had a few new players, but most of the difference came from the fact that we were in a tight pennant race with Detroit. The team we were holding off for first was the Cobb-led Tigers. To win the pennant meant a lot, but to win it over the best efforts of Cobb meant even more. Everybody wanted to beat Cobb—and I do mean everybody!

Compared to the Tigers, our team looked like a bunch of kids, particularly our new infield. I was still at first, but Eddie Collins had taken over at second, Frank Baker at third, and Jack Barry at short. I didn't know it then, of course, but that was to be my last season as the full-time first baseman. It was our pitching staff, though that was keeping us out front. Eddie Plank, Chief Bender, Cy Morgan, Harry Krause, and Jack Coombs was positively the best rotation in the business.

Since we were in the thick of things when Joe returned, none of us had any appetite for dealing with anyone who didn't want to join in the fray with all his heart. We simply didn't have the time or the interest in helping Joe adjust to life in the big city. We were in a race and that was all that counted. I think had Joe jumped in, acted like he cared and really wanted to help the team, and then had gone out and done something about it, he would have been accepted by all of us. A game-winning home run or two would have gone a long way toward making friends, but that's not what we saw. What we saw was a player who acted like he didn't want to be here, a player who acted like he had something more important on his mind than winning a pennant, a player who acted like he didn't care enough about his teammates to put out a total effort.

So, no, Joe wasn't real welcome, but who's fault was that? He had the opportunity. If he didn't want to take advantage of it, that was his problem and he would have to accept the consequences.

**CONNIE MACK** The season of 1909 saw us with new players, new determination and a new stadium. The principle owner of the Athletics and my partner was Benjamin F. Shibe. He made his money as a partner in A.J. Reach & Company, the big baseball equipment manufacturers. We had a good arrangement. Ben owned 50 percent of the Athletics and took care of all the business matters. I owned 25 percent and took care of all matters on the field. It was Ben who arranged for and found the money to build the most up-to-date baseball stadium in the world. Since he paid for it, he got to name it. Shibe Park was a marvel of concrete and steel engineering and the envy of every other team in the league. The official seating capacity was listed as 20,000, but as popular as we were, there was many a game seen by more than 30,000 packed-in fans. We were the class of the American League.

**JOE JACKSON** This time we had a brand spanking new stadium. It wasn't like the old place at all. It had real dugouts instead of benches down each line. It had a giant double-decker grandstand that went all the way around from first base to third base. It even had a roof on it. Down each outfield line was bleachers, but they didn't have a roof or anything. Right in front of the stadium there was a giant tower that stuck up above the grandstand and on top of it was a dome with a whole bunch of flags that was always flying up there.

Inside the tower way up near the top was where Mr. Mack did his business. He could even see out on to the field when we was practicing, so it was a pretty good place for him to have his office.

The stadium looked a little bit like a mill factory from the outside with all the red brick and windows lined up in a row. But on the inside it didn't look nothing like a factory. It was new, and clean and big and quiet. Our locker room looked like it was big enough for two teams.

Across the street from the outfield, there was a long row of two-story houses all alike. Each one had a big window on the second floor and a flat roof above that. On the roofs hundreds of fans could sit and watch the games without having to pay for a ticket. Some of them even had bleachers set up so that more fans could sit. I tell you, I never seen nothing like it anyplace else. For some of our games, especially like when we was playing the Tigers, there was so many people up there that it looked like the houses was about to collapse.

**EDDIE PLANK** If there was the antithesis of Joe on the team, it was certainly Eddie Collins, one of the greatest second basemen in baseball history. He played the position more brilliantly than anyone in the game, other than maybe Larry Lajoie, but by the time Eddie joined us, Larry's best days were behind him.

I always felt Joe and Eddie were the two best players on the team, but boy, oh boy, what a difference. Eddie was real cocky—which is what we called him—while Joe was reticent. Eddie was aggressive, Joe much more passive. The one thing that was somewhat the same was that they were both somewhat aloof, although for different reasons.

I would be surprised if Eddie wasn't Mr. Mack's all-time favorite. Like a lot of us, he was a college grad—Columbia—and we all know how Mr. Mack felt about college grads.

The thing about Eddie is that I thought he was easily the smartest guy on the team—at least baseball-wise. Eddie was always thinking, always plotting, always one step ahead of the opposition—a chess master on the diamond. To put it politely, Joe wasn't always that. Sometimes Joe acted like he was on Mars or someplace—anyplace but in the game, and that really irked me.

**EDDIE COLLINS** The guy who got irritated the fastest about Joe was Eddie Plank. Not that Plank was a mean guy, because he wasn't, but the one thing Plank hated more than anything was somebody who didn't give it his all, and that's what some of us thought about Joe. Looking back on it now, maybe he wanted to be a contributor but didn't know how to go about it. Anyway, in every game Plank pitched, he worked about as hard as anybody. In my way of thinking, he was one of the best pitchers ever. Not the fastest, not the trickiest, and not the guy with the most stuff, but just the best.

He threw with a three-quarter motion and had a sidearm crossfire move to first base. His motion was just different enough that he was an expert at holding men on or picking them off. He'd throw at a guy too, if the situation demanded.

Mostly though, he used his head. He was always trying to outwork and outthink the batter. I think that's what frustrated him about Joe. Joe just didn't seem to want to work like that.

Plank had every angle. Once he got into the late innings, he began counting batters out. "Nine to get," he would say so that we could all hear him. Then "eight to get."

Plank's games took forever. He was the slowest thing on any mound in America and that meant you had to concentrate like the dickens behind him. I don't think Joe particularly liked that. I think he'd rather play faster and just let his instinct take over. Sometimes Plank pitched without fussing, but often he'd only throw the ball after the umpire made him.

Plank loved it when there were two men on and a big slugger up. The better the hitter, the more Plank worked him. Plank would fuss and fuddle with the ball or with his cleats and then maybe talk to the umpire.

His motion was enough to give the batter a nervous breakdown. First he'd throw something the batter couldn't reach with a telephone pole, then follow that with a wild pitch way inside. He'd squint down toward the catcher on the next pitch like he couldn't quite see that far. Then he'd ask for a conference with the catcher and follow that with a couple of pick off attempts of a runner at first. Then suddenly Plank would turn his attention to the fretting batter again, who would in all probability pop up in disgust.

See, Plank tried everything he knew to fool a batter. He used his brain as much as his arm, and he never understood why everyone else couldn't do the same. He used to stare out at a laconic-looking Joe in center sometimes as if to say, "get in the game, or get off the field."

**TY COBB** We had a battle royal going with the Athletics. The guy on that team who always worried us the most was Eddie Collins. We battled each other for the stolen base lead almost every year. He had an unfair advantage over me, though, because he had big sail-like ears that stuck out and when the wind was behind him, it helped propel him to the next base. Of course I reminded him of this at every given opportunity.

By the way, Joe could steal a base, too. In fact, one year I think he had over 40. To be a really great base stealer, though, you had to study the pitcher's moves real carefully. I'm not sure Joe was willing to make that effort.

**EDDIE COLLINS** I respected Joe Jackson's skills, but I can honestly say I never spoke a word to him in my life.

**CHARLIE LEBEAU** Does baseball represent a great cross-section of American life or what? I remember a time when Joe fired a rocket shot to Eddie Collins at second, just in time to tag a sliding runner—the illiterate mill hand and the Ivy League graduate teaming up to make a great play.

**VINCENT ALEXANDER** The 1909 season in the American League was a great one for the fans with the Mackmen and the hated Tigers of Ty Cobb jockeying for first position virtually all season. The unquestioned star of the Athletics was Eddie Collins, who, by the beginning of August, was leading the league in hitting followed closely by Cobb and Lajoie.

Cocky Collins, who couldn't have been more than 5 foot 8, was a skittery, jumpy type of guy. Ironically, he had the same kind of fiery temper and fighting spirit that characterized Ty Cobb, but he generally knew how to keep it in check, whereas Cobb frequently didn't. Collins could steal a base as well as anybody and a lot of people thought he was the smartest second baseman ever. He may not have had Lajoie's grace around second base, but he made up for that by knowing just about everything there was to know about playing the game.

In early August he got the fans all fired up when he challenged a bad call made by Umpire Tim Hurst. I wouldn't doubt it if he started the argument just so that the fans would get more involved in the game. Anyway, Hurst spat in Collins' face, resulting in Hurst being relieved of his umpiring responsibilities by American League President Ban Johnson. But, that's the way he played the game, always trying to find some edge.

With Collins leading the way, the Mackmen stayed with the Tigers game for game throughout the month of August. Then in early September Joe rejoined the team for the first of a three-game series against the New York Yankees. At that point, the Athletics were four games behind Detroit. Knowing that Joe was back, my father arranged for me to be taken to the game by one of his employees. I couldn't wait to see Joe again, for I was sure he was now ready to lay claim to the greatness which so many had predicted for him. It turned out to be one of those end-of-season thrillers which make baseball the magnificent game that it is.

The Athletics got things going in the second inning when Joe singled sharply to right scoring Davis from third. The inning ended, however, when Livingston followed by hitting into a double play. The Yankees scored two in the fourth, but the Athletics rallied for three in their half of the inning on hits by Collins, Baker and Livingston. Jackson had a chance to be a hero, but struck out with two men on. The Yanks, however, came right back in the fifth and tied the game. The damage was done when Frank

Chase hit a ball to the left center field fence. I hate to admit it, but Joe was late in closing on the ball and Prince Hal turned it into an inside-the-park home run. In all fairness, I should say that had Joe played the ball better, he might have held Chase to a double. Be that as it may, that hit turned out to be the turning point in the game and the Yankees went on to win 8 to 6. It was a tough loss for the Athletics because while they were losing, Detroit was picking up a game by beating Cleveland.

Joe got just that one hit in four at bats and made one routine play in the outfield. The fans excused his fielding gaffe by assigning it to the fact that he was probably tired from his long ride north, and quite unused to the spacious outfield after playing all season on the cigar box diamonds of the South Atlantic League.

The next day, I was out at the park again for the second game of the series. I reasoned that Joe would have gotten a good night's sleep and would be ready to show what he could do. I got there early and watched him closely during batting practice. He looked good, even to the point of hitting several pitches out of the park. When the game started, though, Rube Oldring was in center field. Joe never got off the bench.

Eddie Collins was the hero of the afternoon contributing a single, double and homer, and scoring three runs himself as the Athletics beat the Yankees despite a strong game by Wee Willie Keeler. The next day I returned yet again reasonably confident that Mr. Mack would use Joe in the rubber game of the series, but Joe sat while Bob Ganley played center. Once again Eddie Collins was the difference registering a single, triple, and home run as the Athletics easily topped the Yankees while Detroit was idled by rain. The game was a real treat for me, for in addition to the Athletics' win I got to meet George Wright, who was in the stands taking in the game. You may not remember the name, but once he was the greatest player in the game. In 1880 he was the brilliant short fielder for the Cincinnati Reds—the year they went through without a single defeat. Although he had to have been in his sixties, he still had the look of a great athlete.

In retrospect I wonder how much talk there was in the Athletics dugout about Hal Chase, the Yankee first baseman. There was more than a little speculation going around about him at that time, and although he didn't do anything horrendous in the three games with the Athletics, his reputation meant that everybody was looking closely. At one point he got a clean single but was picked off when he rounded first too far. Was this on purpose? Only he would know, but this is what happens when suspicion of gambling is present—everything is questioned.

The next day, the Athletics were scheduled to play two with Boston, but it poured all day and both games had to be canceled. Unfortunately for us, it didn't rain in Detroit and the Tigers were able to take two from Cleveland. The rain finally stopped that night so they played two the next day—Saturday. We had a devil of a time getting tickets for those games, but by now I was committed to seeing as many of the games in this tight race as I could.

I found out later that a crowd of over 31,000 were on hand, a crowd that was one of the largest—if not the very largest—that had ever witnessed a ballgame. The crowd itself was a magnificent tribute to the popularity of the game. Even before the game started, the doors leading to the pavilion were closed, every seat having been sold, while the promenade in the lower pavilion was packed with thousands of enthusiasts who were willing to stand for both games. The overflow in the outfield was the largest anybody could remember, while the concrete wall enclosing the park was fringed by venturesome youngsters including me. There was no way I was going to miss this, whether Joe played or not.

I certainly wasn't disappointed as both games were decided by 1-0 scores. In the first game, Plank out-dueled Cicotte, the Athletics scoring their run thanks to a walk. Joe didn't play in this game either, but he did get his first look at Eddie Cicotte, a man who would play prominently in determining his fate. Joe also sat for the nightcap which was won by Boston. Heinie Wagner won the game in the seventh on one of only four hits off Krause.

Try as they might, the Athletics were having trouble closing ground on Detroit. On the 15th of September they were three games back, but as we all knew, there was still plenty of time left, and we had a number of games remaining with the Tigers. We figured our fate was in our own hands, and all we had to do was stay close and then beat Detroit head-to-head.

People in the stands began speculating on what was happening to Joe.

**TOPSY HARTSEL** When the going got tough down the stretch run, Joe was nowhere to be found except sitting on the end of the bench dumbfaced. We all knew why, although nobody wanted to say it out loud: Joe was a coward, that's all. Certainly other episodes in his life have proven that to be true enough. I'd be willing to bet that he went to Mr. Mack and asked out of the important contests. Mr. Mack wasn't stupid. He knew that having a coward in the lineup against the likes of Ty Cobb and the Tigers would have meant suicide.

**EDDIE PLANK** Joe didn't say anything about not playing, and neither did Mr. Mack, but I think Mr. Mack didn't want to take a chance on losing a game due to some rookie mistake. I think Joe was there for insurance in case one of the outfielders went down.

**CONNIE MACK** Joe didn't need any more pressure on him. Lord knows he put enough on himself without me adding to it. I planned on using Rube Oldring pretty much all the way down the stretch unless something unexpected happened. He wasn't hitting a whole bunch, but he was steady in the field, didn't make many mistakes, and had a good head on his shoulders. As to the speculation in the papers that Joe wasn't playing because he was afraid was just pure bunk. I made out the lineup, not him.

**JOE JACKSON** Sitting wasn't no fun, and hearing people say I was a coward was worse, but what could I do? Mr. Mack decided who played, not me. I was upset about it, sure, but who wouldn't be? I mean, I certainly didn't want to be the guy that made an error that cost us the game, but I would of played if Mr. Mack told me to.

One of the players told the papers that I asked Mr. Mack not to play me, but like a lot of things said about me, that ain't true. I never asked out of a game in my life.

**VINCENT ALEXANDER** When the Tigers came to town for a four-game series starting on the 16th of September, just about everybody who knew what a baseball was whisked on over to the park to try to get a seat. School work be damned! There are some things just more important than arithmetic. It was damp and gray, but that was barely noticed in the rush of anticipation. Long before the gates of the park swung open, the advance guard of us loyal ones blotted out the sidewalk on Lehigh Avenue. When the turnstiles began to click at 12:30, a human stream flowed through and remained constant until after the gong sounded for the start of the game at 3:30.

The grandstand and the bleachers were jammed to capacity while on the fringe, ropes had been stretched out to provide more room for the swelling crowd.

I got in early enough for batting practice and like many of the boys my age, reveled in the opportunity of chasing after batting practice balls hit into the bleachers. In all my years of scrambling over seats for balls, I only once even touched one. I always thought this was strange. I've been to probably many hundreds, or even thousands of games in my life. The odds on that would seem to be astronomical. Nevertheless, the only regular season ball I ever took home as a souvenir, I got during that first game of the Athletics and Tigers series. It was a long drive hit over the wall in dead center. It bounced once, ricocheting directly onto my waiting, but none-too-steady hands. I caressed and protected it like it was the covenant of the lost ark, only more valuable. Of course, you can guess the rest of the story—it was delivered by Black Betsy straight to me. Joe hit it for me, I know he did. I ran off faster than Ty Cobb stealing home and just as guilty, because in those days you weren't supposed to keep the balls. But I did. I gave it to my father in appreciation for his introducing me to the game. For many years it remained proudly on display on a shelf in his restaurant. Then some years later, when it was popular to vilify Joe, it disappeared, presumably at the hands of a scorned and angry fan.

That first game in the Tigers series was, for followers of the Mackmen, cause for great elation. Even when J. Pluvius let drop a few hints that he was on the job before the warfare began, he couldn't halt the invasion of fans. It would have taken a blizzard.

I distinctly remember the electricity in the air that afternoon. As the big double-decked pavilion and the concrete bleachers began to fill up, Eddie Collins, Rube Oldring, Danny Murphy and the other White Elephant hitters tumbled out of the underground runway leading from the clubhouse. A loud and heartfelt cheer welcomed the team.

The crowd was in a festive mood despite the threatening sky and it wasn't long before they turned their attention to the straw lids that a few in the nervy crowd wore in defiance of the decree ordering derbys and Kellys. Scores of summer tiles perished before a bombardment of paper and other missiles while everybody howled good naturedly.

I kept the ball from Joe in my pocket with my hand on top.

Hardly had the battle of the straw hats ended than a fine rain began to fall sending the Athletics to their dugout and the groundskeepers to stretching a waterproof covering over the infield. For a while most of us feared our playful enthusiasm would be short lived and the game canceled. But before long the sky cleared and the game was on, and what a great game it was for the Mackmen.

**JOE JACKSON** I remember thinking during that game how hard it was on a player like Cobb. Everybody was expecting so much from him but whenever he didn't do nothing to help his team he had to listen to all those fans calling him names and throwing things at him.

**DANNY MURPHY** There was a lot of angry feelings because here were two teams that honestly didn't like each other. I mean, face it, nobody liked Cobb, so that meant nobody liked his team either. In the third inning, their big-mouthed outfielder who wasn't even in the game began making rude comments about my Irish heritage from the dugout. Well, I took exception to his obnoxious remarks, ambled over to the Tiger's dugout, and went for him. Not a lot happened as Mullin and several of his teammates pulled us apart. The Athletics, of course, as baseball's unwritten laws would have it, all piled out of the dugout and were on their way to my rescue when peace was restored. I started back to our dugout escorted by Silk O'Loughlin, the home plate umpire. All of the Athletics met me about half way across the diamond. All that is, except Joe. He was barely out of the dugout. I looked at him wondering if he was just slow or a coward.

**VINCENT ALEXANDER** The second game of the series saw The Tigers win behind a brace of walks given up by Krause and seven stolen bases. It looked more like a track meet than a baseball game.

If there were any straw hats left from the previous day, it was certainly no fault of those of us who packed the bleachers. Every man who had the audacity to appear with a summer lid on was soon relieved of it. Everybody roared with laughter as straws were snatched from unsuspecting heads and whirled high in the air, before being tossed from one end of the bleachers to the other.

From telegraph poles, house tops, windows and other points of vantage from which a view of the field could be obtained, you could find eager spectators. I watched a host of small boys scale the fences back of right and left field swelling the crowd beyond official counts. Official figures for the crowd were fixed at 27,814, but I can guarantee you that at least 30,000 people actually saw the game. I was witnessing the largest crowd in the history of the national sport. So, too, was Joe, for once again he had one of the best seats in the house.

The heroes of the game were Chief Bender, who shut the Tigers down on three little singles while striking out nine, and Eddie Collins, who chipped in with three hits of his own and who made a brilliant play on a little chopper by Cobb which, for all the world, appeared to be heading into right field. Collins speared the ball on the full run and threw off balance to Murphy at first to just nip Cobb as he slid spikes up into the base.

The final game of the series was a Monday afternoon affair, and even that was packed. The four-game series attracted more fans than had ever seen a four-game series. Over 117,000 fans turned out for the crucial contests.

In the fourth inning of the final game, Ty Cobb slid into second base with his customary hostility, this time ripping open the left shin of shortstop Jack Barry. Cobb had been walked by Plank and then tried to steal second as Crawford struck out. Paddy Livingston made a perfect throw to second and Barry, covering the bag, got the ball just in time to tag a sliding Cobb. Barry held onto the ball for the out but had to limp off the field with an ugly wound. Stuffy McInnis, the 19-year-old kid had to replace him, and it was his error in the sixth which led to two unearned runs. The crowd got on Cobb immediately, but when he went over to Barry and apologized as the shortstop was limping off, the crowd backed off some. Of course we all remembered the vicious spiking of Baker about a month earlier, so no one was ready to completely forgive him.

Everybody outside Detroit, and probably even some people in that city, hated Ty Cobb, but we all wanted to see him play. We hated him because he was so aggressive and we hated him because he was so good. We also admired him for both of those reasons. Despite all the ill will he generated, there is no doubt Ty Cobb was good for baseball.

The Athletics held on to win the game 4 to 3 and pull within two games of the Tigers. Everybody in the city was excited about our possibilities for playing in the World Series, especially since we had taken 14 out of the 22 games from the Tigers.

It was after the Detroit series that the talk about Joe really amped up. Where was he? Why wasn't he playing? Maybe he could help.

**DANNY MURPHY** To tell the truth, none of us were too upset that Joe wasn't playing. Joe could have used a little of the Georgia Peach in him—just a little, mind you, but something that would have put a spur to his behind, because we sure as heck were in a knock-down-drag-out dog fight.

**HARRY DAVIS** There's no doubt about it, Joe could have helped but instead he sat and sulked.

**DANNY MURPHY** The thing is, we were a real fiery bunch, all except Joe. He just never seemed to have that fire in his belly if you know what I mean. We fought, and we scrapped for every out of every inning of every game, especially when we played the hated Tigers. That's just the way we played then.

After the spiking, Ty, he got a big pile of hate mail, including a whole bunch that threatened to kill him during a game. So what does the Athletics front office do? They hire a lot of policeman and put them all over the stadium to try to keep the situation under control. I'm sure they also let everybody know about it. I don't mean they wanted to see somebody get hurt, but they sure wanted to sell tickets, and this was a great way of promoting interest in the team and the great pennant race. Now as everybody knows, Ty was never shot, but he damn near died of shock in the second game of the series when they came back to town.

**TY COBB** When I was just used to the idea that some crackpot might be crazy enough to use me for target practice, a nerve-screeching 'bang!' exploded behind the right field fence. I must have jumped 8 feet in the air. Later on I found out it was just a car backfiring.

**CONNIE MACK** I wasn't very well acquainted with the Ty at that time. I thought it was just his second nature to act mean on the ball field. He probably got up in the morning with a grouch on and it stuck to him all day. Then during the game, he gave vent to his feelings by making trouble. Such tactics I believed needed to be looked into by the American League, and I made up my mind after the spiking incident that I would see to it that the matter was taken up. Other players had rights as well as Cobb. I know that Cobb had threatened to get Baker, Barry and Collins. He may have been a great player, but he was a pinhead in this respect. It was my belief that baseball should not permit such a malefactor to disgrace it, and I was bound to do something about it. I wanted aggressive players on the Athletics and I wanted some of my players like Joe to become more that way, but I never wanted or asked them to deliberately hurt another player.

**TY COBB** I thought it was real ungentlemanly of Mack to run to the newspapers knocking me. He went around with the salve in one hand and a pile driver in the other and expected to get by with everything. Mack knew that I never spiked a man deliberately, and he also knew that the runner was entitled to the line, and if the baseman got in the way, he was taking his own chances. When I slid I made for the bag. If the man with the ball is in the way he is apt to get hurt. But that is his lookout for he has no business on the line.

Even if he was a great manager, it was a plain case of squeal with Mack, and I told him so. Look at what they did to us in Philadelphia that season when they were seven runs to the good and we hadn't a chance to win. Both Barry and Collins dove into Schaefer and tried to put him out. And Collins did get Stanage and put him out of the game for a week. But we didn't holler.

That is baseball, and if we got hurt we took our medicine and didn't go around crying about it. Collins was all right, he tried to block me off a couple of times, but I dumped him good. He never said a word because he knew that I was right. He went into the bases the same way that I did, and he hurt as many men as I did.

Hughie Jennings, our skipper, also had a mad on about Mack's whining in the papers about me.

**HUGHIE JENNINGS** Anyone who knows Cobb—and I place Mack in that category—knew that Ty was one of the cleanest players in the game despite what some of the sportswriters claimed. His slides to the bases were always forceful but perfectly legitimate. We never squealed if our players were hurt. I thought it was really pretty small business for the manager of a defeated team to cry that the opposing players were trying to disable his boys.

**EDDIE PLANK** A lot of the papers that season referred to us as "Connie Mack and his band of college boys." I don't know if those sentiments got back to Joe or not, but if they did, they could hardly have made him feel very comfortable. The college men were playing. He was sitting.

**VINCENT ALEXANDER** After that big series, the Elephants kept pace with the Tigers, but try as they might—and they did try hard—they just couldn't close ground. Then on the last day of September, they played a doubleheader with the Chicago White Sox. For the first time in weeks, Joe got into a game. He played the entire first game in left field, but he was rusty and it showed. He ended up going 0 for 3 at the plate against the spitballs of "Death Valley" Jim Scott, and he misjudged two fly balls in the field for errors. The Athletics lost the game. In the second game, Joe was back on the bench, but did get one at bat as a pinch hitter. He failed to get a hit as the Athletics lost again, thus ending any chance they had for the flag.

The "what ifs" of baseball can drive a person batty, but I have always wondered what would have happened had Joe rather that Oldring played down the stretch. Not that Rube wasn't a good player, but let's face it, he hit .230 for the season with one home run and 28 RBIs, while the team finished just 3 1/2 games behind Detroit. All season the pitching staff was brilliant posting a team ERA of 1.92, so the Athletics didn't have to score a lot of runs to win. I can't help wondering whether Joe might have made up those 3 1/2 games had he played.

**PADDY LIVINGSTON** It was a lot different in those days. We were gentlemen. Well, maybe Cobb wasn't and a few other guys like that, but most of us were. There was no swearing and cursing in the locker room. There were no scandals.

Even when we were in that terrific fight with the Tigers, we behaved like gentlemen—and that included Joe.

When I made my first communion at the age of 11 while attending St. Patrick's grade school in Cleveland, I made a vow never to drink alcohol and never to use the Lord's name in vain. I'm proud to say I never broke that pledge.

They used to say that you had to be a Catholic to play for Connie Mack's Athletics, but that wasn't true. In fact we had about five or six Mason's on that team. I roomed with one once. At night I'd kneel down next to my bed and say me prayers and he'd get down on the other side. I'd say a Hail Mary and he'd be praying a lot longer than me. Not Joe though. Once I roomed with him on a short trip to Boston, and he didn't say any prayers at all. I don't think he was very religious, but he didn't behave like a heathen either.

**HARRY DAVIS** It was a game against Chicago. Krause was pitching but he was roughed up early and yanked in the fourth. So Mr. Mack sends Joe up to pinch hit. Joe grounds out and I remember thinking to myself that he wasn't ready. Stuff should have hit. Stuff was ready. So I said something to Joe about that after the game, about being mentally ready in case he was needed. "Watch Stuff," I told him. He looked at me as if to say, "Why should I watch another kid who isn't playing?" I talked to him for some time about mental preparedness, about coming off the bench, about learning by watching.

See, you've got to remember, learning the game was different then. Spring training didn't begin until late in March—after St. Patrick's Day. We didn't have long learning sessions in the spring. They didn't teach us anything. What we learned we learned on our own and from the other players. We didn't have coaches. Sometimes the manager coached one of the bases. Sometimes when I wasn't playing I'd coach a base. We didn't have all that sign language going from the manager in the dugout to the coach to the batter.

After that game I decided I'd spend a little time with the kids—Stuff and Joe—teach them a few tricks of the trade. I guess I did such a good job with Stuff that pretty soon he took my job at first Joe, on the other hand, acted like he didn't want to hear my advice, so after a while I stopped giving it. You know, I think really he may have been a bit embarrassed, thinking that because he wasn't educated we had to explain everything to him. That wasn't the case. It was the way baseball knowledge was passed on in those days, that's all.

**IRA THOMAS** We had a lot of characters on that team. I particularly remember Cy Morgan and the minstrel stunts he did on the train, singing and telling end man jokes. Cy was a real odd duck, though. He was always good natured at night, but woke up with the worst disposition in the world.

At breakfast in Chicago one morning he thought the waiter was inattentive. What does he do but gather all the silver on the table and throw it into an electric fan that's whirring on the wall. You never heard such a clatter in your life. But it got everybody service, from the manager down.

We had a lot of superstitious guys, too, but nobody more so than Mr. Mack. He took the same seat on the bench in every park in the league. No one else would dare take it. I recall a time when he was scoring the games with a certain pencil. Well, we went into New York, where Joe Ohl, the road secretary, borrowed the pencil. We were playing a doubleheader that day. We lost the first game. A couple of the players were sent out to find Ohl. They couldn't do it. Then we lost the second game. You should have heard Mr. Mack get on Ohl that night. "Don't you ever borrow another pencil from me," he hollered.

Eddie Collins was another superstitious guy. One day he went to Harry Davis' home for lunch, where Harry's wife happened to serve sliced pineapple for dessert. Eddie went up to Shibe Park and got four hits that afternoon. He figured it was the dessert Mrs. Davis gave him. So he ate sliced pineapple every day for the rest of the season.

We had some good fun, but we played hard, too.

Maybe Joe never got a fair shake, I don't know because I don't know all the details about what really happened in Chicago later in his career. I do know though, that sometimes the fans give the players a bad rap when it's not deserved.

A good example of that is what happened to Jack Coombs—Colby Jack. Jack had a long stride and a terrific sweeping throw. One day he slipped and hurt his groin. He insisted on staying on the mound. On every pitch you could see a wave of agony twist his face. I was catching, so Mr. Mack sent me out to tell him to quit. He wouldn't. He said we were ahead and to let him stay in and win. The manager sent me out a second time to get him out of there. He pleaded to be let alone. But the third time I went to him he consented. Somebody else went in. I think it was Plank. Anyhow, we lost in extra innings.

That night in the hotel, the doctors wouldn't let anybody see Coombs. They said his injury was serious enough to kill him. But the next morning I insisted on seeing him. I went into his room and found Jack and his wife crying.

"Why what's wrong?" I asked. Jack hands me a letter. It's from a fan who wrote "So you sold out the Giants. You're looked on by the fans as a crook!" That shows you how sometimes criticism of a ball player can be so far from being fair. Coombs really risked his life trying to win, only to be called a crook!

**RUBE OLDRING** For whatever reason, Mr. Mack always insisted I room with the Chief—Charles Albert Bender. Everybody in the populated universe called him "Chief," except for Mr. Mack, who insisted on calling him "Albert." When a "must win" game was on the line, Mr. Mack always turned to "Albert" because the blood in his veins turned to ice water and nothing short of a full-scale tribal war could divert his attention from focusing on each batter in turn.

He was an impressive-looking athlete, standing over 6 feet tall, and straight as an arrow. He had huge hands and broad shoulders, and along with his jet black hair and dark piercing eyes, he looked like the fierce competitor he was.

He was smart all right, and a graduate from the Carlisle Indian School and Dickinson University, but he never showed off his smarts. In fact, most of the time he didn't talk a lot, but when he did, he spoke very quietly and slowly with a real deep, low voice. Most of the time when we were on the road, he would stay in the hotel by himself either deeply immersed in a book or sitting quietly in a chair listening to the small talk of his teammates. Sometimes he could be downright moody, or morose. He was a temperamental guy, no doubt about it, and he needed to be handled with a lot of care. I guess that's why Mr. Mack had me room with the sullen man for 12 years.

If you asked the Chief a question, he would look at you penetratingly with those brown-black eyes of his as if pondering the answer over in his mind. Sometimes you had to wait as long as 30, 40 or 50 seconds for a response, and the pause could become embarrassing. Then would come the answer, slow and terse and couched in immaculate English—the language of a gentleman and a scholar.

Now, the irony here was that by far the two quietest guys on the team were Joe and the Chief. Both grew up in conditions of poverty, both were big strong guys, both were loners and both were outsiders. The Chief had a lot of interests, though. He was an expert on tree care and knew a lot about precious stones. He also painted and gardened when he could. Joe didn't seem to have any interests, except maybe hunting. He didn't play golf, or cards, or billiards like the Chief did. But, to everybody's surprise, once in a while we would walk into a hotel lobby and there would be Joe and the Chief sitting off in some quiet corner or alcove, carrying on a real live conversation. About what, we never found out, for every time somebody got near, they shut up. I asked the Chief once, all he said was "nothing much." Well, they were talking about something, but it's remained a great mystery.

**IRA THOMAS** The Chief was as good a pitcher as I ever caught. He had this "talcum-powder" ball he threw when he got into a pinch. What he did was, he would rub one side of the ball against a bag of talcum that he kept in his pocket. He'd get that side of the ball as smooth as a baby's rear end and that would make it drop unexpectedly. He also threw a damn good spitter. Of course, you've got to remember that both of those pitches were legal in those days.

The funniest thing is though, that he seemed to get along with Joe some. Maybe it was because they were both so damn somber.

**EDDIE PLANK** Bender, we called, like all the other players who were of Native American stock, "Chief." The fact that this habit was both disingenuous and offensive never occurred to us. If it did to Bender, he never said so, but I can imagine what he thought.

**JOE JACKSON** The Chief and me got along pretty good. The Chief—that was Chief Bender—was a real Indian Chief, but I forget what tribe. Anyway, he didn't ever get on me—not once. He didn't care where a person was from, as long as they didn't give him a hard time. But nobody much gave him a hard time anyhow because he was tough and looked it.

A couple of times when we was in a hotel after a game or something, and the guys were horsing around, me and the Chief talked about hunting in Pennsylvania. It seems like he knowed everything there was to know about hunting there. He didn't usually talk a lot, but once you started talking serious about hunting, why he'd talk a blue streak. It was kind of our secret, though, because if anybody came over, we just stopped. He didn't want to talk to just anybody about that, but I think he knowed that I knowed a lot about hunting, so I was somebody he could talk to private like.

He told me about rifle hunting in Bradford County near the Colley area which was his favorite place. He talked about the high mountains and woods and how beautiful that area was. He also told me about a place called Sugar Run and climbing a mountain called "Brisky," with full hunting gear, which he said was so hard it separated the men from the boys. Another time he told me about "Tyler," another really steep mountain named after this old man that had just squatted and lived on the mountain and acted like he owned it but he didn't really. He even told me about this mountain called "Dragon," that had real slippery slopes, but it didn't have nothing to do with any fire-spitting animal like a dragon. He said it got its name that way because when a hunter managed to climb all the way to the top of the "Dragon" his rear end would be "draggin." The Chief let out the biggest roar of laughter when he told me that.

We talked sometimes too, about going to the Colley hills part of the state and hunting together.

"You'd like that, Joe," he said.

"I wish I could do that right now," I said.

"I know what you mean," he said, "but they'll be plenty of time for that after the season."

We talked about using heavy 220 grain bullets to cut through brush in the thick part of the woods, but 180 grain bullets out in the open seeing as how they was more accurate there.

"One of the good things about baseball, Joe," he told me, "is that we don't have to work during hunting season. Not many people are that lucky."

At that point I wasn't sure I was going to be playing baseball much longer, but he did have a point.

"And you are going to be with the Athletics a long time," he said. "I've seen that swing of yours. It's as pretty as a white-tail running through an open field in November."

I didn't know how he could say that since I hadn't done nothing with the team to prove that.

He told me we'd make an unbreakable date to hunt that fall, only we never did, and I never went hunting with him.

I don't honestly remember a lot about that month or so with the team that was good, except for talking about hunting with the Chief.

**TOPSY HARTSEL** We had this lucky charm. Actually, it was a lucky dwarf named Louis Van Zelst. Little Louie was this hunch-back guy who was in some kind of accident when he was really little and his body was all out of shape. So he became the Athletics' mascot, and he traveled with the team and even had his own little uniform. When we were going good, some of the guys thought he was the reason. Actually we didn't always believe that, but what the heck, it didn't take much effort to pat his hump. See, that's what you had to do when you were in a slump—pat his hump.

Now Joe, when he first met little Louie, didn't know what to make of him. I told him he had to pat his hump for luck, but he thought we were just making fun of him. That is until he saw some of the other guys doing it. Then every time up he did it too. Since he wasn't getting many hits, I told him he had to learn how to stroke it right. I actually think he believed me.

I'll tell you this: when we won the Series the next year, his hump was damn near wore out.

But if you think that was bad, it was nothing compared to what the Tigers did. Ty Cobb discovered a black urchin he called "Li'l Rastus" who he always wanted around for good luck, but he made sure nobody outside of the Tigers ever saw him with the team. Now, Li'l Rastus was supposed to bring the team luck but once when the team was in the middle of a losing streak and some of their equipment showed up missing, Cobb kicked him out of the clubhouse. So what happened was that Li'l Rastus goes over to the Cubs and sells his good luck to them in the World Series, and they beat the Tigers. Well, Cobb is livid and he gets Li'l Rastus back for the 1909 season.

So when we're playing the Tigers in September, there's Li'l Rastus hiding under the Tiger's bench giving us the evil eye every time we come up to bat, and little Louie Van Zelst running around in our dugout getting his hump patted all the time

**VINCENT ALEXANDER** After the issue of the pennant was decided, Mr. Mack played out the string by using some of his young kids—players like Jackson and McInnis. Joe showed very little enthusiasm for his mop up duties, ending the season with an average of .177. He played in precisely the same number of games as the previous season—five. Hardly an auspicious beginning to his career.

**RUBE OLDRING** It wasn't a happy time for Joe. You could see it in his face. You could see it in his listless shuffle. The thing was nobody had a lot of time or a lot of patience to pay attention to Joe or his problems. If he wanted to play with the big boys, he would just have to begin to act like one.

**HARRY DAVIS** As was the tradition in those days, as soon as the official season was over, we began a "barnstorming" trip, playing against minor league and amateur teams. It was a way for all of us to make a little extra money before heading home for the winter. We played such teams as the Philadelphia Giants, and pickup teams from Trenton and Perkasie. Most of the regulars played in these games—Collins, Oldring, Murphy, Coombs, Plank, Thomas. It was a good opportunity, too, for some of the younger players to get the hang of the way the team operated, and to get a chance to play with the regulars. I expected Joe to go along and get some valuable experience which would stand him in good stead the next season. Surely there was no doubt he would be with the team for the entire season then, his lackluster performance so far notwithstanding.

When we got to Camden for the first game, no Joe. I'm not sure I ever completely forgave him for that. I understood how difficult it was for the kid trying to adjust to life away from home for the first time, and in a big city to boot, but here was a perfect chance for him. The pressure was off. We were playing for fun, and we were getting ready for the next season, a season for which we had high expectations. If Joe wanted to prove to us that he was going to be an important part of our team, here was his opportunity.

Instead of rising to the challenge, Joe took off ... again.

# 26

# I HEARD THEM STORIES

**TY COBB** Baseball is a red-blooded sport for red-blooded men. It's no pink tea, and mollycoddles and anyone who thinks it is had better stay out of it. It's a struggle for supremacy, a survival of the fittest.

**CHARLIE LEABEAU** The thing about Major League baseball around the time Joe was hesitatingly beginning his career is that it had created its own world, a world peopled by rough, aggressive men, which in turn had attracted a following of like-minded individuals. It's not that Joe was the only player who didn't quite fit in, but he was clearly not completely comfortable in that world. Joe was tough in some ways, decidedly not in others.

Baseball was struggling to clean up the image it had created for itself in the 1890s and 1910s. Baseball was flourishing at the gate, but many in the crowds were lowlifes attracted to the game by the violence. John McGraw alone had engaged in enough fights to warrant consideration as a boxing champion. Hundreds of stories were being written about drunken brawls in the stands, violent actions in the dugout, players attacking fans, fans attacking players, everybody attacking umpires. Anarchy reigned supreme. One wag commented, "Yesterday I went to a fight at a baseball park and a game broke out."

At one time or another there were riots in Philadelphia, Brooklyn and

Pittsburgh, all precipitated by John McGraw who, as manager of the New York Giants, subscribed to the theory that the more hated his team was, the more people would show up to see them. Even Christy Mathewson, probably as clean cut a player as you could ever want to find, once punched in the mouth a kid who was selling lemonade behind the Giants' bench, ostensibly because the kid was yelling derogatory comments at the players. "Kid" Elberfield, a Tennessee mountain man who played for a bunch of teams, was known to smash dishes in restaurants if he found fault with the service and once broke a bottle over a waiter's head. And the Cubs--they fought everybody, including themselves when they ran out of players on the other teams. In 1908, when they beat the Giants in a one-game playoff for the league championship, they had to retreat before an angry mob of Giants fans. It took the police to rescue them from a barricaded clubhouse just before they were apparently ready to fight their way out.

Then there was Ty Cobb. He got into more fights than any Tombstone marshal. He attacked players, fans, umpires, porters, cripples. He tried his fists first. If that didn't work, he went for his gun.

Now, I don't want to imply that Joe couldn't handle himself in a fight. He probably could have. He certainly had the size and the physical attributes to take on almost anybody in the game, but that was not his wont. He shied away from fisticuffs which in turn, probably didn't earn him popularity points with his teammates. There was more than one suggestion that Joe was a coward, an accusation that would surface a number of times during his life. If Joe was afraid of fighting, I think it was more a fear of having people getting angry at him. That he hated.

It was about this time that John McGraw invested in a pool hall with Arnold Rothstein, the young would-be mobster. A.R., as he came to be called, was a silent partner, but it was his first connection with a baseball personality. It would not be his last, as Joe was to learn with tragic results.

You can bet your last nickel Joe heard the rumors about Hal Chase. Everybody talked about him in the clubhouse, albeit in hushed tones. If Cobb was the toughest (some would say dirtiest) player in the game, Chase was the most villainous. He was a player without a hint of morality. He gambled and threw countless games without batting an eyelash.

How did he get away with it? Simple. He was as charming a man as anyone could ever remember. Everybody loved Prince Hal. So what if he cheated a little? He was the nicest guy in the world, and any man or woman would be lucky to count him as a friend. He had the dashing good looks of a matinee idol, a smile that could light up a room, and a wit that made him the center of attention in any setting. He dressed to the hilt and ran with the fast New York set. On top of that, he was a brilliant first baseman—some would argue the best who had ever played. He seemed to have everything ... except a conscience.

There were whispers about Chase from the time he first began playing for the old New York Highlanders. Prince Hal had money on almost every game. Balls would roll just inches past his reach, throws would nab him on ill-advised steals, a not-so-fast ball would find him swinging a split second late. Pitchers on the team would be introduced to "friends" with deep pockets who might be able to help them with that mortgage on the house.

The thing is, everybody knew it, but nobody said anything publicly. We knew it wasn't right, but neither was snitching. The players' fraternity said it was OK to talk about him among ourselves, but not to others.

In 1908, the management of the New York team, becoming concerned about the frequency of the rumors, leaked a story to the press that Prince Hal was throwing ballgames, so he hightailed it back to his home in California and played for a few seasons in an outlaw league there.

This became his pattern. When accused of cheating he cried, "How dare you accuse me of such a thing?" smiled with all the charm of a stage hero, and moved on to someplace where he could do it again.

Now get this. Everybody in the world knew he was cheating. They watched him like a hawk. So what happened? The Highlanders brought him back because he was so popular with the fans. Hal showed his undying appreciation by throwing more games, instigating the firing of the manager, and getting himself named the new manager!

Joe, like the rest of us, knew this story, the moral of which was, "It's OK to throw games if you're popular enough."

How much he took it to heart I can't really say. Certainly, though, there was a model right smack in front of him.

**ROGER PECKINPAUGH** I can remember more than a few time when I was a young shortstop with the Yankees that I threw a ball to Chase at first base, and it went by him to the stands and a couple of runs scored.

I'd stand there looking, sighting the flight of that ball in my mind, and I'd think, "Geez, that throw wasn't that bad." Then I'd tell myself that he was the greatest fielder there was, so maybe the throw was bad. Then later on when he got that smelly reputation, it came back to me, and I said, "Oh-oh." What he was doing, you see, was tangling up his feet then making a fancy dive after the ball, making it look like it was a wild throw.

**JOE JACKSON** Of course I heard all them stories about Chase. We all did, but they didn't mean nothing to me. Why should they? Everybody on our team said he was wrong. That was all there was to it.

**CHARLIE LEBEAU** Some people act like Joe came into the pristine world of squeaky-clean baseball, and somehow tainted it. Well, that just wasn't so. Men who called themselves "sportsmen" openly walked around the stands quoting odds to anyone with a spare dollar. Heck, some of the clubs were even owned by known gamblers.

The powers that be in baseball became so concerned about its image with the middle-class fans that they hired private detectives to circulate through the crowds with the aim of ejecting the obvious gamblers. But that didn't matter much, because if you wanted to bet on a baseball game you could find a hundred places in any city to do it. All you had to do was to go to almost any barber shop, shoeshine stand or pool hall, and you could find the morning on the day's games. With that amount of gambling, of course, came the obvious possibility of fixing games. How many players did this? We'll never know for sure, but anybody who didn't know it was going on, either had his head in the sand or was the most naive person on the planet.

**HUGH FULLERTON** Once, Yankee manager, Frank Chance, told a few of us that his first baseman, Hal Chase was throwing games on him. I went to my editor, told him I wanted to run the story. He said, in no uncertain terms, to bury it, that they'd already run so many stories about corruption in the city that nobody wanted to read about it anymore. "Besides," he said, "baseball's as clean as your mother's fresh laundry."

"The hell it is," I responded.

"Well, if it isn't," he said, "and we report it, you're out of a job, because there won't be anything left to report on."

# 27

## I LIKED PLAYING FOR THE PELS

**CONNIE MACK** By the end of the 1909 season two things were becoming increasingly clearer to me. One, it was doubtful that Joe would ever become a prominent part of the Athletics, and two, we were building a team that would be a prominent force in the American League for years to come. Don't think I was losing faith in Joe's ability, because I wasn't, not for a second, but if Joe was incapable or unwilling to make the effort to fit in with the team, then we would move on without him.

Over the winter I talked with Ben Shibe on several occasions about Joe and his future, or lack of same. Ben felt Joe had enough promise to sell him to another team for a reasonable profit. After all, he insisted, we hadn't invested that much in him to that point. But the problem was, I couldn't sell him to another American League team and risk having him decide he was happy enough there to live up to his considerable potential. The thought of Joe teaming up in the same outfield with a Cobb or a Speaker was enough to give me heartburn for the rest of my born days. Ben argued that we should consider shipping him off to the National League. I would have sold my mother before I would have dealt with any team in the National League. To conspire with the enemy was an act of unspeakable treachery and I would have none of it. Ben argued loud and long on behalf of the money, I for the principle.

After protracted and sometimes heated discussions, it was agreed I would try to talk Joe into playing with conviction in Philadelphia. Failing that, we would send him back to the minors.

**LUTHER JACKSON** Joe said over and over again that he wasn't going back to Philadelphia. The more he said it, the more I think he believed it.

Mr. Mack sent a couple of guys down to Greenville over the winter to talk to Joe about his career, but he didn't say much. He didn't have to, his mind was already made up. Joe was going to stay in the South.

**J.C. HATCH** There were more rumors flying than ducks heading south. Joe was going to the Giants to play for McGraw. Joe was going to the Tigers to play next to Cobb. Joe was going back to the Athletics to play first base. Joe wasn't going anywhere.

One thing was for sure, though. Joe wasn't talking and out of his silence sprung enough speculation to keep us engrossed and entertained for the entire winter.

**RICHARD COLZIE** It wasn't long into the winter that we caught wind that Joe wasn't going to return to Philadelphia. Can you believe that? Greenville's most famous son quitting again. What a surprise!

**KATIE WYNN JACKSON** Joe was kind of moody all winter. Like always, he went hunting and fishing with his brothers, and he worked a little in his father's butcher shop, but he didn't seem to be himself. He was even quieter than usual, and sometimes got quite short with people who asked him about playing baseball.

Then around about the beginning of March, Mr. Mack sent a wire asking if Joe was going to report to spring training. Joe's response was short but predictable: "Not interested in playing in Philadelphia."

A week later came another wire. "Report immediately to the New Orleans Pelicans of the Southern League." You would have thought he had just had the cares of the world lifted from his shoulders the way he reacted. He was thrilled. He began running around the village like a little kid. He was a different person from that moment on.

**ANTOINE BEGUE** Joe was about as far removed from the culture of New Orleans as I was from that of the moon. I was born, raised, live, and hope to die in the Vieux Carre area of the city.

It was my distinct pleasure to get to know Joe when he came down to play for the Pelicans. I was employed by the team, my job consisting of a variety of servile duties, not the least of which was indoctrinating "foreign" players into the pleasures of New Orleans life. Joe was a particular delight to me as he exhibited an ingenuous sense of spontaneity and joy at every new sight he encountered, and almost everything he encountered was a new sight to him.

Before he had even unpacked I took him on a walking tour of the Vieux Carre. We passed a long, gangly Negro with a sooty top hat worn at such a steep angle that it apparently defied gravity.

"Mah mule is white, mah face is black; Ah sells mah coal two bits a sack," he sang in a rich deep base.

"Adieu, ramoneur."

"Who's he?" Joe asked.

"A vanishing breed," Mr. Jackson, "a coal peddler in rapid retreat from the advancing army of gas merchants."

As we turned the corner we came upon a myriad of berry men and women.

"Men always sell strawberries, women blackberries," I informed my long-limbed guest.

"Why is that?" Joe asked taking the bait.

"Why? you ask. Ah, it has always been that way. When you get to know us Creoles better, you will realize that the phrase 'It has always been that way' justifies everything."

Presently we came upon a "spasm band," a musical ensemble made up of a variety of cans, pan tops, a soap box, nails and drumsticks, all accompanied by a rag tag collection of little Negro boys dancing up a storm. I flipped them a coin which occasioned a wild scramble for the gold of the realm and an offer to do tricks for a lagniappe.

"What's that?" asked Joe.

"A little gift. Something extra."

Without hesitation several boys began doing hand-walking tricks and exuberant dances in anticipation of supplemental consideration.

We stopped at a snowball wagon for an iced delight. I ordered two strawberry snowballs which we downed with great satisfaction in the warm spring sunshine. I spoke momentarily with an old crone sitting on her front stoop sucking on a corncob pipe. I spoke in Gumbo-French.

"What was that you was talking?" Joe asked.

"Creole talk, Joe. Look at that," I said, pointing to a step two doors down. There on the step was a small white candle burning in the center of a cross made of wet salt. On the end of each arm of the cross, sat a nickel.

"What's that?" Joe said.

"That's a gris-gris," I answered in a whispered voice. "Somebody put that there to bring harm on the people who live in the house."

"Why doesn't somebody just take the money?" he asked.

"Anybody who touches the charm, will have the same bad luck." I told him.

"Really?"

"Absolutely. See all those freshly scrubbed stoops with powdered bricks?"

"Yeah."

"Well, those powdered bricks not only keep away evil spirits, but they also stop witches and ghosts from coming in."

"What do you mean, ghosts?"

"See that house there, on the corner of Royal and St. Ann Streets. That's one of the many houses in the Vieux Carre that are haunted."

"Really?"

"Absolutely. Many an important figure in this city has seen the naked figure of a woman walking up and down on the edge of that roof there. She's always shivering and wringing her hands. Everybody around here knows the story about the beautiful octoroon slave girl more than a century ago who fell in love with her white master. He told her that if she would walk naked on the roof top of that house that night he would become her lover. Well that night was one of the coldest of the year, but the girl, insisting on proving her love, took off her clothes and began walking along the edge of the roof. Before too long she became so exhausted by the cold that she lay down and fell into a coma from which she never awoke. So if you come by here some night and see her, you'll know who it is."

"Are all the houses haunted here?" Joe asked.

"Not all, but many. You see, New Orleans is particularly kind to ghosts."

"I didn't know that."

"Yes, we have many ghosts here, and a considerable amount of Voodoo, too."

"Voodoo?"

"It was brought here from Africa by our ancestors. So the early colonists had to be particularly watchful of trickery. Those Voodoo queens, they knew many things unknown by the white men."

"What kind of things?"

"They could make people die and then bring them to life again."

"They could do that?"

"They could probably make a baseball player lose his legs."

"Could they make a player play better?"

"I wouldn't be surprised, but be careful, Joe."

I liked Joe. He was guileless and honest. I know those aren't adjectives often applied to him, but based on my experiences with him, they are appropriate.

**CHARLIE FRANK** As the owner-manager of the Southern League 1910 New Orleans franchise, I was thrilled to receive a telegram from Connie Mack informing me that Joe Jackson was being sent down to play for our team. In the South, there wasn't a bigger draw, save maybe Ty Cobb when the Tigers barnstormed through. We were a class A league with our share of talented players, but Joe's reputation placed him immediately at the forefront.

Working out the business deal with the Athletics took some doing and a rather protracted series of telegram exchanges with Ben Shibe. While this was going on, we had to legally hold Joe out of spring training practice games. While Joe sat, rumors began flying in the local papers that Mr. Mack had changed his mind and wanted to have Joe sent back to Philadelphia. I'm not sure that was ever completely true, but Shibe did waver a few times during the negotiations. I believed then, and still do that Mr. Mack was having second thoughts. Worried that we would lose him before he ever played in a single game, we finally reached an agreement guaranteeing that Joe would remain with us at least until the Southern League pennant race was decided.

I felt we had a strong team that would be in contention all season, and secretly I worried that we might run away with the race early thereby losing Joe with a good part of the season left. Nevertheless, I wasn't going to do anything to compromise the sport.

Early on I spoke to Joe about this, because I had the feeling that he might have preferred to stay in the South rather than return to Philadelphia. I told him he couldn't lay down ever, that the integrity of the game was at stake and that a professional ball player always plays to win. He said he knew that and I'll tell you this, that is exactly what he did. Joe played like a demon all season.

**ANTOINE BEGUE** New Orleans, as a place for a variety of sporting events, is and has always been unique due in large measure to the particular combination of French and Spanish influences, tempered by the Creole and refined by the Americans. Bull fights and cock fights were popular not all that long ago. My father would tell of blowing garlic and whiskey into the animal's beaks in order to incite the beasts to a greater frenzy of fighting enthusiasm. Dog and alligator fights were not uncommon nor were bear- and bull-baiting contests where spectators would be encouraged to throw stones at the combatants so as to inspire them to greater fury. Street boxing, wrestling, Voodoo dances all are common here,

Growing up in a Creole family as I did, we were early on indoctrinated into the Indian sport of rackets—a violent mix of lacrosse, football, cross-country running and rioting. There was such enthusiasm for the sport among the Creole population that two clubs, the La Villes and the Bayous, were formed thus establishing a rivalry as fervent as any between American college football teams.

Of course, fencing was once the sport *de rigueur* in New Orleans when Creole blood ran hot and all men "of honor" learned how to defend themselves against insults both physical and verbal. Frequent were the duels at St. Anthony's Garden or under the "Dueling Oaks." The most renowned of all the duelists was Jose "Pepe" Llulla who was so prolific with a sword that he apparently maintained his own cemetery for the countless victims of his duels.

At one time, too, we were considered the boxing capital of the world, a title enhanced by a famous battle in the 1890s between Burke and Bowen which lasted almost seven and a half hours and ended in a 110-round draw.

Baseball may lack the danger and violence so often associated with the New Orleans sporting scene, but it has always been popular here. Perhaps it is seen as a respite from the ferocity of our recreational interests. Many amateur and semi-professional teams made New Orleans home during the 19th century. By late in the century, visiting professional teams from the North began playing our Robert E. Lee Clubs at the old Fair Grounds and a two-team league of New Orleans and Mobile was organized by a local patent medicine company. Then in 1901, the Southern Association was formed and the Pelicans became the favorite of the locals. I joined the club in 1905, the year we won our first pennant.

I tell you all of this to make the point that we took our sport very seriously in New Orleans, baseball included. We were ardent in our support and zealous in our defense of aggressive play. When Joe Jackson arrived on the scene he had a reputation for two things: superior natural ability and an indifferent attitude. The former we applauded; the latter we abhorred. I knew Joe would find the going difficult indeed if he played in New Orleans without passion, and conversely I knew that he would be embraced with devotion if he played with zeal. That's the way it was in New Orleans, and that's the way we wanted it.

**CHARLIE FRANK** New Orleans had a long-standing, if somewhat checkered minor league baseball legacy. The Pelican Club had been a charter member of the Southern Association since its inception in 1901, but ran into considerable difficulty in 1905 when a yellow fever epidemic struck New Orleans. In those days we didn't have the medicine to control it, so we had to agree to play all of the remaining games that season on the road. It was tough but the boys pulled together and we played well enough to win the league championship

**HYDER BARR** Once again I found myself on a team with Joe. I had naturally hoped it would be the Athletics, but as fate would have it, we was teammates on the Pelicans, although for very different reasons. I was there because I couldn't help it, Joe because he wanted to be. In two seasons with the Athletics I batted .143 and .079—not exactly numbers to inspire confidence in management, but a lot like Joe's numbers for those years. The difference was that everyone assumed that Joe's statistics was a mistake, but mine wasn't.

Frankie Manush was the other guy on the team I knew, since he played with me and Joe in Philadelphia. I was glad to see a couple of faces I knew. I was even happier when Charlie Frank said me and Joe would be roommates. I always assumed Mr. Mack told him to do that since I was becoming known as a good Jackson babysitter, and again I hoped we would both be called up together—Joe to play, me to take care of him.

Joe was a different person with the Pelicans than he was with the Athletics. With the Athletics he seemed confused and unsure; with the Pelicans he was confident and even cheerful.

Once he even tried to short sheet the bed of Frenchy DeMontreville, our little second baseman.

**CHARLES SOMERS** The Pelicans and the Cleveland Naps had a close working relationship from the start, and in that spring training season of 1910, the two teams trained together and played most of their exhibition games against each other. I owned the Naps, as well as a few other teams, and so I had the opportunity to see Joe Jackson up close. He just about wore out our pitching that spring—Cleveland's pitching that is. He had 20 hits in a handful of games, most of the extra base variety. He was a sweet hitter, that's all there was to it.

I firmly believe that any success I may have had in baseball was due in large measure to my ability to judge other men and pick from the rough, the diamonds which otherwise might have remained unpolished. That was my only definable baseball skill. Joe Jackson was one of those who I was able to so identify and help find his way in baseball.

**CONNIE MACK** Charlie Somers was a truly remarkable man, without whom there might never have been an American League. Back in the stormy days of 1900 and 1901, when the American League was struggling for recognition as a major league, it was Ban Johnson who was steering the boat through precarious waters, but it was Charlie who stood behind the pilot with calm advice and a personal fortune. It was his checkbook that gave Johnson and his associates much of their leverage and strength, yet he was always content to remain in the background. He was a quiet, almost shy man for whom the spotlight held no particular appeal.

**CHARLES SOMERS** I had always been a baseball enthusiast so when there was an opening for a man to get into the game, someone directed Ban Johnson to me. My father disapproved of my involvement in "such a foolish and unprofitable a thing as baseball" and instead suggested I devote my energies to the J.W. Somers Coal Company. Nevertheless, I persisted and, with two partners in Cleveland, purchased the Grand Rapids Club. Because my partners knew little about the game I was forced to take an active part to protect our investment.

A few years later the American League was launched. Ban Johnson saw the opportunity to create a second major league. I knew Johnson was a good honest man and a square shooter. He needed money for his venture and I supplied it.

Before long, I was interested financially in four of the eight American League teams. I owned the Cleveland and Boston franchises outright and had a financial interest in the Athletics. I advanced some money to Charley Comiskey to back his White Sox. I also owned the Pelicans. As soon as I saw Joe, I was determined to get him for the Cleveland club. I had heard the stories about his difficulties with Philadelphia. Perhaps a change of scenery was all that he needed, a fresh start, so to speak.

I queried Connie Mack about his availability, but was told that he had made a deal to let Joe play for the Pelicans, at least for most of the season, and I knew Mack was not a man to go back on a commitment. Nevertheless, I continued pressing my case.

It was obvious that Joe wasn't going to play in Philadelphia, and certainly Mack would rather get something of value for Joe than to let him languish in the minor leagues. Mack had his morals, but he was also a smart business man.

**CHARLIE FRANK** Joe was the sensation of spring training, hitting just about everything that came his way and fielding with an elegance that was the talk of New Orleans from the French Quarter to the waterfront. All of a sudden there was an excitement about the Pels that we had never experienced. Everywhere I went, people were talking about the team, and everyone, it seemed, was buying tickets.

Not every player, no matter how talented, could command the type of interest Joe engendered. Ty Cobb, and later Babe Ruth could, and a few others maybe, but Joe could hold his own with any of them in the interest department. Perhaps his stoical demeanor suggested more than he could deliver on some occasions, but there was something about his quiet elegance on the field that intrigued fans. Even when the stories of his illiteracy surfaced, as they did at regular intervals, they only served to increase his appeal. Joe was a common man with uncommon gifts, and therein lay his fascination.

**HYDER BARR** We had a good team before Joe, but when he joined us, we figured we was unbeatable. One of our pitchers was Teddy Breitenstein. He pitched for a number of years in the big leagues, I think for St. Louis and Cincinnati. By the time he joined us he looked like he was a hundred years old but he could still throw a mean spitter with his old arm. I know he teased Joe something vicious, but he was a good enough guy at heart. Otto Hess was another pitcher we had. He was from someplace in Switzerland. He always said he couldn't understand Joe's broken English, but that didn't matter much because nobody ever understood much of what he said either except, "Ve need Bratvurst. I can't pitch visout Bratvurst," or something like that. Billy Lindsay, our shortstop, was probably Joe's closest friend on the team. He played in the American League with Joe a little bit later on, but didn't stay up for long.

The most popular guy on the team was our big catcher who we called "Frenchy" Lafitte, a true blue New Orleans Frenchman. He was a real hometown hero who didn't hit a lick, but the fans couldn't have cared less. Every time he came to bat, they went wild, and he responded by doffing his cap. He was always telling Joe things like, "You have the right idea, Joe. Don't waste your time learning to read and write English, it's so ... pedestrian. I'll teach you French, the language of love." Then he'd talk to Joe in French, and laugh and carry on as if Joe could understand him. I think this really embarrassed Joe, because every time he saw Frenchy coming he'd try to duck out of sight, but Frenchy was persistent and he'd eventually manage to trap Joe in some corner and begin with the French babble.

I could say I was pulling for Joe to get promoted to the majors, but the hell with that. I was pulling for Hyder Barr, but I knew damn well that Joe was attracting a lot of attention from the scouts, and as long as they were there to see Joe, they would have to see me, too.

**JOE JACKSON** We played most of our practice games against the Cleveland Naps. That was the first time I ever seen Larry Lajoie and it was really something because I remembered all the stories that Charlie Lebeau told us about him. He was kind of old then, but he played every ball and every game like he was in the World Series.

Once he came over to me just after I finished batting practice and said, "Nice swing, kid. Mind if I see your bat?" I gave him Black Betsy and I thought he was just going to look at it, but he took it over to the plate and started taking a couple of swings against one of his pitchers. Now that made me real nervous. I didn't like nobody but me using Betsy, but this was Larry Lajoie and I couldn't tell him he couldn't do that, so I just stood there while he swung and began sweating. If that bat was broke I didn't know what I was going to do. After a few swings, he gave me Betsy back. "Thanks, kid," he said. "That's a good one, take care of it. You know, I wouldn't let anybody else use it if I was you."

**CHARLIE FRANK** Joe was a big part of the reason we got out of the gate so fast. I heard all the stories from Philadelphia about how difficult he was, but I just wrote his name on the lineup card every day as the center fielder and he did the rest. No problems. All season he hit better than anybody in the league and damn near won the stolen base crown. He was an excellent base runner, too. With those long graceful strides of his, he could round first and without slowing be into second before the outfielder knew what was happening. He made a few errors in the field, but most were on balls most other fielders wouldn't have even reached. He didn't have many assists because everybody knew how strong his arm was so they seldom took any chances against him. Joe could do just about everything you needed to do on a baseball field.

**HENRY MANUSH** We had fun that summer. After an exceptionally cold beginning to the season, the weather turned good.

It seems every place we went, Joe was the center of attention—Atlanta, Birmingham, Mobile, Nashville, Chattanooga, Memphis. This was a southern league, followed by southern fans in southern cities. Joe was at home, and Joe was comfortable. Oh, once in a while he'd get annoyed by one thing or another and complain, but for the most part he was at ease.

Sometimes I got the paper and read to him what the reporters were saying about him. Of course, I never did this in public. Joe was real sensitive about the reading thing. Every once in a while a negative comment or two would appear, but I usually skipped that part when reading to Joe. Working with Joe was a little like training a sensitive puppy. Shower him with love and affection and he would do everything asked of him. Criticize in a harsh tone and he was apt to cower or pout. After I figured this out, life around Joe became a lot more comfortable.

**HYDER BARR** I know that if I had had those skills I wouldn't have been playing in New Orleans. If I could have gotten away with killing Joe and stealing his talents I think I would have. It was such a waste, his playing with us. It seemed immoral.

**CHARLIE FRANK** Without question we were the strongest team that season and led the league virtually from wire to wire. Nevertheless the league wasn't as successful as we would have wished owing largely to the lack of competition in the race, really lousy weather early in the season, and a general business recession throughout much of the South. Two things bailed us out—the league's president, W. H. Kavanaugh, had the good sense to impose and enforce a strict salary limit for each team, and the presence of Joe Jackson. Everywhere Joe played attendance rose dramatically. If Joe hadn't yet completely captured the hearts of Philadelphia's fans, he had certainly done so in the Deep South.

Joe made a shambles of the batting race, hitting .354 for the season and winning the batting crown by more than 20 points. To give you an idea of how valuable he was, the next highest average on the team was Frankie Manush who ended up at .256!

**GRANTLAND RICE** When it came time to choose the all-star team for the Southern League's 1910 season I had a few difficult decisions to make such as McGilvray or Swacina at first, but there wasn't any argument about Jackson's status. He was lengths out in front of anybody else in the league.

**JOE JACKSON** I really liked playing for the Pels except for one time late in the season when a big clumsy pitcher hit me on the head with a fast ball. I think he did it on purpose on account of I usually hit him pretty good. I had to sit out a few games with an awful bad headache and blurry eyes. When it didn't get no better after a few games, I started getting worried that something was wrong with my eyesight for good, and you can't be a good hitter with blurry eyes.

Mr. Frank sent me to a doctor who looked into my eyes then asked me to read this sign he had on wall across from where I was sitting. I looked at it, squinted real hard and said, "It says, 'Your eyes are fine, Joe.'"

"Is that what you think it says?" the doctor asked me.

"That's what I hope it says," I answered.

Then I think he remembered I couldn't read the darn sign anyway, because he started laughing. "That's exactly what it says."

"So does that mean I can play tomorrow?" I asked.

He went to his desk and picked up his pen and wrote something on a piece of white paper. "Here," he said and he pinned the paper to the wall. "Look at this and tell me how many lines are on the paper."

I looked at the paper and said, "Two."

"Go home and put this on your wall," he said giving me the paper, "and when you see one line, you can play."

Well, I did just that and in a couple of more days there was one line just as he said, so I started playing again.

The first game back I hit two triples, one double and got a walk. I scored three runs, stole a base, and made four catches in the outfield, one of them on a pretty good running catch, too.

Maybe I should've been beaned more often.

**FRANKIE MANUSH** A particularly nasty line in one of the papers said that hitting Joe on the head created no problem inasmuch as there was apparently nothing in there to damage. That's one story I didn't read to him.

**CHARLIE FRANK** One particular Southern Association game played that summer was of special interest. It was a game between Atlanta and Mobile which Mobile won 2-1. What was of interest about the game, though, was that the entire nine-inning affair took only 23 minutes to complete. What happened was that our league president, Judge William Kavanaugh, decided to experiment by seeing how fast a game could be played, so he asked each team to hustle every minute of the game from start to finish. Players ran on and off the field and apparently swung at any good pitch. There was only one walk and a total of ten hits. Somehow Mobile even managed to reel off a triple play.

The league had seen some good ballplayers like Hugh Hill, Glenn Liebhardt and Tris Speaker, all who went on to careers in the majors. I believed they should be what the league was known for, not some circus act freak baseball speed game. I wrote a letter to Kavanaugh letting him know my feelings. I guess some others did, too, because that was the end of the experiments.

As the season wore on, we continued to increase our lead and as the days counted down toward our clinching the pennant, you could see Joe's demeanor beginning to change. He knew the Athletics had the call on his talents the moment the flag was clinched. Joe was happy in New Orleans. He said he might even live there when his playing days were over. As the specter of Philadelphia began looming larger and larger on his horizon, Joe began to worry. His average slipped some, and his season-long good humor began to turn dour.

# 28

# AIN'T WE GOING TO SEE CLEVELAND?

**CONNIE MACK** I closely monitored Joe's season down in New Orleans. Joe hit well there. Case closed. But could he do the same in Philadelphia? That I intended to find out. A number of things were different for us that season. For one, we were running away with the pennant, and doing it by a wide margin. Our infield of Davis, Collins, Barry, and Baker was being referred to as the "million dollar infield," and was playing splendidly. Our pitching rotation of Coombs, Morgan, Plank, and Bender led our staff to a 1.79 team ERA. Our outfield was the most improved unit on the team, though, with both Murphy and Oldring hitting over .300 most of the season.

So while, I didn't doubt Joe's ability, there really wasn't much room or immediate need for him. Still, I knew how valuable he could be, and I was determined to realize value to our team for all we had put up with in dealing with Joe's waffling behavior.

**TOMMY STOUCH** All manner of speculation began floating around concerning Joe's fate for the remainder of the 1910 season. One frequently reported story had Joe returning to us in Greenville to play for a Mill League all-star team. I certainly would have welcomed him.

What was becoming an annual "Guess-where-Joe-is-going-or-not-going-next" game was in full swing.

**CHARLIE FRANK** Joe came to me and said he wanted to stay in New Orleans. I explained that the rules of baseball were such that if ordered he had little choice but to report to Philadelphia.

He said, "I have a choice to go home, don't I?"

I told him he did if he didn't want to play in the majors ever again.

**CHARLES SOMERS** Despite Lajoie's heroics—he batted .394—the Cleveland franchise was mired in the middle of the pack. Early in June, I made a trip to Philadelphia to talk to Connie Mack about the possibility of trading for Joe. Mack didn't rule it out. I asked him what he would want for Joe. He said "Larry Lajoie" straight up. After I stopped laughing, he said he might consider a trade for Ted Easterly, our excellent catcher. I told him we couldn't possibly let Easterly go for a player who might or might not even show up if we did trade for him.

We sat drinking coffee for some time, discussing Joe's potential which Mack either believed in or wanted me to think he believed in. Either way, I was willing to take the gamble if the price were right. Sometimes a change of scenery could do a player good, and I knew if we had Joe, we wouldn't make some of the mistakes the Athletics made. We would have to treat him with kid gloves, I knew that, but if he were reasonably happy in Cleveland, he could be a great benefit to the team both on the field and at the ticket window.

After a particularly long silence, Mack blurted out, "Briscoe Lord."

"Briscoe Lord?" I repeated. "You just traded him to us last year."

"Well, trade him back," Mack said.

"Briscoe Lord?" I asked again in some amazement.

"Is your hearing going, Charlie?" he asked.

"The guy they call the Human Eyeball?"

Bris Lord was a decent enough player but he was barely hitting .200. He did have an exceptional arm and was a heady veteran, but clearly he was dispensable.

I told Mack we were interested but I wanted to send one of our scouts down to New Orleans for a good look-see at Joe. Mack said to go ahead as there was no hurry since Joe couldn't be moved until the Southern League pennant race was history.

**CONNIE MACK** Of course I didn't want to lose Joe, but Cleveland was in the second division and their best player, Lajoie was past his prime. I didn't see them as being a threat for years to come. It was a good match. Joe could help them if he wanted to, and we could use Lord as a savvy reserve outfielder. He had spent three years with us previously so I knew what I was getting. Cleveland had no idea what they were getting. Besides, I liked Charlie Somers. He was a stand-up guy. If anybody besides us was going to get Joe, Cleveland was a good choice.

**BOBBY GILKS** I was scouting for Cleveland when I got a wire from Charlie Somers telling me to head to New Orleans immediately to check out Joe with a possible trade in mind.

I jumped the first south bound train I could find. I couldn't wait to see Joe again.

Joe welcomed me warmly. I think he was glad to see an old familiar face again. I watched him play a couple of games, and we had some long heart-to-hearts. I didn't expect he'd be excited about the possibility of coming to Cleveland, but I knew he would be even less excited about the prospect of returning to Philadelphia. Cleveland was not Philadelphia I assured him. It was smaller, had more of a sense of community about it, and had a Midwestern feel. It wasn't the South for certain, but it was closer in spirit to the South, than say, Philadelphia, New York, or Boston.

He kept telling me the players in the majors didn't like him. I told him the players in Philadelphia may not have hit it off with him, but that didn't mean the players in Cleveland wouldn't. I didn't pretend it would be all rosy—Joe was a lot smarter than some people think—but I assured him the Cleveland players would treat him with a clean slate. Anyway, they knew him a little from spring training when he tore into them pretty good. He asked about the manager and I told him about Deacon McGuire, and what a great guy he was, and how he didn't feel the need for college players. I talked to him a lot about Larry Lajoie because I knew Joe thought highly of him. I didn't lie to Joe, and I think he recognized and appreciated that.

For days Joe vacillated. Every time I thought I had him convinced, he would come up with another argument against going. All the while, I had the suspicion that Joe wanted me to talk him into going, that he wanted me to make it OK for him to say yes, but it wasn't easy. Day after day we talked without any resolution, but slowly I could see his resolve lessening. Finally when I told him I would go with him, he nodded "OK." He never actually said he would go, but I took the nod as a positive sign and wired Charlie Somers that it looked like Joe would go north with me if the trade were finalized.

**CHARLES SOMERS** As soon as I heard from Bobby Gilks, I contacted Mack and the deal was completed—Joe for Bris Lord and $325 cash. Joe would report to Cleveland as soon as his obligation to the Pelicans was completed.

**CONNIE MACK** Over the years I took a lot of heat for trading Joe, but I knew exactly what I was doing. I knew our players didn't cotton to Jackson, but that wasn't why I traded him. I also knew Joe had great possibilities as a hitter. But at the time things were going none too well for Charlie Somers in Cleveland, and I was anxious to do him a good turn.

**CHARLIE SOMERS** As soon as the *Cleveland Plain Dealer* broke the story, the Cleveland fans immediately began taking an interest in the Southern League race, rooting fervently for the Pelicans to cinch the pennant so that Joe could come and join us.

**BOBBY GILKS** The day the Southern League title was wrapped up I wired Katie and she came down to New Orleans to accompany me and Joe on the train to Cleveland. I figured she would have a calming effect on Joe and would be of help once we settled into town.

We all boarded the train and began heading north. As I expected, Joe began getting a trifle morose the farther we got from New Orleans, but Katie and I did our best to keep him occupied. When we stopped at Memphis, Tennessee, Joe jumped up and said he changed his mind, that he couldn't go through with the rest of the trip.

When I asked him why, he said it was because there just wasn't going to be enough elbow room in Cleveland.

"How do you know that, Joe?" I asked him. "Have you ever been to Cleveland before?"

He insisted that one big city was pretty much like the rest, at which point he stormed off the train. As it so happened, the Pelicans were already in town for a meaningless series against the Memphis squad, so while Katie tried to calm Joe down, I ran and got Charlie Frank from the nearby hotel where he was staying. Charlie talked to him for more than an hour telling him the same things that Katie and I had been saying, but I guess the three of us ganging up on him was more pressure than he could handle so eventually he got back on the next northbound train, and the three of us continued our trip.

Every time the train came to a stop or even slowed down I had to watch Joe like a hawk for fear he would bolt the train once again.

Joe was hard work. By the time we got to Cleveland I was exhausted. For a few minutes Joe sat there like he wasn't going to get off. I was just about to kill him when he got a wry smile on his face, stood up and said, "Come on Bobby, ain't we ever going to get to see Cleveland?"

# 29

# A DARN SIGHT BETTER THAN PHILADELPHIA

**CHARLIE LEBEAU** The 1910 season, like most in the dead-ball era, was dominated by pitching. Cy Young, Walter Johnson, Three Fingers Brown, Smokey Joe Wood, Chief Bender, George Mullin, Rube Waddell, among other notables, conspired to keep the league ERA under 3.00. It was a time for pitchers, and few were the hitters who managed high averages. This, of course, was true for most mortals, Ty Cobb being the exception, although some would argue he was far from being human anyway.

Cleveland was desperate for some batting to complement Lajoie. Enter Joe Jackson. He was joining a team whose starting outfielders were hitting under .220 for the season with a grand total of one home run. If anyone could talk him into actually playing, the argument went, he could hardly fail to help.

**HENRY P. EDWARDS** The Cleveland franchise wasn't exactly a baseball dynasty. They had once finished as high as second in the American League, but that was their greatest achievement. "Poor Larry Lajoie," went the refrain. He gave the team everything he had including his name, but unless the team got some hitting help, they would always be also-rans.

**CALVIN CLARKE** I don't want to say nothing bad about the Cleveland franchise, because I was born and raised in the Emerald City, and I think you got to be loyal to your hometown, but let's face it, they wasn't exactly one of the elite teams in Mr. Johnson's league.

But we was always a baseball town. Going all the way back to 1879 we had a professional team. Then it was a National League team, called, of all things, the Cleveland Nationals. Actually before that, I guess we even had a team in the old National Association, but I don't know nothing about that on account of I wasn't even born then. But I remember the star of that Nationals team who was none other than the great Cy Young. It seems like he won 35 games or so every season. Jesse Burkett, who was called Crab, I reckon because he looked a little like one, was a star in the outfield. Chief Sockalexis, a real honest-to-goodness Indian from some reservation, had about the best outfield throwing arm I ever seen until Joe come along.

With all them good players you would think we should have won all the time, but we didn't. It didn't matter much though, because practically nobody came out to watch the games anyways. Of course, being a kid then, I liked that because that meant you had loads of room to chase after foul balls.

Then after a few years of winning nothing, the Robisons bought the team. There was two of them, Frank and Stanley, and boy, did we hate them. They said Cleveland had lousy fans and didn't deserve a winning team. Now maybe I don't know nothing about running a baseball team, but I can't help thinking that was a pretty stupid thing to do. Insulting your fans can't be a good way to get them to buy your product. See what I mean? Anyway, they got so many people angry by what they kept saying in the papers, that even less and less people came to the games.

See, most people wanted the team to do good but not the Robisons.
So what do you suppose they do? Instead of selling the Cleveland team they bought the St. Louis team, too. So now they had two lousy teams to deal with. They wasn't the first owners to have two teams at the same time, but they was probably the first to have two such bad teams. Lucky them!

Then they got this brilliant idea. Since they were perturbed at the Cleveland fans for not supporting their team, they sent the best players from the Cleveland squad to St. Louis. So Cy Young, Jesse Burkett and a handful of other top-notch Cleveland players found themselves suddenly in St. Louis, and all that was in Cleveland was a bunch of second string players.

The Robisons got even with us, all right. The team they left us with won all of 20 games that season and lost 134. Hell, Cy Young won 26 alone that season in St. Louis and Burkett batted .396. No doubt about it, we got stuck with the worst team in baseball history, finishing 84 games out of first place. Let me give you an idea of how bad they was. Our best pitcher was Cold Water Jim Hughey. He won 4 games that year and lost 30! Our shortstop, Harry Lockhead made 81 errors and the whole team hit a total of eight homers. We had two managers, Lave Cross who won all of eight games, and Joe Quinn, who did much better, winning 12. The guy I remember best, though, was Harry Colliflower. Ol' Harry, he won one game and lost 11. How he won that one was a miracle, because for the season, he pitched 98 innings, gave up 152 hits and 41 walks! He did manage to strike out 8, but those batters must have got something in their eyes because Harry couldn't have broken an egg shell with his pitches.

The average attendance was less than 200! The team was called the Cleveland Misfits, or sometimes the Cleveland Leftovers.

After a while, though, the other owners of the National League got real teed-off because they was all losing their shirts whenever they played in Cleveland. I mean, can you blame them? So what they did was, make the team play the rest of the games on the road. From mid-season on, we never saw our team. Most of the people thought this was a good idea anyways, but I sort of missed making fun of the worst team ever. After all, how many people can say they followed a team that bad? Not many, I can tell you that. We had to read about what was going on in the papers. So the team then became the Cleveland Exiles or the Cleveland Wanderers. I tell you we had more nicknames that season than I can even remember.

The league decided that they had to cut the weakest teams in the league. Presto, Cleveland and a couple other teams were no more.

The year 1900 was a rotten one if you was a baseball fan in Cleveland. If you wanted to see a major league game you had to go all the way down to Cincinnati, or over to Chicago or Pittsburgh, and a lot of us just couldn't do that any time we wanted to.

Then along came Ban Johnson. He was a hard-talking, hard-drinking man who wanted to create a new major league to challenge the National League. For all those years, the National League was the only major league, and since Ban couldn't get control of that, I guess he decided to make a new one so he could run it himself. He took the old Western Association and made it into the American League. They started play in 1901 with teams in

Chicago, Boston, Detroit, Philadelphia, Baltimore, Washington, Milwaukee and yes, Cleveland.

Jimmy McAleer managed the team that first year, and although they wasn't great, they managed to win 55 games and beat out Milwaukee for the cellar. The next year Napoleon Lajoie came over from the new Philadelphia team managed by Connie Mack and we moved all the way up to fifth. Larry was our first real baseball hero in a city that had a bad feeling about itself because of all the bad things that happened to the old baseball team.

When Addie Joss joined the team, he became the second great player we had, and for many years, our greatest pitcher. In 1905, they made Lajoie the manager. Here he was only just 30 years old, and the manager of the team. But everybody respected him, the fans and the players, too. In fact, they liked him so much that they changed the name of the team to the Cleveland Naps and it was called that for many years. In 1908 we won 90 games but just missed the pennant by half a game. Ty Cobb's Tigers just beat us out at the end and Larry took it real personally. The next season he quit as manager saying that he wanted to go back to just playing on account of it didn't look like we was going to win the flag. Deacon McGuire took over as manager but we finished sixth anyway.

Then along comes Joe.

I couldn't wait to see what he could do hitting in front of Larry. For a kid who still remembered the Cleveland Leftovers, this new Naps team looked like the greatest thing to ever happen to Cleveland.

**CHARLES SOMERS** When I replaced Lajoie with McGuire as manager, they called us the Molly McGuires, which at the time bothered me no end. Young was just about through. Joss was slipping some, and Larry was getting along in years and it was only a matter of time. I gave serious thought to rebuilding the team from the bottom up. We had a few very promising young pitchers—Willie Mitchell, a southpaw from down in Mississippi someplace, Freddy Blanding, a righty from out in California, and George Kahler, a kid from downstate.

Then, late in the season we picked up the 20-year-old, Jackson. Even the most dispirited Cleveland fan must have felt, at least, a faint twinge of hope.

**JOE JACKSON** I can't rightly say that I liked Cleveland a whole lot, but I can say it was a darn sight better than Philadelphia.

**KATIE WYNN JACKSON** We got into Cleveland late on a Thursday night, but everybody on the Naps was nice to us from the moment we got there. Mr. Somers even had set up a place for us to stay. It was a nice little house not very far from the stadium with its own kitchen and a little porch out front. It was a trifle noisy what with all the traffic, but it had a long garden along the side and shade trees around it. It wasn't a big place, but compared to living with the Jackson family in Brandon Mill, we had more space than we ever dreamed of.

The good part was that we could walk to the ballpark from the house, and that saved a lot of hassle with learning streetcar schedules. I say "we" because it was my intention to go with Joe to as many of the Cleveland home games as I could. I knew about all the problems Joe had in Philadelphia and I believed that I could help. Of course, I didn't know a thing about Cleveland, or any other big northern city for that matter, but as long as me and Joe stuck together, I figured we could get along just fine.

It was good, too, I think, to have me there when Joe came home, because, let's face it, Joe didn't ever have a lot of what you might call real close friends on teams. He had friends, mind you, but not close like I was.

We didn't have much time to settle, because the next day Joe had to report to the field for a game against the Washington Nationals. I walked with him to the stadium and met Mr. Somers before Joe went down to the locker room to get his uniform and meet the players. Mr. Somers asked me if I would like to stay and see the game and I said I would so he called one of his office boys out to show me up to the grandstand behind home plate. He apologized to me saying that he wished he had a better seat for me but that Joe was the reason why he didn't. I didn't realize that so many people knew who he was, but I guess they did. Anyway, I didn't mind the seat, even if it was in the last row of the stands, because I could see good from there. Mr. Somers told me that I could have that same seat anytime I wanted it, and that I didn't have to pay for it. I knew he was doing that because he thought it would help Joe, having me there. When things weren't going so good, Joe always knew he could look up there and find me.

That first game I think I was a lot more nervous than Joe. I sat in the stands for a long time as the players, one by one, came out on to the field, but Joe wasn't with any of them. I thought oh, oh, he got so scared that he left and went back to the little house. I was just about to leave and go see if I could find him, when he came out on the field. I guess it took some time to get his new uniform and all. It was a brand spanking new white uniform with a big blue "C" on it. When he took batting practice I was afraid that he was going to be so nervous that he wasn't going to hit a thing. But he swung old Betsy like he did at home, and as soon as I saw that, well, it calmed my nerves a whole lot. He hit the ball hard all over the field, and the people sitting around me, they were real impressed. I didn't say anything about being Mrs. Jackson.

Then the game started. Joe was playing center field and batting third. The man hitting right behind him I found out from the little red-haired kid sitting next to me was none other than Napoleon Lajoie. Now I can't say as I knew the names of a lot of the players at that time, but him I knew of, because Joe talked about him many times saying he was one of the greatest players who ever lived. I've been proud of Joe many times for the great things he did on a baseball field, but maybe never more than I was that day. I can't tell you how excited I was to see Joe on the same team as him.

Joe came up to bat in the first inning. There was one out and a man on first base. I really thought Joe was going to have an attack of the nerves before he got to the plate, but as soon as he came out of the dugout the crowd began cheering wildly. The kid with the red hair yelled out, "We're with you, Joe!" He yelled so loud I thought he was going to break my ear drum. I know Joe heard that because he could have probably heard it on the other side of Cleveland. I saw a little smile on his face when he heard it, too. On the first pitch he swung Black Betsy hard and he hit a line drive right at the second baseman which just about knocked him down. The ball jumped out of his glove but he picked it up and threw out the runner going into second base. Joe got to first.

I looked at the kid next to me. "That's the way Joe! That's the way to hit that pill!" he screamed. Well, at least Joe had one fan in Cleveland who would root for him even when he didn't do something spectacular.

On the next pitch Joe stole second base sliding in with a big cloud of dust. "That's the way to run, Joe!" screamed his new fan.

Later in the game, Joe got a hit and made a tumbling catch of a ball in the outfield. Everybody in the stands was cheering madly for him all game long.

After the game we walked back to our new little house. Joe didn't say much, but then he didn't have to. He was so proud. I could see it all over his face. You know, Joe really like to please people. He liked it when they approved of what he did, and that day in Cleveland they screamed their approval loud and clear and Joe was in heaven.

**DEACON MCGUIRE** We weren't gaining any ground in the American League race that year anyway, so I couldn't see any reason not to play Joe the rest of the way even if he was green. I looked at it this way: the team batting average struggled to get to .250, and if it hadn't been for Lajoie's .383 average we wouldn't have even been that good! I think we hit a grand total of 9 home runs all season and one of those was Joe's after he joined us. What could I lose by playing him? If we didn't win my job as manager was going to someone else anyway, so why not?

He came up in mid-September, got in something like 20 games and hit .387 with a slew of extra base hits. In fact, he did everything I asked of him. He stole bases, he threw from the outfield about as well as anybody this side of Wildfire Schulte, and he got such a great a jump on balls hit to the outfield that he ran down shots many other fielders wouldn't even get to.

By the end of the season I was pretty sure Joe could play in the major leagues. The only question was, would he?

**TED EASTERLY** The thing is, Joe didn't listen to nobody. Here he was as raw as an uncooked oyster, and you would have thought he would want to listen to the advice of those of us who had been around the circuit a few times. He didn't though.

I distinctly remember talking to him once about hitting against Big Ed Walsh of the White Sox. All Walsh did was win about a thousand games in his career.

"Walsh shines in a pinch," I told Joe one day while we were warming up before the beginning of a Chicago series. "When he's cornered, Big Ed, he don't take no chances. You will never see him groove any pitch, kid, never. He knows what it means to put that pill in the slot. Instead he sends over a few of those splitters that break a little above or below the knee, and anyone who hits them safe at that angle is lucky."

So what does Joe do? The first game of the series he goes 0-4 against Walsh swinging every time at balls below his kneecaps.

**DEACON MCGUIRE** Joe had a little trouble at first with some of the real good spitball pitchers in the league—guys like Heinie Berger. So he asked me why we didn't have any pitchers like that on our team. I told him that we did, but that I got rid of them. I'm not saying anything against some of the men who mastered the pitch without it affecting them physically, but just the same I preferred hurlers who depended on the good old speed, curve and change of pace. When you have a few spitters on your staff you are always running the risk of having your catchers put out of the business.

**CY FALKENBERG** One day near the end of the season, a number of us were on our way to Bennett Park for a series with Detroit when we had a narrow escape. We were in the second bus when it was hit by a big interurban car. As I recall, we had Graney, and Easterly and Willie Mitchell, and me and Joe in the bus. We probably would have been seriously injured if it hadn't been for the fast action of the motorman. He jammed the car into reverse while the driver checked his horses. The car glanced off the front of the bus smashing part of it and scaring us out of our uniforms. Joe jumped to the street in his cleated shoes, slightly straining his ankle, while the rest of us got out the doors and windows without injury.

Joe didn't want to admit that he was hurt at all, so he played in the game that afternoon but you could see that he was limping a little.

**VINCENT ALEXANDER** One of factors which might have helped Joe adjust reasonably easily in Cleveland was that by the time he came up, the Naps were out of the race, and most of the attention on the team was focused on the torrid batting race between Lajoie and Cobb.

Fueling the competition was a gimmick by the Chalmers Automobile Company. They were offering to the winner of the batting title, a new, 1910 Chalmers auto. This must have had an effect on Joe, too, as he was always enamored of cars. But, of course, he was ineligible for the title as he had far too few at bats to qualify.

**DEACON MCGUIRE** Late in the season we were in Detroit for a doubleheader with the Tigers when Larry and Ty were asked to pose in the automobile which one of them was sure to win. This fella from the Chalmers Company asked them to sit in the car so that he could take pictures of the two great batsmen for an advertisement they wanted to run, but rather than get in the car, they both stood there waiting for the other one to get in behind the wheel. Finally, after some time, Cobb jumped in and Larry followed him.

"I'm not superstitious," said Cobb, "but ..." Larry just smiled at him.

**VINCENT ALEXANDER** Cobb missed 14 games during the 1910 season, including the final two. Likely what happened was that he believed he had the batting championship in hand and therefore the car safely won, so he took the games off rather than risk lowering his average by playing. Making the decision easier for him was the fact that Detroit would finish third regardless of what happened in those last two games. Cobb decided to get an early start on a postseason and left the Tigers with dreams of the shiny new car which he expected to be waiting for him on his return.

In the meantime, the Naps finished up by splitting two games with the St, Louis Browns. What exactly happened in those games is open to considerable speculation, but suffice it to say the honesty and integrity of the game was on display, and according to many was severely compromised.

Perhaps, just perhaps, it was Joe's first real experience with an aspect of the game which was not completely on the up and up. But as I said, that is a matter of some speculation.

**WILLIE MITCHELL** Of course, we didn't want to see Cobb win the car. Larry was one of us and we stood up for our teammates. We didn't like Cobb anyway. Were those last two games on the square? Well they didn't have any bearing on the standings. Let's just leave it at that.

**DEACON MCGUIRE** Here are the facts of what happened in those two games. In the first inning of the first game Larry hits a long drive to dead center which lands just out of the reach of Hub Northern, and bounds up against the fence. Larry legs it out for a triple. Now there are some who have said Hub should have caught that ball. Maybe Joe or Tris Speaker could have caught it, but let me tell you, that ball was hit, and it was hit hard. That was a legitimate hit. There's no doubt in my mind about that at all. What happened after that, however, well, that's another story.

The next time up, Larry looks down the line and sees the Brown's third sacker, Red Corriden, playing back on the edge of the outfield grass. Larry's no dummy so he drops a bunt which Corriden picks up and holds on to it as he has no play at first. Larry's got his second hit.

To all the world, it looked as if the pitcher could have made the play, but he never moved.

Larry comes up two more times that game, and guess what? Each time the third baseman is playing what might best be called a short left field, so Larry bunts, Larry runs, and Red holds on to the ball. Result: Larry is 4 for 4 and there are smiles all-around.

In the second game he comes up five times. Miraculously he manages to get down five bunts, four to Red and then just for variety, one to Bobby Wallace, the shortstop.

After each at-bat, I send our bat boy all the way up to the top deck of the grandstand to check with the official scorer on whether or not Larry was credited with a hit. Each time the kid comes running back out of breath and makes an announcement at the edge of the dugout. "It's a hit, Mr. Lajoie." All except once that is, when he says Larry was credited with a sacrifice. It's a good thing we didn't go into extra innings, because I don't think the kid could have made the run one more time. Those steps were steep.

By the end of the day, Red Corriden's back is killing him from bending down so many times to pick up those bunts, the bat boy's completely exhausted, the players are in hysterics, the fans are howling with delight, but Larry's got 8 hits.

The bat boy is sent up for one final task: get the final averages. He staggers into the locker room. "Cobb .382," he declares. "Lajoie .385."

"You'd better take Corriden for the first ride," somebody says.

"Hell, you ought to give it to him," somebody else says.

Larry lights up a big cigar and puffs like he's really enjoying it.

**CONNIE MACK** The stink that came out of St. Louis from those final two games wafted all the way into Ban Johnson's office. He, like the rest of us, knew that the league couldn't stand for any game not to be played completely on the up and up. It wasn't just a moral position, although it was that, too. It was also a practical one. The league couldn't survive without absolute faith in the integrity of the game.

Joe was only peripherally involved with this episode, but he was certainly aware of the quick and decisive action of the league. Johnson summoned all the principals to his office, including the Browns' rookie manager, Jack O'Connor, the official scorer, R.J. Collins, and Red Corriden.

**RED CORRIDEN** Look, I wanted to remain in baseball for a while, so I had no intention of playing in on Lajoie, and I told Johnson that. All right, I might have gotten some of the bunts, but at the same time I might have gotten a broken nose or lost a couple of teeth. "Lajoie is known as a hard hitter so I played far back."

Look at it this way, my career batting average was only .205. I had to do everything I could just to stay on a major league roster. One of the things I did was, I did what my manager asked me to do.

**TY COBB** I hope you don't think that I was too stupid to know what was going on, but what could I do about it? He was 35 and so popular that they named the whole damn team after him, and I was 23 and played a style of game that didn't exactly endear me to all of my fellow players. But I played the game the best way I knew how and didn't worry about the rest.

So I released a statement to the papers saying that I had absolutely nothing detrimental to say about Lajoie. I insisted the official scorer who gave him eight hits must have known what he was doing. I told everybody who wanted to listen that "If there was a crooked deal pulled off in St. Louis, sooner or later the persons implicated will suffer. That is a question for baseball authorities to take up, but I hardly think there will be an investigation if the commission waits for me to demand one."

Of course, I knew there would be an investigation whether I prompted it or not, and there should have been. Baseball has to be played tough, but it has to be played fair, too. That's something I've always subscribed to, and that's the way I played the game all my life.

**NAPOLEON LAJOIE** About the incidents in St. Louis, I have nothing whatever to say.

**VINCENT ALEXANDER** The Chalmers Automobile Company must have loved the publicity, because every day for weeks, while the controversy simmered, there was a story in the papers about how one of their cars was awaiting the winner of the batting race as soon as things were sorted out.

They finally offered to present a new Chalmers to both Cobb and Lajoie if Johnson would merely declare that the race was a tie. Johnson would have no part of this, and continued his investigation, talking to just about everybody who was involved with the game.

But then, the story which was complicated enough, took an additional twist. The Cleveland paper carried yet another story about the issue, insisting that it wasn't even Collins who scored the game. According to the story, Collins delegated the scoring duties to one of his staff members, E.V. Parrish, and then backed him up all the way down the line.

There were more stories floating around about the batting race than you could read. One apparently had some merit. It said that after the season was over, an official scorer for a game earlier in the season, angered by what he thought was a manipulation of the truth by Collins, or Parrish, changed a disputed Cobb at-bat from an error to a hit. He claimed he scored the game that way originally but neglected to send the score sheet to the American League office. Why I say this story might have had some merit was that right after that, Johnson announced that the final "official" batting averages were .385 for Cobb, and .384 for Lajoie.

Cobb won the car, but the Chalmers Company, which had already received millions of dollars worth of publicity, gave them each a car anyway.

Johnson banned the awarding of prizes for all future league-leading achievements, and caused several heads to roll, most notably those of O'Connor and Harry Howell, a team official who Johnson determined in the course of his inquiry, had repeatedly visited the press box for the purpose of influencing the scorer and who was probably the one who had sent a note to the scorer offering him a $40 suit of clothes as a bribe.

The irony of all this is that years later, upon careful review of all the statistics for the season, it became apparent that Lajoie should actually have been credited with the higher average, based on some discrepancies which had nothing to do with the final doubleheader.

The official records still don't show this, but then, there are a number of things in baseball which aren't quite right.

**JOE JACKSON** President Johnson talked to all us players, but I told him I didn't know nothing about a setup for the car and I didn't. It was the first time I talked to the boss of the league about something not being right, but it certainly wasn't the last.

**CONNIE MACK** I have no way of knowing whether *l'affaire Lajoie-Cobb* made any impression on Joe or not but he may have noticed that everybody pretty much walked away from the mess unscathed. Johnson eventually cleared all of the parties of any dishonesty. None of the players were penalized.

**VINCENT ALEXANDER** The Athletics that year made the World Series, playing against the Cubs. All day Sunday when the final game was being played in Chicago, the excitement was tremendous. The streets all over the downtown Philadelphia were jammed with people and every scoreboard was surrounded with thousands of anxious fans.

The excitement continued until the conquering heroes returned in triumph. It was estimated that at least 50,000 people jammed the area around the Broad Street Station. It took hundreds of police to keep the mob back. When the special train carrying the team arrived at the station, they were met by Mayor Reyburn. The First Regiment Band struck up "Home Sweet Home," and "Hail, the Conquering Hero Comes." The players were hustled into automobiles and taken to the Bellevue-Stratford Hotel where a big banquet had been arranged.

Through a friend of my aunt (who had long since given in to my baseball passion), we were able to get a ticket to what had to be one of the greatest events in the history of our city. After dinner, Mr. Mack spoke, mostly praising his players. He said that a day known as "Davis Day" should be set aside to honor him just as a "Cy Young Day" and a "Lajoie Day" honored those great players. Everybody came in for some praise—Chief Bender, Coombs, McInnis, Plank, Thomas, Topsy Hartsel, Barry, Eddie Collins and the entire outfit. Even the mascot, Van Zelst had good words said about him.

Throughout the speeches, though, I couldn't help thinking about Joe Jackson. I don't doubt that Mr. Mack relished winning the Series partly as justification for trading Joe. He had taken a lot of heat from the press for doing that, and now he was saying, "See, I knew what I was doing all along." I also couldn't help wondering what would have happened to Joe had he stayed in Philadelphia for his entire career, and how things might have worked out for the better—for both Joe and Mr. Mack.

Regardless, he was in Cleveland and we all knew he was in for an uphill battle if he ever thought he would see a World Series victory banquet there.

# 30

## THE NAPS WAS NICER

**CHARLES SOMERS** Our new park, called League Park, opened in April of 1910. It was a concrete and steel structure, signaling the end of the old wooden stadia forever. By the standards of the American League parks, it was one of the smaller ones, seating a little over 21,000. But our fans loved it. It was cozy, inviting, and offered a good view of the game from most of the seats, with the exception, of course, of those behind the steel posts that held up the second deck. But that was a function of the engineering standards of the time, and all the parks had them, so the fans accepted them as a necessary impediment.

League Park suited Joe. I think that was one of the things that piqued Joe's interest right from the start. It had a high wall in right field, only 290 feet from the plate. It was a great target for lefty hitters like Joe. I was with him when he first walked onto the field, and although he didn't say anything about it, I saw a little smile cross his lips when he noticed the closeness of that wall. It was high enough that there weren't going to be a lot of balls hit over it, but it was a great target for a line drive hitter like Joe. Center field was a spacious 450 feet with a lot of room for a speedy fielder like Joe.

**CALVIN BATES** Many a late-hour conversation took place around the tables at the Gem Pharmacy, the all-night drugstore at Superior Avenue and East 10th Street. We regulars tossed around the possibility of the Japanese Army invading the United States, the desperate state of President Diaz's tenuous grip on the Mexican Government, the extra session of Congress, and the Canadian reciprocity agreement. We argued, we cajoled, we demeaned anyone with an opinion different from ours. We stayed until we were too tired to argue anymore, than we went home to sleep some so that we could come back the next night and proffer our opinions again. Down with the Mexican Government. Let the Japs have the entire West Coast and hang their flag on the Golden Gate. There isn't a major league club in California anyway. Forget the high cost of living: President Somers has promised he won't raise the price of admission, and peanuts aren't going to be more than a nickel.

Everyone was talking baseball that spring of 1911. Now I can't tell you I can remember any one given conversation, but the general thrust of our colloquies went something like this:

"I'll tell you this. Larry would hit .400 if he was 3 inches taller."

"He's the same height as Cobb, ain't he?"

"Yeah, and who had a better average last year?"

"One point! What the hell difference does that make?"

"Anyway, it was Larry."

"What?"

"That had the better average."

A week before the season opened, we opined with uncommon unanimity, that the Naps would win the pennant.

"He's got 40 players with him down in Virginia"—the "he" being Deacon McGuire, the manager.

"Don't worry he's going to cut loose the driftwood and build up a machine of speed boys."

"Says you."

"Says McGuire."

"Nobody knows what the team is even going to look like when they open up."

"Kids. That's what they're going to look like. He's going to go with the kids for sure."

"Wouldn't you?"

"Go with the kids?"

"I mean, why shouldn't he? Look, Old Cy has shot his bolt, hasn't he?"

"I hear he can't even get in shape anymore."

"And Joss, too. He ain't what he once was."

"Yeah, who is? Certainly not you."

"Well, at least he's carrying 14 pitchers."

"Not for long, he ain't. Some of them got to be sent to the woods."

"Easterly won't look so peculiar out in the garden chasing the high ones as he did when they first made him a fielder last year."

"I hear Bobby Gilks came in during the off season to teach him to catch flies overhanded without putting so much shock on his arm."

"Why, catchers ain't smart enough to figure that out on their own."

"Don't worry, Gilks is good."

"He better be."

"Anyway, Jackson's going to be Easterly's neighbor out in the grass."

"Somebody should tell him to catch everything he can get his hands on. Forget Easterly."

"I'll tell you one thing, that kid can run, though—Jackson, I mean."

"He'll steal as many bases as Cobb this year."

"More. I'll bet he nabs more."

"He just might."

"Anybody want to bet a buck on it?"

"You taking Cobb or Joe."

"Joe."

I don't recall there being any takers. Of course Lajoie was the one big topic of conversation in Cleveland those days. We all reasoned that unless a baseball miracle happened, Larry would continue to be the shining star on the infield, and the rear admiral and general manager of the clouting brigade.

Here was the image every true Clevelander carried with him: It's a picture of Larry lumbering from the bench. The bases are full and the second man has just whiffed. Larry squats down in front of the stands for a minute. He paws the earth, picks up a couple of bats, weighs them and throws one aside. The he draws a line beside the plate, digs up the dirt with his toe, looks at the pitcher, tugs at the peak of his cap and lets the first one go by. The pitcher winds up for the fatal second delivery. There's a quick swing on Larry's part, wood meets leather and … well, it's the same old story.

What Larry needed, and what we wanted, was some help in the lineup. Someone who would take some of the load off him. This is where Joe fit into our prognostications. He was going to be the other great hitter on the team, or so we publicly stated, and privately prayed.

One thing was for sure, though. We knew that on opening day the stands and the bleachers would be full, and that at the anointed hour, the umpire would step into the middle of the diamond and would pronounce those mystic words that there's no need for me to repeat now, for every baseball fan knows them.

**HYDER BARR** I had a chance to see Joe again during spring training when the Naps came down to New Orleans to play the Pels. There was Joe playing alongside the likes of Lajoie and Stovall and Cy Young, and looking like he wanted to be someplace else, while I was playing with Rohe and Pepe, and I definitely wanted to be someplace else—like Cleveland.

I wouldn't exactly say Joe acted real happy, but he was obviously more relaxed than he was with the Athletics. I few times I even saw him horsing around a little with other players—not a lot like some of the guys, but a little, and that was something coming from Joe.

Yeah, I was jealous of him, I'll admit that, and I'm not sure I ever outgrew it. Although I didn't know it at the time, of course, I would never make it back to the major leagues despite years of trying. I did manage to get in 107 at bats which is more than a lot of people can say, but I can only wonder what I could have done with the talent Joe had. Maybe I would have messed it up, too, but somehow I doubt it.

**JOE JACKSON** The guys on the Naps was a lot nicer than the Philadelphia players. First of all, they didn't have a lot of college guys, and second of all there was a lot of guys more my age.

All during spring training we stayed at this old hotel called the Bentley that had a big wooden veranda on the front of it, and at night most of the players would sit out there and talk about stuff. Deacon would tell these long stories that was so long that sometimes I forgot what he was talking about. He was a tough guy who would show us the scars he got playing and everybody laughed and gave him a hard time about showing off, but it was all in good fun. Cy Young was always talking about his hitting and never his pitching. Terry Turner was always talking about how he had hard luck all the time, and Jack Graney talked about growing up in Canada.

I know I looked like a kid from the mills which is what I was, so one day Ted Easterly and me went into town to do some shopping and buy some fancy clothes. I reckoned that if I looked more like a city slicker, then they wouldn't think of me so much as a country boy.

**TED EASTERLY** After we went shopping Joe came back to the hotel with a snappy double-breasted charcoal gray suit, a dark green pork-pie hat, and two-tone black and white shoes. From then on he was known as the Beau Brummel of the squad. Even the papers picked it up and started calling him that. One time it even said, "Nap's Beau Brummel Jackson, barefooted when he started, is now a fashion plate." I read that to him and he laughed for a second then asked, "What's a Beau Brummel?" I told him to ask Joe Birmingham since he had a college degree.

Joe took the label in good humor, and a lot of the guys started calling him that. From then on for the rest of his career he was a flashy dresser. You should have seen some of his outfits! I think he thought it would help cover up his yokel image.

**CY FALKENBERG** Those nights on the veranda brought the team together a bit. Not that we didn't have arguments, because of course, we did—all teams do—but we were a young team on the rise and for the most part we got along together. The older guys like Young, Lajoie and Joss supplied the experience, the mid-career guys like Stovall and Bradley supplied the tough leadership, and the young guys like Mitchell and Jackson supplied the promise.

President Somers came out on the veranda one night when Joe wasn't there and asked us to try to not tease him too much, because Joe just couldn't take too much of that kind of thing. We didn't anyway. Well, maybe some, because that's part of baseball, but I don't think we overdid it.

**JOE JACKSON** Cy Falkenberg, one of our pitchers was the skinniest guy I ever seen, but he was a real nice guy. He used to sit out on that veranda later than anybody and talk about pitching—mostly giving lessons to anybody who would listen to him about how to throw the emery ball. "Russ Ford of the Yankees started it," he said, "but I perfected it."

He showed me how to do it too, even though he knew I wasn't going to pitch no more. What he done was to put this piece of emery in the heel of his glove and then rub the ball against it.

"All you need is a spot less than the size of a 25-cent piece to make the ball sink or sail, depending on how you hold it," he said.

We went out on the front lawn and darned if it didn't work. After a while I got the ball to move pretty good.

"Any skilled hurler can control the emery ball real good," he told me. "It's just that when less expert hurlers try it that batters are in danger. But you know, Joe, you could be a real good emery ball pitcher if you wanted. Hell, with that arm of yours you could be a great pitcher."

Nobody on the Athletics ever said nothing like that to me—not even once.

**CY FALKENBERG** I got a chance to pitch to Joe a few times in spring training. He was completely impossible for me to figure out. He had no weak spots as far as I could tell. You couldn't play guessing games with him. You know, set him up for a pitch, things like that, because I don't think he was ever guessing up at the plate. I think his system was simple. He waited till the pitch was on its way to the plate. If it looked like he could hit it, he swung. I hated batters like that. You couldn't ever work an angle with them. How did they expect a pitcher to make an honest living if they weren't going to guess up there once in a while? It didn't seem fair. With Joe I think his success was his stupidity, but he was smart enough to know he was stupid. That's why he never tried to think at the plate. See the ball, swing. Bingo, it's that simple.

I'm just glad not everybody in the game was as simple-minded as Joe, or I never would have had a career.

**SIMMY MURCH** I played against Joe that spring. Of course he was then with Cleveland and I was with Chattanooga. After a game down in Tennessee, I asked him how he liked Cleveland. All he said was, "I like it better than Philadelphia," but I got the impression he would have liked hell better than Philadelphia. Man alive, did he ever develop a phobia about that burg!

It was after that same game that I got a chance to talk to the great Cy Young. He was looking his age then, and packing some extra pounds, but still, he was the great Cy Young.

Just as I was about to head back to the hotel, this middle aged guy comes up to Cy and says, "Exactly how many games have you won, Mr. Young?" Ol' Cy, he looks the guy straight in the eye and says, "Why I've won more games than you'll likely ever see." And you know, he was right. I looked it up once, after he retired. He won 511 games and that's more than anybody else ever has or ever will. Now, you tell me. How many fans have actually ever seen 511 games in their whole lives? I'll bet not many.

Years later I heard him say he actually won 512 games, that they forgot to count one. I guess he knows and I don't know as why he would lie about a thing like that since nobody else has even come close. That's one record that's never going to fall.

**DEACON MCGUIRE** As was our custom, that spring we divided the team into two groups—the Naps and the Naplets. Although it was a particularly rainy spring, we had a successful camp. Joe played in just about every game for the Naps. He hit reasonably well and showed he knew how to play in the field.

As the training period grew to a close, I was still somewhat undecided about the batting order. Graney appeared to be the logical man to lead off. I was figuring Turner, a good bunter, to hit second, then Jackson. That would give us three fast men at the top followed by three strong batters in Lajoie, Easterly and Stovall.

The one thing, though, about which I was so unsure as we were about to start the season was Joe. I wasn't unsure about his playing, I was unsure about where he was going to be playing. The way Joe saw it, he had two choices: Cleveland and Greenville. These were his words exactly: "I'll play in Cleveland as long as I can, but if I don't like it real good, I'll be going back to Greenville right soon."

Statements like that make it hard on a manager. With most players, the threat of demotion is enough to keep them in line. But not Joe. He talked about his own demotion like he was looking forward to it.

**JOE JACKSON** Deacon was an OK guy, but the thing that I liked best about that spring training was that Bobby Gilks was with us all the time. He was a scout for the team, but he was helping out with training, so once in a while we got a chance to talk. You know, good old down-home talk that a guy needed to hear if he wasn't going to get all home sicky.

**BOBBY GILKS** Mostly what I did was try to keep his mind off the game when he wasn't playing. We even went hunting one afternoon when Deacon gave him a day off. We spent the whole afternoon together without once mentioning baseball.

**DEACON MCGUIRE** The Naplets were considered more or less the second string team, but every once in a while somebody on it plays so well, that the manager just has to find someplace for him to play on the first string. Joe Birmingham was just such a guy. "Dode," as the players called him was a brainy outfielder. He went to a couple of colleges—Notre Dame and Cornell, I think. Now I didn't feel the need for all these college boys like Connie Mack did, but one or two couldn't hurt just so long as they kept their clever ideas to themselves. Dode had the dope on every American League batter. He studied them like a child did his letters.

I went to Dode and quietly asked him if he would work a little with Joe on learning how to read the batters so that he could position himself better in the outfield. A couple of days later he told me Joe felt he didn't need any tutoring. Later I came to the conclusion that the whole idea was a mistake—sending Dode to him, I mean. Putting Joe together with a college boy probably just reminded him of the Athletics, and that was the last thing in the world I wanted to do.

The two Joes—Jackson and Birmingham—had two of the best outfield arms in baseball. A couple of times I saw them in the field "dueling" with each other on throws home. They never said anything, but you could see what they were about. Jackson's throws became legendary, but I remember once when Dode nailed Bobby Wallace streaking from third to home on a long fly. The throw was so sensational that a tape measure was brought out to measure the distance. It was three hundred and seventy feet.

Maybe Joe didn't have a lot of things to say to Dode, but they sure could relate to each other when they were throwing balls from the field.

**HENRY P. EDWARDS** I was the stringer for the *Cleveland Plain Dealer* when Joe came along, and I guess I saw about as many of his games in Cleveland as anyone. I particularly remember that 1911 season as one in which the Naps entered the race with unbridled optimism—a condition I might add which was unique for the team. McGuire was proclaiming loudly that the team had a chance to wave the pennant over League Park. I was somewhat more cautious, predicting instead a third place finish. It looked to me as if Hal Chase's New York Highlanders and Connie Mack's Philadelphia Athletics were the class of the league, with Detroit and Cleveland contesting for the third spot.

This is how I sized it up on opening day. The infield of Stovall, Lajoie, Olson, and Turner was solid and second only to the infield of the Athletics. The outfield corps of Graney, Jackson, Easterly, Birmingham and Griggs, although young, had great potential assuming Jackson lasted the season.

The year before, the Cleveland club had absolutely the worst catching staff in the American League. Game after game was lost because of indifferent work behind the plate. Cy Young looked ready for the discard pile until Ted Easterly was shifted to the outfield. Ted was a splendid batter, but as a big league backstop he failed to deliver and much of Young's ineffectiveness the year earlier was probably due to Ted's inability to catch the grand old veteran.

Addie Joss once told me he believed pitchers were 80 percent of a baseball club. He should have said that batteries are 80 percent of a club, for without good catchers, pitchers, particularly those lacking experience, cannot show their real form. But with Land and Smith coming into their own, the 1911 catching staff looked greatly improved.

Without Joss Cleveland had an excellent string of pitchers. With him in form, Cleveland had potentially one of the best rotations in the business. But until he recovered from the accident that prevented him from pitching at all during the 1910 season, I was unwilling to include him in the team's list of assets. Nevertheless, a roster which included Kaler, Mitchell, Young, Falkenberg, Blanding, West, Krapp, and Gregg had to be considered a strength.

McGuire had the youngest team in either league, and one has to be forgiving with young teams, for they are wont to make mistakes, but if the management and the fans were willing to suspend judgment while this team jelled, I was sure it would prove to be an entertaining and successful team.

With that said, the biggest question still remained Joe Jackson. He showed at the end of the 1910 season what he was capable of, but he would have to produce in a big way if this team was going to contend. Would he hold together for the full season?

One afternoon I was sitting in the stands down in Alexandria, Virginia where the Naps were putting the finishing touches on spring training. I was with most of the other writers who were covering the team at the time and we were all speculating on the upcoming season. We all pretty much pegged Jackson to join Cobb, Lajoie, Speaker, and Collins at the head of the list of American League hitters. Then, as if he were making a pronouncement from on high, the influential sportswriter, Hugh Fullerton, boldly wrote: "A man who can't read or write, simply can't expect to meet the requirements of big league baseball as it is played today."

There it was—a statement out in the open that reflected what a lot of people were saying in private. Fullerton's words were delivered with such an unsavory finality that they stayed with me, and then came back with shattering potency nine years later when Fullerton leapt at the opportunity to make sure that his prophesy came true.

# 31

# WE WAS LUCKY TO PLAY THE GAME

**CALVIN BATES** OK, I admit it. I am, and have been since childhood, a dyed-in-the-wool, rampant, ring-tailed Cleveland baseball fan. In 1911 I was one of the millions of masculine maniacs who yearly tossed perfectly good straw "Kellys" high in the air during the excitement of opening day, a day which rivals in importance the assassination of the president, a declaration proclamation of war, or the announcement that John D. was a candidate for executive chief of the United States on the Socialist ticket. Opening day meant the democratic hobnobbing of bootblacks and bankers, bartenders and brokers; the visual appearance of small boys' idols; and a liberal interchange of the coin of the realm.

But the opening of the baseball season in those days had another, deeper, darker side—a side which brought sorrow to thousands of happy homes, made prevaricators of hitherto perfectly honest men and caused a dearth of office boys which threatened to bring the business of the nation to a standstill—to wit, the death of grandmothers. Each summer's loss of the dear old ladies was viewed as a season which, during its open months, rivaled the yearly slaughter of other game. In fact, so great was the death of grandmothers, that it was estimated upon competent authority, that something like 40,000,000 succumbed yearly to the rigors of our summers.

My grandmother on my father's side died for the first of many times that 12th of April 1911, and I brazenly admit that I watched Jackson, Lajoie and the rest take the field that warm spring day with nary a tear in my eye.

I became in time, what we called in those days, a "bug." A bug is a parasite, a maniac and a pest—men, women and children, rich, well-to-do and poor—who at work or at play, awake or asleep, at home or away, eat, sleep, think and talk baseball.

To all bugs, opening day was sacrosanct, and to a young boy mourning the first death of his dearly beloved grandmother, the lineup of Graney, Turner, Jackson, Lajoie, Easterly, Stovall, Land, Olson and Blanding has been etched permanently in memory as the greatest team in history, the decidedly contradictory record notwithstanding.

**HEINIE BERGER** Here's the thing about Joe when he come up at the end of the '10 season. He hit pretty good, I'll say that. Sure, .387 ain't chopped liver but you got to look at the circumstances. The race was over by the time he showed, so the pitchers, they wasn't trying that hard no more. I mean why kill your arm for games that don't matter? It wasn't a real test so Joe's average don't mean nothing. Besides, every pitcher in the league figured that once they discovered his weakness, they would make him look foolish.

So when the '11 season rolled around and Joe was still with the team, we all figured it was just a matter of time before the bottom fell out on his batting average. Every pitcher in the league, and I do mean every, began trying all sorts of pitches on Joe in order to find the holes in his swing.

Another thing you should know is that ballplayers have really good memories about some things. Things like being yellow is one of them. If a player ever shows signs of yellow, or gets the reputation of being a quitter, he is going to come in for a lot of razzing from his teammates, and you can count on that. Now whether he was yellow or homesick when he quit the Mackmen is something I can't answer but I can tell you that the word got around every locker room in the league that it was a case of the yellows and that was all that counted. Joe was yellow. That was all there was to that, and nobody dared to say anything else, because if they did, then they would be considered to be siding with a coward and so that made everybody suspicion them.

What was being said about Joe was that he would quit again under fire when the going got hot. Lots of fellows made fun of Joe's '10 swat average, and said that as soon as he got into his first batting slump he would catch the first flyer for the sunny South.

One pitcher, and he was a big star, too, but I don't want to tell you who he was because that could get him in trouble, he made a bet in the winter books that Joe wouldn't hit .250 in '11.

**GEORGE STOVALL** I doubt if any ball player ever started a season under more difficult situations than Joe did in 1911. The players were convinced he would hoist the white flag under fire, and absolutely nothing got the angry juices flowing more than the thought that someone was a coward. Cowardice was positively un-American. It was contrary to our way of life and not to be tolerated. The players rode Joe hard.

"Honestly, what made you quit Connie by the light of the moon?"

"I understand, you have a keeper, Joe, so no one will kidnap you."

"A couple of more days without any hits and you will head south for sure."

"Isn't that your mommy I hear calling you home, Joe?"

It was relentless. Game after game, day after day, Joe heard these and hundreds of like comments. It almost became a contest to see who could come up with the wittiest Joe Jackson put down. Not all the players joined in the festivities, of course. I don't ever remember Ty Cobb doing it, for example.

Joe tried to "be one of the guys" by firing back a witticism of his own and sometimes he hit the mark, but usually his barbs fell short. Joe had a sense of humor, but he was never the fastest wit in the game.

The difference between Philadelphia and Cleveland, as I understand it, was that in Philadelphia it was his teammates who caused most of the problems, but with us it was mostly the other players. I can't say he was ever exceptionally popular with our players, but I think they realized his value to the team, and for the most part, they left him alone. Oh, they would sometimes play pranks on him, or set him up for jokes, things like that, but they didn't directly attack him.

As the season went on, various pitchers put forth theories about Joe's hitting weakness. One successful twirler said it was a floater that would make him look foolish. The words were barely out of his mouth when Joe smashed two hits off the right field wall on the pitcher's floaters. Another veteran insisted that a low curve on the inside corner would do the trick every time. One afternoon Joe drove one of those low curves over the wall in Washington. A fast one at his head would scare the daylights out of him and then an outside curve would find him bailing out was another prominent theory which failed.

**VINCENT ALEXANDER** Since I could no longer see Joe play on a regular basis, I became even more of a confirmed box score aficionado. I followed his exploits carefully in the papers and went religiously to the park when he came back to play the Athletics.

The Naps opened the season with a four-game series against the hapless St. Louis Browns. Expectations were a bit dashed as the two teams split the series. Cleveland was hoping for better, although one game was called in the ninth due to hailstones with the bases full of Naps and no outs. Joe got five hits in the series and in the third game, made a brilliant running catch.

**DEACON MCGUIRE** On the morning after one of those first St. Louis games we were in the hotel eating breakfast when President Somers comes in.

"Addie is dead," he said directly.

News spread through the hotel like wildfire. Addie Joss had been left down in New Orleans to get his arm in shape with the hope that he would be back with the team in May. That was probably more hope than reality, but nevertheless, that was the plan.

The news hit the boys hard because Addie was a genuinely popular guy. In all the years I knew him, I never heard him knock another player. In fact, he went out of his way to help the young kids with words of encouragement even as his career was fading. One of the things I always regretted was that he didn't have more of a chance to work with Joe. I know he could have helped.

Addie had just reached his 31st birthday a couple of days before. Of course, as soon as we heard, the first thing we all thought of was the times he fainted. The first time I remember him doing that was in 1908, the day after he pitched a perfect game against the Chicago club. The following night we left for St. Louis to play a series of three games. To win all three meant the pennant for us. But just as he reached Union Station he fainted onto the floor. We called for a doctor, but by the time he came, Addie had recovered and the doctor said it was probably just something he ate. Despite the incident, when Lajoie called him to come to the rescue of Berger the next day, he pitched seven strong innings of an overtime contest. Then, maybe 10 days before he died, we were in Chattanooga for a spring training game, and he passed out again. Looking back on it, we should have done something else for him, but he came around pretty quickly and said he was all right.

Dr. Castle said that Addie had the tubercular germs in his system since about the middle of February, and that there was nothing that anybody really could have done.

When we talked about it, we all remembered how he wasn't eating well that spring, and how he was getting skinnier than he usually was. We started calling him "Slats."

The funny thing is, I was playing whist in the lobby with a couple of the guys when President Somers gave us the news. Whist was always Addie's favorite game. He could beat the daylights out of any of us any time he wanted.

**HENRY P. EDWARDS** Was Addie Joss a great pitcher? Most assuredly so. Heck, he ended with a 160-97 record and a lifetime ERA of 1.88. There were pitchers who had greater speed, pitchers who could throw a more deceptive curve, but everything considered, there have been few pitchers who have had the right to be considered in the same class as Joss.

Like Mathewson, Joss considered pitching an art. He learned early in his career that speed and mechanical skill alone were not always enough. To his natural mechanical ability he added all the power of his brain. Eight full seasons he pitched for Cleveland winning more than 20 in four of those years and 19 in another. Even in his last year, when his arm failed him, he broke even, which is more than his club could do.

**CY YOUNG** I never met a fairer or squarer man than Addie. I was pretty close to him so I was really upset when I heard that such a hale, hearty, and grand fellow as he should pass away so early in life.

**CY FALKENBERG** When Addie died like he did it made us think twice about our own lives. I had only been with the club a short time when it happened, but I can honestly say I never had a better friend in my life, and there wasn't anything he wouldn't do for a friend.

**DEACON MCGUIRE** The day after he died we heard that he was going to be laid to rest in Toledo. So I immediately asked President Somers to contact Ban Johnson, to have Monday's game postponed so that the team could attend the funeral together. We also chipped in and had a big floral token sent to the Joss' residence.

**CHARLES SOMERS** To say the least, I was shocked when I received a telegram from Johnson saying: "The Cleveland-Detroit game will be played Monday as scheduled." This despite the fact that he had postponed a game two years earlier when Mike Powers died.

I met with McGuire and we came up with a plan. If we couldn't get Johnson to change his directive then I would instruct the manager to allow all the older members of the club to go to Toledo and leave the game to the younger players. It was agreed that Stovall, Lajoie, Turner, Birmingham, Young, Easterly and Falkenberg would go to the funeral.

As it turned out, there was so much pressure on Johnson to postpone the game, that he eventually capitulated, and 18 members of the club attended the services. Billy Sunday, the former great ballplayer turned evangelist presided at the Masonic Temple in Toledo.

I know it sounds like a cliché, but the fact is, there wasn't a dry eye in the room.

**CY FALKENBERG** Most of the players made the trip down to Toledo for Joss's funeral. Even some members of the Tigers were there. Joe Jackson was nowhere to be seen. Now I know he hadn't known Addie for a long time, but if he wanted to be accepted by the team as surely he must have, then not supporting his brothers at the funeral of one of the most loved men in the game, was a poor way to go about it.

The next day we played lethargically in a game against the Tigers. We were all pretty emotionally spent. Joe was in his usual place in the lineup, but you could tell the boys felt a little differently toward him.

**JOE JACKSON** After the funeral of Addie Joss I found out some of the players were miffed at me for not going. But I wasn't the only player who didn't go. Scotty Olson, for example, he didn't go neither, but nobody said nothing to him about it.

The reason I didn't go is that I never been to a big city funeral and I didn't know what you was supposed to do so I thought the best thing was to not go and do the wrong thing. Besides nobody really asked me to go, so I thought maybe they didn't want me to.

**TED EASTERLY** On opening day in Washington, President Taft threw out the first ball from the stands to Dolly Gray, the Washington pitcher, and started a tradition. Anyway somebody saw a story about this in the paper and mentioned in the locker room that Taft threw the first pitch to Gray. Now I could be wrong, but it was my distinct impression at the time, that Joe didn't know who either of them was.

**DEACON MCGUIRE** When we secured Joe Jackson we all thought that, if the stars were in the right alignment, we might have picked up a hitter who could in time challenge Ty Cobb as a hitter with a high batting average. What we didn't expect, however, was a hitter who would not only rival Cobb, but Cobb's power-hitting teammate, Sam Crawford as well.

A little while back we had reconstructed League Park with the express purpose of stopping Crawford from hitting his cannon shots over it. What we did was have workmen build a wire screen on top of the right field wall. But the 45 foot wall and screen did little to deter the Detroit slugger. In an early game against the Tigers he smashed one over the wall which was 290 feet from the plate. Somebody figured out that the ball traveled 350 feet.

But in the second home game of the season, Jackson comes up and hits the first pitch of Roy Mitchell so hard that the large crowd let out an audible gasp as the ball sailed well over the wall and the "Crawford Fence." They measured that one at 386 feet! It was, by all accounts, the hardest hit ball yet seen at League Park.

Joe was the hero of the first two home games. In the first he electrified the crowd with a spectacular throw that caught Jimmy Austin at the plate, and then in the second he hit that tremendous shot over the wall.

Joe was off to a great start. The crowd loved him, and so far no one had heard him even murmur a word about retreating to South Carolina.

**TED EASTERLY** Somewhere around the end of April we're playing Chicago, and one of their players hits a high fly to me in right field. It was that time of the year when the right garden was one hell of a sun field, and it was almost impossible to pick up the ball well. Anyway, I muffed the damn thing. So, Joe, who's playing next to me in center comes over and says something about how to shade my eyes better. I mean it wasn't exactly like I was butchering everything out there, so I didn't exactly appreciate Joe trying to tell me how to play the game.

Then, a little later in the game, Matty McIntyre of Chicago does the exact same damn thing. I look over at Joe on the bench and say, "Why don't you go out there and show him, Joe?" I don't think he liked that any better than I liked him telling me what to do.

The next day I lost another ball in the sun, but this time, Joe didn't say a word. Well, at least he's learning, I thought to myself.

**DEACON MCGUIRE** A couple of weeks into the season and Cy Young comes down with something awful. I called, Dr. Castle, the team doc and he says he doesn't think Young in dangerously ill, but that he has a severe case of acute bronchitis and that he will be out for up to a month. This got some of the players a little nervous. Joe must have asked me four or five times if the doc was sure Young didn't have the same thing as Addie. I assured him, but boy did he shy away from Young for the longest time.

**TERRY TURNER** We followed an early series against Detroit at home with another in Michigan, so the teams traveled together to Cleveland on an all-night trip across the lake on the D. & C. boat. Joe didn't like boats very much. First he got nervous when we got out of sight of land, and then when the lake got a mite choppy, he got sicker than a dog. He spent the entire night at the rail so I didn't think there was a chance he'd even play the next day. But to his credit, he was in the lineup within hours of our landing.

**GEORGE STOVALL** It seems like every time the Naps played Detroit, the only thing any of the sportswriters could find to write about was this supposed battle between Joe and Ty. "Cobb Outbats Joe Jackson in Game"—stories like that. Cobb gets a home run in a game against us once and Joe goes hitless, and to read some of the stories, you would think Joe was hitting .085 for the season. The fact was he was batting close to .400, but it seemed like if he didn't out-duel Cobb every game there was something wrong with him.

**JOE JACKSON** I heard one day that Ty Cobb's pet bat was broken in batting practice by Stanage, their catcher. Ty had to play the whole game with a borrowed bat.

Me and Ty, we had our own special bats and a lot of people didn't understand how important they was to us. But, I would have loaned Betsy to Ty if he asked me. He would of understood the importance of taking care of an important bat.

**BOBBY GILKS** After Addie Joss left us, and Cy Young got sick, the only veteran pitcher on the squad was Cy Falkenberg. Of course, Larry Lajoie was still playing every day, but most of the other regulars were young. This probably helped Joe adjust some. It wasn't like he was the only kid.

The problem was only Joe, and Larry, and Ted Easterly did much hitting early in the season, so almost every game was a struggle.

**DEACON MCGUIRE** At the beginning of innings while the catchers were putting on their gear, I would warm up the pitchers. Once when we were playing the Detroits some fans behind the plate started giving me all holy heck—because we were winning!

Now I reckon this takes a little explanation. See, in Cleveland we had a store called the Gelm and Selzer Drug Company. It was over on Public Square. Anyway, they had this deal which they advertised in the papers. If you bought five El Pino cigars for 25 cents on the day of a Cleveland home game and then we didn't win the game, well then, you got all 25 cents back and, as they said, "you will have had five good smokes free."

Now in this particular game I finish warming up Falkenberg to their mocking comments. The first batter up is Schaeffer and he gets a hold of one and sends it on a trip which is apparently going to take it over the center field wall. But Joe gets on his horse and runs it down just before it's about to clear the wall. Well, you should have heard these cigar-smoking blockheads get on Joe. Poor Joe, he didn't understand what all the abuse was for until I explained it to him. I also gave the folks at the Gelm and Seltzer Drug

Company a piece of my mind. We had enough trouble keeping the fans on our side with without this kind of nonsense.

**CY FALKENBERG** One day, maybe a month into the season, McGuire walks into the locker room before a game against the Chicago team and announced like he was telling us the weather, "Well boys, I'm not your manager any longer, but I do think that with some good field generalship and a lot of hustle on your part, you can still be a successful club. I wish you well."

**DEACON MCGUIRE** I surrendered my leadership for the exact same reason Larry turned over the reins two years earlier—because I was sorely disappointed in the club's performance and I honestly believed that someone else might have a better chance to change the way things were going.

I gave the issue a lot of thought before deciding what to do. Then came one rainy afternoon game against Detroit in which we pounded out 13 hits but still lost the game 14-5. We just played bad ball. We made five errors and even though Joe got four hits we were embarrassed. In the seventh inning I tried to get umpire Dinneen to call the game on account of the bad weather but even that didn't work and he made us wade through to the gory finish. There was almost nobody at the game anyway, so our embarrassment wasn't seen by a whole lot of people but I went home mighty depressed. My resignation was on President Somer's desk when he arrived the next morning.

"If that's the way the situation looks to you, Deac," said Somers, "I will accept your resignation. I would like to have you stay on with us, though, as a scout."

Without hesitation I said I would.

**CHARLES SOMERS** It's probably fair to say that Deacon didn't have much of a chance to show his managerial ability as we were committed to trying out a large bunch of kids. Still when I got his letter of resignation I was a bit relieved, because I liked Deacon and I didn't relish the thought of someday having to fire him.

I was determined to take my time in finding a manager. I wanted someone who would stick with us for the long run, and who would be capable of helping us move up the ranks. I was willing to wait for such a man if necessary, but I wanted a man of the caliber of Mack, Clarke, McGraw or Chance.

Until I could find such a man, I appointed George Stovall as acting manager with the full understanding that he would be replaced when I found a permanent successor.

**HENRY P. EDWARDS** As soon as the word got out about McGuire, the guessing game as to a successor began in earnest. Fielder Jones, Bill Donovan of the Tigers, Bill Bernard, manager of the Nashville Southern League club, Harry Davis of the Athletics, and Joe Birmingham and George Stovall of the Naps were some of those mentioned. But most of the names were easily eliminated. It didn't seem likely that Donovan would be released by Detroit since his pitching days seemed far from over. Moreover, he was being coached to take Jennings place when Hughey retired to devote all his time to the practice of law. Joe Birmingham had many supporters for the vacancy as he always enjoyed the reputation as a brainy player, and his work as manager and captain of the Naplets on the training trip was a mark in his favor. Still he was young, and although Hal Chase was just as young, I think the feeling was his time would come to manage, but it wasn't just yet. Bill Bernhard was considered scarcely aggressive enough, and it was very unlikely Harry Davis would be available until, at the very earliest, the end of the season. There had been, for a couple of years, considerable talk of Davis as a Nap manager, but it was said Connie Mack wanted him to continue as a member of the Athletics for the time being.

It was my feeling, and I think of most of us covering the team, that if Somers learned he could get Davis the next year, he would let Stovall finish the season, and then make the switch during the offseason.

One of the issues clouding the picture was Joe Jackson. He was already a budding star, and clearly he was someone who could be a mainstay of the team for years to come. But Joe had a terrible time in Philadelphia, and who was the captain of that team? Harry Davis to be sure. Would that be a problem if he came over to the Naps, or would that be an advantage? Speculation was rife.

**JOE JACKSON** George Stovall wasn't nothing like Mr. Mack who could get riled up once in a while, but mostly he was calm and quiet. Now George, he was riled up most of the time and he was always yelling and carrying on about something, but you know, the funny thing is, most of the guys liked him anyways.

**GEORGE STOVALL** The first time I met Joe I told him a story about years earlier when I was playing for the Portland club out on the coast. This big fellow named Ferguson made three deliberate attempts to bean me with the ball.

I called his attention to this and also made a few other remarks. He replied that after the game he would get me. I told him if he thought he was man enough to try, the place to pull off such a stunt was the clubhouse. And sure enough when I went to the clubhouse I found him waiting. We had quite a little debate. Neither of us were orators, but we used such arguments as occurred to us. These arguments consisted of right swings, left jabs and uppercuts. Along toward the last of the debate he became unable to answer my arguments, so I dragged him into the dressing room and wiped the blood off his face with a towel.

I think Joe got the picture.

**CY FALKENBERG** Stovall was something. He set the tone in the clubhouse and pity the player who came in for his wrath. Larry Lajoie found this out the hard way. A couple of years before Joe came over from the Athletics, Larry, who was our manager then, got the team together in the clubhouse and began enumerating our deficiencies. Now George took particular offense at something or other—I can't remember exactly what—and responded by getting up from his chair and using that piece of furniture as a weapon breaking it into several pieces over the head of the fulminating manager.

Lajoie, unused to such a rebuttal to his argument, charged out of the room and pledged to the assembled press that under no circumstances would he again play on the same team with George. Despite his vitriol, in time he cooled off, and eventually the two became friends.

I bring this story up because it looked for all the world that Joe too would feel the wrath of Stovall, who was, in every respect a product of the old school of ball playing. He was tough, unbending, uncompromising, yet he was generous to a fault. He was totally devoid of snobbishness, cared nothing for popular favor, and could be impulsive to the point of rashness. In short, he was a complex man, but clearly the team leader in the clubhouse. If Joe was going to be successful with the Naps, he would have to win the favor of Stovall.

**BILL KLEM** George Stovall was a menace to all of us in the umpiring fraternity. It was our sworn job to maintain the integrity of the game by enforcing the rules without prejudice or favor. The sanctity of our position had be honored at all costs, or the game would degenerate into chaos and eventual elimination. Occasionally a player comes along who needs some convincing--George Stovall for instance. In a game in which Ferguson was umpiring, George took exception to a call by spitting into the face of the arbiter. Everyone was shocked at the audacity of the act with the result that he was suspended for three weeks by Ban Johnson.

When somebody asked him why he spit on Ferguson, he answered, "Well, you see, we had a very fussy groundskeeper and he wanted to keep the field in good order."

**GEORGE STOVALL** They got it wrong about Joe and me. Everybody said he was difficult in Philadelphia and maybe he was, but that didn't mean diddly to me. If he played hard for me that was all I cared about, the rest was history and I didn't give a damn about history. Everybody said he was stupid, that he couldn't read and write, that he was totally uncultured. Well, who cares? I'm against the literary kind of ballplayer anyway. If I had a watch to be fixed I wouldn't hire a carpenter and if I was looking for a first class outfielder I wouldn't hire a sporting editor.

**CY FALKENBERG** Although in many ways they were polar opposites, Jackson and Stovall were probably more similar than either one ever cared to admit. They both responded to their world with primitive instincts. Neither one filtered his emotions very carefully through the screen of societal propriety—Joe because he never learned how, George because he refused.

**CHARLES SOMERS** When Deacon resigned, the morale on the club quickly disintegrated. Things were not going well on the field, and this just added to the confusion. My first choice to replace Deacon was Harry Davis, first lieutenant to Connie Mack and one of the acknowledged masters of the fine points of the game. Everybody knew he was near the end of his playing career but his availability was unclear.

I contacted Mack immediately. He was gracious, said yes, Davis would be a great manager, and that he wouldn't stand in the way of him going to another club to manage, but that he doubted that he was ready to quit playing quite yet. He did say he would discuss the possibility with his captain and let me know within a couple of days. Two days later he wired saying Davis appreciated the interest but that he would be finishing the season as a player. Mack furthermore hinted in subsequent conversations that as soon as Davis had finished schooling young Stuffy McInnis in the art of playing first base for the Elephants, he would be ready to leave and manage another club.

That gave me hope that he might be available the following season. I'm not sure any of us thought that George, given his fiery temper, would be particularly successful at managing, but we were gambling that he could, by dint of his strong personality, keep the team headed in the right direction until we could lure Davis into the fold.

I knew that the only reason Joe was even on our team was that he was running from the Athletics as fast as he could. At the time I still wanted Davis because I thought he was right for us, but the nagging question of Joe's response was lingering.

Much to our surprise, Stovall quickly proved to be a manager of considerable proficiency. The players liked his firm leadership style and a general sense of affable camaraderie developed in the locker room. Furthermore, he demonstrated a keen sense of baseball tactics.

**TERRY TURNER** Yeah, Stovall was a good guy. He was tough but he was fair, and that's about the best you can expect from a manager.

He used to come into the locker room all the time and say, "Two kegs of beer if we win boys, and one keg anyway." We liked that kind of thing in a manager. It made him look like one of the guys.

**GEORGE STOVALL** My managerial style was very different from McGuire's and come hell or high water, I was going to be true to that style. McGuire believed that the Naps only chance of winning anything was to play the best players from the start and stick with them to the bitter end. He was always tinkering with the lineup like he was trying to find the perfect one.

Well, let me tell you, no such thing existed on that team. I knew that with the exception of Falkenberg we were going to have to rely on the kid pitchers, that for some outfielders every fly ball was going to be an adventure, that the quality of our catching and shortstopping was an unknown. In short, I knew that in order to win in the future we were going to have to be patient with the kids by letting them play and that meant losing some games that we might otherwise be able to win with some of the veterans. I knew we weren't ready to play in the Series, but I also knew that we might someday if we could develop our young players. They, like Joe, had the ability. What they needed most was self-confidence.

**WILLIE MITCHELL** What Stovall did better than anybody else I ever played for, was that he let you play, and even when you made a mistake, he didn't yank you, or scream at you in public. Even when I got into one of my wild spells when the plate looked like it was dancing all over the place, he left me in until I worked my way out of it. That was a great confidence builder.

I think he was good for Joe, too, because if anybody ever needed his confidence built up, it was Joe.

**VINCENT ALEXANDER** As well as Jackson hit from the beginning of the season, when Stovall took over he went on an even stronger tear with several long hitting streaks and a couple of game-winning late-inning home runs. When fans talked about the great hitters in the American League, they were beginning to add Joe to the likes of Cobb, Collins, Lajoie and Speaker. By early June, here's the way the batting race shaped up: Cobb was batting .415; Collins, .408; Jackson, .402; Speaker .383; and Lajoie, .378. The interesting thing is that, with the exception of Lajoie who was 36, the others were all under 25 and yet to reach their peak of athletic ability. That Joe seemed younger than the others was undeniable, but it certainly looked like this group would dominate the game for years to come. These were the young lions on whose shoulders lay the future of the league.

**JOE JACKSON** Once when we was eating dinner, Cy Falkenberg brought his younger brother by for a visit. The kid's name was Gordon and he could throw real good for a 13-year-old because he showed us that after we finished eating. Everybody said the kid was going to play in the majors just like his big brother. Now that got me thinking about Davey and just how good a player he was and how it would be nice to have him play with us in Cleveland. So I talked to Mr. Somers about this and he said he would write a letter to Davey and ask him if he would like to come up to Cleveland to visit us. I figured he could show off just as much as Gordon Falkenberg could and maybe even better.

It was good having Katie around, but having Davey too, would be great.

**GEORGE STOVALL** The bench jockeys had a field day with Joe—not our players, mind you because I wouldn't have none of that—but guys on the other teams. They took Joe's quiet ways for a sign of weakness, and of course, everybody knew he couldn't read or write, so every joke in the world that anybody could think of was thrown at Joe. I sat him down and told him not to pay attention to any of them, that if I ever saw him get upset when somebody said something nasty to him, I would kick his ass from one end of the field to the other. But by the same token, every man on the team would stand behind him if it came to that.

I told the players, too, that I didn't want to hear any cracks about Joe—no rube jokes or no moron jokes or they would have me to face. Most of the older guys like Cy Young and Larry Lajoie, they were above that kind of thing anyway, but you know how it is with young players. Besides, the longer Joe stayed with the team without hightailing it back to the sticks, the more everybody came to realize that he could maybe help us go all the way.

But the jockeys on some of the other teams, they were something else. I suspect some of them were doing it because they were ordered to do it by their managers, but regardless, they rode Joe pretty good.

"Hey, is it true, Joe, that you lost your brains when a butterfly kicked you in the head?" "Hey, Joe, I hear you are a fugitive from a brain gang." "Joe, if they ever put a price on your head take it." Lines like these and a thousand more. Some of these jerks must have stayed up late nights thinking these things up.

After a while, Joe learned to give some back a little. I remember once when Nixey Callahan, the White Sox outfielder, was riding Joe something vicious from the bench and Joe came over and laughed at him. "You're another one of those fellas after my nerve," he said. "Well keep on after it. I like to have you fellas chase me. I know I'm a good player when the whole pack of you are after me. I didn't know if I would make good before the season started, but I'm certain now."

Once I heard him call out to a heckler in the stands, "Hey, big mouth, how do you spell triple?"

Of course, some of our guys would say things when Joe wasn't around though they learned to keep their mouths shut when he was there. But I know it still hurt. Even when Joe began giving it back you could see how it bothered him.

Once I asked him about not being able to read. I asked him if he ever tried to learn. He said he never tried, so as far as I'm concerned, that don't mean he was stupid. I've always thought there were a lot of guys in baseball no smarter than Joe.

**HENRY P. EDWARDS** Of course I heard all the disparaging remarks being hurled at Joe and I'm not sure I would have been able to handle them as well as he did, but I'm sure some of the credit has to go to Stovall. He had a way of keeping the players all pulling together.

I wasn't going to jump on the Joe-baiting Bandwagon. He was showing himself to be a great player, and as long as he was doing that, I saw no reason to criticize him in public.

Let me give you an example from his first full season in 1911. The Naps were playing the Red Sox and Joe, batting third, came to the plate four times. He lined a single to right his first time up but was thrown out stealing. In the fourth he worked a walk and eventually participated in a double steal, scoring Cleveland's first run. In the sixth he would have been an easy out at first had he not worked a trick and got away with it by causing Williams to drop the ball. While the Red Sox were arguing the play, Joe stole second base. He scored a pitch later. In the eighth Joe hit the ball high up on the right field screen for a double.

In the field he also distinguished himself, chasing far into right center on two occasions to make fancy catches of drives hit by Williams and Lewis, while in the ninth he went deep into center to catch a terrific smash off Hooper's bat.

When he had games like that, all I could do was praise him.

**TERRY TURNER** For a country boy, Joe sure fell in love with the automobile. The whole country was beginning its love affair with the car. "Autoists" as drivers were then called were starting to drive their cars to games. At first they would park on Quinby and Linwood avenues but then they started parking them right outside the stadium. President Somers even had to hire special policemen to take care of the cars. Mostly they had to stop the small boys in the area from constantly sounding the horns because the neighbors were complaining.

After games, Joe liked to go outside and look at the cars, and of course, the proud owners loved to have a famous baseball player pay attention to them. Sometimes they would even give him rides home. Joe was like a kid looking at new toys. Later he owned many of them. I even remember newspaper ads that he posed for. "Famous Slugger Buys Second Oldsmobile" ran the headline across the top while at the bottom of the ad Joe was quoted as saying "The Oldsmobile Eight for me every time." Of course, he couldn't read it himself, but according to him, he got paid pretty good for that sort of thing.

**CHARLES SOMERS** Like most of the cities in the League, Cleveland was barred from scheduling Sunday games. But like most owners, I knew that Sunday ball would be a good moneymaker for the team. Remember, there were no lights then, so all of our games had to be played in the afternoons, and Sundays were ideal for that. During the week, fans had to take off work if they were to see a game, but on the weekends, well, that was when we could expect our biggest crowds.

Of course, the issue wasn't a simple one. Sunday blue-law legislation went all the way back to a Virginia statute from early in the 17th century. But the times were changing, and there was an ever-increasing swell of popular interest in Sunday games. Most churches weren't against baseball. Many even sponsored teams in various amateur leagues, but Sunday ball either violated religious principles or competed with churches for Sunday attendance, take your pick. Only three cities had a history of allowing Sunday games—Chicago, St. Louis and Cincinnati.

Luckily for us, Mayor Baehr of Cleveland was both a Naps fan and a supporter of Sunday games, so after a number of years of politicking, we came to an arrangement whereby we could experiment with a few games on Sunday. We would let the fans tell us if they approved or not. On Sunday, May 14, 1911, we opened the gates at League Park for the first time on a Sunday.

The response was immediate and overwhelming. Nearly 16,000 fans, the largest crowd of the season showed up for our game with the New York club. Since hundreds of them were women, I had every spectator handed a dodger on which was printed a warning against boisterous rooting.

We were all slightly apprehensive lest some fans opposed to Sunday ball should create a disturbance. To that end we even hired a large squad of special policemen for both inside and outside the park.

Mayor Baehr himself attended the game as did many of the city's dignitaries. It was probably the most orderly crowd ever to see a game at League Park.

The loudest cheer came when Joe stroked a triple with the bases loaded in the third inning.

I knew right away that Sunday ball was in Cleveland to stay. Detroit and Washington also added Sunday games about that time, and, of course, the others followed suit eventually.

**JOE JACKSON** Some of the fellas griped a little when we started playing on Sundays, but I didn't. I wasn't going to go to church anyways, and playing a game on Sunday was a darn site better than sitting around Cleveland.

**CHARLES SOMERS** That season we went to a new ball with a cork core. Everyone referred to it as the "lively ball." Popular baseball conversation of the day centered on a debate as to whether we should continue to use the new ball or go back to the old one. Frankly, I preferred the old ball as we had a number of pitchers hit that season by batted balls. It seemed to me as if the pitchers were having a harder time getting out of the way of the faster flying balls. But then every time I expressed that opinion, someone would bring up the names of Bill Bernhard or Red Donahue, both of whom suffered broken fingers from batted balls before the lively ball was even dreamed of. Regardless of what I felt, it was clear the fans preferred the "lively ball."

Players like Joe and Ty were tearing the seam off the ball, and fans loved it. I maintain, however, that Joe and Ty could have hit any kind of ball. Joe in particular, had he played longer, would have hit a ton of home runs as the ball was changed yet again about the time Babe Ruth checked in. Joe would have been one of the greatest home run hitters in the game had he been born 15 years later.

**SILK O'LOUGHLIN** I was in favor of the lively horeshide, but I don't think it accounted for the heavy hitting that season. I felt at the time the hitting was a product of two factors. First, many pitchers were not working up to the usual standards. This also accounted for the unusually long games that season, many of which were running close to two hours. Secondly, there was a brace of good young hitters lead by the likes of Cobb, Jackson, and Wildfire Schulte of Chicago who led the game in home runs with the gaudy figure of 21, the highest total since 1899.

**JOE JACKSON** Just when I was starting to feel a bit comfortable playing for Cleveland, darned if I didn't get a broke finger.

We was playing Philadelphia and Cy Morgan was pitching against us. In the second inning we had the bases full with two outs when I come to bat. On the first ball pitched I swung but had my first finger broke for my effort. After the game, Mr. Mack come over and told me he was sorry I got hurt.

Dr. Castle, the team doc, he looked at my finger and said it was a little cracked and that I shouldn't play for a while. Now I knew that wasn't good, because Larry went out of the lineup the same day and so did Griggs.

It was really the first time I was injured since I come up but I knowed somebody would think I was faking it. There's always somebody willing to think the worst if they got the chance.

The finger hurt a lot more than I let on, but just the same I went to all the games while I was out.

**DEACON MCGUIRE** As soon as Joe and Larry went down, I was called into President Somers office for a meeting with him and Stovall. The manager said we needed a couple of new players right away. They figured Larry might be out for up to a month and no one was sure just how long Joe was going to be sidelined. The plan was to use Birmingham in center for the time being but to look for another outfielder capable of playing center so Birmingham could be developed into a third baseman.

As soon as Joe heard I was out looking for another outfielder, he started to get nervous, and began talking about how much better his finger felt. Fear of losing a starting slot is the best doctor I ever saw.

Joe got even more irked when Ted Easterly read him a story out of the paper one day when Joe was not playing. It was about a player named Jack Flannagan an outfielder on one of the teams in the Cleveland Baseball League, a minor league with some pretty good players. Anyway, the story went that Flannagan made a remarkable throw of 435 feet.

When Joe heard this he got angry. He never said he was the greatest hitter in the game—although that was said about him by many others—but he was real proud of his throwing arm and any hint that somebody else might be better evoked his ire. This fact, which was well-known to his teammates, was used to get his dander up on numerous occasions. I don't know what Ted's reason was for reading that particular story at that particular time, but I assure you, it was premeditated.

**CONNIE MACK** I never saw a team hit by as many injuries as that 1911 Naps team. I want to tell you that no club could be expected to win when hit by as many injuries as they were, but I'll tell you this, the fella they missed most was Joe Jackson. Larry, too, of course, but Joe was beginning to be the player they counted on most in critical situations.

Was I becoming sorry I let him go? I was sorry Joe wasn't playing for us the way he was for Cleveland, but I still wasn't sure he ever would have played that way for Philadelphia.

**VINCENT ALEXANDER** When Joe's finger mended sufficiently for him to get back into the fray, he rejoined the starting nine and without missing a beat, picked up hitting where he left off. In fact, if anything, he was better, his average ever rising nearer the .400 mark. He also continued making circus catches in the outfield and running the bases wildly.

One of the joys of the season for me was monitoring the battles between

Wabash George Mullin, the premier pitcher of the Detroit club, and Joe. Before the season began, Mullin brazenly declared, "A player who pulls away from the plate as Jackson does is not a real hitter. Jackson is bat shy. The pitchers know it now and will throw a ball at his head, then three over the outside corner and he will go to the bench." He went on to predict that he would strike him out oftener than Joe would get safe hits off him.

The first 14 times Joe batted against the Tiger pitcher, he got six hits for a .429 average, and struck out only once. After that, Mullin was known to lead the "Joe Jackson heckling club," and for the remainder of his career, never, as far as I know, ever had a kind word for or about Joe.

**GEORGE STOVALL** In June I decided to make a change in the outfield, sending Birmingham to center, moving Joe over to right and putting Ted Easterly on the bench despite his solid batting statistics. The reason I did this was because I felt we needed another experienced man out there who knew the batters. Jackson was a much better outfielder than the other two, but he had been a big leaguer for only a short period of time and wasn't particularly proficient on going back on the ball.

With Birmingham in center, I figured not only would the position be well taken care of, but he would be in the position to give Jackson and Graney some valuable coaching, for there was no player in the country more capable of teaching outfielders.

**TED EASTERLY** There was only one reason I lost my starting job—Joe Jackson. We were playing the Athletics in a Saturday game when Ira Thomas came to bat in the bottom of the twelfth inning. Joe calls over to me, trying to tell me where to play Thomas. I didn't appreciate the suggestion at all and told Joe so. I also stayed right the hell where I was. After all, I had been in the league three years and I knew a little about positioning.

Now, of all the luck, Thomas hits a little fly that lands where Joe was telling me to play and Barry makes it to third and eventually scores. All right, it looks like I was wrong, but I had played Thomas the same way before and made the outs. So which position was right? If outfielders were right all the time, no batters would ever get any hits.

After the game, Stovall tells me I'm benched.

"From now on, Joe, just shut the hell up," I tell him in the dugout. "I don't need help from you—especially you,"

**TERRY TURNER** It was better when Joe didn't try to tell somebody else how to play the game like he did that time with Ted. Nobody wanted to be told how to do something by Joe.

**JOE JACKSON** That first day with the new lineup we looked pretty good. Between us in the outfield we got seven hits against Washington. In the first inning, after Graney singled and Olson walked, I came up and hit the first pitch, a big sweeping drop, and hit it over the right field wall. It hit a brick building way across the street. A lot of people said it only went that far because it was a "lively ball." Well, if that was the reason, how come that building didn't have ball marks all over it?

**VINCENT ALEXANDER** Sometime in the middle of the season, the Washington Nationals put out press about a promising young outfielder from down in Telford, Tennessee by the name of Clarence Walker. The kid whom they called "Tilly" had been playing on the Spartanburg team of the Carolina Association. He was hitting close to .400, fielding well, and by all accounts running the bases like a frightened deer. Tilly, they said, was a second Joe Jackson. What was remarkable about this is that here they were comparing the kid to Jackson, who hadn't yet played one full season in the majors. Of course, Tilly wasn't the only player to be compared to Joe during his career, just the first. I know it was meant as a compliment, but the comparison carried the implication of "dumb Southern hick" along with the obvious baseball skills.

**CHINK YINGLING** I was on the pitching staff of the Naps when the season began and started six games for them. I even played center field once when Joe was out with the bum thumb. Then they dumped me just like that—sent me down to the Toledo club. They always worked me in the cold weather, while I needed hot weather to get going right.

Of one thing I was certain. I did not ever care to return to Cleveland again. Sooner than go back to the club I would quit baseball, or pitch semi-professional baseball around Dayton. I told Somers that, too, and I told Joe that he better be careful, that he better look out for himself because baseball wasn't going to do it for him. I always remember that conversation with Joe and wonder what would have happened to him if had listened to me.

**JOE JACKSON** Everybody knowed about Cy Young on account of how he won so many games, but he didn't pitch for us until in the middle of that summer. It was against Boston, his old team, so of course he wanted to pitch real good, and he did, too. It rained pitchforks all game, but I made one pretty good catch and I got a couple of hits, and we won the game. And the darndest thing was that all game, Boston tried to bunt on Cy but he fielded every bunt on that wet grass and a couple weren't easy chances neither. He knew exactly what he was doing out there. Yes, sir, he surely did!

The funny thing is, he is one of the greatest pitchers to ever play the game, but mostly I have memories of him as a fielder.

**GEORGE STOVALL** Come the middle of June and it began to look like we were going to have to carry on all season without Larry Lajoie who was out with a severely pulled muscle in his side. After maybe a week on the bench he came into my office one morning before a game and announced that he felt first-rate but on further questioning, admitted that there was still considerable soreness when he moved. We went down on the field where I watched him work out lightly and it became clear right away that he couldn't make any kind of twisting motion. Granted, he was 36 but you wouldn't have known it by the way he was playing before the injury. I didn't see any reason why he couldn't play another 4 or 5 years if he didn't do something dumb like playing with a serious injury, so I sat him down.

While he was out, Neal Ball would have to play second, and while he could field the position, he certainly wasn't in Larry's class as a hitter.

This meant more of the offensive burden would have to fall on Joe's young shoulders and I wasn't sure if he could handle that. Look at him cross-eyed and he acted like you cussed him out or something. Read him a trivial criticism from the papers and he looked like he was devastated. I knew that if he didn't develop a tougher skin he wasn't going to make in the pressure-driven big leagues. But how do you teach someone to do that? I didn't know for sure, but I knew I was going to have to try for the team's sake, as well as for Joe's.

I went to Larry and asked him to help—to help Joe become a tougher ballplayer.

"He knows how to play, George," Larry said. "Leave him alone and he will be a great player."

"Not that," I responded. "Help him become a professional ballplayer. He needs to learn how to get along with the guys. He needs to learn how to get his laundry done, when to leave for the train station, how to play cards, who to tip, where to find a decent cup of coffee in New York, which is the best beer to order in Boston."

"What do I look like, skip, a miracle worker?"

"I haven't found anything yet you couldn't do well," I answered.

"Except how to say 'no.'"

From then on, if Joe had a real friend on the team it was Larry. That's what a true team player he was. If he couldn't contribute on the field, he would do what he could from the bench, and what he did might have saved Joe's career.

**NAPOLEON LAJOIE** Joe wasn't at all like the way some people wrote and talked about him. I mean if you read all that garbage you might think he was devil complete with horns. He wasn't. Maybe he didn't make all the right decisions in his life, but, hey, who did?

I went out to eat with him many, many times, and let me tell you he didn't sit around talking about robbing banks or beating up little kids. What we talked about was things like hunting dogs for grouse and where to play Ty Cobb, what you could do to try to hit Walter Johnson, the merits of the lively ball, and what was wrong with the lousy streetcar service in Cleveland, anyway?

**JOE JACKSON** I was really hoping that Davey was going to come up to Cleveland. I always knowed that he was a better player than I was anyway if only someone would give him a chance. Then I got a letter from Katie while we was in New York which Larry read to me saying that Davey just got married and would be staying in South Carolina. I was real surprised because I didn't know nothing about getting married, and the letter didn't even say who he got hitched to. I was hoping on him being with us for the rest of the summer.

We had a day off in New York, though, that was pretty fun. Manager Stovall took 12 men over to Paterson, New Jersey to play an exhibition game and the rest of us got to stay in New York, so what we did was we all chipped in and hired a car for the day and we drove around the city from morning to dinner time. New York had a lot of interesting things to see, and I think we seen them all.

**CY FALKENBERG** I'll say one thing about Joe, he played hard and he didn't complain when things got rough out there. In that way he was a little like Ty Cobb. But that's about the only way.

The comparison between Cobb and Jackson went on all season as Cobb batted over .400 right from the get go, but could never quite shake loose from the challenge of Jackson. It was a great battle!

**GEORGE STOVALL** About the end of June, President Somers signed Abbot Mills, a third baseman who had been the captain of the Williams College team. He was a highly-regarded rangy left hander. A number of teams had tried to sign him for some time, but Abbot, who everybody called Jack, refused to sign a professional contract until his responsibilities to the Williams team were over.

Connie Mack was proving that you could mine the colleges for good infielders. He had Collins and Barry, and then there was Devlin of the Giants, Grant of the Reds, and Larry Gardner of the Red Sox.

We were eager to see Mills—all of us, that is, except Joe. He treated Jack like he had leprosy. Mostly he gave him a wide berth, but it was obvious that he felt suspicious of anybody from the college ranks. I'm sure this was a holdover from his days on the Athletics when he had more than one run-in with an academic ball player. Jack was a nice kid, but he didn't go around every day quoting Carl Sandburg in the locker room. To Joe I guess he represented all that was distasteful from his earlier experiences.

I was afraid this might set Joe off on one of his retreats again, but as it turned out, Jack didn't stick. I know Joe was relieved when he saw the kid packing his things.

Incidentally, it was about that time, too, that we signed a little shortstop from down in some one-horse town in Kentucky. The kid's name was Ray Chapman, and although he didn't come up until the next season, he was destined to become one of baseball's truly tragic figures.

**CHARLES SOMERS** We decided to hold an Addie Joss day on July 24, an open date on most teams' schedules. What we planned to do was to invite enough top American League players to create the greatest team ever assembled. They would play our Naps in a game for which we would offer subscriptions to patrons who would be willing to pay more than what was usual for a seat. The proceeds would go to the Joss family.

It wasn't the easiest thing in the world to arrange, because the club owners had to be contacted and their consent given to use their players, and the players had to agree to come and play without pay on what would otherwise be a rest day for them. The response to my requests, though, was overwhelming and most players asked, agreed to play. We attracted an all-star team, the likes of which had never been assembled on any field for a single game in the history of the sport. We had Tris Speaker, Sam Crawford, and Ty Cobb starting in the outfield. The infield featured Hal Chase, Eddie Collins, Bobby Wallace and Frank Baker. Our pitching staff consisted of Russell Ford, Jo Wood and Walter Johnson.

What wouldn't I have been able to do with a team like that every day? Add to that our own stars, and you had what some papers were calling "the first great galaxy of diamond stars."

More than 15,000 people showed up to watch and we raised more than $12,000 for the Joss family including contributions from some of the umpires like Silk O'Laughlin, and managers like Connie Mack.

Speaker, Collins, and Cobb led off for the all-stars with hits and they were never headed. They won 5-3, but the score didn't really matter. What mattered was that we paid tribute to a great player and a great man.

**JOE JACKSON** We played a charity game for Addie Joss with a lot of big stars like Ty Cobb in the game. It was supposed to be a day off, so we wasn't excited about playing, but we did anyway and it turned out to be a lot of fun. Germany Schaeffer was a good player, but he was a really funny announcer who walked around the field with a big megaphone announcing the players in funny ways. Like once, when they changed catchers, he said "Street of Washington, better known as 'Gabby' is now behind the plate."

Before the game started the photographer had all the stars lined up so that he could snap a picture, but Germany, he jumped up, grabbed the camera bulb and yelled, "Now, boys, just one smile." That cracked everybody up. During practice he even played first base for our team, but what he did was sit on the bag with his legs crossed and make everybody throw real low to him.

After the game, a writer told me that George Jackson was being called up to the Boston Nationals. George was a cousin of mine but I didn't really know him. First of all, he was younger than me, and second of all, he lived in Texas. The writer kept asking me questions about him, but I didn't know what to say, so finally I walked away. I just wished it was Davey Jackson instead of George Jackson.

**TED EASTERLY** We were sitting around the locker room during one of those interminably long rain delays where the umpires couldn't make up their minds whether to call the game and send us home or wait all day for the rain to stop. Graney's reading the paper and he sees a story about how the *Mona Lisa* was just stolen from the Louvre gallery.

"For four hundred years she has baffled her admirers with her world famous 'inscrutable smile,'" Jack read. "Not a vestige of a clue was left by the person or persons who took it and the search of every nook and cranny of the Louvre only brought to light the valuable frame in which the picture hung and the glass that covered it."

Now just by coincidence, Joe is sitting next to Jack, so Jack turns to him and says, "Can you believe that, they pinched the damn Mona Lisa?"

"Nah, I can't believe that," says Joe.

Now I'm telling you, me and Terry Turner are across from them and we hear this, and we almost choke. Joe wouldn't know the Mona Lisa from Jenny Lind. He wouldn't know whether the Louvre was a museum or a cat house.

For the next 15 minutes or so, all the conversation was about "The Mysterious Lady of the Louvre," and conjecture about who might have stolen her, the consensus being it must have been some low-life German.

Never once did Joe let on he didn't know what the hell we were talking about. He even threw in a couple of "that's rights'" and an "uh huh" or two. At least it was entertainment for a dull, drizzly afternoon.

**CY FALKENBERG** One thing that helped the batters in those days was what they called "Turtle-Back" baseball diamonds, diamonds that had the mound raised above the rest of the field. If they found that, they always leveled it. The damn league was always working against the pitchers and in favor of the batters. I'm not saying guys like Joe, and Larry, and Ty wouldn't have had those high averages if they batted in later years when they raised the mound, but I doubt if their averages would have been as high. Sure, Joe, Larry and Ty were good, but not as good as they thought they were.

**JACK GRANEY** One day we were getting ready for a game. A reporter comes in saying that the Polo Grounds—that's where the Giants played—had completely burned down during the night because a fire started in dried peanut shells under the grandstands.

"I guess it was really something," the reporter said. "They even tried to check the flames with hand grenades."

That led to considerable conversation about why they would try to use grenades. Then, from someplace, some wise guy rolls a phony grenade into the room and it comes to a stop right under Joe's feet. Well, he dives for cover and, of course, the whole room breaks up.

"You'd make a helluvuh soldier, Joe," somebody says.

"I'm not going to be no soldier," Joe responds.

"Where's your patriotic feeling?" somebody else asks.

"I got plenty," Joe says. "Don't worry about that."

I always remembered that incident when all those questions about Joe's patriotism came up later.

**EDDIE COLLINS** Joe took a lot of abuse from the fans even when it wasn't his fault.

Let me give you an example. Once when we were playing Cleveland, with Joe at first and Birmingham at bat evidently the hit-and-run signal must have been flashed because Joe began running as Bender started to deliver the ball. Birmingham, in an attempt to carry out his part in the play, swung at the ball and lifted a little pop fly to Baker at third. Joe was over half way to second by the time Birmingham hit the ball. Since I was playing second, and Barry short, we took in the play in an instant. I raced to second ahead of Joe as if to receive a throw from Baker at third. I made wild gestures and yelled at Baker, "Second, Baker, second." At the same time, Barry yelled at Baker, "Hurry the throw, Harry." All of this was designed to make Joe think the ball was on the ground, and it worked perfectly. Joe stopped once as if in doubt, then hurried on. So, to continue the ruse, we shouted at Bris Lord in left field, so that Joe would think the ball got through Baker and was on the ground in left field. Joe stopped again, now totally confused. Naturally, the Philadelphia rooters were having the time of their life over Joe's dilemma, and there was no one they would rather see in trouble on the paths than Joe. The noise they were making was deafening which just further compounded the confusion. Joe didn't see his mistake until he saw Baker throw the ball to Davis at first and the umpire wave both men out.

**JACK GRANEY** There were so many locker room tricks played on Joe that after a while he couldn't tell a trick from the truth.

During the season, Deacon McGuire who was then scouting for the team, comes up with a kid he says was one of the fastest runners and best fielders he ever seen. He finds this phenom playing for Victoria, British Columbia out in the Northwestern League and signs him. Well, one day Deacon brings the kid in and introduces him to the fellows in the locker room.

"This here is Ten Million," he announces. Now the truth, as we found out was that his father, Judge Million, actually named him Ten Million. There was no nickname about it. That was his real and only name.

Only, Joe, he thinks Deacon's trying to put one over on him, since that's what he was used to all the time. The kid stuck around for a while before being farmed out, and never did make the squad, but for all the time he was with us, Joe went out of his way not to have to talk to him. He just knew that everybody would laugh at him if he called him Ten Million.

Everybody but Joe had fun with his name. The paper even ran a jingle about him:

The Naps have bought a fielder
Of the soothing name Ten Million;
Now it's up to Barney Dreyfus
To unearth some guy named Billion,
Then perhaps our mister Somers
Can excavate a trillion.

**CHARLES SOMERS** In August we had to release Cy Young. It was one of those real difficult business decisions that had to be made. He was the only pitcher to have won 500 games, but he had only won three that season. I hated to do it, but I could see the end was near even if he couldn't.

He was so popular with the fans, but I knew we had a new star in the making in Joe Jackson.

**CY YOUNG** I was sorry that things did not break so that I could have kept on in Cleveland, but I knew I wasn't finished with baseball.

I was in good condition, and honestly, my arm was as strong as it ever was, so I knew that I still had a few years of good pitching in the old whip. None of that "back to the farm" stuff for me. I stayed with the boys in Cleveland working out until the Boston Nationals decided they could use this old farm boy.

**JOE JACKSON** It didn't seem right, letting Cy Young go like that, but it made me think about how lucky we was to play the game, because someday we was all going to be let go like that.

**CHARLIE LEBEAU** Apparently Joe behaved himself pretty well during his first full year in the majors, he certainly had numerous examples that season of how management dealt with obstreperous behavior. Several popular and successful players, like Joe Tinker and Sherwood Magee, were suspended for the season. Tinker, the future Hall of Famer, was exceptionally popular with the fans, but in one game two Texas league pop-ups dropped into short left field with Tinker playing shortstop. Now, Frank Chance, the manager thought both balls should have been caught by Tinker who made no effort for either.

When the team returned to the bench Chance asked Tinker why he didn't go after the ball. Tinker's response was reported as being, "If you don't like my style of ball playing, why, you know what you can do." Chance's response, without an instant's hesitation, was to impose a fine of $150 and suspend him for the rest of the season.

Even though the fans interceded and demanded that Tinker be reinstated, which he was, it still illustrates the point that in those days, management didn't take much from the players.

**WILLIE MITCHELL** We generally got along pretty well, that Cleveland team, but we weren't exactly choir boys. I mean we had our share of late nighters, and we got into a few scrapes.

One time in particular we got a little more than we bargained for. Me and Fred Blanding, Gene Krapp, and George Kaler made a pitchers' night of it. After a dance in Silver Lake, we were escorting two young Kent ladies to their homes. On the streetcar, all the seats were occupied, but we saw a man taking up two—one for himself, and one for his luggage. It turns out he was an actor, so I guess he was used to special treatment. His name was Nat Haines in case you ever heard of him.

Anyway, we asked him very politely if he would make room for the young ladies. He said he wouldn't. Just then, the motorman stuck his head in the door and told us it was OK to throw his luggage on the floor. As George reached for one of the bundles, Haines yelled, "Don't you touch that package. That cost me $5."

George put it down, but when the motorman again said to throw it on the floor, Fred reached for it only to have Haines swing at him, but miss. Of course, that set off Fred. He unleashed a right cross to the actor's chin knocking him across the car.

When the car got to Cuyahoga Falls we were arrested by a marshal who, had we been a bunch of train robbers, couldn't have been more agitated.

Haines threatened to bring a civil suit against us but since he first offered to settle for $20, we tried to get him arrested on the charge of attempted blackmail.

Since we were held overnight and almost missed the game the next day, Mr. Somers was perturbed to say the least, but eventually everything got straightened out.

Fighting wasn't all that unusual though. I remember Grover Land who once hit a gatekeeper at Cleveland League Park breaking the victim's nose. A warrant was issued for his arrest on an assault charge, but he skipped town before the warrant could be served. And Ty Cobb practically had a career as a boxer.

I can't remember Joe fighting anybody, but he sure could have caused some damage if he had.

It was common to see ballplayers getting into fights back in those days.

I remember one fight in particular. It happened over in the National

League, so we didn't actually see it, but we sure did talk about it in the locker room. Deacon told us about it, and I know Joe was there because I recall him being as shocked about it as I was. I don't recollect Joe actually fighting much, but he sure was intrigued about stories of fights.

This particular fight took place between Bill Dahlen, the manager of the Brooklyn Club, and an umpire named Charles Rigler. It seems the fight started when Artie Wilson, the New York catcher, hit a towering home run into the right field grandstand with one out in the ninth inning to win the game for the Giants. As soon as the ball landed in the upper tier, Dahlen charged from the Brooklyn bench yelling that the ball was foul. Rigler said he saw it clearly all the way and that it was fair.

Dahlen rushed at the umpire shaking his fist in Rigler's face. The crowd began screaming. Then, all of a sudden, Rigler hauled off and threw a vicious right cross to the chin of the manager. Dahlen recovered quickly, struck back with his own shot, and the melee was on. The fighters continued swinging madly at each other as the teams began running toward the action. Close on their heels came hundreds of spectators who rushed past the gray-coated special policemen and onto the field. Most of the crowd avoided the actual fight but ran around the field on a wild rampage. Cries of "Smash him again Rigler," came from the New York fans, while hundreds of Brooklyn rooters implored Dahlen to "Soak him, Bill," an expression popular at the time. It was total chaos.

Eventually the Pinkertons' got control of the situation and escorted the combatants back into the clubhouse. The fans stayed around for a long time waiting for the pugilists to come back out. It was a better fight than many had seen in the ring for some time.

Dahlen was known for being one of the worst umpire baiters in the game and had only the day before been released from a three-day suspension inflicted by President Lynch for a run-in with umpires in Brooklyn.

When things like this happened, the stories quickly made the rounds of all the clubhouses in the league.

The day after the ump decked Dahlen, Ty Cobb, in the fourth inning of a game in New York, leaped into the seats in left field and proceeded to beat up one of the spectators who apparently made some remarks not to Cobb's liking. Ban Johnson immediately suspended Cobb, but the Detroit players came to his support and sent an ultimatum to Johnson saying that if the suspension wasn't lifted they would strike. The ultimatum was signed by all the Tigers except manager Jennings. Their argument was that the penalty inflicted on Cobb because he defended himself from an unwarranted attack by a rooter was uncalled for and unjust.

In our clubhouse there was considerable talk about this. Some thought Cobb got his just deserts and his teammates were supporting him only because they needed him on the field. Joe, I know, sprung to his defense in an unusually eloquent appeal from him.

"Ty, he don't attack nobody unless somebody said something real bad about his family," Joe said. "It ain't right for him to be punished for something he didn't start. It just ain't right."

Somebody else whispered Joe was just trying to protect another good ol' southern boy. That may have been very true.

The next day, the Tigers did in fact pull off the first big strike in major league baseball. They refused to play a game against the Athletics. In their place was a team of ringers who lost 24 to 2. Ironically, one of the ringers was a 25-year-old kid who went by the name of William Maharg. He played third base during the game, but he played a much bigger position in Joe's life a few years later.

Johnson rushed to Philadelphia to warn the Detroit players that if they didn't play the next day they would be blacklisted. Still the players refused. It was only when Cobb himself requested that they return to the field that they consented. Ty was reinstated with only a $50 fine. The other players were each fined $100.

Cobb claimed that what finally provoked him was the fan calling him a "half nigger." Now the fact is, a lot of players could sympathize with him on that one. Ty may have been a racist, but you have got to remember that southern kids were brought up that way in those days. Joe may have felt that way, too. I really don't know. Certainly he was raised in a time and in a place where he might be expected to have racist feelings, but in all the years I knew him, I can't remember him ever exhibiting particular sentiments in that direction.

**HENRY P. EDWARDS** There must have been something about that 1912 season that got the blood of the Naps all roiled up. A few days after the Cobb fight and strike, the Naps got into an altercation all their own.

Rumors reached me at the paper that a battle between Willie Mitchell and their captain, Ivan Olson, had taken place. The story went that the two players quarreled in a cab on their way to their hotel after a game in Boston, Mitchell receiving a bad gash over his right eye. Apparently members of the team met secretly and demanded that Olson be deposed from his captaincy and Joe Birmingham made captain as soon as he recovered from his illness.

The day after the rumors started I saw Mitchell. He showed the results of an accident all right, as his head was plastered and bandaged. Willie, however, claimed that he and Olson were merely fooling around and that he hit his head against the cab door. Olson told the same story, as did manager Davis. I ran into Joe and asked him. His very politic comment was, "I think you'll have to ask the manager that."

I asked him why he said that, and he responded: "Because that's what he said I should say."

That's one thing I learned about Joe. Ask a question and you got an answer.

**HARRY DAVIS** There was absolutely no truth in those rumors. Olson and Mitchell did not fight, and Olson was not deprived of his position as captain. The club had a captain and his name was Ivan Olson. Stories like that made me angry. They didn't do the club any good. I know where they started, however. They were told by Ed Hornhorst after he had been released.

**JOE JACKSON** Willie Mitchell and Ivy Olson once got into a big fight and so we had to have a big team meeting and try to settle it on our own. Willie and Ivy were busted up pretty good, but we kept it to ourselves like good teammates should.

**TED EASTERLY** One day a Captain Matsuda from Tokyo, Japan, came to spend time with us. He wanted to learn how we played the game. He told us that little kids all over Tokyo were playing baseball. He called it an "honorable game," which seemed like a good thing to call it. Of course, he said all this through an interpreter. I don't know who set him up for this, but when the interpreter wasn't around, he turned to Joe and for the longest time spoke to him in Japanese. Joe didn't know what to think, he just kept trying to get away.

"What's the matter, Joe, you got something against the Japanese?" Willie asked him.

"I don't got nothing against them," Joe answered, "except I don't know why this guy's bowing at me all the time."

**TERRY TURNER** Several times during the course of the year some preacher would talk to the players. One preacher in particular, Reverend Dr. S. Edward Young, was a big ball fan and he loved to talk about how St. Paul would attend baseball games if he were around. I guess he thought it was a way he could get the players to pay more attention to him.

He talked about things like the chaplet which the Great Umpire in the skies, the Lord Righteous Umpire, would give players on judgment day. I thought he was pretty silly, but maybe some of the players took notice, I don't know.

I distinctly remember, however, one sermon when he said that an evil hour came to the ball field two-thirds of a generation before when gambling and hired defeats and dishonest victories almost ruined the game. But now, he insisted, the players were taught honor with the slightest infraction meaning expulsion from the game. St. Paul, he assured us, wouldn't permit dishonesty in his games.

Joe was there for that sermon. I know, because he sat next to me, and I so clearly remember him pretending to read from the Bible during the appropriate part of the service.

**VINCENT ALEXANDER** Cleveland ended up third that year, but they sure had their share of highlights. They won 10 in a row at one point and stayed close most of the year. Gregg was terrific, winning 23 games and posting a 1.81 ERA. Lajoie dropped off a bit to .365 which still would have been a highlight in almost anybody else's career. But it was Joe who stole the limelight. All he did in his first full year in the majors was hit .408, only a few points short of Cobb. During the course of the year his average never dropped below .360. He also had a 37-game hitting streak and was second to Cobb in hits, doubles, slugging average, total bases and runs scored. For good measure, he hit 7 home runs in a season which saw Frank Baker lead the league with 9. In almost any other year he would have been regarded as the greatest hitter alive. The only problem for Joe was that he had to do it with the older, more experienced Cobb around.

**TY COBB** It was because of my wits that I won the batting championship in 1911, although, near the end of the season it appeared that I would surely lose it. It seems like every year I had some worthy challenger for the crown—Crawford in '07 and '08, Collins in '09, of course Lajoie in '10. In '11 though, I faced my toughest test, this time from a kid—Joe Jackson.

On the field he always flashed a smile in my direction and greeted me with a "Hiyuh, brother Ty." We Southerners always felt a kind of connection with each other anyway.

The last series of the season was in Cleveland, a six-game affair. I waited in the clubhouse until Jackson had finished his batting practice. I had given one of the clubhouse boys a buck to tip me off when he was done so that I would be ready and waiting for him.

Joe walked in a little sweaty and when he saw me, gave me his customary "Hiyuh, Brother Ty. How you been?"

I got the coldest look I could muster in my eye, stared off into space, but said nothing. Puzzlement replaced the grin on his face.

"Gosh, Ty, what's the matter with you?"

As I turned and walked away, Joe became even more confused. He followed me down to the end of the long bench they had in there.

"Get away from me, Joe!" I snarled and stormed out.

Every inning after that I made sure to pass close to him, each time giving him the deep freeze.

"Gee, what's wrong, Ty?" he said the first few times I passed him. But I never answered him. Not once. After a while he gave up asking, but he kept looking at me with those sullen, deep-seated eyes of his. He was hurt. I could see that, but as I've said a million times, baseball is a tough sport and you've got to be tough if you want to be the best.

I kept this up throughout the series, and Joe became so hurt and confused that he completely collapsed at the plate allowing me to rally and not only catch Joe in the batting race, but pass him and thus win my fifth consecutive batting crown.

The moral here is that it helps if you help them beat themselves. Now I know some people think that what I did to a fine fellow like Joe was unusually cruel, but it's all part of the game. The psychology of hitting is as important as the physical aspect, and since I had to fight all my life to survive, I learned all the tricks—all the fair tricks. I didn't cheat Joe, and I didn't cheat anybody else, but I took every advantage the rules gave me. If Joe wasn't up to it, well, he should have learned from that experience.

**VINCENT ALEXANDER** We've all heard or read Cobb's account of how he duped Joe into losing the batting race in 1911. In fact, it was one of his favorite stories. Over the years the story has been used again and again to prove that Joe lacked character, that he folded in the face of any crisis, that he cowered under pressure, and that he was too stupid to understand what Cobb was doing to him.

That would perhaps be an acceptable argument in favor of the "characterless Joe" theories except for one fact: the story isn't true. Cobb made it up. Oh, I know it's been printed in various versions umpteen times, but that doesn't make it so. The fact of the matter is that as brilliantly as Joe hit that season, he was never ahead in the race. Cobb got off to a blistering start and never cooled down. For much of the season he was batting in the .450 range. Joe managed to narrow the gap several times, even threatening to overtake Cobb, but he never did. There was simply no day in the entire season on which Joe led Cobb in batting. Close, yes; lead, no.

Another problem with the story as Cobb claimed: there was no six-game showdown at the end of the season. Early in October, the Tigers came to Cleveland for a three-game series with Cobb comfortably leading Joe. In the series, Joe actually out hit Cobb getting three hits in eight at bats while Cobb got three hits in 10 at bats. After those games, Cleveland headed to Chicago, and Detroit to St. Louis. In a repeat of what he did the previous year when he was dueling Lajoie, Cobb sat out the final games, thus protecting his average at .420. Joe played the first game against St. Louis, and collected three hits, and then with third place clinched for the Naps, sat out the meaningless last game. It had been a long season and Joe had various minor injuries, so sitting out seemed to make sense. Joe finished 12 points behind Cobb and couldn't have caught him anyway unless he had an unbelievable game that went well into extra innings.

Cobb's story was pure fiction, but in time, it helped to reinforce the image of Joe as "dumb yokel." Like so much else that was written about him, this just ain't so.

**GEORGE STOVALL** Sometimes we had pickup games at the end of the season where a select team would play the league champion, sort of as a way of helping them prepare for the World Series.

Near the end of the 1911 season it was decided to field such a team, and there was talk of Joe and Larry, being on that team. But I wouldn't allow it because we were scheduled to play a seven-game series with Cincinnati after the regular season was over. This was for the unofficial championship of Ohio, and since Cincy won four of the seven games played the previous season, I felt we needed to seek revenge. When I told them they couldn't play, it was real obvious Joe was relieved. I don't think Larry cared one way or the other, but Joe, he didn't need any more pressure on him, so he was delighted.

# 32

# I PRETTY MUCH HIT WHAT THEY THROWED

**KATIE JACKSON** Among the good memories of Cleveland are those of me and Joe at the West Side Market over on 25th and Lorain Avenue. We always carried two shopping bags and brought them home full.

Any time we were in the area we could find the Market by looking for the tallest thing around—the Market clock tower which rose above everything in the neighborhood. Inside it was always crowded. Everybody, all the vendors, they knew your name. "Hello, Joe, Hello, Mrs. Jackson" as we walked between the booths.

In case you're wondering, nobody called him "Shoeless Joe" then. That didn't happen until later when Joe got into trouble, and they used that to suggest that he was still such a rube. No, in the Cleveland days it was just plain "Joe."

The Market had hundreds of little stands selling just anything you could want to eat, and the good part was, all you had to do was point to get whatever it was you wanted. Joe didn't have to feel out of place. He could point with the best of them.

Lots of people just hung around, and some of them—mostly kids—recognized Joe so he would stop and talk a while about the team or what it was like hitting against Walter Johnson, then we would move on down the crowded isles. These were the working people of Cleveland, and around them, Joe always felt comfortable.

I remember the smells, too—sauerkraut in big barrels, sausages of all shapes and sizes hanging from hooks, sheep's milk cheese in big blocks, candied ginger, oregano, and juniper berries in all shapes of jars.

We particularly liked Mrs. Pulaski's thick black bread. As soon as we got close to her stand, she handed us a loaf already wrapped and tied in string. "For the baseball player and his pretty wife," she said in an accent so heavy we wouldn't know what she was saying if we hadn't heard it so many times. I doubt if she had any idea who Joe was, but that's how it was in the Market. It was a little like a family and a little like the South—or at least it felt that way to us.

Sometimes we stopped and got a hot dog and a root beer for a nickel each. We would stand and eat at the counter watching the little girl washing every cup and plate and heavy root beer mug by hand.

If we needed a bottle of milk it was fun to go to the Market to get it. Now if you need a quart of milk you get in a car and drive to a supermarket. All the fun is gone.

**CALVIN BATES** I don't think Joe ever really loved Cleveland but what made the city tolerable was that it was an industrial city with a lot of semi-skilled laborers not unlike the mill towns of the South, only a lot bigger.

Cleveland was a city on the rise as an industrial power. Iron and steel and foundry and machine shops were at its heart. Most of my family worked in the auto parts business, an area in which Cleveland ranked second to no other city, including Detroit. My father and brothers all made things like electric starters, which when they worked, were great additions to the automobile, and all sorts of auto related devices such as tow ropes, tire patches, dusters, and the bulb horns which frightened horses and bicycle riders.

Joe loved cars, particularly the powerful and noisy Winton and Stearns gasoline models, but I know Mrs. Jackson preferred the quiet and more refined Baker and Rauch & Lang electrics which could frequently run up to a hundred miles without recharging. Automobiles in those days were raising so much dust that street after street had to be paved.

As much as Joe loved cars, he also loved gadgets, particularly the new electrical ones, and as electricity was becoming the illuminant in many homes, electrical appliances were being invented and marketed at an astonishing rate. Seemingly, Joe bought one of each. Cleveland offered all kinds of ways of separating Joe from his money.

Joe bought electrical appliances and lots of clothes. He was becoming something of a dandy. At the beginning of the season, he could be found around town wearing high-waisted, pinched-back coats and narrow trousers. Summer was officially marked by the opening of the straw-hat season. Joe wore straws with buzz-saw brims and colored bands and in gusty winds even sported a silk cord to anchor the hat to a buttonhole. Like the gentlemen of Cleveland, he wore linen-like paper collars which were thrown away after wearing them for a day or two.

Joe may have not loved the city, but he sure liked the benefits the city offered.

**KATIE JACKSON** One of the things we liked to do in Cleveland was go to the motion pictures—or at least I did, and Joe went along without complaining. Sometimes if it wasn't too crowded, I would read the captions to him, other times he just watched the action, which was about all you needed to do to follow the story anyway.

We saw stars like Gloria Swanson, Rudolph Valentino and Max Sennett and Joe's favorite, John Bunny. We laughed at Fatty Arbuckle, Mabel Normand, Charlie Chaplin and the cross-eyed Ben Turpin, and we were thrilled by the actions of Pearl White and William Farnum. I can still remember pictures like "Cheyenne," "The Bird on Nellie's Hat," "San Antonio Hearts," "Flowers Love Me" and "The World is Mine."

Once we went for a moonlight cruise on the *City of Erie*. Mostly, though, Joe played baseball, and that took up most of his, and much of my time.

**VINCENT ALEXANDER** When the 1912 spring training season had begun, no one was sure Joe would show up. By the time the season ended, he had proven himself to be one of the brightest stars in the baseball galaxy. He was among the league leaders in all important offensive categories.

He also led the league in taking abuse from other players. Had he not been the great player he was, he very well might have done what a lot of people expected—bolt for home.

**CALVIN BATES** The big question of the Cleveland hot stove league that winter was, what would Joe do next year? And that included the possibility that whatever he did, he might do it someplace else—like South Carolina. Conversations went something like this:

"He can hit, though, there's no question about that."

"We need to be lenient. I mean what if he doesn't get off to such a great start again."

"He can't match what he did last year. Can't even come close. That's an impossibility."

"A buck says he doesn't get within 50 points of what he did last year."

"Yeah, but that would still put him around .350 and that ain't all bad, not bad at all."

Joe kept the league engaged all winter.

**KATIE JACKSON** We moved into a nice little apartment on Lexington Avenue, near the right field wall of League Park. It took us a long time to get used to the noise on the street, which I swear never stopped. I always wondered what people found to do on the streets in the wee hours of the morning.

Most of the time when Joe wasn't playing we stayed in the apartment, because as he was becoming more famous, it was difficult to go out.

Sometimes people thought it was funny to make rude comments about Joe's illiteracy. Oh, he never said much about it, and I never even acknowledged the comments. I think Joe appreciated that, but I know it hurt him.

I tried to cook like we ate in the South as much as possible. We led a pretty quiet life actually, which was the way we both wanted it.

I went to most home games, always sat in the same seat which was in the last row of the grandstand directly behind home plate. The papers said it was because I was superstitious but really I just wanted to get away from the people who were saying nasty things about Joe.

After one of the other wives showed me how to keep score, I started keeping my own score book for all of Joe's games. That is until the seventh inning, when I left to head home and fix dinner so that when the game was over Joe could come home right away and eat. Most of the other players I know went out to restaurants, but that wasn't as easy for us. Joe felt uncomfortable when I had to read the menu and the bill to him.

**NAPOLEON LAJOIE** It wasn't long before me and my wife became good friends with the Jacksons. We had them over a few time and even went to movies and summer band concerts—things like that.

You always had to be a little careful with Joe. It didn't take long to figure out that if we were at a concert or something, I could always read the program and then find some excuse to talk about it without sounding patronizing. The worst thing in the world was to say something like "let me read that for you, Joe." Joe hated that, and I can't say I blamed him much. Sometimes me and my wife would even sit down before going out with them and figure out how to handle the potentially embarrassing situations which were likely to come up during the evening.

Look, Joe wasn't the only famous and successful athlete without a stellar education: Jack Dempsey never got through grade school; Babe Ruth had little formal education. I think those two more or less accepted their state and were at peace with it, but Joe was desperately sensitive about his illiteracy and always tried to conceal it from strangers. Once he became an important fellow with social and business obligations the embarrassment became agonizing. In a way he was like a blind man: he knew of the existence of rare and beautiful treasures but he couldn't enjoy them.

I remember one particularly disturbing cartoon which ran in one of the papers while Joe was still in Philadelphia. It showed a stupid-looking hick running for a train out of Philadelphia saying "I'd rather be a clod in Greenville than a millionaire here."

But make no mistake about it, the Jacksons were good people—down-to-earth, and straightforward. Katie was a real sweetheart, and very pretty. She was perky with a wonderful smile and sparkling blue eyes, and she was a very fashionable dresser. They must have spent a goodly part of their salaries on clothes, because the two of them were the best dressed couple on the team.

I guess we were about their closest friends on the team, and I'm proud of that. I'd like to think that I was a good influence on Joe, and helped in some way to make his time in Cleveland reasonably tolerable. I only wish I had been around him later when maybe I could have helped him avoid some of the problems he fell into. Perhaps it wouldn't have mattered. Who knows?

**VINCENT ALEXANDER** Going into his second year, Joe's potential was as great as anyone's then playing the game. In his first year Joe had flashed across the horizon of the American League like Halley's comet. His .408 average and 41 stolen bases were better figures than Cobb, Lajoie, Speaker, or Collins were able to put up in their first full seasons.

It's no wonder the Cleveland fans were excited about the possibilities for their future. With Lajoie and Jackson on the same team, the potential was staggering.

**JOE JACKSON** Pretty much I hit whatever they throwed at me, but one pitcher in particular almost drove me nuts, and that was Walter Johnson. No other pitcher ever treated me as shameful as him. My batting average went into shock every time his name was even mentioned.

**CHARLES SOMERS** I didn't make money as a businessman by making un-businesslike decisions, and one of the things I knew was to protect your assets. Joe was an asset who needed some protecting. So I did everything I could to make Joe as comfortable in Cleveland as possible. The front office went out of its way to make Mrs. Jackson feel welcome. When she asked for the same seat, we gave it to her. When she needed some help in buying new furniture, we provided it. When she wanted to go along on a road trip, we made the arrangements. We understood that keeping Katie happy meant keeping Joe happy. She was always pleasant and helpful when we needed her assistance in getting Joe to some public relations function or similar event.

Ernest Barnard was general manager of the club when Joe arrived and we had a long talk about handling Joe. At first Ernie was hesitant to treat Joe differently from the others. He felt that would create dissension on the club, but as Joe began to establish his value to the club, he began to see things a little more my way. It was Ernie's idea to room him initially with Bill Steen on road trips. Bill was a decent fellow who didn't seem to mind handling Joe's mail, answering his wires and reading him the menu in restaurants and in dining cars. He got so good at it after a while, that he could discuss the various items on the menu with such casualness and interest that often the waiter didn't even realize what was going on. Bill even wrote the letters back to Katie that Joe dictated to him.

No, Joe wasn't treated the same as all the other players, and maybe some of them did resent that, but that's the way it had to be, and that's the way it was.

Once I even went to Joe and offered, as I know Mack had done earlier, to hire a tutor to teach him to read and write a little.

"No, Mr. Somers, I don't want to do that," he said.

"But why Joe?" I asked. "It's not that hard and it's got to make things go easier for you if you could do at least some of your own reading."

"I just don't want to, that's all," he answered.

"If you're worried what other people might think about you learning at your age, why, I can arrange it so that nobody will know. You've got my word on that."

"I'm not going to do it, Mr. Somers," he stated with great conviction and finality.

I spoke with Joe about many different things, but I never saw him so absolute about anything as he was about this. He never said why, and he never discussed it. It didn't make any sense to me then, and it still doesn't, but I guess I can't put myself in his position. Maybe he was afraid he couldn't learn.

**CY FALKENBERG** People often asked what kind of a fellow Joe was. When he didn't have his uniform on, he was every bit the gentleman. He was mild mannered, didn't seem the least affected by his success, talked in a low tone with a soft southern accent that was so pleasant that it sometimes made me wish he was more talkative.

He gave the umpires little or no trouble. Even when he thought he was done wrong by an umpire, the most he usually showed was a slight turn of the head.

Was Joe stupid? I'm not sure how to answer that one. I knew Joe only as a player, and I knew nothing about his mental ability in other areas of life. I do know, however, that time and again he demonstrated that he was a bright ballplayer. In order to do the things he did on the field, he had to be able to think quickly.

**DEACON McGUIRE** The possibility of night baseball became one of the big baseball topics of 1912. Mr. Comiskey of the Chicago club hired a guy who patented an electric light system. He spent weeks installing big lights at White Sox Park and then one night in August he turned them on and as everybody said, "turned night into day." What they had were 20 powerful lights, 10 on the roof, and 10 on the ground. The rumor was that we would be playing night ball one of these days, but I'll tell you that made our outfielders a mite nervous.

"It ain't going to work," insisted Ted Easterly. Ted, of course, had enough problems just trying to catch the damn ball during the day.

"Don't seem right," said Joe. "Playing ball in the middle of the night just don't seem right to me."

I don't think Joe really took to the idea of any change anyway. He was an old-fashioned player who learned the game as a young kid and played the same way all his life.

"It don't matter what you want," I said over and over again. "It's the owners like Comiskey who decide what the game will be."

**GEORGE STOVALL** Joe wasn't exactly a very scientific type of player. That was a phrase you heard a lot in those days: "scientific baseball," or as it was sometime called, "inside baseball," a style of play using such tactics as squeeze plays, hit-and-run plays, delayed steals, pitchouts and decoy plays.

Complicated signals were important. In "scientific baseball" nearly every play is signaled to every player on the team. This involved a most intricate set of signs and wigwags which had to be changed constantly. It has been claimed that one reason that the Athletics hit the Cub pitchers so hard in the 1910 World Series was because the shrewd Indian, Bender, had detected the signal code of Chance and Kling and tipped off the batters from the coaching line. Bender or one of the other Athletics pitchers was constantly on the coaching lines when they weren't pitching.

McGraw, manager of the Giants, was considered the best of the "scientific managers," and although his style was quite different, Mr. Mack also was considered to be a good strategist.

Some writers argued that if Joe couldn't learn to read, how could he possibly learn the intricacies of "scientific baseball?" Joe was something of a "hit the ball, throw the ball, catch the ball" type of old-fashioned player, but I can't honestly say that he missed any more signs than the rest of us. Oh, some players like Eddie Collins got a reputation as a good "scientific base stealer" but on the whole, most of us played the game the way we were asked to. Joe was probably no better or no worse than most of us at following signs and doing what the manager asked.

**CHARLES SOMERS** I desperately wanted to have someone at the head of the team to take charge just as McGraw and Connie Mack did, and as much as I wanted Stovall to be that man I didn't think he really had it in him. I felt I needed a man big enough in baseball wisdom to buy and release players on his own account, a manager who would take the initiative and run the team without involving me. I had half a million dollars tied up in baseball and I wanted a high-priced manager to run my baseball business.

The man I still wanted was Harry Davis, but I remained concerned with Joe. I wasn't exactly sure what his relationship was with Davis when he was with the team, but I knew he still harbored considerable ill will toward his Philadelphia experience. So I called him into my office.

"Joe, I want to ask you what you think of Harry Davis," I said.

"I think George is a good manager," he responded, obviously aware of the situation.

"So do I," I said, "but, look, if he isn't managing here, he'll probably get the job with the Red Sox or Browns—the Sox more likely."

"That wouldn't surprise me," Joe said.

"Davis will make a good manager, don't you think?"

"Probably."

"He's a smart baseball man, isn't he?"

"You bet. He's real smart."

"You played with him, Joe, any problems you can think of?"

"Gee, Mr. Somers," he said, "I really can't think of any."

Joe went up a notch in my estimation after that meeting. I gave him every opportunity to criticize Davis, but he wouldn't do it. He valued and respected authority, and he could be one loyal son of a buck.

**WILLIE MITCHELL** I had more than my share of things in common with Mr. Jackson. Like him, I was a true son of the South, only I hailed from Mississippi—Sardis, to be exact. I doubt if it was a whole lot bigger than that mill town where Joe grew up, and probably not a lot different either. We were southerners and unless you were one of us, you couldn't know what that meant. It's more than a matter of geography, it's a matter of attitude and temperament.

Me and Joe, we were the same age, or just about. The "just about" part comes from the fact that Joe didn't ever seem to be exactly sure.

We both loved to hunt more than anything, maybe even baseball.

There the similarities ended though. I was a graduate of Mississippi State. I may have been the first player from Mississippi in the majors. At least I am going to continue to claim that until and unless somebody proves me wrong.

Joe was, of course, a star on the team. I was something considerably less. I always put up good ERA's, but lousy won-loss records. What I did have, though, were bushels of strikeouts. I was in love with the wonderful sound of a bat scything through air hitting nothing.

Anyway, getting back to Joe. For the first few years on the team we got along well. I took an almost avuncular interest in him standing up for him on more than one occasion. Then came the war and I was the first American leaguer to enter the army. I saw active duty in France and was injured in a gas attack there. Although the injuries weren't serious, they did delay my release from the service. By the time I did return, I had a whole new opinion of Joe.

**TERRY TURNER** The only guy I ever seen who acted like he almost liked spring training was Joe. And you know why? I think it was because he was in the South. Or maybe it was because he knew what came next—the North.

Oh, I know when you're a young player you think spring training is going to be riding in fancy Pullmans, easy exercise in the warm sun without the pressure of a game, plenty of good southern cooking, and lots of fun with the guys.

But it wasn't really like that. What it was like was managers yelling at you, stiff muscles and hard work. We kicked about the grub, sang songs at night, and listened to the same old tired stories year after year.

But Joe, I never heard him complain about spring training like the rest of us did. He went about his training without saying much. Still it didn't seem right not bitching. It made it seem like he was different from us and some of the guys didn't cotton to that too much. So what they did was, they waited until he was sound asleep one night, then they took this bucket of warm water, and when his arm was hanging out over the side of the bed, they put his hand in it. As anybody who has ever tried it knows, that makes the guy wet his bed.

Man alive, was he ever embarrassed! As far as I know, he never found out what happened, but I doubt if he ever forgot it either.

We had to do something to make spring training interesting.

**WILLIE MITCHELL** There was a couple of neighborhood bars not too far from the stadium where we went after games to tip a few. Most of the players wasn't very heavy drinkers, but a few beers or a couple of shots would go a long way toward making a lousy game seem better.

Joe didn't come with us often. He could drink a little, though. He wasn't no lush, not by any stretch of the imagination, but he had his own bottle of stuff. Somebody kept sending it to him from his hometown. Every few weeks or so, he would get a heavily wrapped package. I think it was from one of his brothers. Anyway, it was triple-distilled corn whiskey. At least that's what he said it was, but I never tried it. I stuck with my beer and chaser. I heard when he invited players over to his house that's what he served.

I don't think Joe and the Mrs. did a lot of what you would call formal entertaining, but I know that corn whiskey stuff was a real southern drink that he liked a tad.

**TED EASTERLY** Some fan gave Joe this big, loud, obnoxious, multicolored parrot. Joe kept it for a while. He brought it into the clubhouse a few times. What a pest! Its entire vocabulary was limited to screeching, "You're out," and "You're lousy O'Loughlin."

One writer insisted that it could read better than Joe and had a better vocabulary. If there was a bond between them, it was understandable. They could share their ignorances.

**TERRY TURNER** The story went like this:

George Stallings had heard of the great hitting ability of a raw country youth named Jackson who was down in old South Carolina. Stallings was seated on the porch of the village hotel one evening when he heard a hue and cry. Looking up the street, he saw, approaching on the run, a big raw boned kid who was lifting his enormous bare feet and putting them down again one after the other in the yellow dust with precision and speed. Pursuing him was a big crowd of men. The landlord came out on the porch and smilingly stood watching the pursuit,

"Say, landlord," said Stallings, "what is this—a lynching party?"

"Nope," replied the grinning boniface, "the folks are only tryin' to put a pair of shoes on Joe Jackson."

The story made the rounds angering Joe something bad.

**SILK O'LOUGHLIN** In all my years as a young umpire in the bush leagues I took my share of rough handling from just about every angle, but none of the stuff handed to me down there compared to what I took from the press after a game I officiated in Cleveland.

"We understand that umpire O'Loughlin," the story read, "is very kind to his mother. We are very sorry he ever left home. His place is back with his mother."

Somebody read it aloud in the Cleveland clubhouse, and most of the players had a good laugh at my expense. Most, but not all. The next day Joe came up to me and said he was sorry about the story and that I shouldn't take it too seriously. You know, I really believed that he was sorry.

**JOE JACKSON** One day in spring training, this guy from the league office came into the clubhouse to talk to us about spikes. He said he thought the spikes many of us was using was too large. He said that when he was playing they was only half as big and just as good. I don't know for sure when exactly he was playing but ever since I played they was the same length. He insisted that the spikes we was wearing in them days was what he called "murderous spikes."

Now, of course, the first thing that we all thought of was Ty Cobb, and how he always slid into the bases with his spikes up all. And the year before in the World Series when Snodgrass of the Giants spiked old Frank Baker twice.

It didn't matter, we told this guy, we wasn't about to change because we needed those spikes to get a good footing in the outfield, but he kept telling us he wanted our help in getting the league to change the rules to make the spikes shorter.

It was one of those times when everybody on the team stood together against the league. I guess I had a little something to do with that because I cried the loudest. I didn't want to make no changes. I was going good, and I didn't want to change nothing.

**HARRY DAVIS** It was tough to leave Philadelphia and Mr. Mack, but when the opportunity came to manage, I jumped at it.

As I took over the Cleveland club, I figured we had a good shot at second place. Oh, I kept telling the press that we were prepared to win it all, but actually I figured we had a realistic chance for second and, if all the breaks went our way, an outside chance to take it all. The way I had it figured was this: we were the club Philadelphia had to beat to win its third successive pennant. As far as I was concerned, we had a better ball club than either Boston or Detroit, the two clubs likely to be our strongest challengers.

Detroit lacked pitching. They might have rated an edge at first and short, but not in the outfield where we had Butcher, Graney, Jackson, Birmingham and Ryan. Crawford of the Tigers was 32 and was probably at the tail end of his prime.

Some thought that the Red Sox had the strongest outfield in the league with Speaker, Lewis and Hopper, but I didn't think that they had any batters in the class of Lajoie or Jackson.

We opened the season at home against Detroit. I chose Willie Mitchell to open for us against George Mullin, the Tiger's 18-game winner from the year before. As luck would have it, Cobb came down with a terrible cold on the day of the game, and although he played, he was clearly not himself. He went 0 for 4 and we won 3-2 in 11 innings. Joe was our leading hitter, going 3 for 5.

The largest crowd in the history of the park turned out for the game, and they got their money's worth. Before the first pitch Nap Lajoie was presented with a box of flowers and a diamond studded key chain.

Butcher, Jackson, and Ryan started for me in the outfield.

This looked to me like our strongest lineup but it left out Joe Birmingham. My plan was to use him in a reserve role, and to have him in the coach's box as much as possible. According to all accounts, he was the best strategist on the team, and he knew the players. I planned to use him much as Connie Mack utilized Topsy Hartsel for a couple of seasons.

**JOE JACKSON** I made up my mind I was going to go after Ty Cobb that season in three ways: As a batter, a run-getter and a base runner. Even the year before if Larry wasn't injured so much, I think I would have beaten Ty as a run-getter.

Don't get me wrong, Ty was a great ball player and all, but I thought I could get more hits and score more runs than he could. Oh, maybe he could steal more bases than I could, but I knew I could give him a battle for that honor, too.

In 1911 I was mostly a right field hitter. I made a few hits to left or center, but most of my safe drives went to right. So, in spring training the next season I switched my batting style a little. They got to playing me in right so I was determined to mix them up and hit as much to left as to right. Now and then I wanted to sandwich one in to center.

I know a lot of folks didn't figure I thought of things like that, but I sure did.

**HARRY DAVIS** We caught a little luck early on in the season when Cobb refused to play a game because of a quarrel with a hotel clerk. It seems one day he left the Detroit club in a huff after getting into a row with the management of the Chicago Beach Hotel. He packed his bags and took the 10:40 train to Detroit.

We were set to play them again in a couple of days, but by the time we got to Detroit, he was back with the team.

**CHARLES SOMERS** We were scheduled to open Navin Field, Detroit's great new park. Detroit planned big doings, including a parade, speeches on the diamond, some celebrity throwing out the first ball, and a banquet in the evening. But, the best laid plans of men .... It rained for days, and it looked like we might have the entire four-game series rained out.

The Detroit baseball club spent several hundred thousand dollars in constructing the new plant. Had it spent maybe $2,000 more and purchased a large tarpaulin, such as we used in Cleveland, we might have played the opening game as scheduled.

After several days sitting around the hotel, it finally cleared enough for us to get in one game, albeit on a soggy field.

Harry was undecided about whether Joe would play or not. His arm was a trifle sore, the result of cutting lose too early in the damp season. In addition, he had a terrible cold. Harry said "the only way that Joe can be kept out of the game is by hiding his uniform."

"I believe," Joe said, "that there are over 100 hits in that uniform. I ought to get that many in 75 games. My cold has made me not too good, but as quick as we get a few warm days I'll get better again."

That said it all about Joe a far as I am concerned. Joe played in that first game in Navin Field, and he played well.

**JOE JACKSON** In the fourth inning of a game against the Tigers in late April I came up against Sleepy Bill Burns. Now Sleepy Bill wasn't much of a pitcher. I think he won one game that whole year. Anyways, he threw an inside fastball that hit me flush on the right elbow, and hurt like hell. I dropped immediately to the ground and Doc White came out to look at me. He said it wasn't broke, but I couldn't stay in the game.

Later in the locker room he said that it looked to him like one of the muscles in my arm was tore away from the bone. He also said that he was afraid that the ball had pressed my "crazy" bone against this tube in my arm that supplied some kind of fluid to the elbow joint. He ordered an X-ray examination for when we got back to Cleveland, but told manager Davis that I wouldn't be able to play for at least a week.

Now, there were two things really strange about that night. First of all, it was the night the Titanic sank, so getting your arm hurt didn't seem that important when so many people lost their lives. Second, the man who almost broke my arm, Sleepy Bill Burns, broke a lot more of me a few years later. He was one person who I wish I never saw.

**WILLIE MITCHELL** Joe got a particular kick out of a photo that was taken of the Tigers during the 1912 season. It seems the Tigers were lined up in their new ball yard for a group photograph one Sunday afternoon. A panorama camera was used. Cobb was fourth from the left end. Cobb, the instant the lens passed him, dashed to the rear of the machine and dug for the other end of the line. He arrived in time to take up a position at the side of Manager Jennings and in the photograph appears there as smiling and as composed as he showed in the fourth place from the left.

I tell you, when Joe saw this, he just cracked up and couldn't stop laughing. You would have thought that was the funniest thing anybody had ever seen.

"I knew Ty was fast," Joe said, "but I didn't know he was that fast."

**HENRY P. EDWARDS** It was, undeniably, a problem-ridden year for the Naps. To claim that they had more than their fair share of injuries would be a gross understatement. Nowhere was the injury bug more apparent than with Lajoie himself. Here was the great player who was struggling to remain in the lineup. At 37, staying healthy was becoming his biggest challenge. He had missed quite a few games in 1911 due to a variety of injuries, but had worked hard during the winter to get back into shape. He was really looking forward to the new season, but early on he reached for a wide throw and felt a sharp pain in his back. He threw down his glove in disgust and walked to the bench. There was some fear that he might not ever play again. The next day on his return to Cleveland he was met by the team doctor at Union Station. Dr. Castle sent him home to South Euclid after strapping his back tightly with adhesive plaster.

He was laid low for some time. When he did return, he had barely gotten warmed up when he received a telegram saying that his mother was seriously ill, so he left right away for Rhode Island to be with her. He returned some days later only to go out with a spike wound. While recuperating from that, his mother passed away and again he left the club.

When he returned from the funeral he went back into the lineup briefly, but after being bruised by a batted ball his left leg became badly infected. This was indicative of the way the entire season was going—high hopes going in, but great disappointments along the way. First base was a problem all season. Davis started with Eddie Hohnhorst there, but he didn't hit his weight, so he tried Lajoie there for a time but, as I said, he kept going down. Joe Birmingham played first some, and Davis himself even took a turn there, but it was clear to all, including the manager, that his best playing days were well behind him. Finally, he brought Art Griggs back, and he played reasonably well.

Catcher was another problem. Steve O'Neill, Ted Easterly, and Paddy Livingston all suffered injuries. Jack Adams was given a shot, too, but while he was a decent enough receiver, he didn't hit. Davis then picked up Freddie Carisch, and, of course, given the way things were going, he quickly went down after a foul tip split open one of his fingers.

Davis was juggling his lineup every day. The only player to see action as a regular all season was Jackson. As the season opened, Lajoie was the clear star of the team; by season's end in was Jackson. By early June he was batting .342; by July 7th, .401. He already had amassed more than 100 hits and led the league in slugging, just ahead of his old teammate, Frank Baker. To look at the American League batting leaders on that date was to look at a list of some of the all-time greats. Jackson's .401 was followed by Cobb's .395, Speaker's .388, Lajoie's, .378, and Eddie Collins' .328.

Jackson was the workhorse of his team, consistently playing well even when hurt. At one point in June, Davis said that Joe was playing with the worst charley horse he had ever seen. In mid-July he bruised his hip badly sliding into second, but he stayed in the lineup. The injury-riddled team needed him, and he knew it.

Despite Joe's heroic efforts, the team was sliding down the standings slowly but steadily. In mid-May they were in third behind Chicago and Boston. By mid-July they were in fifth struggling to keep pace with Detroit, while Boston was showing signs of running away with the flag.

Rumors were rife that Somers was running out of patience with Davis.

**DANNY MURPHY** I was still with the Athletics when Harry took over at Cleveland. We all liked Harry, and since things weren't going too well for him, we decided to do something to show our appreciation. So one day before a game with the Naps, we called him over to the plate and gave him a present—a real nice silver table service that we had all chipped in for. He thanked everybody for it including Joe which was a little awkward because none of us had thought to ask Joe to be a part of the gift.

**WILLIE MITCHELL** It was a lousy season by any standard, most of which I have thankfully forgotten about, but I do remember one particular crazy play. For the first time since he was a member of the Cleveland Club, Lajoie had the experience of seeing an opposing pitcher give an intentional walk to the batter ahead of him. Talk about insane! I mean, remember Larry was still hitting over .375! There were two outs with Graney on third and Olson on second. Jackson was the batter and he had already tripled and singled earlier in the contest. When Quinn, their pitcher, fell behind in the count, he threw two deliberately wide ones to Joe sending him to first and bringing up Larry.

All Larry did was to drive in three runs, but it shows the respect which Joe had earned from opposing pitchers. Walking him to get to the great Lajoie, well that said it all to me right there.

**HARRY DAVIS** Injuries can't be an excuse when a team is going badly. We just weren't playing like we were capable of, so I held a team meeting to let them know how I felt. I told them in no uncertain terms that I was disgusted with their showing to date. I told them they were playing without enthusiasm and that if things didn't change pretty damn fast, there was going to be a major shakeup in the team.

"With a few exceptions, you have quit dead," I shouted at them. "In the spring I patiently waited for the weather to improve, excusing your lack of form on the bad conditions, but I can no longer be patient. The weather is good now, but where is the ginger? You have lost your nerve, and a team in this condition cannot win games. Clevelanders want more than a team that can hold its own with second division clubs and I intend to give it such a team. I can't do it with players putting up the article of ball that you have recently."

The trouble with speeches like that is that it doesn't go for everyone. Larry for instance. I never knew him to give less than his best. Never.

**TED EASTERLY** Harry got on us pretty good, and he had a right to, but he was always making excuses for Joe. He didn't want to believe that Joe goofed up as much as any of us. I guess when you're hitting .400, a lot of sins go unnoticed.

I remember after Harry's big speech everybody on the team went out and knocked themselves out trying to turn the thing around. I got so worked up in one game that I got tossed after I politely informed umpire Dinneen that he didn't know the difference between a balk and a broiled lobster.

It was my way of trying to get things stirred up a little. I couldn't hit .400 but that didn't mean I wasn't going to do everything I could. Harry didn't see that though. He never did. He protected Joe and Larry and jumped all over the rest of us. I'm not sure that is the best way to lead a team.

**HARRY DAVIS** I did what I could. I moved players, benched players, brought up players from the minors. Still we settled into the second division and showed few signs of moving up.

I wanted us to play more aggressively—steal, hit-and-run, that sort of thing. The problem was, we didn't really have a great base runner on the team. Joe was probably the fastest, but he was never what you would call an excellent base stealer. Terry Turner was fast, but he was so darn recalcitrant, I felt like I had to push him off the base to get him going. Olson was quick enough, but you have to get to first before you can steal. As for the others, Lajoie, Griggs, Graney and Birmingham, there wasn't one who could get arrested for exceeding the speed limit.

**TERRY TURNER** You could tell how frustrated Harry was getting as the season went on. Joe was pretty much carrying the team when Larry was out, but the rest of us were struggling.

One afternoon in Philadelphia, where he was still a big favorite, Harry got into a loud argument with an umpire. So loud, in fact, that the ump got a police escort to drag Harry off the field. Now, that's major league frustration.

The next day was his birthday, and we got him a cake, but he got a bigger present from Ban Johnson—an indefinite suspension.

**HENRY P. EDWARDS** The Chalmers trophy competition was still around, but no longer in the format it was when Lajoie and Cobb battled for the car. The company had created a trophy commission, with 11 newspaper men from the big-league towns doing the voting for what amounted to a most valuable player award. I was one of them.

As the season progressed, there was considerable speculation as to who would win it  Cobb more or less eliminated himself. First he got into trouble in a Chicago hotel. Later, the Detroit team went on strike because of his actions and then in one game Ty was in such a hurry to climb into his street clothes he neglected to be on hand when it was his turn to bat in the ninth inning.

With Cobb practically out of the running, most of the attention turned to Tris Speaker and Joe Wood of Boston, Ed Walsh of the White Sox, Frank Baker of the Athletics, Clyde Milan and Walter Johnson of the Nationals, and Joe Jackson.

The odds-on favorites were Speaker and Jackson. Both were having great years. Both hit over .375 just about all season, and between them, they led the league in just about every slugging category—doubles, triples, home runs.

My support was for Joe, because in covering the team every day, I saw what he meant to the franchise. Speaker, though, got the majority of the support, largely because he had his team in first place virtually all season, and so the spotlight was always on him.

There was no doubt, however, that these were two superb players at the height of their playing prowess.

**HARRY DAVIS** It became apparent that I was going to have to find some new blood.

One of the players we brought up in August was a skinny, 21 year-old shortstop from down South—Beaver Dam, Kentucky as I recall. Ray Chapman had been playing for Topsy Hartsel who was then managing down in Toledo. Topsy said he was the class of the American Association. He was at the top of the league in just about everything. He was hitting .329 and had stolen 45 bases. Surprisingly, too, he hit for some power.

He proved right away that he could play in the big leagues. I worked him in at shortstop and he ended up hitting over .300 for us.

He was also a hell of a nice kid. I made sure he and Joe got together some since they were both southerners, and I figured Joe could help him settle in some.

**JOE JACKSON** Ray was a real nice kid and he could play good, too. There was probably nobody on the team that was faster than Ray. I know once he even won a loving cup for being the fastest player in circling the bases. I think he did it in 14 seconds.

He was smart, too. I know many times he would go over and steady the pitcher when the pitcher got riled or something, and he was always thinking about ways to win the game. He was a big help to the team as soon as he come up.

I never roomed with Ray, but we did go out together a few times and had a good time.

**HENRY P. EDWARDS** Davis made some smart changes as the season went on, but the team seemed listless. During the month of August, the team won only eight games and lost 17.

Who was to blame? That's what the fans of Cleveland were asking.

Should the team be entirely rebuilt? Or should there be a change in the management?

It was the lethargic playing that caused many fans to lose heart and remain away from League Park. They realized there was a radical fault with the club but the big question was, were the players overrated? Or was Harry Davis a failure as a manager?

There were plenty of opinions on both sides. Joe was spared most of the criticism. It was generally believed that he was doing everything he could, except maybe providing leadership. But that was never Joe's strong point.

**TED EASTERLY** Look, there was a lot of friction in the clubhouse that season. Most of it didn't make the papers, because we tried to keep those things to ourselves as much as we could. The fact of the matter is, though, that Harry never really got the respect of the players like he should have.

To my way of thinking, Davis was a driver, not a leader. He didn't seem to know the difference between pulling and pushing. He drove Joe and that worked because Joe didn't respond to anything less subtle, but for many of us who had been playing for almost as long as Davis had, we needed leadership, not criticism.

Harry had the habit of blowing up in the dugout before games which didn't exactly inspire us to go out and win for him. He got frustrated and the more frustrated he became, the more he screamed at us. He called us quitters, which wasn't true. All that did, was set us off against him. I mean, couldn't he realize that calling a player a name in the papers isn't a good way to get a player to want to win for him?

Harry made a lot of mistakes. The first was in spring training when he refused to make Joe Birmingham captain. Joe had been of great value to George Stovall in the previous season and deserved the chance, but when he didn't get it, his game went downhill a little bit. I think he was just damn disappointed, and I don't blame him. Instead Harry made Olson captain, and that didn't sit well with us. First of all, he wasn't as smart a baseball man as Birmingham, and second, he wasn't playing worth a damn.

The fact is, Davis had never been a manager before and he did so many things to get us angry with him, that I don't think he ever really had a chance to put a winning team on the field.

It was a frustrating season.

# 33

# IT WAS THE EASIEST MONEY I EVER SEEN

**VAUGHN GLASER** I knew the language of the stage, not the diamond, but I also knew a bit about the language of money. The way I had it figured was that vaudeville audiences would pay to see baseball players on the stage—you know, get a more personal look.

Mike Donlin was the first player of note I signed. For several winters his name flashed prominently over playhouse entrances all around the circuit. After that other players figured out there was a buck to be made on the boards in the offseason. The problem was, a lot of the guys who offered me their services couldn't hit .250 if their life depended on it and that wasn't who the audiences wanted to see. But eventually the bigger names came around and I began doing a brisk booking business.

One of my biggest early acts was the Pearl Sisters in the company of no less renowned diamond heroes as the Athletics trio of Jack Coombs, Chief Bender and Cy Morgan. I got $2,500 a week for that act and that was nothing to sneeze at in those days.

The act was called "learning the game," and a key feature of it was that the players appeared in the exact same uniforms that they played in. At least that's the way we advertised it, and if it wasn't exactly the God's honest gospel all the time, well, chalk it up to the magic of the stage. Kathryn Pearl and Violet Pearl, headed up the act with help from Morgan. Cy was known as the "Minstrel Man" and had worked before as a singer. He spent time coaching Coombs and Bender. Even during the season you could see him working with them in the dugout between innings. I think he really liked it—teaching the others I mean. Coombs took the stage right away and showed unusual ability. Bender's chief claim to theatrical fame was his famous smile.

**JACK COOMBS** Right after I defeated Mathewson at the Polo Grounds in the 1910 Series, two vaudeville agents approached me at the Hotel Somerset with a proposition to break away from the Pearl Sisters act and join another. They said I could bring Bender and Morgan along with me and they offered me a bigger salary but I turned them down flat. A fella's got to honor his commitments. That's the way I look at it. Another time some guy offered me $800 per week for the entire winter burlesque circuit. I turned it down because I had given my word to a Cuban promoter that I would make a trip to Havana for $500 and expenses.

**VAUGHN GLASER** Rube Marquard of the Giants was another flinger who trod the boards. He did a baseball monologue about his part in the World Series. I also put a quartet of Boston Americans together: O'Brien, Bradley, Gardner and McHale. O'Brien was particularly good having spent his winters as a vocalist in moving picture theatre shows. Charley Dooin, manager of the Philadelphia Nationals, and his stage partner Jim McCool also did well because of Dooin's singing voice. Chief Meyers, who sometimes teamed with Christy Mathewson and May Tully had good success with an Indian monologue. The audience always loved Indian bits. Mathewson, though, gave up the stage after a short stint. I think His Highness felt a little above it.

Germany Schafer, who was a natural comedian, carried his diamond humor to the stage with great success. Joe Tinker, the Cub shortstop was another pretty fair Thespian, particularly when he worked with Jules von Tilzer. "Doc" White, the White Sox pitcher, did well as a monologue artist.

I tried like the dickens to get Frank Baker, the home run hitter of the Philadelphia Athletics, to go out on the circuit, but he turned a deaf ear to all of my pleas. He had a family and home in Maryland and steadfastly insisted on returning there every winter. Marty O'Toole I tried to sign when he was the highest priced player, but he spurned me then, and when his career went into reverse he came back wanting to sign, but by then he had little marquee value so, of course, I turned him down.

Without doubt, though, the three biggest sensations in my stable of ball playing actors were the irascible John McGraw, the tempestuous Ty Cobb, and the enigmatic Joe Jackson.

**JOHN McGRAW** I made my stage debut at the Colonial Theatre on October 28, 1912, a memorable date in Theatre annals to be sure. It was a matinee performance, and as soon as I stepped through the curtains, the audience erupted into thunderous applause. It so startled me that I lost my composure for a brief moment before regaining my wits and beginning. It was a hell of a lot tougher facing that kind of audience than a baseball crowd, I can tell you that. At least on the field you had a slew of players to share the attention, but on the stage it was just you and a lot of faces staring back at you. There was no dugout to hide in.

The title of my monologue was "Inside Baseball" so I talked a little about scientific ball as I knew it, which I described as nothing more than three or four players working together to fool the opposition. I talked about Christy Mathewson, saying "There never was and never will be another pitcher like Matty." I told amusing stories and never failed to get a laugh with any of them. Mostly what the audience wanted to hear was my take on other players, and Joe Jackson was as requested a topic as any player in the game. Joe had quickly established himself as a figure of intrigue. Although I was managing in a different league, everyone knew I held an opinion about everybody. Joe had the talent, I told the audience, but I didn't know about his heart. Still if he applied himself he could go a long way. "But, my friends," I said, "that's a mighty big 'if.'" Joe was a player everybody loved to feel smarter than. That was big part of his popularity.

**VAUGHN GLASER** Between the 1911 and 1912 seasons, I scored what was up to that time, my biggest coup. George Ade had written a play called "The College Widow" which I thought could be a box office winner with the right cast. Oh yeah, there were plenty of actors around who could fill the bill, actors being a dime a dozen in my business, but I was looking for someone . . . special. Ty Cobb was special.

I approached Ty with the idea not really knowing what to expect. Ty was immediately receptive, but wanted to change two things—money and the role. Ty was a good businessman, always trying to get the edge. Nobody could put anything over on him. Not on the field and not in life. The lead role in the play was a football playing son of a railroad president who attends a Baptist college. The father returns from a trip abroad to find the boy a football hero of a rival Methodist college, a situation created by the president's charming daughter who had induced him to remain.

On learning that his son has been the chief architect of the winning game against the Baptist college, the father gets off the funniest line of the play when he bellows, "Well, you're a hell of a Baptist."

Someone once said it was the only time Ty Cobb took that kind of abuse from anyone without striking back. Ty was a Baptist but in this particular case he was being paid to take it, and Ty loved to be paid, maybe more than anything else.

We agreed to rewrite the play as a baseball play. I got Paul Armstrong, the well-known play doctor, to do the revisions.

Ty was to be a star outfielder, a brilliant hitter and daring base runner—an easy piece of casting to be sure. In the ninth inning of the crucial game against the Baptist college he would come to bat with what else but the bases loaded and his team down by three runs. Well, I hardly need to tell you what happens next. All the girls and college boys were to gather around and adore Ty who would lean on his bat in the happy, careless, but threateningly alert way he had, and absorb the adoration for which he will be paid. In the end, of course, it is announced that everything is arranged between Tyrus and the president's daughter at which point the curtain would come down, the audience would go home happy, and we would go home a little wealthier for the experience.

When Ty agreed to do it I knew we had a winner. I had known Ty for a number of years and I knew he was far from being the rowdy he was often painted. All that talk about using his spikes to cut down players, for instance, was overdone. Part of it was for advertising purposes, for there are many people who will go to a ballgame only when they think there's going to be trouble. Part of it was inspired by jealousy. But all of that was beside the mark. The point is that Cobb was an intelligent man who had plenty of fire and spirit and wasn't afraid to work hard to become an actor.

He had no training that fit him for the stage, but in "The College Widow" he didn't have to do much acting. In the business the part he played is known as a "walking part." About all he had to do was come onstage and be himself. He was young, lithe, good looking, famous, and that pretty much was what was required, provided he could read his lines decently, and he could. He didn't make anybody forget Booth, or Edmund Kean or Forbes Robertson or even Eddie Foy, but I'll tell you something I've never said before, at least in public: I wasn't at all sure he didn't have a "Hamlet" in him that would surface sometime after his hitting stroke deserted him. Had he committed himself to it, I do think he could have managed it. Ty was one of those people who, once they set their targets, never stop until they hit the mark.

The Georgia Peach was popular enough in Detroit and the North, but once we got down South with the show, well, you should have seen the reaction. The audience sown there thought more of Tyrus than they did of President Taft.

Now what made the show so popular was Cobb, but it didn't hurt any that we also had in the cast, one Joseph Jefferson Jackson, the shoeless wonder.

I mentioned the idea one day to Ty, almost as a passing joke, but he thought the idea had merit.

"Why not," he said. "The two greatest southern stars together on the stage. I kind of like it. Besides, playing next to Joe, I'm bound to look good."

I think that's what he liked about the idea. He thought the slow-witted Joe would make his performance positively inspired by comparison, and he wasn't far wrong. That and the fact that he knew we'd sell more tickets. Ty had a real nose for the dollar.

We figured Joe couldn't possibly memorize lines no less read them, so we found a good little part for him without any. Mostly he had to stand around and look at Ty. To tell the truth, he was pretty bad, but what the hell, he sold tickets and that, after all, was what the show was about.

Later I came in for criticism from some bleeding heart types who said I was just exploiting poor Joe, that he was nothing but a side-show freak! You bet I was. That's what a promoter does, but remember, I didn't make him do it. I offered him decent money and he said yes. Besides, face it, Joe was a bit of a freak in some ways so if he could make a few bucks off that, why the hell not?

Working with the two of them couldn't have been more different. Ty checked the books every night, and if there was a dime out of place, he called me on it. Joe took what I gave him every week and never asked a question. Ty challenged everything he was told, Joe followed every order to a tee.

They got along pretty well though—Ty and Joe—even though Ty and the others in the cast sometimes lost patience with having to explain everything to him. I mean it was a pretty complicated business this touring theatre routine. We played eight performances a week and were always on the go, moving from town to town from theatre to theatre. To keep things moving along smoothly, the general manager of the company would post a sheet every morning listing the day's schedule—things like checking out of the hotel, meeting at the train station, checking into a new hotel, sound check in the new theatre, speed-run through rehearsals, meal breaks and lots more. Naturally, somebody had to read all of this to Joe. Sometimes they had to remind him several times during the day. Once he missed a performance in Wilmington because he was late for the train down from Baltimore. All of this wore on the company some, but we managed to get Joe through the season somehow, and we all made a few bucks in the process.

**JOE JACKSON** When I was playing for the Pels down in New Orleans, I got to see real vaudeville shows a couple of times and I thought they was lots of fun. So when Mr. Glaser told me he would pay me to be in one of his shows with Ty Cobb and I didn't even have to say nothing, well that was the easiest money I ever seen in my life. I mean I got paid to play ball and that wasn't easy, but standing on a stage and looking at Ty and getting good money to do it was.

I asked Katie what she thought and she said it looked like a better way to make money during the winter than going back to Greenville and working in Father's butcher shop or in the mill again. So that's what I did.

**DAVEY JACKSON** When Joe didn't come home after the 1911 season, we was all a bit miffed, thinking he was acting like a big shot. But now when I think of it, I probably would have done the same thing so I can't blame him too much.

**DEACON McGUIRE** We were all surprised to see Joe go on the vaudeville circuit after the season because we thought he'd skedaddle back to South Carolina at the drop of a hat, but the fact that he didn't meant, I guess, that he was losing some of the homesickness. It looked like we had a good chance of seeing him again next season.

# 34

# I HEARD THE SPEECHES

**CHARLIE LEBEAU** Never before in this land of the free had we known an entity such as organized baseball. It was a trust which owed its very existence to the fact that it had been able to secure an absolute monopoly of flesh and blood. Its power derived not from its real estate holdings or from its franchising ability but from its dominion over the men who drew the money to the box offices—the players. Its hold on the players was absolute and unconditional.

Seventy years earlier, the game was being played by "gentlemen" organized into sporting clubs. Its financial implications were minimal, limited mostly to the dues of its members and the expenses of putting on matches. There was little to recommend it to those with capitalistic entrepreneurial instincts.

Then in the late 1860s came the advent of that odd duck known as the semi-professional. Ostensibly he was as pure an amateur athlete as anyone since the days of the naked Greek wrestlers, but in practice he was often nothing but trouble in cleats. Semi-professional baseball was a scandal-ridden. cheat-driven game someplace just the other side of boxing and horse racing. Paid but a pittance, the players were easy prey for the gamblers who were attracted to the game like flies to cow dung.

Any time an athlete is poorly paid, the opportunity for him to add to his coffers by discretely influencing the outcome of a game is likely to come his way. So it did to the semi-pros, resulting in a myriad of scandals, semi-scandals, and an assortment of mayhem from which the game barely escaped.

Escape it did though, thanks to that aggregation of marvelous whiskered athletes known as the Cincinnati Red Stockings who convinced enough people to pay to see them have fun that they eventually deigned to call themselves professional baseball players. Of course it didn't hurt that one year they played 57 games, winning 56 and tying one. Fans are always more willing to pay for winners.

Then in 1871, the National Association of Professional Baseball players was formed, signaling the death knell of the semi-pro. The idea was to make the game better. It didn't. The organization was run by players but players are players because they possess certain skills, none of which are necessarily related to organizational abilities. They professed intentions of grappling with the twin evils of gambling and intemperance, but their efforts were as disorganized as they were futile.

It was whispered—and not all that quietly either—that at some games as much as $20,000 was being handled on bets. It was claimed and believed that certain star players could be "handled." In a show of bravado but little tact, the president of the Association, a squat second baseman for the New York Mutuals, even created a minor riot by accusing several known gamblers of trying to "buy" the players! Everyone knew it was being done, but you weren't supposed to say so. That seemed to be a bigger sin than the gambling act itself.

Chaos reigned. Riots were common, liquor was freely sold at games, teams kept their dates only if convenient, and most of the players lived from hand to mouth on the gate receipts which they divided after each game.

Enter William A. Hulbert and associates who formed the National League with the expressed intent of creating order out of chaos and profit out of investment. To do so they immediately lifted the burden of business administration off the shoulders of the players leaving them to do what they did best—play ball.

Now we had an employer/employee relationship, and as one might expect, the employer set the rules to his advantage and even gave himself a whip to see that the rules were followed. Nobody, but nobody argued that the whip was unneeded.

Hulbert and his buddies recognized that they needed an iron-clad system to restrict players from jumping ship at the first showing of a $50 note, said practice being the norm at the time. Many a team was all but wrecked by a rival manager's offer of a few dollars to defect to another team. The new league decreed that the punishment for contract-jumping would be expulsion with no hope of reinstatement. At the same time, a ban was placed on the sale of liquor at the parks and a full-scale attack was leveled at the gamblers.

The new league acted quickly and decisively by heaving out of the league, two of its most powerful and prosperous clubs—the New York Mutuals and the Philadelphia Athletics—for neglecting to make western trips and play out the schedule. Soon after that, the league fired its first real salvo at the gamblers. Hulbert obtained proof that four of the best players on the Louisville team had been in collusion with gamblers. "Gentlemen George" Hall, Bill "Butcher" Craver, Al "Slippery Elm" Nichols, and Jim "Terror" Devlin were said to be the culprits. When Devlin confessed, Hulbert banned all four from baseball forever. The players cried that they only threw the games because their owner had failed to pay them their salaries, but public sentiment was decidedly against them, and the ban remained.

**JIM DEVLIN** We weren't getting paid, that's all there was to it, so we thought we had to do something so that we could live. I mean you can't live on nothing, now, can you?

I tried to get back into baseball, but nothing doing. One paper called us "slippery roosters, artful dodgers, eels of a superlative degree of lubrication, little jokers whom now we see and now we don't—a bad crowd."

We were real stupid to have done what we did, but we certainly paid the price for it.

**CHARLIE LEBEAU** Devlin was a particularly tragic figure who begged for years to get back into the game. He even begged club owners to let him become a groundskeeper. He died a few years later at 34. Several papers wrote that he was a perfect example of the fruits of crookedness. It was the first big baseball scandal.

I always meant to ask Joe if he knew about the Devlin affair. I'd like to think he didn't.

**CHARLES SOMERS** Allegations of impropriety continued to be leveled during Joe's time in Cleveland. Everywhere he turned he heard stories about someone trying to make a fast and easy buck off the game. Ticket scalping during the World Series became a big issue. It was illegal but thousands of fans were engaging in it and all were making money. At one point a warrant charging grand larceny was sworn out by a William Gordon for the arrest of Walter Calvin, alleged to have embezzled $1,050 for speculating purposes. Calvin claimed he would get 50 tickets for each game from Harry Davis. Before the Series opened, Gordon sent a certified check for $1,050 made out to "Capt. Harry Davis, Philadelphia Baseball Club." Gordon never saw the tickets.

There was, of course, no charge against Davis. If a player could make an extra buck on the game, legal or not, nobody seemed to object.

Of equal concern were the constant and insidious inroads into the game by professional gamblers. A severe threat was posed to the game when in 1912, the Western Commission Company, a poolroom concern operating out of Newport, Kentucky, announced it was inaugurating a scheme to take wagers on baseball. It immediately sent price sheets all over the country quoting the odds-on the chances of the National and American leagues as well as on the American Association.

Now I don't have to tell you that this immediately got the attention of the club owners as well as the league officials. This pretentious play by the ring of gamblers who had been taking bets on horse racing for some time came as a big shock to all of us. We knew without even discussing it, that if gambling took hold of baseball it would signal the end of the game. Betting on horses who can't react to the bets is one thing, but betting on men, with all their imperfections is quite another. We had to squelch this plan and squelch it fast.

One problem which immediately arose was that since the gambling operation was centered in Kentucky, we were powerless to take any legal action, for in fact we had no jurisdiction over any betting that took place outside the ballparks. Nevertheless, we could not and would not sit still for this scheme.

At a hastily-called owners' meeting I averred that any move to put the game on a par with horse racing would bring disaster. Chairman August Herrmann of the National Baseball Commission took up the cudgels immediately. He told us that the Western Commission Company had already secured a lease on a building in Newport and they had acquired a prominent lawyer to represent them.

Herrmann managed to get telegraph companies to promise not to deliver telegrams to members of this company and a promise from the express companies to refuse packages to them. If they try to use the mails, he assured us, the United States would move against them in the federal courts.

Herrmann was a great one for bombastic speech giving. "It will be made plain to all," he announced, "that gambling and baseball are incompatible; that no real friend of wholesome, clean sport will sanction gambling on this sport, and that anyone placing his money is doing so without protection from anyone connected with organized baseball."

We all agreed that stringent measures had to be put in place to make sure that the players understood that they must have nothing to do with men or their agents who make wagers on ballgames. To that end I called a meeting of the Cleveland players and I talked at some length of the dangers of associating with known gamblers. All the players were there, including Joe, when I said that anyone caught in the company of such men would invite scandal and that ballplayers, who had worked to keep the game honest and above suspicion, would have to look to the character of their associates.

I told them how in 1876, President Hulbert of the National League found it necessary to blacklist several players on the Louisville club for throwing games. I told them point-blank, "Keep away from any person or persons connected with betting. Failure to do so will result in you being thrown out of the game."

I can't tell you who in that room took me to heart, but I can tell you this: they were all there and I spoke more than loud enough for all to hear.

**THOMAS J. LYNCH** I was president of the National League when the Newport betting syndicate sprang up and while I was concerned about it, I never really believed it would take hold. I felt that any baseball fan who took the time to read over the odds and quotations would see that it was simply another one of those sure-thing, quick-touch affairs and would toss the paper into the wastebasket and think no more about it. The baseball public knew a lot more about the game than it did 20 years earlier and understood that it was perfectly on the level.

I gave interview after interview stating emphatically that it was absolutely impossible to make baseball crooked. The game itself was straight and the least suspicion of underhanded work would be easily detected. A player of 1912 wouldn't dare to consort with gamblers. The penalty would be too great. He would be banned for life, and what gambler could offer a player inducement enough to make him take a chance that would mean the loss of his livelihood? Only a very, very stupid one is the only answer to that question.

**TED EASTERLY** Oh, we heard all kinds of speeches that year about gambling. We all thought the speeches were pretty stupid. We sat there and listened because we had to, but we knew what we were doing, and no owner was going to tell us how to behave off the field.

I know lots of guys that put down a bet or two on a game once in a while and the world didn't come to an end.

**JOE JACKSON** I sort of remember Mr. Somers giving so many speeches about gambling that after a while you kind of stop listening. Besides, I don't know anybody on that team that was really interested in gambling.

**CHARLES SOMERS** Let me be real clear about this so as to set the record straight. Everybody on that team heard me say on numerous occasions, that any player caught associating with known gamblers would be barred from the game for life.

Maybe the key word here is "caught," and maybe some of them thought that since they were skillful enough at playing the game, they were skilled enough to avoid getting caught.

At any rate, there was enough pressure put on the syndicate that after a while, they announced they were retiring from taking bets on baseball. With that, questions about the integrity of the game were put aside—temporarily.

**THOMAS J. LYNCH** About the time of the betting syndicate hubbub, another issue concerning the integrity of the game arose. Horace Fogel, owner of the Philadelphia club in the National League, made some public statements which cast doubt on the honesty of the game. The most damaging was a statement that in September of the previous year, after the Giants had defeated the Phillies in both games of a doubleheader, the National League was fixed for the Giants to win and that several umpires were giving all close decisions to the Giants.

The league took immediate action against Mr. Fogel and excluded him from further participation in League activities.

The message should have been clear to fan and player alike: the institution of baseball had become strong enough to withstand any threat to its integrity.

Unfortunately, a few people either didn't hear, or didn't believe the message.

# 35

## I CAME IN SECOND AGAIN

**JACK GRANEY** During spring training for the 1913 season, everybody on the team got a letter from Ban Johnson, the American League president, saying that no players were going to be allowed to write articles for papers.

I read the letter to Joe.

"It is not the intention to infringe upon the rights of players, but alleged expert criticism and ball playing do not mix. I would not mind so much if the players themselves wrote the stuff which appears in the newspapers throughout the land, but in the great majority of cases the players never see the stories to which their names are appended until after they have been printed. These writings frequently have been an injury to the league and if it can be done—and I think it can—no American League player will be allowed to write these criticisms in the future."

Joe got a big kick out of that letter.

"Damn," he said cracking everybody in the clubhouse up, "there goes my career as a writer."

Then we got another letter saying that any player known to have signed newspaper contracts will be summoned before the league and told they will be heavily fined if their names appear signed to baseball contracts.

"I wonder how much they'll fine me?" asked Joe again showing an unusual sense of humor about his illiteracy.

**HENRY P. EDWARDS** At the beginning of the 1913 season there was a flap about the reporting of baseball games in the papers. The argument was started by Charles A. Comiskey, owner of the Chicago White Sox. He came out arguing for what he called "clean, plain English reporting" and against "the vernacular which obscures facts and wearies the reader who wants to know merely who won the game and how it was done. For this," declared Mr. Comiskey, "plain prose English, such as Milton or Macaulay might have used, suffices."

But it doesn't. Every sport has its own peculiar vocabulary, but there is none among them that boasts the rich, crackling, onomatopoetic morsels that the describers of diamond doings have evolved. Baseball slang was developed for descriptive purposes.

On the other hand, there are the Joe Jacksons of the world, for whom that kind of argument might have been in a foreign language. For Joe, the simple facts were enough. He understood winning and losing, and what batting averages meant. I always wondered, though, if he wasn't missing some of the great pleasures and nuances of the game precisely because he didn't have a vocabulary sufficiently detailed or flexible enough to describe it, even to himself. After all, doesn't the scope of our thinking depend to some extent on the scope of our vocabulary? And isn't vocabulary expanded by our reading?

**JOE JACKSON** In the winter Mr. Somers sent a contract, which me and Katie went over real careful. At first we decided to ask for more, but the more I thought about it, the less I really wanted to hold out, and I knowed I couldn't go to spring training unless I had a signed contract so I signed it and sent it to the club. I think Katie still wanted me to get more, but I figured there would be other years to do that.

The first part of the spring training was down in Pensacola, Florida, then we all went up to New Orleans. I always liked that town and me and Katie, we talked about settling down there when my playing days were behind me.

**HENRY P. EDWARDS** As the season was about to begin, the Cleveland fans were speculating not so much whether Joe Birmingham, their new manager, would make good, but whether Lajoie had enough left to help.

It was clear to everyone, that Larry and Joe were the heart and soul of the team. Larry was as beloved a figure as the Cleveland sporting world had ever known, and Joe, while not of that stature, certainly had proven himself as a premier player. No longer were there questions about Joe's ability to play in the big leagues. Oh, there were still plenty of questions about his intelligence, but certainly not his talent.

**CHARLIE LEBEAU** Many players carried bundles of superstitions about bats. One I remember who was particularly absorbed with these superstitions was Monte Cross, a pretty fair shortstop around the turn of the century. He used to study the positions of the assorted bats sprawled out in front of the bench. If the handles of any two were crossed, he knew that his team would lose the game. If the ends of several of them stuck out beyond the others, that indicated the number of runs they would score that inning.

Some players like Cincinnati's Billy Bottenus believed implicitly that every bat contained a certain number of hits and no more. The trick was to know when to discard a bat because the hits were used up.

I know at one point Joe had 18 bats and he treated each one of them as if they were people. I can remember "Old Ginril," "Big Jim," "Caroliny," and, of course, the great one, "Black Betsy." Each bat had certain attributes as well as certain shortcomings and limitations.

I once heard Joe say of "Big Jim:" "He's coming along good for a young feller, but I ain't got much faith in him. Trouble is, he ain't been up against big league pitching very long."

At the end of one season I came upon Joe busy packing his black bats into several carrying cases. Joe insisted he was taking them home to South Carolina with him for the winter because, "Anybody with any sense knows that bats are like ballplayers. They hate cold weather."

He also collected hairpins. He would pick up every pin he could find until his pockets bulged with them. If his hitting happened to fall off, he would complain the "charm" had worn off and he would throw out the whole lot of them. When he found another one—the rustier the better—he knew his batting would pick up and he would start a new collection. And you know what? It usually did.

**JOE JACKSON** Going into the 1913 season I was happy with what I had done, but still there was something in the back of my mind about wanting to settle down some day. I was on the go ever since I was 15 years old and though I enjoyed traveling with the team, I was looking forward to a time when Katie and me could get away from the bustle and hustle of it all. I started dreaming of going back down South and buying a farm someplace far from the whirly-twirly of city life.

**JACK GRANEY** One day just before the season was about to start, Bill Blackwood, who was secretary of the club, was quarantined with a case of small pox. Word came down that we might all have to get vaccine shots. I never saw Joe run so fast in my life. He was out the clubhouse door like he thought he was Ty Cobb streaking for home plate. The reason I know this is because I was right on his heels. That always struck me as amusing—two big guys afraid of a little ol' needle. Joe and I got a big kick out of that later.

I remember another funny thing happening with Joe. Well, it wasn't really funny, but at the time it set us off laughing. One day we heard that Fred Perrine—everybody called him "Bull"—an umpire in the league for a number of years, had been committed to an insane asylum. Now Joe, who had had a couple of run ins with Bull at first started laughing when I read the story to him, but then he stopped suddenly.

"That's not really funny, is it?" he asked.

"No, it's pretty sad, if you want to know the truth," I said.

We thought about that for a moment, then we both started laughing out loud again. We just couldn't help it. But we didn't mean anything by it. Joe wasn't a mean guy, and neither was I, but something just struck us funny about an umpire locked up in a loony bin.

**IVY OLSON** Some writer who couldn't find anything better to do with himself one afternoon came into the locker room while we were waiting out a rain delay and wanted to know what each of us planned to do during the next offseason. Doc Johnston said he was going to build a new house to replace the one that burned to the ground a few weeks earlier; Terry Turner was going to take care of his invalid wife; Cy Falkenberg was going to stay in Cleveland and run a bowling alley. Several of the players indicated they planned to travel—Johnny Bassler to Australia, Jack Graney to Japan. Ray Chapman had the best answer, though. He was going to spend the winter working as a sewer inspector in some dinky town in Illinois. Lajoie said he was going to spend the winter watching hockey games and shoveling snow.

Joe said, "I am going to work out one hour each morning so I can keep my batting eye in shape." And he meant it. It was probably also the most inventive thing he could come up with.

**JOE BIRMINGHAM** I had reasonable expectations that we would at the very least finish in the first division. In spring training, however, we didn't show much evidence of it. At one point we were down in New Orleans and we played a series with our minor league affiliate, the Pelicans. Well, to put it mildly, they thrashed us good. One of our problems was that after Joe and Larry, our batting fell off dramatically. In this series they didn't hit and we didn't win.

Returning to the De Soto hotel after the final game, I found a note which had been slipped under my door. It was apparently from a disgruntled fan.

"Your team is rotten. I never saw such a bunch of boobs on a ball field in my life. If you finish above last place it will be a big wonder to me. The only player you have who doesn't stink is Joe Jackson."

They always did like Joe in New Orleans!

**BAN JOHNSON** There was a lot of talk in 1913 about the length of the games. Although most games were completed in under two hours, some ran as much as 2 1/2 hours or even longer. Accordingly, I issued instructions to the umpires calculated to shorten the games. As was the custom, umpires waited for balls hit into the stands to be tossed back and placed in play again. I asked for the patrons of the game to assist by handing balls hit into the stands to the ushers instead of throwing them onto the field and the balls to be returned to the umpires between half innings.

The thought was that a faster game would be a more appealing game to our public.

**JOE BIRMINGHAM** The Baseball Players Fraternity supported the idea that the baseball fans of America wanted to see the games shortened. The argument went like this: it was a bad year financially for baseball, and the fans were not as enthusiastic as they had been in previous years, so it was up to the players to make the game as attractive to the public as possible. We all know a long drawn out game, especially when the result is determined in the early innings, loses much of its attractiveness.

President Fultz of the Fraternity visited the teams and gave a long speech in the locker room.

He told the players that they needed to hurry to and from positions, and avoid unnecessary arguments with umpires. He also said that pitchers needed to consume as little time as possible in preparing for their delivery. He called slow games, a "growing evil."

**JOE JACKSON** President Fultz told us to make the games go faster, but baseball just ain't a fast game. That's one of the good things about it. I thought fans came out to the park because they wanted to see a game. If they was in such a hurry to get home, why did they come out in the first place? Me, I liked to play baseball and had no interest in seeing the games made shorter. I would have played all day if I could of. All that stuff about shorter games was poppycock if you ask me. Make the games longer was what I wanted to do.

**JOE BIRMINGHAM** One of the things that I figured we could do better that year, was steal bases. Ray Chapman was an excellent base stealer, and Doc Johnston wasn't too bad either. Joe had the speed, but he never really applied himself to the art of stealing, so that spring I talked to Larry about challenging Joe in the speed department. I thought that might get Joe a little more motivated.

Larry went up to Joe and told him flat out that it was his intention to steal more bases than Joe that year.

"I'll show some of these American League catchers whether I'm slow or not," he announced, "and I'll certainly steal more bases than you."

The year before Joe had stolen 35 bases, and Larry 18, so he had a ways to go before he could catch his considerably younger teammate. It was a great idea, and for a while Joe applied himself to studying the pitcher's motions a little more closely. During the season though Larry could only manage 17. Joe ended up stealing 26. What I should have done, of course, was have Chapman offer the challenge.

Joe often took things literally. He beat Larry because that's what he had to do, and he was satisfied with what he had done. I think though, in hindsight, base running is the one area where Joe never quite lived up to his potential.

**JOE JACKSON** You know what I remember most about the opening day in 1913? The team picture. What was so odd about that is that there was this superstition that a team never had its picture taken on opening day. Never! It was considered bad luck, but the manager said, "Nonsense, you lose games because you play bad ball, not because you had your picture taken on opening day."

Since he was a new manager, I sure hoped he knowed what he was doing.

**JOE BIRMINGHAM** It was obvious that the key to the club was the health and productivity of Jackson and Lajoie, and both looked fit and ready. Our infield was better than it was the year before, and our pitching and catching staffs compared favorably with the other teams in the league.

I avoided making any public predictions at the beginning of the season. I had no intention of venturing out on a limb by going on record and stating what I thought we would cop. If I would have said I expected us to win it all, then the press and the fans would have held me to that, and anything less would have come down on me. If I would have said I didn't expect us to do well, then the players would have come down on me. Either way, I lose.

Actually, however, I figured that if Joe and Larry stayed healthy, we had as good a shot as anyone.

The season opened with a 3 to 1 win over Chicago. Joe got three extra base hits. In the second game, he went 0 for 4 and we lost. It looked to me as if that was going to be the story all season long.

**JOE JACKSON** One thing that drove me crazy that season was all the games called before we was finished because the other team had to catch an early train to another city.

Some of us complained a little to Mr. Somers and he took it up with the league. Anyway, the league said that they wouldn't let that happen no more. I know once we played Detroit Friday morning and then again that afternoon, and then after that Detroit had to catch a train to St. Louis for a Saturday game. Well, the Friday afternoon game ran long, so instead of calling the game, they made them get a special train so they could get to St. Louis. We was all glad about that.

**IVY OLSON** Once we all went out to look at the new cars. Joe was particularly fond of the Cole 6-60. So was Birmingham, for that matter. The two Joes, they were among the first players I remember who owned their own cars. Not that they ever took any of us for rides or anything.

**BAN JOHNSON** In 1913 I had to clamp down on the rampant use of profanity by the players. I suspended quite a few that season for profane and vicious language on the playing field. Foul language is obviously always going to be a part of the ball player's stock and trade, but when it gets back to the public we have a problem.

Joe, I must say, never got busted for bad language. Not that he didn't use it, but he had enough problems with his public image as it was, so he was pretty careful in public.

**JOE BIRMINGHAM** Thanks to Joe we got off to a great start and were running neck and neck with Philadelphia for most of the early going. Gone was the tentative, starry-eyed youth of a season or two ago, replaced by a confident, modestly aggressive, brilliant hitting outfielder. He may not have been as secure in his relationships with the public, the press and the fans, but he certainly had come into his own as a superlative player.

Joe never gave me any problems other than when he lost concentration in a game, which he did from time to time.

I seldom had any long conversations with Joe because that just wasn't his style, but right from the start he seemed to accept me as a manager. I say that because that was not the case with everyone. When you come up through the ranks as a player and then you move up to managing the same guys you once played with, well that occasionally caused some conflicts.

**HENRY P. EDWARDS** The Naps got off the snide better than most of us expected. Joe Birmingham seemed to have gotten the players' attention and Jackson was positively on fire. He was primarily playing right field with player/manager Birmingham patrolling center.

Lots of hitters maintain high averages in the early days of the season, only to have the average plummet as the season wears on. Joe, however, kept his average well above .450 as the season headed into the warm days of summer.

I remember one particular game that combined all the essentials of farce, burlesque, melodrama and tragedy. The St. Louis Browns supplied the burlesque, the Naps the comedy, Umpire Ferguson the tragedy, and George Stovall, then the manager of the Browns, the melodrama.

Angered that his own error at first base had given Cleveland the lead, the boss of the Browns took exception to a strike called on him by Umpire

Ferguson. He argued the point so forcibly that he was ordered from the grounds. As he went he pulled Ferguson's cap off the umpire's head. Five minutes later when the inning was over, he allowed his temper to carry him too far. Walking back on the field ostensibly to get his glove, he spit on the umpire's shoulder as he was passing.

The Naps picked up on this and for the rest of the game reminded the umpire of his travails.

"It's not raining is it Ferguson? You look a little damp."

"I was thinking of spit shining my shoes, Ferguson. What do you think?"

I remember Joe's contribution: "You're the spitting image of a good ump, you know that?" Joe always tried to join in on these witticism competitions.

Of course, Stovall was fined and suspended.

Joe related a story once to me about a time during the winter when he was visiting relatives some 40 miles from Greenville. Some college boys nearby were playing a practice game. Joe asked if he could take part. Nothing doing. They coldly told him they did not have any time to waste on showing a rube like him the finer points of the game.

The next day, Joe asked them again. This time the college boys were short a man. They consented. When asked what position he could play, Joe replied: "I could play that position between second and third base I think."

In the third inning he came to bat. The pitcher threw one right down the middle. Joe swung. As the ball disappeared over the trees in right field, Joe threw down his bat and walked off, yelling: "There, blast you. I'm Joe Jackson and I hit over .400 in the American League."

**CLARK GRIFFITH** To win a pennant, a club has to use brains, and that Nap team with Joe as its leader seemed to forget what brains were good for on the baseball field. They got away with a lot of poor baseball because of their batting, but ultimately their bone-headed plays caught up with them. Joe was perfect for the Naps, and they for him. It was one of the most talented, but dumbest teams I ever saw.

I was managing Washington in those days, and I can tell you that nobody liked the Naps. They seemed to be a low-class bunch of dumb athletes. All except Larry, of course. He was the class of that organization. Ray Chapman, too, I guess he was OK. Joe was the most talented, but stupid. The rest of them, well they just didn't act like a quality team.

**JOE JACKSON** In the middle of the season this sports writer wrote a long story saying that Jack Graney got into a fight with a bunch of guys from the team. Some people, they liked to say that there was a lot of trouble on our team, but there really wasn't. Oh, not all of the guys got along real good, but it wasn't like we was fighting all the time.

I'll tell you what happened with Jack and his fight. What happened was that Jack was riding on a street car, reading his paper, but he didn't notice that his paper was rubbing up against the neck of the man sitting in the seat in front of him. This man, who was maybe 250 pounds or more, got annoyed, grabbed the paper out of Jack's hands, and threw it out the window. Ol' Jack he could get his dander up real easy and he started to swing at the man but then he noticed that the man was wearing glasses, so he stopped. He was still mad so what he did was he grabbed the man's hat and throwed that out the window.

When they started shouting at each other, the driver stopped the car and the two of them got off but kept jawing at each other in the street. Jack begged the stranger to take his glasses off, but the man was too smart for that. What he did, though, was to swing at Jack, and hit him in the cheek, making one of his eyes all red. Jack started wrestling with him to get his glasses off, but before he could do that, a policeman came along and stopped them. When the policeman asked me what happened, I told him and he let Jack go.

Now that's what really happened, not what you might have read in the papers.

Ballplayers lots of times got into scrapes like that, but usually when the writers got hold of the story, they made it into something it wasn't.

**JOE BIRMINGHAM** One problem we had that season was that when Larry was out, opposing pitchers took advantage of that to walk Joe. We were in effect, deprived of both of our great players and put the burden of driving in runs on Buddy Ryan, who followed him in the batting order.

This is often what happens when you have one great hitter like Joe in the lineup and nobody to protect him. Joe didn't like it one bit, and he let me know about it all right.

**JOE JACKSON** I thought I could win the batting title except I wasn't getting the same chances to hit the ball that Cobb was. The only chance I had to get any hits was when no one was on. I think the big leagues ought to pass a rule either stopping the passing of a batter on purpose or to let each runner on the sacks to advance a base.

**JACK GRANEY** I don't know why exactly, but some teams just had it in for other teams. That's the way it was between us and the Red Sox. When we got together, it was like oil and water. We just didn't mix.

After a game in early May, both of us teams were walking toward the clubhouse and then, out of nowhere, all holy hell broke loose. To this day, I don't know what even started it. All I know is that fists were flying and everybody was fighting everybody. Harry Hooper, and Tris Speaker, and everybody else was in it, and it took the umpires to come along and put a stop to it. Finally, we all went into our own locker rooms and things settled down for a while.

President Johnson sent somebody down to investigate. The first guy he got hold of was Jackson and he asked him what happened.

"I didn't see nothing," Joe said.

"Where'd you get that black eye?" the man asked him.

"Nowhere," Joe said.

"What do you mean, nowhere?"

"I mean I don't remember."

"You don't remember where you got the shiner?"

"I surely don't."

"Let me prompt your memory. How about a fight with Red Sox players?

"I don't think that was it," Joe said.

Say what you want about him, but loyalty was big in Joe's book.

**JOE BIRMINGHAM** A few days after the fight with the Bostons, we're playing them again in Beantown. Now we all thought that the recent unpleasantness was a thing of the past. We had no idea we were being led into an ambuscade. By the time the game came to a close, two Naps had been badly spiked and another had been injured by a pitched ball.

Chapman was the worst hurt. Sliding into the plate in an eighth inning attempted steal, he was severely spiked by their catcher, one of the spikes sinking clear to the bone. Unfortunately, Chapman was not wearing one of the shin guards with which all of our infielders were fitted before coming to Boston. He wore them on the first two games of the series, but thinking peace had been declared left them off at the wrong time.

Olson was also spiked, Engle turning the trick as he slid into third base in the 10th inning. Ole had the ball waiting to tag the Boston runner and there was no occasion for such a deed but he deliberately leaped, spikes up, into Olson.

Lajoie was the victim of a bean ball when he was hit by Joe Wood. Larry declared Wood hit him on purpose and swore he would get revenge before the season was over. As a rule when a pitcher hit a batter in those days, he was quick to offer his apologies and express a little sympathy. Nothing like that came from Wood. He merely turned his back, so Lajoie walked up to within 20 feet of the mound and informed him that he had something coming before the season was over.

Late in the game, they threw one right at the head of Jackson. He was quick enough to get out of the way—barely. From that point on, we made it our mission to see that they didn't win the pennant.

**JOE JACKSON** On the first day in May, I got a call from Katie back in Cleveland that she had gotten a telegram from my sister saying that my father was very sick. He was in the hospital but that was all that she knew. She said that she would let me know if she got any more information. I thought about going home right away, but that didn't seem like the right thing to do unless we found out that he wasn't going to live or something.

Once I started playing in the big leagues I didn't see my father much. Even when I went home for the winter I didn't see him a whole lot. He still ran the butcher shop and that kept him pretty busy. And he always had his hunting. Nothing would have kept him away from that. He never saw me play in the majors because he didn't travel away from South Carolina. I think even more than me, he didn't like the big cities. Of course, he couldn't read either, and since he didn't have no teammates to travel with, that made it pretty difficult.

That was one of the hard things about being on the road all the time. You couldn't leave and go home when things like that happened unless it was a real emergency. Still I knew if I had to go home, Mr. Somers would say it was OK as long as I got back as fast as I could.

**HENRY P. EDWARDS** Things took a turn for the worse in June. The club began losing games they should have won and morale was worsening. Matters weren't helped when Ban Johnson, responding to a report from the umpires who had a run-in with Birmingham, publicly called the manager incompetent. Actually he said, the "boy pilot" was incompetent, which certainly didn't help the young manager's waning confidence. I don't think Birmingham had turned 30 yet when he was appointed manager, and here he was, trying to manage a team which had shortcomings while playing himself in the outfield. Lajoie, Carrish, Turner, Falkenberg, and some of the others were all older than he was. It couldn't have been an easy task.

Jackson was 23, just coming into his own and playing brilliantly. Certainly no one could blame him for the team's problems. He was the first player in either league to reach 100 hits and was playing superbly in the field despite one game in which he made three errors behind Vean Gregg. The pitcher must have thought he was jinxed because in another game Lajoie also committed three errors in a game he was pitching.

Birmingham began burning up the phone lines in an attempt to engineer a trade, but everyone he talked with wanted Jackson. Although the manager continued to talk, he was extremely leery of including Joe in any deal.

**JOE JACKSON** One thing a manager could count on was having Joe Jackson in the lineup just about every day. Like every player, I got banged up a few times, but nothing really serious.

One day in June I got hit in the ear by a pitch thrown by Rath of the Chicago club. It knocked me down all right, and it stung pretty good, but it wasn't thrown all that hard. Still, my hearing was a little screwed up for a few days, and the doc made me wear a bandage, but I didn't miss much. I would rather go the park and play a game than sit home any day. Isn't that what a ball player is supposed to do

**TERRY TURNER** One Sunday in the midst of our prolonged slump, we actually had an off day in New York, and it was a Sunday to boot. Birmy told us we should all take the day off and relax. It was his way of trying to get things turned around. Man, we were out of the hotel like a shot. Cy Falkenberg chaperoned a bunch of Izaak Waltons who went out to the cholera banks. I guess the title of the fishing grounds failed to scare them away. Birmingham, Olson, and Mitchell spent the day touring Long Island in an automobile.

I went with a bunch of the boys, including Joe, to Coney Island. Man alive, you should have seen that rube's eyes light up when he saw what that place had to offer. Coney Island wasn't exactly South Carolina.

The day after our outing we went back to our old ways, however, losing games we should have won.

**VINCENT ALEXANDER** On the verge of his fourth anniversary as a major leaguer, I decided to look at Joe's averages in the various parks. Up to that point in the season, his average at home was .441. In the Windy City his record was .419 and in Detroit and Boston it was an even .400. On his visits to St. Louis, he was hitting at a .303 clip; at the Polo Grounds his record was .333. In Philadelphia he was hitting .133!

Now the question is, can an attitude about a city affect performance to that degree? In Joe's case it certainly looked as if it did.

**JOE JACKSON** I was leading Ty in the batting race most of the season, but it wasn't easy. Every time we played the Tigers it seemed like he was getting two, three hits a game. Then once—I think it was late July—we played three doubleheaders in a week. Does that ever take it out of the legs! The amazing thing is that we actually won all three! Somebody said it was a record.

**JOE BIRMINGHAM** One extremely important game against Boston was played late in the season. We had recovered somewhat from our mid-season slump and were hot on the heels of the Boston team in the pennant chase. We eventually lost the game 2 to 1, due in part to sloppy play by Joe. First he overlooked a chance to take second on Carrigan's throw to center, even though Chapman made it to third. Then he stopped at second when Lajoie singled to left, despite the fact that the ball was fumbled by Lewis. To offset these bits of lethargy, he hustled slapdash for home when Johnston lined to Hooper, thus allowing Hooper to double him off second. Joe sought to make the best of the situation by cutting across the diamond, but even then, Hooper's throw to Engle at first, beat him to the keystone sack. It was just this kind of play that led others to jump on the "Joe is stupid" bandwagon.

Joe wanted no part of anything I had to say, so I backed off. I think he knew. Anyway, sometimes leaving him alone was the best way to get him to do the right thing.

**IVY OLSON** Late in the season we were scheduled to play a three-game series in New York. We finished a game in Boston and were about to board the train for New York when our traveling secretary came running into the station with a telegram from the manager of the Hargrave Hotel in New York informing him that the cold weather had driven all of his regular guests back into town and that he would be unable to take care of us as on our previous trips.

The secretary rushed to the telephone and tried various other metropolitan hotels without success.

"They're all full up," Blackwood, our traveling secretary, announced dejectedly. "It looks like we're going to have to sleep at the Polo Grounds or take refuge with the Salvation Army."

"You ready to join the army, Joe?"

"No!" he shot back. It was clear he didn't have a clue what the Salvation Army was, but I'll never forget the shock on his face when he thought we were bunking with the army.

**HENRY P. EDWARDS** There were two hot races down the stretch in the American League. The race for the pennant featured Connie Mack's Philadelphia team headed by Eddie Collins and Frank Baker, Clark Griffith's Washington team led by Chick Gandil and Walter Johnson, and the Cleveland team of Larry Lajoie and Joe Jackson. Philadelphia was in front much of the way, but the other two teams were fast on their heels.

The batting race featured, as expected, Ty Cobb and Joe Jackson. Joe led the way almost all season, but he couldn't ever open up a secure lead on his southern rival.

When the dust settled from the race, Joe came in second to Cobb—again. He ended up with a .373 average to Cobb's .390. He led the league in slugging average, doubles and hits, was second in total bases and batting average, third in runs scored and triples, and fourth in home runs. It was perhaps the best all-around performance by anyone in either league that year.

The team finished third, behind Philadelphia and Washington, and immediately joined the alibi competition. The Red Sox, champions of 1912, were out of the race because of accidents to players. Washington was more or less crippled. Chicago was deprived of the services of Ed Walsh, its great pitcher and Detroit was weakened. St. Louis was a joke while Philadelphia had a suspect pitching staff. Such being the situation, why did Cleveland lose, asked the fans?

After the regular season was over, the Naps played a seven-game series against Pittsburgh. The games ran concurrently with the World Series games between Philadelphia and New York. It was an opportunity for the American League fans to see the great Honus Wagner and for the National League fans to see Larry and Joe. Cleveland won the series, thanks in part to an absolutely brilliant piece of fielding in the third game. In the 11th inning when Wilson hit a short fly into right field. Jackson raced in, snagging the ball an inch from the ground, turned a complete somersault, but got up with the ball securely in his hand. The crowd in Pittsburgh gave him a tremendous standing ovation.

No one could blame Joe for the disappointing ending to the season. He was as steady as a rock from April to October. As good as he was in 1911 and 1912, in the world of baseball you have got to put together a string of great years if you are to be considered one of the truly outstanding players in the game. He had now put together a three-year major league average of .381. During that same time only Ty Cobb had a higher average.

Joe was now clearly one of the very best players in baseball, and he was still only 23!

# 36

# I DIDN'T REALLY WANT TO LEAVE

**AMES A. GILMORE** Following the 1912 season, the ballplayers, feeling they were getting the short end of the stick from the owners formed the Fraternity of Professional Base Ball Players. The aim was simple: cut up the economic pie differently, giving the players a larger share and the owners a smaller one. The problem for the Fraternity was that, since there was no imperative to do otherwise, the owners simply ignored them.

About this time, a number of successful businessmen, myself included, got together to form a new league. Baseball could be a money-making proposition if handled properly, so we were able to corral enough men with enough cash to create the Federal League. After all, why should Ban Johnson have all the fun? There were enough millionaires left for our own party—Charles Weeghman, who made a fortune with a chain of Chicago restaurants; Otto Steifel, the wealthy brewer from St. Louis; Philip De Catesby Ball, who made a cool fortune selling ice-making equipment; Harry Sinclair, the oil tycoon. They were all men of money and not averse to making more.

So we created the league and began collecting players and managers with the promise that we would pay them better than organized ball—and we did. Our first success was in nabbing George Stovall as player-manager of our Cincinnati team which quickly became our Kansas City team.

Organized baseball responded just as we assumed they would. They panicked! Ban Johnson boldly announced that he would not take back a single man who jumped to our league. He said he wouldn't even talk to them! They didn't know how lucky they were.

Our first big coup occurred when we landed Joe Tinker, the famous shortstop. Then the war was on. We would have signed even more famous players, but many were afraid of Johnson's blacklist, and they were being persuaded by their owners that we couldn't make good on our commitments.

Then the biggest defection of all—the great Walter Johnson. After he won 36 games in 1913, Washington upped his salary to $10,000. This for the greatest pitcher in the game! The next winter Johnson turned down their offer and signed a three-year deal with us. Some of the fans were shocked to learn that the great pitcher was interested in money. What a surprise!

There's no doubt about it, we tore a great rent in the grand old game.

**CY FALKENBERG** I've always felt Joe should have come with us over to the Federal League. We asked him on several occasions, and I know he was tempted, but in the end he stayed put. Look, he was being taken advantage of by the system as much as anybody. Somers was using him to his own gain and poor Joe just went along with it, but he could have increased his own value greatly by using the leverage of the Federal League. He was bringing the crowds into the park, no doubt about that, but he wasn't making anything compared to his value to the franchise. Had he come with us to the new league, I have no doubt that he would have profited greatly which probably would have spared him the need to do what he did later.

Anyway, the reasons which led me to join the Federal League are very simple. At the age of 33, I found myself with a wife and two children to support, my active baseball career drawing to a close, and the first chance I had to make an unusually good salary. Any reputation I could hope to gain was already won. On that reputation I rested any demands I might consistently make for a better salary. And at that time of life, a baseball player knew that his days were numbered. and whatever of this world's goods he would retire with from the good old national game he would get in that brief and uncertain interim which stretched between 33 and finis.

My relations with organized baseball were, I suppose, about on a par with most other humble employees of King Baseball. I had my own grievances, some of which, I flatter myself, were not wholly of my own thinking, and doubtless I was not always right or reasonable in my dealing with the magnates. In any case, I will not say that I left the American League without a regret, for that would not be true. There is some sentiment in baseball, in spite of all the talk to the contrary. But my going was not a matter of sentiment. I felt that whatever preference I might have for organized baseball, I owed a more immediate debt to myself and my family.

Organized baseball never showed the players any sentiment. All things considered, they treated us in a fair, but perhaps not a generous way. I owed organized baseball no extraordinary debt of gratitude.

None of us were being paid what we should have been—not me, not the last guy on the bench, and certainly not the fellows like Joe, and Ty and Larry, players the fans paid good money to come out and see. I know the remark is often made that even then the ball player made more money playing a kid's game than he could have in any other profession. Perhaps in many cases, that is so. Certainly Joe couldn't have made anything even close working in the mill, and that surely would have been his destiny had he not been born with extraordinary athletic skills. But to say that a man is a major league player, is to say that he belongs to a group of four or five hundred athletes who possess special skills that let them rise above the ordinary, and like in any other profession, they should be paid accordingly. Most players drew salaries no more than those of moderately successful salesmen.

I talked over the matter of salary with Mr. Somers, sometime in December. He had sent me a contract which was certainly not satisfactory, in view of what I had done. So I dropped into the office to chat with him. We began by talking about the contract in good faith, but we got nowhere. Mr. Somers seemed unable to see my arguments and gradually the conversation tapered off to discussions about the weather and the situation in Cleveland and how the new draft rules would affect the standing of the club. And so I left, knowing as little as I did before.

In January, Larry Schlafly came to Cleveland. We had played together on the Washington club and he was interested in joining the Buffalo team of the Federal League. Of course he felt very enthusiastic over prospects in the young circuit. I will not deny that I was interested in what he had to say, and though I was by no means persuaded to throw away my limited future on a wild goose chase, I investigated and found that conditions were as he represented them. Fortunately, this opportunity came much sooner than I had anticipated. I received, together with several other members of the

Cleveland club, including Joe, an invitation to visit Mr. Gilmore, president of the Federal League.

My first meeting with him was not what I had expected. When he began to talk of thousands of dollars with as much apparent indifference as I would show in talking of dimes, it looked at first blush like loose business talk. But when he proceeded to make me a concrete offer for three years, at a salary double anything I could hope to get from Cleveland, after carefully going over the terms of the contract, I signed it.

As soon as I returned to Cleveland, I found that the news of my actions had proceeded my arrival. Mr. Somers naturally sent for me, and I had various conferences with him during the early spring. If I had made a mistake it was too late to rectify it. Mr. Somers took the position that the new league would not last, and that my contract would go up in smoke. Then he proceeded to make me an offer which was a few hundred dollars more than he had offered before, but it still thousands less than the Federal League offer.

Of course, Mr. Somers could hardly have paid me a salary out of proportion to that which he paid other members of his club, without either creating jealousy or substantially increasing his payroll.

I also talked to Joe at some length, and so did some league officials. They even went down to Greenville during the offseason to talk to him there. Joe said he felt he owed something to Mr. Somers. I think it was more likely that he just didn't want to consider moving to another strange city. Perhaps if the league had had a franchise in the Deep South he might have been more interested, but as it was, the team interested in him, Cincinnati, was the Southern-most city in the league. Incidentally, Ted Easterly and Artie Krueger were on that team, both of whom Joe knew from Cleveland, and George Stovall was the manager, so he certainly would have been with some of the guys he knew, but Joe wouldn't commit. It's too bad, because he would have been paid what he was worth, even if it was only for a couple of years.

**AMES A. GILMORE** We were interested in Jackson, sure we were. We were interested in anybody who could attract fans, and Joe proved he could do that. I even sent Lloyd Rickart, our secretary, down to some hick town in South Carolina where Joe was wintering. I figured Joe would be a lock cinch to land. All Lloyd would have to do was wave a pile of money under his nose and he would follow as spring does the winter. He couldn't count it, so that wouldn't be a problem. As long as it was green he was bound to take it.

Lloyd got back a few days later and said Joe refused the offer. We were dumbfounded. Lloyd opined that he wasn't smart enough to know a good offer when he saw one. I figured maybe Lloyd wasn't smart enough to know how to talk him into it.

**JOE JACKSON** I was interested in the Federal League, sure, and they offered me a lot of money, too, but I didn't really want to leave Cleveland and start all over again with a new team. Mr. Somers told me the new league would never last, and that I might not be able to come back to the American League if I jumped. That was good enough to me, and he was right about the league. It did fold after two seasons, but they let a lot of the players back in anyways. Some of the players from the league like George Mullin from Detroit, and Hal Chase from New York, and Danny Murphy my old teammate from Philadelphia, they jumped, and then jumped back again when the league folded. Maybe I would have made more money if I done that, too, but I was loyal to Mr. Somers because he treated me right.

# 37

# IT WAS A SAD SEASON

**CHARLIE LEBEAU** The 1914 season was memorable for a number of reasons: it was the year Babe Ruth made his major league debut by pitching seven innings as the Red Sox beat Cleveland; it was the year the New York team officially became known as the "Yankees," then hired the 23-year old Roger Peckinpaugh as its manager; the season the rule was instituted saying that a runner got three bases if a fielder stopped a ball by throwing his glove or hat at it; the season Eddie Collins led the American League in batting average and Tris Speaker in just about every other offensive category. It was also the year Cleveland, which had lost Cy Falkenberg to the Federal League, fell to the basement despite another stellar performance by Jackson.

**HENRY P. EDWARDS** All winter, baseball dominated the papers with its war with the Federal League. Stories had it that organized ball was going to form a third league to add to the National and the American as a way of fighting the potential inroads from the Feds. Most smart baseball fans believed that there weren't enough good players to go around for that many leagues, but still the stories persisted.

Another story which got a lot of press at the time was a story that Joe turned down a bonus of $8,000 if he would affix his signature to a Federal League contract. One baseball wag suggested he balked when he was asked to sign his name; another suggested that the mistake was not showing him the money in pennies, for had it been shown to him that way, he would have swum up Niagara Falls to get it.

I didn't like those stories and didn't think they were fair to Joe. The fact is that he had already shown the willingness to give up contractual money when there were other issues at stake for him. In 1908, for example, when still a raw recruit, he decided to bolt the Athletics and head home to South Carolina. That decision cost him postseason prize money which the team went on to earn. No, Joe wasn't driven by money, although he did have a love for the things it brought.

He could, and did, always negotiate a decent salary for himself, but he was never paid as one of the game's best. That distinction in 1914 went to Tris Speaker who signed a two-year contract for a whopping $37,000. Joe made maybe half that, despite the fact that his skills and contributions were on a level with Tris.'

**JOE BIRMINGHAM** I don't want to suggest that we were snake bit or anything, but a signal of how things were going to go that season came in Athens, Georgia during a spring training game. Our shortstop, Ray Chapman, busted his ankle good. I remember him crying as he was being carried off the field on a stretcher. I wanted to cry, too. All spring he had been our most enthusiastic player, and a damn good shortstop to boot. I was counting on him to team with Larry and Joe as the mainstays of our club. As it turns out, he wasn't out all season as the doctor said he would, but it was an example of the luck we ran into.

I thought that since we were assured of the services of Blanding and Kahler on the mound, we would be a much better team than in 1913. It was a hustling team, and you don't keep that type of team down for long.

Our two veterans, Lajoie and Turner reported in great shape. We had Olson to step in for Chapman, and a much improved Doc Johnston. Our catching staff was strong and our pitchers excellent. Our outfield with Jackson, Leibold and Graney was among the best in the league, and Jackson was one of the best players in the world.

The high hopes of the spring, however, didn't last long.

**JOE JACKSON** I had a real good spring in 1914, and I was looking forward to the season. Birmy kept saying we had a real shot at the pennant, and I guess most of us believed him. But then, a lot of bad things began to happen. First Chappie went down with a busted leg, then Stevie O'Neill, he got real bad blood poisoning from getting spiked and had to spend a spell in the hospital. Then Steen, he broke his hand, and Leibold and Graney both missed a bunch of games with twisted knees, and even Birmy was out when he tore some ligaments in his side. Josh Billings, one of our reserve catchers got hurt so bad in a game against the White Sox that he had to go to the hospital and for a while they was afraid they was going to have to do a serious operation on account of another case of blood poisoning. Our clubhouse looked more like a hospital ward than a baseball room.

What happened was that we got off to a real bad start and found ourselves in the basement almost from the get-go.

One thing happened though that was really pretty funny when you think about it. Mr. Somers, he's a pretty sharp cookie, and one day in April, he got the best of the law. It seems this deputy sheriff come out to the park when we was in St. Louis to look for Freddie Blanding who had a lawsuit slapped on him by the Kansas City Federals of the Fed League. They claimed that he signed a contract with them and so he couldn't play no more for us.

Now the sheriff, he was watching the game from the stands, just waiting for Freddie to come out on the field so that he could slap him with the suit. But Mr. Somers, he sent Secretary Blackwood out to sit next to him. When the announcer called out that Collamore had replaced Mitchell, Blackwood said loudly to a friend sitting next to him, "What is that fellow giving us? That isn't Collamore pitching, it's Blanding."

The deputy sheriff took the bait hook line and sinker. He jumped out of his seat and ran down to our bench to stop the man he thought was Blanding from escaping. When he found out he was tricked he got awful mad and ran back up to look for the man who gave him the bum steer, but by that time Blackwood was long gone.

Freddie wasn't even at the park. The fact is, Mr. Somers said he might have to be kept out of St. Louis all year so he couldn't be served with no papers.

**HARRY P. EDWARDS** The team got off to a lousy start, then they deteriorated. All but Joe. He hit with a consistency that marks the great hitters in the game. For much of the season he was hitting about a hundred points above anybody else on the team. Even Lajoie was showing signs that he was nearing the end of a very productive line. He struggled to keep his average above .250. This once lissome, graceful batter was losing some of his bat speed and agility.

It was up to Joe to carry the team, and he certainly did everything he could. It just wasn't enough.

**JOE BIRMINGHAM** On the road Joe roomed with Billy Steen. The two of them seemed to get along pretty good. Billy was an interesting guy. He would tremble at the very sound of a base hit, sometimes absolutely going to pieces. Once the tide of a game started going against him, he would set up a howl for help that had a steam siren beaten four different ways. Like a good many other twirlers I have seen, Billy was a wonder when he was winning, but if he wasn't, look out.

He was a big right hander with a good spitter and two or three other very deceiving pitches. He had decent control except when attacked with the chilblains. Then his control disappeared, and he couldn't seem to keep the pill out of the groove. It was best to derrick him before he blew up completely.

Billy helped Joe by reading what he needed; Joe helped Billy keep his composure. Joe had a pretty even temperament and seldom ever got real riled up like Billy. I think they were good for each other.

**STEVE O'NEILL** Like Joe, I came from a large family, only mine was an Irish family that moved to Minooka in Western Pennsylvania in 1885. When I say large, I mean large. There were 15 of us kids, and like everybody in that area we went to work in the mines as soon as we were able. Not many of us ever finished school, but we had enough schooling to get by.

Four of us boys made it to the big leagues. It would have been five and tied us with the Delahantys except that my brother Paddy threw out his arm when he was five. He managed the awesome Minooka Blues, an amateur team that never lost a money game. It was also the team that sent the four of us to the big leagues. Mike was the first to get a shot. He started as a pitcher with the St. Louis Nationals under the name of Mike Joyce because he had put in a short time playing college ball and he used a false name in pro ball so he could guard his amateur status if he had to return to college ball under his real name. But St. Louis not only kept him, they also agreed to sign our brother, Jack. Since both of them were born in Ireland, they exchanged their signs in Gaelic. Needless to say, nobody ever stole their signs.

Because we had a lot of similarities in our backgrounds, I spent some time talking with Joe. We both had ball-playing brothers, and we both worked as laborers—he in the mills, me in the mines. We spent many a night talking about our families and about hard work. Joe was always a straight guy as far as I could tell. What you saw was what you got.

Joe may have been out to lunch half the time, but he did have a pretty good sense of humor. He didn't tell a lot of stories himself, but he sure enjoyed a good one when he heard it. I specifically remember telling him this story once.

The McNallys lived next to us O'Neills out in Minooka, a town probably smaller than Brandon Mill, but had no telephone. Mike McNally was playing with the Yankees then. Every evening my mother would call the morning paper in Scranton to get the Cleveland score. Mrs. McNally used to raise her window and call out at the appointed time every evening to find out how the Yankees made out, too. But she was very polite about it. She would first ask:

"And how did your boy Steve's team do today, Mrs. O'Neill?"

"Cleveland won today, Mrs. McNally," my mother told her one night. "Now isn't that foine?"

"It is indade, Mrs. O'Neill, and whom did they bate?"

"New York," my mother said.

"Oh-oh," said Mrs. McNally ... and she was so taken back, she released her grip, the window fell and broke one of her fingers.

Of course, it was a good thing in those days that the Yanks and the Indians didn't have to play a World Series, for it might have wrecked the long friendship between those fine neighbors, the McNallys and the O'Neills of Minooka, Pennsylvania.

Joe really enjoyed that story.

**NEMO LEIBOLD** I seen Joe play a lot. I can say that because I was on the Cleveland team with him when things wasn't going so good, and then later on the great Chicago team when things was. I played next to him in the outfield for an awful lot of games.

We was exactly the opposite kinds of players. I was a leadoff hitter who was hard to pitch to; Joe was a big cleanup hitter that always seemed to hit the ball hard someplace. He covered a lot of ground in the outfield, but I made sure he knew that anything that come my way was mine. I was in charge out there, and he knew that.

I never had no truck with Joe, but I never had much to do with him neither. We had an understanding in the outfield, but both of us kind of went our separate ways as soon as the game was over.

During that 1914 season when we stunk up the joint, he was about the only player that had a great season. But then, he almost always had a great season. He was a good player, I got to admit that, but as a guy, well, as I said, I never had much to do with him.

**JOE JACKSON** I played with Nemo on two different teams. He was a scrappy little fella who I guess was named after a comic strip character called "Little Nemo." He was called that on account of how small he was.

He stayed in baseball a long time, as a manager, but then, late in his career he was throwed out of baseball for decking an umpire. When I heard about that, I wanted to talk to him, but I didn't know how to get in touch with him.

I guess we had more in common than either of us knowed.

**JOE BIRMINGHAM** One day in the middle of the season with us stuck in last place, George Stovall stopped by to see me. By then he was manager of the Kansas City Feds.

"I came over to see if you didn't want a couple of ballplayers who might get you out of last place," he said to me.

"Don't need them, George," I told him. "We will get out just as soon as Gregg, Steen, and O'Neill are all right and that won't be long."

"Tell you what," he went on, "I'll trade you my entire pitching staff, and throw in an infielder or two for just one of your players."

"You can't have Jackson," I laughed, "and that's that."

**BILL STEEN** We were playing Chicago. Wood was on first and Olson on third when Umpire O'Loughlin made a big mistake. Wood took a long lead off first and drew a throw that allowed Olson to score, Wood dashed back to first and slid into the bag as Weaver threw wild to the plate. As Wood lay there sprawling in the dirt, Birmy, who was coaching at first, ran over, slapped him on the shoulder, and yelled for him to pick himself up and run to second. Umpire O'Loughlin called him out, saying that Birmy had violated some rule that says a coacher can't touch a base runner.

We all thought that was probably right. It was Joe who told Birmy that the rule only applied to the third base coacher, and that there was no penalty if the first base coacher did. Unfortunately for us, Joe told him too late, and the play stood.

How in the world Joe knew that, and none of us, including the manager and the umpire did, I'll never know. I asked Joe about that once and all he said was, "I don't know how I knowed, I just did." That was Joe, all right.

**HENRY P. EDWARDS** Writing about the Naps that season was not easy. Finding positive things about which to write was almost impossible. There was, however, considerable attention given to stories about baseball pools. Because a crackdown was ongoing, gamblers were being arrested weekly. Surely there was talk in the clubhouse about this. Most baseball players talked about little else but the game when they were together.

**BILL STEEN** It's tough when you're losing all the time. The clubhouse turns sour, and nerves get edgy. People start getting on each other, because no one wants to take blame.

Birmy was doing everything he could think of. He even got suspended in the middle of the season when he got into a run-in with Umpire Dineen. He charged out onto the field and started screaming to Dineen about a called strike on Chapman, but he was thrown out of the game for his troubles. Then fans started throwing pop bottles at Dineen and the game had to be stopped while they were picked up. Luckily for the ump, the fans didn't have any better control than our pitchers, and none of them hit him. The next day, Ban Johnson announced that Birmy was suspended indefinitely. What he was doing, of course, was trying to get us riled up enough to play better, but it didn't really work.

When we had to come up with somebody to manage the team for a few days while Birmy was gone, somebody said we should let Jackson manage. Nobody took the suggestion seriously, but you know what? I'm not so sure he wouldn't have done a good job. No one would expect him to run a giant corporation, but a baseball team? He knew the game, no doubt about that. Granted, he couldn't fill out a lineup card, but he could dictate one.

Birmy tried just about everything that season to get us kick-started. Once, when we were in St. Louis for a doubleheader, they set a time limit of

5:45 o'clock to begin the second contest since both teams had to catch trains for other cities after the game. The first game lasted three hours and three minutes, which in those days was a heck of a long game.

The second game didn't start until around 4:45 and we jumped out to an early lead. Then in the fourth inning, St. Louis rallied and took the lead 4 to 3. At that point, Birmy told us all to use stall tactics. When Joe came to bat, he pretended like he had something in his eye and couldn't hit until he got it out. Umpire Evans, though, was wise to the tactic and warned us to cut out the nonsense. Then he got angry and said that there was an unwritten law saying no matter what the time limit agreed upon, the umpire can insist that any inning that starts has to be finished. He insisted that the umpires usually allowed seven or eight minutes to an ordinary half inning and that there were eight minutes to play when we came to bat for our final essay. Heck, Joe took longer than that to get the speck out of his eye.

Evans made us finish the inning, so Birmy filed a protest. Of course he lost, but as I said, he was trying everything.

**HENRY P. EDWARDS** In the middle of July, the Baseball Player's Fraternity declared war on the club owners and announced that the players would go out on strike. President Johnson responded that if the players dared to carry out their threats, he would close all the ballparks for the remainder of the summer, cut off the salaries of the players, and impose heavy fines on the players before the parks re-opened.

The announced cause for the strike was a player named Clarence "Big Boy" Kraft who had come to Brooklyn that season from Nashville. Nashville claimed the player on a waiver technicality. Baseball decided that he should go back to Nashville.

Kraft balked at going back to a Class A club for a meager salary when a Class AA club like Newark was willing to keep him for a larger salary.

Since he was a member of the Baseball Player's Fraternity, they took up his cause. The president of the Fraternity put out a release saying: "They boys have espoused Kraft's cause as eagerly as they would have that of the greatest star, which is somewhat contrary to the selfish light in which they are often wrongly placed."

The strike was finally averted when the Newark Club agreed to buy Kraft from Nashville.

**JOE JACKSON** All that talk about a strike scared us good, but we knew we had to go along because us players had to stick together. I didn't want to strike at all. First of all, I needed the money, and second I was playing good and I didn't want to lose what I had going. Besides, none of us even knew who this Kraft fella was. It would have been one thing if it was somebody like Larry, but it was a player who came to bat in the majors maybe three times in his whole life.

**JOHN K. TENER** In 1914 I was serving as Governor of Pennsylvania and as President of the National League. It was my opinion then, as it is now, that baseball players are neither miners, hod carriers, nor ditch diggers. Baseball players are professional men, and professional men do not strike.

I was glad when the strike threat over Kraft was settled. I knew though, that we had to prepare for war. The fundamental differences between the owners and the players were not something that was going to go easily away.

**HENRY P. EDWARDS** The specter of a strike brought forth all manner of questions concerning baseball labor issues. It would have been easy to accept Mr. Tener's pronouncements as accurate were it not for other lingering issues. The fact is men whose professional status was unquestioned—doctors and musicians for example—had struck many times.

**JOE JACKSON** When the strike threat was over, we all got back to playing ball, only we didn't play no better and we never got out of the cellar. I batted .338 for the team, but the next highest was .275 by Ray Chapman. It was a sad season.

Then one day I got a telegram from Davey saying that Father had died. Mother was strong and I knew that she would carry on without him, and even though I wasn't home much, she had plenty of family around her. I went back to Greenville for the funeral. I didn't cry or nothing, but I felt a real sadness because I realized that even though I never saw him much, my life was going to be different from that point on. I just didn't know at the time how different.

# 38

## I HAD THIS FUNNY FEELING

**JOE JACKSON** During the offseason I sensed that nothing was going to be quite the same for me again. I know that sounds funny—like I could tell the future or something but that's not what I mean. It's just that I had this funny feeling all the time.

**KATIE JACKSON** Naturally our life revolved around baseball. Our friends were baseball players, our activities were dictated by baseball schedules, our conversations were mostly about baseball issues. Out of necessity, I became something of an expert on the game.

I didn't care what the official scorer said, I credited Joe with a hit when it was a clear, unambiguous hit. The official scorer at Cleveland was known to be a "homer." Questionable hits were often awarded to Cleveland players, and errors for the home team were hard to come by. It became a joke between us.

"Why didn't you give me a hit on that one?" Joe would sometimes say with reference to a particular play.

"Because the second baseman should have had it," I would reply.

"Not even Eddie Collins could have gotten to that one."

"I could have gotten to it with one leg in a cast."

"In a pig's eye."

Joe once complained to a reporter, "She won't even give me a hit unless I poke the ball a mile away from a player. I've almost got to get a home run to get credited with a hit by my official scorer. She's a pretty good judge, but we can't always agree on my hits."

I still have most of those scorebooks, and as far as I am concerned, they better represent Joe's actual achievements than the "official record." Of course, that's only true for the first seven innings of any game, because after that, I was on my way home to fix dinner. We ate out sometimes, but mostly we ate at home, because, with all things considered, it was just easier on both of us.

Once in a while we went out to one of the fancier Cleveland restaurants with the Lajoies. Joe would usually say something like, "I think I feel like a big steak tonight," and when the waiter would come by he would ask what was the best steak they had, and then tell the waiter that is what he would have. The Lajoies knew exactly what that was about and they let it go without any reaction at all. They were fine folks. Occasionally Larry would see something particularly interesting on the menu, something he thought Joe might like so he would announce something like, "That venison here is about the best I ever had. No way I'm not going to have that again." Joe would take his cue and say, "Yeah, I think I'll do the same."

Like Mr. Mack had done earlier, Mr. Somers offered to pay for reading and writing lessons for Joe, but Joe wouldn't have any of it. He didn't want to be embarrassed by the process, or by the possibility that he might fail in the attempt. Of course, he wouldn't have. Everyone around him learned as children, and Joe was apprehensive about trying to do so as an adult, particularly since he was so in the spotlight so much. It was hard enough on him when people referred to him as stupid, but can you imagine what he would have felt were it know that he tried to learn but failed?

Throughout our years in Cleveland, Joe remained unusually popular with the young fans. He had his own youthful rooting section out in the bleachers who cheered his every move and followed his every exploit.

The Cleveland newsboys had a longstanding tradition—an annual newsies' game. Part of the tradition had the newsies choose two of their favorite Naps to serve as umpires for the game. You guessed it. Joe was always one of them, and how he did love it! He had the time of his life. Being the newsies' idol was a role he relished.

**JOE JACKSON** Mr. Somers was a good baseball owner and he took care of his players good, too. One thing I remember is that we couldn't play Sunday ball in Washington then, and when we played the Senators over a weekend, we made the jump back to Cleveland for a Sunday game, then back to Washington Sunday night. There never was a time we made that jump that Charley Somers didn't come down the aisle of the train and give all the players $20 gold pieces. He was all right, that Mr. Somers. If he would have been my owner for all my career, things would have been a lot different.

**CHARLES SOMERS** After Joe established himself as a bona fide star, I gave him his own drawing room on our train trips. He didn't ask for it, I gave it to him as a symbol of his importance to the team. I thought Joe would appreciate the gesture. Of course, some of the other players took umbrage at this, but that's the way the system worked. The stars were rewarded at a level above the average player.

Katie accompanied Joe on many road trips, sometimes with that parrot of theirs which you could hear squawking two cars away.

Joe was one of those players who liked to relax. He could lay back and look out of the window all day without ever feeling the need to occupy himself with anything more strenuous. Some players had to be active all the time. They played cards, or they joked or read or sang songs. Not Joe. He had an easy (some would say lazy) demeanor and he appeared to be as happy doing nothing as anyone I ever knew. He was the antithesis of Ty Cobb in that respect. In his movements he tended to be slow, and his speech had a drawl to it that naturally made everything he said sound measured and deliberate.

Joe didn't rush anywhere except around the bases.

**HARRY DAVIS** Like a lot of people, when I first met Joe, I bought into the "Joe is stupid" thing. The more I got to know him, though, the more I realized he had a head on his shoulders, and a pretty decent one at that. In fact, he had as level a baseball head as I ever saw in the game. He had a head for things outside of baseball, too. As I could tell, he was doing all right for himself.

**GERTRUDE TRAMMEL JACKSON** Joe bought a good-sized house out in West Greenville. I remember the house well, because for a while

I lived in it with Mother and Father. During the winter when he wasn't playing, Joe came down, along with Katie, of course and lived there with us. Those were really good years.

It was a big brick, two storied house, set back from the street on a wide green lawn with large shady trees.

Mother did most of the cooking, but when Katie was home, she chipped in some.

Joe was a celebrity in Greenville, but he didn't go around making a big deal about it. Mostly he did the same things he did before he became famous. The only difference was that the kids from the area constantly followed him. He was a regular Pied Piper.

Since everybody around here wanted to see him play, and few had, he formed a barnstorming team. Of course he made a few bucks on this at the same time.

**JOE JACKSON** Between seasons I put together a barnstorming team to tour around the South. Joey and Davey agreed to play the outfield with me. The twins, Ernest and Earl were our first and second basemen. Luther played shortstop, and Jerry third base. Two of my cousins also played. Pinky Jackson who lived down the road a couple of miles played some in the outfield, and Wade pitched. He wasn't too bad neither! I had a devil of a time finding someone in the family who wanted to catch, but eventually we turned up a distant relative big enough and good enough to handle those chores. The Jackson family was in the baseball business!

**DAVEY JACKSON** Playing on those barnstorming teams was a ball. Everybody in the little southern towns where we played showed up to see Joe. But all us Jacksons got a lot of support from them fans. We played mostly on the weekends. The traveling got a little long at times, but I think all of us loved it, including Joe. He was the attraction, but there wasn't much pressure on him to have to perform. The people were just glad enough to get to see him in the flesh, and if he did something good, well that was just an added bonus.

We made a couple of bucks for playing a game, and we had a lot of fun. I don't think I ever seen Joe so happy in all his life. It was too bad Father couldn't see us all together like that once, but then again, he was never all that interested in baseball.

We were never what you would call a real close family, at least not like some others I know, but we had a lot of good times together and the Jackson's baseball team provided some of the best

**LUTHER JACKSON** We played in towns all over the South, and we played pretty well, too. Of course Joe was the star attraction, but we all got a kick out of being Joe's brother. That made us sort of famous, too and besides, we were good enough to win most of our games, and that made it fun.

When Joe did something great like hit a long home run, or make a really good throw, the crowds went wild even if they were rooting for the other team. They liked being able to say that they were there when Joe did this or that. A little place like Greenville didn't have a whole heck of a lot to be proud of most of the time, so when somebody like Joe came along, they made the most of it.

**KATIE JACKSON** After Joe had that success with the show he did with Ty Cobb, he figured he could do it again only this time by himself. So one winter he toured all over the South with a show they called "Joe Jackson's Baseball Girls." It was pretty silly, if you ask me, but there was enough singing and dancing and funny business, that I guess they could sell tickets. Anyway, the highlight of the show was Joe's monologue. The producer of the show talked to Joe a few times, and then he wrote out Joe's speech for him. I read it aloud a bunch of times so that Joe could learn it. Not word-for-word mind you, but close enough that it made sense. It was pretty sappy but everybody said they liked it anyway. What Joe did was, he talked about his childhood in the mills, and how he started his career in baseball, and that sort of thing. He laid on the sob story pretty good, but that's the way the producer wanted it.

The newspaper critics said it was terrible, of course, and they weren't all that wrong but they also said he lost his shirt on the show which wasn't right at all. I think some of them wanted to use the story as another example of how dumb he was, implying that he wasn't smart enough to figure out the business side of the deal. It may have lost money in a few of the smaller cities where it played, but when it got to Atlanta for a two-week run, it made plenty. The show played to full houses every night, and the audiences loved it.

**JOE JACKSON** "Joe Jackson's Baseball Girls" did so good for us that me and Katie actually talked for the first time about retirement. Not right then, of course, but maybe in a few years. It seemed to me that I could make a lot of money in show business if I wanted to, and in some ways, it was a heck of a lot easier than playing ball. But, Katie, she argued that as soon as I stopped playing baseball, the audiences would stop coming to see me onstage. As usual, she was right.

**JOE BIRMINGHAM** Joe was getting so involved in some of his offseason activities that they were beginning to get in the way of his ball playing. I reminded him that without baseball none of the rest of that stuff would matter.

When Joe failed to show up for the start of spring training one season because of his "show business" commitments, I hit the ceiling and fined him plenty, hoping that would get his attention.

Joe had this ridiculous idea that he actually could have a career in show business.

The problem was exacerbated by the fact that while he was "trodding the boards" he was neglecting to stay in shape.

**KATIE JACKSON** Doggone if I didn't get angry with Joe a couple of times when he put more time in on the vaudeville circuit than he did on getting ready for the season. Joe had to watch his diet a little, because he had a tendency to put on weight if he was not careful. Traipsing around the South with a troupe of show folks wasn't exactly helping his baseball game. After all, baseball was our livelihood, not show business, and no matter how much fun the life of the stage may have appeared, it wasn't going to support us in the long run.

It was about this that we had our first real fights.

**JOE JACKSON** At that age I thought I could roll out of bed any day of the week, grab a bat and hit .400. It never dawned on me that it would ever be any other way. Katie got on me some about not staying in shape in the winter, but that's not what was really bugging her. That's just what she said. What was bothering her was that I was on the road away from home too much. What I tried to get her to understand though, was that I had to do that while I could because the life of a baseball player ain't all that long, and you got to strike while the iron's hot.

**KATIE JACKSON** When word got back to me that Joe was spending a lot of time with one particular actress in the show I hit the ceiling. I worked hard to make a good home for Joe, even if he wasn't in it much, and I wasn't about to let him run around with some chorus girl.

I wired Joe to come home immediately. I got a wire back saying he still had some dates to play and that he had to finish with his contractual agreements. Joe Birmingham called me wanting to know when Joe was going to appear at spring training.

I told him I honestly didn't know.

"Mrs. Jackson, I think you should try to influence him to get to spring training right away," he said.

I told him I would.

"Because it would be in both of your best interests," he insisted.

"What do you mean?" I asked.

"I think we both know the answer to that one."

Right away, I thought to myself, "My God, everyone knows what Joe's up to."

I called Joe in his hotel in Georgia and told him he had to report to spring training right away. When he said he had to stay with the show on its tour through Georgia, we had words. We both got pretty angry, I admit that, and I think we both said some things we shouldn't have. Anyway, Joe hung up saying there was nothing to discuss.

But there was something to discuss. I don't know if I was more angry, or more hurt. We were always a team, me and Joe. I handled the business affairs, he handled the batting. We discussed all the options when it came to his career. I read the contracts and we discussed at great length any and all the choices we had to make. We were as much a team as Tinkers, Evers and Chance. So, of course, I was hurt. Why shouldn't I have been?

He just laughed when I asked him about the chorus girl and said there was nothing to it, but of course there was. Too many people knew about it for it not to have been true. I'll never know exactly what went on between them, but I do know he was paying attention to her and not to me.

I called Joe back the next night and again we argued, and again he said he was going to finish the tour. I didn't know what to do, but I did know our relationship was in danger and so was his career.

Davey knew of a lawyer in town and suggested I see him. I was just angry enough to do it. Davey was real supportive of Joe, but he was annoyed too, that Joe wasn't paying enough heed to his career so he thought seeing the lawyer might get his attention.

I went down to see Herb Cameron, a Greenville lawyer who handled a lot of business for the local folks—wills, divorces, real estate deals, those sorts of things. He had a nice little office over the hardware store right in the center of town. It was the first time I had ever been to see a lawyer and I was nervous about it. It was unfortunately, not the last time, but lawyers always made me nervous.

Mr. Cameron was a round man with a big mustache. I told him about my problems with Joe. Of course, he knew all about who Joe was, and I got the impression he liked being involved with a celebrity. He asked me if I wanted to pursue divorce proceedings. That word "divorce" hit me like a load of bricks.

"I wasn't thinking about that," I told him.

"Then exactly what is it you would like me to do for you?" he asked.

"Make him to come home, or at least go to spring training," I said.

"That's tricky."

"That's why I need a lawyer," I said.

"Because we're tricky?" he asked.

"I didn't mean it that way."

"Well, if you didn't, you should have."

What he suggested was that he send a telegram to Joe saying that I was considering divorce and would proceed to do so unless he returned home immediately. He went on to explain that he would start the action in Cleveland, Ohio since that was our legal residence and because divorces were illegal in South Carolina.

Now, understand, I never filed for a divorce. I just threatened to do it to try to get Joe to come home so we could get this mess straightened out.

Mr. Cameron sent the telegraph, but Joe didn't answer at all. I don't know, maybe he didn't believe it, or maybe he had his own lawyer who told him this was a lawyer trick. So, Mr. Cameron suggested I go see the sheriff and swear out a warrant to have Joe brought back. Since Joe was acting like an idiot, I decided to take the lawyer's advice.

I went down to City Hall to see Sheriff Conway, who had been in office for as long as I could remember.

**JOE JACKSON** I knew Katie was sore, but I had an agreement to finish the tour in Atlanta, and I have always done the right thing by my agreements. Some lawyer called and said he was Katie's lawyer and that she would divorce me if I didn't come home right away. That didn't sound like Katie to me. That sounded like a lawyer to me.

I didn't do nothing about his call, but then while I was sitting in my hotel room before a matinee show I heard a knock on the door.

"Joe, it's Sheriff Conway," he said through the door.

Now I didn't have no idea what he was doing in Atlanta so I got up and opened the door for him.

"Sure is a nice hotel room, Joe," he said. "It looks like you're doing right well for yourself."

"Can't complain, Sheriff," I said. "What in the world brings you all the way down here?" I thought maybe he come down to see the show or something.

"I came down for you, Joe."

"To see the show?"

"To take you home."

"I ain't going home. I got a show to do."

"Then after the show."

"What for, Sheriff? It ain't illegal to be in Atlanta, is it?"

"I got a warrant for you, Joe. Sworn out by Katie. It says you got to come back with me."

"Katie?"

"She swore it out."

"It says you've been lavishing too much attention on one of your Baseball Girls."

"Is that some sort of crime?"

"Might be."

"No it ain't. Besides, you know damn well I can't read that thing."

"I'll be glad to read it to you."

"How do I know I can trust you?"

"Doesn't look to me like you got a lot of choice. Now, come on, Joe, don't make trouble for me. I'll help you pack your things if you want, and we can get the next train back to Greenville and get this whole thing settled."

"What if I don't go?" I asked.

"Then I'll have to arrest you, and I don't think you want that."

"What's she doing this for?"

"You two will have to work that out."

We talked like that for a while and then I said I'd go along seeing as how he said I didn't have no choice. I thought about telling him I wasn't going to do nothing until I talked to my lawyer, but I didn't really have one.

Now the truth is, there was one of the girls in the show that I spent some time with. You know, dinner and that sort of thing, but it was nothing like Katie was saying. Because of my baseball playing and my stage appearances, I had lots of chances to go out with other ladies. I could have done that almost any night if I wanted to, so Katie really was pretty lucky that I did as little as I did.

After I packed my things, me and Sheriff Conway, we started walking over to the train station.

"Well, all I want to know is, was she worth it, Joe?" the sheriff asked.

"What are you talking about?"

"The little lady you were fooling around with? Was she worth costing you your marriage?"

"You don't know what you're talking about, Sheriff."

"Everybody knows."

"Like hell they do! They don't know nothing."

"I knew you were stupid, Joe but I didn't know how stupid."

Maybe he had a right to get me to go back home, but he didn't have no right to call me names like that. What happened after that was that we got into this big argument right in the middle of the street, so what he tried to do was put his handcuffs on me, which he had no right to do. I mean you can't put a man in handcuffs just because he's arguing with you. What made it even worse was that there was all sorts of people watching. None of them probably knew who the sheriff was, but most of them darn well knew me.

"You're not putting them things on me, Sheriff," I told him. "You got no right to do that."

"I got any damn right I want," he shouted as he grabbed me by the arm.

I was real angry, I'll admit that. I swung and hit him on the side of the head, and then when he came back at me, I hit him again, and he went down to the street. I walked away with him lying there. He wasn't hurt serious or nothing. I knew that. I didn't hardly hit him hard at all, but he wasn't the biggest guy in the world, so he just dropped down.

I didn't know what to do so I done nothing, just kind of walked around Atlanta. I thought about going back to where I hit the sheriff, but I didn't know if that was a good idea or not. I figured some people might be out looking for me. I was still angry, and maybe a little scared, too, because I knew that hitting a sheriff wasn't a good thing. I thought about a lot of things to do. I thought about calling Katie. I thought about calling Joe Birmingham down in spring training. Your mind races a lot when you're in a state like that.

After a long time, I decided to walk to the station and get a train back to Greenville. I was lucky because there was a train leaving almost right away. I got on it and rode the long trip back to Greenville. I got there the next morning and went right to the sheriff's office. Sheriff Conway was already there. I guess he caught a train back right away after our little fight. He was still mad at me, but he didn't say much. I was back in Greenville and that's what he wanted all along wasn't it? He didn't press charges about the fight or nothing, but he did say I had to put up a bond on account of the charges made by Katie. Davey came down and we took care of that.

Sheriff Conway said that I should go right home to see Katie if I didn't want no more troubles, so that is just what I done.

She was plenty mad and I was probably pretty bull-headed. Anyway, she said she was getting tired of me being gone all the time, and that I didn't appreciate all the things she did for me. We didn't fight a lot, Katie and me, but when we did, we could both be a mite stubborn. After we talked about it for a while I could kind of see her side of the story a little bit. Finally I agreed to leave for training camp on the first train in the morning and she agreed to drop the charges.

The rest of the show was canceled and that caused some problems, but in the long run I know I done the right thing.

The whole mess wasn't that big of a deal really, but the way the press wrote about it, you would of thought we was fighting forever. And the fight with Sheriff Conway they really exaggerated. One paper said that he was "badly battered." That was a laugh! He wasn't even cut. I don't even think he was hurt. At least he didn't say he was. That was just another example of how the press made up things when they didn't know what they was talking about. That wasn't the first time that happened, and it certainly wasn't the last.

# 39

## I NEVER WANTED TO LEAVE

**CHARLES SOMERS** The 1914 season had been a disaster for the Naps as a team, and for me personally. Our last place standing all season cost us thousands of fans and cost me almost everything I had. As a result, in December my interests in the New Orleans, Waterbury, Connecticut, and Portland, Oregon clubs were placed in the hands of a committee of bankers with the aim of restoring financial stability to those enterprises. I maintained full control of the Naps, but I was on shaky financial grounds.

The bankers determined that my liabilities were $1,750,000 and therefore asked my creditors to accept reduced collateral trust notes. The plan was designed to give me a little more time in which to meet my obligations.

I was determined to remain as President of the Naps and to discharge the club's liabilities as they arose. I was equally determined to give the Cleveland fans a real team, one which would be in the pennant race from the start. Although urged by many to replace the manager, I knew it was not Birmingham's fault that we had fallen so precipitously.

Since Lajoie's season was a disappointment, I thought about moving him while I could still get something for him. Jackson was a treasure who, at his young age was a valuable commodity. I had no real interest in losing Joe, but I also knew that the Federal League was hot on his tail, and they were waving around lots of green stuff.

**HENRY P. EDWARDS** The 1915 season saw a Cleveland club reeling right from the opening bell. The impossible had just happened: Larry

Lajoie, the brilliant second baseman who had given everything he had to the club—including his name—was sent unceremoniously packing back to the city of brotherly love. Clevelanders were in shock. Napoleon Lajoie was the Naps. The thought of seeing him playing in any other uniform seemed, well ... traitorous.

**JOE JACKSON** I couldn't believe it when Mr. Somers sent Larry to Philadelphia. I mean I just never thought something like that could ever happen.

I was sitting in a little coffee shop one morning having breakfast when Larry come in and told me the news. I think he was in shock, too.

"I've been fired," he said just like that. No introduction or nothing.

"What are you talking about, Larry?" I asked him.

"Somers sold me."

"Quit joking me, Larry," I said.

"No joke, Joe."

I could see how hurt he was. He was trying to act like it didn't matter none, but that wasn't the truth at all. He was hurting plenty.

"I figure I got a few more decent seasons in me," he went on, "so I expect I'll go play for Mr. Mack. Did you know I played there a bit in 1901? Anyway, I expect I can live with it for a while if I have to, and I guess I have to."

When we lost Larry I lost a real friend, and the team lost one of the greatest players I ever seen.

Me and Katie went down to the station to see Larry and his wife off and when they got on that train for Philadelphia, I knew again that nothing was going to be the same that season.

As soon as Larry left, guys from the Federal League they come to talk to me again about going over. They said Mr. Somers was having big money problems. Me and Katie talked about it, but we just couldn't see ourselves leaving Mr. Somers. I mean he was always good to me, and we were pretty settled into Cleveland by then.

**JOE BIRMINGHAM** We decided to go with Wamby—Bill Wambsganss—as our second baseman. Now he was a pretty fair player, but he was only 21 and a long way from being Napoleon Lajoie. He ended up batting less than .200 for the season although I couldn't complain about his effort.

As soon as Larry was gone, we all thought it would be best not to have the team still called the Naps. How would it look if the team was named after a player on another squad? I don't know if anybody ever thought about that when they decided on the Naps as a name. Anyway, we had a team meeting with Mr. Somers and decided to change the name of the team to the Indians. For a while we thought we might call ourselves the Spiders, but most of the men felt Indians suggested toughness. Indians were ferocious and that's how we wanted to be thought of.

**NEMO LEIBOLD** Man, was things ever crappy in that Cleveland clubhouse. Everybody was on everybody about everything. The pitchers wasn't pitching, the hitters wasn't hitting, nobody was fielding, and absolutely nobody was coming out to the park.

It didn't help either that Larry was gone because he was always a good guy in the clubhouse, a real leader type. Now Joe was the most outstanding player on the team, but he never could do what Larry done. The guys just didn't look up to him the same way as Larry. Oh, he didn't bitch much like some of the rest of them, but he didn't stop them either. I guess nobody really would have listened to him anyway even if he would have tried.

Birmy, he did what he could, but when you ain't hitting or pitching there's not a whole lot a manager can do except cuss quiet and yell loud. Still, we was losing, and everybody knew what was coming next: changes.

**CHARLES SOMERS** Sometimes, when teams are going bad, the best recourse an owner has to make a correction is to change managers. I liked Joe Birmingham and thought he was doing a pretty good job considering all the problems the team had, but when we got off to such a poor start, I felt I had to make the change.

I called Birmy into the office in mid-May and told him. He really didn't seem all that surprised. I guess he had been around the game long enough by that point that he could see it coming. He asked if I would let him resign and I said I would. He then asked who was going to replace him. I told him Lee Fohl, a coach with the team. He didn't respond to that at all.

I thanked him for all of his work on behalf of the team as a player and a coach. He was all misty-eyed when he left the office.

The next day he announced to the press that he was retiring from the game—"for the good of the team," he said.

**JOE JACKSON** Lee Fohl wasn't the kind of manager who said much to his players. Heck, he didn't say much period, but he did get the team playing a little better after he took over. Not great mind you, but better.

**NEMO LEIBOLD** Lee Fohl was a tough Dutchman. He was a catcher as a player but he didn't get very far in the game. He was about the quietest man I ever knew, and why Mr. Somers thought he would make a good manager is beyond me, but you know he wasn't all that bad. You know what they say— still waters run deep.

**VINCENT ALEXANDER** About mid-season, rumors began floating around that Joe was about to be traded, but the Cleveland club denied them vigorously. Vice President Barnard was quoted in several papers as insisting that Joe was not going to be traded or sold to any club under any circumstances.

**CHARLES SOMERS** Here was the situation regarding Jackson: My financial affairs were in bad shape, I could not pay Joe more, and I wouldn't have been surprised to lose him to the Federal League. The only solution: sell him for as much as I could.

But it wasn't just the money. For two seasons I had been experimenting with young players, hoping to find some comers among them who would build up my team. I needed money badly, to be sure, but I also needed players.

I knew that Comiskey, an old associate of mine, could afford Joe. So, with considerable sadness, I let him have one of the very best players in the game for $31,000, and three players.

**VINCENT ALEXANDER** Charles Somers must have desperately needed operating capital because what he got for Joe was a lot of money—$31,500—and three unexceptional players. The best of the group was Braggo Roth, an outfielder with no power but decent range. He ended his career with a .284 lifetime batting average. The other two were outfielder Larry Chappell whose entire major league career lasted all of 109 games, and "Big Ed" Klepfer, a pitcher who won 21 games in three plus years in Cleveland.

**CHARLIE LEBEAU** In the 1915 season, Charles Comiskey of the White Sox, shocked the baseball world. In quick succession, he acquired

Eddie Collins from the Athletics, and then in the middle of the season, Joe Jackson from the financially strapped Indians.

There was an immediate outcry from fans in Philly and Cleveland. The deals seemed to smell of unsavory business practices.

All of a sudden, Chicago had assembled the greatest team on earth.

**CHARLES COMISKEY** My side of the Joe Jackson deal was very simple. Charley Somers and I started the American League together. We were old friends, so when he needed to dispose of Jackson he wired me informing me of the prospect. I made him a good offer and he accepted. That is how I acquired Joe Jackson.

It looked like a good investment to me. Jackson had been a wonderful player for several years, but an owner always takes a gamble in buying a star. Nevertheless, I reasoned Jackson would be worth a great deal to our club, and I paid a great price to get him.

As for the criticism that a strong club ought not to be strengthened at the expense of a weak club I have only this to say: When an owner leaves the annual league meeting he no longer considers the benefit of the league as a whole, but rather his own individual needs as a club owner. He goes on the theory that his associates are doing the same, that all are striving to build up the best club they can.

My sole ambition was to give the people of Chicago, who had supported me loyally all those years, the best club I could gather together. They had come to my park and paid to see my team when it wasn't a good team. They stood by me when times were hard, and I wanted to stand by them. That, and only that is the reason I bought Joe Jackson.

**BAN JOHNSON** The Jackson trade was bitterly criticized, particularly in New York, where it was felt that I wasn't doing enough to help the American League team there—and yes, I know it needed help. The fact is, I did try to help them. When Connie Mack decided to dispose of Collins I suggested to the owners that they secure Collins for New York. But at that time they did not attach the importance to the deal that I did. They had an opportunity to bid for Joe Jackson, but Mr. Comiskey was willing, upon first notice, to pay substantially for Jackson.

**VINCENT ALEXANDER** Charles Somers was hurting. He was losing money, losing fans, losing patience. It should have come as no surprise when he traded/sold Joe to Chicago, but of course, to Joe's legions of fans it was a shock. Clevelanders were angry; they had lost their one great player.

During his tenure in Cleveland, Joe had certainly done his part. His batting average while there was a robust .374. Of his 937 hits, more than 400 of them had gone for extra bases. Joe was the franchise, and without him, Cleveland fans lost faith in the future of the club.

**CHARLES COMISKEY** Before we consummated the trade, I met with Joe and his wife, and after explaining the situation carefully to them, got them to agree to an iron-clad contract lasting through the 1918 season.

Joe's wife did what little negotiating there was. I assured her that Joe would do better with the Sox than with the Indians because the club was in much better financial shape. She seemed to understand that.

I wasn't going through with the trade until and unless I had a signed contract first.

It was obvious they were not happy about the prospects of leaving Cleveland, but eventually I convinced them that the club would do everything possible to help make the transition a painless one.

**JOE JACKSON** I never wanted to leave Cleveland, but I didn't have no choice really.

**VINCENT ALEXANDER** As the 1915 season began, two overriding issues were on the minds of baseball fans: the impact of the Federal League, and the war being waged against baseball gambling.

The 81 former major leaguers who were lured to the new league were their immediate stars. Teams were operating in Baltimore, Brooklyn, Buffalo, Chicago, Kansas City, Pittsburgh, St. Louis and Newark. They built and renovated ballparks; they attracted new fans. They were also losing money. By the end of the season, they were gone.

All over the country, the headquarters of baseball pool operations were raided by police and hundreds of men were arrested.

By the end of the season, most of the baseball talk was centered on the team being built in Chicago. Charles Comiskey was stockpiling outstanding players. He looked to be building the next great team in baseball.

If, if, if. If Somers had more money, if he hadn't sold Joe, if it hadn't been to Chicago …

# 40

# EVERYBODY WAS ANGRY ABOUT SOMETHING

**VINCENT ALEXANDER** Joe came over to Chicago in late August and made his Sox debut in a doubleheader against New York. In the first game Chicago prevailed in an 11-inning affair then dropped the second contest 3 to 2. Joe played no part in the victory, and ended up with only one hit on the day.

A couple of days later, he made the first payment on his expensive price tag, when he tripled in the 11th inning scoring Eddie Collins with the winning run.

For most of the remainder of the season, he batted fourth in the lineup, just after Collins and in front of Felsch and Weaver. It was a strong lineup, and although he didn't post a great batting average that season, he did manage to make a handful of brilliant fielding plays in the outfield that brought the Chicago fans to their feet and sent the sportswriters scurrying for adjectives to describe them.

**JOE JACKSON** Playing in Chicago was never as much fun as it was in Cleveland. It seemed like everybody on the team was angry about something. It was more like a job than a game, if you know what I mean. Guys like Eddie Cicotte, and Buck Weaver, they didn't act like they was ever having fun, and maybe they wasn't.

I asked Mr. Comiskey if he would consider sending me back to Cleveland, but he said he wouldn't.

Baseball's a game, ain't it? And games are supposed to be fun. Well, it was becoming less fun all the time.

**KATIE JACKSON** I wasn't crazy about leaving Cleveland, but I knew, like all baseball wives know, that being traded was part of the game. In time, though, I came to like Chicago—maybe even more than Cleveland. We had adjusted to city life to a certain degree, and although we understood that when Joe's playing days were over we would return to the South, we had learned to become comfortable in the big cities of the North.

We took a nice apartment not too far from the ballpark and had all of our things moved from Cleveland. I went to most of the home games, and some of the road games, too. I guess I went to more of them than the other wives did, because they started calling me "The White Sox Girl," and pretty much everybody knew who I was.

**EDDIE COLLINS** I had not seen Joe play much since he was traded away from the Athletics five years earlier. Now, reunited on the same team with him again, I was reminded of what kind of special player he was.

I always thought players could be placed into one of three categories: those with overconfidence, those with a lack of confidence, and those with excessive nervousness. Overconfidence can cause errors in the field because of lack of application. Lack of confidence can easily cause a player to freeze at the plate when puzzled by the pitcher or at least the pitcher's reputation. Excessive nervousness, however, I considered to be the talented player's worst enemy.

When Joe was with us in Philadelphia, he certainly was a nervous and frightened young man. By the time I caught up with him again in Chicago, he was considerably less so.

Baseball is a mental game, make no doubt about that, and confidence is half the battle. Thus a weak team that is winning is harder to beat than a strong team that is losing. A fresh young pitcher can be harder to hit than an experienced one who is uncertain of himself. One team is helpless before a pitcher that a weaker team pounds all over the field. A batter is unable to get a hit off one pitcher, yet can hit the same kind of ball from another pitcher. There are scores of retired players or players who have been returned to the minors only because they lost confidence in themselves.

Joe, I think, always lacked some confidence in himself but it was his nervousness which caused him the biggest problems. As he became used to the major leagues and the big city life playing major league ball demanded, he became a much better player.

When he first came over to Chicago, he didn't hit particularly well although he did have some big hits. I believe nervousness created by the new situation and surroundings was primarily responsible for that.

I assumed that once he relaxed some with the new team, his contribution would increase significantly.

**CHARLIE LEBEAU** In Cleveland the kids had been deprived of their idol and refused to be comforted even when Somers brought in Tris Speaker to occupy the pedestal. In Chicago, the kids had swarmed to Joe. He walked the streets with flocks of them at his heels. After games, they would wait to see him emerge from the grounds and fought for the privilege of carrying his bats.

Many of them he called by their names, and sometimes, after the heat of a fierce game, he would stop at the vacant lot near the park and toss the ball around, or draw a practice ball from a pocket and throw it to them. Sometimes he would hit a ball far over the railroad tracks while the kids watched awed and breathless. For days the pitcher who had thrown the ball strutted among his friends as a genuine celebrity.

**RAY SCHALK** One day during a rain delay we got into a big argument in the clubhouse. Somebody—I think it was Collins—said that the present day outfielders couldn't throw like the old timers. We were always hearing how the old players were supposed to be so much better than we were, but I think that was just a lot of bunk. Anyway, somebody said they seen George Van Haltren throw out runners at first base after they hit balls to him in right field. Somebody else said that Harry Niles nailed 39 runners from the outfield when he was playing with St. Louis in 1906, and then Mike Mitchell was supposed to have matched that a few years later. Somebody brought up Fielder Jones, and Jimmy Fogarty and Bill Lange, and even Mike Kelly way back when.

But we had Ty Cobb, and a lot of people don't remember how good he threw. And so did Tris Speaker and Joe Birmingham and Clyde Milan. Well, the argument went on for some time and then it stopped raining and we went back out to play. It wasn't two outs later that a ball was hit to the wall. Jackson raced after it, picked it up and threw a strike to Blackburne at third. Well, I tell you, everybody on the team broke into a big grin. The old-timers, they didn't have nothing on Jackson in the throwing department. Nothing at all.

**HAPPY FELSCH** One day late in the season, me and Joe were sitting in the lobby of a hotel in Washington waiting to go to the park for a game that afternoon, when in comes a man named Arthur MacDonald. He was an advocate of what in those days was called "scientific baseball," a term that was thrown around a lot, although no one knew exactly what it was supposed to mean.

He sat down next to us and told us he had done studies on major league baseball players.

I probably insulted him when I interrupted and asked what he did for a living. He said that he was a criminologist. I suggested that scientific baseball was a strange area for a criminologist to be involved in.

"I consider baseball one of the greatest moral tonics for boys and young men," he said. "It directs the surplus physical energy of youth into the right channel, for otherwise this energy might be employed in wrong ways which are detrimental to moral and physical life. Baseball is one of those fundamental educational forces of prevention whose power and utility are not realized until it is taken away."

Then without invitation he started giving us all these statistics.

**ARTHUR MacDONALD** According to my studies, players under 5 feet 11 inches in height are better batters and fielders than those who are taller, and the superiority is greater in batting than in fielding. Thus the taller men, who bat for an average of .250 or better, are but 43 percent of the whole, while the shorter men have a percentage of 62.

Moreover, the average player is 5 feet 9 1/2 inches tall, pitchers average a fifth of an inch of 6 feet; catchers 5 feet 10 1/2 inches; and shortstops only 5 feet 8 1/2 inches. Catchers are the heaviest at an average weight of 178 pounds and shortstops the lightest at 167 pounds.

When it comes to batted balls, you may be interested to know that twenty percent of fair batted balls result in safe hits, and of all the balls batted, 20 percent are fly balls, 51 percent grounders, 20 percent bunts and 9 percent line drives. Line drives, of course, are the best balls to hit, as 77 percent result in safe hits. Only 8 percent of grounders go for hits, 45 percent of bunts, and 20 percent of fly balls.

**HAPPY FELSCH** After the windbag left I asked Joe what he thought of his statistics.

"I don't think nothing of them," he said. "He don't play baseball, so he don't know. When the pitcher throws me the ball in a place I think I can hit it, I swing as hard as I can and try to hit it as far as I can. The rest takes care of itself."

If there ever was a Joe Jackson quote that summed up his approach to the game, that was it—he swung as hard as he could and the rest took care of itself.

**CHARLES COMISKEY** After the 1914 season I decided we needed new blood to manage the team. It was a tough decision. Jimmy Callahan hadn't done a bad job, but I thought the team could do better. The problem was that Callahan was an idol of the South Side faithful, and the man I wanted to replace him with, Clarence Rowland, was a young bush league manager with the Peoria Distillers of the Three-Eye league—not exactly a big league operation.

Rowland was a scrappy little manager in the Hughie Jennings mold. He abhorred rowdyism and would not permit it on the part of any player. He was also a smart handler of pitchers, and a good developer of young players.

I thought the young fellow was a good choice although lots of persons took the trouble to inform me otherwise.

I believed that the 1915 team had the class and the manager to win the pennant. When we got Jackson, I knew we did.

**PANTS ROWLAND** When I took over the Sox, I was 35 and without major league experience as player, manager or coach, but I knew baseball, and I knew players. I must confess, though, that I never saw the Polo Grounds in New York before we played our first game there.

While as a minor league manager I developed several winners, I never dreamed that I would receive a major league engagement until the moment Commy asked me to. The offer nearly took my breath away.

It was a good team—that 1915 squad. I tried to help them by offering encouragement, and by keeping them in good spirits. It was my aim to work up dual feelings of confidence and aggressiveness.

All of this was made easier by Eddie Collins. He was a splendid fellow as well as one of the best players in the game. He quickly became my right arm in everything, especially in exerting the proper influence among the players. Collins, as a field captain, inspired the players with gameness and a fighting spirit. Yet, he was never looking for the limelight. If anything, he was a bit too modest.

Collins immediately made Buck Weaver a better shortstop by teaching him the meaning of inside baseball.

We also had Happy Felsch, another potentially great young player, and Ray Schalk, the best catcher on top of the earth. Our pitching was strong with Red Faber, Jimmy Scott and Eddie Cicotte. But it was when we added Joe Jackson to what was already a fine and talented team, that many people—me included—figured that we were on our way to something pretty great.

**RAY SCHALK** Eddie Cicotte, the stocky pitcher, was always known as a smart hurler—maybe not the one with the best array of pitches, but one who always used his head, who always tried to outsmart hitters. Over the years he had developed a freak curve, a "knuckle curve" he called it. He threw it with his fingers doubled and his thumb grasping the ball. It floated to the plate in a lazy fashion, then broke fast. It was an effective pitch which he had worked on for a full two years before daring to use it in a game.

The first day Joe joined us, Eddie threw him batting practice and became thoroughly frustrated. Joe didn't play guessing games at the plate, and that's what Eddie counted on. Eddie wanted a hitter to guess along with him so that he would have a chance to outwit him. Joe wouldn't go along, and as a result, kept hitting pitch after pitch on a line to the outfield.

**EDDIE COLLINS** Pants Rowland, despite the colorful nickname, was one of the most businesslike managers in all baseball. He never bawled a player out for a mistake or tried to anger his players hoping for a better effort. He cajoled and jollied men instead.

Right away I could see that difference in the way he handled Joe. Perhaps had Pants been his manager earlier in Philadelphia, the history of baseball in that town would have been different. Joe was intimidated by Mr. Mack; Pants played Joe like a violin—encouraging, urging, prodding when necessary, but never criticizing.

**CHARLES COMISKEY** Rowland came in for a lot of criticism, especially early on, some of it justified. He was raw, inexperienced, and prone to listen to too many people. He was getting advice from everyone. For him to learn how to separate the valuable advice from the worthless would take time. While he was learning, he was losing games.

**JOE JACKSON** A lot of people got on Pants about being so young. Sometimes they called him the infant manager.

To show what kind of a fellow he was, all you had to do was look at what happened in one game against the Red Sox. Big Jimmy Scott—sometimes he was called "Death Valley Jim"—was pitching for us and he let go a high hard one that caught Tris Speaker on the side of the head. Tris went down like he was shot and didn't get up for several minutes because he was out cold. When he come to, he went down to first base, but he was real shaky on his legs. So, Pants, he goes over to the Boston skipper and he suggests that he puts in a runner for Tris, but that he would let Tris come back in the game later, which is exactly what happened. The only thing is Tris came back in but only lasted an inning or two because of his headache and had to come out again. Anyway, that shows what kind of a fellow Pants Rowland was.

He was also one hell of a good manager in my book. I would say he was the best manager I ever had. He knew how to get good results out of a bunch of fellows better than any leader I ever seen, and I think a lot of the other boys felt like that, too. If anyone on the club ever tried to knock Rowland, he would have been mighty lonesome.

Did he know baseball? Well, I should say he did. He knew it from the bench to all parts of the diamond and he knew how to talk it in the meetings. He proved to us that a man didn't have to have played baseball in the big leagues to know how to manage a big league club.

Sometimes writers in Chicago asked me if I was disappointed in not leading the league in hitting. You bet I was, and I'll tell you why. I wanted to do it for Rowland's sake, and if I did do it, he would of deserved the credit.

I never seen a single time after I joined the club that the players didn't give Rowland their best effort.

**PANTS ROWLAND** I spent a considerable time patting Jackson on the back and telling him he was the greatest natural hitter that ever came down the pike, which was true. He needed and responded to that sort of motivation.

Hell, I even roomed with him on some road trips.

He may have been without an education, but I'll tell you, he was smarter than many I met with one.

"Gentleman Joe" a writer called him. And he was.

**CHARLES COMISKEY** By adding Jackson and Collins to our team, we increased our expenses significantly. We had to win games—period. Crowds paid to see winning teams.

The finances in those days were fairly simple. It cost us something in the neighborhood of $1,500 a game to run the club. The way the turnstile money was split was that the visiting club received one-half of the bleacher admissions and 25 cents on every other seat. That meant for all 75-cent seats, the home club kept 50 cents, and on the dollar seats they got 75 cents. All the quarter and half dollar admissions were divided.

Say we had a crowd of 10,000. About 5,000 would be in the bleachers. They would pay into the gate $1,250, or $625 for each club. We might sell about 2,000 50-cent seats which would yield $500 for each club. Another 3,000 fans would buy better seats at an average of 75 cents which would give the visiting club $750 and we would get $1,500. We might get another $100 by selling box seats at $1. That would make the total receipts $4,600 which would be divided $2,725 for the home club and $1,875 for the visitors.

The problem was a crowd of 10,000 was the exception, not the rule. In order to break even or make money with the high-priced team we had, we had to win to attract the big crowds, because in those days, the gate receipts were just about all we had to rely on.

Wining the pennant was damn near a necessity if our expensive team was to survive.

**EDDIE CICOTTE** The thing you have to understand about Charles Comiskey is that he was a liar. In the press he consistently exaggerated his financial dealings. For example, he claimed he was paying Joe $10,000 a season. He said this over and over again in the press. Joe told me he never made more than $6,000. Comiskey claimed he had one of the highest payrolls in the league, but the fact is he had one of the lowest. He even skimped on the meal money he gave us. Every other team got $4 per day; we got $3. In every way, he was cheating the players, and then talking big to the press about his expenses.

One of the first things I did when Joe joined the team was to take him aside and fill him in on the cheapskate owner. Joe listened. He didn't say much, but I know he understood. Just about all the guys on the team hated Comiskey. Joe needed to know this.

**CHARLIE LEBEAU** Make no mistake about it, Comiskey was a smart man, a very smart man. He was also a bit of a prevaricator, not to mention con man.

He was a born and bred Chicagoan who never became more than, at best, a mediocre major leaguer. That did not stop him, however, from promulgating several self-promoting myths. Probably the most frequently repeated one had him originating the practice of playing away from the bag at first base. The fact is, first basemen had been playing off the bag since 1883, when the rules changed to disallow the one bounce catch on foul balls.

**EDDIE COLLINS** I know there was a lot of talk about Comiskey's penurious ways, but the fact is, he paid me well. I demanded and got a $15,000 a year, five-year contract. The Federal League was, after all, a boon to us all when it came to contract negotiating.

**EDDIE CICOTTE** Of course Eddie Collins, the fair-haired boy of the team, was treated differently than the rest of us. He was a college graduate and so could have earned a lot outside of the game. The rest of us couldn't do that, something Comiskey took advantage of.

**JOE JACKSON** Most of the guys seemed to hate Mr. Comiskey—not Collins and Schalk so much—but just about everybody else.

The guys didn't spend much time together either. It was like nobody trusted nobody. They pretty much played the game and then went home, which was all right with me. The only thing was, it was never a very friendly place.

**CHARLIE LEBEAU** Charles Comiskey was a piece of work, He was a proud, stubborn man who controlled others by dint of his dynamic personality. A big round-faced man with an ever ruddy completion, he used and abused his intimidating presence.

Early in his career while still managing he became acquainted with a Cincinnati sports writer named Byron Bancroft Johnson, and it was Comiskey who brought Ban Johnson into a management position and eventually to the founding of the American League.

The players, press, public, all loved to tell Comiskey stories. He was a larger-than-life personality who loved the spotlight and encouraged the stories.

One of the most famous had him in a Chicago eatery one night ordering a lobster. When it was brought to the table, Comiskey complained to the head waiter that a claw was missing.

"It happens often, Mr. C." said the waiter. "Lobsters get into fights, you know. This one lost a claw."

"Take it away," roared Comiskey, "and bring me the winner."

Quite some years ago in a postseason championship between the White Stockings and the American Association St. Louis Browns, he forfeited the second game when he pulled his team off the field in protest of umpire Dan Sullivan. In the seventh and final game of the series, the teams combined for 27 errors after which both teams declared themselves world champions.

Earlier in his career, he was involved in an ugly situation. It was in 1901, a time when the Baltimore Orioles did their spring training in Hot Springs, Arkansas. They stayed in a grand hotel with a host of useful bellboys, one of whom was a light-skinned black man who went by the name of Charles Grant. As it turns out, Grant was a pretty fair ballplayer who had played for a Negro team in Chicago the previous year.

Now, the hotel staff was in the habit of playing ball in their off hours, and the outstanding player was clearly Grant. John McGraw, who was managing the Orioles saw him playing one afternoon and immediately tabbed him as having major league abilities. McGraw, never one to miss an opportunity to pick up a great player, tried to pass him off as a Cherokee Indian. He even gave him a new name—Tokohama.

When Comiskey got wind of McGraw's ploy he became irate. "I'm not going to stand for McGraw bringing in an Indian on the Baltimore team," he screamed. "Somebody told me that the Cherokee of McGraw's is really Grant, the crack Negro second baseman from Cincinnati, fixed up with war paint and a bunch of feathers."

Despite Comiskey's protestations, Grant and McGraw tried to get away with their ruse by insisting that Grant's mother was a Cherokee and his father a white man. They didn't get away with it for long, but Comiskey never forgave McGraw for the deception. What probably irked Comiskey even more though, was that he didn't think of it first.

Comiskey was irascible and devious, but he could also be charming—mostly when he was reaching into someone's pocket. They called him the "Old Roman," although nobody is really certain how the moniker became attached. Nevertheless, by 1909, when he opened his new stadium, Comiskey Park, the nickname was so well established that he decorated his private box to resemble the emperor's box at the Roman Coliseum.

It's no wonder that the players resented his penny-pinching approach to their salaries. Looking up at the "Old Roman" in his fabulous private box while they were treated so poorly galled them.

That Joe never got close to him is not surprising; that he played for him at all, is. The fondness that he felt for Charles Somers, never transferred to Comiskey. It was an uneasy relationship from the outset.

**HAPPY FELSCH** Comiskey like to have drove us nuts. He spent a lot of money on making himself look good, but very little on us players who had to do all the work.

It was an unhappy club really, and we spent a lot of time griping about things—almost everything in fact—but mostly what we griped about was Comiskey.

**CHARLES COMISKEY** I'll tell you this about that season, poor umpiring cost my club seven or eight games. It seemed to me that Rowland was being made a mark. For example, in one series in Detroit, umpires called a bunch of balks on my pitchers. My guys made the same motions in St. Louis, but there were no calls. In Boston they beat us out of a clean triple play, and when Mayer was hit by a pitched ball, they didn't let him have first base because, according to the umpire, he didn't make a strong enough move to get out of the way of the pitch. Then they chased Rowland when he went out to protest. He had a right to do that, and I would expect him to do it. He assured me he did not swear until after he was thrown out of the game.

Why was all this happening to us? It was my belief that there was antagonism about picking up Jackson, and we were paying the price.

**VINCENT ALEXANDER** Joe ended up playing 46 games that season for the Sox and 82 for Cleveland. He hit a cumulative .308. For Chicago he hit only .265 in 162 at bats, but nobody, including Joe seemed worried. It wasn't unreasonable to assume that it was going to take him a little time to adjust to his new surroundings and new teammates. Despite his relatively low average, he still managed to place fourth in the American League in runs batted in and in slugging percentage. He had five home runs that year, which was only two shy of the league leader, Braggo Roth. Ruth was still a few years away from becoming a full-time outfielder.

Chicago was happy with Joe. Comiskey even went so far as to claim that Joe was "the greatest straightaway hitter in baseball."

Despite dreams of a championship, however, the team came home in third place, behind Boston and Detroit. Nevertheless, they won 91 games, and added, in Collins and Jackson, two of the game's greatest players. Hopes loomed high for the 1916 season.

# 41

# YOU COULD FEEL IT IN YOUR BONES

**JOE JACKSON** One day Happy Felsch comes into the locker room waving a Chicago paper around saying that the paper says somebody shot and killed Red Faber. Red was a big pitcher on our team, so everybody just kind of sat there in shock.

Then he told us the rest of the story. Mr. Comiskey owned a big hunting preserve someplace up in Wisconsin. A big moose with a bad temper lived on it. Mr. Comiskey called the moose Red Faber on account of he also had a bad temper. It was the moose that was shot and killed by the brother of a boy who was attacked by the moose.

That was one of the only times I can remember us laughing in the Chicago clubhouse.

**KATIE JACKSON** One of the best things about Chicago was Jackson Park. It had a nice paved walk which ran along the lake. Me and Joe sometimes used it when there weren't too many people around. Jackson Park—not named for Joe—also had several baseball diamonds on it, and a few times, we stopped to watch the young boys play ball.

Chicago also had the White City Amusement Park which included two dance floors and a roller skating rink, and the Midway Gardens where lots of Chicago folks went to dine, dance and wile away summer evenings.

The thing I remember more about Chicago than anything else was the electric street railway system which ran all over the city. There wasn't anyplace we couldn't get to by electric car if we wanted to. Joe loved to drive, but in Chicago, taking an electric streetcar was so much easier. They even had trolley cars that worked as rolling post offices, carrying mail from the neighborhoods to the central post office and sorting it while the ride took place.

The main part of the trolley system was the downtown loop. It was mighty noisy, but it's what we took if we wanted to go shopping downtown.

The Loop had something for just about everyone. Michigan Avenue had the swanky shops with the latest fashions from New York and Paris. The wholesale produce market was over along South Water Street. On State Street there were plenty of penny arcades, saloons, burlesque palaces and vaudeville theatres.

There was always something to do in Chicago, and me and Joe did a lot of it. As long as we were in Chicago, we tried to make the best of it.

**VINCENT ALEXANDER** That was quite an old stadium—Comiskey Park. I take it Comiskey had this thing about ballparks being symmetrical. Maybe he didn't have much imagination, I don't know. Anyway, when he opened his new park in 1910, he made damn sure it was just that—362 feet down each foul line, and 440 feet to straightaway center.

There were bleachers in right and left fields, but none in center. The grandstand was covered, and on a good day it was said they could squeeze in 32,000 fans, 7,000 of whom could buy 25-cent bleacher seats. Comiskey wanted to attract the working class which made up most of the local neighborhood.

I'm not sure if this was part of the original equipment or not, but I remember visiting the park later and noticing that the foul line markers in the outfield were flattened fire hoses painted white. Old Comiskey could save a buck when he had to.

**PANTS ROWLAND** It was a decent team, that 1916 bunch. With Buck Weaver, Jack Fournier, and Eddie Collins in the infield, and Shano Collins, Happy Felsch, and Joe Jackson in the outfield we had a solid starting lineup. Ray Schalk was an outstanding catcher, and with Red Faber, Eddie Cicotte and Reb Russell, we had three strong starting pitchers.

Realizing that we needed more pitching, we picked up a good little lefthander—Lefty Williams. Lefty had good stuff and a surprisingly good fastball especially when you consider how small he was.

It wasn't long after we got him, that he and Joe became good friends. It became a standing bet among those of us who knew them that whatever Joe did, Lefty did, too. They were neighbors in Chicago, having rented places near each other, roomies on the road, and as it turned out, their wives became such good chums, too.

**JOE JACKSON** Right away, me and Lefty Williams hit it off. His real name was Claude, but most of the time everybody just called him Lefty because that's what he was—a left handed pitcher.

He was a good roomie because he didn't care a lot about anything except playing baseball. I mean, he didn't make no big deal about reading stuff for me if it was something important.

He was a good roomie, I'll tell you that. The bad stuff that happened later, well, that was something else, but as a roomie, he was the best I ever had.

**LEFTY WILLIAMS** Oh sure, it was a pain in the neck once in a while, doing stuff for him because he couldn't read, but most of the time I didn't mind really.

We talked a lot about baseball. He told stories about playing in the mill leagues and I told stories about all my minor league experiences, which were many.

I was born in Springfield, Missouri and began playing professional ball with the Springfield club in the Kansas-Missouri League and then with Nashville in the Southern Association. I also played in the Appalachian League and for Sacramento of the Coast League, and for the Salt Lake Club.

I also had short stints with Brooklyn and Detroit, so you can see I had a lot of baseball stories I could tell.

Of course, when I joined the club, Joe was already a big star but the thing I liked was that he didn't treat me no differently than anybody else. That was the thing about Joe; he didn't care about how big a star you was or nothing, but about how you treated him.

**PANTS ROWLAND** The team was never what you would call a close-knit group. Oh, there were a few small cliques on the team but not a lot of real team unity. Eddie Collins was pretty much his own man, although sometimes he hung around with Ray Schalk or Red Faber. Buck Weaver and Happy Felsch didn't get along with those two at all but they pretty much stayed to themselves anyway. Joe and Lefty, of course seemed to be inseparable, but they didn't associate too much with the others.

I tell you, I never saw a team quite like it.

**LEFTY WILLIAMS** Sometimes, me and Joe, we would go out and have a beer together. Now, neither one of us was what you would really call a big drinker, but once in a while, after a tough game or something we would go out for a drink, or sometimes, he would break out some of his special brew.

Once this guy from the Players' Fraternity came to the clubhouse to give us a speech about how players shouldn't drink.

"It would be a great thing if you players retired earlier and omitted beer drinking," he told us. "Of late years there has been a decided change in the behavior of you players, I know that. Years ago it was taken for granted that you would spend your money like a sailor and care little about your physical welfare. But you have seen many of your fellow stars of the diamond have short careers because of intemperate habits. Men, the Fraternity urges you to curtail the use of beer or ale except with meals. A cold glass of beer after a game when you are still heated from the energy on the ball field, is a bad thing for your health. Indigestion and low spirits invariably follow these careless habits. At best, a ball player's career is short. Conserving energy is the only thing which will prolong your diamond career. Temperance will add years to your time on the playing field."

Me and Joe were so impressed with that speech that as soon as the game was over, we went out immediately for a few beers.

**PANTS ROWLAND** Joe seemed more relaxed when we reported for the 1916 season than he did at the end of the '15 season.

I remember one particular incident which happened while we were down in Oklahoma City for a spring training game. We hadn't played for several days owing to a deluge which had hit that whole part of the country. Then, when the rains stopped long enough for us to get in some hitting practice, the players had a lot of pent-up energy. One of Joe's wallops sailed far over the wall and into the kitchen of a bungalow across the street. That was one of the longest balls I ever saw hit. It brought everything on the field to a standstill as everybody just watched in awe.

I know Joe didn't hit all that many homers in his career—at least not by the standards of a few years later when Ruth and company changed the nature of the game—but he was capable of uncorking a long shot with the best of them.

**CHARLES COMISKEY** Going into the season, we figured we had as good a chance for the pennant as anyone.

The fans must have agreed with that assessment too because we had more than 31,000 spectators at our opening game against the Tigers. It was the largest opening day contingent in our history, and although we lost the game 4 to 0, it suggested that my investment in the high-priced Collins and Jackson might have been a wise move after all.

**JOE JACKSON** Fans can be funny sometimes. When I went back to Cleveland for a series, every time I came up they gave me applause, but then after the game several fans were waiting for me outside the clubhouse just to tell me that they were happier with Tris Speaker.

We didn't get off to a good start like everybody thought we would, but we stayed close to the top all season. We kept waiting for a big winning streak that would put us clear out front, but it never came.

**BAN JOHNSON** Too many bean balls were being thrown that season. In one particular series, I saw Joe Jackson thrown at five times, but he never backed away. Now I was loath to believe that any player in the game would deliberately injure another, but I was of the growing belief that pitchers were throwing more and more at top players like Jackson. So I put forth a plan to give the batter two bases whenever he was hit in the head by a pitched ball. Comiskey agreed with me. After all, he had a great deal of capital invested in Collins and Jackson. President Ebbets of the Brooklyn National League Club argued that a batsman be given his base any time the pitcher tries, in the opinion of the umpire, to hit the batter in the head.

We kicked the ideas around for a while, but obviously nothing came of it. Nevertheless, I have always believed that baseball should do more to protect its star players.

**PANTS ROWLAND** The 1916 season saw us in the chase all the way, but in the end, we came in two games behind Boston which repeated as American League champs. They surprised us all by winning despite giving up Tris Speaker to Cleveland after a salary dispute. They had a terrific pitching staff led by the young Babe Ruth who won 23 games and the ERA title at 1.75. Cicotte came in second to Ruth with an ERA of 1.78.

You know, it's not out of the question to argue that Ruth was the best southpaw in American League history. Even in the World Series that year, he outshone everyone. He gave up a first inning run, then pitched 13 scoreless frames in two Series games.

We were all disappointed in coming in second, but you couldn't blame Joe for that. He rebounded brilliantly from the lackluster tag to the 1915 season, and finished with a .341 average, trailing only Speaker and Cobb. He topped the majors by collecting 21 triples and 293 total bases.

If there was any doubts about his ability to produce in Chicago, he certainly put those doubts to rest.

**JOE JACKSON** Everybody was saying that the White Sox was one of the best teams anybody ever seen. Then why didn't we win?

I'll tell you this: long before the season was over, I began wanting to get home real bad. Something was wrong with that team right from the beginning. Like my daddy used to say, you could feel when something was wrong. You could feel it in your bones. It's like when you're hunting. You just know it, that's all

# 42

## WE SHOULD OF BEEN HAPPY

**JOE JACKSON** It was in 1917 that I won a big old loving cup for a long-distance throwing contest in Boston. Me and Katie lugged that cup around from house to house for a long time.

All the best players from both leagues were at a field in Boston for a charity all-star game. The throwing contest was what they did before the game.

I didn't even know I was in it. Cobb and Speaker slipped around and entered me. I was sitting out by the flagpole and when they called my name I picked up the ball and throwed it to home plate and that was the winning throw.

The National League won the game on a double by Rabbit Maranville but I thought we had the prettiest ballclub I ever did see stacked together. We had Stuffy McInnis and George Sisler sharing first base. Eddie Collins at second, Everett Shott at shortstop, Buck Weaver at third, and me, Cobb and Speaker in the outfield. Hank Severeid, Ray Schalk, and Stevie O'Neill was the catchers.

Walter Johnson started off for us, and the second pitcher was a spitball hurler for the Yankees. I can't remember his name, but he was a good one.

Now that was a baseball team!

**BAN JOHNSON** Concern arose during the winter of 1917 that the major league players might go out on strike. The issue, believe it or not, was the playing conditions of minor leaguers, a sentiment stirred up by the Baseball Players' Fraternity.

I met with the owners several times over the winter to detail strategies should such a strike materialize. However, as we neared the beginning of spring training, most of the established players got cold feet and signed. By the time the spring games began, 85 percent of the players had signed, and virtually all of the stars like Collins, Jackson, Speaker, and Cobb were in the fold.

The big concern on everyone's minds during that winter was the escalation of the war in Europe. The papers were filled with the stories of extensive casualties in the battles of Verdun and the Somme offensive. U.S. neutrality had been imperiled by the sinking of the Lusitania, and although we remained apart from the fighting, it was obvious that it was only a matter of time before we became involved.

Patriotic sentiments were running high, and a number of players felt that they should immediately enlist for military service when we did enter the fray. Many fans felt players owed it to their country to enlist as they were young and fit, and thus potentially good soldier material.

League officials and owners were unanimous in their resolve to support the war effort when the time came. We agreed that any player in the American League desiring to enlist would be granted immediate release and their roster spots held open. Not only that, but we would also look to the welfare of their dependents. Baseball is, after all, as American as apple pie.

We determined that the league would not suspend playing in the event of war. "Normalcy" at all costs was essential for the spirit of the country. It was also essential for the continued popularity of the game. And we had precedent. The National League, during the Spanish-American conflict continued its schedules.

The New York club put forth a suggestion that certain hours be set aside during the training season for military drill. It would be a good example in military preparedness he argued. We agreed. The game must go on, but it must go on in the spirit of the times.

On behalf of the league, I made application to the government for the appointment of expert United States Army Drill Sergeants to accompany the eight clubs to the spring training camps as military instructors.

Most players demonstrated an admirable patriotic spirit—most, but not all. Joe Jackson, for example, irrevocably hurt his image with the public by his actions. I'm sure that some of his later problems stemmed from this time.

**EDDIE CICOTTE** Some army officer got the bright idea to offer cash money prizes for the best drilled team in the league. The winning team was to get a $500 prize and a prize of $100 in gold was going to go to the sergeant who instructed the winning players.

Since Comiskey was the stingiest owner in captivity, some of us joked that winning that prize was the only way we were going to get any additional money all season.

**EDDIE COLLINS** Before every game, we not only took batting and infield practice, but we took military drill practice as well.

None of us really took the idea seriously at first, but that changed once we started drilling. Most of us had never had the advantage of a single military drill in our lives, yet it soon became apparent that the discipline of the ball field was a great help. The coordination so necessary for successful teamwork translated well to the drills.

Some people said that the calisthenics and setting up exercises would throw off the muscular balance of the player. If anything it turned out to be a help. We were more fit for ball playing after a week of drill than we would have been without it.

The bats made a good substitute for a rifle.

Sergeant Smilley was our assigned taskmaster and he put us through the mill. Oh, some of the boys resisted at first—one of our new players, Chick Gandil mostly—but once the public started seeing us doing it, we shaped up.

There was, however, more to the drills than the mere manual of arms, squads left and right, and so on. After the first few days it was apparent that every man in the line felt a certain responsibility not to be shown up.

No more patriotic a bunch of fellows could have been found in those days than the ballplayers—at least the great majority of them. We knew military drill was serious business that might come in good stead once we entered the war.

It was hard work to make the American public realize that war was at our door, but many of us understood that if the small part the White Sox took to bring this to the public's attention was successful, then that would have paid for all the extra work the drilling entailed.

I can still see Joe out there marching like Sargent York, with his long loping strides and serious face. I don't recall him complaining too much, but on the other hand, I don't think he was overly excited about it.

**BAN JOHNSON** The U.S. entered the war on April 6—just as we were about to open our season. From that point on we redoubled our efforts to prove that baseball was synonymous with the spirit of America.

The issue of players enlisting or being conscripted into the service arose immediately, and although I had no assurances from the government, I had reason to believe that if the proposed conscription law became operative, it would not be applied to the players in the league until after the season ended in October.

All the teams other than the Boston Red Sox had become proficient in military tactics, and I expected them to catch up quickly. The service we were providing to the country was, I believed, extremely valuable, and it didn't seem likely that anyone in the government would want to alter that.

On the other hand, I knew that the public would look askance at any player who indicated he didn't want to fight. Accordingly, I put out the following press release:

"General Barry knows all about the efficiency of our earnest and patriotic players who want to become real soldiers, so that they can ably fight for the United States Army. The players who are great athletes will make splendid soldiers. I expect to see all the unmarried ones in Uncle Sam's army next fall, as they will be kept at work drilling under the command of army sergeants until autumn."

I just hoped to God I was right.

**LEFTY WILLIAMS** A lot of talk floated around the locker room about the draft that was supposed to be coming in. Many of us who fit all the criteria—we were the right age and we were not married. Me, Red Faber, McMullen and Leibold were the most obvious ones to go. Guys like Risberg and Weaver were married, so it looked like they were safe. Joe was over 29, and everybody was saying they weren't going to take guys over 25. Besides he was married.

Still, nobody knew for sure what was going to happen.

**JOE JACKSON** First we drilled with baseball bats, which must have looked pretty stupid, but later they gave us real rifles. Now, a lot of the boys didn't exactly know what to do with a rifle, but I did, so I showed some of the others at least how to hold one.

**I.E. SANBORN** I was covering the Sox for The Chicago Trib during that season. Some people who doubtless lacked patriotism themselves tried to insinuate that baseball arranged the military features at its games merely to increase its own patronage.

Although it is true the attendance may have been increased by some of these patriotic pageants, the increases were wiped out by the expense of arranging and decorating for them.

Comiskey set aside 10 percent of his share of the receipts of every game at their park for the military. Clarke Griffith of the Washington team donated baseball outfits to the soldiers and sailors.

In some cities, the entire receipts of some games were donated to engineer corps.

The nation's need for funds was recognized by the American League's subscription of $100,000 to the first issue of Liberty bonds.

In most ballparks, soldiers and sailors in uniform were admitted free. Some games were played by big leaguers at camps and training stations for the benefit or entertainment of men preparing to go to France.

In every conceivable way, baseball showed its red white and blue colors during the war. It's just a real shame, a few players—Joe Jackson among them—sullied the reputation of an otherwise patriotic sport.

**EDDIE CICOTTE** Yeah, I know Comiskey donated a lot of money to the Red Cross except he did it for the wrong reason. Comiskey wasn't a patriot; he was a self-serving, money-grabbing businessman. He wasn't as interested in the war effort as he was in making himself look good. It was all a public posture,

Believe me, the players weren't blinded by his phony generosity.

**LEFTY WILLIAMS** Early in the season the papers said June 5th was the day set by President Wilson for the draft registration, so Mr. Comiskey arranged for all of us Sox who was eligible for the draft to go down to the city clerk's office together to register. Although most of us didn't live in Chicago we all went down there under what they called the absentee clause of the Army bill because our schedule had us on the road for registration day.

Of course, Mr. Comiskey arranged for plenty of publicity for what we did.

My roomie, Joe Jackson, and I spent many nights talking about this, but he was luckier, because he was married and older. Still, neither one of us really wanted to be sent to France. I mean, can you imagine Joe in Paris? He had enough troubles in Philadelphia.

**CHARLIE LEBEAU** Of course Joe was leery about going into the army. The issue of his illiteracy would have come up all over again. I'm sure he was frightened of the prospect of being given some important information—like how to use a hand grenade—in written form, and not being able to deal with it at all. And, of course, he must have broken into a cold sweat at the mere mention of going to Europe.

I'm convinced Joe was more frightened of the army than he was of the war.

**BUCK WEAVER** Three of us went down to take army physicals in August—me, Hap Felsch and Chick Gandil. We all passed but claimed exemptions on the grounds that we were married and had dependents.

As far as I know, Joe never appeared for his physical.

**PANTS ROWLAND** The war was on everybody's mind, of course, but the game had to go on. It was a good healthy outlet and a good substitute for the tension caused by the war issues.

We had been disappointed in the 1916 season results, and everybody was committed to better results in 1917. We simply had given up too many runs that we shouldn't have. So, to remedy that, we went out and picked up two sweet fielders: Swede Risberg and Chick Gandil. Both knew what to do with the leather.

Gandil, in particular made a big difference. He was a rangy first baseman, who it turned out, inspired confidence in the whole infield by his ability to handle throws that would have gone through Fournier the year before. We had even played Joe there a little when we got him. He probably could have succeeded there, but it was a shame to waste his speed and arm. We needed him in the outfield.

Risberg helped, too. Although he was only a kid and hadn't played a lot of short before, he picked up the position quickly, and before long he was an outstanding fielder.

Everyone in the organization believed that with these two players added to what we already had, we were sure to win the pennant.

**I. E. SANBORN** It looked for all the world, as the season began that nothing short of a spate of serious injuries could stop the Sox. Remember, the year before they had missed the pennant by just two games.

This was a solid team with a set lineup at all but one position. In Gandil they picked up a first baseman of skill and experience, and although he had a loose knee, he had not missed many games in his career. Risberg had all of the qualities for a shortstop: speed, good hands and a fighting spirit. Weaver, having been moved permanently to third, looked to be on the verge of stardom. Eddie Collins anchored the infield, and there were few men who ever played it better.

They also had a couple of superior spare parts for the infield. McMullen could play second, third or short, and do it well in a pinch, and as a bonus he was a decent hitter.

Defensively there was nothing lacking in left or center field with Jackson and Felsch on the job as they were a great pair of outfielders capable of bagging anything they could get their hands on and of inspiring fear in base runners. Only right field was a question mark, but Rowland had his choice of Leibold, Murphy, Shano Collins and perhaps a couple of others.

At catcher, Ray Schalk, the Litchfield pepper pot led the league's catchers in all-around play.

The pitching staff returned intact from the previous season, and although it didn't boast a marquee hurler like Johnson or Mathewson, it was a well-balanced staff made up of dependable pitchers. Faber, Scott, Williams, Cicotte, Benz, and Wolfgang made up a formidable, if not overpowering staff.

The team opened at home against the Browns. It was a balmy day for which Comiskey had prepared by decorating his stadium with more American flags than I supposed there were in the world. Everywhere I looked, from the scoreboard, along the bleachers, pavilions and grandstand, it was a circle of red, white and blue. Special boxes were draped with United States flags in honor of Major General Barry, and Captain Kennedy, the distinguished guests of the day.

Fans were on hand early for the military drill. Nearly 25,000 were there when the White Sox marched out between grandstand and pavilion clad in regulation army uniforms and each shouldering a Springfield rifle. A roar fairly drowned the band which was trying to furnish a quickstep for the Sox to march by.

After Sergeant Smilley brought his men to rest in front of the grandstand, Major General Barry briefly inspected the ranks and complimented the sergeant on the showing of what had been a raw bunch of military rookies only six weeks before,

The Sox were then presented with a regimental flag as a gift from the Chicago Board of Trade. After disappearing for a short period, the White Sox reappeared clad in their baseball uniforms and went through more military drills, winding up with brief setting up exercises, using the more familiar bats.

The crowd loved it, loved the patriotic spirit, loved their ballplayers showing the flag.

**JOE JACKSON** Man alive, that was the strangest opening day I ever seen. We spent more time acting like make-believe soldiers than we did real ballplayers.

Then the game started and it began raining, but we played in the mud anyway and lost 6 to 2. I only got one hit, but I felt like I was in good condition helped by the drilling and was looking forward to the season.

Everybody said we had a good chance to make the World Series, and that was something I really wanted to do. The only thing was, this team still didn't get along together very good, but maybe that didn't have to stop us from winning the flag. Liking each other and playing good together are two different things.

**PANTS ROWLAND** The 1917 season saw us duking it out with Boston all season with Cleveland nipping at our heels. Our hitting was keeping us at or near the top. With Collins, Jackson, Felsch, Gandil, and Weaver hitting in the middle of our lineup, we scored more runs than any other team in the majors. Our pitching staff led by Cicotte's 28 wins posted the lowest earned run average in the American League. That's a hard combination to beat. Score more runs than anyone else and give up fewer, and you damn well should win the pennant. Mostly my job that season was filling out the lineup card, and then watching the game.

**I.E. SANBORN** As far as the fans were concerned, the Sox really had three great star players: Cicotte, Collins and Jackson.

Cicotte pitched brilliantly all year. He led the league in wins while posting a 1.53 ERA and striking out 150 batters. He completed 29 games that season, finishing behind only Babe Ruth and Walter Johnson.

Perhaps because of his great record, he was accused of using various kinds of dope to make the ball do funny stunts. Several teams hypnotized themselves into the belief they couldn't touch Cicotte with a telephone pole. Notable among them was Tris Speaker, who became the leader of the campaign to have Cicotte's delivery called to the attention of the United States government inspectors on the ground it was interfering with the batting averages of loyal American citizens.

Eddie Collins' batting average was down a little bit from previous seasons, but he played a brilliant second base, and he played it every day. He stole 53 bases, walked 89 times, and was unquestionably the leader of the team on the field.

Jackson's average slipped to .301 but his slugging average was among the highest in the league and he hit consistently in the clutch.

Cicotte, Collins, Jackson: three great players, three completely different individuals.

**PANTS ROWLAND** Cicotte was a crafty veteran who relied more on gray matter than muscle matter. Everyone accused him of throwing the shine ball. The pitch was a myth, but it was a myth Eddie encouraged. Some of the other teams claimed he was 45 years old and therefore it was impossible for him to suddenly become a winning pitcher. The fact of the matter is, he became a great pitcher when he decided to get in shape.

Eddie used to be a beer guzzling roly-poly type. Then one day he got the message, lost a lot of weight, worked himself into shape, tuned up his knuckleball, and became a huge success.

He could be downright surly and probably more concerned with his own record than with the team, but he could pitch.

Eddie Collins was smart. He was smart in baseball, and he was smart in life. He was like a second manager, and I was damn glad to have him out there. When Collins made a suggestion, I listened. Off the field, however, it was quite a different matter. Some players resented his I-holier-than-thou attitude and let him know it. Cicotte, Risberg and Gandil in particular. As far as I know, the latter two never spoke to him. Gandil apparently became furious with Collins over a rough play at second base when Collins was with the Athletics. Risberg went along because he was a stooge for Gandil.

Collins was without doubt more respected than liked. Connie Mack claimed he was the greatest second baseman who ever lived, and Connie, remember also had Nap Lajoie on his team for a few years.

The man they called Cocky Collins was a jug-eared, long-nosed, thick-lipped, brilliant but aloof player.

The only real friend I think he had on the team was Ray Schalk, our hard-boiled catcher.

Back in 1912, when for once the Athletics did not win the flag, I remember some of his teammates turned on Collins for accepting $2,000 from American Magazine to pen a series of articles on inside baseball. In them he explained how opposing pitchers were tipping off their pitches. Needless to say, this did not go down well with some of the As.

One aspect of the game where he unquestionably excelled was in salary negotiating. He was a master of the art form, and as a result made about twice as much as anyone else on the team. This, of course, did nothing to endear him to his mates.

Joe Jackson was neither in Collins' camp nor in Cicotte's but he could be influenced by either one. Joe could be manipulated, and Cicotte was a master manipulator.

In hindsight I should have seen signs of the coming troubles. What is clear now, however, is that the team was split into two groups—the Cicotte/Gandil faction, and the Collins/Schalk faction. Cicotte and Gandil would spit on their grandmothers if it were in their best interests; Collins and Schalk would help them across the street.

Joe was a pawn who could be moved by either side. He seldom exerted himself in off-field situations. He probably felt he couldn't.

**JOE JACKSON** Everybody was mad at everybody most of the time. The locker room was tense with a lot of people not talking to a lot of other people. The only thing is, we were winning, so nobody made much of the problems off the field.

**CHICK GANDIL** I was the new guy on the block as far as the Sox were concerned, but I had been around for a few years before heading for Chicago, so I figured I knew a little about how a team was supposed to be run, and let me tell you, on that team things were screwed up. So I spoke up. I spoke up for what I thought was right.

Let me give you an example. Smack in the middle of the season and the fight for the flag, Comiskey comes up with this plan to send us from Philadelphia to Detroit for a game in Jungletown the next Sunday to play off a postponed game for no other reason than to grab some extra Sunday receipts and then back to Philadelphia again. You can see why we weren't in a particularly gentle mood.

This when we needed every ounce of fight to keep the lead we had in the American League pennant race.

Look, we were facing a tough series with Boston lasting four days, then we had to have a night jump into Philadelphia on Thursday to begin a series of five games in five days against the Athletics. We were counting on a Sunday's rest to steady the pitching staff which was already showing signs of wearing out.

Instead of that, Comiskey told us we were expected to make a hurried getaway out of Philadelphia on Saturday, ride all night and part of Sunday, play a game in Detroit, then board an early train out of Detroit, ride all night and part of Monday back to Philadelphia, then tackle the Athletics who would have been resting over the Sabbath. On top of that, the weather was hot, very hot, so we all knew that it was going to be impossible to make that trip and preserve any energy at all.

That was just one of a million examples of the kind of treatment we were receiving at the hands of Comiskey.

We had a team meeting, and some of us bitched about the schedule—me, Cicotte, a couple of others. Collins, said it was not up to us to set the schedule, that our job was to play baseball. He made me sick with his sanctimonious preaching.

I asked Joe what he thought.

"I really don't know," he said.

"What do you mean you don't know?" I asked him. "You got a brain in your head, don't you?"

"Yeah, I got a brain," he responded angrily.

"Then what the hell do you think?

"About us going to Detroit and then right back to Philadelphia?"

"Yeah, that's what we're talking about, isn't it?"

Joe looked around the room like he was looking for an answer from someone else. Then Lefty jumped in.

"Look, let's just play baseball, OK."

"That's what I'm trying to tell you," I said. "We're in the middle of a hot race, and we can't play our best ball if Comiskey has us running all around the country so that he can make a buck, can we?"

"Why don't you just shut the hell up!" chimed in Schalk.

"You guys are just a bunch of weak-kneed cowards, that's all," I said.

That's the kind of stuff that went on all the time on that team. There were those of us who were willing to stand up for our rights, and those who weren't.

Another time, while we were still in spring training, we stopped off in a god-forsaken place called Horton, Kansas.

It was raining cats and dogs when we got there, but Comiskey insisted we play the local team despite Rowland's plea that we be allowed to continue to St. Joseph.

Assurances from management that our hotel arrangements had been taken care of proved false. The dash to the hotel included a narrow escape, as our machine was hit amidships at a street crossing by a jitney driven by a veterinary surgeon dashing madly to answer a call. After the thrilling ride, no breakfast was to be had at any price because none of us were expected.

In the drenching rain we were obliged to forage for food. All of this was so Comiskey could get the receipts for a lousy game that was never played. That was typical of the way he ran his operation.

**JOE JACKSON** When we was in New York, we had a fire scare in the hotel. Well, it wasn't really a fire, but it looked like one. Somebody said what really happened was that an ammonia pipe burst but the fire alarm sounded so we all had to leave the hotel in the middle of the night and go out into the rain.

I got a bad cold from that rain and got sick to my stomach on the train coming over that night. I tried to play the next day, but had to come out of the game.

Gandil thought I was just trying to take the game off which I wasn't, but we got into a pretty good argument about it. I hardly never missed any games, so I didn't appreciate his saying that I was loafing, but there was no keeping some of the boys on that team happy.

One day, too, a kid who didn't have the price to get into the game, tried to climb a ladder outside of the park, but he fell off and died. Gandil said the only reason he was there was to see me play, but I don't know if that was true or not. Anyway, it was the kind of thing he would say. Another thing I remember about that season was that Weaver and McMullen got drug off to court for something that had to do with a fight on the day some gamblers tried to break up one of our games against Boston. Somebody from the team had to go bail them out.

Things like that were happening to us all year—one problem after another.

One good thing, though, was that Fred Clarke who used to be the manager of the Pirates, invented these sun glasses which screwed on to the peak of your baseball cap. Boy, was they ever a help. I was never without them after that.

**EDDIE CICOTTE** I remember one particular game that season when Joe's failure to see a cinch double play in the sixth inning was responsible for our loss. With runners on third and second and one out, Miller popped a little fly to short right. Jackson made an easy catch of it and there was no chance for the runner on third to score, but Joe threw home absolutely deaf to the yells of Collins at second, where Pipp would have been doubled up easily because he thought the fly was going to fall.

This gaffe was pointed out to Joe who took the criticism personally and sulked the rest of the week. Look, we were just trying to make the team better, but Joe, he had real thin skin.

**JOE JACKSON** Even though we was arguing a lot of the time, we was still playing pretty good ball. Once in the early innings of a game against Detroit, Heilman lifted a high foul to the stands. Weaver dashed over, jumped on the concrete step leading to the grandstand next to the Detroit dugout, reached over and made a terrific, falling catch. That was one of the best catches I ever seen made by a third baseman and showed the kind of ball we was capable of playing when we wanted to.

We also won a game by forfeit that season even though the score was tied 3 to 3 in the 10th inning. We was playing Cleveland and umpire Owens called Jack Graney out for interference on a play that the Indians scored three runs. The Indian players made a joke of the game by bellyaching so much that Owens lost patience and finally stopped them by forfeiting the game which was just fine by us.

That was the year, too, that they brought back the Bull Durham signs like they used to have. They was on the outfield fence, and every time you hit the sign with a fly ball in a game, the tobacco company gave you $50. That wasn't a lot of money, but it was fun trying to do just the same. I came close a couple of times, but never did hit it.

**I.E. SANBORN** By early September, the White Sox were out front of the Red Sox by some six games and thinking about the World Series. The game which seemed to have clinched it for them came on September 8th, against the Indians.

Eddie Cicotte with four days rest pitched a whale of a game, holding the Tribe to four singles. Collins, Jackson, and Gandil did the telling stick work in the winning third. Collins started the attack with a single, Jackson peeled off a double that would have been longer had Graney not knocked it down on the run, and Gandil sent Joe home with a single.

The combat was preceded by a review of more than 6,000 local soldiers and sailors who gathered in response to the invitation of President Comiskey to accept a gift from the Woodland Bards' Association—a complete set of baseball uniforms for each local military unit. For nearly two hours prior to the game, the men who were going to blaze the trail to France paraded around the playing field accompanied by rousing band music. The crowd of 15,000 who had arrived early for the big demonstration, cheered loudly.

**JOE JACKSON** It started to look like we was going to make it to the Series, except that all sorts of people were saying that the Series might be canceled that year on account of the war.

**BAN JOHNSON** America was preparing to send 2,000,000 men to France, and I knew that baseball had to be seen as willing to do its share in the battle—anything else would have been organizational suicide. I realized that if the government called the new conscription army to colors in September as rumor had it, then we had to be prepared to wind up the championship race immediately and turn over 200 well drilled players to the army.

**PANTS ROWLAND** Although there was plenty of talk about canceling the Series, we had to play as if it were going on as scheduled. By mid-September, it looked as if we were going to face off against the Giants, a strong and formidable machine, a hard-hitting organization, brilliant on defense, and smart and alert on the bases.

Interest in the championship was strong from the start, with scalpers going all the way up to $7.50 for a $5.00 box seat.

Johnson decided that if we made it to the Series, it would be held in two-game segments, beginning on October 5. The place for holding the first game was to be determined by lot. However, President Johnson decided that should New York win the toss of a coin for the first game, he would ask the Giants to waive their rights and play the first game in Chicago, as the competition was scheduled to begin on a Sunday, and Sunday ball was not played in New York.

These were the plans. The only question was, would there be a Series at all?

The players were antsy as we headed down the stretch, and the tension created by the uncertainty, only made the clubhouse discord worse.

**HARRY GRABINER** My office was camouflaged like a post office before the final week of September. We must have gotten 3,000 to 4,000 requests for tickets every day. As White Sox team secretary, it was my job to deal with them. Who says the war diminished interest in baseball? If anything, it heightened it. Baseball was a great relief from the tensions of war—a safety valve if you will.

At Comiskey's insistence, we did everything we could to cut down on the scalping. We even went so far as to try to get the name and address of every purchaser of every reserve and box seat for every game, and then we would be in a position to let the public know the names of fans who scalp tickets by advertising them in the newspapers at the club's expense.

It seems as if one of the net results of war was the opportunity to increase the price of everything except possibly a few luxuries, among them baseball. It was still possible to see a major league baseball game for 25 cents.

**CHICK GANDIL** We ended up winning the pennant by 10 games. Now it was well known to everyone in and around baseball that the Red Sox had offered each of their players $1,000 if Boston had captured the flag.

So when we took the flag we expected a similar bonus from Comiskey. On the train ride home after we clinched, the Old Roman made good. He gave us a case of cheap Champagne to share among the whole team—one lousy case.

I guess we shouldn't have been surprised though. I mean after all, this was the man who charged us 50 cents a garment to clean our uniforms. When some of us balked at that, he had our uniforms taken out of our lockers and cleaned. Then he docked our pay for the cost.

Talk about an owner without class! Is it any wonder he ran into the problems he did?

**JOE JACKSON** Me and Ted Jourdan were the only Southerners on the team unless you count Reb Russell from Texas. Ted was a young kid from New Orleans who didn't get to play much and I didn't really get to know him. Most of the boys on the team went their own way. I was just glad I was married and had Katie. I don't know what I would have done without her.

We had more nicknames on that team than I ever seen before. Scott was "Succotash;" Schalk was "Cracker;" Felsch, "Hap;" Gandil, "Chick;" Risberg, "Swede;" Benz, "Blitzen;" and I was known as "General," or "General Jackson." Only the papers called me "Shoeless." Nicknames sound friendly, but this was not a friendly club. It looked like there was going to be a Series after all. We should of been happy.

# 43

## THERE I WAS ON A CHAMPIONSHIP CLUB

**CHARLES COMISKEY** Chicago went baseball crazy. It was the first championship Chicago had won in 11 years. On the eve of the Series, my biggest problem was where to find enough tickets for the friends and fans who wanted to see my boys. We had requests for more than 200,000 tickets in a park which would seat about 32,000. I didn't know it was possible to lose so many friends in so short a time. Letters of protest inundated my office. There was more talk on the street about how to get tickets than there was about who was going to pitch.

**JOE JACKSON** We was supposed to have a practice game against Cleveland the day before the Series was supposed to begin, but it rained so hard that the game had to be called. Instead we went into the clubhouse and listened to a lot of speeches on how to lick the New Yorkers. Mostly we listened to Eddie Collins, Eddie Cicotte and Kid Gleason, one of our coaches.

I guess we was all a mite nervous on account of all the talk about the Series. I never seen nothing like it.

We was set to play the first two games in Chicago and then leave at 8 o'clock Sunday night on a train that got into New York at 6 o'clock Monday night. I wondered if New York was going to be as hepped up on the Series as Chicago was.

**I.E. SANBORN** Boiling all the World Series dope down to the bone, I figured it was a 50-50 proposition. There were so many ifs of vital importance that the issues were shrouded with uncertainties. The big bettors—the gamblers who lived by their wits—left the Series practically alone and what wagering was done was largely a matter of sentiment or local pride. That's how even the teams appeared to be.

I gave the edge in the infield to the White Sox, but only slightly. I figured Collins and Gandil gave them that edge. At catcher, the White Sox had a decided advantage with Schalk, but if he got hurt, the Giants' backups were stronger.

Cicotte was the one dependable man on Chicago's slab staff, but he could not win the Series alone and in postseason events in the recent past, pitching had been the determining factor.

The outfield, though, was the most intriguing unit to figure. Based on past performances, I had to rate Felsch superior to Kauff by a wide margin. The right field spot, the weakest on both teams, was about an even break. That left it up to leftfield. Joe Jackson versus. George Burns. Burns was an excellent little outfielder and a good hitter, although not with Jackson's power. He was fast, stole quite a few bases from his leadoff spot, and was excellent defensively. Then there was also the issue of Joe's nerves. Would he feel the exceptional pressure as he did when he first came up with Philadelphia? This was a question being asked, and with some justification.

All things considered, as the Series was about to begin, I had to give the edge to Burns.

**VINCENT ALEXANDER** I was not about to miss the opportunity to see Joe play in the Series, so, mustering every penny I could beg, borrow or steal, I made my way to Chicago—without tickets. My only choice was to buy from scalpers, an expensive option for one with limited resources, but given my passion to see the games, a necessary one.

A man named Waterfall, who operated out of the Palmer House, it turned out, had the rarest of commodities—grandstand seats. These were almost impossible to come by as most scalpers were offering only three-game box seats for $50. Waterfall, though, knew someone who knew someone who knew someone I met on the El. The tickets were not for public sale but were reserved for "regular customers."

"If I can talk him out of some," my train-riding acquaintance informed me, "they'll go for $15 for a complete set of pasteboards."

Comiskey had sold them for $4.50, but I had no choice. Unfortunately I was not one of the lucky ones to get a set. Joe Jackson's biggest fan was out in the cold.

I did, however, come across a White Sox patriotic button. In the center was a baseball with a rifle across it. In the top space there was a picture of Comiskey, at the left a bullet, at the right a baseball, and at the bottom a pair of white socks. I still have that button.

**I.E. SANBORN** Much was being made of the manager match ups. John McGraw, Little Napoleon, was already in his 18th year as a manager, and that followed a long career as a player. Without doubt, he was one of the most influential figures in the history of major league baseball.

His rival was a manager who never played in the major leagues. When Comiskey announced three years earlier that he had engaged a bush leaguer whose first name was Clarence, the baseball world smiled and said that any man with a name like that would never do in big circles. His only claim to fame was that he once led the Peoria club to a minor league title, a fact which occasioned even more laughter. Peoria always drew a laugh anyway as the place named in a popular song about being the town where theatrical troupes get stranded and where the ghost always walks.

Was he up to the challenge? Would his pitchers come through? Would Joe Jackson hold up under the pressure? These were some of the questions as the Series was about to begin.

**CHICK GANDIL** Get this. Just before we started playing, Commy and the league officials decided it would be a good idea if the players and the clubs involved would invest anything they made from the Series in the second issue of Liberty bonds. It would be a real service to the Liberty Loan they said.

Now that's fine and dandy for someone with Commy's money, but most of us had families and things in mind for our shares.

**VINCENT ALEXANDER** On the street and in every crowded hotel lobby, White Sox and Giant fans talked volumes about the chances of both clubs. McGraw and Rowland both insisted the night before the games began that they did not know who would pitch the opening game. The chess match had begun. Most of the sentiment was on the side of a match-up between Ferdinand Stubblefield Schupp, the Louisville Kid and the knuckleball-throwing Eddie Cicotte.

In Chicago there seemed to be just as many ways of pronouncing Cicotte's name as in Philadelphia. Some called him Cheekotee, others warbled it Cy-Kot, while Cicotte seemed to think that his name should be pronounced See-Kot. Any way it was pronounced, he was the likely starter.

I went over to the park to see the teams practice the day before the first game, but the weather was bad and the field wet, so neither manager cared to risk turned ankles or broken legs. The players were sentenced to worrying about what the experts had written about them. All except Joe, of course. He was spared that trial.

Despite the rain, I was one of hundreds of fans who braved the weather and formed a line outside the bleacher gates. I arrived early, hoping to get the place of honor among rabid bugs. I found, however, that there was one fan ahead of me, so I edged into second place.

The rain fell so heavily that we had to resort to umbrellas, raincoats, and even blankets to protect us during our long vigil. Most of us were well bundled up, and prepared to try to catch a few winks.

During the long cold hours of the night some waiting fans started fires to keep warm. A change in the weather at midnight brought a full moon. Every hour brought hundreds more to the line.

A surprisingly large number of women were among us. At one point an automobile took its place in line, and the five occupants slumbered on the cushions until morning.

Many a fan was overheard to say he (or she) would do the same thing over again that night and would willingly take his place outside the gates as soon as the day's last fly had been caught.

The wise undertaker who brought 500 chairs to rent to the standers was on hand early in the morning. It was an orderly crowd, and on only one occasion, when the police changed the direction of one line and the iron fence around the playground gave way under the stress, was protection necessary. At 10 bells sharp the bleacher and pavilion ticket windows flew open with a bang and those of us who were lucky enough to get tickets started streaming into the park singing "The End of a Perfect Night." Four lines led up to the two arteries to the unreserved seats. The long lines that straggled out for blocks surrounding Comiskey Park passed through the turnstiles.

The supply of tickets ran out before the end of the lines were near the gates. Late comers who had remained at home for breakfast were turned away to hunt electric scoreboards.

**PANTS ROWLAND** The day the World Series began I realized the two greatest ambitions of my life—winning the American League pennant and getting to the Series.

The boys appeared confident, if somewhat anxious.

Before the game, Commy came into the locker room and, like a general inspecting his troops, looked the boys over carefully. He told them the ambitions of his lifetime were at stake in the Series. He told them that he knew deep down in his heart that they would win if they played the ball they were capable of playing.

Some players listened attentively, others sneered derisively behind his back.

**VINCENT ALEXANDER** It was bright and warm and gave the women fans just the chance to display their fall finery.

Throughout the stands there were patches of color, purple being the most popular. Many of us wished we had left our overcoats behind.

Managers Rowland and McGraw must have had their pictures taken a thousand times. Most of them were of them shaking hands, to which one woman sitting next to me remarked, "Oh, I thought those men knew each other before. How interesting."

I watched Joe pose a number of times. If only I had one of those photos.

One noticeable thing about the ball field at Comiskey Park was the grass didn't seem to be as green as it was in Philadelphia.

The loudest collection of fans were the Woodland Bards, the famous organization of White Sox fans who had waited for years for this occasion. The Bards were, without doubt, the most rabid baseball fans in the world. They even had a clubroom right at the park, so that when the Sox won a game, they could sit around and win it all over again.

The Sox were the first to come running out onto the field, and they received a great welcome from the crowd. Rowland, Cicotte, and Collins seemed to be the crowd favorites, but Joe came in for his fair share of vocal support.

During batting practice, Joe poled several long shots to the outfield wall.

When the Giants ambled onto the field to a meager scattering of applause shortly after 12:30, they appeared to be a dejected, mournful group of athletes.

The first play of their practice was a grounder to Zimmerman, and when he missed the ball, the White Sox fans roared with delight.

The Sox were all togged out in new cream colored uniforms, and the white hose which they usually wore were replaced by socks of red, white and blue. The Giants wore uniforms of battleship gray decorated with purple, and they sported new sweater jackets of autumn brown.

The happiest person at the game looked to be the mascot, young Clarence Rowland, Jr., son of the manager.

**I.E. SANBORN** In the opening game, a prodigious home run by Happy Felsch sailed deep into the left field bleachers giving the Sox a one-run victory.

The Giants were baffled by the knuckle balls of Eddie Cicotte.

Joe was hitless in three at bats, but may have saved the game with his defensive heroics. In the seventh inning with one out, Walter Holke, the Giants' first baseman, raised his team's hopes with a resounding single to right. Lew McCarty stepped to bat, having already smacked a three-bagger earlier in the contest. He caught hold of one of Cicotte's floaters and smashed a low, hard liner to left field. It looked as if it would drop too short for Jackson to reach, but General Jackson ran as I had never seen him run before. Holke, at first base, started to race toward second. On came Jackson as the ball settled closer and closer to the ground. Then he dived headlong toward the spot where he thought the ball would drop. As he tumbled forward, the ball fell into his outstretched hands.

It was a remarkable catch that undoubtedly saved the game.

**KATIE JACKSON** The Sox wives went to the Series games. Mrs. Weaver, who was a very pretty lady, wore a seal skin coat and a bright red turban. Buck must have been able to pick her out of the crowd without much trouble. She talked a lot about everything but baseball. She said she and Buck were going to go out west someplace up in the mountains and live in a hunter's log cabin as soon as the big games were over.

Mrs. Cicotte brought her little baby who cried and fussed some, but really wasn't too bad. She had her older daughter there, too—Miss Rose she called her. She was 10, and she ran around near the players bench most of the time. In one of the games she was given a huge bouquet of American roses by someone.

Mrs. Schalk kept score and announced all sorts of things about the game. She knew a lot, too, but not quite as much as she thought. She wore a purple coat with a small black hat.

Mrs. Lynn was a quiet charming little woman with a lovely voice. Her husband was a backup catcher so he didn't get to play much, but just the same, she was there all the time. Her little boy, Vernon, watched with her. She said she left her two- month-old baby with a nurse at the hotel and that she was impatient to get back.

Mrs. Williams sat next to me, and we followed the game pretty closely. We knew more about baseball than most of the people in the stands did. We talked a lot out loud about the games which made some of the men around us laugh, but we didn't care.

**CHARLIE LEBEAU** I went up to Chicago to see the Series, but mostly to see the young boy I used to tell stories to down in the mill village.

Well, I tell you, Chicago was something. Every hotel was packed to the gills. Fans came from every part of the country. One man I met at the Congress Hotel came all the way from Tampa even after he had been notified his application for tickets had not been honored.

Loop hotels put overflow guests on cots, and every restaurant, it seemed had a waiting line out the door.

"Reminds me of a national convention," remarked a politician as he surveyed a milling crowd in one of the big loop hotels. "I've been visiting around at all the hostelries, and it's all the same story—all full of bugs—baseball bugs I mean. Down on Michigan Boulevard I heard a fellow from Nevada fighting a hotel clerk for a room, while other fellows were hollering for a chance to double up."

"A little man in a black suit stepped up and asked if anyone knew where he could get a ticket to one of the games. A half dozen bystanders edged in, thinking a little inside information was about to be imparted. No one answered."

A man swung by humming and clapped a friend on the shoulder.

"Know him?" the politician asked quizzically. "He's got tickets for every session. He's going to see and hear everything from the nominating speeches to the last pop bottle thrown at the umpire. Now that disconsolate looking guy over there comes up with the home delegation expecting the bush league boss to fix him up with the gate passing equipment after arrival. He hasn't found his friend and he won't."

According to a story widely circulated after the first game, Polly, the newsboy who ran a stand on the northeast corner of Madison and Clark streets supposedly cleaned up $4,000 on the first game. Apparently, Polly sent out a number of newspaper peddlers to get tickets, sold them at scalpers' prices, and bet the money on the Sox at odds of 7 to 5.

The next day, I passed by his corner and he was there selling papers just as if he had not made a penny, so I don't know if the story was true or not, but a lot of people said it was.

It was a great time, and I was pleased to be there for Joe.

**CHARLES COMISKEY** To give you some idea of the popularity of this Series, The Chicago Tribune switchboard supervisor told me that all records for phone calls were broken by baseball fans who called for updates on the games. Something like 25,000 calls a day were registered by the eight girls who devoted their entire time to allaying the anxiety of fans. Apparently there were a lot of out of town fans calling, too, because the number of long-distance calls was amazing.

**VINCENT ALEXANDER** After another long, but dryer evening vigil, I managed tickets for the second game, too, It was a beautiful Sabbath day, more like July than October, and as before, the park was filled to overflowing. The game featured Red Faber throwing for the Sox, and Ferdie Schupp, the Giants' big winner going for McGraw's boys.

It was a noisier game than Saturday's, but the undercurrent of respect and fear that Chicago fans had for Heinie, Zim, Herzog, Kauff, Schupp and the other supposed McGraw stars had completely disappeared.

With the game tied 2 to 2 in the second inning, I happened to look over into the Old Roman's box and noticed that he was not sitting with his wife and friends, but was standing on the steps of the main entrance to the grand stand, shifting from foot to foot, wiping perspiration from his face. But then that all changed.

The Sox rallied to a 7 to 2 win, largely on the strength of Joe and Black Betsey. They had a perfect game at the plate—three hits and a base on balls. Joe was, without doubt, the hero of the left field bleacher crowd. Every time he took his place in the left terrace, he was greeted with a storm of applause. On that day, Joe could have had anything he wanted in Chicago.

In the fourth inning Weaver and Schalk opened with singles. After Faber popped out, Leibold drilled a hit to center which sent Weaver home. Then McMullen followed suit scoring Schalk, and Collins did the same plating Leibold.

Perritt was pitching by that time. He wiped the perspiration from his brow and looked in to see who was up. It was none other than General Joe Jackson. Herzog and Fletcher came in and whispered to Perritt. They had also whispered to Schupp and to Anderson, the two pitchers who had preceded Perritt. The whispering apparently was of no value. He turned his battery of curves on Jackson. Joe picked out one he liked and lined it out to right field, where the beleaguered Robertson, who was already panting like a deer that had run 20 miles, ran after it. But by that time McMullen and Collins were already at the water cooler in the dugout.

At the end of the inning, the Giants walked to the bench looking just as jolly as a crowd of invalids taking their constitutional on the lawn of Doctor Killium's Sanitarium.

Faber pitched well all day, surrendering only eight hits. He was, however, considerably less successful as a base runner. To be honest about it, he made one of the stupidest plays ever seen in a World Series game when he tried to steal third. Since the game was already locked away by that point his marble play was greeted with considerable merriment.

**JOE JACKSON** That second game was one of the best games I ever had. We was all pretty excited after that. So excited, in fact, that Pants got carried away when he turned on the hot water in the shower and steam gushed out and burned his hand so bad that it had to be slathered in oil.

Some of the people waiting outside the clubhouse when they saw the bandages, thought he was faking so that he didn't have to shake hands with everybody that was waiting. A big old sheriff though grabbed his hand and shook it so hard that the manager cried out in pain.

**CHARLES COMISKEY** Joe was the fan's favorite after the first two games of the Series, no doubt about it. Collins was still the team's biggest star, but Joe was the hero of the moment.

On Monday we had maybe a thousand local fans show up at the park for the third game—a game which was being played in New York. It still amazes me that anyone who would follow the game closely enough to stand on line at the break of dawn for a ticket, wouldn't know the location of the third game of the Series.

One of the team's few officials who stayed behind in Chicago went down and gave them the bad news, at which point most dispersed and went to where they could get the returns over the ticker. Then, of course, when they found out the game was postponed on account of rain, they were really disappointed.

**VINCENT ALEXANDER** I followed Joe and the team to New York, and although, like everybody else, I hated to see the rainout, I nevertheless enjoyed the opportunity to get some much needed rest.

I had tickets in New York thanks to a cousin with connections, but rain checks were the order of the day. On Broadway, I noticed that rain checks were going for $5 to $10, some fans betting that the next game was also going to be rained out. It also turns out that someone had produced counterfeit tickets that looked just like rain checks, and scores of duped fans were buying them thinking they could walk right into a grand stand or bleacher seat for the next game.

It seemed just as hard to buy a reserved seat ticket in New York as it did in Chicago. Scalpers were doing great business. Several speculators had big display advertisements in the newspapers. All one needed to get a couple of boxes was an unlimited bank roll.

The place where a lot of the scalping was going on, interestingly enough, was on the elevated trains. Speculators armed with a fair assortment of rain checks and tickets plied their trade until the grounds were reached and then, retracing their journey, boarded a following train.

Like thousands of others I went to the Polo Grounds on the possibility they might get the game in, but at 1 o'clock sharp, the official announcer came out with his big megaphone and said the game was off.

Two men were arrested outside the park for trying to sell their places in the line waiting for bleacher tickets. Imagine getting arrested for trying to sell your place for a rained out game!

The Woodland Bards, who came 250 strong on the same train with the team, were making things lively.

The odds were reported in the papers each day and anyone wishing to bet a couple of bucks certainly didn't have any difficulty in finding someone to take his money. The Sox were favored to take the first game in New York. The Chicago rooters, however, wanted even money on that bet, while the New York fans argued that they should get odds as the advantage was clearly with the Sox.

**PANTS ROWLAND** We were staying at the Ansonia Hotel while waiting for the Series to get restarted. Having won the first two games, we were eager to get on with it, and although we were all a bit weary from the long train trip, we would have preferred not to have the delay. We wanted to get at the Giants while we still had the momentum.

The happiest player at the hotel was undoubtedly Happy Felsch. By dint of his home run, he received numerous gifts from admiring fans—a couple of Liberty bonds, a new suit of clothes, several dozen pairs of socks, some new shoes and neckties and even, believe it or not, a block of stock in a new airplane concern.

Joe, too, got a slew of presents, but even in those days, home runs drew the most attention.

I was even approached in the lobby by a booking agent and asked if I would accept a contract for a 12-week turn on the vaudeville circuit. I said I would let him know later, but wondered what I would be offered if I won the whole Series.

**VINCENT ALEXANDER** The next day dawned bright and sunny.

Before the game, they had a ceremony for Corporal Hank Gowdy, former catcher for the Boston Braves, and hero of the World Series in 1914. He was the first player from the major leagues to have enlisted. He was called to the plate, and presented with a wrist watch.

In the stands, young men circulated asking for contributions for the soldiers in France. There may have been a baseball game on, but we were not allowed to forget there was also a war on.

A few enthusiastic fans who couldn't get tickets stayed outside the grounds during the game and even when they couldn't determine exactly what happened, when the crowd inside cheered, so did they. The only man who was able to see the game well without paying was the one who came on tall stilts. A few fans succeeded in reaching the roof of the elevated station from where they managed to catch a partial glimpse of the action. A couple of other daredevils climbed two steel towers, risking life and limb in their exuberance to see the Giants rehabilitate themselves.

There wasn't a sign of a ballplayer until nearly 12 o'clock, and then, Jim Thorpe, the renowned Indian athlete who had worn a Giant uniform on and off for several seasons, made his way across the field receiving the greetings of friends. It was not long before the Giants appeared in their home white uniforms.

Benny Kauff, who had distinguished himself by not getting a hit yet in the Series, was presented with a gold-handled cane, but it was announced that the prerequisite to permanent possession was that he must get a hit in the Series.

Fifteen minutes before the game started, Mayor Mitchell, flanked by a cordon of police, came from the gate under the scoreboard and walked across the field to his seat behind the New York dugout. The appearance of the Mayor was the signal for the first bit of concerted cheering. He tossed out the first ball, and a second later had it back in his possession after Benton had made one toss across the plate.

**I.E. SANBORN** Game three saw Eddie Cicotte return to the mound. This time against Rube Benton. The game was scoreless through three, then New York pushed two across in the fourth.

The Sox didn't mount a serious challenge until the ninth. With two out, Eddie Collins beat out a roller down the first base line. That in itself didn't look terribly alarming to the Giant faithful, but General Jackson was coming to bat. If the General could get hold of one, the game would be tied. The Giant fans held their collective breaths; the Sox fans were exhorting Joe with everything they had.

It was a tense moment. Many in the huge crowd rose to their feet to watch the mighty slugger match brawn, if not wits, with the pitcher who had been in complete control of the game. But, had he run out of steam?

Kid Gleason, Rowland's right hand man on the board of strategy, danced up and down at third base, while Rowland, on the first base coaching line, was reminding Eddie Collins to be prepared to take off as soon as Joe hit the ball.

Benton, aware of the danger in the situation, took his own sweet time. The first ball he sent to Joe was twisting so fast that when Joe swung hard enough to pole it into Eighth Avenue, the result was only a long foul. Again Joe set himself at the plate. Again Benton, cool and cautious, delivered up a curve. Joe brought his bat back far over his left shoulder and unleashed a vicious swing. The bat cracked against the ball and it shot high into left field near the foul line. Fletcher raced out from short and at the last second, snared it and raced into the clubhouse with the souvenir.

Final score: Giants 2, White Sox 0.

**BUCK WEAVER** After the game Ban Johnson, announced that he had volunteered for military service in France. He said that he had offered his services to the government, but in what capacity he didn't say, explaining that the offer had not been accepted.

What a joke! The players just laughed at the hypocrisy of it. But we had more important issues in front of us—like winning the Series.

The League announced that the players on the winning team would get 60 percent of $152,888, which means they would divide $91,733. The players of the losing team would divide 40 percent, or $61,155.

We had 26 players eligible to share in the money, including Manager Rowland and Coach Gleason. It wasn't real difficult to figure that if we won, each of us would get $3,528. If we lost, we would get $2,352. That meant we were playing for an extra $1,175.

The way Comiskey treated us this was something we desperately wanted. And we talked about it, too. We talked as a team about these figures, and vowed we would fight to the end for the extra dollars--not for Comiskey, but for us.

**I.E. SANBORN** For three innings of the fourth game, Faber and Schupp pitched remarkable ball, and it looked as if the battle were going to settle into a pitcher's duel pure and simple. When the Giants broke through for a run in the fourth, the crowd began to josh the Sox. They called Rowland and his men bush leaguers and called for the Chicago leader to go back to the Three-Eye League.

The Sox never mounted a challenge. Joe took the collar and his teammate did little better, combining for only six singles and a double by Collins.

Benny Kauff, the shrinking violet—that's what they called Benny in jest because he had more brazen assurance than a banty rooster—boasted before the Series that he would do something to make the name Benjamin Michael Kauff go ringing down the corridors of baseball fame. Well, in that game he came close by hitting two home runs leading the Giants to a 5-0 victory.

**JOE JACKSON** People said we was a depressed team after we lost the second game but I think we was more angry than depressed. We really thought we could win four straight, and when that didn't happen, well, we had to look at it different, that's all. We didn't score for 22 innings which meant that we was probably due.

The Giants caught the first train after game four back to Chicago, but we didn't go until a little later on account of the long speech given to us by Gleason. He kind of bawled us out and I guess we deserved it. Ray Schalk screamed a little, too. Manager Rowland he, didn't yell or nothing, just went over calmly what we had to do to win—mostly get some runs.

**I.E. SANBORN** Manager McGraw seemed to be in doubt right up to the last minute about his choice of pitchers for the fifth game. Perritt, Schupp, and Sallee all warmed up before the game and in spite of the cold weather, he picked Slim Sallee.

The fifth game brought miserable baseball weather, so cold that spectators and players alike shivered in the wintry blasts.

Reb Russell, pitching for the Sox, was wild as a hawk at the start. He seemed to think that the plate was somewhere near the Giants' bench. He lasted three batters before Rowland rushed from the bench waving his arms as if he were trying to flag a freight train. Reb understood what he meant and took the shortest route to the dugout. Williams and Danforth were warming up but Rowland had them there only to fool McGraw, for when Reb was yanked, Cicotte suddenly jumped into view and went out to take up the pitching burden.

Despite their ace's best efforts, New York was up 5 to 2 in the seventh, and the Sox fans were worried. Collins opened the inning by lining out to short, but Jackson and Felsch followed with solid singles. Gandil drove in both runners with a double to right. Weaver than grounded to first with Gandil going to third. After Schalk walked, Rowland sent in Byrd Lynn as a pinch hitter. But before he could do anything, Schalk and Gandil took off on a double steal. The Giants' catcher bluffed a throw to second but instead threw to Slim on the mound who turned and promptly threw the ball into center in an attempt to nail Schalk. Gandil scored tying the game at five.

When the Sox came to bat in the eighth, the fans went wild. I had never seen Chicago so riotous in my life. The Sox players, led by Ray Schalk, were doing an Indian war dance in front of their bench, throwing blankets and bats and gloves and balls into the air. The fans in the stands were all up on their feet waving hats and White Sox pennants. Out in the bleachers, boys and men had to be restrained from jumping onto the field.

Shano Collins walked up to bat wearing a half-ashamed expression. No one on the team expected to be seeing Sallee again that inning after what had happened in the seventh, but there he was on the mound with his Eiffel Tower figure staring down to his catcher. Collins slapped a single to right and then was promptly sacrificed to second by McMullen. Again the Sox expected McGraw to pull his battered pitcher, but again, no move from the manager.

The other Collins, the man who McGraw considered the most dangerous World Series performer in the world came to bat. Amid thundering cheers, Eddie Collins blistered the ball to center field scoring Shano Collins with the run which put the Sox in the lead.

No one could figure why Sallee was still in there. The Sox were swinging at first pitches and hitting them hard. Jackson came up and promptly smashed a single to right sending Collins racing around third. Collins scored just ahead of the throw, Jackson alertly taking second. Finally, the Giants sent in Perritt, but it was a case of too little, too late. Felsch's single sent in Jackson with another run.

The final score was 8 to 5. Jackson had contributed three hits and played flawlessly in the outfield on a frigid day which saw three errors committed by the Giants, and six by the Sox.

**EDDIE COLLINS** After the fifth game I was approached by John P. Crozer, a millionaire backer of the Upland team in the Delaware County League to play an exhibition game against his team after the Series. I had no interest whatsoever, until he mentioned a guaranteed dollar figure—$10,000.

He said he had engaged Chief Bender to pitch for his team and asked me to assemble a group of Sox for the competition. One of the players I approached was Jackson. At first he said he wanted to get back home as fast as he could after the Series, but when I told him it was going to be worth $833 to him, he consented. The other players were Schalk, Williams, Cicotte, Faber, Benz, Gandil, Weaver, McMullen, Leibold and Felsch.

In those days $833 meant something to a player.

**I.E. SANBORN** Travel was the order of the day as the teams were obliged to head right back to New York for game six. The scene aboard the train as it went flitting through the peaceful Sabbath Mohawk Valley landscape was remarkably quiet. Almost without exception, the passengers were persons connected temporarily or permanently with the game—baseball writers, baseball players and baseball officials. So, was baseball the prevalent topic of conversation? It was not.

In the club sleeper the White Sox mainly laid curled up in languid heaps with windrows of discarded Sunday newspapers piled about them. The officials who were connected with Mr. Comiskey's operation shut themselves up in staterooms to smoke and doze. The newspaper men were scattered through the cars, some engaged in that phase of literary endeavor so dear to the heart of true newspaper men—filling out expense accounts—and the rest deeply concerned with industriously doing nothing at all. The fonts of inspiration had run dry as bones.

No one was talking about baseball, past or impending. No one apparently was thinking about baseball. Seemingly all had ceased to wonder why McGraw had permitted Sallee to say in there long after the Sox had begun to pound the earth out from under Slim's long and slender feet. It appeared that this was destined to remain one of the unsolved baseball puzzles of the ages. The ways of a great manager were past finding out.

**VINCENT ALEXANDER** With the Giants coming home to play such a decisive game, I assumed the crowd would respond with the same vigor as they had for earlier games, but there was no great rush for seats early in the day. The scene around the Polo Grounds was relatively peaceful and serene, although by game time the park seemed to be full.

I watched Joe come out for batting practice with the other players and kept my eyes riveted to him as he took his swings. He had acquitted himself well in the Series up to that point and looked to be his normal self. I was hoping he would prove to be the critical difference before the Series was over.

**I.E. SANBORN** Rowland sent Faber out for game six; McGraw, Benton. There was no score going into the fourth.

Eddie Collins was the first up that inning and he slammed a grounder down to Zimmerman at third. Heinie threw the ball away at first and Collins raced to second. Jackson lifted a routine fly to Robertson in right, but he dropped it like a hot potato, Collins going to third. Benton then grabbed Felsch's bounder back to the rubber. He looked over and saw Collins several yards down the third base line, ran over and chased Collins back toward the bag then tossed the ball to Zimmerman. Collins stopped on a dime and set sail for home, Zimmerman chasing him all the way. It was no contest. Collins reached home ahead of the now embarrassed third baseman. Jackson and Felsch were also on the bases, remember, and they had enough time to go just about anywhere they pleased while Zim was playing chase. Jackson ended up at third and Felsch at second.

It looked for a moment as if the Giants were going to form a posse and haul Zim to the tar barrel. Thousands of spectators were anxiously waiting to volunteer should their services be requested.

Gandil followed by walloping a hot single over first base which rolled out to the concrete wall while Jackson and Felsch scored. Gandil was thrown out trying to stretch his hit into a double.

The Giants made the most of Red Faber's wildness in the fifth, and a whale of a three-bagger by Charley Herzog gave them a couple of runs.

The Sox held on to their one-run lead until the top of the ninth when Weaver scored an insurance run.

The Giants had one more chance left. In the last of the ninth, Dave Robertson, who had been the Giants hitting hero up to that point was hit on the hand and given a free ride to first. The Giant fans came alive. Holke slapped a grounder to Collins at second. Eddie thought about trying to get Robertson, but instead wisely threw to Gandil at first for the out.

Without doubt, Collins was the shining light of the Sox. Not only did he hit and field well, but he performed like a general on the battlefield. Throughout the Series he could be seen signaling Jackson and Felsch to shift slightly in the outfield for each batter or running to the mound to whisper instructions to the pitchers.

With Robertson on second, Collins again went to the mound and conferred with Faber. Whatever he said, it must have worked, for Faber, clearly tiring, marshaled enough energy to fan Raridan.

Out of desperation, McGraw sent up Lew McCarty to pinch hit for the pitcher despite the fact that he was still suffering from a wrenched shoulder. McCarty slashed a grounder at Eddie Collins and the Sox were world champions.

As the disappointed crowd surged onto the field, McGraw, who had been coaching at first base rushed onto the diamond, elbowed his way through the howling mass of spectators and grasped the hand of Pants Rowland. Here was a picture. McGraw, one of the oldest and craftiest leaders in the game, squeezing the outstretched mitt of the bush league manager from Peoria. There were tears of happiness in Rowland's eyes as McGraw grasped his hand. He was happier still when McGraw told him he had won with a team as game and fair as he had ever played against.

**VINCENT ALEXANDER** It was Eddie Collins with his foxy base running who took the hero's wreath for the Sox, but I wasn't there to see Collins, as brilliant as he might have been. I wasn't there because I was a Chicago White Sox fan, I was there because I was a Joe Jackson fan and Joe Jackson played well. He ended up with a .304 batting average, 4 runs scored, 2 RBIs, a base on balls, a stolen base and a world championship. Not bad for an illiterate ex-mill hand!

**JOE JACKSON** Of course, everybody was real excited in the clubhouse, slapping backs and shouting and everything. Mr. Comiskey came in and said a few words but it was so noisy I didn't really hear what they was.

Now maybe I didn't jump around and yell and shout as much as some of the other boys, but I guarantee you I was just as happy as anyone. A lot of people said I wouldn't never play in the major leagues, but there I was on a championship club, and I played pretty good, too.

**CHARLIE LEBEAU** After Heinie Zimmerman chased Eddie Collins over home plate with the first run in the final World's Series game, I noticed that Captain Herzog of the Giants talked to Umpire Evans. Herzog was not protesting, however. Here are his exact words as later reported in a number of papers: "Bill, did you ever see anything like that? I have $1,700 riding on this ballgame and that's the shortest run for $1,700 that I ever heard of."

I bring this up only because of what happened a couple of years later. See, even the players were betting on games.

There was talk, too, that McGraw left Sallee in the game so long because of pressure from gamblers. Anyone who knew McGraw, though, probably didn't seriously subscribe to that theory. What McGraw did to deflect any criticism directed toward him was to complain loudly about Buck Herzog's play. His second baseman, according to the manager, didn't make a reasonable effort on several ground balls. Although he didn't come out and say it, the implication wasn't lost on anyone—Herzog was purposely trying not to win. McGraw traded him as soon as the Series was over.

**I.E. SANBORN** The Sox and the Giants locked horns again the day after the Series in an exhibition game played out in Long Island for the benefit of the soldiers at Camp Mills. This was the one game sanctioned by the League and played with its blessing.

The White Sox beat the Giants just as neatly as they did in the big pageant.

Germany Schaeffer went along with the players, and arranged with the umpires to pull a hysterical stunt in the ninth inning. Umpires like Bill Klem, who have never been known to smile, consented to a bit of horseplay, and sure enough when the ninth inning came around, Schaeffer went in to play third base for the Giants. As soon as he got in, he and Fred McMullen, the Sox third baseman, gave an imitation of Heinie Zimmerman. The soldiers roared with laughter.

The only Sox player of note not there was Joe Jackson.

**CHARLES COMISKEY** A cheering crowd of 5,000 rooters stormed the La Salle Street train station to welcome home the champions. When the train arrived at 4 o'clock, the crowd broke through police lines, and, accompanied by two brass bands, swarmed around their heroes.

Some fans hoisted Pants to their shoulders and carried him into the street. Traffic was blocked for more than 20 minutes while the crowd sought to shake hands with the players.

With the exception of Eddie and John Collins, Mel Wolfgang and Urban Faber, all of the team was there.

There was great merriment and lots of speech giving. The fans let Jackson know how much they loved him. He returned their praise with typical modesty.

Although none of us knew it at the time, winning that Series was the high mark of his career. He would never again hear cheering like that. He would never again stand unblemished at the top of his profession.

# 44

# I FIGURED IT'S WHAT I SHOULD DO

**JOE JACKSON** After the Series and all the celebrating, me and Katie stayed in Chicago for a few days to take care of a couple of things like the apartment. In fact, I was one of the last players to leave for the winter.

Each of us players put some of the money we made in Chicago Liberty bonds. Joe Benz, one of our pitchers, he kept only $69.32 for himself and put the other $3,000 into the bonds. Even the umpires, they put $1,000 each into bonds.

I put a little bit in, but me and Katie had more important things to do with our money. We had a new house in New Orleans. Ever since I played down there with the Pels, I liked that city. It was big enough to have a lot of interesting things, but it wasn't so big that you got lost in it.

Anyway, we had a nice house on the waterfront not too far from my sister Lula who moved down there when she got married. We paid $10,000 for it.

Actually it was Katie who organized the buying of the house and arranged everything with the lawyers. It was a pretty big house with three bedrooms, so Mother and my little sister, Gertrude came down to live with us. We spent more time in the Chicago apartment than we did in the New Orleans house but when we was down there we felt real comfortable. It was a southern house in a southern city, and we was southern folk.

People knowed me in New Orleans since I played there, but after we won the Series, why, it was different. Everybody expected a lot more then. Winning doesn't always make things easier.

One thing it made easier, though, was making more money. That's mostly what we did that winter—made money. Actually, Katie made most of it, but it was because of my name.

We bought some other property in the area, and we owned part of a pool room. We also organized a new "Baseball Girls" show which played in a number of vaudeville houses, only I wasn't in it this time.

I also did a couple of newspaper and radio commercials, for Oldsmobile automobiles. They paid real good for not a lot of work.

I was the guest of honor at big dinners and vaudeville shows.

It was a good time, that winter. A very good time for the Jacksons.

**I.E. SANBORN** Joe was proving to be a good business man. He invested prudently and monitored his investments carefully. Oh, I know Katie was a big part of that, but look at how many baseball men weren't as successful with their finances as Joe was—with or without enlightened wives.

Joe was no fool.

**CHARLIE LEBEAU** The war raged on into 1918, and the public consciousness about it escalated considerably. If the war continued for much longer, everyone understood that luxuries would have to be curtailed, and to some, baseball was a luxury.

But baseball crowds were big during the war, and naturally the owners were reluctant to shut down operations. So they decided to embrace the patriotic spirit, wave the flag and keep the parks open. They even opened enlistment booths at some parks.

A few players enlisted, a handful of others were conscripted, but generally, major league rosters remained little affected by the war.

There was lots of jingoistic talk by the players, but few of them went to get measured for uniforms.

**JOE JACKSON** It seemed like every week, Katie read a different letter from home telling us that another one of my brothers enlisted and might get sent to France any day. Imagine how that made me feel. One day in spring training I told Katie that I thought I should join up, too and go with my brothers.

**KATIE JACKSON** It didn't make sense, Joe going into the army. First of all it looked to me like he was going to be exempt anyway in that he was the sole support of me, his mother and his sister, Gertrude. Since we all lived together in Savannah, no one could argue that the sole support issue was a ruse. Secondly, if he had to, it would be far better for him to take a job in what they were calling "essential work." That is, work related to the military needs of the country, but work that was done here at home.

We talked about this at some length. At first, Joe said he should enlist, but I don't know how much he really believed he should do that or how much he thought it wouldn't look right if he didn't. Anyway, we batted that around for a few days. His mother and sister both agreed with me. I guess not too many mothers would want their sons to go to war if there were other choices, and Joe definitely had other choices.

**CHARLES COMISKEY** There was a lot discussion—some of it heated—among the 16 club owners about how to deal with the exigencies of the season. What we all agreed on, however, was that there would be no curtailment of the playing season, no slashing of the player limit, nor limitation of the training season. We wanted to present the public with the idea that there was no cause for alarm.

We decided to open the season a week later than usual but to play the 154-game schedule which had been the standard for years. We agreed on a plan for the collection of the war tax. We would collect 3 cents on bleacher seats, 5 cents on pavilion seats, 8 cents on grandstand, and 10 cents on box seats.

**LEFTY WILLIAMS** Who do you suppose was the first one on our team to announce that he was going to enlist? You guessed it! Eddie Collins. Figures, right? Despite the fact that the club paid the Philadelphia Americans $50,000 for him three years earlier, he announced in the middle of the winter that he was enlisting. And remember, he was making $15,000 a year—a whole lot more than any of the rest of us.

**CHARLES COMISKEY** During the winter meetings in New York, I put forth a plan for major league club owners to make partial payments of salaries to dependents of players who were drafted or enlisted. Exhibition games could be played during the season for such a cause, and I knew this would be given a hearty support by baseball fans.

Needless to say, not everyone was so willing to contribute.

**PANTS ROWLAND** Since we didn't know exactly what was going to happen to the season, or even for sure if we were going to have one, I sent a letter to all the players during the winter suggesting they begin daily exercising so as to be in condition for the season in case spring training trips had to be abandoned on account of the congested railroad conditions.

As far as I know, it was the first time major league players had ever been asked to train at home and report in good physical condition.

**JOE JACKSON** I wasn't crazy about the idea, but I stayed with the team and went north with them to start the season. It was pretty much the same team we won the Series with, but the war had everybody nervous and nobody really knowed what was going to happen.

I felt good and got off to a good start. Through about the first three weeks of the season I was hitting .354, had a home run and 20 RBIs.

**CHARLIE LEBEAU** It was in late May, or early June I think, when Provost Marshall General Crowder issued a "work or fight" order, mandating that all draft-age men enter either the military or essential industries. Baseball was explicitly ruled "non-essential."

This meant that all able-bodied men between the ages of 21 and 30 had until July to get jobs in essential work or face mandatory military conscription. Baseball officials tried to get special exemptions for the players but when they were turned down, players began to join up in droves. By the end of the season, at least 75 American League players were in the service, and as a result, the pennant races were determined largely by the number and quality of players lost. Some teams fared considerably better than others in this regard.

Only two White Sox players opted for essential service—Joe Jackson and Lefty Williams.

**KATIE JACKSON** I had a number of communications with the Greenville draft board, most of which I did not tell Joe about. At first it looked as if they were going to give him an exemption, then probably because of pressure on them from local citizens, they changed their minds and classified him 1-A.

Although no one told me so directly, I got the distinct impression that some of the local folks who had sons conscripted, lobbied to get Joe classified as they did. The argument went that he was just a mill worker like the rest of them. He just happened to be able to swing a bat better than they could. It was an argument hard to argue with.

I know it was a Saturday when we got the notice that Joe was to appear before the nearest draft board for examination. It said that he would probably be called sometime between May 25 and June 1.

I talked to some people back in the Brandon Mill, and they gave me the name of a shipbuilding company up in Delaware that was designated as "essential." I told Joe about it, but he still had this idea that he should join up, so I talked to his mother. When she suggested that he should consider the shipbuilding job, he reluctantly relented.

I called the company. They were thrilled at the thought of having the World Series hero, Joe Jackson, working for them. Not the least of their interest was in having Joe play for their baseball team.

**PANTS ROWLAND** Joe came into my office and informed me that he had accepted a position with the Harlan & Hollingsworth Shipbuilding Company at Wilmington, Delaware, a subsidiary of the Bethlehem Steel Corporation.

"I guess I won't be playing with the Sox no more this season, skip," he said bluntly.

I figured right then and there any chance for the pennant was gone.

**LEFTY WILLIAMS** Joe was my friend. It's as simple as that. Our wives were such chums that what one knew, the other knew. So when Joe jumped to the shipyards I told him I would go, too.

Now, I didn't have to do that, because I had an exemption. I did it because of Joe and because I thought it would be a good thing to do for the country.

**JOE JACKSON** Working in the shipyard wasn't all that different from working in the mill except that it was a lot hotter. But, to be fair about it, most of the time I didn't really work much in the plant. Most of the time I played baseball for the company.

**CHARLIE LEBEAU** Once when I was down in Wilmington, I stopped by the shipyard to see how Joe was doing. The yard was like a city onto itself. It was a warren of mismatched buildings and long-necked cranes that rose from the mud flats of the water.

I don't know for sure, but I would guess there were maybe 30,000 men and women working there—mostly men, of course. Everything looked oversized. It was a bustling, febrile place of fences and guarded gates, of cranes and machines, and during the war at least, it never stopped, never even slowed down.

Looking at the men who worked there, I thought Joe must have been reasonably at home. The yard appeared to be peopled with the unlettered and untaught, with drifters and failures, farmers and others living on the borderline of subsistence. It seemed to me that most of the workers were those who in peacetime worked primarily as semi- or unskilled labor.

Joe, as it turned out, was spared most of the heavy and dangerous work. He was a celebrity, and as such, was accorded the privileges such a status warranted.

But he also played an important role within the culture of the wartime shipyard. The pressures to meet yard quotas were great, so much of the workforce put in lengthy hours—sometimes as many as 60 to 75 per week. Only Sunday was a day off. Since the areas around the shipyards themselves offered scant little in the way of wholesome entertainment, the steel companies encouraged and supported the playing of baseball. In a manner not unlike the mill leagues of the South, the steel leagues offered a healthy release from the pressures and drudgery of the factories and shipyards.

It's quite reasonable to conclude that Joe and his fellow players provided a healthy and valuable—perhaps even essential—service to an industry vital to the American war effort.

Joe, I think understood that, but he also understood that not everyone else did.

**HOWARD HOLLINS** We had in the steel leagues during the war, some of the best dammed ballplayers you ever seen. We had major leaguers, minor leaguers and some who didn't play in either but were better. We had shipbuilders with arms of steel and legs like pistons. We had some kids in the outfield who would run through outfield walls if necessary. These men played for fun, not for money; they played to win, not to become famous. Well, to be accurate, some of the players were paid—maybe as much as five hundred dollars a week—but they was exceptions. Most of us got squat—other than satisfaction, of course.

It was called the Bethlehem Steel Baseball League, and it was one hell of a league. We played tough, and we played fast, and we didn't cheat. The major leagues should have been so good!

I played catcher for the Harlan club, and let me tell you, we had some players on that team. Jeremy Helligson could throw as hard as Walter Johnson, I swear it. Only he didn't have The Big Train's control, that's all. And Andy Koussof, he handled short as well as Ray Chapman ever did. He would have played in the majors after the war, except that he had an accident in the plant and screwed up his back. And we had Joe Jackson. Let me tell you this about Joe: the Babe said he copied his swing from Joe. That says it all.

Now, I never got the chance to play in the majors because I had to go to work in the plant while I was still a kid, but I could have if I had the chance, and I know a little about the game. I know, for instance, that Joe Jackson was the greatest natural hitter who ever swung a bat. See, the thing is, he had a set style, a grooved swing. That's why he never got into a batting slump. His swing was so perfect that it never came apart. Years later, a kid named Ted Williams came along and people said the same thing about him—that he had a natural swing. But it wasn't as good as Joe's. When he got into a slump he had to work like a dog to get out of it. He was good, but he was no Joe Jackson. I seen them both, and I know a little about hitting.

Joe was the star of the league, but as I said, we had a bunch of men who could play, so he didn't dominate the league or nothing. He was good, but so were we.

**JOE JACKSON** The way I looked at it, everybody needed to do what they could do best if we was going to win the war. Some people were needed to fight, some to organize the fighting, some to make the tools of fighting. The best thing I knowed how to do was play baseball, and if I could do that in a way that helped, well, then I figured that's what I should do.

Many Sundays I took the train over to Reading to play in Red Cross charity games. I paid my own way over there, too. For the last game, they said there was four thousand fans watching. I won the game with a home run, so I felt pretty good about that, and I guess we earned a pile of money for the Red Cross.

I led the league in hitting at .393, which is less than I hit two times in the American League, which I guess tells you how good the steel league was. And it wasn't just the steel workers and their families who came to the games, lots of regular folks did, too. We were a real attraction during the war.

We had some good players that knew what to do on a diamond, not just me and Lefty, but some good players. Howie Hollins, our catcher, once took a guy's teeth out who tried to score against him on a close play. The guy's mouth was all bloody, but he didn't say nothing. He just got up and went out and played second base without front teeth.

I got banged up good a couple of times, too, but I kept playing. I didn't want nobody to say Joe Jackson wasn't as tough as the other players, or that I was sloughing it instead of going into the service. I'll guarantee you playing in that league was as hard as any basic training.

We played all over the place. We even played a game in the Polo Grounds in New York where I played in the World Series.

Sometimes, too, the Harlan team loaned me out to other teams and I played for them.

I did my part. Believe me, I did my part.

Our team made it to the championship series which we won when I hit two nice homers in the last game. The fans got so excited about that, that they threw all these coins down on the field for me, and they had to stop the game for a long time to pick them all up.

**CHARLIE LEBEAU** Why did Joe go down to the shipyard in the first place? That's a question a lot of people asked. Remember, this was a very patriotic time. Healthy young men were expected to fight. Anything less was ... well, it was considered cowardly. So, why didn't Joe do that?

I suspect there are two answers to that question. The first lies squarely with his wife, and perhaps, mother. There's no doubt that they put pressure on him to work in the shipyards. But so too, did millions of other mothers whose sons went off to war despite matronly tears.

The other reason, I firmly believe, is that Joe was afraid. Not any more fear of fighting than any reasonable young man would harbor, but a deep-seated fear of the problems a life in the army would bring him. I think he was afraid of being ostracized for his illiteracy. Never mind that there were others in the service who shared that condition. That could not provide solace for an intrinsic fear. He had succeeded in putting the issue behind him for the most part, but not before suffering in the process. He didn't want to go through that again. Baseball and the army were both male societies, and neither known for its sensitivity.

I'm sure he was afraid that he would be given army material to read that he couldn't, material that left unread, could jeopardize his or perhaps his mates' lives. As time went on, I can imagine him exaggerating these conditions in his own mind to the point of virtual paralysis. No, a baseball diamond at the shipyard was a decidedly better alternative, albeit one that was to create problems for him—again.

Joe, it seems, was singled out by the press for special treatment—again. Not only was he stupid, he was also a coward. So went the refrain in paper after paper. Editorials lashed out viciously at Joe. They attacked his lack of courage, lampooned his morals, derided his decision. Never mind that there were others who chose essential service over military service; never mind that many players who chose to join the army spent their entire service careers playing exhibition games for the troops. Joe became the poster boy for cowardice.

Joe couldn't, wouldn't, didn't fight back. He was the illiterate hillbilly with no backbone.

Most of the vicious attacks—anonymous, of course—capitalized on the "General" Joe Jackson nickname which had become popular. One in particular I remember went, "Either the fighting blood of the Jacksons is not as red as it used to be in the days of Old Stonewall and Old Hickory, or General Joe of the Chicago White Sox concluded there were enough of his family in the war already, for he has fled to the refuge of a shipyard, hoping thus to escape service."

There were references to earlier escapades of so-called cowardice, particularly the time when he fled Philadelphia for the South Carolina hills. There were suggestions, too, that baseball fans would not be pleased to see Joe back in a major league uniform when the war was over.

**CHARLES COMISKEY** I went public with my sentiments about Jackson. I had to. I had to let the Chicago public know where I and the Chicago White Sox organization stood on the issue of patriotism. I told the public that there was no room on our club for players who wished to evade the army draft by entering the employ of shipbuilders, and that there was a good chance that the "jumpers" would not be taken back into organized baseball.

The public had to know the White Sox and baseball stood for wholesome American values. If they didn't we would be out of business in one inning.

I said then, and I'll say now, Jackson made a mistake. He should have gone into the military. He had made a lot of money off this country, and he was popular with the kids. What kind of idol shirks his responsibilities to the public like that?

Once the war was over, we could deal with the issue of Jackson and Williams in an altogether different way.

**CHARLIE LEBEAU** The thing you have got to remember is that what Joe did was perfectly legal. He had options open to him, and he chose one. That was his right. It was also what was done by hundreds of thousands of other young men. The fact that he was a celebrity magnified the issue, but it didn't change the facts.

**KATIE JACKSON** We stayed down in Savannah during the time Joe was in Delaware, but don't for a minute think that we didn't see what was going on. People sent us the papers with the attacks on Joe. They were ugly, and they were wrong. Joe worked hard during the war, and he worked within the law.

Joe was a target because he couldn't read or write. It's really as simple as that. Who were the real cowards? Men like Joe who worked in the war industries, or men who wrote those anonymous editorials in eastern papers saying he was a slacker?

**ALFRED VON KOLNITZ** I had a short career in the major leagues in what you would call a "utility" player role. I played for Cincinnati in the National League, and Chicago in the American League, and at one time or other, played every position but pitcher and second base.

I got to know Joe a little bit—not real well, but a little—when we were both on the 1916 White Sox squad. He was, of course, one of the stars of the league; I got into 13 games. When the war started, I was one of the first to go, figuring that I might have more success in the military than I was having in baseball. I could see the writing on the wall, and it was saying my playing career was going to be short and undistinguished. I also had a very German name which was creating problems for me at home—home being, by the way, Charleston, South Carolina.

I told Joe what I was going to do, and he wished me well and said we'd hunt the South Carolina fields one day. We promised to stay in touch, but never did.

I kind of took to the army life, rose to the rank of major—I think the highest rank achieved by any player—and stayed on when the war was over. I never saw Joc again, but when the attacks on him started I got real angry.

People forget how hard Joe worked to get out of the mills in the first place. That, in itself, took considerable courage. Then he dealt with the mockery over his illiteracy, and he dealt with it with great class. I've been in those mills; I've seen the workers up close. Many of them couldn't read and write. Why should they have to learn? They were never going to get out of the mills in the first place, and they knew that. Reading and writing didn't get you anything in the mill.

Joe went on to have a successful career outside the mill despite his great handicap. That took fortitude; that took courage.

Joe wasn't a coward. He was attacked because he was an easy target, and because small-minded writers got great delight out of attacking a famous man who responded by saying nothing.

**JOE JACKSON** Of course I didn't like the things they was saying about me. Why would I? But I figured the best thing to do was to play for the Harlan team and keep my mouth shut. If I talked back, they would only write more bad things. Sometimes the best answer is no answer.

The guys in the shipyard, they didn't say nothing, but I know they read the papers.

The Jacksons were fighting in the war all right, and I was working on ships. The Jacksons aren't cowards. That's all I have to say about that.

I kept hearing that Mr. Comiskey wasn't going to let me come back to the Sox after the war, and that worried me a lot, but other people said he wouldn't do that, so I didn't really know where I stood.

**CHICK GANDIL** The guy leading the parade against Joe was Comiskey. He kept saying he didn't want a slacker to come back on his team. But you know what? He was doing that for one reason only. He was a cheapskate. He figured he could get Joe cheap after the war that way. I mean, how could Joe refuse any offer he made if he was threatened with expulsion? Joe would be so thrilled to be let back into the game, that he would sign for anything.

Comiskey never let a chance go by to get a player on the cheap.

**CHARLIE LEBEAU** "General Jackson in Full Retreat," they wrote when Joe went to the yards. They didn't write about the other players who did the same; they didn't write about the players in the service who never came near a rifle. They picked on the yokel, and it made me sick.

He will go down in history as the most famous slacker of the war, and that's a shame, because he didn't deserve that.

While all the flap about Joe simmered, the war continued and so did baseball.

Ty Cobb, everybody's favorite fighting ballplayer, announced he would quit baseball for the duration of the war and enlist. He said he had been reading the casualty lists and it made him feel that his place was in the thick of the big fighting overseas. He declared that baseball was good for the entertainment and morale of the people, but that he wanted to shoulder a gun and serve his country "in the best way possible." He made this announcement at the White House, after which some wag commented that maybe since Joe couldn't read the casualty lists, he didn't feel that way. He offered publicly to read them to Joe if Joe thought that would help.

General Pershing offered his opinion that in the matter of grenade and bomb throwing, the Americans quickly became proficient because it was a skill similar to what they learned by playing baseball. One paper opined that Joe didn't know he would get to throw things in the army, and maybe if someone told him that, he would volunteer.

In the middle of August, major league baseball announced that arrangements had been completed for bringing an all-star team from the United States under the supervision of John McGraw. They were to play a season at the American centers in France against a team selected from former major league players then in the army under the management of Hank Gowdy. The game was to be played for the entertainment of American wounded.

An editorial in one of the papers suggested that Joe Jackson be left at home as he would probably faint at the sight of blood.

Collins had passed his physical, and gone to boot camp at Paris Island, South Carolina, as a member of the Marine Corps. Someone suggested they tell Joe about the South Carolina camp, and maybe he would change his mind since he seemed to be homesick for that neck of the woods. They also pointed out that Collins was 31 years old, was married and had two children.

**CHARLES COMISKEY** The Emergency Fleet Corporation declared that ballplayers must be placed on the same footing as all other workmen, and that yards that offered high salaries to obtain their services would not be reimbursed by the corporation.

It was the debate around Jackson that caused this, and rightfully so.

**BAN JOHNSON** Before the war was over, 227 major leaguers served in the armed forces, and three players were killed in action, including Eddie Grant, the infielder and former captain of the Giants who was killed in the Argonne Forest of France. Grover Alexander served in the trenches of France with an artillery unit and was wounded badly enough that he was never the same after he returned home.

Even Branch Rickey served, and he had four children. He commanded a unit over there that included George Sisler who was one of his Lieutenants, and Ty Cobb and Christy Mathewson, who were both Captains. They could have put together one heck of a baseball team from that unit!

Mathewson was exposed to poison gas that fouled up his lungs pretty bad, and he only lived a few years after that.

Baseball contributed to the war effort, no doubt about that.

During the seventh-inning stretch of the first game of the Series that year between the Red Sox and the Cubs, the crowd was surprised when the band struck up The Star Spangled Banner. It was quite a moment. At first nobody knew quite what to think, then slowly fans here and there around the stadium began to sing along. Finally everybody joined in. At the end the spectators exploded into thunderous applause. So thrilling was the moment that the performance was repeated at every game of the Series, and a new American tradition was begun. Baseball and American patriotism were forever linked.

That a few players like Joe Jackson lacked the courage to wave the flag when they could, did nothing to demean the great game. The fans knew the reality.

**CHARLIE LEBEAU** Baseball did everything it could to promote itself as a patriotic institution, but the reality was quite something else again. Baseball was really only interested in business as usual, which meant profits. Oh, of course, the Comiskeys and Johnsons of the game put on a show of patriotic fervor, but they did so because they had to. Anything less would have been financial disaster. They did everything they could to protect themselves. Under pressure from the government they reduced the number of games in the season, then they cut salaries accordingly. They lobbied mightily for designating baseball an "essential industry," so they wouldn't lose players to the armed forces, and they derided players like Joe Jackson for not being patriotic enough. The fact is their position was based on pure hypocrisy and the desire to protect profits. Joe was a pawn caught in the middle of a public relations campaign.

**PANTS ROWLAND** First Joe, then Lefty, then Eddie left the team. Then one day in July, I gave Hap Felsch his pay check and he told me he was quitting the team to accept a position in Milwaukee where he was going to play semi-professional ball.

Needless to say, we were going no place fast in the pennant race. We finished the year in sixth place and with real questions about the next season, not the least of which concerned Joe and the likelihood of his returning to the game.

The season was shortened somewhat after continuous rumors that it would be terminated in the middle of the summer. The War Department's "Work or Fight" order was executed in mid season, but baseball was granted an extension until September 1. The powers that be in the game decided that because September 2 was Labor Day and therefore not what they called "a legal day," that they would play through the holiday with a series of doubleheaders in an attempt to wring every last dollar out of an otherwise difficult financial season.

The Series was another question altogether and seemed in doubt until Secretary of War Baker finally gave his approval for the Cubs and the Red Sox to play a World Series since they were on top when the season was brought to a close.

Boston won behind the brilliant pitching of Carl Mays and Babe Ruth, each of who won two games. Comiskey Park again saw a World Series as they chose to play the games there rather than in the smaller National League Park. The argument was that 10 percent of the receipts were going to go to war charities, thus the need for the larger venue.

My only thoughts as the Series concluded were about the next season. Would the war be over by then? Would Eddie and Lefty and Joe be back? Would Happy? Would Comiskey let Joe rejoin the club, and if he did, what would be the reaction of the fans? It was a winter of unsettling questions.

# 45

# I JUST WANTED TO KEEP PLAYING

**CHICK GANDIL** While Joe and Eddie and the others were away, things sort of fell apart on the team. Me and Swede and a couple of the other boys were sick and tired of being screwed by a lousy owner. Trying to get a decent contract out of him was a real pain in the behind. But he continued to pay his "pets" well, while the rest of us were paid like we were garbage collectors. For example, Eddie Collins made $5,000 in 1918, and what does Comiskey do? He give him a $2,000 bonus on top of that because he liked Eddie. Joe made $6,000, and Ray Schalk, he made more than $7,000. But most of us got diddly. I got $4,000 despite hitting more than 50 points higher than Schalk the year before. Swede was making $2,500, and Felsch, who hit over .300 got $3,750.

So there were two groups on the team: the "haves" and the "have nots;" the players Comiskey liked and the players he didn't. The "have nots" seldom talked to the "haves," and never associated with them if we could avoid it and we generally could. We didn't even really play with Collins if truth be told. We played next to him. Oh, we threw the ball to him when that was necessary, but when it wasn't we didn't. Even in warmups sometimes, we just refused to throw the ball to him. After all, if he was too good for us then he didn't need us warming him up. Usually he did that with Schalk. The two of them deserved each other

Look, I'll admit it, I didn't like Collins and his high-handed ways and most of the other boys didn't either. It was no loss to me when he went into the Marines. He should have re-upped.

Joe was sort of in between. He made good money, but he wasn't with the "haves" group. I knew that if he came back to the team, he was going to have to choose sides. He was either with us or against us, the choice was his.

If you're getting the impression that this was not a jolly team, you're right. It was a divided, bitter team, and for that I put the blame smack dab in the lap of one Charles A. Comiskey.

**CHARLES COMISKEY** I know what some of the players were saying about me and the club, but the reality was that the 1918 season was a disaster for the game in general and the Sox in particular. Sure, baseball was a great outlet for tensions, but much of the public consciousness was on the war, and as a result the attendance dropped significantly—about 40 percent, in fact, and that is the real reason the season was shortened.

The players take no financial responsibilities for losses, the owners do. We take all of it, and we pay the players their contracted salaries whether we make money or not. When we lose money it comes out of our pockets, not the players. They only stand to gain by the game, never lose.

So we had to do something about the 1918 season's losses. First on the agenda was an appeal to the government for the release of players in the army for the scheduled opening of the next season on April 23rd. This, by the way, was no different from what the heads of large corporations and business houses were doing. The war had ended during the winter, but discharges were coming slowly. We needed our stars if baseball was going to rebound financially. As we approached spring training, men such as Grover Cleveland Alexander, Hank Gowdy, Eddie Collins, and Rabbit Maranville were still in the service. The Cincinnati club was holding up the naming of a manager owing to the absence of Christy Mathewson who was still in France.

Another thing we did was to exercise the "10 day clause." What this meant was that technically we released every player in the league, but all the owners reached a "gentlemen's agreement" that we would not touch each other's properties. We then went about the business of re-signing our players, many at more reasonable salaries.

Then there was the issue of Jackson and Williams, our two army dodgers. They had not distinguished themselves during the war, still they were good ballplayers, and good ballplayers put customers in seats. On the other hand, if our fans were angry and/or disappointed with them, then perhaps having them on our team would prove to be a drawback.

Then offers for Jackson came from the Yankees and the Red Sox. They were decent offers, too—more than decent actually. There was some thinking that Jackson would fare better in another environment where there had been less criticism of his shipyard retreat.

We decided to talk to some fans, to test the waters so to speak. We heard some resistance to bringing him back, but on the whole, I think everyone realized how valuable he could be and the thought of going back to the World Series was not farfetched.

I sent Jackson a contract for $6,000. He immediately returned it signed and without comment.

**JOE JACKSON** When I got out of the shipyard, I was pretty depressed. After all the things he said about me, I didn't know if Mr. Comiskey was going to let me back on the team or not, and if he didn't I didn't have a lot of choices if I wanted to keep playing ball which I did. When the contract came in the mail, I gave it to Katie right away to read and when she said she thought it was OK, she signed it for me and I ran it over to the post office that same afternoon and sent it to Chicago. I doubt if the team ever got a contract back that fast before.

**PANTS ROWLAND** One day soon after Christmas, I got a call to meet Comiskey in his offices. I assumed we were going to talk about the makeup of the team.

Heading over to the office I was afraid that he might be going to tell me that he decided not to bring Joe and Lefty back, a decision I was more than willing to argue with even though arguing with the Old Roman was usually a waste of time.

The news, however, was worse than that. Comiskey fired me on the spot. He said that I had lost control of the players, whatever the hell that was supposed to mean.

I never expected this. In four years as Sox manager I had won 339 games, lost 247 and won a World Championship—hardly a lousy record. The only year we came in lower than third was the year in which we lost so many players to the service.

He has never satisfactorily explained why he did it, but I believe I know. A lot of players were speaking ill of him, and he felt I was at least partially responsible for this. I was close to the players, yes. But he brought on the anger himself. Of course, it was easier to blame someone else and I was that someone. Managers are always easy targets.

There is no question about the club being a divided group, and there is no question that there was a lot of anger and bitterness, but he was wrong if he thought I was the cause—dead wrong. My job was to win games and I was doing that. To hold me responsible for the animosity against him was ridiculous.

That was the end of my major league managing career, and if I sound a little bitter about how it ended, I guess I am, and I can't say in all honesty that I was either surprised or shocked by what happened to the team after I left. I'd like to think that had I still been there, the players would have trusted me enough that I could have headed off the terrible fate that befell them.

**JOE JACKSON** I couldn't believe it when I heard that Manager Rowland was fired. I didn't want to have to learn to work with another manager, but it was Mr. Comiskey's team and he could do anything he wanted with it which is what he did. I never got a chance to say goodbye to Pants because by the time we showed up for spring training he was gone.

Kid Gleason who replaced him was a very different kind of guy. He was peppery and excited all the time. He hollered at the boys a lot, but he knew what he was doing. I guess that's what Mr. Comiskey wanted—somebody that could shake the team up some.

**KID GLEASON** My take on Joe was that he was one hell of a ball player, but my job as I saw it was to make all my boys better no matter how good they was to begin with. Take Joe, for example, I thought he could be even better if I lit a fire in his pants. I think the game came so easy to him that he sometimes forgot that he had to work at it. I mean, put Cobb's fire into Joe's belly and there was no telling what he might of done.

One night, not too long after I was made manager, I took Joe out to get a drink and something to eat. Then after a little more to drink than I had planned, I lit into him. Not too rough, you know, but forceful enough for him to get the message.

"They can't bring back the old kind of game, not the way we played it.

Know what I mean?" I started out. He said he knew what I meant but he didn't.

"No, siree. Know how I used to play second base?" I continued. "I'd let 'em slide into the bag, then kick them off and slap the ball down on their conks. Yes, sir. Kick 'em right off the bag. That's the way we put 'em out."

I figured rather this was better than lecturing Joe, which he probably wouldn't take too kindly to.

"Take the pitchers. You never see a pitcher nowadays running in front of a man when he's going to second or third, do you? Well we did it when I was pitching. Any time a man tried to steal I'd run over in front of him and slow him up. If a pitcher did that today folks would think he was crazy."

We was getting a little tight, so I was probably talking too loud but I continued on anyway.

"In the early 90's when I was still a pitcher with the Phillies, I won 36 games. You bet I did. A year or so later, they moved the pitcher's box back farther from the plate and that put a lot of pitchers out of business. They either lost their control or couldn't last out a game. At the old distance, a fellow could pitch every other day if he was tough. When I won 36 games with the Phillies I pitched every other day—had to. We had only 15 men. The reason the hurlers can't work so much now is because of the pitching distance—that and the fact that they ain't so tough as we was."

We was there maybe a couple of hours—me talking and Joe listening. He didn't say much. Hell, he didn't say practically nothing, but he did listen. Ol' Joe was always a good listener.

"Joe, you can play for me just as long as you play hard every day, and you play to win every game. That's all I ask."

Hell, it's what I did and I didn't see no reason he couldn't, too.

"Baseball, it's a wonderful game, and it will be good to you just like it's been good to me, Joe. Play the game on the square and it will be square with you. Know what I mean?"

He said he did.

**CHARLIE LEBEAU** The Kid was amazing. When he began his career he was maybe the worst pitcher in the history of professional baseball. He lost his first game 15 to 0, and then it got really bad. He had a pet curve that didn't and a fast ball that wasn't. He finally won a game but he gave up 18 runs in the process. The Kid wasn't smart enough to know when to quit. He kept throwing and the batters kept hitting. For some unknown reason he landed with the Phillies at just the right time. No sooner did he get there, when some players revolted as part of the formation of the Brotherhood League. Since the Kid refused to go along with the players, he was one of the only pitchers left on the squad, so he pitched just about every other day.

He was so stubborn that eventually he started winning and actually turned into a halfway decent pitcher—not as good as he claimed he was, but decent.

After a couple of years he was dealt to the St. Louis Browns. The only trouble was that Gleason and the manager, Chris Von der Ahe, didn't always see eye to eye about everything. Actually, they didn't agree on much of anything. The manager's strategy for dealing with his irascible pitcher was to fine him—again, and again and again. One season the fines amounted to $500, quite a hefty sum in those days.

On one occasion he picked up his pay envelope and found himself $100 shy of expectations. With his Irish blood at a full boil he rushed down to the manager's office with murder on his mind. He charged in to find the mild-mannered skipper sitting with his feet on his desk and a big cigar in his mouth.

"Hello, Kid, how you vas?" he asked with a big innocent smile on his face.

"Look here you big fat Dutch slob," roared Gleason, his fists doubled. "If you don't open that safe and get me the $100 you fined me, I'm going to knock your block off."

Von der Ahe had the safe open in a heartbeat, but the animosity between them continued unabated.

**I.E. SANBORN** The words most used to describe the Kid were "gruff" and "grizzled." Take your pick. He was from the "play hard or else" school of baseball, and nobody wanted to find out what the "or else" meant.

The interesting thing about this is that Joe managed to get along with every manager for whom he ever played, including the difficult Kid Gleason.

**JOE JACKSON** I went to spring training not knowing what to expect. I didn't know Gleason, I didn't know how Comiskey was going to treat me, and I didn't know what my teammates was going to say.

One of the first players I met when I got there was Chick Gandil. He told me about Fred Toney, a pitcher in the National League who was from down in Nashville. He was given a jail sentence, said Chick, for trying to evade the draft.

Most of the boys though, they didn't seem upset about me not going in the army. I thought maybe Eddie Collins would, but he didn't really say nothing about it. He was in the Marine Corps stationed in Philadelphia during the war, but he didn't say much about that either.

Ray Schalk asked me point-blank why I didn't fight, so I asked him why he didn't.

"I had an exemption," he said.

"Was that legal?" I asked.

"Completely legal," he said.

"Yeah, so was working in the shipyards," I told him.

He didn't say nothing after that.

Gleason acted like he didn't want to talk about the war. What he wanted to do was to teach good baseball. He worked a lot with each player showing him how to do certain things the way he wanted them done. For example, we had a young kid pitcher named Jack who couldn't field his position very good, so Gleason had us bunting at him for hours. That's the kind of camp we had that year down in Mineral Wells, Texas, a place that was hot and rainy most of the time.

He divided us up into two teams—what he called the Regulars, and the Goofs. The Regulars had most of the players who won the Series on it, the Goofs were mostly the reserves and the rookies. We pounded them pretty good.

One newcomer to the team who was on the Regulars was Dickie Kerr. He was a little left-handed pitcher who looked like he was going to make the team from the first time I seen him. He just had that look.

He told us stories about how he used to be a boxer up in Milwaukee and how he played football there, too.

"At first, the big boys didn't want to play baseball and football with me because I was too small," he said. "They told me just once too often that I was a little shaver, so I walloped the lad who said that. After that I played with them all the time."

He looked more like our batboy than our pitcher, but he always had a sunny, smiling look, until he got mad and then he could be awful tough.

The rest of the team was pretty much the same—Weaver at third, Risberg at short, Collins at second and Gandil, who everybody was now saying was the best first baseman in the league, at first. Me and Happy Felsch were in the outfield with either Leibold or Shano Collins or Murphy. Schalk was the catcher and Cicotte, Faber, Williams, and Kerr did most of the pitching. McMullen was our utility player.

I wasn't sure what kind of major league shape I was going to be in after playing for the shipyard for a year. Face it, it wasn't like I was going up against Walter Johnson every day and we didn't play all that many games neither.

When we stopped in Memphis for a game on the way up to Chicago and I knocked out two long triples and two singles. I figured I was ready.

**I. E. SANBORN** The Sox were a hard team to dope out at the beginning of the season. Gleason had the same outfield, the same infield, the same wrecking crew at bat. The new manager had the same premier catcher. There were questions about the pitching staff, but there were in 1917, also.

The bigger question in my mind was whether they would be able to offset their faults in base running and their inability in other ways to make the most of their strengths. But if anyone could get through to them, it was Kid Gleason.

It was obvious that Gleason was working hard to inject "baseball sense" into the rank and file.

**JOE JACKSON** I was real nervous for our first home game of the season. I just wasn't sure how the crowd would greet me. Eddie Collins could see how I was, and he told me not to worry about it. Then when we ran out onto the field for batting practice, there was already a lot of people in the stands. Well, I'll tell you, it was something I'll never forget. A whole bunch of my fans, they got together and brought a band with them and as soon as we came out onto the field they started playing and cheering like mad. They was marching through the stands with big banners and carrying on real loud.

When I came to bat for the first time, out came a group of fans up to home plate and they stopped the game for a few minutes while a lady gave me a beautiful gold pocket watch—and it was a good one, too.

The crowd started chanting, "Give 'em Black Betsy, Joe! Give 'em Black Betsy."

**CHARLIE LEBEAU** As soon as Comiskey saw the fans' reaction to Joe—not just in Chicago, but around the league—he pulled one of the most incredible about faces in baseball history. That hypocrite had the gall, to announce that he was so pleased he had not listened to the critics who had pushed for Joe's removal from the team.

"Joe's no slacker in my book," went the new shameless litany.

Clearly Comiskey had underestimated Joe's fan appeal, just as he had overestimated his own ability to influence public opinion.

Everyplace he went, the fans let Joe know they supported him. He was back, and so were his loyal fans.

Had he not been such a good player would they have been so supportive? Probably not.

**CHICK GANDIL** We got off to a good start that year—particularly me and Joe, which I know made some of the other boys angry.

Early in the season Comiskey held what he called "Honor Day," in which anyone in any military or Red Cross nurse uniform could get in for free. He also specially invited 2,500 wounded "heroes" from nearby hospitals.

Now I didn't have anything against helping out the soldiers but here was Comiskey showboating again at our expense and I was peeved. I figured when we were up for a new contract that he would claim he just didn't take in enough at the turnstiles to pay us more. And did he ever!

**LEFTY WILLIAMS** By the end of April we had moved into first place. Cicotte and me were pitching good, and Joe, Gandil, Schalk and Collins—Eddie, not Shano—were tearing up the league at the plate.

**SWEDE RISBERG** One day while we were in Cleveland, thieves broke into our clubhouse at home and stole all of our left-handed gloves, several sweater jackets, and a number of other things. About the only thing they didn't steal was the bases.

When we got back into town and found out about it, some of us went to Comiskey and asked him to replace our lost things as it was his clubhouse from which they were taken. He refused. He didn't give us one red cent. I mean, even if he had given us anything, it would have sent a message that that he cared a little about his players, but no, he was his usual I-don't-give-a-damn-about-anybody-but-myself skinflint owner.

It wouldn't have taken much.

**HAPPY FELSCH** Trying to negotiate a contract with the Old Roman was a real treat. He had a standard line which I think all of us heard at one time or another: "Look, I started with $50 a month in 1877 and look where I am now." If he thought that was supposed to be inspirational, he was delusional.

**CHICK GANDIL** On the road we got the exorbitant sum of three dollars per day in meal money. Now I didn't do a scientific poll or anything but I'll guarantee that was less than players made on any other team. I know things were cheaper then, but three dollars? With the reserve clause in place there was nothing we could do about it. We were stuck with the team that owned us until we were either cut lose or until Judgment Day, whichever came first.

Once during the 1918 season we had a players meeting where we talked about going out on strike because of the way Comiskey was dealing with us. Joe and Eddie weren't with us at the time because of wartime commitments and they were two of the highest paid. The rest of us, though, talked about it a lot. It was generally known that we drew the largest crowds, larger even than the Giants, but were being paid like we drew the smallest. We talked about walking out but then didn't for the simple reason that we just didn't have any real clout. Comiskey could have brought up minor leaguers or done anything he wanted.

We were nothing more than chattel. Play for whatever we were offered, or not play at all. That meant in effect, we didn't have any real choice.

**I. E. SANBORN** One afternoon when I was about to do a short piece on Joe, I asked him to come up to the press room. You should have seen his eyes pop out when he saw the spread laid out for the writers. Comiskey was never chintzy when it came to the writers. We had an endless supply of bourbon and food prepared by a special chef and it was all laid out on a long table.

As soon as Joe came in, I realized I had made a mistake. The penny-pinching owner the players knew was a different man with the writers. He treated us with a generosity the players never saw.

Joe didn't say anything, but he had to have thought about the discrepancy.

Comiskey was a smug, portly, penurious man, a man not without considerable charm, an imaginative executive who built a successful team on and off the field. You would think he would have known what effect he was having on his players. Apparently not.

**VINCENT ALEXANDER** Rumors were flying all year about the rancor on the club, but despite that—or maybe because of it—the team was winning. Williams, Cicotte, and Faber were all pitching well, but it was Joe who was the star of the show. Through much of the season he was leading the league in hitting and dreams of winning the batting championship must have been floating in his head.

**BUCK WEAVER** I remember times when we were playing important games and we'd go out to the ballpark early and take infield and sharpen our spikes till they were like razors. The only guy who didn't do it was Eddie Collins. Why? Well, he was a different type of ballplayer. He never went in for that sort of stuff because he figured they might come back at him and he would get hurt. He was a great guy to look out for himself. If there was a tough runner coming down to second, he would yell for the shortstop to take the play.

**JOE JACKSON** We was an odd group of players on that team, no doubt about that.

Freddie McMullen pretty much went his own way. What I mean by that is that he didn't pal around with anybody really. He wasn't a good hitter but he could field good on the infield so he was a valuable bench player.

Buck Weaver, some people said was the best third baseman in the game, but he wasn't always. He used to strike out too much and make plenty of wild heaves into the grandstand.

He told me once how his father was a Pennsylvania iron worker who liked to hunt more than work which reminded me of my father. When he realized that he could chop wood better left-handed he learned to switch hit. He was a flashy fielder who was real quick around the bag. He was so fast actually that not even Ty Cobb would try to bunt against him, and Ty was the greatest bunter who ever lived.

Buck was full of pepper. He would take on just about anybody. Once he called McGraw's team a bunch of yellowbellies and said to McGraw that he had the guts of a canary bird.

Buck was a college boy so we didn't have much to do with each other, but I never had any trouble with him, and I don't think he ever had any truck with me.

Dickie Kerr was the coolest little rooster you ever seen. I mean he didn't act nervous about anything. Maybe that's because he started as a professional boxer who learned to take a beating and give it back. He was one tough little cookie. I pretty much stayed away from Dickie not because I was afraid of the little guy but because I don't think he liked me much.

Swede Risberg was our shortstop. He wasn't the greatest hitter who ever come down the pike, but he was a great fielder and a real fighter. He was the type of player we used to call a scrapper. Me and him got into it a little bit a couple of times, but mostly we didn't have no problems.

Chick Gandil's mother and father both come from Switzerland which is maybe why he thought he was better than everybody else. Chick was something of a loudmouth, and maybe a little bit of a bully. He said what he thought and he didn't give a darn if you liked it or not—particularly where Mr. Comiskey was concerned. Like, for example he was always saying he was making only $4,000 a year, while Jake Daubert, the first baseman for Cincinnati was making $10,000 and he wasn't nearly as good, which he wasn't. When he didn't like something I done either, he said that, too, but I knew that was just Chick.

Before he started playing professional ball, he earned his living as a boilermaker driving home rivets. He always said he was proud to have been a working man just like me, and like me, he didn't have much of an education, although he did have some. He said that when he was not yet 17, he jumped a freight train heading for Amarillo, Texas because somebody told him they was looking for semipro players out there. It wasn't true, so he moved on to some little town down in Mexico which he said didn't have no laws or policemen. He played for the local team and did some boxing on the weekends, and when he wasn't doing that, he took a job as a boilermaker down in the copper mines.

He was a good enough player that somehow he ended up on the White Sox, but he always reminded me of a rough boilermaker from the mines. He was married, but that didn't seem to stop him from acting pretty wild.

The two things I remember most about Chick are that he was always smoking a cigarette, and he didn't really have any friends, and didn't seem to care. He wasn't close to anybody on the team which is the way he seemed to want it.

Happy Felsch wasn't always as happy as his name. Actually, we called him "Hap" which seemed better for him anyway. He played next to me in center field and he had good speed and a strong arm, but not as strong as mine.

Everybody knowed Eddie Collins was the captain and leader of the team. He was smart and he was a great fielder and hitter. Some of the guys, too, thought he played more to make himself look good than to make the team look good. Maybe he did. I don't know for sure. Anyway, he was the boss on the field and everybody knowed that.

Ray Schalk didn't exactly look like a catcher, but he sure played like one. Most men at that position, at least back then, had big bulging arms and legs and usually a big chest, and they were either tall or broad so that the pitcher would have a big target to shoot at. But Schalk, he wasn't none of those things, and when he ran to back up first or third, he ran as fast as any infielder. Believe it or not, he actually made putouts at every base, and that means second, too. I remember one game when a little fly came into center field. Hap took off after it, but it dropped in front of him. Ray figured it would, and he ran out to the pitcher's mound and when the ball fell safe, he yelled to Eddie who threw the ball to him in time to tag the runner. I saw him work that play a number of times.

He loved to run all over the field, and he could throw as good as any catcher I ever seen. He stole his share of bases, too

One thing about Ray, he never liked to come out of a game. I seen Ty foul one back once that caught Ray on the collar bone. It not only knocked him down, but it knocked him out cold. The trainer ran out on the field and they had a heck of a time bringing him to. They had to use artificial respiration and even oxygen. When Ray finally come around, he insisted on staying in the game.

Once two sportswriters were standing on the field in front of our bench. Now nobody was paying any attention to them at all, so one of them said to the other that he would bet a dollar that if he rolled a baseball into the dugout, none of us would even notice except Ray. The other writer took the bet and the second the ball hit the dugout floor, Ray was on it like a cat. That was Ray. You could never get anything by him.

He was really good friends with Eddie Collins. The two of them used to talk baseball all the time, because both of them said they wanted to be managers someday.

Ray was a smart baseball player. He told the pitchers what to throw, and if they didn't follow his instructions there was hell to pay. We didn't call him Cracker for nothing.

**RAY SCHALK** If I had any success in the game at all, it was because of Gleason. Tough, rough, and ready gentleman that he was, he sold me on the idea that a little fellow didn't have to give too much ground to the big bruisers. The Kid wasn't an oily talker, he wasn't one of those percentage figurers, he didn't possess a master mind. But he was sharp and he was inspiring. What a wonderful little man he was.

**I.E. SANBORN** Ironically, what probably doomed the team was their own success. We kept hearing about dissension on the club, but they were winning so no one paid much attention. Looking back on it, I wish we had made more of an issue of their problems. The reality is, though, in those days we writers didn't delve deeply into the personal lives of the players or emphasize their off-field problems. Mostly we wrote the positive stories the fans wanted to read, and told the uplifting sagas of success and accomplishments.

**JOE JACKSON** We had a few fights in the locker room that season. The biggest one was between Chick Gandil and Eddie Collins, and it took a lot of guys to pull them apart. I don't know for sure what started it, but it probably wasn't much.

Swede and Schalk got into it once too, but we had so many scruffs, that one wasn't nothing special.

**VINCENT ALEXANDER** Any thoughts that Joe had lost some of his spark after a year in the shipyards were quickly put aside. He was playing some of his best ball.

I got a chance to see one regular Sox game that year and as luck would have it, was a great one. It was a 1 to 1 tie going into the last half of the 10th inning of a game against New York. About 30,000 fans began howling as Joe came to bat. He delivered as ordered by hitting a heroic drive far and high over the right fielder's head. The crowd screamed as the ball sailed and sailed and finally dropped into the right field bleacher for a home run.

**KATIE JACKSON** Joe was playing well, but there was so much strife on the team, that he was always on edge.

We tried not to talk about it. On our days off we went to the movies, which Joe liked or took long walks, which he didn't like so much but he did for me.

Sometimes on those walks we stopped by and watched Chicago Baseball League games. I guess it was one of the most organized amateur leagues in the country, or at least that's what they said.

The league was made up of both white teams and black teams like the Leland Giants. It may have been the first time we ever saw Negroes play ball. Joe watched the game from the back where he wasn't recognized. We stayed for the whole game, and I think Joe enjoyed himself by letting off a little steam.

Now, you've got to remember, we were both from the South and we were brought up with a certain attitude toward Negroes. That attitude was ingrained in us since we were little, and it didn't disappear easily, if ever at all. I can't say Joe wasn't prejudiced some. That just wouldn't be true. But I remember him watching the game that day with enjoyment, and never did he even mention, during or after the game, that they were Negro players.

Joe appreciated a game well played and that game was.

**I.E. SANBORN** In front since July 10th, the Sox nailed down the pennant on September 24th. In that game against St. Louis, it was Joe's single in the ninth inning which put his club into the World Series. For the second time within the space of three years, and the fourth time in the 19 years of American League history, the pennant in the junior league went to the Sox.

They were a speedy aggregation led by the aggressive Gleason and played as good ball as the best products of the American League in years gone by. Neither the great Athletics of 1911-13-14, or the Red Sox teams of 1912-15, had Gleason and he made the difference in more than just a few games that season.

As the season wore down, writers and fans alike were touting the Chicago White Sox against the Cincinnati Reds. Everyone agreed that the key was going to be the pitching, and that Gleason would have to call on Cicotte up to three times in a long Series.

The line on the Series went something like this.

The Reds certainly had more depth at pitching

At catcher, it was no contest. Schalk was one of the better catchers in the hectic history of the game. He would be opposed in the Series by Bill Rariden, but Schalk not only had a better throwing arm, and knew how to hold up his pitchers better, but he was a much, much better hitter.

At first base, the veteran Jake Daubert, had an edge over Gandil as a fielder, but not as a hitter. At second base, Eddie Collins had a clear and decisive edge over Morrie Roth. At third, both Heinie Groh and Buck Weaver were strong-hitting veterans, but the nod went to Weaver inasmuch as he was a shade more clever in the field than Groh. Kopf and Risberg were about equal at third.

In left field, the Reds used a number of different players, while the Sox relied primarily on Nemo Leibold. Regardless of who the Reds chose, Leibold had the edge. Eddie Roush and Happy Felsch patrolled center for their respective teams. Felsch was one of the best defensive fielders in the game, covering almost as much territory as Tris Speaker, but he was not in the same class with Roush at bat. In right field, Joe Jackson loomed head and shoulders above Earle Neale. For the season Joe hit.351 and led the team in virtually all offensive categories including batting average, RBIs, hits, doubles, triples, slugging average and total bases.

Such was the thinking on the eve of the Series. But there were rumors—odd, disturbing, recurring rumors, rumors which threatened to change the face of the game forever.

# 46

# I ALWAYS SAID NO

**HUGH FULLERTON** Let me try to put this as simply and clearly as I can. The fix was on. The goddamed World Series was fixed! Every dog on the street knew it, knew it before the Series began, knew it during the Series, knew it afterward. The operative word here is "knew," not "thought," "guessed," or "suspected." We knew.

The "we" here speaks of almost everybody directly involved with the game. The players, even those not in on it, knew. Comiskey knew. Gleason knew. The shoeshine boy in my hotel knew. My ancient uncle Alfred knew.

The Series was fixed. So what? It wasn't the first time. You might as well make a buck on the game. Everybody else is. What's wrong with that?

**SHORTY SCHIRALDI** I used to put a buck or two down on a pony or a dog now and then, and if a situation came up on the diamond that looked like it was worth a 10 spot or so, well I'd do that, too. Nothing too big, you understand, just enough to make it interesting.

Then one afternoon before the 1919 Series I'm at Joey's getting a haircut, and maybe a tip or two, because Joey's a talker not to mention a listener.

"The Pale Hose are three to one," Joey says.

"No shit, Sherlock," I say. "Tell me something I don't know."

Of course the dammed Sox are three to one. The high and mighty ones should roll over the Queen City pretenders.

"No contest. Lousy bet," I say. "Gimme a pony instead."

"Not so fast, Shorty," says Joey without missing a beat.

Now I'm interested.

"Never bet without the skinny," Joey says.

Now I'm real interested. "What have you got?"

"Take Cincinnati."

"No shit?"

"Can't miss."

"You got it straight?"

"Directly from Sport Sullivan," Joey assures me, "and he's a personal friend of Gandil."

"Gandil, he in on it?" I ask with real surprise. "Gandil, man, that's big. You sure?"

"And several others."

"Yeah, who?"

"Kcy players. That's all I know."

"Gandil! I don't believe it.

"Himself."

"Gandil! I'll be damned!"

"Put the farm on it."

"You got this straight, Joey? I mean don't hang me out there to dry."

"Do I ever?"

"Doerie in the fifth last Saturday."

"Horses don't listen so good sometimes, but Gandil does."

I gave Joey a quarter for the haircut and a fiver for the tip. The tip was better than the haircut.

What Joey said sounded good to me—real good. A guy could do OK with this kind of information, but I wanted to check it out before I put down anything with more than a couple of zeros at the end of it. I went around to Paulie's where a guy could get down some serious green if he wanted.

"Cincinnati money's all over the place," says Paulie's flunky Sammy.

"So what are we talking about now?" I ask trying to control my excitement.

"We've gone from 7-10 to 5-6 overnight," Sammy offers without looking up from his paper.

"I hear it's even money in places," I say.

"Wouldn't be surprised. Might even get to 9-10 by first ball."

"Might be worth waiting," I say.

"Might be."

"Paulie, take 5 G's?" I ask.

"You wouldn't be the first."

Something was up. No doubt about it. I checked the morning paper. It said that there was an unconfirmed report that Cicotte's arm was sore, and that the sudden support for the Reds was nothing short of startling. Perfect! Cicotte's sore arm story was all I needed to hear. If there was a fix on there had to be some cover up. I bought it, hook line and sinker.

The next morning I was sitting on Paulie's door step when he opened. I got 5 G's down and I got it at even money!

There's nothing like a good barber to make a guy look and feel great.

**SPORT SULLIVAN** Yeah, I'll tell you how it went down. Why not? It's water over the dam now. Gandil, he's the one who jump-started the whole thing. I had known him for a number of years. You know, traded him a good cigar once in a while for dope like the starting pitcher for the next game had a sore arm—stuff like that. Not really big info or important inside tips but all the same it helped a little in my business. My business was gambling. I never did too much with baseball, because unlike say horse racing, baseball had so damn many variables that it was hard to get an edge and an edge was what we were all looking for.

Gandil was in the Hotel Buckminster in Boston with the team. Now the boys usually stayed in posher joints, but a couple of the Sox had gotten into a fight in their old hotel and busted up the place pretty good. They were cordially invited to find another hotel.

So one day I get a message from Gandil that he wants to see me in his room. I don't remember the exact date, but it was maybe three, three and a half weeks before the Series was scheduled to start. I'm figuring he's got some dope on an ingrown toenail for a reserve outfielder or something equally as useless, but I had the time so I go to his room anyway. I got a kick out of Chick. He liked to think he was some kind of big shot, so a few times I introduced him to people like George M. Cohan or Harry Sinclair and he ate it up.

I get to his room and he's alone. We do the normal obligatory chit-chat for five minutes or so before we get down to serious business. I mean you can't meet somebody like this and then come right out with "I got a deal for you." You've got to talk about things that don't count for a few minutes—weather, some acquaintance or something just as stupid.

"Spit it out, Chick," I finally said. I can see you got something on your mind. Maybe it'll be worth my time. Who knows? What have you got?"

Now I'm expecting "Weaver's got a sprained wrist he's hiding and can barely swing the bat," but instead he blurts out, "I can put this thing in the bag."

"What are you talking about, Chick?" I ask him. "Put what in the bag?"

"The Series," he says with the sanctity of a man being sworn in as Pope.

"You got the Series?" I ask wanting to make sure I heard this straight.

"I can get it," he says.

"How you going to do that, big guy?"

"I can get enough of the guys to go in on it."

"Like how many?"

"Enough."

"The whole Series, you can't do it with just a couple, you know, you've got to have a bunch."

"I can get them."

"And you've got to have some pitchers. You can't do it without pitchers."

"Leave the details to me," he insisted.

Now, I didn't know whether to believe him or not. Chick didn't always deliver on his word, but I was interested enough at least to keep the conversation going.

"Who do you have? I asked cutting right to the crux of the issue.

"I can get who I need, trust me."

"Chick, I trust you, but what makes you so sure you can get to the right guys?"

"This is a real unhappy team, Sport. Real unhappy. They hate Comiskey. They'll do anything to get back at him."

"But this is the Series we're talking about," I insist. "We're talking about guys' careers if they're caught."

"I can get them."

I'm still not sure, but I'm willing to go along with this, at least for a while. "What's it going to take," I ask him.

"A lot. At least fifty. It has to be worth it for the boys and it has to be upfront."

"Why me?" I ask.

"You're the only one I know can raise that kind of money."

I wasn't sure I could, but I believed he believed I could.

The conversation went on like this for a few more minutes then I left saying I'd see what I could do and then get back to him. I walked out onto the street feeling like somebody had just kicked me in the stomach. Being in on some fix of a lousy horse race was one thing, but the World Series, that was a whole other matter. Oh, I know baseball games had been fixed before, but never, as far as I knew, the whole damn Series. Still, if Chick was right, and if he could deliver, there was a lot of money to be made. A lot of real easy money. The only thing was, I knew this was going to take more than just me to pull it off.

**CHICK GANDIL** We spent a lot of our off-field time bitching about Comiskey—most of us anyway. Then one day in Boston, a guy I knew casually, named Sport Sullivan, comes up to me and suggests I get a few players together to throw the Series.

I don't care what the creep said later, he's the one who brought the idea to us, not the other way around. Let me be clear about this: He approached me, I didn't approach him. He's the liar.

"You're the leader of the team, Gandil, you can do it," he says. "I can pretty well assure you I can get some real money together if you can deliver."

"What's real money?" I ask him.

"More than you've ever seen from Comiskey," he says, "a lot more."

Oh, and he wasn't the first one to make the proposal either. The idea to throw the Series came from the gamblers, not the players. But it wasn't a bad idea. Comiskey owed us and the only way we were going to see our rightful share of the profits was through the back door, through people like Sullivan and his cronies, and it wasn't the first time something like this was done. The history of baseball was rife with player abuse. It was a classic case of labor conflict between management and workers, and it wasn't all that different from workers blocking factories to get what they were worth. Sometimes you just have to do what it takes to get justice.

The first guy I turned to was Cicotte. He was the key. The World Series back then was a nine-game affair, so he would pitch two, maybe three of the games, and, of course, he was capable of winning them all. I talked to him a couple of times about the idea and knew that he was interested from the get-go. He was one of the most underpaid players on the team, and one of the most interested in maintaining a good lifestyle. He said he'd come in for $10,000 which was a hell of a lot more than I had talked to Sullivan about, but I agreed, figuring we'd work out the details later.

**EDDIE CICOTTE** I'll admit it, I hated the son of a bitch Comiskey. I won 29 games in 1919, and that cheap bastard wouldn't even cough up six grand. Yet one bad season, one unlucky injury, and I knew I'd be out. That's the way the game worked. The players brought in the crowds, the crowds brought in their money, and the owners kept most of it. The players were getting screwed by the owners, and none more so than those of us who worked for Comiskey. He was getting rich, while we were being screwed.

Thoughts of getting even were dancing in my head when Gandil comes to me and begins talking revenge.

"What are you going to do, shoot the bastard?" I asked him.

"Worse," Gandil answered.

"What's worse, dismemberment?" I asked, with thoughts of a juicy murder on my mind. Saying that I want to be clear that, yeah, I did have thoughts of murder, but I never would have done it. They were fantasies, and who hasn't fantasized sometime about bumping off somebody we were mad at?

"Throw the Series," Gandil came back.

"You're out of your mind," I said without a second's hesitation.

"There's money in it. Big money."

"I don't care how much money's in it, I don't want any part of it," I insisted.

Gandil was cagey, though. He knew I had bought a farm up in Michigan and he knew I was having a tough time with the mortgage. I guess I didn't make any secret about that. Anyway, if Comiskey had paid me even close to what I was worth to the team, I wouldn't have had those problems, but he didn't, so I did. I was getting pressure from the wife, too, so Gandil was singing the right song. Only I wasn't interested. Well, I was interested, but not enough to go along with any kind of fix. That wasn't right, and I knew it. Baseball was good, even if some of the people in it weren't.

Gandil kept at me over a number of weeks—always pushing the money angle, always telling me it was nothing more than what Comiskey owed me. After a while, every time I saw him coming toward me, I went the other way. I didn't want the temptation.

"You can name your own figure," Gandil said at one point. "Name a figure that you think is what Comiskey owes you. Come on, Eddie, be realistic. Fair is fair. Who do you think is making the money for this franchise? You, maybe more than anybody. Comiskey owes it to you. All we're going to do is take what's owed to us, that's all. It's what's right, Eddie, and you know it."

I didn't ask him about how he expected to pull this off, or who else he had with him, or thought he could get. I didn't want to know. All I knew was it was wrong, no matter what Chick said.

Chick was relentless. Over and over he hit me with his arguments, and over and over I resisted.

Then one day I got a letter from an attorney threatening me with foreclosure if I didn't come up with back payments on the farm. I know I shouldn't have been in that position in the first place. I knew we spent too much money on trying to keep up with the Joneses, and I knew we hadn't always managed our finances properly, but that letter got me mad. In my mind I took out my anger on Comiskey. That night, on a Pullman heading for Chicago, Eddie approached me again.

"Ten thousand dollars," I said. "Cash. Before the Series begins!"

That was it. A moment of anger I've regretted the rest of my life.

**CHICK GANDIL** After Cicotte fell in line, I went after the others I thought would go along.

Risberg came next. He jumped in without any hesitation and brought his buddy, Freddy McMullin. As a utility player, I knew McMullin wasn't going to be much of a help, but he and Risberg were pretty tight, so I didn't want to upset the apple cart. Besides, the more players I could guarantee Sullivan, the better chance we had of attracting the kind of money we were going to need.

**LEFTY WILLIAMS** When Chick came to me with his plan, I didn't believe he was for real. This sounded to me like another one of his harebrained ideas that would never see the light of day. He could talk big, but I didn't believe most of it. Look, guys were always talking about doing something to get back at Comiskey, but it was just hollow bravado that kept us all thinking we were making progress against the evils of management.

He came at me a couple of times saying he had Cicotte and Risberg, and could get a couple of other guys like Joe and Buck. I asked if he had talked to them yet; he said to leave that to him, and that it was no problem. I still didn't believe him, but to get him off my back, I said I'd think about it.

**CHICK GANDIL** In late September, we had a meeting in my room at the Ansonia Hotel at Broadway and 74th Street in New York. Despite what some of the fellows have said to save their hides, we were all there—all eight of us, me, Cicotte, Williams, Felsch, Weaver, Swede, McMullin and yes, Jackson.

I laid out the details as I knew them to be at that time. I told them about the eight grand up front from Sullivan, and I assured them we'd all be paid before the games.

I know this sounds like it should have been a real somber meeting, but to tell you the truth, it wasn't really. What I remember mostly is that we drank a little, laughed a lot, and generally enjoyed the thought of screwing Comiskey.

We talked a little about how we were going to accomplish the task. We talked about the creative art of making an error without making it look intentional. We joked about bonuses for the guys who could leave the most men on base or hit into the most double plays while swinging the hardest. Felsch even confessed to how he used to get hit on the head with fly balls as a kid and suggested he could resurrect his act with great aplomb. We were having a great time at Comiskey's expense.

I don't remember Joe saying much, but then, that was his style. Lefty offered a few mild protests, but I knew when the chips were down, he'd come along.

Later on all sorts of people have asked what we thought about the issue of getting away with our plan. The answer is simple: we didn't. Why should we? Hadn't Hal Chase thrown dozens of games, and wasn't he still around? Hell, they even promoted him to manager after he was discovered. Hadn't players thrown games since bases were posts and gotten away with it? Wasn't the connection between baseball and gamblers as old as the game itself? Was anybody really looking? Besides, how could anybody really tell if an error or a fat pitch was intentional? You couldn't. You could guess, but that's all. Players make errors all the time. It's part of the game. Pitchers throw fat pitches every time out. It can't be avoided. Baseball is played by men, and men are prone to err.

**JOE JACKSON** Sure, me and Lefty heard talk that there was something going on. I even had a fellow come to me one day and make me an offer. It was on the 16th floor of a hotel and there was four other people there, two men and their wives.

I told him in front of everybody, "Why you cheap so-and-so! Either me or you—one of us is going out that window."

I started for him, but he ran out the door and I never saw him again. Those four people swore to that at my trial later. Absolutely there was a lot of talk, but I didn't know what was going on.

**CHICK GANDIL** Apparently the word about our plans got out to the money people pretty quick, because before long Cicotte set up a meeting with me and Sleepy Bill Burns who had heard about Sullivan's attempt to round up the cash. Sleepy was a retired player who I met briefly when he was up with the team in 1910 for a cup of coffee. He wasn't much of a pitcher, but he was a real character. He had some kind of a hang-up about riding on trains, which he said stemmed from witnessing holdups as a kid. At any rate, he would always carry this pistol with him when we were traveling, and he'd keep it under his pillow when he was sleeping. Anytime someone made a noise around him, he'd whip out the gun and level it in the direction of the sound. Needless to say, we gave him a wide berth. Come to think of it, maybe that's why he looked sleepy all the time—he was up all night waving that damn gun around.

Anyway, at this meeting, Sleepy Bill said he could do better than anything we might get from Sullivan and asked that we hold off on any deal until he could contact some of his own money people.

I talked to the guys, and everybody agreed we should consider his offer.

"Let's take bids," laughed Felsch.

That wasn't such a bad idea. Here we were now being courted by some of the best gambling interests in the country. There are worse positions to be in.

I told Burns we could alter the outcome of the Series for an even

$100,000, and when he didn't even blink, I knew we were set for business.

We were going to get what was due us yet!

**BILLY MAHARG** Sometime in September, I received a wire from Sleepy Bill inviting me to go hunting with him on his ranch someplace in the God-forsaken hills of New Mexico. I should have known something was up. Bill was far more interested in money than he was in deer, or whatever the hell they had down there in the desert.

He told me he needed some backing for a fix of the Series. At first I thought he was pipe dreaming, but then he got down to details, and he named names. That was the key for me. He said he had eight players and he told me who they were. I grilled him a little, but he seemed to have the story straight. He said he wanted $100,000 to be paid in installments of $20,000 before each game then divided among the eight players involved. He didn't say "equally," but that's what I took him to mean.

"I'm thinking eight men, ten grand each. Nobody'll go along without upfront money and once they get that … well, you know they're in for good. Nobody but nobody would dare cross a gambler who put up that kind of dough. They know there would be … consequences.

He asked if I could help with the money.

"Are you kidding?" I asked. "If you got the players, I'll get the bucks."

"I got the players," he assured me.

"Locked in?"

"Tighter than a vice."

If he was on the straight, he not only had the players, but he had the right players—players who could really change the course of a game. Baseball was trickier than say football or basketball, or certainly boxing. In boxing you only needed to get to the fighter, in football the quarterback, and in basketball one, maybe two key players, but in baseball you needed a bunch of players and the right players at that.

I knew a little about baseball having played briefly for the Tigers and Phillies a few years back. Since then I had been making an honest buck as a gambler. I told Burns that I'd head right for Philadelphia, put the money together in a breeze, and then wire him with the details.

I took the next train to Philly and called on my contacts. I struck out big time. They said they couldn't raise that kind of money that quickly.

I don't know if that was really the truth or that they were afraid of the Series because of the exposure it would get. This was a tricky deal, because, assuming Burns had the players he said he did, you still had a situation where everybody was going to be watching what was happening. A guy's gambling career could go down the drain in a minute if the deal blew up. Still at the same time it was a chance to make your mark if the deal went through smoothly. I mean a guy could be known in the right circles as the man who fixed the Series, and that could be worth plenty down the road. You could be known as a big time player overnight. I was willing to take that risk because I thought the payoff could be worth it.

I headed to New York, met with Burns again and said, "Look, I've got a better idea. Why don't we contact A.R. himself?"

"Can you get to him?" asked Burns as if he were in awe.

"Yeah," I said. "I can get to him."

Just like that I was playing in the big league again. I just hoped to stick around longer than I did before.

**HUGH FULLERTON** Rumor had it Arnold Rothstein was behind the fix. The man known simply as A.R. was the king of the gamblers. There was no one higher in the muddied echelons of underworld gambling than A.R. He had made a fortune gambling on just about anything that involved chance, and more than a few that didn't. The story goes that he began his illustrious career by stealing his father's money and gambling with it. The family was Jewish and the father, a highly respected public-spirited benefactor, was devout enough that he would take all his money and jewelry and place in a dish in the house before heading off to the Temple for Friday evening services. Young Arnold, who did not get along with his father, would pocket the money, gamble with it all night, and then replace the capital before his father picked it up again. That was his beginning, but from there he went on to make contacts in the right political circles and to expand his interests. To the father who said he was no good, Arnold responded by becoming incredibly successful in his own way.

It was said A.R. had a genius for numbers, could figure odds in an instant, and never bet unless the numbers were leaning his way. It was also said that he could make the numbers lean a little if necessary. He was a mythic figure among New Yorkers. To the players he was akin to a god; to the police, above harassment; to the public a mysterious and romantic figure.

If A.R. wanted to back the fix there is no doubt he could. There is also no doubt that he was smart enough and well enough connected that if he did back it, the connection to him would have been invisible—totally impossible to trace. And you can bet on that.

**BILLY MAHARG** Me and Burns went out to the race track when we knew A.R. would be there. I had an introduction from a mutual friend in Philadelphia. He was surrounded by his boys so I gave a note to one of them. A message came back: wait in the restaurant.

So we did that, and after quite some time, one of his boys came around. It was Abe Attell, the boxing champ known as "The Little Hebrew." He couldn't have been more than 115 pounds if that, but he was one of the toughest little prize fighters in the world. In his prime he whipped many a heavier fighter on his way to becoming featherweight world champ. There was a lot of talk, though, about fixes in some of his fights and so eventually he was suspended. I didn't know he ran with A.R., but I wasn't all that surprised when I saw him come into the restaurant.

"What's the pitch?" he asked.

I told him we had the Series, and wanted to talk to A.R. about backing it.

He asked me who we had and I told him.

"You guaranteeing you got Cicotte and Jackson?" he asked.

"Absolutely," I said.

"What about Collins?" he asked.

"Not him," I said, "but we got enough without him. We don't need him."

I knew this was a test question. If I had said Collins, he would have walked immediately. He damn well knew Collins was out of the question. Joe was another issue, though. He wasn't quite sure we could get him, and to tell you the truth, I had some questions about that myself.

I told Attell I would like to talk to A.R. personally about the plan, but he said he would relay any message. I really wanted to meet A.R. It would have been a big thrill for me, but I wasn't about to take on the Little Hebrew despite his size.

"I'll get back to you. Tell me where," said Attell.

I told him we were staying at the Ansonia. "What do you think?" I added, "Do you think he'll go for it."

"I'll give him the message" he said, and walked out.

**ABE ATTELL** I gave A.R. the deal Maharg and Burns laid out. He listened as he always done then said, "I'll let you know." That's all he said, but you didn't argue with A.R.

So I thought to myself, if he's not in, why not give it to somebody else and keep a little piece for myself? If it don't work, I got nothing to lose.

I thought right away of Hal Chase. He was in New York and if anybody knew if it could work or not, he was the guy.

So I meet with the great first baseman and he says "Yeah, it can work. If you got the guys you say, it can work." He ought to know, right? Here was the world's greatest fixer of games and he says it will work.

I asked him what to do. He says to press A.R. personally. I asked him what he wanted out of the deal and you know what he says? He says, "The right to bet."

Now here was one smart cookie. He's on the in, but he's in the clear, so he puts down some big money and cleans up. He was in a great position.

**BILL BURNS** When Attell shows up in the Ansonia lobby he comes with good news. He says A.R. is going to back the whole thing. I asked him how much and he said the whole one hundred grand, but only if we kept his name completely out of it, and that if we didn't, we would pay the bill. I didn't have to ask him what that meant.

"Don't try to contact him in any way," he said. "If you so much as even try, the deal's off. Do you understand that?"

I assured him I did. I could understand why A.R. wanted to stay in the background. That's why he was A.R.

"I'll handle everything, do you understand that?" he asked again, and again I assured him I did.

"I'll bring the money. I'll be your only contact."

"I understand," I said before he could ask again.

**EDDIE CICOTTE** One night when I was sound asleep in the hotel, the phone rings. It's Sleepy Bill. He says everything's all right, that the money is in place, and that the deal's on. I was still half asleep so I mumbled something about that being great and went back to bed.

**HUGH FULLERTON** I keep hearing Billy Maharg referred to as "the ex-major leaguer" as if he had a real career. Well, his career consisted of all of two major league at bats, without ever reaching first base, which, come to think of it, kind of sums up his life, too.

Incidentally, maybe Maharg wasn't his real name anyway. Ever notice that Maharg spelled backward is Graham? I've often wondered if maybe he got himself into trouble early on and had to change his name. That thought certainly isn't inconsistent with what we know about his sleazy life.

**ABE ATTELL** Rothstein could back this whole scheme with the loose change in his pocket if he was so inclined. It was my intent to incline him.

We met in the back room of a little restaurant where he often did business. The waiters there were very discreet. I laid out the plan as I knew it. The very fact that he was even sitting down and talking to me meant that he hadn't completely closed his mind to the project.

A.R. was allergic to small talk. We got right down to serious business as he peppered me with questions.

Who's in? How are they going to do it? What's the split? Mostly though, he kept coming back to the same issue: how many people know about this? I didn't know all the issues, but I gave it to him as straight as I could. A.R. wasn't a guy you wanted to give bum answers to.

"What about Jackson?" he asked, "You sure he's smart enough to get the message?"

"Gandil says he won't talk," I assure him. "He's mostly that way anyhow."

"There's no question about him being in, is there?"

"Gandil says he's got him."

"And Cicotte, too?"

"For sure."

"What about Williams? You're going to need two pitchers in a nine-game Series."

"He's shaky, but I think he'll be OK."

"Who's his closest friend on the team?"

"I think Jackson."

"That's good."

"Very good."

We went on like that for some time. A.R.'s a very thorough man. "I don't gamble," he once said. "I only bet on sure things."

I know he was concerned with the secrecy angle. A lot of people were already in on this, but then it would take a lot to pull this off. I think he was intrigued with the challenge. Fixing the World Series could only add luster to his already legendary status. And it couldn't hurt me either. Being known as the guy who worked with A.R. on the Series, I'd be set for life.

He ended the meeting by saying he'd take the matter under advisement. I took that to mean "yes" if all the ducks were in a row. I agreed to catch up with the team in Chicago and check with Gandil on the specifics and then get back to him. Just to be sure, he sent one of his boys with me.

**CHICK GANDIL** I met with Attell when we returned to Chicago. We met in my room at the Hotel Warner. He had a guy with him who listened to the whole conversation but said nothing. The guy was introduced as a "Mr. Ryan," but that obviously was an alias. I think maybe it was Rothstein himself.

Sullivan said it was Rothstein's plan to win the first game so that the odds on us would go up. After that we could lose the Series anyway we saw fit, just so long as we made it look good.

Attell gave me 10 $1,000 bills as a show of faith, and said the rest would be paid in installments.

I said, "The deal was $80,000 up front. That was the deal."

"We need a guarantee," Sullivan said.

"What? How? How can we guarantee anything other than giving you my word?"

"Eighty grand is going to take some collateral."

"You think I'm going to run off with your money? Where am I going to hide?"

I could see a little smile break on "Ryan's" face.

**ARNOLD ROTHSTEIN** I had absolutely nothing to do with the White Sox fix of 1919, and have nothing to say about the matter.

**EDDIE CICOTTE** By this time, some of us were getting a little nervous. It wasn't that long till we began the Series, and we kept getting mixed stories. First it was Sullivan, then it was Sleepy Bill, then it was Maharg, then Attell but nothing seemed to be straight. All of them were somehow involved at some level. The whole thing was getting out of hand. Then Chick said

Rothstein was ultimately the man in charge. Still, I thought going into this thing that it was going to be real simple: we manipulate the Series, the gamblers make a few bucks because they know what the outcome will be, they pay us for our efforts, and we make the money owed to us in the first place. But it was getting more complicated and I didn't like it.

**CHICK GANDIL** As the Series drew close everybody was getting a little edgy. We had lots of talk but very little green stuff, and that was the deal—money up front. Nobody wanted to be in on a thing like this, with all the risks involved, and then not see the money. The risks were huge, the money had to be guaranteed, that's all there was to it.

**LEFTY WILLIAMS** The day before the Series was to start, I went to Gandil and said I wanted out. No, I said I was out.

"You're a sucker, Lefty," he said, "nothing but a sucker."

"I'm out," I repeated.

"The hell you are," he shouted. "You're in just like the rest of us, whether you want to be or not."

"Say what you want, Gandil, I don't want any part of it."

"It's too late for that."

"Like hell it is."

"If anything happens, Lefty, I'll say you were in, so you might as well come along."

"You son of a bitch," I shouted at him.

"We're all sons of bitches, Lefty, didn't you know that?"

**CHICK GANDIL** Cicotte was all right, I thought, but I wasn't so sure about some of the rest of them. I didn't give a damn about McMullin, but he seemed to be committed anyway, maybe more than any of them. Who knew what Weaver was thinking? One minute he was in, the next out. I didn't trust him at all. Joe I had to keep working on. He and Collins were the big hitters on the team, and we needed one of them. Since Collins was definitely out, that meant Joe had to be in.

We had a number of meetings and Joe was at most of them, but because he didn't say much, it was hard to know what he was thinking. Most of the guys on the team you couldn't bully. Joe you could bully.

"Look, you stupid bastard," I told him, "You were at that first meeting. You agreed to it like everybody else, so you're in."

"Gee, Chick, I don't know anymore," he whined.

"What's not to know? You don't have a choice."

"About the whole thing."

"Are you getting screwed by Comiskey, or not?"

"I guess I am."

"You guess you are! You're getting screwed more than anybody. You ought to be getting what Ty's getting, and you know it."

"I know it."

"Name two players in the league better than you."

"I know what you mean."

"This is the only way to get what's yours."

"You really think Comiskey owes me more than anyone?" he asked with that stupid smile of his.

"Of course. So does everybody else."

"If that's the case, then I think I should get more than anybody else."

"What are you talking about?"

"I want $20,000."

"The deal was 10."

"But I'm worth more than anybody."

For a stupid jerk, Joe sure could be smart when he wanted to. I told him he would get 20. What was he going to do if he didn't get it? Go to the press? I figured I'd worry about the details later.

**SHORTY SCHIRALDI** What I found out was that A.R. was taking all sorts of money on Chicago. Most of it came from important "respectable" people who had no idea what was going on. Of course they bet on Chicago. Chicago was one of the greatest teams anybody could remember seeing, maybe better than some of Mack's Athletics teams of a few years back.

A.R. was raking it in.

**SPORT SULLIVAN** Attell comes to me with 40 grand. It's obviously from A.R. only he never says that. I'm to take it to the players as the down payment. I had heard it was supposed to be 80 but Attell says 40 is it.

Now I had the 40 Gs in my pocket and the Series in the bag.

I always knew I would make it to the big time someday. All I needed was a break. Now, suddenly I was smack dab in the middle of it. What to do?

A.R. made his money by always having an edge, didn't he? Why couldn't I do the same?

That $40,000, put down on Cincinnati, even at modest odds, would be a hell of an edge. Let the players wait for the bulk of their money. Give them $10,000, make them play the Series first, and then pay them off. There wasn't a lot to lose here—as long as they did what they said they would. That was my only gamble, but I was convinced Chick had it right and they would go through with it.

I had to be careful getting the money down. I didn't want to throw up any smoke signals. I went to a couple of contacts I had in Chicago, but I couldn't get decent odds. I could only get it down at even. That meant only one thing. A.R. had beaten me to the punch. But that was good in a way, too. If he had big money down, then that meant he was sure this thing was going to work. A.R. didn't take chances.

I'll tell you, I've never been so nervous in my life turning over that 30 grand. If this didn't work I'd have one pissed off Arnold Rothstein on my tail, and that didn't seem like a real good idea.

**CHICK GANDIL** Sullivan showed up with $10,000, that's all.

"The deal was all up front, Sport. It's that or no dice."

"You know whose money this is, don't you?"

"I don't care if it's the Pope's, I want it all now. That's the deal."

"You're lucky to get any of it up front! Just who the hell do you think you're dealing with!"

"You. I think I'm dealing with you, Sport.

"This is the deal."

"It's not what we agreed to."

"It's what we're agreeing to now. Look, somebody on your team has leaked the whole thing."

"What are you talking about?"

"The odds are dropping all over the place. Somebody's talked."

"Nobody's talked! What do you think they are, stupid?"

"You tell me."

"Nobody talked."

“Check it yourself,” Sport said.” Check the odds, you’ll see.”

“I don’t give a damn about the odds,” he answered. “I care about the money you promised.

“You’ll get it. Every penny of it. As soon as the Series is in the bag, you’ll get the rest.”

“I’ve got to give $10,000 to Cicotte now or he won’t go along, and you know damn well, no Cicotte, no deal.”

“I just gave you 10, didn’t I? What’s the problem?”

“What’s the problem? You’re the problem. Your word’s the problem. It’s no damn good, you welcher.”

**SPORT SULLIVAN** I knew damn well that the odds had dropped because of the money A.R. was taking, but I wasn’t about to tell Gandil that. When I showed up with 10 instead of 40, he flew into a rage. I thought at one point it was going to come to blows.

I kept thinking, how would A.R. handle this? Be forceful, but stay in control.

**CHICK GANDIL** I thought for a minute we were going to get into it right then and there.

“Tell your players to keep their mouths shut, Gandil,” he screamed. “Keep your mouths shut and this thing will work.”

“Not if you don’t keep you word, it won’t.”

You’ve got what you’re getting up front. Now just do your damn job.”

With that he walked out, leaving me with a hollow feeling in my stomach that we were now locked into this and there was no backing out. It was one thing to talk about this late at night in a hotel room, it was another to now have to do it.

Suddenly I felt sick.

**EDDIE CICOTTE** I was thinking of the wife and kids and how I needed the money. I told Chick I wanted the cash in advance. I didn’t want any checks. I didn’t want any promise. I wanted the money in bills. I wanted it before I pitched a ball.

The day before I went to Cincinnati, I put it up to Chick squarely for the last time, that there would be nothing doing unless I had the money.

That night I found the money under my pillow. There was $10,000. I counted it. I don't know who put it there, but it was there. It was my price. I had sold out Comiskey; I had sold out the other boys; sold them for $10,000 to pay off a mortgage on a farm.

Later I told the boys I would lose the first game if I had to throw the baseball clean out of the park.

**CHICK GANDIL** The next day I got a call from a Chicago sports writer who said he heard the Series was fixed and did I have any comment? Was he kidding me? Who was this moron anyway? Did he really think that if I knew anything I was going to give him the story?

"Where did you hear that crazy story?" I asked, and hung up.

Now I was beginning to really worry. I kept trying to think of a way out. I didn't think, "Excuse me, Mr. Rothstein, but we've changed our minds" was going to work.

From then on I ate little, slept less.

**KATIE JACKSON** As the Series got closer Joe came home often and said that there was a lot of talk from the players about getting even with the skinflint, Comiskey. He even said he was at some meetings where the subject of fixing the games came up, but I'll tell you this for sure, Joe thought it was just talk. You know how guys are about things like that. They'll talk big, but mostly that's all it, just talk.

I'll tell you how I know this is true. During all of this, Joe slept like a baby. Don't you think if he knew a fix was on, he would have been nervous about it? Don't you think I would have known?

**JOE JACKSON** Yeah, there was lots of talk about fixing the games, and yeah, I was there when some of it was going around, but I never agreed to do nothing. That's a fact.

**SWEDE RISBERG** The only thing was we didn't have the money up front that we were promised. I wanted to bet it all. Why not? If there was even more money to be made, why shouldn't the players get a piece of that, too?

I called some friends in St. Louis and told them what was happening.

Even though I had little money to put down, I thought I might as well let in a few friends so that they could get something out of.

**HUGH FULLERTON** The odds kept dropping as more and more people were included in the loop. You would have thought that men smart enough to fix an institution as visible as the World Series would have been smart enough to know that if the odds dropped too precipitously—and that's exactly what they did—that somebody would have spotted the fix a mile away.

**ABE ATTELL** When the team got to Cincinnati, I met with the players in Cicotte's room at the Sinton Hotel. There were seven of them there. The only one missing was Jackson. I asked about that.

"Don't worry, he's with us," said Gandil.

"Then where is he?" I asked.

"He's with us." Gandil said and then quickly changed the subject. "Where's the money?"

"Lose in five." I told them. "That's what we want. Five games, not a sweep."

We talked about the order of games and finally decided Cicotte and Williams would lose the first two since they would surely pitch those. Dickie Kerr was scheduled to pitch the third game. Since they couldn't control that game, they would find other ways to lose the game.

"No problem," assured Gandil.

They hated Kerr, so they wanted to be damn sure they didn't get a win for him.

Cicotte would pitch again in the third game. That one they would win. They were a cocky lot about their playing. They never even considered the possibility that they might not always be able to win on command.

"We'll win the fourth," said Cicotte. "That way I can use it in contract negotiations for next year."

Everybody agreed that was a good idea. They would lose the fourth, and we'd all go home happy. All except Comiskey.

**LEFTY WILLIAMS** Things were getting more confused than ever. We weren't sure who was coming up with the money—Rothstein, Sullivan,

Attell, Burns? How much were we getting paid, and when. The story changed every time we met.

I should have seen it coming. We all should have, but Gandil kept telling everybody everything was OK, that this is the way deals like this always went down.

Everybody was tight.

**HUGH FULLERTON** In retrospect, here's how things shaped up on the eve of the first game.

Eight players were to a lesser or greater degree involved in a plot to throw the World Series, even though the details of the plot were unclear.

The players, all members of one of the strongest teams in American League history, were idols of millions, and with the exception of McMullin, all were stars on the team, and highly respected players. All except Cicotte were still young enough to expect better seasons ahead with concomitant raises in salaries although all were already being paid well by the standards of the day.

Cicotte, was one of the best pitchers in the game, arguably second only to Johnson in terms of effectiveness. He had already had seasons of 28 and 29 wins behind him and was closing in on 200 career victories. He had thrown a no-hitter and had a 1.82 ERA for the 1919 season. He was at the top of his formidable game.

Gandil, was a big, rangy first baseman with soft hands and great range. At 31 he was at the peak of his career which had already seen him hit over .300 twice. He wasn't the best first baseman in the league—that honor would have to go to George Sisler—but he was a solid player who contributed much to the success of the team.

Swede Risberg, was a 25-five year-old fielding whiz just beginning to hit his stride in his third season. He had an arm like a rifle and awed everybody with his intensity and hustle. His future looked great and everybody expected him to be the glue to the Chicago infield for years to come.

Happy Felsch, was coming into his own as a dominant center fielder. Just 28, he could patrol center field as well as anyone in the league this side of Speaker and Cobb, and he consistently hit in the neighborhood of .300.

Buck Weaver, was the sweetest fielding third baseman in the game. Already in his eighth season, he was still only 29, but he played the game like he knew every nuance. He played with a smile, and in so doing he was a darling of the fans. He was as popular as anyone on a team of popular players.

Lefty Williams, just 26 was on his way to sure stardom. He was getting better by the year capped off by a 23-11 year in 1919. His career ERA at that point was under 3.00. Like the others, he was looking at a bright future.

Only one, Fred McMullin, was not a star. He was a utility infielder who filled in at short, third or second as needed. He was 27, and still waiting his chance to become a regular. Of all the players involved, he had perhaps the least to lose.

Then there was Joe Jackson. All he had done in his career to date was prove that he was not only one of the greatest players in the game, but one of the greatest players to ever have played major league ball. And I say this, fully cognizant, of my earlier opinions that he would never make it. Did he ever prove me wrong! At that point he had a lifetime batting average of .350 with the prospects of many more years of high productivity to come. Only Ty Cobb and Rogers Hornsby ever managed higher career averages, and that's pretty good company! He hit over .300 in the 1917 World Series. There was little reason to think he would hit anything less in 1919.

There was so much to lose, and relatively little to gain by throwing the Series. Joe, probably had the most to lose, but they were all vulnerable.

Didn't they think about that? Apparently not. Apparently what they thought about was money and revenge, in what proportion I suppose depended on the individual.

**SWEDE RISBERG** Of course I knew what we were doing was wrong. I wasn't nuts. But at the time we rationalized it. I never would have done it alone, but everybody else seemed to be OK with it, so I went along.

I really didn't think we would get caught. If Hal Chase got away with it, there was no reason to think we wouldn't. I reasoned that the only person who would really get hurt was Comiskey, and that was all right with me. Besides it was only a game. In the long run it wouldn't matter whether we won or lost. It wasn't a world war, it was a stupid game, that's all.

I had visions of spending the money. I had visions of the next season and another World Series appearance, a World Series we would play to win, and maybe more after that. When you're an athlete playing on a top team, you see only more of the same. You don't think about the team coming apart. You don't think about the misplays, you think about the game-winning plays.

Sometimes in the middle of the night I would wake up scared. But I always rationalized myself back to sleep. There were too many other players involved in the scheme for all of us to be wrong.

I knew, though. Deep down I knew.

**EDDIE COLLINS** We heard the rumors, all of us on the team, but nobody ever said anything to me directly. They damn well knew better. Me, Ray, Dickie, Nemo and the others, we wouldn't have given that lot the time of day.

I really believed it was just talk, big talk from little men. I didn't have any trouble believing they would think of such a stupid idea, I just didn't think they were dumb enough to carry it out. In my wildest flights of imagination, I can't conceive of a scenario how they could have gotten away with it. I guess they had better imaginations than me.

The only one I feel even the slightest sorry for is Joe. He wasn't the bad egg the rest of them were, or maybe he was and I just didn't see it. I sincerely doubt it, though.

**EDDIE CICOTTE** I should have known things were going haywire when the day before the Series began I stopped to get a shoeshine. The kid shining my shoes recognizes me immediately.

"How are you going to do it, Mr. Cicotte?" he asked.

"What's that?"

"Throwing the games," he said.

"What are you talking about?"

"I hear there's a fix on."

"Is that what you hear?"

"That's what I hear."

"Well you're listening to the wrong people, kid."

"Everybody's saying it."

"Shut up and shine the damn shoes."

I had been nervous. Now I was downright panicky. The deal had to be called off. There was no question about that. Too many people knew. The deal had to be called off.

**CHICK GANDIL** I was in my room trying to get some rest, which I might add, was not easy, when Sullivan comes barging in without knocking.

"Some of the players are saying the deal's off," he bellows.

"Who? Who have you been talking to?"

"Lefty, Eddie, it don't matter."

Now I'm beginning to think we need to call it off, too. Everybody was nervous and real edgy. Hell, we were scared.

"Well, maybe it is," I said.

"I wouldn't call it the best policy to double-cross Rothstein."

"Get out of here, Sullivan!" I screamed. "Get the hell out of here! I'll take care of the players. You just make sure the money's there."

I was so angry, I sprung up and started shoving him through the door and out into the hall. Except deep down I knew he was right. We couldn't turn back now.

I sat on the edge of the bed for a long time trying to think what to do. Go to Rothstein, give the money back, tell him I couldn't deliver the players. I wanted to think that would work, but I knew better. Like everybody else I had heard the stories about double-crossing gamblers, and about Rothstein's organization.

For a time I thought about going to Gleason and telling him the whole story. But what? What then?

**EDDIE CICOTTE** None of us could sleep, I'll tell you that. Every person I looked at in the street I thought was looking back at me like he knew what was up. I walked around the city till the sun was almost up. I kept looking for something to take my mind off what was happening— anything at all. But it was hard. I could think about something else for maybe about a few seconds, then wham! There came the thoughts about the fix again.

I got phone calls. We all did. Anonymous calls saying things like, "Don't even think about double-crossing us." Some took the other side, "Don't do it, don't do it."

My world was unraveling. Usually a baseball player's life is all neat and tidy. Everything is organized for him. Pitch every fourth day, when I'm told, where I'm told. Train schedules are arranged, hotels are booked for us. The schedules are set. We just follow along. But those days just before the Series were becoming a nightmare of disorganization.

My instincts were to run away, to find someplace where nobody ever knew me. My thoughts flew momentarily to Europe. I could take a boat to England, find a little place in the countryside, maybe even learn cricket.

Ultimately, I don't know which would take more courage, staying and doing the deed or running. What once seemed like an ingenious plan for justifiable revenge, was turning into a convoluted plan of sheer folly.

When we talked about it originally, it seemed like a game—get the big, bad owner game. Now it was turning into something much more serious, something that could even be life-threatening.

**LEFTY WILLIAMS** I was rooming with Joe in Cincinnati like I always did.

"Joe, I don't like it," I said to him.

"I don't understand what's going on, Lefty."

"I don't either, but I think we need to get this straight for once and for all. We've got to get everybody together. We've got to get this sorted out."

**SWEDE RISBERG** The whole plan, the whole idea, was like a giant snowball rolling down a hill. It was on its own, out of control, and it was rolling up everybody in its way. Nobody was controlling it, nobody was in charge, but once it started moving it was impossible to stop until it got to the bottom of the hill. It was that bottom of the hill that I was afraid of.

**CHICK GANDIL** Lefty and Joe came into my room late on the night before the first game saying they wanted to talk. I figured everybody did so I got all of us together.

If I had to describe that meeting in one word I would say "angry." Nerves were tight. Everybody, and that includes me, was upset.

There was a lot of talking, mostly people talking on top of each other, and there was some name calling, too. Lefty said I was a liar, that I hadn't told them the whole story all along. I assured him I told the story as I knew it, but I didn't always know what the money men were up to.

At some point, we talked about calling it off, but I could see how Cicotte felt about that. He already had a chunk of the money, and if I knew him, he probably already spent it.

I kept arguing that it was too late, that we had a commitment from everyone, that we had to go forward. Lefty said he didn't make any promises about anything, so did Buck, so did Joe.

Cicotte got up and screamed that they did. "You damn well said you were in. We all heard it. All of us heard it."

"I talked about it. That's all I did." Insisted Buck. "That's damn site different than saying I'd do it. That's different. It's not the same thing."

"Don't give me that crap," yelled Cicotte. "Don't try to dump it on us now like some yellow, coward!"

"Calm down." I said. "That's not the point here. That's not the point at all."

"Yeah, then what the hell is the point?" demanded Lefty.

"The point is we've got to figure out where to go from here," I said.

"Home." Joe said.

"That won't work, Joe." I said. "Maybe that worked for you in the past, but it won't work now. You can't hide from these guys, I don't care where you go."

After more shouting and arguing we came to a new position. Whether we said it no not, I think we all agreed that there was far too much suspicion floating around for us to throw the games without getting fingered for doing it. That was a bone-chilling, sobering conclusion, but there it was with all of its ugly manifestations. We were going to get caught, and we damn well knew it.

There was more name-calling finger-pointing, and blame-fixing—mostly at me I might add.

I came up with the only solution I could think of. We would have to win the Series, something all of us thought we could do.

"They'll kill us," said Lefty.

"Maybe, maybe not," I responded.

"We could return the 10 grand," said Felsch.

"I don't think that would help," chimed in Cicotte.

We discussed this for a long time, weighing all our options. I argued that Rothstein wouldn't dare do anything since he wasn't in a position to do anything about the cash. Besides, what's $10,000 to Rothstein? It's pocket change, that's all.

By the time the meeting ended, we had agreed that that's exactly what we would do—win the Series.

**LEFTY WILLIAMS** Who's he kidding, Gandil? I don't know what the hell he thought happened at that meeting, but I left more confused than ever. One thing I knew, though—we were up the creek without a paddle.

**JOE JACKSON** Just before the first game, I went to Mr. Comiskey's room to talk to him. I felt awful about everything and wanted to tell him, but I couldn't rat on the guys. That I couldn't do, because a player has got to respect his fellow players. That's the way I was taught and that's the way I acted then and ever since.

Mr. Comiskey lived in the big suite on the top of the hotel. Maybe he even owned the whole hotel, I don't know about that.

"What is it, Joe?" he asked. "You're not nervous about the Series, are you?"

"Nah, I ain't nervous," I said. "But I don't feel too good."

"Why what's the matter?"

"I don't know, I just don't feel too good."

"You'll be fine once the games start."

"I think you should keep me out of the Series."

"Are you crazy? We need you, Joe. You and Eddie, you're the backbone of this club."

"I think it would be better if I didn't play."

"Why? What aren't you telling me, Joe?"

"Nothing. I just don't think it would be good if I play, that's all."

"I need a better reason than that."

"Tell the newspapers you just suspended me for being drunk, or something, but leave me out of the Series and then there won't be no question."

"Question? Question about what?"

"I don't know. About anything."

But he still refused.

There was somebody else in the room who heard the whole thing—Mr. Fullerton, the sports writer.

**HUGH FULLERTON** Comiskey had heard all the stories. He knew what Joe was talking about, but he wasn't about to let him off the hook.

**CHARLES COMISKEY** Not for one second did I believe the rumors. The players weren't that stupid, not even Jackson. Fix the World Series! The very thought was ludicrous. But what about the shift in the odds? I assumed that Cicotte's sore arm was the cause. That was certainly a plausible reason for the shift.

**JOE JACKSON** Yes, I knew about the fix because Gandil asked me to be a part of it. In fact, he asked me several time, but I always said no. Buck Weaver, he didn't take no part in the fix either, but just like me he knowed about it.

As things turned out, I would have been better off to have refused to play.

# 47

## I KNOWED I WAS TRAPPED

**HUGH FULLERTON** The night before the game a threatening, gray, leaden sky hung over the stadium as if it were a presage of things to come. If you tried hard, and not everybody was willing to do that, you could smell the stench.

**VINCENT ALEXANDER** By scrimping and saving everything I could from my restaurant earnings, I was able to again see the Series. I was just hoping it wouldn't go the full nine games because that would stretch my resources to the limit and maybe beyond. I got one good break, though, when they let us sleep on the benches in the ballpark. It seems there were so many people in the city for the games that there weren't enough hotel rooms, so rather than creating havoc, they opened the gates to everyone with tickets. They even supplied police to watch over everybody and make sure nothing got stolen. Hotel? Who needed a hotel? I'd rather sleep in a baseball park any time.

The Reds were a good team, and Cincinnati had a long history of baseball success going back to Red Stocking teams of the last century who once went through an entire season without losing a game. But the Sox, led by Joe and Collins, and with Cicotte, Williams, and Kerr doing most of the pitching, well, I couldn't see anybody stopping them that year.

Who would pitch the first game for the Sox? Stories were going around that Cicotte's arm wasn't entirely sound. After all, he had pitched more than 300 innings already that season. Many businesses in the city were closed so that their employees could go to the games. Since all games were completely sold out long in advance, many fans were going to have to watch the results from large scoreboards put up in front of the newspaper offices, and in several halls and theaters around the city. One of the biggest hotels even installed a scoreboard in its ballroom where it could handle a large crowd at $1.00 per.

The police were out in full force and many of the streets were closed to automobile traffic because the number of machines in town was incredible. Colorful bunting and banners hung everywhere.

Since I had spent the night there, in what was undoubtedly better than any hotel the city had to offer, I was privileged to watch the teams warm up and take batting practice in the morning.

I watched Cicotte warm up with Schalk, and I saw Williams and Little Dickie Kerr limber up with Big Bill James.

The Reds were particularly animated as they worked out under the guidance of the famous pair of Chicago infielders, Joe Tinker and Johnny Evers. Evers was first lieutenant to the Manager, Pat Moran, and he apparently had been scouting the Sox for weeks, delivering to his manager what was supposedly the most complete set of notes on an opposing team that anybody had ever before created. There was no better tactician in the game than Evers.

The day turned out to be a squelcher, particularly for those of us sitting on the hot pine planks out in the bleachers, and more than one fan wistfully eyed the covered stands and the better-heeled fans sitting in the shade, but we wouldn't have given up our seats for anything.

Redland Field looked wonderful, clean and spiffy befitting an event of this caliber. Temporary stands had been built to handle some of the demand for seats, so the whole park could accommodate about 35,000 fans.

During batting practice, a cadre of policemen stationed themselves at five-yard intervals around the outfield, to make sure that the youngsters who were chasing the balls, didn't interfere with the players. Several times young boys got through and managed to get away with balls. This brought a mighty roar from the fans. When one policeman forced a young man to give the ball back, the crowd erupted into a chorus of boos.

Once, Joe let a hard hit ball go directly through his legs with only a perfunctory effort to stop it. The ball went right into the hands of a young fan whose smile was equaled only by Joe's.

A story going around the stands was that a prominent businessman had bet $5,000 at even money on the Reds to win the Series. He apparently claimed that he was prompted more by local pride than by cool judgment, but he was so enthusiastic about Moran's team that he was willing to lose that amount.

Tickets for the opening game were as hard to get as gold nuggets. A man sitting near me said he paid $140 for the pair. Government agents came around when they got wind of that, trying to get a line on the men who were profiting by scalping, but this man wouldn't give out the name. They let him keep his seats though.

I was one lucky son of a gun. Or in hindsight, maybe I wasn't.

**WALTER QUINCE** I was a bellhop at the Sinton Hotel and I tell you, we was mobbed like I never seen before. The whole place was crazy but I made more tips in them days than I ever thought possible.

The Sinton was the center of all the activity. The Sox was all staying there, the leagues officials, they was all there, everybody was there. Senator Warren G. Harding, he had the entire bridal suite to himself, and governors of a whole bunch of other states, they was there, too. If you wanted to see celebrities, the hotel lobby was the place.

All the Sox players, when they come in, they had to sign our register like all the guests, but I seen it myself, all the players signed but Joe Jackson. His signature was done by Lefty Williams. I was watching closely, so I can tell you that as a fact.

We all heard that there was something up, that there was something fishy going to go on in the games. So when I got the chance to carry Joe's bags up to his room I asked him point-blank.

"I'm not involved, kid, don't ask me," he said.

That's all he said, so since he didn't say there was nothing going on, I took my tips and put them on the Reds, the best bet I ever made.

**CHRISTY MATHEWSON** Since I had pitched in 11 games in four World Series, someone figured I should write some articles about the Series. I never heard about any kind of fix, and I think if I had I wouldn't have believed it anyway. The people I knew in baseball were good, clean men who played hard and believed in the code of fair play. I believed that then, and I still believe it. If there were a few who violated that code, they were a minuscule exception. Baseball was and is a clean game.

On the eve of the Series I had it figured to go at least eight games.

**DUTCH RUETHER** I was scheduled to pitch the first game. I was in my first full season in the majors having missed out on most of 1918 because of military service. I was coming off the best season I was ever to have. I won 19, lost just six and posted a 1.82 ERA. I wasn't exactly a household name like Eddie Cicotte, but I wasn't chopped liver either. Still I was awful nervous warming up before the game. It didn't get any easier either when, in batting practice, Joe poked three balls halfway up the bleacher seats. Nobody had ever seen that happen before, so you can bet it got my attention.

Evers said there was no single right way to pitch to Joe, that he hit mistakes a mile. My only hope was to try to mix them up and not throw anything fat.

**JOE JACKSON** Everybody was horsing around before the game to try to make it look like they wasn't nervous, but we all was. I felt like I was back on that train to Philadelphia with my stomach all in knots.

I walked over to the manager beside the dugout.

"I don't feel good, Skip." I said. "I don't think I should play today."

"The only way you're not playing today is if you're in a coma," he said, "and even then I might play you."

"I don't want to play, and you can tell that to the boss, too."

"You're playing, Joe, you're playing," Gleason said walking away.

I didn't know what to do. I was trapped.

I looked up in the stands for Katie. She looked as nervous as I did.

**SWEDE RISBERG** "Count me out," I said to Gandil as we walked toward the dugout.

"Look at Comiskey, that son of a bitch is smiling," Gandil said and turned away.

I didn't trust Gandil. I didn't trust him at all.

**VINCENT ALEXANDER** About a half an hour before the game began, six army officers, each missing a leg lost in the recent action in Europe, were helped onto the field to be introduced to the players. They shook hands with many of them, but I noticed that Joe wasn't there. I think he was afraid a veteran might say something. He was probably right.

An elderly man in a Navy lieutenant's uniform came out of a box near the Sox dugout and was escorted across to where the band sat. When he got close they burst forth into "The Star Spangled Banner" while he stood at strict salute. When it was over, he picked up the baton and led the band in a stirring, emotional version of "The Stars and Stripes Forever." The crowd, already at a high pitch of excitement, went crazy.

"That's Souza!" somebody behind me cried out.

The crowd stood and applauded for a long, long time. Patriotic feelings were still running high and the emotions of the moment were intense.

I took out my scorecard, dutifully wrote in the starting lineups, and sat ready to record every play in what I was anticipating would be a great Series.

Finally, the moment arrived. Ruether took a half a dozen warm up balls and signaled that he was ready. Shano Collins stood in as the opening batter. After taking two balls and a called strike, Collins lined the next pitch into center for a clean single.

"Not already!" moaned somebody sitting near me.

After Eddie Collins forced Shano at second on an attempted sacrifice bunt, Buck Weaver came to bat. Collins was nabbed at second trying to steal, then Weaver hit a shot into left center upon which Roush, the Reds great center fielder, made a remarkable one-handed running catch.

So far, so good for the Reds fans. They had escaped the first inning without damage.

Much to the relief of Sox fans, Cicotte took the mound in the bottom of the first. The consensus of the fans around me was that he looked like his old self warming up.

On his second pitch he hit Rath in the back. Daubert followed with a single to right center, sending Rath to third. The fans went wild as Heinie Groh stepped to the plate. Make that "Henry" Groh as he had changed his name to avoid connections with his German heritage. After almost being decapitated by a Cicotte fast ball, he drove the next ball deep to left field where Joe hauled it in and fired to second, seemingly in one motion, holding Daubert on first while Groh scored.

**JOE JACKSON** When that first ball come my way I knowed I had to make a good play on it because I didn't want anybody to think I wasn't trying.

**VINCENT ALEXANDER** With Roush at the plate, Daubert tried to steal second, but Schalk's throw to Risberg beat him by a step. Cicotte proceeded to walk Roush, but he got out of the inning by coaxing Duncan to ground out to Risberg who made a perfect throw to Gandil at first.

The inning was well played. Oh, Cicotte was a little on the wild side, but it was only the first inning, and anyone would have been a bit nervous.

Joe led off the second by hitting a hard grounder to Kopf who fumbled the ball then threw wide to first. Joe turned on his speed, legging it to second. Felsch laid down a perfect sacrifice bunt sending Joe to third. Gandil brought him home with a Texas leaguer to left on which Roush just barely failed to make another spectacular catch. Gandil attempted to steal second, but he too was thrown out on a strong throw. Risberg walked, but died on first when Schalk flied out.

The bottom of the second was uneventful as Cicotte set the Reds down in order.

When Cicotte came to bat in the third, he received a scattering of applause from the Sox faithful. He struck out, which was business as usual for the light-hitting pitcher. Ruether got out of the inning without giving up anything.

In the bottom of the inning, Cicotte walked Ruether, then made a nice play to throw out Rath on his sacrifice bunt. Joe fought the sun then made a solid catch of a high fly off the bat of Daubert. Cicotte got out of the inning without any damage.

In the top of the fourth, Weaver tried to bunt his way on but was just nipped at first. Still it was a good surprise tactic and the Sox fans let him know it. Jackson and Felsch each harmlessly grounded out.

To this point there were no reasons to question any aspect of the tied up well-played game. Most of us were just waiting for the Sox to explode.

In the bottom of the fourth Cicotte seemed apprehensive as he took the mound. He scanned the field minutely, giving the outfielders particular attention. This is exactly the note I made at the time, not a comment generated after the fact. He opened the frame by getting Roush to hit a deep fly to straight away center which after a long run Felsch caught. After almost getting hit by Cicotte's first pitch, Duncan lined a shot over Eddie Collins' head for a single. The next batter, Kopf hit a bounder to the box which Cicotte gathered in and fired a perfect strike to Risberg covering second who quickly relayed it to Gandil at first in an effort to get the double play. The umpire, Billy Evans called Kopf safe on a very close play. The Sox fans booed the decision and Gandil put up a perfunctory argument, but, of course, the decision stood. Neale followed with a shot up the middle. Risberg, playing him perfectly, raced over like a deer to scoop up the ball but he couldn't get it out of his glove in time to get the runner. It was a good play, though and went as an infield hit. Risberg got applause for his effort. Wingo crashed the next pitch into right for a single, scoring Kopf and breaking the tie.

Now Cicotte seemed to work the hitters very carefully, and very slowly. Ruether, the pitcher was up next, and it appeared that Cicotte wasn't going to take him for granted. The fact is, Ruether was always a good hitter for a pitcher and even hit over .300 a couple of times. He was a good-sized guy who played a number of games at first base because of his hitting. It didn't look to me at the time as if Cicotte gave in to him at all, but rather Ruether jumped on a good pitch and sent it to deepest left center which, by the time Felsch tracked it down, was good for a base-clearing triple. The crowd went into a frenzy of joy, while the Sox infielders went into a conference on the mound.

Maybe his arm is tired went the murmur.

**ABE ATTELL** I was sitting down the third base line wondering when something was going to happen. A triple by the opposing pitcher looked like maybe it was. I looked into the bullpen where Gleason had Roy Wilkinson starting to warm up. Gleason wasn't in on it so I didn't want to see him too early, unless, of course, it was the plan to win the first one. I wasn't sure about that but I was sure I didn't trust these players any farther than I could spit into a hurricane.

**EDDIE CICOTTE** I kept looking around at the other guys. It was becoming clear: nobody wanted to look bad, nobody wanted to make the first mistake. Maybe there were double crossers everywhere. Wouldn't it be nice to get a share of the split without ever having to do anything? Then they could say, "What me? I'll stand on my record. I played good ball in the Series. You can look it up." Or maybe everybody was just waiting for somebody else to start.

**CHICK GANDIL** I think everybody was pretty much figuring that since Eddie already had his $10,000, it was up to him to see that he earned it.

**VINCENT ALEXANDER** After two low ones, Cicotte got the next ball up and Rath drilled it just past Weaver's outstretched hands into the corner for a double. The noise was so loud in the stands I could hardly concentrate on the scorecard. When Daubert followed with a single to right, Gleason went berserk. He came flying off the bench calling for Cicotte to come into the dugout. Now they were both irate, Gleason at Cicotte's performance, Cicotte at Gleason's apparent attempt to embarrass him in front of the enormous crowd.

Half the people in the park could hear it.

"Cicotte, you're out of there!" he screamed.

**HUGH FULLERTON** Cicotte had gone two and two-thirds innings, thrown 23 balls and only 9 strikes, given up 6 runs on 7 hits, hit one batter and issued two walks. It was hardly an inspired performance. Still, there were the stories of the tired arm. Ruether certainly didn't look tired, but then he was a lot younger and had thrown considerably fewer innings during the season.

If there was any questionable play so far it might have been the botched double play attempt, but then maybe it was just a little slow in developing.

The jury was still out.

**KID GLEASON** I didn't like it one bit. Either Cicotte was dogging it like the rumors said he would, or his arm was tired which he should have told me about. Either way, I was livid.

I looked down at Joe sitting alone on the end of the bench remembering our earlier conversation.

"Don't you dare," I remember thinking to myself. "Don't even think about it."

**VINCENT ALEXANDER** The kid, Roy Wilkinson, relieved his more prominent teammate and got the next batter to hit a little fly to center. Hap Felsch raced in and made a spectacular catch to end the inning. But the damage had been done—five runs and six hits off Cicotte.

Maybe it was his arm.

Gandil led off the fifth with a solid line drive to center for a single, but that was all the Sox could muster. In the bottom of the inning, Risberg made the play of the game. Kopf, the Red's little shortstop, smacked a hard grounder over second base, but Risberg was off with the crack of the bat, and sprinting at full speed, grabbed the ball with one hand, then still at a full run, fired a perfect strike to Gandil at first to get the speedy runner by an eyelash. Even the Reds fans had to cheer.

In the next inning, Joe swung at Ruether's first pitch and hit a little squibber back to the pitcher who fielded it cleanly and raced toward the bag, sliding in a split second before Joe. Eddie Collins and Weaver got hits but the Sox failed to score. In the bottom of the inning Ruether got his second hit of the game proving that it wasn't only Cicotte who found out that this was one pitcher who could hit.

In the Cincinnati half of the seventh, the Reds scored twice more off Wilkinson, helped in part when Gandil dropped a throw from Weaver.

**HUGH FULLERTON** I was watching the game like a hawk. Any sign of suspicious play, was grist for the speculation mill. Gandil's error. He should have caught it. He had to stretch a bit for it, but he had made that catch a million times. Still, if he was going to err on purpose, why there? They were well behind in the game and Ruether was pitching well. There seemed to be neither reason nor purpose for it there.

Maybe he was trying to show Cicotte that he was going to do his share. The only problem with that was, it didn't square with his personality at all. Gandil was a taker not a giver.

**VINCENT ALEXANDER** Gleason sent McMullen in to hit for Wilkinson who had fared little better than Cicotte. His line read, 5 hits and two runs in 3 1/3 innings. With two strikes on him, McMullen smashed a solid single to center, but the Sox failed to score.

In the eighth inning, Grover Lowdermilk, who had replaced Wilkinson, surrendered a run-scoring triple to Ruether, who had surprisingly become not only the pitching star, but the hitting star of the game as well.

About the only time the crowd quieted down for a moment was when Jake Daubert was hit in the head by a Loudermilk curve and dropped in his tracks at the plate. Players rushed from the dugout and picked him up, but he was OK in a few minutes and continued in the game.

Joe led off the Chicago ninth. I desperately wanted to see him get a hit. He had played flawlessly in the field, but as yet, had done nothing at the plate. The first pitch was a called strike. On the second, he unleashed Black Betsy and hit a towering fly to deep right field. Greasy Neale shaded his eyes, reached up and made the catch.

Final score: Cincy 9, Chicago 1.

**CHRISTY MATHEWSON** Not even the most ardent Cincy fans expected this—a rout. But credit had to go to Ruether. He showed a good fast ball, a pretty fair slow curve, and a Cobb-like bat.

In the third inning of the game, Hugh Fullerton, who was sitting next to me, asked, "Do you think Cicotte was right?"

I replied, "No, because if he had his usual stuff the Reds would be making more foul tips."

I realized, though, that Gleason must have thought he was right because of his strategy in the first inning. After Shano Collins singled, he had Eddie Collins, one of world's best hitters in a pinch, lay down a sacrifice bunt. The only reason he would have done that was if he thought it was going to be a low-scoring game, if he thought Cicotte was going to keep it close.

After the game I saw Tris Speaker. "Don't forget," he reminded me, "Cicotte's last three games of the regular season were bad. This was his fourth in a row."

Suddenly Cicotte became the biggest question mark of the Series.

**HUGH FULLERTON** Of those rumored to be on the take, only Cicotte looked lousy. Gandil got a couple of hits, McMullen and Weaver one each. Joe didn't do anything but then neither did Schalk, and Eddie Collins went only 1 for 4.

All that aside though, they lost the game. That after all, was the point, wasn't it?

**JOE JACKSON** I was mad after the game. All I know is I played as good as I could and didn't do nothing wrong. I don't know about Eddie. He's the only one who can tell you whether he was trying his best, but I think he was. I think we just got beat, that's all.

In the locker room after the game, it was pretty quiet, except that Gleason kept staring at me like he was angry or something.

"What did I do wrong?" I asked him.

"You tell me, Joe." he said.

"I didn't do nothing, that's what."

"Yeah, you sure didn't do nothing, Joe."

"Tomorrow."

"Tomorrow what?" he asked.

"You'll see."

**SHORTY SCHRALDI** After the game the odds jump to 7 to 10 making the Reds the favorites. That's okie-dokie with me because I got my money down early and big.

Good ol' Eddie Cicotte. That bum's going to make money for both of us yet.

You got to remember, now, that betting was all over the place. Any poor slob could place a bet, and most of us did. John Doyle's Billiard Academy for example took in all sorts of coin on the game, and the papers even had reporters there to report stories on the largest bets and things like that.

One guy bet that Chick Gandil would outhit Jake Daubert and that Eddie Roush would do that to Joe Jackson. Those bets were at even money. One pretty smart guy bet that Eddie Cicotte would not finish the first game.

Gambling wasn't looked on as illegal. But fixing games, that sure as hell was.

**CHRISTY MATHEWSON** If the White Sox went on to lose this Series, I knew it wouldn't have been the first time the favorite didn't prevail. Look at the Athletics in 1914. They were an 8 to 5 favorite over the Braves. The Giants, too, we were favored over the Athletics and the Boston Red Sox.

Nevertheless, it was far too early to call this one.

**KID GLEASON** Cicotte! I wanted to face Eddie eye to eye and have him tell me without blinking that he gave his damn best out there. That son of a bitch had better not lie to me, or I'll kick his ragged butt from one end of the locker room to the other.

I went looking for him as soon as I could race my 53-year-old body into the room. I might have been half his size, but I'll tell you I was twice the man. As soon as I got there the clubhouse boy told me that Cicotte had already dressed and left the stadium.

Well, I went nuts. I didn't want to lose on any count, but I certainly didn't want to lose because some coward tanked it. If that's what he did, I wanted a piece of him and let the devil take the consequences.

Ray Schalk too, I guess he had heard the stories, and he was frantic.

"He shook off too many signs, skip," he said, "and I want to know why."

I didn't know for sure if anything was up, but I wanted answers. Anybody involved in any kind of a fix was going to sit down for the rest of the Series, even if I had to grab a uniform and play myself.

**CHICK GANDIL** I knew Gleason was on to something, but he didn't say much. He steamed a lot, but he didn't say much.

We tried to win that game, we just didn't that's all. That happens in baseball, you know.

**ABE ATTELL** The only damn problem I had after that first game was counting all the damn money. I was raking it in, and no matter what happened from then on, I was set.

I love baseball. It's a great game.

**JOE JACKSON** I talked to Larry after the game. Lajoie had never played in a World Series. I just hoped he didn't hear nothing, because I didn't want him to think I was involved with it.

"It's a long Series. You'll get them tomorrow, Joe," he said.

"Yeah we will. We'll get them tomorrow, Larry," I said even though I knew Lefty was pitching and that might not be so easy.

"Because I got some money on you boys, Joe," he said. "Now don't let me down."

"Well, you know how it is, Larry," I said.

"I'm counting on you."

I felt sick to my stomach. Larry was my friend.

"I'm counting on you," he repeated.

**KID GLEASON** That night I got telegrams—a bunch of them, all from people I knew around the country. They all said about the same thing. The game was fixed. I read them all and I saw the game, but I didn't believe it, or maybe I wanted to not believe it.

It was late, but I went flying down to Comiskey's room and shoved the telegrams under his big nose.

"Look at them Commey" I said. "They can't all be wrong, could they? How can they all be wrong?"

What I wanted was for him to tell me that they were all wrong, that he had an explanation for them, that all the stories were a crock.

Instead, he looked at me calmly and said, "I'll look into it."

That's the best he could do? Say he'd look into it?

I thought to myself that he'd better damn well look into it, and he'd better come up with some answers fast.

I stormed out and went back to my room, but certainly not to sleep.

**CHARLES COMISKEY** The stories, the allegations were mounting. The thing is, though, I had no evidence, no hard evidence. Gambling stories were always all over the place, and they were often exaggerated, so it was hard to know what to really believe. All I can tell you is that the hotel that night was alive with rumor and conspiratorial activity.

I've heard people say for years, "Comiskey knew." I didn't know, I suspected, and the distance between knowledge and suspicion can be light years.

Gleason came up late that night with a fistful of telegrams—suspicions. I asked him if he had any real evidence. He admitted he didn't. I couldn't act on suspicion I told him. Bring me evidence and I'd do something.

This wasn't the first time I'd heard stories about Gandil on the take. I could imagine him as the ringleader. He always wanted to be in charge, but he was a whiner, and an argumentative one at that. Risberg, and Felsch too, somebody told me a year or two earlier were on some gambler's payroll, but that also could have been some gambler's wishful thinking. Risberg was a real hothead who got into more fights than any player we had. Felsch usually had a dumb-looking smile on his face, hence the nickname, but I always thought underneath, he was anything but the happy warrior he portrayed.

These were bitter, ungrateful men, who made a good living playing a game, but never appreciated what they had. It wasn't too far of a stretch to imagine them involved in despicable acts of betrayal. But, the rumor that threw doubt on the whole story for me was, that Joe Jackson threw his lot in with these thugs. I just couldn't, no matter how hard I tried, picture him in this mess. He had neither the guile, nor the cunning to do it, and he had, oh so much to lose if he were caught.

**BAN JOHNSON** Charley Comiskey and I didn't always see eye to eye. The fact is by the time the 1919 Series rolled around, we hadn't spoken to each other in I don't know how long—a couple of years maybe. Frankly I didn't care if we ever spoke again.

So imagine my surprise when I answered a knock on my hotel suite door at 3 a.m. and there he was, in all his glory and pomposity. Only he had John Heydler, the president of the National League, with him as his mouthpiece. As I was neither accustomed to, nor fond of, nocturnal visits, I told them to get to the point immediately. Heydler recounted his conversations with Charley concerning allegations of impropriety in the first game.

I wouldn't know what to do with myself during the Series if it weren't for the rumors of game-fixing. They were about as ubiquitous as mosquitoes on a hot Cincinnati summer's night—and about as bothersome.

"Is that what Charley told you, John?" I inquired.

"Yes, and I believe him," he said.

"My, my, now if that isn't the whelp of a beaten cur, I don't know what is," I said rather pleased with myself.

Seeing Charley in trouble did not exactly break my heart, but I wasn't buying a damn word of it—not at that point.

I ushered them politely but forcefully out the door, went back to bed, and slept exceedingly well.

**HUGH FULLERTON** Had it not been for the childish and interminable petty squabbles between these two powerful men, this whole sordid issue might have been dealt with expeditiously and effectively right from the start. But no, they were more interested in making the other one wrong than in determining what was right, a pattern not wholly unknown among men of influence.

**CHICK GANDIL** Comiskey didn't say squat to me, or as far as I know, to any of the others, but I heard he was running around like a wild man trying to collect information. Had he come to me saying he heard rumors, I would have come back with the old "Who hasn't?" line and walked away. But either he wasn't smart enough, or courageous enough to confront me.

That night I got threatening phone calls, telling me I better go through with it as agreed. Go through with what? I didn't have the money we agreed on, and as far as I was concerned, we were out of business.

**EDDIE CICOTTE** That "I tried to win" baloney spooned out by Gandil to anybody hungry enough to swallow it makes me sick. I don't know what he was doing, but I had my money and I wasn't about to lose my fingers over a few grand.

**BILL BURNS** We met with Gandil the night after the first game, me and Maharg, and Attell. Gandil was sweating the money thing, so I flashed a telegram from A.R. guaranteeing the money in full. He bought it, only it wasn't really from A.R. I sent it to myself.

**RAY SCHALK** Williams was tabbed by Gleason to start the second game even though he was one of the guys who wasn't looking anybody straight in the eye.

"Lefty," I said to him, "I'm watching you today closer than a hawk tracking a rabbit. You flinch, and I'm going to notice. You fart and I'll smell it. After the game, I'm going to tell you how many times you blinked—each eye separately, and both together!"

"I don't know what you're talking about," he said.

"Oh, yes, you do," I said to him about 3 inches from his face.

"I'll do my best, Ray," he said. "You know me."

I stayed looking right at him. "No, I don't think I do."

**VINCENT ALEXANDER** The city went wild after the first game. You would have thought they had the Series already in hand. They had to win four more, but from the noise, and parades and fireworks during the night, I'm not so sure all of them knew that. I even saw a mock funeral parade pass by, a stuffed effigy of Eddie Cicotte, securely placed atop a cardboard bier.

For the first time, I noticed the grimy factories which seemed to ring the outside of the stadium in sharp contrast to the irrepressible beauty and classic symmetry of the white-striped green field. I realized how fortunate I was indeed to be a participant in what was shaping up to be perhaps the greatest series ever played. At least, that was my feeling at the time. I am an unabashed, unrepentant optimist and feel truly sorry for those who aren't. Life is much better on the sunny side, and yes, I did use the word "participant" rather than spectator, because I have long understood, that we, the fans, play an important part in what goes on between the lines. It is not only our money which pays the salaries, but our fervor which drives the players.

I watched Joe warm up. He looked less tense than the day before. Perhaps the first game jitters were gone.

Williams was scheduled to go up against Slim Sallee, probably Cincinnati's best pitcher, and a brilliant control artist. Sallee's stock-in-trade was the shine ball.

The game was played on yet another warm, muggy afternoon. Sallee got out of the first inning giving up nothing more than a walk to Eddie Collins.

"Well, that's his quota for the game," said Reed, the man sitting next to me, and now a companion-in-arms.

Nice fielding plays by Felsch, Risberg, and Eddie Collins took care of the Reds in the bottom of the inning. Williams looked his usual self.

Joe led off the second by looping liner into short center. Roush, charging fast, tried to make a shoestring catch but came up just short and the ball got past him for a double. Joe stood on second, and if I was reading his expression correctly, looked greatly relieved. Felsch, who was up next, surprised me by sacrificing Joe to third. Gleason again was playing like he thought this was going to be a low-scoring game. Neither Gandil nor Risberg, however, could get him in, so the threat ended there.

When Roush came to bat in Cincy's half of the inning, the crowd let him know how much they appreciated his play in the first game. After the first two pitches were well wide, Schalk trotted out to admonish his pitcher with what looked like extremely animated conversation. The umpire had to finally break up the confab and get the game started again.

**RAY SCHALK** "Remember, I'm watching you, Lefty," I said when I went out to the mound in the second inning, "and I don't like what I'm seeing."

"I'm OK, I'm OK," he kept repeating.

What I didn't like was that he was continually shaking off signs. I was in my eighth season with Chicago, and believe me, I knew how to call a game. If he was thinking about doing anything funny, I wanted to be on top of it right from the start.

"Pay attention to me, damn it. I know what I'm doing," I told him.

"So do I Ray," he said.

"I sure as hell hope you do."

"Just catch the damn ball, that's what you're being paid for," he said in a whispered shout.

"Yeah, I know what I'm being paid for," I told him. "What I'm not so sure about, though, is what you're being paid for."

The umpire interrupted our little chat. So what does Lefty do but proceed to walk Roush.

If looks could kill, he wouldn't have lived to see the next batter. I began throwing the ball back to him harder than he was throwing it to the plate, partly to make a point, partly out of anger. We got out of the inning on a nice play by Eddie Collins.

**VINCENT ALEXANDER** Schalk led off the next inning looking like he was still angry. He swung at a Sallee offering with such ferocity that he drove it high onto the roof of the left field pavilion, but it was just foul. He was only about 5' 9," and hadn't hit a home run all season, so this quickly got our attention.

"Boy, who's he mad at?" asked Reed of no one in particular.

He swung hard again and hit a liner into right center, but Roush came up and made the play.

Williams followed with a single to left, but that was all they could manage for the inning.

**LEFTY WILLIAMS** Going back to the mound I turned toward Schalk and said, "How many hits you got in the Series, Ray?"

He didn't answer.

**VINCENT ALEXANDER** Joe and Buck caught routine flies in the bottom of the inning and Neale struck out. Williams looked in control. Gleason was probably right. This had all the markings of a tight, low-scoring affair.

The fourth inning opened with ringing singles by Weaver and Jackson. Joe was 2 for 2.

Weaver again sacrificed, sending Weaver to third and Joe to second. Gandil then hit a wicked grounder to Daubert on which Weaver tried to score, but Daubert's throw beat him easily. On the play Jackson alertly took third while Gandil legged it to first. With a 1 and 1 count on Risberg, Gandil stole second standing up. A nice, aggressive play. Both runners were stranded when Risberg lifted a fly to short right.

**HUGH FULLERTON** The game going into the bottom of the fourth was a well-played, tight defensive struggle. Williams looked sharp, and the team was making all the plays behind him. I was waiting for something fishy to happen.

I didn't have to wait long.

**VINCENT ALEXANDER** Williams threw two wide balls to Rath, before Gandil trotted over to the mound apparently cautioning his pitcher to be careful.

**KID GLEASON** I wasn't crazy about Gandil talking to Williams any time, but especially when he was on the mound.

"Just throw strikes, Lefty," I called to him from the dugout.

Lefty was a smart pitcher, always painting the corners, seldom giving the batters much to hit, and never giving in to them. He had good control, too. I doubt if he averaged two walks per game—not Sallee's control, but good control.

**LEFTY WILLIAMS** Gandil comes over and says, "Easy does it, Lefty."

His meaning was clear.

I was pitching well. I didn't mind losing, if that was the inevitable, but I was dammed if I was going to stink the place up.

Nothing fat I kept telling myself, nothing fat. Make good pitches and if they got a hit or two, or a couple of walks … well, they didn't win almost a hundred games during the regular season without having some hitters on the team.

**VINCENT ALEXANDER** Williams walked Rath, but the little second baseman walked a lot so that was no big surprise. Because he could steal a base now and then, Williams watched him carefully. On the second pitch, Daubert dropped a bunt down the first base line, which Williams scooped up and threw to first to get the out as Rath scampered into second.

The next batter, Groh, had two strikes on him before he foul tipped one back to Schalk, but the catcher couldn't hold onto it, so Groh got another life and walked. After two straight balls to Roush, Schalk again headed to the mound hollering at his pitcher all the way.

**RAY SCHALK** "You throw strikes, damn it, or you'll have me to face in the locker room," I shouted at him in a hushed voice. I knew Roush was their best hitter, but I wasn't going to let him back off.

"You and me after the game, Lefty," I challenged him. "Just you and me."

The little coward didn't say a word, not a damn word. I probably looked pretty stupid to the crowd, flailing around like an angry idiot, but at that point I didn't give a damn. I just wanted to get out of the inning without any damage.

As I stormed back behind the plate, I looked over toward the manager.

"Don't go too long with this bum, skip. He's tanking it," I hollered.

**VINCENT ALEXANDER** I never heard a crowd so loud in my life as when Roush, after his conference with Schalk, hit Williams' first pitch into short right center. Felsch made an incredible one-handed pickup of the ball and fired on the run to Schalk at home, but barely too late to catch the sliding Rath.

Granted, I was a long way from the plate, but it sure looked like a fat pitch to me.

Roush attempted to steal second, but a perfect throw from Schalk and a good tag by Risberg nabbed him. With two outs it looked as if the Sox might survive the inning. But Williams lost sight of the strike zone again and walked Duncan. Even from where I was, you could see Schalk still fuming and fussing behind the plate. On the first pitch to him, Kopf drilled one all the way to the left field fence scoring Groh and Duncan. Williams got out of the inning when Neale grounded out to Collins, but the damage was done. The Reds had scored three runs on two hits and three walks.

The crowd was ecstatic, thriving on the euphoria of the moment when, between innings, a plane appeared flying only a few feet above the grandstand roof. As it passed over the field, we saw a figure suddenly fall from the plane and land with a sickening thud near third base. Screams went up all over the stadium. A policeman raced out from behind the dugout to the side of the victim, then without even bothering to resuscitate it, picked up the prostrate figure, and bore it off the field. It was a stuffed dummy, bringing both great sighs of relief as well as laughter from the crowd. The dummy apparently provided a comfortable cushion for the policeman's ample backside as he spent the rest of the sunny afternoon sitting on the dummy in front of the third base stands.

Gleason wasn't laughing, though, and neither was Schalk. But all wasn't lost yet. They still had time. Joe was swinging the bat well, and Eddie Collins hadn't yet begun to hit like everybody knew he would in time. With those two in the lineup, you could never be too far out of a game.

**HUGH FULLERTON** It looked to me that no sailor ashore after a six months' cruise was ever more generous than Williams was. He was simply a better pitcher than that.

If nothing else, the game seemed to be setting a world's record for most pitcher-catcher conferences. Schalk was wearing a trough into field between the plate and the mound, but to little apparent affect.

I kept my eyes on the other alleged conspirators. Joe was playing well, so were the others. The only slight chink in the armor of respectability came in the fifth when Risberg raced in from deep center to attempt a shoestring catch on a little pop fly off the bat of Rath which he just missed, but the ball rolled past him for an error. Honestly, it was a questionable call that had no impact on the outcome of the game.

**VINCENT ALEXANDER** Between innings I remember my eye was caught by an enterprising movie camera operator perched on the top of the left field pavilion. I couldn't help thinking that this great series, or at least part of it, would be caught forever on film, and that no matter the outcome, these players would in some ways be immortalized.

In the sixth, Joe fanned. The mere sight of the great hitter striking out brought almost as much pleasure to those assembled as the falling dummy. Weaver crushed one against the left field wall for a double and advanced on a Sallee balk, which for some reason, Weaver found extremely funny. Or at least something did, because he laughed all the way to third. The inning ended on a brilliant play. Hap Felsch got hold of a fast ball and sent it on a line to deepest center field. Roush, off with the crack of the bat, sprinted after it and with his back to the plate caught it over his shoulder just as he careened off the wall. It took him a couple of seconds to shake the cobwebs, but he got up, holding the ball aloft, and trotted off the field to a standing ovation.

Cincinnati scored another run in the sixth on a hit and a walk, but Chicago came back with two in the seventh thanks to singles by Risberg and Schalk and a crucial throwing error by Neal. In the inning, Williams looked exactly like a pitcher trying to hit when he struck out swinging at two pitches which were well out of the strike zone.

In the eighth, Joe hit a smash into the hole between second and first. Daubert managed to get to the ball on a nice play, but threw past Sallee covering first allowing Joe to get to second on the error. Still it was his third hit of the game. Felsch left him there, though, when he lined out to Groh. In the final frame, Felsch made a sparkling running catch of Roush's fly ball doubling up Groh. All Chicago could counter with was a single by the hot-hitting Gandil as they went otherwise quietly in the ninth.

**JOE JACKSON** The locker room after the game was like it was after the first game, everybody was mad except they was more mad. Ray Schalk was steaming, mostly at Lefty, but there was no way to tell if he walked those guys on purpose or not.

**RAY SCHALK** I damn well knew we were in trouble. I confronted Gleason in the runway leading to the locker room.

"Who was that bean bag out there today, skip?" I demanded. "That wasn't Williams. That wasn't Lefty. Lefty doesn't walk those guys. No way Lefty walks those guys."

"What do you want me to say, Ray? What? He was a little off, but he didn't pitch that bad."

"We lost, ain't that bad enough? How bad do you want it to get before you do something?

"What do you want me to do, Ray? What in the hell do you think I can do about it?"

"Talk to Comiskey."

"I did."

"Talk to him again."

"I don't know anything now I didn't know before."

"Yeah, you do. You know you've lost two World Series games."

"But I don't have any proof."

"He kept changing my signs in the fourth. He wouldn't throw the damn curve. He wouldn't throw it once."

"All that proves is he's stupid. It don't prove he's a crook."

"Does to me."

"I'm going to talk to Williams," Gleason said. "I want to see what he has to say for himself."

**KID GLEASON** As soon as I got to the locker room I set sail for Williams, but there, sitting on his fat ass, puffing a big cigar and looking real pleased with himself, was Gandil.

"Gandil, you sure had a good day today," I said to him between clenched teeth.

He looked up at me with that little stupid looking grin of his on his face. "So did you, Kid."

Well, at that I lost it. I wasn't going to have that big fraud making fun of me in front of my boys. I dove at him, getting my hands on his neck before Joe, Eddie and a couple of others pulled me off. In the heat of the moment I probably would have strangled him.

**CHICK GANDIL** Gleason looked ridiculous. We didn't play that badly, but I suppose he felt he had to make a grandstand show for appearance sake, so he decides to take me on in the locker room. Eddie actually had to pick him up and carry him away like a bag of groceries. I couldn't help laughing. The little guy didn't take kindly to that.

**CHRISTY MATHEWSON** A lot was made of the six walks Williams surrendered, but when you look at the game more closely, you have to admit that there was more to it than just that. Williams gave up just 4 hits, while the Sox managed 10, and from where I was perched, it looked like he made a fair number of good pitches, particularly on the outside corners.

If you didn't know better, and you were just looking for a scapegoat, you might have to look at Neale, whose wild throw let in two runs, or Edd Roush who was caught in a trap and tagged out after a foolish attempt to go to second.

In fact, the Reds hadn't played particularly well. Twice unsuccessful hit and run attempts ended in double plays, and their fielding looked tentative. On the other hand, Chicago fielded superbly. At one point, Roush was nailed attempting to steal by one of the prettiest plays of the series. Schalk made the throw on a hard straight line to the bag. Collins came forward to take the throw in front of the bag so that he could try to catch the runner on third going home, but when the runner saw Collins move up he retreated to the bag, whereupon Collins immediately dropped to the ground allowing the ball to go through to Risberg who applied a perfect tag to nail Roush.

So after two games, the leading hitters for Chicago were Jackson, Weaver and Gandil. Chicago had committed two errors, neither of which resulted in runs being scored, Cincinnati, made three which were much more instrumental in permitting runs.

Two days earlier all the Cincy fans could dream of was taking a game or two from the mighty Sox, now they were dreaming of a World Championship.

**ABE ATTELL** I tell you, that Williams was some kind of genius. He figured out a way not only to lose the game, but to look great doing it. That takes skill, and brains and motivation. Lefty supplied the brain power and the pitching skills, I supplied the motivation.

It looked to me like that they planned to pass the blame around so no one would take too much heat. First it was Cicotte, then Williams, and then maybe Jackson and Gandil. Pretty smart for a bunch of greedy ballplayers. Pretty smart.

**HEINIE GROH** To this day I don't think we got the recognition we deserved for our play during the Series. Don't forget we ran away with the National League pennant. Eddie Roush led the league in hitting, and our pitching staff led the league in ERA and gave up by far the fewest runs in the league. We had the best fielding percentage in the league and committed something like 70 fewer errors than anybody else.

So give us some credit. We were no cream puff, and we were up against the likes of Eddie Collins and Joe Jackson, and I don't care what you say, Joe played like a demon.

**RAY SCHALK** I still had unfinished business with Williams, so as we were leaving the stadium I went looking for him. The best I could find was the south end of a man heading north. I chased him up a ramp, caught his yellow tail, and got in a couple of good licks before we were pulled apart. One of the guys doing the pulling was Joe.

"What's the matter, Joe, afraid I'm going to hurt your meal ticket?" I screamed at him.

"No, my roommate," he answered.

I don't think I did much damage to the gutless wonder, but it felt good. It felt real good.

**JOE JACKSON** After the second game we took the 11 o'clock sleeper back to Chicago. During the whole ride I wished I was going back to Greenville to do some hunting with my brothers. Everybody on the train was nervous and nobody was having fun. There was no singing or card playing or storytelling.

Eddie Collins came over to talk to me for a bit. The funny thing is, what he talked to me about was mostly hunting. He ended up by saying, "Just make sure you know who your real friends are, Joe. Who would you want to spend time hunting with if you had a choice? Think about it."

I said I would.

**CHICK GANDIL** Now things were all bollixed up. What we had were a lot of promises. What we didn't have was a lot of money. When we got back, Burns came into my room at the Warner Hotel and asked what our plans were for the next game. I asked him what his plans were to get us the money. I got the usual shuck and jive but not the money. I told him to let us worry about that, but he kept insisting he needed to know how to bet the next game. Right then I realized how small time he was. The big guys, the real gamblers, they wouldn't bet individual games, they would bet the Series as a whole. So I told him we had a meeting and the guys agreed the next game would go just like the first two. He never bothered to ask what the hell that meant. As far as I was concerned, it meant we were going to try to win, but to him, of course, it meant another loss, but frankly, I didn't give a damn.

He asked who was at the meeting. I told him all the players were there. He specifically asked about Joe and Buck, implying he didn't think they seemed to be going along with the plan. I told him not to worry about them. "Money talks," I told him.

Of course, there was no meeting. We weren't about to be seen together. Hell, at that point we were barely talking to each other for fear it would raise more alarms than were already sounding.

How could we lose the next game with Kerr pitching he wanted to know.

"That busher?" I said. "Who do you think wants to win a game for him?"

Of all the guys on the team that I couldn't stand, that little midget stood on the top of the list. He was a phony, a pretentious little goldbrick.

"Maybe it would be better to win," he said. "It would make the odds on the Series better."

I told him we'd take care of the games, the gambling details, those were up to him.

**LEFTY WILLIAMS** That was pretty much the end of serious talk between us. I figured it was every man for himself, that each of us had to do what he wanted to from then on, and I knew what I wanted to do. When Schalk came after me that settled it. I wanted nothing more to do with him or anyone in his merry band of hypocrites. No pompous little catcher was going to tell me how to call a game. I'd done all right without his help before and I could do it again.

What I wasn't at all sure about, though, was Joe's commitment. He kept saying, "I don't want to talk about it."

I began figuring ways to insure his involvement.

**BUCK WEAVER** On the way to Chicago I asked Joe what he was doing.

"I'm playing baseball, what are you doing?" he replied.

"I'm playing baseball, too," I said.

**SHORTY SCHRALDI** I got a real kick out of what happened in the lobby of my Chicago hotel. All sorts of bets were going down in every corner of the lobby, but what do the police do? They arrest a bunch of guys for scalping tickets! Actually, they were a bunch of Internal Revenue agents and their deputies, who came running in and collared the bad guys.

They claimed one of the men they arrested sold $16 tickets for $75. Now get this! The charge they were arrested on was not registering as ticket brokers. Federal war tax regulations say you can make a profit of 50 cents on each ticket, but any profit above this must be split equally with the government.

Here we are with betting going on all over the place on a rigged Series, and these poor slobs get pinched for making a couple of bucks on a ticket sold to people who are willing and anxious to pay that! You figure it.

**VINCENT ALEXANDER** Special trains brought me and a ton of Redland rooters to Chicago for the resumption of the Series. Their bright red banners were very much in evidence.

A friend had gotten tickets for me, so I was set, but by noon, thousands of fans jammed the thoroughfares around 34th Street and Shields Avenue. Certainly they did not think the Sox were out of it yet and they were determined to show their support for Comiskey and his boys. But they knew, too, that this, the third game, would be the most crucial game of the series so far. The Sox could not afford to lose. They knew Dickie Kerr was a good pitcher, but not the equal of Cicotte or Williams. Still, Joe's bat had come alive again, so that was cause for optimism.

I even got to see Jack Dempsey, the great heavyweight champion who sat in the stands and rooted loudly for the Sox. Special boxes were decked out for the array of dignitaries—governors, mayors, senators. I even spotted Judge Kenesaw Mountain Landis. At the time I didn't know who he was, but later, when his picture was in every paper because of this Series, I recognized him as the man I saw in the box with Governor Lowden.

Marines in their bright, starched dress uniforms posted themselves at the head of each isle, barking military-like instruction to those looking for their seats. Salvation Army lassies were in every section pushing their collection boxes into the laps of new arrivals.

The left field bleacher crowd gave the Red outfielders a good-natured razzing during their warm up and booed them loudly when they refused to toss balls into the stands.

There was one fan had a piercing klaxon that could be heard in every corner of the park. He let loose with ear-splitting shrieks every time a Chicago player made a particularly good play. Pity those sitting next to him.

During batting practice, a group of singers and a small band took up a position in the third base box and began entertaining the crowd. That is, until Joe sent one on a line between two of the singers who scattered madly to get out of the way.

When Dickie Kerr made his first appearance on the field, a Reds rooter, shouted, "What's that kid going to do? Carry the water pail?"

They said Kerr was 5' 7" and 155 pounds, but he didn't look even that big. The Reds rooters kept on him while a photographer lined him up for pictures with Ray Fisher, the Reds starting pitcher. Truly, they looked like father and son having a picture post card made to send home to the folks.

You couldn't say, "Richard Henry Kerr did this or that," or even "Dickie Kerr did this or that." It was always "Little Dickie Kerr," as if "Little" was a part of his name.

Anyway, Little Dickie Kerr came out of the chute firing strikes and set down the side one-two-three in the first inning.

Greasy Neale made another superb catch in the bottom of the inning and Fisher got out of the inning unscathed.

Joe opened the bottom of the second with a ringing shot to left, for the Sox first hit of the game. Bedlam broke loose before the ball even touched the ground. Bells, tin horns, and noise makers of every variety joined with the voices of the crowd to make a tumultuous din.

"I just hope Gleason doesn't make Felsch bunt again," said a fan sitting behind me.

But he did, and when Hap pushed the third offering for a bunt, it was fielded cleanly by Fisher, but thinking he had a shot at Joe heading for second, he threw the ball into center. Not expecting this turn of events, Joe stumbled rounding second, but righted himself and made it to third a split second before the ball arrived. On the throw, Felsch took second. On the very next pitch, Gandil drilled a single past Rath to right field, scoring both runners.

The reaction of the fans is hard to describe. Suffice it to say, the place went wild. It was truly an exhilarating moment. Even the bat boy got involved, throwing bats high in the air.

The Sox settled for just those two and Kerr went back to his job of shutting down the Reds. Meanwhile, the Chicago batsmen continued to knock out hits. Eddie Collins and Weaver singled in the third but failed to score. In the fourth, Risberg tripled to right when Neale overran the ball, then scored on a Schalk carom shot off the shins of Fisher.

Joe singled again in the sixth, but was thrown out attempting to steal second.

**KID GLEASON** Maybe, just maybe, I thought, the boys got the message. We were playing well, damn well, and little Dickie Kerr was pitching his heart out. This was the White Sox I knew. This was the team I expected to see on the field.

I should have been thrilled. I should have been having the time of my baseball life. Why then did I still have an uneasy feeling?

I was waiting for what? I didn't know, and I didn't want to know.

**VINCENT ALEXANDER** The Sox seemed to be all fired up when they came out for the eighth. They seemed to be a renewed team.

Fisticuffs almost broke out when Weaver and the Reds third base coach, Jimmy Smith got into a shouting match about something. Eddie Collins charged over from second to come to the aid of his third baseman, but the umpire, Billy Evans stepped between them before blows could be landed.

**EDDIE COLLINS** I was the captain. It was my responsibility to come to the aid of our players, so when Smith and Weaver got to name-calling, I ran over to third. Apparently Smith was saying something to Weaver about the rumor that he was involved in a fix. I neither knew nor cared at that moment whether the stories were true, I was going to back my teammate to the hilt until and unless something was proved. Besides, Jimmy Smith, a utility infielder was the official goat-getter of the Reds. I knew Moran sent him out there to try to stir up something to get his team fired up.

I was determined to set an example of hard and fair playing. The rest would have to take care of itself.

**VINCENT ALEXANDER** In the eighth, Adolfo Luque, the pride of Havana, came on for the Reds. The Cuban right hander wasn't a heck of a lot bigger than Kerr, so now we had a battle of two little guys. After he quickly struck out Leibold, the Sox right fielder got into a war of words with Groh, but again, Evans came between them before it could escalate into anything further.

In the top of the ninth Smith and Schalk exchanged a few words in anger.

We all began to wonder what got into the Sox that they were all of a sudden playing with intensity.

Kerr was in control the entire game and was never in what you would call real trouble. He got the final out of the game by inducing Groh to lash a grounder to Weaver, who broke into a grin so big you could see it from the top row.

Kerr had thrown a 3-0 shutout putting Chicago back in the race whether they wanted to or not. The Chicago fans now believed their team could come back.

As the crowd headed out, there were predictions a plenty that Cicotte would pitch the next day and get revenge.

**CHRISTY MATHEWSON** There was considerable speculation about the next day's pitcher. There was some talk that Gleason wouldn't risk sending his wild man, Williams back to the hill. Stories resurfaced that Cicotte's arm was in no shape to tackle another game so soon.

There was no dismissing the job Kerr did. He gave up only three harmless hits, struck out four and walked only one. He was ably assisted by Risberg, who made several excellent plays on slow rollers, handled all 10 of his chances flawlessly, and threw beautifully. Joe led the way with two hits and a run scored.

**HUGH FULLERTON** The big question, of course was, what the dickens was going on? There were three reasonable explanations. The Sox were playing the best they could, which meant winning only one of three, or they threw the first two then won the third to make it look good, or they won it to influence the odds.

Were I a betting man, I would have put a deuce on the latter. Hell, maybe a couple of deuces.

**KID GLEASON** We won the damn game, that's all I cared about. Call me Pollyanna, but I actually had thoughts that maybe the players saw the bright light of reason, that maybe we could win the whole thing after all.

I looked at Joe. I thought I saw a hint of a smile.

**RAY SCHALK** They should have given Dickie Kerr the Medal of Honor for what he did out there. He played his heart out. He fought on every pitch, used his head in every situation, and he did it with that bunch of gutless bums behind him.

One thing I made sure of was that everybody saw me congratulate him in the locker room. I was big. I was loud. I was positive. Not that anybody in that room didn't know where I stood, but I thought I would make the point again, and again and again if necessary.

There were thousands, maybe millions of people who were following the Series content in their hearts that what they saw on the field was on the up-and-up. Anything less was criminal.

**KATIE JACKSON** I was happy to have Joe back in Chicago, but I could tell something was wrong. Joe could get nervous before big games, but he appeared more so than usual. He was extremely quiet. When I asked him what was bothering him, he insisted there was nothing wrong. When you know somebody as long as I had known Joe, you can sense when things aren't right. I put it down to the pressure he was under and to the undeniable conflict within the team.

**BILL BURNS** Why I ever believed Gandil about anything is one hell of a question. I lost on that game, and I lost big. Gandil couldn't be trusted. Maybe none of them could. All they did was stand around and watch the little midget make them look like idiots. I was steaming.

I confronted Gandil and Cicotte and told them that the deal was off.

"Sorry, it's all out on bets," Cicotte snarled.

You could have cut the tension in that room with a knife. The players weren't playing straight with us and I wanted out. I told Maharg the deal was off.

**SPORT SULLIVAN** After the third game, Gandil told me the deal was off after the third game, that he couldn't hold the players together anymore.

That was out of the question. I had told Rothstein everything was going according to plan, and I was no more about to double-cross him than I was to jump in front of a moving streetcar.

I asked Gandil if he could get the players back if I came up with more upfront money.

"That would be a start," he said.

It didn't look to me like all of the players were cooperating anyway. Joe, for instance, was playing particularly well, and Weaver, too. Maybe money in their pockets would change their attitudes.

**VINCENT ALEXANDER** Comiskey Park, despite being located in an area known as the Stockyards District, was actually a very pleasant stadium, surrounded as it was by tall trees and attractive residences. As was my wont, I got to the stadium early enough to watch the boys warm up. I was able to stay with a friend in Chicago which was certainly more restful than the planks of Cincinnati, but somehow lacked some of the excitement and comradery I was used to.

During batting practice Sherry Magee and Walter Ruether, two Reds who weren't likely to see much action in the coming game, entertained the crowd with lively dancing accompanied by a band and singers pouring out their lyrics through large megaphones.

Then I saw Ruether taking batting practice. Maybe Moran is planning on using him as a pinch hitter I thought. Why not? He was the leading batter in the Series.

**KID GLEASON** I didn't know where we stood exactly, but if any player was dirty, I didn't want him on the field.

I went up to Cicotte. "How's the arm?"

"My arm is fine, Kid, it's always fine. I didn't get the best record in the league this year with a bum flipper."

"How about your head?"

"Head's fine."

"And your heart?"

"Raring to go."

I would have started Big Bill James if Cicotte had given me any reason to doubt him, any reason at all, but he seemed ready and downright anxious to get back in there. The question was why?

"A lot of people are counting on you, Eddie," I reminded him.

"Oh, don't I know it."

**VINCENT ALEXANDER** The fans brought tin pans and a wide variety of noise-making contraptions to help the comeback attempt.

Rath opened with a single on a little blooper but Cicotte got out of the inning easily.

It was still scoreless in the second when Joe came to bat. He was still the crowd's favorite as you could hear by the cheers he got as he carried Black Betsy to the plate. With one strike on him, Joe lashed a drive to right center for a solid hit, but when Roush let the ball get by him, Joe made it into second for a double.

As was now becoming his pattern, Gleason had Felsch lay down a sacrifice bunt. Once again he did it perfectly and Joe took third. After Gandil, who had come through so well in game three, popped up, Risberg worked Jimmy Ring, the Reds pitcher for a walk, and then took second on a passed ball. With first base open and the pitcher up next, Ring wanted no part of Schalk, and intentionally threw his fourth wide pitch to load the bases. Ring, who was pitching in his first Series game looked bewildered. The Sox rooters went wild as Cicotte stepped to the plate.

**KID GLEASON** I thought about using a pinch hitter for Cicotte—maybe Shano Collins. Cicotte wasn't much of a hitter, and if, heaven help me, he was planning on having another one of his wild streaks like in the first game, it might be a good idea to get him out of there before the temptation got to him. But it was really too early to pull a pitcher.

I wrestled with the thought for a couple of long moments then turned my back as Cicotte walked to the plate. I didn't know if I had just made the stupidest decision of my brief managerial career, or the wisest, but it was the correct baseball move.

I was letting the rumors effect the way I was thinking about moves on the field. That wasn't baseball.

**VINCENT ALEXANDER** With the count at 3 balls and 2 strikes, Jackson, Risberg, and Schalk all took off with the next pitch. Cicotte slashed a grounder to Rath, and the second baseman easily threw him out at first ending the threat.

The Reds seemed a little shaky in the third. Ring hit Collins on the hip with his first pitch, then Rath fumbled a sharp grounder by Joe for an error. Felsch stranded the runners however when he took a vicious swing at the first pitch he saw, hitting it right at Heinie Groh.

Cicotte was pitching well, demonstrating how he posted the highest winning percentage in baseball that season. The Reds were getting nothing off him, not even long outs, but the Sox batters weren't coming through in the clutch despite some sloppy Cincinnati fielding.

With one out in the fifth, Duncan slapped a high bounder off Cicotte's glove. The ball rolled toward the third base line where Cicotte retrieved it and, in his haste to try to nip the speedy Duncan, bounced the ball past Gandil. Schalk, alertly backing up the play, raced after the ball holding Duncan on second. On the next pitch, Kopf lined a single to left sending Duncan to third. When Jackson saw him round the bag, he unleashed one of his rifle shots to home in a way that only Joe could do. The throw was perfect. It was straight and right on line to Schalk, but Cicotte, apparently thinking he could intercept the ball and catch Duncan off the base, reached up with his glove and deflected it back to the stands behind the plate. Duncan sped in from third with the first run, while Kopf took second.

Cicotte looked shaken by the sudden turn of events. He certainly should have let the ball go through, but under the circumstances I could see why he might have thought that trying to get Duncan at third was the right thing to do.

**KID GLEASON** How could I have been that stupid? Cicotte had only made three fielding errors all season and here, in one inning alone, he had made two. Still, I had to admit he was pitching well, and we should be expected to score more than one run.

**RAY SCHALK** That was it, I thought to myself. This cretin is going to pitch as brilliantly as he always did, but he's going to throw it with his glove.

I stormed to the mound.

"Why didn't you let that go through?" I asked.

"I thought I could get Duncan at third. That's pretty obvious, isn't it?"

"That's not what's obvious, Eddie. What's obvious is the stink around here."

**VINCENT ALEXANDER** The next batter, Neale, lifted a fly ball directly over Joe's head in left. Joe got a good jump on the ball and raced back after it, but it fell inches beyond his outstretched glove, scoring Kopf with the second run.

**JOE JACKSON** Some people said I was playing too shallow against Neale, but remember, he was a left-handed batter who usually pulled the ball to right. I was playing him right, only he got lucky on an outside pitch and just blooped it over my head.

**VINCENT ALEXANDER** The Reds continued their sloppy play in the bottom of the fifth when Groh threw low to first on a little roller from Leibold but got out of the inning without any damage. Ring was up to the task however, and with the exception of harmless singles by Gandil and Felsch, he shut down the Sox the rest of the way.

You would have to say Cicotte pitched well. He gave up only five hits, struck out two and walked none. But Ring pitched even better, surrendering only three hits, one each to Jackson, Felsch and Gandil, and three harmless bases on balls.

**HEINIE GROH** We weren't surprised by Jimmy's performance, and don't give me that garbage about how it came out of no place. He was a big, strong kid from New York who pitched in bad luck all season. I say "bad luck" because at one point during the season, we didn't score a single run in any of his four starts. Two of his shutout defeats were by 1 to 0 scores.

The front office promised him $1,000 bonus if he won 15 games, but we didn't have an owner like the penny-pinching Comiskey, and Jimmy got his bonus even though he came up a couple of games short.

He was a fighter, that's why he won that game. He never gave in to what the papers were calling the "Murderer's Row." In only one inning, the sixth, did they hit the ball hard. Felsch busted a long one, but the wind held it up and Duncan made the catch.

**CHRISTY MATHEWSON** I couldn't help feeling a little sorry for Eddie Cicotte. He was driven from the first game, but asked to get back in there and show what he could do. In his second outing he worked with his old-time cunning under a baking sun. Suddenly the wind changed and a cold breeze came up from Lake Michigan which probably chilled his old soup bone. Believe me, I know how that could harm a pitcher his age. In the fifth inning Duncan hit one to Cicotte. He had to make a quick throw to first, and threw wild. Without that one play, it might have been a different game.

**RAY SCHALK** In the locker room after the game we all got to meet two old players from the Cincinnati Reds of the 1860s, George Wright and Cal McVey. I guess they were on the Chicago team at some point, too.

Charles Murphy, who was once President of the Cubs, presented McVey with a check for $50. Murphy announced he would ask all the baseball men to contribute to a fund for the heroes of the past. Sounded like a good idea to me. McVey said he worked every day in a lumber yard out in California someplace.

It was nice meeting them, but I couldn't help wondering if the game was as good as it was back when they played. They specifically asked to meet Joe. Here were these two old men who asked to meet Joe Jackson without any idea of what was going on.

**CHICK GANDIL** Finally Sullivan said he was going to cough up another 20 grand. I figured Cicotte already had his so I'd split the rest up among those who were still earning it. Williams and Risberg for sure, and probably Felsch, too. McMullen wasn't even playing for Pete's sake, so I wasn't about to include him in. Weaver, as far as I was concerned was out. I wasn't sure which way Jackson was going.

**CHRISTY MATHEWSON** The question of the day: Who Gleason would send to the mound for the all-important fifth game—James or Williams. James was a big veteran right-handed thrower who had pitched well for a number of teams in the past. But Cincinnati hit better against righties. Common baseball sense said to go with Williams, the lefty. After all, hadn't he started more games than anyone in the league that year? Hadn't he come close to leading the league in strikeouts while winning 23 games?

Without Williams they wouldn't have been in the World Series, but still in the back of everybody's mind was the memory of his game two wildness.

**KID GLEASON** I couldn't tell about Williams, so I was leaning toward James, but when the next game was rained out I changed my mind. The extra day of rest, I thought, might be all Williams needed to get over his wildness.

**CHRISTY MATHEWSON** It looked to me like Gleason was being outgeneraled by Moran. As far as I was concerned, Chicago was playing overly conservative baseball. The hard-hitting Felsch being asked to sacrifice so often was a good example. They weren't playing the kind of aggressive ball that got them to the series. Jackson was leading the team in hitting which wasn't surprising, but where was the captain, Eddie Collins? The team looked like it could use some leadership from him, and a few timely hits wouldn't have hurt either.

**EDDIE COLLINS** I've sat through more than my share of team meetings, but I don't remember any more vividly than I do the one we had in the locker room during that rain-enforced day off in Chicago.

Everybody was apprehensive, edgy, unsure of how to act. We were down but not out. We were a great team which wasn't playing great ball. Nobody knew that more than me.

Some fingers were pointed for bad plays, but it wasn't an angry meeting, it was a nervous meeting.

I distinctly remember watching Joe. If there was something going on I didn't know about, I might see it in his face. Joe wasn't real good at hiding things. I watched him all during the meeting. He fidgeted, he fumbled, he looked down. He inspected the leather in his glove like he was looking for something in the wrinkles. He never looked into Gleason's eyes, or anybody else's for that matter.

I watched him more closely than a batter looking for signs from the third base coach. "Come on, Joe," I whispered inaudibly to myself. "Show me what's going on."

What I wanted to see was a sign, a clear sign that everything was all right. There was no way, of course, that Joe could have done that short of standing up and saying it, but I kept hoping, waiting, watching.

I knew nothing was going to be said out loud. But it didn't have to be spoken to be communicated.

Joe was playing well, so he didn't have to hang his head. All the same, I was looking for an "all's clear" signal.

Were we playing the best we could and still getting beaten? I could handle that. Or were some of us not playing our best? I needed to know.

**KID GLEASON** I told them the Reds were the luckiest team I ever saw.

"They won the second game purely on luck," I told them, "and they won yesterday by the sheerest kind of fortune. Eddie was good yesterday. He got them out in eight of the nine innings, yet they were able to win on a couple of errors Eddie wouldn't make again in 40 games. They say it is better to be born lucky than rich."

**CHRISTY MATHEWSON** The meeting resembled a conference at German G. H. Q. after the Yanks had Ludendorff on the run. I believe General Ludendorff claimed it was bad coaching at third base which stopped the Germans from scoring at Paris. Gleason wasn't so sure.

"The Sox figure they can take Ruether the next time he starts," said a baseball man standing next to me at the meeting.

"And the Germans figured that the Americans didn't count in the war until they got into it," I told him.

**CHARLIE LEBEAU** As fate would have it, I was sent to New York for my last mill trip. The kid that I had told stories to years earlier was now in his prime, and playing for the world's best team.

I went where so many other New Yorkers went to follow the game—Times Square. It wasn't Comiskey Park, but it was the next best thing. I was told that not even on election night or New Year's Eve had so many people crowded into Gotham's busiest triangle. From the moment that Lefty Williams threw his first pitch to Joe's final at bat, all eyes were fixed on The New York Times scoreboard. I couldn't prove it, but it seemed to me that there had to be more people standing there that afternoon, than there probably were sitting in Comiskey Park. They filled Broadway and Seventh Avenue right out to the car tracks, leaving only a narrow lane for the trolleys. In the windows of the Claridge and the Astor I could see spectators watching every move of the white ball on the green background, some using field glasses to get a better view. Fans began to collect near the Mayor's Committee huts and the navy recruiting tents long before game time and while the little white ball warmed up in a series of trial flights over the miniature diamond.

My main interest, of course was Joe, but I couldn't help being fascinated by the hold the Series had on the population of a city which didn't even have a team represented in the event.

The scoreboard was a fascinating thing to watch. As far as I could tell, it took five men perched on a platform on the outside of the Times building to run it. One of the five, of course, was the telegraph operator, in direct and constant contact with the ball field. It seemed he was getting a detailed description of every play which he then immediately read off to the others. The man who controlled the flight of the ball, was also apparently a telegraph operator, because it looked like he was confirming every message before actually putting the board into action. The ball itself hung on nearly invisible wires which made it possible to move it in any direction.

A third man was in charge of the base runners, and he moved the white metal squares along brown paths by the simple process of turning a crank. This man and the ball operator were well coordinated in their actions, making the ball and the runner arrive at the right base at just the proper instant, bringing a spontaneous "out" or "safe" from the lips of the crowd.

The other two men on the platform were responsible for the box scores on both sides of the diamond and for the proper registering of hits, runs, errors, outs, balls or strikes, and the announcement of a fly or a sacrifice. All the figures were pushed into place by hand. There was also one innovation which The Times bragged didn't exist anyplace else in the world. It was a system of marking each player as he came to bat, by an electric light.

**VINCENT ALEXANDER** Hod Eller pitched the fifth game for Moran's team. He had won 20 games that season, one of which was a no-hitter against St. Louis.

Williams opened the game by walking Rath.

"Here we go again," was the collective moan of the Chicago fans.

Daubert laid down a pretty bunt along the third base line. It would have rolled foul had Schalk listened to Weaver's call to let it go, but instead the catcher picked it up about an inch from the line and got Daubert at first. Rath made it to second. It looked like maybe Williams' wildness was going to cost him another run, but he got out of the inning thanks to a perfect throw by Felsch to Weaver, and a nice play when Williams covered first and took a toss from Gandil.

Eller must have been watching Williams because he opened the game the same way—he walked the first batter. Eddie Collins grounded to Kopf at short and when the umpire called him out at first on a close call, Collins erupted in a frenzy of anger. I thought at the time he was probably just trying to get his players fired up, because he'd had that play called on him hundreds of times with nary a word.

Quite surprisingly, Aldolfo Luque began warming up beyond right field. Apparently Moran didn't like what he was seeing from Eller. He must have been even more concerned when the next batter, Weaver, hit one back through the box which baffled Eller and went into center for a single. Now there were two on, one out, and the Sox had two of the most dangerous hitters in the league coming up—Jackson and Felsch. The partisan Chicago crowd desperate to see the Sox come back, began roaring. It was the loudest moment of the Series. Get a jump on the Reds here, they all figured, and the Series could turn their way. The crowd was on its feet as Joe strode to the plate.

On the first pitch, Joe swung Black Betsy with everything he had, but missed, the effort spinning him completely around. The crowd was unforgiving.

"Give me a bat," cried an elderly man behind me, "I could do better than that."

From the stands, Eller's pitches didn't look that hard to hit. He wasn't that fast, but he was tricky. When a player swings hard at a smoking fast ball and misses, the fan in the crowd can see and appreciate that, but not these dinky, little, slow pitches. Anybody should be able to hit them. But, of course, any player will tell you, that these can be the hardest of all to hit.

When you are a great player, people expect great things on every play. It was unfair to Joe. He was playing well. He was doing his part for the team, but where was the help? He couldn't go it alone.

Joe took another hefty swing and a high fly shot up over the infield like a geyser. Groh settled under it, and waited seemingly forever for the ball to return to earth and plop in his glove.

The crowd turned so ugly that at a word from a leader they would have taken Joe out and boiled him in oil. As he returned to the bench, Joe must have heard the boos.

Eller waited as the outfielders shifted, then got Hap to fly out to Duncan in left. The rally was over, and the fans worried anew.

Both sides went quietly in the next two innings. When Williams came to bat, he got applause from the partisan crowd, who figured he was back on track.

Risberg let one get past him in the fourth, but Williams quickly got out of the jam. When Roush came to bat in the inning, Williams let go a fast ball at the outfielder's head. Roush dropped safely to the ground, but got up angrily staring at the pitcher.

**RAY SCHALK** When Lefty decked Roush he looked like a different pitcher—in control and confident. I was holding my breath.

**VINCENT ALEXANDER** A couple of pitches later Roush lost his grip on the bat, sending it sailing out to the feet of Williams. Lefty picked it up and threw it right back to Roush. The Sox looked more animated than they had, but the game was scoreless entering the sixth.

A few days earlier they were calling Lefty names not even Joe heard in Philadelphia. But now, they were ready to nominate him for sainthood. All was forgotten.

Then came the sixth inning.

In the top of that inning, Eller led off with a long blast to the fence in front of the bleachers. Felsch raced over and retrieved the ball, but his high throw glanced off Risberg's glove, allowing Eller to get all the way to third.

**CHRISTY MATHEWSON** My attention was piqued in the sixth inning when I saw Felsch shading over toward right against Eller. There was a hole between him and Jackson in left wide enough to send a regiment through. It was difficult to understand why the Sox figured Eller as a right field hitter.

I could think of only two reasons for playing Eller as they did. Either the scouting report was lousy, or Felsch wanted to give him a big hole to hit into. I wondered to myself if Felsch was smart enough to set it up that way. He could run after the ball like a deer, but if he couldn't catch up to it ... well, you couldn't blame him for that, could you?

Then again, if Gleason didn't want him to play there, why didn't he say something? Why didn't he move him over? This was only one of many things that weren't adding up.

**VINCENT ALEXANDER** For a pitcher, Hod Eller was another outstanding hitter. He hit .280 for the season, an average which included a home run, three doubles and as many triples.

With the infield playing in to try to cut off the run at the plate, Rath dropped one over Collins' head for a single, scoring Eller with the first run of the game.

**RAY SCHALK** I went out to the mound. "Don't give up on me now, Lefty," I said. I was firm but not angry.

"Watch for the sacrifice," is all he said.

"Just don't give him an easy one to drop."

"Oh, and Ray," he said to me as I turned and started back to the plate, "listen to Buck this time."

Lefty was always a wise guy. That's one of the reasons I didn't like him.

**HUGH FULLERTON** I picked up my field glasses to get a close look at Williams. I wanted to see his eyes, to see deep into them, to see what was going on there. What I saw was a man beginning to wilt like a morning glory in the sun.

**VINCENT ALEXANDER** After a called strike he didn't like, Daubert sacrificed Rath to second. Groh then walked.

Maybe Williams was fighting his control again. Maybe with first base open and one out, he purposely walked Groh setting up a force play situation. Certainly he didn't want to give Daubert anything good to hit.

Roush followed with a high, hard drive to deep center. Felsch started in for a second, then realizing the ball was hit harder than he thought, raced back. The ball landed just outside his reach, then in his haste to pick it up, he slipped and fell to the ground. By the time he righted himself and threw the ball to Collins, Groh had rounded third. Collins fired a strike to Schalk at home, but Groh slid in under the catcher's tag and the umpire called him safe.

Schalk immediately flew into a fit of frenzy. He leaped at the umpire over the prostrate form of Groh. The umpire stepped back in an attempt to avoid the onrushing catcher who bumped into him anyway, then quickly waved his right arm signaling that Schalk was out of the game.

Schalk tried to swing at the umpire, but by that time, Gleason had his arms locked around him. It looked for a moment that there was going to be a free-for-all as the players spilled onto the field, but despite taunts and threats, things quickly cooled down.

I'm not sure that Gleason, despite his protestations, didn't admire the gutsy little catcher for putting up a fight when maybe some of his other players weren't so committed.

Groh, Jimmy Smith, and a couple of others mocked Schalk's pugilistic efforts and roared with delight when Schalk had to take off his mask and head to the locker room.

Byrd Lynn took Schalk's place behind the plate, but with Schalk gone, one of Gleason's best players was no longer a factor in the game.

**RAY SCHALK** Yeah it was stupid getting thumbed, but I was mad, only I don't know who at more, the ump or Williams. I didn't like anything about the game, not the officiating, not our lack of hitting, not our sloppy fielding, and sure as hell not the pitching. It was just as well I wasn't around to see the lousy finish.

**VINCENT ALEXANDER** Duncan lifted a fly to left. Joe made the catch then fired a perfect strike to Lynn in an effort to catch Roush who had tagged up at third. The throw was there in time, but Lynn, who probably wasn't even warmed up yet, dropped the ball and the run scored.

Cincinnati had scored four runs on three hits, one error, some sloppy play and one ejection.

**HUGH FULLERTON** That was enough! At that point I had become officially disgusted. When Felsch makes two stinko plays like that in one inning, what's the use? It was then that I knew my suspicions were no longer that.

I've seen bums, and I've seen bums, and Felsch was a bum.

I didn't blame Lynn. He looked as nervous back there as a first timer at the door of a whorehouse. I just wondered if he knew what the hell was going on.

**VINCENT ALEXANDER** In the eighth inning, still down 4 to 0, Gleason sent in Eddie Murphy to bat for Williams. Williams had given up only four hits in eight innings, but oh, that sixth inning. Murphy struck out, and the side went down one, two, three.

Erskine Mayer, the veteran right hander, came on in the ninth. He was greeted by a wicked grounder off the bat of Edd Roush to Eddie Collins, but the captain fumbled the ball for an error. Duncan drew a pass on four balls before Larry Kopf switched over to the left side against Mayer and sacrificed Roush to third and Duncan to second. Neale then grounded to Risberg who threw him out at first as Roush scored and Duncan took third. Mayer got out of the inning without giving up anything else.

In their last chance, Weaver crashed the first pitch he saw to the fence in right center for a long triple. Then Jackson came to bat. He had a decidedly determined look on his face. Eller delivered the first pitch. Joe swung hard, probably too hard. It looked like he was trying to get all five runs back with one swing. He grounded to Kopf who got him at first for the final out of the game.

Joe was whitewashed, but so was most of the team. They managed only three hits, two by Weaver, one by Schalk before he was tossed. Eller was great. It was said that Eller was a trick pitcher who got his hops and spins and twists with a shine ball. Whatever it was, he had it working that day.

**CHRISTY MATHEWSON** The classic question in a game like this is always, were the batters bad, or the pitching great? I suspect the Sox underestimated Eller's cunning and trickery. But it was the showing of the White Sox outfield which puzzled me after hearing so much about their great work. Their fielding was not up to the advertisement. Felsch obviously misjudged the ball hit by Roush, and Jackson seemed to be slow to react to one ball hit directly over his head.

**KID GLEASON** What can I say? I was disgusted. The press surrounded me like Custer at Little Big Horn.

"Something is wrong, "I told them. "I don't know what it is. The team that won the pennant for me this summer would have made about 15 hits off Eller in August. It wasn't the same team that faced him today. The Sox are in a terrible batting slump. It is the worst slump a team ever had. Sometimes I feel like going up and hitting myself. All I know is to come back with Dickie Kerr tomorrow, then if he wins, maybe I'll have to pitch him the next day, too. Hell, maybe he'll pitch every game we ever play again."

**CHICK GANDIL** After that game we were told that all the players on the winning team would get $5,000 each, the losers $3,254 each. My quick mind told me then that we were playing for $1,746. That didn't seem like a whole lot of motivation, particularly considering the numbers we had been throwing around earlier.

**SWEDE RISBERG** We were playing the games like we needed to, playing good ball most of the time with only a slip up here and there. I got a real kick out of Collins booting that one late in the game. Maybe some people would start looking at him, too. He always acted like he was king of the hill, but he wasn't hitting worth a damn, and he wasn't fielding so hot either. I thought he might take some of the heat off us.

We were expecting Sullivan to make another delivery before we headed back to Cincy but we saw nothing. Like everything else in this whole business, nobody was doing what they said they would, when they said they would. It was a real mess. The money wasn't there. Even if it was, Joe and Buck didn't seem to be doing a damn thing to earn their shares, and

McMullen wasn't even in the games except for one lousy pinch hitting appearance.

We hopped the night Pullman to Cincy and tried to get some sleep. All I could think was this thing was such a mess that unless I saw some real money, I was going to play ball the best I could. The rest would have to take care of itself.

Look, I felt crummy enough about being involved in this mess to begin with, but I sure as shooting didn't want to take the blame and then head home on the short end of the deal.

**VINCENT ALEXANDER** We took the same train as the players back to the Queen City, but, of course, in different cars. We didn't get in till about 7 in the morning, so unless they slept a lot better on the train than I did, I knew they were going to be tired for that afternoon's game.

They headed directly to the Sinton while I went back to my friends in the bleachers.

Before the game a band played energetic popular songs and after each verse or chorus, the bandsmen shouted in unison the name of a Cincinnati player and then rendered more music in his honor. Thousands of bleacherites joined in the chorus.

The game began with Ruether and Kerr as the opposing pitchers. Ruether got out of the first inning giving up only a single to Weaver.

In the bottom of the inning policemen were summoned to remove a group of spectators sitting on the grass back of home plate. The first cabin fans had to watch the rest of the game from high up in the stands. With one out Heinie Groh lashed one of Kerr's offerings into right center for a long double. Roush followed with a sizzling grounder to Risberg who acted as if the ball was on fire. He booted it over toward second as Roush reached first. Groh meanwhile, rounded third too far, and was nailed by Risberg on a strong throw to Weaver. Groh put up a stink to the umpire, but, the inning was over.

Risberg misplayed another ball in the next inning when he failed to come up with Duncan's slow roller, but nothing came of it.

In the bottom of the third with still no score, Daubert managed a single. After Groh was called out on strikes, Daubert took off for second. Schalk's throw was low and in front of the bag, and Collins slipped trying to come up with it. Roush over slid the bag and Collins tried to get him coming back, but the umpire called him safe. Eddie was usually one of the slickest, most graceful fielders in the league, so his gaffes in this Series, were becoming a cause of concern. Kerr drilled Roush in the kidneys with the next pitch. The Reds were suddenly in business with men on first and second. Duncan wasted no time in lashing a double to deep center scoring Daubert and Roush with the first runs. Kopf fouled off the first pitch then hit a long drive to deepest center field. The ball was hit well, but high enough for Felsch to track down and corral. Kerr was out of the inning but he had given up a pair of runs.

I saw Gleason begin to pace in the dugout. If Kerr couldn't get it done, who could?

Felsch lashed a single to center past Rath in the fourth, but that was all the side could muster.

In the Reds' half of the inning, Neale opened up with a long triple to deep right field. Cincinnati was shelling Kerr.

**EDDIE CICOTTE** At one point Gleason looked over at me.

"What are you looking at me for, Kid?" I asked. "I told you these guys could hit."

Every time they launched one off Dickie, it took some of the pressure off me.

**VINCENT ALEXANDER** There was an element of luck in Neale's hit, though, because the ball took a mischievous bounce out of the reach of Shano Collins. Still, it was hit hard.

**CHICK GANDIL** Neale was looking so hard at the ball bouncing away from Collins that he never stepped on first, so when the ball came back in, I had Kerr run over to touch the base. The umps huddled but said nobody saw it, so they let Neale stay on third.

After all, the game has got to be played according to the rules, doesn't it?

**VINCENT ALEXANDER** Ruether, who had already proved that he could hit, drove a pitch right down the third base line scoring Neale. The next batter, Rath, sent a grounder to Risberg, who elected to go to Weaver in an attempt to get Ruether going to third, but the ball hit the runner squarely in the back and bounced off into foul territory. Roush took advantage and scored. Risberg screamed bloody murder to the umpire, claiming Ruether had deliberately thrown out his arm so the ball would hit him. The umpire didn't buy the argument which was reasonable considering the ball never hit the arm. Rath promptly stole third, the ball getting away from Weaver on the throw from Schalk.

It looked like the Reds were going to score again when Daubert sent a fly ball deep. Rath tagged up and raced home on Joe's catch. Joe unleashed a bullet throw to Schalk which just caught the second baseman at the plate.

**KID GLEASON** Kerr was getting hit, that was obvious, but what was I going to do, bring in Eddie or Lefty? Dickie was a tough little cookie, so I decided to go with him as long as I could.

**VINCENT ALEXANDER** Risberg and Schalk opened the fifth with walks, then Kerr got a scratch infield hit off the glove of Kopf. Just like that the Sox were back in the game. The bases were loaded, and the top of the order was coming up. Shano Collins lifted a fly to Roush. Risberg started home after tagging up, but Roush's throw was on the mark so Risberg wisely retreated. Eddie Collins then followed with another fly to Roush. This time Risberg scored.

**CHRISTY MATHEWSON** Make no mistake about it, there were some prize bonehead plays in the Series. There were times when neither of these teams looked much like the two best teams in baseball, but the play of Kerr's in the fifth inning takes the cake.

When Collins hit that fly to Roush for the sacrifice, Kerr took off for second, apparently oblivious to the fact that Schalk was standing squarely on top of the bag. Schalk began waving frantically for his battery mate to reverse his ground and head back to first before he gummed up the works, but the pitcher had his head down and didn't see him until he was practically on top of the bag. He stopped dead in his tracks, and Groh easily put the tag on him instantly killing what once looked like a very promising situation.

If you didn't know better, you might have thought Kerr was out to lose the game on purpose.

**VINCENT ALEXANDER** Kerr looked rattled when he returned to the mound. His first three pitches weren't even close, but then he settled down and got out of the inning despite another terrible play by Felsch. Duncan drove a fly to deep center which completely befuddled Hap. He was playing in when the ball was hit. He started to run back, hesitated, turned around, misjudged the direction of the hit, and finally muffed the catch.

**HUGH FULLLERTON** I had to laugh at Felsch.

"Maybe they should call him Happy the Clown," I said to anybody close enough who cared to listen.

Of all the players, Happy looked the most ridiculous. Couldn't an athlete as gifted as he was, at least make his attempts look real?

He was a buffoon, a happy, sad, buffoon. Next to Tris Speaker he was supposed to be the best defensive outfielder of his day, but in this Series he was not only having trouble catching routine fly balls, but he was looking ridiculous in the attempt.

If Joe was involved in this, though, I have to give him credit. I guess hezmust have been smarter than Felsch after all, for he maintained his impassive demeanor and played with the grace befitting a great outfielder.

**RAY SCHALK** I couldn't resist the sarcasm.

"Nice play, Hap," I said to him as he returned to the dugout.

"I like the way you looked like a statue on second last inning," he responded. "Couldn't you think of any place to go?"

I thought about slugging him on the spot, but it didn't seem to matter much any longer.

**CHARLES COMISKEY** What was once a nettlesome bother was now turning into real concern. Hap didn't make plays like that—ever. It was time to do something, but what?

**VINCENT ALEXANDER** Weaver led off the sixth with a single when Duncan and Kopf, afraid of running into each other let the ball drop between them. Joe followed suit with a line single as Weaver scored. Then

Felsch quickly lashed a double to the fence in left center, Jackson scoring all the way from first.

At this point, Moran yanked Ruether and sent in Jimmy Ring. An uneasy silence suddenly fell on the crowd. Were the mighty Sox finally waking up? This was the kind of hitting they had expected.

Schalk got Felsch home with a single but Ring got Kerr to ground to Groh for the final out.

The score was still tied at 4 when Joe just missed by an eyelash of making a sensational shoestring catch on a sinking liner off the bat of Morrie Rath, but Kerr got out of the inning without giving up anything else.

In the eighth Joe got to second after walking to lead off the inning, but was doubled off second when Roush made an excellent catch of a ball that Joe, as well as well as everybody in the park, thought was going to drop in for a hit.

At the end of nine, the game was all knotted up. Kerr had battled back, and although he was frequently in trouble, the Sox were still in the game.

Weaver started off the 10th by dropping a Texas leaguer into left. He got a double out of it when Duncan overran the ball. He would have been better off playing it on one bounce and holding Weaver to a single, but the Reds had been playing aggressively the whole series so I guess he thought he had to take the chance.

What Joe did next surprised everybody. On the first pitch he turned and bunted, but the ball went foul. The Sox counted on his power, not his bunting prowess, so I figured after one failed attempt, he would go back to swinging away. However, after letting the next two go for balls, he turned to bunt again. This time he laid a perfect bunt down along the third base line, and beat it out.

**CHRISTY MATHEWSON** I have to admit, Joe's bunt caught me off guard. Certainly no one expected him to be able to do that, so if he wanted to, he could have easily pushed the ball foul or missed it altogether, and no one would have thought him the worse for it yet he laid down probably the best bunt of the series.

**VINCENT ALEXANDER** Weaver got to third on Joe's bunt. Gandil then followed with a solid single to center scoring Weaver with the go-ahead run.

Kerr got the Reds in order in the bottom of the inning, and the Sox picked up their second win.

**CHRISTY MATTHEWSON** You could have seen better games played on city parks for free—and it wasn't just the Sox. The Red's infield slipped around like they were playing on a frozen pond. Duncan and Kopf played "I got it. No you got it," in the outfield and while they stood around like a couple of lawyers arguing about it, the ball dropped in for a charity two-bagger.

The crowd's opinion of the bantam weight hurler, Dickie Kerr went up and down like the mercury in a thermometer on the back of a cross-country train. The Reds hammered him for 11 hits, but he battled back and showed grit when he had to. Of course, he also committed a ludicrous piece of base running so ludicrous that it will go down in baseball lore along with Fred Merkel's boner and Fred Snodgrass's $30,000 muff. Kerr acted like he was the victim of sleeping powder.

Well, at least they scored some runs for the crowd. In the games up to that point, runs had been as scarce as rooms in Cincinnati hotels.

If nothing else, the game put a lot of confidence back into some of the discouraged White Sox fans who suddenly were dreaming of beating Sallee in the next game and taking the entire traveling baseball hippodrome skedaddling back to Chicago.

**KID GLEASON** I told the press we had hit our winning stride.

"We're coming back" I boasted to the reporters. "We're going to win this whole thing, boys and you can print that."

Then I turned to Gandil. "That's right, isn't it Chick?" I wanted the reporters to hear his answer.

"You said it, Kid," he responded flashing that big smile of his.

**BUCK WEAVER** You know at that point I honestly wasn't sure if the others were playing to win or not. It was that confusing, but after Kerr's second win there was a different attitude in the locker room. I thought I sensed a feeling that they could win, and maybe would—if they tried, really tried.

I knew this though: I knew the next game was going to be real interesting.

**JOE JACKSON** Little Dickie, he pitched good in them two games, he pitched real good. Nobody could blame him. I was trying hard to help, but maybe I was trying a little too hard.

**VINCENT ALEXANDER** The next morning, the city was deluged with a new load of Sox fans fresh off the morning train from Chicago. They dashed frantically from hotel to hotel looking for rooms and from scalper to scalper looking for tickets. If the Reds fans were losing faith, the Sox fans certainly weren't.

The momentum had shifted. Chicago was back in the mix of things and the Reds fans knew it, so much so that they stayed away from the next games in droves. Even though they needed but one more win, the feeling was that they were fortunate enough to have won the games they did. Deep down they knew Chicago was the better team, and there wasn't a rush to be part of the inevitable funeral ceremonies and the pinning of the lilies and white ribbons on the body.

By game time, the stands were only half full, if that. It was an amazing demonstration of cowardice on the part of the fans who only a day earlier were screaming with delight from every seat in the park.

Maybe the band said it all when every time the Sox came out on the field, they were accompanied by strains of musical sarcasm such as "She May Have Seen Better Days," and "Please Go Away and Let Me Sleep."

**SHORTY SCHIRALDI** Now get this. There were more rumors floating around the park than hot dog wrappers on a windy afternoon in Chicago. There was even one that said the Reds had bribed some of their own players to lose that last game so they could stretch the series out for more gate revenue.

Of course that was ridiculous, but if you listened long enough you could hear just about anything. Everybody had some cockamamie theory—everything from the Sox choked, to the Sox were dogging it, to the Reds were dogging it, to the whole thing was arranged by the baseball powers before the series began.

It was a real circus for the bettors and the money was all over the place. The papers were even reporting bets of $60,000 and more being placed on certain games. You bet depending on what "information" you had.

**KID GLEASON** Eddie was being shown up by Kerr, and I knew he couldn't stand the little guy. Maybe that would motivate him.

"Throw one ball away at first, and I'm going to throw you out of the game," I said to him as he was warming up.

"Me, Kid? I got great control today. I can feel it. You just watch."

"Oh, I'll be watching." I told him.

"I knew I could count on you, Kid."

He could be a real sarcastic son of a bitch when he wanted to.

**VINCENT ALEXANDER** When Sallee threw the first pitch the sparse crowd let out a cheer which sounded downright anemic compared to the previous days. They became even quieter when Shano Collins led off with a solid single into left and Eddie Collins sacrificed him neatly to second. After Weaver flied out to deep center, Joe stepped to the plate. It was a perfect opportunity for him to make a big contribution. I wanted him to just relax a little and let Betsy do the talking. I wanted him to be the hero who brought the Sox back.

With the count on him at 2 and 2, Joe lashed a hard single to right easily scoring Collins from second. The Reds fans moaned the moan of seeing the inevitable. Jackson overran the base, but got back safely when Daubert bobbled Rath's throw. On the first pitch he saw, Felsch dropped a perfect bunt toward third and beat it out. Gandil came up with a chance to add to the lead but ended the inning by forcing Felsch at second.

**KID GLEASON** I said something complimentary to Joe as he trotted back to the dugout, I don't remember exactly what, but I remember his face lighting up like a kid who just got a told by his father that he did something good.

Just as we were about to take the field, I told Hap to switch positions with Shano. Let's face it, Hap's fielding had been, well, let's say mediocre.

Hap looked at me like I was crazy.

"Don't look at me that way," I said. "Play right. You can do that, can't you?"

He said 'yeah' like he meant 'no,' but I knew he could play anyplace in the field if he wanted to, but who the hell knew what he wanted to do.

He was having trouble with the sun I told the press after the game. It was a good excuse.

**VINCENT ALEXANDER** Cicotte got applause from the Chicago fans when he came to bat in the second. Apparently the Chicago fans were less fickle than the Reds fans.

Eddie Collins uncharacteristically let a ball go right through his legs for an error in the bottom of the frame, but the Reds still were not touching Cicotte.

The bottom of the third started like the first. Shano Collins opened with his second hit of the game. Then Eddie Collins reached first when he hit a little grounder that forced Shano at second. Weaver tried to bunt. Gleason was nothing if not consistent. He fouled the first two off then rapped a grounder to Kopf who got Collins by stepping on second. Weaver, though, was called out at first when the umpire upheld a protest that Collins had interfered with Kopf at second. Both Collins and Weaver exploded in the face of the umpire, screaming wildly that Collins' slide was within legal bounds. When the argument ended, Collins stormed back to the dugout. Joe came up and jumped on the first pitch shooting another single to the outfield which again scored Shano Collins. The Sox settled for the single run.

**RAY SCHALK** When Cicotte opened the third by almost taking Sallee's head off with a high inside fast ball, I immediately went to the mound. I didn't want him to get away with what he did in the earlier games—pitch well for several innings, then blow up in one and lose the game.

"Calm down, Eddie," I told him.

"I am calm," he said.

"Then quit trying to rearrange Slim's face."

"I didn't like his look."

That was the kind of attitude he had when he was on his game. I loved it.

**VINCENT ALEXANDER** With one out in the fifth, Eddie Collins singled to center, and Moran immediately sent Fisher down to warm up. On the first pitch, Weaver grounded to Groh, who became confused, let the ball roll behind him, then ran around in circles looking for the ball. The wonderful red machine which had played so well earlier was coming apart. Jackson followed with a grounder to Rath who booted the ball setting up a bases-loaded situation for the new right fielder, Felsch. Hap sent the Sox fans into ecstasy when he smashed a hit into center scoring Eddie Collins and Weaver and sending Jackson to second. Fisher came in to end the threat.

In the bottom of the inning Ruether was sent in as a pinch hitter, but he popped out to Weaver.

In the sixth inning Luque went to the hill for the Reds. Dolph's presence on the team was an interesting side note to the game. A few years earlier, the Reds signed a pair of light-skinned players from Cuba, and when questions arose about their backgrounds, the teams' management assured everyone they were "as pure white as Castile soap." Now they had Luque, the Pride of Cuba, and the first Latin player to appear in the Series. He was light-skinned enough that they could get away with it.

Luque gave up a double to the hot-hitting Shano Collins but got out of the inning without surrendering a run.

Cincinnati managed to nick Cicotte for one run in the bottom of the sixth thanks to hits by Groh and Duncan.

The normally slick-fielding Eddie Roush dropped an easy fly in the eighth, but the Sox couldn't cash in.

**ABE ATTELL** Watching these two teams go at each other you had to wonder who was trying to throw the series. I mean if you didn't know, it would have looked like maybe it was the Reds. They fumbled and bumbled their way through the Series. You would have thought the ball was on fire the way they handled it, or maybe I should say didn't handle it.

I wasn't all that concerned though. I had confidence that Chick and the boys could out-bumble the Reds.

**VINCENT ALEXANDER** In their last at bat, and still down 4 to 1, Kopf opened with a long fly ball down the left field line that was slicing foul all the way. Joe got a good jump on the ball, reaching it and the railing at the same time. He stretched his long arm out for it and went tumbling headlong over the railing and into the temporary seats which were set up in anticipation of overflow crowds. It looked for a moment that Joe might have been seriously hurt, but he got back to his feet to the cheers of the crowd. Although his effort went for naught, the spectators appreciated his all-out attempt.

The Reds got a couple of men on, but Cicotte got Rath to fly to Felsch ending the threat and giving Cicotte the well-earned victory.

The Reds looked and played like a nervous team. The Sox looked like ... well, the Sox.

**CHRISTY MATHEWSON** Cicotte looked like the comeback player of the series. He kept his cool and pitched well, particularly in the clutch. Over and over again, the Redland hitters tried to rattle the pitcher by protesting that he was using a foreign substance on the ball. But Eddie never flinched, and every time he rubbed the ball on his uniform to try to get a smooth spot, the Reds seemed to get upset and worried. It was a great psychological ploy.

The Sox looked spirited throughout. In fact Gleason showed so much confidence in his pitcher that not once did he leave the dugout.

Moran, on the other hand, was a picture of dejection. When Sallee was lifted and came trundling back to the bench, Moran bowed his head and began nervously tearing up a piece of paper. Somebody commented he looked like a distracted old schoolmaster who wanted to keep the whole class after school and give them a licking. They deserved it.

On the way back to the hotel I passed a newsboy shouting, "Reds give away the ballgame." That they did.

**SHORTY SCHRALDI** What a difference a few hours made. Just the day before the Cincy fans were laughing at the poor slobs who bet on the White Sox. Now the odds had once again shifted, making Chicago 7 to 10 favorites to win the eighth game. Oh, the Red fans were still smiling but the smile was more like the whistle of the small boy passing a graveyard.

**KID GLEASON** I told the press, "The Sox played magnificent ball, outguessed the Reds, outbatted them, outplayed them and Cicotte outpitched them."

**HUGH FULLERTON** Well, now I was vacillating. This was getting very interesting. Where once I was sure the fix was on, now I had questions. Don't misunderstand. I wasn't sure it wasn't on, but something seemed strange about this whole smelly mess.

One thing for sure. I wouldn't have missed the next game for all the money in Rothstein's pockets.

Then everything changed in an instant. A friend, a gambler, tells me "All the money's shifted to Cincinnati."

I don't gamble. I never did. So I ask him, "Yeah, what does that mean?"

"The fix. It's back on," he says.

"How do you know?" I ask.

"Money don't lie," he says. "Gambling money never lies."

"Maybe it's just hunch betting," I suggest.

"Yeah, and Rothstein's an angel of mercy."

"It could be legit. I mean, after all, Williams is up again."

"The first inning. Watch the first inning. It's going to be big," he insists.

"Is that what you hear?"

"That's what I hear."

**SPORT SULLIVAN** You can bet your sweet bootleg I was worried. I didn't know what in the hell was going on. The damn Sox, they didn't look good, they looked great!

If I could have gotten my hands on him, I would have choked to death that bastard Gandil, and I would have done it slowly, too. I trusted him to control the boys but obviously he couldn't control water in a glass, let alone other players. He talked big, but talk was easy. Delivering, that was another thing.

I didn't know what to do. I briefly thought about running, but I knew I couldn't go far enough or fast enough. I thought about suicide, but that looked like a lousy option to me.

I went to A.R. because I didn't know what else to do. He said I'd have no problems as long as the series ended on the next game.

"Forget how it looks," he said. "I don't want it to go to nine."

A.R. wasn't one to argue with. When he said something like that, no matter how simple it was, that was that.

Except it wasn't that simple. How the hell was I going to guarantee anything? I couldn't get a damn thing out of Gandil, and I didn't even know who was still in on it.

The only edge I could figure was Williams. Maybe I could get to him. But what if he didn't go the next day? What if Gleason was scared off by Lefty's first two games? What if he gambled and went with Faber? That scared the daylights out of me. I was more worried about Faber than anyone.

**KID GLEASON** Faber was my ace in the hole. We were down 4 games to 3. With Faber's spitball, he was a gopher's worst enemy, but he was hobbling on a bum ankle and hadn't pitched in a while.

I asked him if he could go. He said he'd try if I really needed him, but he couldn't put any weight on his ankle. That pretty well sealed it. If you can't put weight on your ankle, you damn well can't pitch.

He had served in the navy during much of the previous season, and came back in rotten shape. If it wasn't for the lousy navy overfeeding him, he would have pitched that eighth game.

It was going to have to be Williams.

**LEFTY WILLIAMS** During the night before the eighth game, I got a phone call. This guy said if I didn't lose the next game something bad would happen to my wife.

What the hell was I supposed to do? Run to the cops? Cops who probably had their last paycheck on the game, tell them I was supposed to throw it?

Not a chance. Not a snowball's chance in a Chicago summer's day.

**KID GLEASON** I told the team Lefty was pitching. I told them that I expected them to play their hearts out, and that if they didn't I would tear them out. I told them that if I even suspected any of them of laying down, or even leaning like they was going to lay down, I would pull them from the game, and I would do it in the middle of an inning if necessary, and I would do it so loudly that every person in Chicago would hear it whether they were at the game or not.

I told them I would embarrass them in public the likes of which they had never seen before, and that they would forever be branded as quitters.

"Hell, I'll play myself if I have to. I'll pitch to Comiskey if I have to, but I'll give it everything I've got to the last out, and anybody who doesn't want to do that can get out of the room right now, and I'll even help you pack your equipment!"

**JOE JACKSON** The Kid, he was real fired up before the game. He started out angry, and then he started cussing and swearing and carrying on something awful. I thought he was going to have a heart attack or something. He threw a stool, then he threw a bench, then he said he'd throw anybody in the room who got in his way, only nobody did.

I wasn't too worried though, because I played good in the last game and he seen that.

What was going to happen, I had no idea, because the last time I spoke to any of the players in on the fix was a lot of days before.

I just wanted the Series to be over so I could go home.

**EDDIE CICOTTE** The thing was, guys had done things in the first seven games, and nobody noticed. Nobody said a damn thing specific—not the papers, not the league office, not Commey. One thing we were proving was you could throw a series without anybody being able to prove a thing. Even if they did, hell they couldn't do anything about it. Hal Chase was living proof of that.

Everybody makes errors sometimes. Nobody ever played the game perfect, and nobody can ever tell if you muffed one on purpose or not. Oh, they may think they did, but all you have got to say is, "Gee skip, I gave it my all, honest I did. It just took a bad hop, but we'll get them next time."

Say that with the right look on your face and you can get away with it.

And don't tell me this didn't happen, because I know it did.

**VINCENT ALEXANDER** Although I was fast running out of funds, I managed to scrape together enough to take yet another Pullman back to Chicago eagerly anticipating game eight.

The weatherman said it might rain for the game and it certainly looked like it early on. It was cool, and quite windy. So much so that Gleason had his troops out early for a session of high infield pop fly practice. Little whirlwinds of dust were swept up from the base paths, forcing the players to shade their eyes from the dust.

I was out in the right field bleachers where several fans were terrorized by a big green flagpole above us which bent precariously in the wind.

When Williams took the mound, the crowd gave him a big ovation.

The Reds wasted little time. The second batter up, Jake Daubert, lashed a line drive to center which Leibold just barely missed making a shoestring catch. Groh immediately followed with a sharp single to right, sending Daubert to second.

**RAY SCHALK** All I could think was, oh no, here we go again. With my arm I motioned for Lefty to bear down, then looked toward Gleason on the bench.

"Get him out of here now!" I mouthed.

Gleason sent Big Bill James down to the right field foul territory to warm up.

Lefty's first pitch to Roush was very high. I walked the ball out to the mound faster than Lefty had thrown it to me.

I looked at him with fire in my eyes, slapped the ball in his glove, turned, and walked back to the plate. I didn't say a word.

I was sick to my stomach.

**VINCENT ALEXANDER** After his brief conference with Schalk, Williams threw two perfect strikes to Roush, but the second one was smashed down the right field line for a double, scoring Daubert and putting Groh on third. After fouling one back and taking one wide, Duncan slashed a double over Weaver's head, scoring both Groh and Roush.

Gleason immediately waved James into the game. Williams had thrown 15 pitches and was already down three runs.

**SPORT SULLIVAN** That was too early I thought. Williams shouldn't be out of there in the first. There was still too far to go.

**VINCENT ALEXANDER** James didn't fare a lot better. He surrendered a walk, a hit, and another run before getting out of the inning.

The Sox were down four runs before they even got a chance to hit, and the fans wondered out loud how their team would react. It didn't take long before they answered the question for themselves. Leibold opened by smacking a single to left.

The crowd liked what they saw, but Moran obviously didn't. After only one batter, he sent Ring out to warm up. Clearly both managers were going to use every weapon at their disposal.

With the count one and one, Eddie Collins doubled off Duncan's glove, Leibold going to third. The stands were in a turmoil. Weaver swung hard at a pitch, sprawling in the dirt as he struck out. Joe popped up and Felsch struck out. Suddenly the crowd was silent.

In the top of the second, the Reds picked up where they had left off. They scored another run on hits by Groh and Roush. Roush's was a long double off Jackson's glove.

Chicago got the fans' hopes up again in the bottom of the inning when they got two men on, but they were unable to push a run across. Then in the third Joe came up with two outs and the bases empty. He watched the first pitch sail wide. The second one was belt high on the outside half of the plate. Joe swung with that beautiful naturally graceful swing of his and drove the ball on a line toward the right field bleachers. The ball couldn't have been more than 12 feet off the ground the whole way. It cleared the railing, hit the edge of one of the bleacher steps, bounced straight up into the air, and then into my cupped hands. Joe had a homer, the Sox had a run, and I had a souvenir—a second Shoeless Joe home run ball!

Well, I can't begin to describe the thrill that gave me, or for that matter, the reaction of the crowd. I have never, to this day, seen anything like it. That hit set off a wild, joyous, spontaneous reaction. You would have thought the Sox had just won the championship. Even some of the Reds supporters in the crowd cheered Joe as he glided easily over the base paths.

I have long considered that an act of manifest justice. I thought of myself as Joe's biggest fan. It was right that he hit that ball to me.

My eyes were admittedly still moist as the inning concluded without any more scoring. But Joe's shot brought confidence to the faithful and concern to the Reds.

**SPORT SULLIVAN** Joe's home run made me instantly more nervous—if that was possible. What the hell did he think he was doing? The big, stupid rube couldn't even get a simple order straight.

**VINCENT ALEXANDER** Cincinnati pushed another run across in the fifth on a triple by Kopf and a run-scoring single by Neale.

In the sixth, the Reds jumped on James again. After giving up a single to Eller and a walk to Rath, Gleason sent in Roy Wilkinson to replace him.

It seemed that Cincinnati had their bats working this day. They were swatting everything the Sox threw their way, and it didn't matter who was doing the throwing. It didn't help that Schalk threw wide to Weaver pulling him off the base for an error which left the bases loaded. Roush singled off Collins' glove scoring Eller and Rath, and Duncan singled sending in yet another run before Wilkinson could get out of the inning.

Cincinnati got to Wilkinson for another run in the eighth. Time was running out for the Sox.

In the eighth Joe laced a double to deep right field scoring Collins and Weaver. He damn near had his second home run. Gandil sent Joe home with a triple off the fence in right field, then scored himself for Chicago's fifth run when Roush muffed Risberg's little fly to short right center.

Wilkinson got through the Cincy half of the ninth without any problems.

Chicago came to bat in the bottom of the ninth five runs down and the Series on the line. Some in the crowd hightailed it for home. Those who stuck around watched nervously.

Eddie Murphy was sent in to bat for Wilkinson. Eller hit him in the hip and he took first. The Sox were still alive, but barely. Leibold lined a hard shot to deep center. Roush dove for the ball, did a complete somersault as he hit the ground but came up with the ball in his hand. It was truly a spectacular catch. Collins followed with a single to center, and then right away stole second. Chicago had men on second and third with one out. Could they get back in the game and the Series with a big inning? The crowd was becoming restless.

Weaver skied to deep right. Then it was Joe's turn again. He already had a double and a home run in the game. Could he possibly deliver more?

Joe took two strikes. He was looking for a pitch he could drive out. The third pitch was a ball. On the fourth he swung hard and popped it foul into the stands behind third. The next pitch was low, but with two strikes on him, he couldn't let it go. He swung, trying to lift it over the infield. The ball bounced twice, then right into the hands of Morrie Rath at second. The little Texan scooped it up and then in one slick move fired to first to get Joe and end the most incredible World Series in baseball history.

# 48

# I PLAYED MY HEART OUT

**JOE JACKSON** I played my heart out against Cincinnati. I set a record for the most hits in a Series. I made 13 hits, but after all the trouble came out they took one away from me. Morrie Rath went over in the hole and knocked down a hot grounder, but he couldn't make a throw on it. They scored it as a hit then, but changed it later.

I led both teams in hitting at .375. I hit the only home run of the Series. I handled 30 balls in the outfield and never made an error or allowed a man to take an extra base. I threw out five men at home and could have had three others, if bad cutoffs hadn't been made. One of them was in the second game Eddie Cicotte lost, when he made them two errors in one inning. One of the errors was on a throw I made trying to cut off a run. He deflected the ball to the grandstand and the run came in.

That's my record in the Series, and I was responsible only for Joe Jackson. I can't positively say that I remember anything out of the ordinary in the Series. I mean anything that would of turned the tide. Well, there was just one thing that didn't seem quite right, now that I think back over it. Cicotte seemed to let up on a pitch to Pat Duncan and Pat hit it over my head. Duncan didn't really have enough power to hit the ball that far, if Cicotte was bearing down.

Williams was a great control pitcher and they made a heck of a fuss over him walking a few men. Swede Risberg, missed the bag on a double play ball at second and they made a lot out of that, too. But those was things that could happen to anybody. You just can't say out and out that they was shady baseball.

There was supposed to have been a lot of big gamblers and boxers and shady characters mixed up in it. Well, I wouldn't have recognized Abe Attell if I stepped on him. Or Arnold Rothstein either.

They write a lot about what a great team we was that year. It was a good team. You can't take that away from us. But it wasn't the same kind of team Mr. Mack had at Philadelphia from 1910 to 1914. I think that was the greatest team of all time. Our team didn't have but two hitters in the .300's. Eddie Collins, as fine a man as there ever was in baseball, and me. It wasn't a hard-hitting team, not the kind they made out it was.

It was a good ball club, but not like Mr. Mack's.

**CHICK GANDIL** Total hits favored Cincy only 64 to 59, and each side committed 12 errors. Though I hit only .233, remember it was still seven points better than our star Eddie Collins, and two of my hits knocked in winning runs.

Oh, our losing to Cincinnati was an upset all right, but no more than some of the other Series I could name. Mind you, I offer no defense for the thing we conspired to do. But I maintain that our actual losing of the Series was pure baseball fortune.

**VINCENT ALEXANDER** Just to set the record straight, Joe's batting average was 71 points higher than he hit in 1917, and higher than any of the everyday players. He had more hits than anyone. He had the only homer. He had more total bases than anyone.

And what about the other players on his team? Collins hit only .226 and committed two errors. Nemo Leibold could only manage .214; Shano Collins, .250; Felsch, .192; Gandil, .233; Risberg, .080.

For the victorious Reds, Rath hit only .226; Daubert, .241; Groh, .172; Kopf, .222; and the National League batting champion, Edd Roush, .214.

Any suggestion that Joe was not playing his best is ludicrous. That assumes he could hit better than .375 had he really been trying. Absurd! Nobody but nobody had a higher lifetime batting average in the Series to that date than Joe's .375.

Let's look at what some of the greatest hitters in the history of the game managed to hit in the Series pre-1919. Tris Speaker, .290; Ty Cobb, .260; Sam Crawford, .240; Honus Wagner, .230.

Joe didn't have a good Series, he had a great one.

And let me add this, too. I had heard nothing about Joe being involved in any kind of fix before or during the Series and I saw nothing in the Series that raised the hint of suspicion.

**TOPSY HARTSEL** I wasn't surprised when I heard all them reports about Joe being involved in the fix. But then everybody said look at what he did, look at how well he played, so how could he have been involved? The way I figure it, Joe was too dumb to be a good fixer.

**KID GLEASON** We were a better teams than the Reds, period. Something was wrong.

**BILLY EVANS** Maybe I was just a blind umpire. Certainly I've been accused of that and worse, but I worked that Series, every inning of every game, and all I can say is that Series looked all right to me.

**JOE JACKSON** Like all the players, me and Katie was staying in the Lexington Hotel. The night after the last game, while Katie was washing up in the bathroom, Lefty Williams came in. I could see he'd been drinking and I could smell it on his breath, too.

"What is it, Lefty? What do you want?" I asked him. I didn't really want to talk to him about the game or nothing. All I wanted to do was get packed up and head south. I wanted to get out of Chicago bad.

He had a couple of envelopes in his hand.

"Here, this is for you," he said.

"What is that?" I asked.

"Some of us players sold the Series to a couple of gamblers." he said.

"I don't want nothing to do with that," I told him, "and I didn't have nothing to do with that."

"Don't matter," he told me. "We told the gamblers that you were part of it, so you might as well take it."

He threw the envelope on the bed.

"I don't want that." I told him.

"Buy yourself a new suit, Joe. Hell, buy yourself a whole closet full of suits."

"You've got some nerve using my name with the gamblers without asking me. That ain't right. Now you're going to get me in trouble and I didn't do nothing."

"Don't give me that crap, Joe. You knew exactly what the hell was going on."

"Just get out of here Lefty. I'm going to tell Mr. Comiskey everything."

"Who the hell do you think is going to believe you? Who do you think is going to believe a stupid farm boy who can't even sign his name?"

"Get out of here, Lefty. I'm warning you."

He got out fast, just before Katie came in.

**KATIE JACKSON** When Joe told me what Lefty had said, I was really upset. It sounded to me like they were trying to get him involved even though he wasn't. People sometimes thought they could take advantage of Joe and maybe sometimes they did, but Joe was a lot smarter about those things than a lot of people realized.

I told Joe that was a terrible thing for Lefty to do and that he should do something about it right away.

He said he was going to see Mr. Comiskey in the morning.

I opened the envelope. There was $10,000 in it in—some fifties, mostly hundreds.

**JOE JACKSON** The next morning I went right away to see Mr. Comiskey, but Mr. Grabiner, who was the secretary or something for the team, he told me that Mr. Comiskey wasn't feeling well.

Then he said, "Go home Joe. We know what you want."

But I didn't think he knowed what I wanted at all, so I showed him the money and told him what Lefty said, then I asked him what I should do about it.

He told me to go ahead and take the money home with me, and that Mr. Comiskey would get in touch with me later.

Then he slammed the door in my face.

**LEFTY WILLIAMS** If a lot of people thought we were all talking to each other about this thing, they got another thing coming. After some of those early meetings, we hardly talked about what was going on at all. After I saw Joe in his room when I gave him his money, I didn't talk to him again for a long, long time.

**HUGH FULLERTON** The way I had it pegged, this was going to be the last World Series, and a sad way it was to end a great tradition. The powers that be in the national pastime must surely have seen that its pride and joy was sick indeed, and euthanasia the only way out.

**CHARLES COMISKEY** Some kinds of scandal seem always to follow a big sporting event like the World Series. These yarns are manufactured out of whole cloth and grow out of the bitterness of lost wagers. We all had heard the stories that a few of the boys had succumbed to the imprecations of gamblers, but I didn't know that for a fact, so I put out a public plea.

"I believe my boys fought the battles of the recent World Series on the level as they have always done, and I will be the first to want information to the contrary. I will give $20,000 to any one unearthing information to that effect."

If I got the goods on any of my players I would see that there was no place in organized ball for them—ever.

**JOE JACKSON** I scooted back south about as fast as our car could chug. The farther away the better for me. Down in Savannah nobody would bother me about the Series. I was even thinking about not going back.

The one big mistake I made was, I had the envelope Lefty gave me. I never should of done that, but Mr. Comiskey wouldn't listen to me to give it back, so I didn't know what else to do.

After I got to Savannah I found out that Mr. Comiskey wasn't going to send our World Series checks until he found out what happened. I would of been glad to tell him if he would of bothered to listen. We was supposed to get $3,000 which I was counting on so I wasn't exactly too unhappy to have the $10,000.

**LUTHER JACKSON** That winter we visited with Joe and Katie in Savannah. I was glad to see Joe and all, but I could tell he was bothered by something even though he wouldn't say what. I asked him a couple of times, and Katie, too, but they didn't want to say nothing and I always figured a person should be allowed their privacy if that's what they wanted.

We went fishing a lot, mostly up the Savannah River, even a couple of times way up above Augusta, and we visited some of the old Civil War sites and things like that.

One day Joe said he particularly wanted to go out to a Bethesda orphanage to meet with the kids. That didn't seem like the best thing to do during your offseason but I said I would go along. When we got there the kids was real excited to see Joe, like they always was. Joe started talking about what it was like being a famous baseball player and all, and then all of a sudden, Joe said he had to go and he almost ran out of the place like it was on fire. That didn't make no sense at all to me at the time but I could sure see Joe wasn't his old self.

**KATIE JACKSON** We didn't talk about baseball that winter. It was a scary feeling though, as if we kept expecting somebody to come knock on the door late one night. Every time the phone rang we both tensed up. Every time we looked at the mail we were afraid we were going to find something we didn't want to see. It was a very difficult winter, probably the worst winter of our lives.

Even though Joe hadn't done anything wrong, we both knew he had talked to the boys enough that he was going to have a difficult time explaining his innocence. We were hoping the whole thing would go quietly away, but I think we knew better.

My one pride and joy that winter was the new Singer sewing machine Joe promised me. I went to the Singer shop and picked out the one I liked and the man said he would have it brought around to the house so that I could give it a real try out. Then the New Home Sewing Machine Company found out about this and they also sent over a machine for me to try out. Well, the two companies were so eager to have Mrs. Joe Jackson as a customer, that they even each began cutting their prices below the other one. I really favored the New Home one the best, but Joe thought the Singer had a better reputation and would probably last longer. Then all of a sudden, the Singer man came and took his machine away, and he was kind of mean about it, too. I couldn't figure out why.

I found out later that right in the middle of our negotiations he heard something about Joe and the Series. From that point on, he didn't want to be associated with Joe any more.

As I said, it was a difficult winter.

**CHARLES COMISKEY** Fullerton was publishing articles every other day about the supposed fix. I didn't know for sure who was making money out of this except for him, but he was sure stirring up a mess. So I hired a detective. What else could I do? I told him to find out what he could and report back to me as soon as possible. I certainly didn't want to go into a new season with this mayhem hanging over my head.

During the course of the offseason he reported back to me periodically, but what he gave me wasn't worth a plugged nickel. He said Cicotte was quoted as saying "Don't worry about me. I got mine." Big deal. Gandil apparently was spending money like it was going out of style but all that proved was that I paid him too much for the season.

I specifically asked him about Jackson.

"As far as I can tell," the detective said, "Joe is spending the winter hunting—down around Savannah."

"What does that prove?" I asked him.

"He likes to hunt."

The detective wasn't much help.

**JOE JACKSON** The more the winter went on, the more I figured everybody was forgetting about what happened in the Series. Every day that went by without hearing nothing from the league or from Mr. Comiskey made me feel a little better.

I was hoping the 1920 season could begin like 1919 never happened.

# 49

# PLAYERS DON'T RAT

**CHARLIE LEBEAU** The season of 1920 was one of remarkable change, arguably the single most influential year in all of baseball history.

A new ball arrived on the scene, one that completely changed the way the game would be played from then on. The two manufacturers of major league baseballs, the A.J. Reach Company for the American League and Spalding for the National League, each switched to an Australian yarn which had qualities that allowed them to wind the balls tighter, resulting in balls which were harder than those used previously. This meant that they would travel farther and faster than the old ones, and instantly the home run became an important part of the game. You have got to remember that before 1920, home runs accounted for very few of the runs produced as the emphasis was on "scientific" baseball. But after 1920, the home run became *de rigeur* for the serious ball player and he who could hit them in profusion became lionized.

Enter Babe Ruth. Actually, re-enter Babe Ruth, for in January of 1920, Babe Ruth became a Yankee and with the move, a full-time outfielder. Here was a player who knew how to take advantage of the new ball. And did he ever! In that season alone he hit 54 home runs, not only surpassing his own record of 29, but also that of any other team in the league.

Some people forget that Ruth was a heck of a pitcher before he gave that up for the greater rewards of home run hitting. He had a record of 90 wins and just 39 defeats not to mention a string of 29 consecutive shutout innings in World Series appearances. If it wasn't for that Australian yarn, he might have gone on to become one of the greatest pitchers ever.

But it wasn't just the new ball that made such a difference in 1920. There were a couple of other changes that also helped. The rulers of the baseball realm decided that they would outlaw such trick pitches as the shine ball and the spitball. Oh, they let 17 pitchers continue to throw these pitchers because they had used them for so long that they didn't want to take their livelihood away from them. What they did was to grandfather in a rule which allowed them to throw these pitches legally, but nobody else could, and then when their careers were over, that was it, nobody else could throw them again. The result was that the league ERAs went up dramatically. Still another change was the practice of keeping clean balls in play all the time.

All of these moves led to unprecedented hitting outbursts. I have no doubt that had Joe been beginning his career in 1920, he would have been a prodigious home run hitter. He had the size, he had the swing, he had the power. He could easily have developed the uppercut swing that drove balls over walls. I don't know that he would have hit them like Ruth, but he would have hit plenty. No doubt about it.

**KID GLEASON** Re-signing players for the 1920 season proved to be ridiculously difficult. You would have thought these guys had just swept the Series the way they were demanding more money. Do you believe the gall?

I was having a hell of a time starting spring practice. I didn't have the players. Gandil was demanding $10,000. Jackson, Weaver, Cicotte, Risberg, were all unsigned. Even Dickie Kerr wanted more money—and after only one year in the majors to boot. Well, at least he won something in the Series. That was more than I could say for those other bums!

Early on in spring training, the only veteran signed was Eddie Collins.

**CHICK GANDIL** I was out in Pasadena for the winter. The way I had it figured, the farther away from Chicago I got, the better off for both me and the club. With my feelings for Comiskey, well let's say murder was not out of the question. He sent me one contract that was a joke, so I sent it back to him with a joke written on it that I'm sure it raised his already-high blood pressure a few notches on the old pressure meter. What he made on the Series, win, lose, or draw was enough to keep his family clothed and fed for the next hundred years—at least.

I had an offer to manage a club out in Idaho. Now you tell me how they could afford to pay me more than Comiskey. I mean I was going to manage a bunch of potato farmers and make more than I would have playing for the mighty Chicago damn White Sox! You figure it!

The only way I wanted to see that old skinflint again was in a pine box.

**KID GLEASON** One by one the guys began straggling back into camp. Everyone except Gandil. They all wanted more money and some of them got it, but, of course, in the back of everybody's mind was the thought that they already had gotten all they deserved and more.

Nobody talked about the Series in spring training that I heard. It was more like business as usual—two groups of guys that didn't like each other, and some who didn't like the owner even more. But I had a job to do, and I was going to do it.

When Joe finally reported I made it a point to ask him if he felt he was ready to play. He said he was, and he said it like he meant it.

**BAN JOHNSON** We decided to hire detective agencies in each of our cities to keep track of the known gamblers and any contact they might have with players.

If Jackson or Cicotte or any of the others even smiled at a gambler then we were going to have a picture of it on my desk in the morning.

**KID GLEASON** Maybe the second or third game of the season Joe's in left field and somebody in the stands throws a bottle at him.

"We don't want no cheaters on this team," the guy yells.

He didn't have much of an aim. Didn't even come within a couple of feet of Joe, but Joe could have been hurt if he was a better thrower. So some judge gets all riled up about this.

"A man who throws a bottle might sentence a player to six months in the hospital," he announces. "I recommend that we sentence any such person to six months in jail."

Now that's what I call justice. A guy who throws a game gets nothing. A guy who throws a bottle gets six months.

**EDDIE COLLINS** We got out of the gate like Man o' War. We were playing like everybody said we should and although there wasn't a lot of camaraderie, we were at least not in open warfare. Having Gandil gone certainly didn't hurt.

Shano Collins was playing first base, and while he may not have had Gandil's finesse around the bag, he was doing a credible job. Collins and Collins manned the right side. It was confusing for announcers, but successful for the team.

Joe picked up right where he left off the previous season pushing .400 early on. Weaver was hitting well, I was too. Everything was looking good and nobody was talking much about the recent past.

**JOE JACKSON** We was in a pretty good race with Cleveland when one day they was playing against the New York Americans. Carl Mays, the submarine pitcher for New York, he throws one in too close to Ray Chapman and little Chappie, gets hit right on the side of the head. Well, he goes down right on the spot. They took him off to a hospital for a brain operation, but he didn't make it. He died on the operating table that night.

Boy, did I ever feel bad about that. Chappie was a good guy and I liked him a lot when we played together in Cleveland. He was about the fastest guy around and a great hitting shortstop.

It had to make you think about how dangerous baseball could be.

Mays, he always threw inside. That's how he made his living, but some of the boys, they didn't like him at all because he kept doing that. Players on the Detroit and Boston clubs voted not to play in any games that Mays pitched in. That was kind of funny when you think about it because Ty Cobb was one of the players that shouted the loudest about Mays when everybody said he was such a dangerous player. The league stopped that, though and Mays continued to pitch.

**CARL MAYS** I didn't throw at Chapman on purpose. That's all there is to that. The fact is that an injury to "Chick" Fewster, a club mate in Jacksonville the previous spring had affected me very much. So much so that I had been unable to pitch close to batters for some weeks afterward and I attribute some of my bad pitching that year to my keeping the ball too far outside.

Chapman was one of the hardest men to pitch to. He was little and crouched very low at the plate. In the fifth inning of that game I pitched him a straight ball inside just above the waist. I expected that he would drop as Ruth did when the pitchers threw in close to the big fellow to drive him away from the plate. Instead he ducked and the ball hit him.

**CHARLIE LEBEAU** A lot of people think Chapman was the first professional player to be killed by a baseball, but that just isn't so. He was the first major league player, but not the first professional. Around 1910, I know Kirk Hageman hit and killed a player up in Grand Rapids, and Johnny Dodge, a promising young player, was killed in 1916 while he was playing for Mobile.

I'm sure Chapman's death affected Joe like it did just about every hitter in the game.

**KID GLEASON** There was some talk on our team about not taking the field against Mays again but that was coward talk. I told our guys we would face Mays anytime he was sent out there and that we would go after him just like any other pitcher.

Not too long after the incident, we made a trip to New York for a three-game series against the New Yorkers, and Mays was lined up against Cicotte in the second game. We lost in extra innings, but nothing exceptional happened. Oh, a couple of hecklers got on some of our players a little for being a bit loosey-goosey in the box, but Joe came in for special attention because to some, Joe would always have the "coward" label firmly affixed.

**EDDIE COLLINS** You better believe we were all shocked when Chappie died but we also knew the race must go on and they were a formidable team with or without Chapman. Still, we had to believe we had a little leg up going down the stretch.

If it hadn't been for the grand jury I think we would have run away with the whole thing.

**HARTLEY REPLOGLE** In 1920 I was an assistant State Attorney in Illinois, and acting on requests from Charles Comiskey and other baseball officials, I convened a grand jury for the purpose of investigating corruption in baseball—not just the 1919 Series, but any hint of intentional wrongdoing.

Initially we looked into a report that a player on the Chicago Cubs offered Rube Benton, then a pitcher for the Giants, $800 to lose a game to the Chicago Cubs. Then we turned our attention to the not-so-quiet whispers of the White Sox fix. All summer, stories continued to surface and they didn't go easily away.

Comiskey had offered money for proof of a fix but had come up empty-handed. Still the stories persisted—too many stories from too many sources to be readily dismissed. It was said six to eight members of the Sox were involved. Depended on who you talked to, the names varied.

It fell on me to get to the bottom of the issue once and for all. For the good of the game, we simply had to either find and punish the guilty or clear the names of the implicated innocent.

We began with a rumor about Rube Benton. That seemed like a simpler issue than the Series fiasco.

**RUBE BENTON** Here are the facts as I told them to the grand jury.

On the evening before the game in question, Buck Herzog, Hal Chase, and myself stopped in a cafe near La Salle and Madison Street.

Buck and Hal asked me if I wanted to make some "easy money" but no amount was mentioned by either of them.

I asked them what they meant. They said they wanted to see the Cubs win the game with the Giants the next day, and that it rested entirely with me. Of course I refused to consider the proposition.

Then Buck left us and Hal and I went to our hotel.

Anybody could look it up and see that the Giants won that game by a score of 6 to 3.

I didn't know anything about the rumor of crookedness among the other clubs.

That's all I had to tell the grand jury. That is the end of my story.

**BAN JOHNSON** To make a bad situation even worse, rumors began circulating that the White Sox would not dare win the pennant in 1920 because the managers of a gambling syndicate had certain Chicago players on their payroll and had forbidden it.

The gamblers were said to have backed Cleveland heavily, in what was turning out to be an extremely tight race.

I talked to Joe and Buck and a few of the others about this but, of course, they denied it. I wanted them to know, however, that I was watching, and I was.

Our biggest worry: if we didn't force the gamblers out of the game, there would soon be no game to worry about. If that meant we might be unfair to one or more players in the process, then so be it. The survival of the game would just have to take precedence over the rights of the individual. It was a matter of the greatest good for the greatest numbers.

**JOE JACKSON** One time when I was playing with the Spinners I remember I was running for a low line drive in short center. Well I dived for the ball but misjudged it some and landed on the ball. It pushed so hard into my stomach that it just took all the breath out of me. For what seemed like forever, I couldn't breathe. It was about the worst feeling in the world. I thought I was going to die right then and there and I've never forgotten that feeling.

Well, when I heard they was putting a jury together to investigate the 1919 World Series, it was just like that feeling all over again.

I don't know why they just didn't leave it alone. We was all playing hard. Bringing all that stuff up again just made it hard to concentrate on baseball.

**HARTLEY REPLOGLE** It was our intention to call a long list of witnesses—men outside the game who allegedly had knowledge of, or active involvement in the Series fix. The players we would call last when we had a better idea exactly who was involved and who wasn't.

One of our first witnesses was Abe Attell, the ex-boxer. He spewed out a long, convoluted story of deals, counter deals, sub deals and cross ups, the upshot of which went something like this: he claimed the deal was for $100,000 in installments of $15,000 after the Sox lost the first game, $20,000 on the morning of the third day, $25,000 on the fourth morning, and the balance after the Series ended. He swore, however, that in actuality only $15,000 was ever turned over because he claimed to have personally held out on the rest.

Then later in his testimony he came up with slightly different numbers. He was anything but a reliable witness.

It was his understanding that five White Sox players were in on the deal, and that four members of the team were known to be honest beyond question. Two pitchers, two outfielders and an infielder were involved. He refused to name them.

**CHARLES COMISKEY** The way the whole thing was handled was a complete farce and for that I lay the blame clearly at the feet on one man—Ban Johnson. Had he acted decisively and with conviction this thing wouldn't have dragged out forever in the press like it did, and baseball would have been spared any more humiliation than it already had. But that wasn't his style, was it? The fact is I had told Gleason to yank any ballplayer who did not appear to be doing his best. Then I heard a story that a gambler in East St. Louis had been crossed by other gamblers and had lost $5,500 on the Series. He said he would tell the story of the alleged frame up if he could get his $5,500 back.

I sent Gleason to East St. Louis and offered to pay the money to the man in question if he would give me the information, but to no avail.

All the while Johnson did nothing, and I do mean nothing.

I had faith though, that the investigation would be thorough in its scope even if it took long night sessions as the grand jury had promised.

**H.H. BRIGHTMAN** I was foreman of the Cook County grand jury investigating alleged baseball gambling. It was a long, grueling process, believe you me, with scores of people interviewed, often with lots of conflicting evidence. You would think that if you asked someone under oath to tell a story you would get an accurate one, but we heard so many versions of stories that our heads were spinning. Everybody was out to be the good guy in his own story.

Anyway by late in September, while the pennant race was still going strong, we had the name of the man we believed had arranged the fix. He was Arnold Rothstein of New York, a well-known turf man. We had him subpoenaed along with a William Burns, former Chicago American and Cincinnati National League pitcher, and several other well-known boxing gamblers.

We also had the names of three players we thought were involved.

**EDDIE COLLINS** By late September, we were in the middle of one of the tightest races of our baseball lives. On August 25$^{th}$, with 9 games to go we were tied with Speaker's Cleveland men in the win column, but three down in the loss column.

Then came the bombshell from which we never recovered. The papers that day printed the names of the players they believed were involved in the fix: Weaver, Felsch, Williams, Risberg, Gandil, Cicotte, McMullin and Jackson.

We never recovered. What was supposedly one of the greatest teams in history was through in a complete freefall.

**HUGH FULLERTON** There it was for all and sundry to see—the names of the guilty, in capital letters. For a nickel anyone could read the names of the villains, could call down upon their heads the wrath of whoever oversaw such transgressions, could swear eternal damnation upon the souls of the infidels.

Make no mistake about it, there was one name which stood tall above the rest, one Joseph Jefferson Jackson. The others were baseball players. Joe was more. He was an American icon, a backwoods illiterate rustic who rose to the top through hard work and dedication, the very image of the American dream.

The other might—just might—be forgiven, or better yet, be forgotten. But not Joe. Not Shoeless Joe, the war dodger.

**BUCK WEAVER** Unless you have been through it like I have, you have no idea what it's like picking up the papers every morning and seeing that somebody else has called you a crook or a liar, or worse.

Joe wasn't spared either. Maybe he couldn't read, but he sure as hell wasn't deaf.

Even though we didn't do anything to throw those games, Joe and me, it was the roughest time of my life, and I suspect of his, too.

I didn't want to talk to anybody, didn't want to look them in the eyes, didn't want to know what they were thinking. Everybody I saw on the street, I thought was talking about me.

My crime, my only crime was talking to some rotten apples about their illegal schemes. I did not throw the 1919 Series. Neither did Joe. What they did to us was as wrong as what Chick and Lefty and the others did. They ruined our lives.

**J. C. HATCH** When word got back to Greenville about Joe's being implicated in the fixing scandal, it was as if a pall had descended over the entire area. Joe was ours. His successes were our successes. His triumphs were shared by us all. Well maybe I should say "most" rather than "all" for there are always those who are jealous of the successful. Most of us followed Joe's career like he was one of our own sons. We were a small town without a lot of things to brag about, but we had Joe and he had carried our flag with honor and grace. In a big city he would have just been another example of a successful citizen but in a little village, largely uneducated and hardworking, he represented the possibilities few even dreamed of.

At Harrison's and just about every other place in town, Joe was once again the primary topic of conversation. Most didn't believe he could have been involved, some feared the worst but prayed for the best. A few said they could see it coming.

Once they convened that grand jury, there were stories in the papers every day, and everybody in town followed the saga as if it were another installment in one of those never-ending, long-running stories the Sunday paper carried.

**LUTHER JACKSON** Some people in town, they wanted to see Joe fail, and they liked it when the papers started saying he was a cheater.

**HARTLEY REPLOGLE** Our list of subpoenas began to look as long as the Manhattan telephone directory. It might have been easier to have made a list of those who were not going to testify. One aspect of these hearings was made very clear to us: no Chicago players would be called until after the season was over.

No sooner was that determined than Ray Schalk came to me and said he wanted to come before us and tell us what he knew without waiting for a subpoena.

Like so much of what we heard, Schalk offered no hard evidence. What he said, in essence, was that he didn't believe some of the players were trying their best in the series, and he named names.

**JOE JACKSON** Ray should never have gone to the grand jury the way he done. Players don't rat on other players, especially when they don't even know what the truth is.

**KID GLEASON** I had games to manage, and this jury business was nothing but one long distraction. I announced to the press that I knew nothing of any player throwing the series and had no intention of saying another word on the subject.

This wasn't exactly true, but for my part, I had to get the attention of the team back on the pennant race and off legal issues.

Late in September, we played a crucial series against Cleveland. Dickie Kerr went out and won the first game for us with another of his gutsy performances, but we dropped the second despite a good performance by Red Faber. In the final game of the series, Joe took matters into his own hands, slamming out three hits, including a long home run over the right field fence. Joe raised his average to .387 and brought us to within a half game of Cleveland.

**VINCENT ALEXANDER** On September 26th, Eddie Cicotte pitched a strong game beating Detroit 8-1, but the Sox were unable to pick up any ground as Cleveland topped St. Louis. Joe was 0 for 4. The next day, the Sox still trailing Cleveland by 1/2 game faced the Tigers again. It was their final home game of the season. Dickie Kerr and Hooks Dauss were locked in a scoreless pitching duel when, in the sixth inning, the Sox broke through for two runs. After Dauss hit Weaver, Eddie Collins and Joe each knocked out long singles driving in the runs. Those two runs held up the rest of the way as the game was played in a brisk one hour and 15 minutes.

It was the last major league game Joe ever played.

# 50

# EVERYBODY WAS TALKING

**EDDIE CICOTTE** After the stories hit about Billy Maharg's testimony before the grand jury, where he supposedly laid out the whole bollixed up mess, I went to see Comiskey. I went all the way out to his house and told him Maharg's story was pretty much on the mark. I told him who was involved, or at least who was in on the meetings when we made the plans.

Everything was coming down on us pretty hard, and there were as many different stories being written in the papers as there were people writing about them. We couldn't go anyplace without being pressured about the Series. We couldn't talk to the press, we couldn't talk to other players, we couldn't eat a meal in a restaurant without somebody saying something about the fix. I was so nervous all the time that I thought the best thing was to tell my story and get it over and done with. There was no hiding it any more. The sooner I could tell the truth, the sooner the pressure would be off, and the sooner I could get on with my life. Other people had been involved in crooked games and had gone on to successful careers. It wasn't that big of a deal. It wasn't as if I had assassinated the president or something. I didn't play my best in a game, that's all. I wanted to get it behind me as fast as I could.

The old skinflint took it better than I thought. He listened quietly as I told him what happened. I didn't know the whole story, because it got so screwed up, but I told him what I knew. When I was done, he said that he would set up a meeting with Alfred Austrian, the attorney for the White Sox, and that there was nothing to worry about, that the team would look out for me, that as long as I was a member of the White Sox, they would represent me legally in court on any baseball-related issues.

He called Mr. Austrian and we arranged to meet him at his office right away. It was clear that here was an important attorney. I could tell by the expensive-looking downtown offices. I was still a little shocked that Mr. Comiskey was taking this all as well as he was.

Mr. Austrian's exact words were: "Don't worry. We will take care of you. Everything will be all right."

He asked me about the other players involved, and I told him. I told him Chick, Swede, Happy, Lefty and Freddy. I also told him Buck and Joe because they were involved with it whether they did anything wrong in the games or not.

He told me it was his advice to sign the waiver of immunity that he put in front of me. He was representing my best interests he told me, so I signed it.

As you might imagine, I didn't sleep much that night, so I was pretty tired when at 11:30 the next morning Mr. Austrian met me in front of the Criminal Courts Building. He said that he appreciated me coming down without having to be subpoenaed. I told him I just wanted to tell the truth and get it all over with. He said he could understand that.

I waited in this waiting room for a while with Mr. Austrian. He didn't say much, just to not be too nervous and tell the truth.

"As my lawyer, do you think I should not answer some things?" I asked him.

"My advice is to tell the truth. We'll see that everything works out all right," he said.

After a while someone came and asked me to follow him into the courtroom.

"Go ahead," said Mr. Austrian. "I'll talk to you later."

"Aren't you coming with me?" I asked really shocked.

"You'll be all right," he said and walked out the other door.

**H.H. BRIGHTMAN** Cicotte's testimony was hard to listen to. He became extremely emotional telling us his version of what had happened. Several times during his testimony he cried.

"My God! think of my children," he said. "I never did anything I regretted so much in my life. I would give anything in the world if I could undo my acts in the last World Series. I've played a crooked game and I have lost, and I am here to tell the whole truth. I've lived a thousand years in this last year."

Then he told us how he accomplished the deed.

"In the first game at Cincinnati I was knocked out of the box. I wasn't putting a thing on the ball. You could have read the trademark on it when I lobbed it up to the plate. In the fourth game I deliberately intercepted a throw from the outfield which might have cut off a run. I muffed the ball on purpose. Another time in the same game I purposely made a wild throw."

He went on with a few other examples like that. He sounded like he knew exactly what he was talking about. None of us were really surprised by what he said because we had heard so many stories and rumors but to hear it live from the mouth of such a famous player, well that was quite another thing. It was a very emotional morning in court.

He told us Chick Gandil was the ring leader but that they had been double-crossed and never received all the money they were promised.

It was truly an amazing spectacle—Cicotte's testimony. The room was jam packed but other than Cicotte's hushed words, there wasn't a sound to be heard.

When asked what other players were involved, he had a hard time spitting their names out. He took a long time between names, and said them so quietly that he had to be asked to repeat them louder. Joe Jackson was one of the players he said was involved, but he said it like he wasn't real sure. When questioned about that, he said he never talked individually to Jackson about it himself, but that Gandil insisted he had and claimed Jackson was in on it and since Gandil was the organizer, Cicotte assumed he knew what he was talking about.

**JOE JACKSON** My stomach was jumping around like butterflies on a spring morning. I didn't know what to do. Every place I went people were talking about the fix. I wanted to talk to Katie, but she was back home in Savannah, and I didn't know who to trust. I didn't have nobody to talk to.

Eddie was with the grand jury but I didn't know what he was saying. I was afraid maybe he was saying I throwed some of the games. Some people wanted to believe that. I knowed that as well as I knowed my name.

There are probably things in everybody's life that they would change if they could, and I would change going to them meetings about throwing games if I could. I would do anything to go back and not go to those meetings, but at the time I didn't think nothing about it. I didn't think anything would happen.

When I heard about Eddie talking, I went to this bar where I sometimes went to have a drink. I didn't know what else to do.

This was kind of a quiet neighborhood friendly type of bar, and although Billy, the bartender, knowed who I was, he usually just let me drink in peace and didn't bother me about baseball or nothing. Back in the corner there was a booth where a guy could sit without being seen by anybody else in the bar, so that's where I went.

Billy came over with my usual drink without me even having to ask for it.

"I didn't see you, Joe," he said. "But I'm around if you need anything. If you need anything, I'll be here."

"I need another drink" I said.

"Done," he said and returned to the bar to get me another.

I was never a real big drinker, not what you would call a serious drinker, like some of the boys, but that day, I had more than just a few.

I didn't know what else to do. Not that liquor made it any better really, but it was all I could think of.

If Eddie was talking then the whole story would be out, but what story? Everybody had a different one. I kept thinking that maybe I should go and tell my story like Eddie was doing. At least then it would be told right. But people didn't always believe what I said because I didn't talk like a college professor or something.

I would have talked to Ty, but I didn't know where he was. Ty was a man who got himself into trouble a couple of times, and he got out of it.

The more I drank and the more I thought about it, the more different stories kept coming into my head. Maybe we was going to be sent to prison. Maybe they was going to take away my house and do something to Katie

When Billy came back over with a drink I said to him, "I didn't do nothing, Billy, but they're saying I did."

"Aw, nobody believes them," said Billy. "They're all leeches. You're the one that plays the game. They just want to make money off of you, that's all. You're the one that plays the game, and you play it maybe better than anybody else has ever played it. You're the great Shoeless Joe, don't forget that."

"They want to get me, Billy," I said. "That's what they want to do."

"They won't touch you, Joe. You're the one that brings fans to the games, not them. You're too famous for them to do anything to. Why, can you imagine what your fans would do if they try to do anything to you?"

"I have a lot of fans, don't I, Billy?"

"Of course, you do."

"But not like Babe Ruth."

"You have millions of fans."

"And I've been a good, clean player."

"They're not going to touch you, Joe. Maybe some of the other guys, they're not as important as you to the game. Maybe they'll get them, but not you, Joe, not the Great Shoeless Joe. Never. No way."

Billy was all right.

I got pretty stiffed that night, but that was OK because the next day was a day off. I woke up the next morning with one helluvah hangover but more confused than ever.

I didn't know what I was going to do all day. I didn't think talking to any of the other players was a good idea but for a while I thought about trying to get a hold of Lefty, only I didn't do that.

I figured since I was already hungover, I might as well make myself another drink or two. Things couldn't get a lot worse.

I saw Happy and Swede later that morning. Happy sure didn't look like his name no more. I didn't exactly talk to them, but Swede looked at me like he would kill me if he could. "Nobody's singing around here, Joe, understand?" he said.

I didn't say nothing, but I knew what he was talking about. Except it looked like Eddie was.

I made another drink and headed for the White Sox offices. I didn't know what else to do. I figured the White Sox needed me to keep playing for them so they would look after me. Why wouldn't they? I played good for them and we were in the middle of a hot pennant chase.

I needed to talk to somebody who would tell me what I should do.

When I got to the offices, Mr. Comiskey was there. I told him I needed to talk to somebody about what was happening. He took me right away over to an empty office in the courtroom building where Mr. Austrian was. He had on a gray suit with a vest and a big gold chain hanging across the front. He was the big shot lawyer for the team. That made me feel a little better right away. I needed somebody on my side who knew how to handle things like was going on. I didn't know how to do that. Why should I? I was from a mill town in South Carolina, and I never learned about those things. Maybe somebody like Eddie Plank or any of them other college boys had that kind of training, but I never did.

"Joe, I'm here to help you," he said.

That's what I wanted to hear. That's exactly what I wanted to hear.

"Are you going to confess, Joe? Is that's why you're here? You want to confess?"

I told him that I didn't have nothing to confess, that all I wanted to do was to tell what I knowed. I told Mr. Austrian that I tried to do that right from the start. I told him about trying to talk to Mr. Comiskey when I got the money, but how he refused to talk to me about it. I told him that I tried to give the money back, but I was told to go ahead and keep it. I told him about how I had Katie write letters to Mr. Comiskey, but I never got no answers.

Mr. Austrian said that the White Sox would take care of me, but that it was important that I told the truth. I told him I was telling the truth.

"Eddie Cicotte has already told the jury everything, Joe. He's told them the whole story from start to finish. It will go bad for you if you don't tell the truth," he said.

"Did he say I was involved?"

"He did, Joe. He said you were involved. The jury knows the whole story."

"But I wasn't," I insisted. "I talked about it some, I'll admit that, but I didn't do nothing. I didn't do nothing to throw that Series. Look at the record."

Then he said something that at the time I thought was real strange seeing as how he was representing the team and all. He said he didn't watch the Series, that, in fact, he didn't watch baseball at all.

So then I told him he could ask anybody who knowed anything about baseball if it looked like I throwed the series. I played about better than anybody and that was clear to everybody who knowed anything at all about the game.

"Everybody says I'm going to get into trouble, Mr. Austrian," I told him, "and that ain't right, because I don't deserve to get into trouble."

"You're not going to get into any trouble if you tell exactly what you know," he said, "because that's the only way we've got to protect you—by telling the truth."

I told him I'd tell the truth, but I wasn't sure if everybody would believe me.

"They'll believe the truth."

"Some people think that because I can't read, that means everything I say is wrong."

"You work for the Chicago White Sox Baseball Club, Joe, and we take care of our own. Mr. Comiskey is an honest man, and he wants to treat his players fairly."

That should have told me something right there, because we all knew that wasn't always true.

"Why are they doing this?" I asked him. "Why are they making all this trouble?"

"The State doesn't want you," he said. "The State wants the gamblers. They want to get them out of baseball once and for all. It's the gamblers, Joe, they're after, not an outstanding player like you."

He said, in fact, the State would really appreciate my help in cleaning out the gamblers, that I was doing the State a big favor. He said I would be more popular with the fans than ever for helping to get the bad guys out of the game.

I didn't know nothing about grand juries or subpoenas or indictments or things like that I told him.

He said he would take care of me. He said that several times, but he also said I was going to have to testify to the grand jury. Then knowing I couldn't read it, he put a piece of paper in front of me, and handed me a pen.

"Just sign it, Joe," he said. "I need it for the hearing."

"What is it?" I asked.

"Don't worry about it, Joe. It doesn't change a darn thing. It's just a formality. If you hadn't come in today I would have called you in to sign it in a couple of days. But since you're here now you might as well sign it now."

"I don't want to sign nothing until Katie reads it."

He asked if she was outside the room. I told him she was in Savannah.

"We can't wait for her to get here. Just sign it, Joe."

We were in this big empty room, and I felt like I just wanted to run out the door and go as fast and as far as I could.

"It's something all the witnesses sign. Now just sign it and let's get on with this."

"I don't think I should until Katie reads it," I told him again.

"Look Joe," he said to me over the top of his glasses, "do you or do you not want me to keep you out of trouble?"

"That's what I want," I said.

"Then either sign it now or find yourself another lawyer. I've got better things to do than argue with those people I'm trying to help."

I drew my signature. Mr. Austrian picked up the paper and walked out of the room.

**CHARLIE LEBEAU** No one will ever convince me that Joe's fate was not determined by that meeting with Austrian. If he had honest legal and moral advice I believe he would have come away from what followed relatively unscathed. As it was he was a confused, slightly inebriated, unsophisticated young man, who once again, could not adequately sift through the advice being leveled at him.

Austrian was an impressive, articulate and extremely clever high-priced attorney. Of course Joe was swayed by his arguments. Joe was looking for an answer and Austrian gave him one which on the surface, looked like it was heaven sent, an answer to a prayer.

That Austrian was a liar and a masterful manipulator probably never crossed Joe's mind. The package was too perfect—the air of authority, the language of knowledge, the guise of respectability.

If you ask me, it's Austrian and Comiskey who should have suffered the punishments of the damned. Their sins were far greater than Joe's. They portrayed themselves as saviors, then they fixed the game in a way Joe never dreamed of, and lied their way to admiration.

All Joe did was play his heart out in the series and then tell the truth, or at least he tried to tell the truth.

**HARTLEY REPLOGLE** Austrian brought Joe down to the judge's chambers and told us Joe was ready to talk. Judge MacDonald warned Joe that he would put up with no shenanigans in his courtroom. As if he were talking to a little child, he asked Joe if he understood that. Joe answered that all he wanted to do was tell the truth.

Joe looked like he had slept in his suit and smelled like he might have fortified himself with a drink or two before his ordeal. He hardly looked like the man of heroic stature who roamed the outfield as if he were born to it. Maybe celebrities never live up to their glorified images, I don't know. But Joe looked almost pathetic. He was terrified. There is a certain satisfaction we lawyers sometimes take in bringing someone to their knees in front of an open-mouthed jury. I'll readily admit to that, but seeing Joe sitting in the judge's chambers frightened of the unknown and totally alone, I decided then and there to take it easy on him. There would be no glory in beating him down any further than he already was.

**JOE JACKSON** Walking towards that courtroom was like walking down a long tunnel lined with millions of people. Flash bulbs was popping all over the place so that I had to cover my eyes with my hands. Everybody was shouting questions at me all at the same time. It was loud and noisy and confusing. I never played in no stadium that was so loud and rowdy in my life. Or as angry either.

**HUGH FULLERTON** As he walked the gauntlet to the courtroom, Joe hung his head and covered his face with his hands. Replogle did his best to try to keep the cameramen at bay. They forcefully refused, punctuating their objections amid a volley of flashes. Jackson cursed newspapermen, gamblers, and baseball as he fled to the security of the jury room. Or maybe he didn't and I just imagined he should have.

**HARTLEY REPLOGLE** Joe took the stand looking more like a frightened German soldier at the bottom of a foxhole than he did a heroic athlete, which at that moment he clearly was not.

I began by asking him perfunctory questions about his background, his early years in baseball, things like that—anything I could think of to try to get him to relax a bit. He answered the questions in a slow southern drawl that was all but inaudible at times.

The room was packed and hot, but everybody and I do mean everybody, was attentive to his every word.

Since it looked to me as if everyone in the room was suspicious that Joe had been drinking, I broached the subject indirectly.

"Do you drink much, Mr. Jackson?" I asked.

"Now and then, but I don't make no regular practice of it," he answered.

"Do you get drunk?"

"No, sir."

This brought a few audible smirks from the assembled.

"Have you been drunk since you have been with the Chicago White Sox team?" I continued.

"Yes, sir."

"During the playing season?"

"Yes, sir."

"Where?"

"Atlantic City."

"You were not playing?"

"Off days," he volunteered.

"Did Mr. Comiskey or Mr. Gleason know you were drunk at the time?"

"I don't judge they did, no sir."

"Who was with you when you got drunk?"

"Claude Williams, John Fornier and myself."

"That was some years ago."

"A couple"

"You haven't been drunk since?"

"Not what you would call drunk, no."

It appeared to me that Joe was going to be both forthright and polite. I danced around the subject of the Series for some time, which in retrospect I guess probably just made him more nervous although certainly that wasn't my intent.

"Who was your best chum on the team?" I asked him. "Who did you go with on the club?"

"Mostly Williams and Lynn. I hardly ever pal with any of them except those two."

"Who did Gandil pal with mostly on the team?"

"Risberg."

"Who did McMullin pal with mostly on the team?"

"I cannot recall who McMullin roomed with."

"Who did he go with?"

"You would see him with Charlie and sometimes Chick, quite a bit."

Finally I got down to it. I asked him if he was present at a meeting at the Ansonia Hotel in New York with the other players in question some two or three weeks before the Series began. He said he was not although this directly contradicted testimony we had earlier heard.

I asked him if his contract with the Sox called for him to make $6,000 as had been generally reported. He said that actually it was $8000.

"What part of the money did you get when you were sold by Cleveland to Comiskey?" I asked, trying to raise a response consistent with what we had heard—that some of the players by participating in the fix were attempting to exact revenge against a penurious Comiskey.

"I think they gave me $1,000 out of the sale," Joe responded.

"That's all you got out of it, just $1,000?" I prompted again.

"Yes."

"Do you know how much Mr. Comiskey paid the Cleveland Club for you?"

"I do not, no, sir."

"You knew it was a big sum of money, did you?"

"So they said."

"You were satisfied with $8,000 a year, were you?"

"That's all I could get out of them."

"Did you get $8,000 in 1919?"

"I believe they gave me $6,000."

"That also includes all your expenses on the trips, doesn't it?"

He admitted his salary covered railroad fare and room and board on the road, but he didn't suggest he was angry about that.

"You were pretty well satisfied with that weren't you?" I asked stating the obvious.

"They wouldn't give me any more, that's all you could get. I was pretty lucky to get a contract like that with them when I come over here."

I continued the questioning by asking him about a meeting we had heard about that supposedly took place at the Warner Hotel. He insisted he was not at that meeting either but that he heard about it from Williams after the fact.

"He told me about it," Joe said. "He said the gang was there, and this fellow Abe something and Bill Burns."

Joe continued to insist he was not privy to the meetings of the other alleged fixers, but that he knew about them and he knew of their plans for the series fix.

"They asked me would I consider $10,000?" Joe said. "And I said no, then they offered me twenty."

"Who mentioned it first to you?" I asked.

"Gandil." Joe responded without missing a beat.

"Who was with you?"

"We was all alone."

"What did he say?"

"He asked me would I consider $10,000 to frame up something and I asked him what? And he told me and I said no."

"What did he say?"

"Just walked away from me, and when I returned here to Chicago he told me that he would give me twenty and I said no again, and on the bridge where you go into the club house he told me I could either take it or let it alone because they was going through with it."

Joe said he talked to both Gandil and Williams and that his understanding was that they were offering him $20,000 if he took part in the fix.

"And you said you would?" I asked him very directly and clearly.

His answer was a simple, "Yes, sir."

"And you were to be paid $5,000 after each game, is that right?

"Well, the Abe fella was supposed to give the $100,000. It was to be split up and paid to Gandil, I believe and $15,000 a day or something like that, after each game."

"At the end of the first game you didn't get any money, did you?"

"No, I did not, no, sir."

"Then you went ahead and threw the second game, thinking you would get it then, is that right?"

When I questioned him further about this he seemed not to really know whether anybody actually threw a game or not. He knew that possibility was discussed. He knew some money had changed hands. He knew there was a major screw up on the gambling issue. He knew it was uncertain going into the Series exactly who was going to do what for how much. I think he also had genuine confusion about how much he was actually involved. It seemed to me, that if Joe was telling the truth, he was involved to some degree, but that he really didn't know the whole story. He was either never fully informed or he failed to fully grasp exactly what was going on with this whole sordid affair. It was like he had some of the pieces of a giant jigsaw puzzle, but he had no idea what the picture was supposed to look like when all the pieces were in place

"Did you ever talk to Buck Weaver about it?"

"No, sir, I never talked to Buck Weaver very much."

"Did you know at the time Buck was in on the deal?"

"They told me he was; he never told me himself."

"Who told you?"

"Chick told me."

"Did Mrs. Jackson ever talk to Mrs. Weaver about it, that you know of?"

"No, sir, not that I know of, no sir."

"Is Mrs. Jackson a friend of Mrs. Weaver's?"

"They are all chummy there on the ball ground. Most of the ballplayers' wives sit together."

"Who did Mrs. Jackson sit with most?"

"Mrs. Williams and her sit together."

"Did Mrs. Jackson talk to Mrs. Williams about it?"

"Not that I know of."

"Did Mrs. Williams ever talk to Mrs. Jackson about it?"

"They never talked about it when I was around. I don't know what they did when I wasn't around."

I was doing my best to try to adopt a non-threatening persona, but make no doubt about it, Joe was taking it as a threat. Several times before answering a question he looked around, as if he were waiting for help, but if he was expecting Austrian or some other White Sox attorney to step to the fore, he was sadly disappointed. They were nowhere to be found. Joe was alone in the chair. I suspect more alone than he had ever been.

I began pressing him a bit about Atell and Burns. He insisted he never met Atell but he had been acquainted with Burns briefly while Burns was still a ballplayer. He admitted he talked with Burns on the day the Series began. I asked him about the conversation.

"How is everything? I asked him," Joe said. "And he said everything was fine. Then he told me about this stuff and I didn't know so much. He walked away from me. I didn't know enough to talk to him about what they were going to plan or what they had planned. I only knew what I been told, that's all I knew."

I decided it was time to move on to the critical questions. I asked him point-blank if he was ever paid any money to throw the Series. At the time I was neither sure of the correct answer or whether he would supply one, although without counsel to confer with, I should have had no doubt.

He brought the room to a dead silence by stating clearly that he had been given $5,000. He said the money was given to him by Lefty Williams in his hotel room at the Lexington Hotel.

When I asked him who was in the room at the time he said that he was there alone when Williams came in, but that Mrs. Jackson was in the bathroom.

"What did you say to Williams when he threw down the $5,000?" I asked.

"I asked him what the hell had come off here," Joe said.

He then went on to tell me that he thought the whole thing was a cross up.

"You think Gandil may have gotten the money and held it from you, is that right?" I asked.

"That's what I think. I think he kept the majority of it."

When I asked him what he did with the money he said he put it in his pocket.

"What denominations, in silver or bills?"

"In bills."

"How big were some of the bills?"

"Some hundreds, mostly fifties."

"Did Mrs. Jackson know that you got $5,000 for helping throw those games? I asked.

"She did that night, yes," said Joe.

"What did she say about it?" I continued.

"She said she thought it was an awful thing to do. She felt awful bad about it, cried about it for a while."

"Did it ever occur to you to tell about this before now?"

"Yes. I offered to come here last fall. I would have told it last fall if they would of brought me in."

I asked him if he was talking to us now of his own free will. He insisted he was, but looking at him, he looked more like Joan on the way to the fire than a man acting on his own volition. I asked him what he did with the money and he told a story about going to the team's office but being told to go home.

"Did you ever ask Williams where he got this $5,000?"

"Yes."

"What did he say?"

"Up at Gandil's apartment, he said."

When I asked him who he thought came up with the idea of the fix in the first place, without even stopping to think he responded that he thought it was Gandil. He said he thought Burns and Abe first approached Gandil.

"He was the whole works of it," Joe offered. "The fellow that mentioned it to me. He told me I could take it or let it go, they were going through with it."

"Did you tell anyone you wanted out?"

"I said I was not going to be in. I would just get out of that altogether," Joe said.

"Who did you tell that to?"

"Chick Gandil."

"What did he say?"

"He said I was into it already and I might as well stay in. I said, 'I can go to the boss and have every damn one of you pulled out of the limelight.' He said it wouldn't be well for me if I did that."

"What did you say?"

"Well, I told him any time they wanted to have me knocked off, to have me knocked off."

"What did he say?"

"Just laughed."

"When did that conversation take place?"

"After the fourth game. I met Chick Gandil and his wife going to the 12th Street Station. They got out of a cab there. I was standing on the corner."

It appeared to me at that point in the questioning that Joe had been approached by Gandil and others to throw the Series, that he knew of the conspiracy and of the conspirators, that he had been given $5,000 toward that end. The big question then remaining was, what, if anything did he do to help lose the Series?

"Did you do anything to throw those games? I finally asked him directly.

"No sir."

"Any game in the Series?"

"Not a one. I didn't have an error or make no misplay."

"Did you bat to win?"

"Yes, sir."

"And fielded the balls at the outfield to win?"

"I did."

"Supposing the White Sox would have won this Series, the World Series, what would you have done with the $5,000?"

"I guess I would have kept it. That was all I could do. I tried to win all the time."

On further questioning, Joe seemed unclear about exactly what was done by whom to lose the games. I asked him if he could recall any specific plays or incidents in any of the games that would indicate the games were being lost on purpose.

"No, sir, I didn't see any plays that I thought was throwing the games," he insisted. When I went through the lost games one by one he mentioned a couple of possibly suspect things—Cicotte's cutting off a throw to the plate in the fourth game, the wildness of Cicotte and Williams. He seemed genuinely to not know exactly what was going on in the games with reference to purposeful misplays.

When pressed, the only other thing he could come up with was a possible botched double play attempt by Risberg but he couldn't remember in which game it occurred.

"It looked like a perfect double play," he said. "And he gets only one, gets the ball and runs over to the bag with it in place of throwing it in front of the bag."

"After the Series was over," I continued, "did you have any talk with any of these men?"

"No, sir, I left the next night for Savannah, Georgia."

"Weren't you very much peeved that you only got $5,000."

"No, I was ashamed of myself."

"When was the last time you saw and talked to Chick Gandil?"

"It was on the following morning after the Series was over, that day in Comiskey's office, waiting in there."

"What did you say to him at that time?"

"I told him there was a hell of a lot of scandal going around for what had happened. He said, 'To hell with it.' He was about half drunk. I went on out and left that night."

"Did you ever talk to Happy Felsch since that time, about those games?"

"Yes, I know I did. I told him they would have him down before the grand jury before long, the way things looked."

"What did he say?"

"He said all right."

"Do you know whether or not he received some of this money?"

"I don't know that he received any more than what the boys said."

"What did the boys say about him?"

"They said each fellow got so much money."

"Did they say how much?"

"$5,000 I understand."

I asked him in turn about each of the alleged fixers and whether he ever talked to them about how much each man got. He said Cicotte admitted he got more—$10,000.

"Did you talk to McMullin?

"Very little. I never talked to Mac any more than to just say hello."

"Did you ever ask him how much he got?"

"Yes."

"What did he say?"

"Never made me any answer, he just walked right out."

"Did you ever ask Charlie how much he got?"

"Yes."

"What did he say?"

"Asked me how much I got."

"What did you tell him?"

"Told him."

"What did he say?"

"He said, 'I guess that's all I got."

"Did you believe him at the time?"

"No sir. I think he was telling a damn lie."

"What did Williams say when you asked him?"

"He said he got $5,000."

"You think he gave you the truth?"

"No sir, I do not."

"What do you think?"

"I think those fellows cut it up to suit themselves, what little they did have."

"Who is this?"

"This gang."

"What gang?"

"Charlie."

"Who else?"

"McMullin and Williams."

"Who else?"

"Cicotte. They were gambling."

I noted at the time, that he continually omitted Weaver from the list of conspirators. It also seemed, from Joe's testimony at least, that he wasn't really a part of the clique that fixed the Series, that he wasn't ever part on the inner circle. I asked him if he had heard from Gandil since he had been on the coast. He said he had not.

"Have you talked to Claude Williams about it since the Series."

"We have talked about it once or twice, yes."

"What did you say to him and what did he say to you?"

"We were just talking about how funny it looked that Gandil didn't come back. He must have made an awful lot out of it. Crossed up the boys. We both decided he crossed them up."

"You think now Williams may have crossed you, too?"

"Well, dealing with crooks, you know, you get crooked every way. This is my first experience and last. I told him what a damn fool I thought I was, and he said the same thing, so we just let it go at that."

"Do you have any suspicion about the White Sox, any of the players throw any of the games this summer?" I asked slightly switching the subject to address rumors we had heard with some consistency.

"Well, there have been some funny looking games," he admitted.

"Where?"

"A couple in New York, this last Eastern trip looked bad, but I couldn't come out in the open and accuse anybody of throwing them games."

"Was anything whispered around the club that you know of, that you should beat New York and then drop these games for these other teams so that Cleveland could win?"

"No, sir, I never heard that."

"Did you hear anything to the effect that if the White Sox would take second place and get part of the World Series money because you won second place in the pennant race, that you would make more money than if you won the pennant and won the World Series?"

"No, sir."

"Did any of the other players tell you that?"

"No, sir, never told me that."

"Did that ever occur to you, yourself?"

"No sir. I wanted to win, this year, above all times."

"Why?"

"Because I wanted to get in there and try and beat some National League club to death. That's what I wanted to do."

"You didn't want to do that so bad last year, did you?"

"Well, down in my heart I did, yes."

All in all Joe was on the stand for about two hours I would guess. He was exceedingly nervous, but unlike some of the others we questioned, he was very polite. He answered all my questions. Did he tell the truth, the whole truth and nothing but the truth? That's a question that lingers after every testimony ever given.

**HUGH FULLERTON** Joe walked out of that courtroom looking actually rather pleased with himself. I don't think he had any idea what he had just done.

**HARTLEY REPLOGLE** When it was over, I saw a slight smile cross Joe's lips. He was in much better shape than when he went in. I think he was actually relieved. He told his story and lived through it.

"I got a big load off my chest," he announced. "I'm feeling better."

"No questions," I told the anxious reporters, he's gone through beautifully, and we don't want him bothered," I said.

The crowd outside the Criminal Court building cheered and jeered as he rode off in the company of bailiffs.

**HUGH FULLERTON** While Joe related sordid details to stern-faced men, there gathered outside the big stone building a group of boys. Their faces were more serious than those who listened to the shame of the nation's sport. There was no shouting, no scuffling. They did not talk of baseball or of anything else. A great fear and a great hope fought for mastery within each kid's heart. It couldn't be true.

After an hour, guarded like a felon, Joe emerged from the door. He did not swagger. He slunk along between his guardians, and the kids with the wide eyes and tightening throats watched. And one, bolder than the others, pressed forward and said, "It ain't so Joe, is it?"

Jackson gulped back a sob. The shame of utter shame flushed his brown face. He choked an instant.

"Yes, kid, I'm afraid it is."

**JOE JACKSON** I guess the biggest joke of all was that story that got out about 'Say it ain't so, Joe.' There wasn't a bit of truth in it.

There wasn't any words passed between anybody except me and a deputy sheriff. When I came out of the building, this deputy asked me where I was going, and I told him to the South Side. He asked me for a ride, and we got in the car and left. There was a big crowd hanging around in front of the building, but nobody said nothing to me.

If some kid would have asked me that, though, I would have looked him directly in the eye and said, "No, it ain't so."

**HARTLEY REPLOGLE** The next to testify after Joe was Lefty Williams. He made a clean breast of his relations with the deal.

He told pretty much the same story as Joe, only in a little more detail. He seemed to know more about what was going on during the affair than did Joe.

"I went to Gandil's room," he told us. "There was the money laying—or two packages laying, two envelopes laying there, and Gandil says, 'There is your dough.' I picked it up and went down to a taxicab and went back to the hotel, where I went right in and threw half of it on the bed. Some of the folks was in the bathroom or in the bedroom—I won't say which. We had a big suite there. But I went in the other room and said to Joe, 'There is supposed to be half of it.'"

"Did you know what games the Sox were to lose for all this money they were getting?" I asked him.

"Why they were supposed to lose the first two to Cincinnati and I never did hear whether they were to lose or win the one with Kerr."

"You knew half of the money was to go to Jackson."

"Yes."

"Gandil told you so, didn't he?"

"Yes, sir, Gandil told me 'There is five for yourself and five for Jackson and the rest of it has been called for."

"Now did anyone ever speak to you about any more money after any other game?"

"They never said a word to me. Nobody asked me about money or any other game at all."

**ALFRED AUSTRIAN** Questions were being thrown around as to whether legal action was possible against the accused players, or whether simple expulsion from the game was the extent to which we could proceed.

The fact is, a number of legal precedents which made it possible to indict and prosecute both players and gamblers on a charge of conspiracy to injure the business of the employers of the players. There are at least two different counts on which each of the White Sox players named in true bills voted by the grand jury could be prosecuted.

The first is conspiracy to commit an illegal act. Without question the public paid admission prices to see honest baseball played, thus the conspiracy to throw the games cheated the public.

The second was that the men conspired to injure the property of Mr. Comiskey, which consisted of contracts worth more than $200,000, the drawing power of the team to attract crowds to games, and other losses of goodwill which I estimated at the time to be worth about $300,000.

By entering into the conspiracy, the players destroyed $500,000 worth of Mr. Comiskey's property. Bill Veeck, president of the Cubs, had told me in his office that he would have given Comiskey $75,000 for Buck Weaver's release prior to exposure, but after that he would not have him on the team.

Could anyone say that men could enter into a conspiracy to destroy $500,00 worth of property and not be subject to the law?

When Cicotte came to see me he said, "What can they get on me?"

I asked him, "Don't you feel you've been crooked?"

He said, "I do. It's been burning in me ever since it happened."

"If you've been crooked I can find the law which you have violated," I told him.

It made little difference that the case was unusual. There was a case more than 200 years ago in which a man named Orbell was indicted for cheating in a foot race.

There was plenty of legal basis not only for indictments but for prosecution.

Bishop's Criminal Law states that for workmen to conspire to violate their own contracts with their employers or to persuade others under contract to do the same is a crime.

The thought of seeing Joe and the boys in jail didn't please me but I was committed to that course of action because it was the correct thing to do—both legally and morally.

**HARTLEY REPLOGLE** By late September we had heard enough testimony to issue indictments against seven players and one former player. The specific charge against the eight was "conspiracy to commit an illegal act," which was punishable by five years imprisonment or a fine up to $10,000.

**CHARLES COMISKEY** As soon as the indictments were handed down I knew I had to immediately suspend the seven players who were still on the roster. I had to take this action to protect the integrity of baseball and to save the White Sox franchise.

I sent identical letters to Risberg, McMullin, Felsch, Weaver, Williams, Cicotte and Jackson:

"You and each of you are hereby notified of your indefinite suspension as a member of the Chicago American League Baseball Club.

Your suspension is brought about by information which has just come to me directly involving you and each of you in the baseball scandal resulting from the World's Series of 1919.

If you are innocent of any wrongdoing you and each of you will be reinstated; if you are guilty you will be retired from organized baseball for the rest of your lives if I can accomplish it.

Until there is a finality to this investigation it is due to the public that I take this action even though it costs Chicago the pennant."

That was the exact wording of the letter as written by Alfred Austrian, attorney to the club.

**VINCENT ALEXANDER** When I heard the news I went into a state of total denial. It was a frame, or it was a mistake, or it was a misprint, or there was some other yet-to-be-determined explanation which would be made public at any moment. What it wasn't, was true. That was not something I believed, it was something I knew. In my heart I knew it.

The others maybe, but not Joe. Joe was a hero. They were just good ballplayers. There is a difference. Heroes don't cheat. It is one of the fundamental precepts of heroism.

As soon as I read the story of Joe's testimony in the Philadelphia paper, I called my cousin in Chicago and had him send me a copy of the *Chicago Tribune*. A few days later I was able to read the story they printed. After all, they were there.

I read it carefully, word by agonizing word. I will never forget it. The story said on the stand Joe claimed he got involved in the deal through the influence of Gandil and Risberg but got only $5,000 which was handed to him in Cincinnati by Lefty Williams. When he threatened to talk about it, Williams, Gandil and Risberg said, "You poor simp, go ahead and squawk. Where do you get off if you do? We'll all say you're a liar. You're out of luck. Some of the boys were promised a lot more than you, and got a lot less."

That's exactly how the *Tribune* quoted Joe. It went on: "And I'm giving you a tip. A lot of those sporting writers who have been roasting me have been talking about the third game of the World Series being square. Let me tell you something. Some players done their best to kick it but little Dick Kerr won the game by his pitching. And because he won it these gamblers double-crossed us for double-crossing them."

"They've hung it on me. They ruined me when I went in the shipyards. But I don't care what happens now."

"He was also quoted as saying, "Now Risberg threatens to bump me off if I squawk. Swede is a hard guy."

Years later, when I was able to get my hands on the official grand jury testimony, there weren't even any comments roughly close to these.

It's possible Joe made these comments outside of the official hearing—perhaps on his way out of the building. Perhaps he didn't make them at all. Perhaps they were as fabricated as the "Say it ain't so, Joe" story.

All I know is this: all the papers had him saying different things, none of which appeared in the official transcripts.

**CHARLES COMISKEY** No sooner had I announced the suspension of my players than I received a telegram from the owners of the New York team:

"Your action in suspending players under suspicion, although it wrecks your entire organization and perhaps your cherished life work, not only challenges our admiration but excites our sympathy and demands our practical assistance. You are making a terrible sacrifice to preserve the integrity of the game. So grave and unforeseen an emergency requires unusual remedies. Therefore, in order that you may play out your schedule and, if necessary, the Worlds Series our entire club is placed at your disposal. We are confident that sportsmanship will not permit you to lose by default and will welcome the arrangement."

Of course, it was impossible to take them up on their offer as American League rules prohibit the transfer of a player after July 1 without the clearing of waivers. Nevertheless, I think the offer stands as a sincere gesture of the respect the league had for my decision. The thought of Babe Ruth playing in a Chicago uniform was, however, tempting if only for a fleeting but intriguing moment.

**EDDIE COLLINS** The night after Joe's appearance before the grand jury, we got as many players together as we could for a celebratory dinner. Most of the boys were there. Red Faber and Ray Schalk couldn't make it but both telephoned during the dinner to express their happiness over the clearing of the air. You have no idea how good it felt to get all this out in the open. We had been carrying it around for almost a year, this heavy weight, this burning anxiety.

In the middle of the dinner, Gleason got up and brashly announced, "This thing has come to a head and I'm glad of it. I've been working on this affair with Mr. Comiskey for a long time and it has kept us under a tremendous strain. The men on my team are real men and real ballplayers and we're going to win the pennant and then the World Series in spite of this scandal."

What a catharsis! It was one of the most joyous moments of my baseball life.

**CHARLES COMISKEY** When I reached my office on the morning after the suspension, I found enough letters and telegrams to fill two barrels. Baseball officials, players, and fans from all parts of the country had sent their sympathy and congratulated us on the manner in which we had cleared the team of the accused players.

The boys who were left were clean; they had never sold a game and they never would.

Me, Gleason and Harry Grabiner met to work out a new batting order. We put on good faces but we knew it wouldn't be easy overtaking Cleveland without the likes of Joe, Eddie and the others. We decided to move Shano Collins from the outfield to take over third base. Harvey McClennan, who had hardly played at all that year, moved in at shortstop. Ted Jourdan was given first base. Our new outfield consisted of Nemo Liebold, Amos Strunk and Eddie Murphy, the pitching staff of Faber, Kerr, Tex Wilkinson and Shovel Hodge.

They weren't exactly a murderer's row, but they were honest.

**CHICK GANDIL** After the 1919 Series, me and my wife packed up our things and headed to Los Angeles where we bought a house. Later that spring I went to St. Anthony, Idaho to manage a team out there but returned shortly as my health seemed to be suffering in that climate. For a while I played baseball in Bakersfield and for a few other teams in Southern California.

We were on our way to New Orleans when my appendix burst and I had to go into a hospital in Lufkin, Texas and have it removed. It was while there that I heard about the mess breaking in Chicago. Reporters moved in like vultures at the sight of a dead longhorn. In one way I was lucky. I had the hospital announce that I had nothing to say as I was not permitted by my doctor to have any visitors. A couple of days later I quietly slipped out the back door.

I felt bad for the other boys who had to face the music in Chicago, but they had the same choices I had. They could have gotten out when I did.

**HAPPY FELSCH** If you say anything about me don't make it an alibi. The beans were spilled and I knew I was through with baseball. But I took the gaff. I got my $5,000 and I suppose the others got theirs, too. I was as guilty as the rest of the boys—we were all in it.

I wish I'd kept out of it—I guess we all felt that way afterward. All that stuff about us pulling games during that 1920 season, though, was foolishness. We tried to be square that year.

My coin was put in my locker at the club. I don't know who put it there. We were double-crossed on it—it was to have been an even split. I thought Gandil was the fixer, but I wasn't sure. I have heard since it was Attell.

It happened that I didn't have any chances to throw any of the games. Whether I would have carried out my part in the deal if I had the chance I don't know.

The whole deal seemed so easy when we fell for it—we were expert ballplayers and it would have been a snap for us to get away with it. But you can't get away with it all the time—because while you can fool others you can't fool yourself.

I got $5,000. I would have gotten that much on the level if the Sox had won. I was out of baseball—thrown out because I was crooked.

I didn't know what I was going to do when my career came to such an abrupt halt. Go to hell perhaps. We all sold ourselves and our jobs—the only jobs we knew anything about. We had gotten in return only a few dollars while a lot of gamblers had gotten rich. It looks like the joke was on us, doesn't it?

**CHARLES COMISKEY** After the suspension of the players, I didn't see any of them again for some time, except in legal settings. All except Buck Weaver, that is. He demonstrated some courage, I'll say that for him

He asked for an interview which I granted. He was very upset, he said, about the suspension.

"I was not a part of it, Mr. Comiskey, I promise you that," he said almost crying. "I knew about it and I know I should have said something, but I was afraid to."

He insisted he did nothing to throw any of the games and that he took no money. I asked him who else was involved. He said he only knew what Gandil said but everybody knew Gandil was a liar. When I asked him specifically about Joe he said he didn't know if Joe was involved or not but that he doubted it very much.

"Anyway, he played good ball for you, Mr. Comiskey. He tried to win the Series for you."

After a while the scene got embarrassing. He was sniveling and begging like a pauper at the foot of a king.

I told him there was nothing I could do, that the matter was in the hands of the legal system.

"You could put me back on the team. I'm a victim of circumstances, Mr. Comiskey, not a cheater. I could help you win the pennant."

"Sorry, Buck. I just can't do that. This thing is bigger than just you. It's the integrity of the game that's at stake."

He left my office in a state of extreme depression. Had I heard that he had done something violent to himself after that I would not have been surprised.

**HAPPY FELSCH** To add an exclamation to an already ugly joke on us, the Internal Revenue Bureau announced it was going to take legal action against any of the players who admitted they received money from gamblers but didn't claim it on their tax returns.

I mean, maybe Joe was the only one of us who you could excuse. You would have thought the rest of us were bright enough to have avoided the incredibly stupid actions we took.

**HARRY GRABINER** The irony is that the players who remained loyal to the team in the Series, and who then were kept on the roster for the remainder of the 1920 season, probably ended up making more money that year anyway. The league regulations gave to the second and third place finishers in the pennant race, a share of the World Series pool. But I guess if they were stupid enough to go along with the plan in the first place, they certainly weren't smart enough to figure that out.

**JOE JACKSON** Damned if I did, damned if I didn't. I told the truth, but things didn't get a lot easier like I thought they would. One minute I thought I was going to play again, the next minute I thought we was going to jail. One minute I thought the White Sox was going to help us, the next minute I thought they was against us. One minute I thought it was going to all blow over, the next minute I thought it was the end of all of us.

Katie come up when she heard about my testifying. She said I done the right thing in telling, but she was scared just like me because we didn't know what was going to happen next. That was the very worst part—not knowing what was going to happen. If they told me I was going to have to go to jail I probably would have been able to deal with that, but I didn't know from day to day what was happening. I hoped, though, with all my heart that because I told the truth and all that they would let me come back and play the 1921 season. Katie said that might just happen and I thought so, too. After all, all I ever did was play to win, and then I told the truth. I didn't see as how they could keep me out of the game very long for that.

I'll tell you what the hard part was. The hard part was watching the team lose the pennant and not be able to do nothing about it.

**VINCENT ALEXANDER** The White Sox played out the season with a makeshift lineup. The Indians though, edged out the Sox for their first pennant in 39 years of competing.

Chicago just wasn't the same team. In fact, they would never really recover.

I wondered about Joe, wondered if he listened to the games on the radio, wondered what he was thinking, wondered if I would ever see him play again.

**EDDIE PLANK** In some ways I think Joe was the lucky one of the bunch. He didn't have to go home every day and read about his perfidy in the papers. He probably understood less of what was happening than the others, and in that there may have been some salvation.

In public there was considerable antagonism against the players and against the team. Some people argued that all the games played that year by the White Sox should be thrown out, and that they shouldn't participate in the sharing of the World Series money.

Any time the players appeared in public they were booed. The American public was angry. They would not forgive any of the players. Not even Joe.

**BAN JOHNSON** It was as if we had discovered that Daniel Boone had been bought by the Indians to lose his fights in Kentucky, or that John Paul Jones had thrown the *Serapis-Bonhomme Richard* battle for British gold.

On city corner lots, in small towns and country villages, on diamonds improvised by farm lads in the stubble field, millions of boys have spent the energy of their growing years in the wild hope that someday they, too, might take their places in the fellowship of the big league elect. Most of them eventually outgrew the ambition but it did them no harm. Then suddenly they found that some of their heroes were only crooks, and contemptible crooks at that. They did it for their wives and children, or to lift a mortgage from the old farm they said. They had scruples about going in, and their guilty knowledge was an awful load on the conscience, but they all kept quiet till they had been found out: then they did what they could to get off easily by betraying each other.

**JOE BIRMINGHAM** I must say that the one player who came over as the most sympathetic was Happy Felsch. At least he appeared to be genuinely sorry for what he did, and he didn't make up any lousy excuse like needing the money for the wife and kids.

I was kind of pulling for Joe to come out with something like that. I mean, I played with the guy for a few years and I don't believe for a moment that he was capable of thinking up something so nefarious. My guess is he went along without realizing what was happening until it was too late. Those other guys weren't big stars like Joe. They didn't have nearly as much to lose.

**CHARLES COMISKEY** Right after the banishment, I got together with Barney Dreyfuss, owner of the Pirates; John McGraw, Vice President of the Giants; and William Veeck, President of the Cubs.

We drew up a plan with resolutions to be signed, and sent it to every club owner on both the major and minor league levels. The plan called for a complete reorganization of professional baseball, the chief aspect of which was the removal of the game from the hands of the owners, player, and officials and returning it to the public, where we believed it belonged.

The plan called for a tribunal composed of three of America's most important men, with absolute power over both major and minor leagues, to take control of the game. The men would be representatives of the public.

This was the only way we knew to restore trust in the game. All of us involved with the game were suspect to the public, and rightly so.

# 51

# WE SAT THERE FOR MORE THAN A MONTH

**CHARLIE LEBEAU** On November 12th, 1920, the major league owners gathered in Chicago for a critical meeting to select a commissioner, a czar of the game, a high pooh bah of the national pastime.

The owners fought bitterly, argued incessantly, and screamed loudly about each proposed candidate. Then the name Judge Kenesaw Mountain Landis was thrown on the table and things really got hot.

**BAN JOHNSON** I did not want Landis. I'll admit that now and forever. I got five teams to agree with me—the loyal five, Cleveland, Detroit, Philadelphia, St. Louis, and Washington. The others, claimed they wanted a strong figure and nobody could argue that Landis wasn't strong. The problem was he was too strong for the good of the game. I was afraid baseball would become about him, and not the great game it was. Comiskey led the group favoring him. It was a grandstand play of the first order. Suddenly Comiskey was positioning himself as the game's white knight, but don't forget it was he who got us into the mess in the first place. Had he acted decisively when he first got wind of the fix, this whole thing could have been avoided.

**VAUGHN GLASER** Landis was a piece of work, I'll tell you that. He was a great actor, a regular Booth. When he tried cases he played a role akin to that of The Lord High Executioner. He sat on the bench in flowing black robes, his studiously unkempt long silver hair catching the light just right, his demeanor almost god-like. He played to the crowd—especially those in the balcony. All eyes in the room were focused on him. Everything in his hands became props and were used to dramatic advantage. William Jennings Bryan had nothing on him. Neither did Barrymore—John or Lionel.

Landis never blinked. His steel-gray cold eyes cut like razors. His very carriage and costume suggested all that was good and worthy in the rugged individualism of frontier justice.

He was riding into town in his leather duster with two guns strapped to his waist and his hat pulled down low. No one would dare question his judgments, and everyone knew he would clean up the town just as he promised, because the judge always did exactly what he said he would.

Hadn't he already taken on the mighty Standard Oil Company and brought them to their knees? Wasn't he the judge who had sentenced a small-time bootlegger to the unheard of term of two years in the Federal pen?

The very name, Judge Kenesaw Mountain Landis, sounded like American values etched in granite, and values are exactly what baseball was in sore need of.

He was right out of central casting.

**EDDIE PLANK** The good judge had a record of always siding with management against labor—read players—when it came to a confrontation. No wonder Comiskey and the big boys wanted him. The fact that he often put himself above the law seemed to be of little if any consequence. The fact that he was a bigot seemed to be ignored. He was against what he called "sissies," which seemed to mean anyone who was cultured.

As soon as I heard of his appointment I knew the boys were in trouble. Fairness would give way to image making, and the image of Joe as a barefooted, stupid, cheating hick was not going to sit well with the gunslinger.

I figured we were in for an interesting time. I didn't figure wrong.

**CHARLES COMISKEY** By and large the owners supported me in my desire to bring in Judge Landis. We needed an image of integrity and principle, and the good judge offered that and more. Of course Ban Johnson and a few of the other owners were frightened by the specter of such a dominant individual. With Landis in charge, Johnson's role in making the decisions which governed baseball would be greatly reduced. We knew that and he knew that. It was carefully calculated.

Johnson was continuing to be a cause for concern. He was drinking more than was good for either him or the game, and some of us thought it was time to, let's say, reduce his influence.

We offered the judge $50,000-a-year to become Commissioner of Baseball. He accepted on the proviso that he be granted unlimited powers to do whatever he felt was in the best interests of the game.

His first order of business—clean up the game. Return it to the wholesome sport it once was, if not in practice, then at least in perception.

**HUGH FULLERTON** Here's the kicker. Despite the fact that he sat on the bench for a number of years and presided over several landmark cases, "Judge" Landis wasn't a trained judge. He wasn't even a trained attorney. He didn't have any formal legal education. In fact, he never even went to law school. To quote the judge, "I'm not a college graduate and I'm proud of it."

So how did he get appointed as a judge you ask? Good question. It seems he skillfully managed a gubernatorial campaign for Frank O. Lowden, and as a reward was appointed judge of the United States District Court for the Northern District of Illinois. He was appointed by President Theodore Roosevelt.

**KENESAW MOUNTAIN LANDIS** The only thing in anybody's mind then was to make baseball what the millions of fans throughout the United States wanted it to be. I vowed that if I caught any crook in baseball, the rest of his life was going to be a hot one.

**GEORGE GORMAN** I was assigned to handle the prosecution in the case against the alleged conspirators. Everybody knew about the case, but I had not followed it any more closely than reading the never-ending newspaper stories.

What I knew when I began preparing for the trial was that Eddie Cicotte, Joe Jackson, and Claude Williams had confessed their share in the affair to the grand jury, and that Oscar Felsch was quoted in newspaper stories as confessing to reporters, but that Felsch, George Weaver, and Swede Risberg had officially denied that they were guilty and had hired counsel. Jackson and Williams had also been quoted in several stories as saying that they would be back in baseball the next season. Charles Gandil, who was already out of the game, was saying nothing.

**KATIE JACKSON** Waiting for the trial to start was probably the worst part. Joe, like all the other players was under court order not to leave the state. He was scared, yes, and maybe a little confused, and a lot lost, and he had absolutely no idea of what was expected of him or what to expect from himself.

Other than an occasional visit from Lefty, he pretty much stayed clear of the other players. Sometimes at night we took walks when there weren't too many people on the streets.

I've got to admit Joe was drinking a little, sometimes a little too much, but under the circumstances, who could blame him?

Eventually, a guy he knew helped him open a little pool room over on 55th and Woodlawn, across from the university. It was just a small place with a few tables, but a lot of the students would go over there and shoot pool, probably because it was Joe's. I know university students and Joe don't seem like a very good mix, but some of the students liked to say they played pool with Joe Jackson. Actually he wasn't there much, but I guess they dropped in with the hope that they might catch a game with him.

People were saying a lot of bad things about him, and Joe knew it, but people are less likely to say bad things when you're in their house, and that pool room was, in a way, Joe's house.

He had some guy run it for him, and it was really the first time Joe ventured out into business on his own. Joe had a pretty good business sense. As long as I read the contracts to him and took care of some of the details that needed tending to from time to time, he was fine. He knew what a buck looked like and he knew how to take care of one when he had it.

Anyway, this wasn't a big moneymaker, but it was something to do, and it was in Chicago where he could do it.

**HUGH FULLERTON** As we were all waiting for the arraignment and then the trial to get under way, the story took yet another shocking turn. George Gorman, the primary prosecutor for the state announced that, somehow, apparently like magic, all of the grand jury records had mysteriously disappeared. Presto! Vanished into thin air, the testimonies of

Jackson, Cicotte and Williams among them.

Imagine that! When asked, Gorman appeared to be as shocked as anyone. "Why, I have no idea what could have happened to them." He said, or words to that effect.

**HARTLEY REPLOGLE** I know a lot of people speculated that I made off with the records in one kind of a political gambit or another. All I can say to that is, "Hogwash!" I worked hard in the grand jury hearings and I wanted that work to pay off. The last thing I wanted was for those records to be unavailable.

I know also that a lot of people thought I was too soft on the players, Joe in particular, but I got the evidence we needed and I got it through what I judged to be humane methods. You don't think the players were humiliated enough without my having to add to it?

I did my job. I did it well. I didn't tamper with the evidence. I will say, though, that I had my suspicions. I am not making accusations you understand. I am just saying I had suspicions. I always wondered about Alfred Austrian. Just wondered, mind you.

**GEORGE GORMAN** I'll tell you this, sports fans: no records, no evidence; no evidence no conviction. It doesn't get any simpler than that. You don't need a Harvard Law degree to figure what was coming next.

Oh, of course every fan in the country "knew" what happened to the records, only everybody knew something different.

If nothing else, we were supplying the off season fan with his daily entertainment. Heck, even non-baseball fans were following the melodrama in the papers.

I wasn't crazy about the roles we were playing, though. There was the good judge, the crooked players and the bumbling attorneys. There were the caring owners, the duped fans and the incompetent prosecutors.

I did what any good attorney would do under the circumstances. I filed a motion called *nolle prosequi* which is fancy legal mumbo jumbo for stalling for time while you figure out what the hell to do next.

**KATIE JACKSON** While Joe was waiting around for the courts to find their records and to begin the trial, he was approached by some men to play on a barnstorming tour with a few of the other players who were also waiting for the trial to begin. The court said they had to stay in Illinois, but if a few games were played in neighboring states nobody would say much about that.

Joe realized how much he missed baseball. He played on that barnstorming tour like his life depended on the games. He played with a passion and zest the likes of which I had never seen before.

Ironically they called their team the Black Sox, a name they later regretted as that name became associated with all the worst in the game.

**JOE JACKSON** We was playing baseball again and that felt really good. Then after a while, the word got out about us, and some stadium owners wouldn't let us use their parks because they said we was a bad influence. They stopped us from playing on what they called "moral grounds." Even when we did play, sometimes we was booed. So finally we just broke the team up and we all went home.

Organized baseball could really carry a grudge when it wanted to.

The trial was on again, off again. Every day we heard something different. I don't know what the problem was exactly, all I know is that the damn thing took forever to get going.

**BUCK WEAVER** They called them the Black Sox, but actually the real name of the team was the Major Stars. Joe, Happy, Lefty, Swede, and Kenny all played on the team with a few other fellows who weren't as good. I didn't join them even though they asked me to. I wasn't guilty of anything and I didn't want to be associated with them. Actually I thought Joe would have been wise to avoid them, too, and I told him that on a couple of occasions, but Joe wasn't always known for making the wisest of decisions.

The team was backed by George K. Miller, a wealthy area investment broker, and several of his cronies.

The team got into trouble almost immediately when several teams complained about playing against crooked players. Later that spring they formed a different team called the South Side Stars and played Sunday games in a little park on the South Side—that is until the city council got involved and pulled the license of the park because Joe and the boys were playing there. While they were playing, though, it was some kind of spectacle. I went down once out of curiosity and sat in the back of the bleachers where nobody recognized me. I saw Joe drive a homer over the center field fence that didn't look like it was going to come down until the next fall. It was quite a treat for the spectators. Some of them cheered, and some of them booed, but all of them went home saying they saw the great Joe Jackson up close on the day he hit a gigantic home run.

**JOE JACKSON** That spring there was a new baseball league being started. It was called the Continental Baseball League, or something like that, and they sent this man over to talk to me about joining them, but I figured I still had a good chance to play with the Sox again, or maybe they would trade me to another major league team that wasn't in Chicago, so I told him I appreciated the offer, but no thanks.

**HUGH FULLERTON** All spring while everyone waited on tenterhooks for the trial to begin, the good judge continued to keep himself on the front page with his posturing and pronouncements.

"Now that I am in baseball, just watch the game I play," he said.

Any time the scandal began to lose its hold on the public, you could count on him to redirect attention to where he thought it belonged.

**B. J. SHORT** I was one of the team of attorneys representing three of the accused players—Jackson, Weaver and Williams.

We decided to throw up every possible obstacle that we could think of. That was part of a calculated ploy to confuse the issues as much as possible, and thereby put doubt in the minds of the potential jurors, who, even though not yet selected, were likely reading the papers daily.

Prior to the trial we ran the three players in and out of court like a parade.

My everlasting image of Joe is one of a man looking like a little kid dressed by his mother for Sunday school.

First we petitioned the court for a bill of particulars setting forth in detail the charges on which our clients were to be charged.

When we appeared in court for that, the room was packed to the gills. I heard Buck lean over to Joe and say, "They ought to build bleachers and charge admission."

In the petition we presented, Williams and Jackson asserted that they did not make any admission of game throwing as they were said to have made before the grand jury. Remember, the records were lost.

Some of these sessions got downright heated. Once a member of our team took a good swing at the baseball magnates. We knew they were going to have to be portrayed as villains if we were to have any chance.

"They lead the public to believe a player gets about $10,000 or more a year and here we find out that they get $2,600. At the end of the season they have nothing left but a chew of tobacco, a glove and a uniform."

All during these protracted, and highly-charged legal pyrotechnics, the three ballplayers sat utterly bemused, confused and disheartened.

**HUGH FULLERTON** While the legal jockeying-for-position was still going on, a long series of trial dates were set and subsequently postponed. Finally Landis announced that the players were all put on the ineligible list which meant that the players would have to show a "clean slate" if they ever hoped to play major league ball again.

The implications of this were great, although I'm not sure how many people appreciated that at the time. What he was really saying was that the high commissioner of baseball would have to approve their reinstatement regardless of the outcome of the trial.

In other words, Landis was playing god with respect to their futures. I knew right then that they had better start wearing out their knees in prayer.

**CHARLES COMISKEY** It didn't matter that Landis put the men on baseball's ineligible list because they were already on mine.

That spring, even before the trial started, I formally released all the players involved. This meant, of course, that the seven players were free to be signed by any other team in the major or minor leagues. I was confident, however, that none would dare.

**HUGH FULLERTON** Landis, Comiskey, and Johnson entered into an "I'm-holier-than-thou contest" to see who would ultimately take credit for cleaning up the sport.

**GEORGE GORMAN** At my instigation, police in various cities around the country began arresting men indicted by the Cook County grand jury. Not the players, they were all in Chicago, out on bail, but others who were suspected of being involved in the fix.

One of the first to be arrested was Hal Chase, the former major league player, whose name came up every time anybody put the words "gambling" and "baseball." Together. Police caught up with him in San Jose, California which was, I believe, his hometown. However, no sooner was he arrested, than he was released on a writ of habeas corpus. He got out on the grounds that a proper warrant had not been sent for his arrest. Chase certainly knew his way around the legal system. He should have. He had enough practice.

Others were more difficult to track down. Our information indicated that Attell was in Toronto, Sport Sullivan in Montreal, Bill Burns on a farm near Juarez, Mexico.

Attell, however, was later taken into custody at Broadway and 42nd Street in New York. He was picked up by members of the pickpocket squad. He immediately offered to turn state's evidence and tell all in exchange for complete immunity against any and all charges relating to the 1919 Series.

**HUGH FULERTON** Finally, one sunny day in late June, the preliminaries for the trial began. The courtroom was jammed with writers, fans, and a menagerie of curious on-lookers. The former players, all nattily attired, gathered in small groups. Cicotte, Williams and Jackson sitting together, but conversing little. Risberg and Felsch sitting apart from them. Gandil sat alone. It was easy to figure out why.

Weaver came in a bit later, passing by the others as he took his seat away from everyone else. It was obvious he was being ignored. Word was that it was because he had refused to play independent ball with them. He chatted freely with friends in the stands but not a word or even a look was passed between him and the other players. Take that Buck!

McMullin was conspicuous by his absence, but his attorney averred that he would make a bee-line from the West Coast whenever the court indicated it was necessary.

On the first day, the specific charges against the players were read aloud. They were all charged with conspiracy to do an illegal act and conspiracy to defraud. Under Illinois law it was explained conviction could result in either a jail or penitentiary sentence.

Early on, most of the action was limited to legal verbal gymnastics. It appeared to most of us without legal training that attorneys for both sides were trying to drag out every legal technicality to gain advantage for their side. The arguments became so heated at one time that Joe was heard to exclaim: "Those are certainly smart men, and that lawyer of mine is one lawyerin' bird. They better not get him riled up."

His lawyer, Ben Short argued that the state "came into the court limping and lame, and knew that its case was a failure."

"If it wasn't a failure," he said, "you'd have the real leaders of this conspiracy here—the men who made millions—and not these ballplayers, who were reputed to get big salaries, but most of whom got practically nothing."

"We've got the real leaders," replied George Gorman who was heading up the prosecuting team.

Each of the players entered a formal plea of not guilty.

I couldn't help wondering what position Joe would have been in had he been fairly represented at the hearings by Ben Short. Weaver, too, for that matter.

**JOE JACKSON** During the lawyer talk, I couldn't help thinking the funny thing was that since we wasn't allowed to play ball no more, everybody wanted to see us play. We all signed one-year contracts with the independent team and gave the owners an option for four more years. I was making more money than when I was playing for the White Sox, and that's a fact. I was also making some dough on the pool room, especially after I brought in Lefty Williams as a partner.

The others was doing pretty good, too. Buck Weaver, he was half owner of a drugstore. We was a little mad that he wouldn't play ball with us on the weekends, but he said the store took up all of his time which I didn't really believe.

Eddie Cicotte, he had a good farm near Detroit and he said he was also interested in a garage somewhere over there.

Swede and Happy, they also did something to make some money, but I'm not sure what. I think mostly though that they counted on baseball for their living.

**GEORGE GORMAN** The trial itself began with the tedious task of interviewing prospective jurors. A long line of veniremen were examined and questioned as to whether they personally knew any ballplayers, if they ever played ball, attended professional games, saw the 1919 World Series, or opposed professional or Sunday baseball. They were asked whether they thought baseball an honest game, whether they took part in baseball pools, bet on games, or would be influenced by the fact that all the defendants were not on trial.

One man, a machinist, claimed that although he was a former semi-professional ball player in New Jersey, he had never heard of the baseball scandal. He was dismissed immediately as a likely liar. One would have had to have been a troglodyte not to have known about the scandal.

**EDDIE COLLINS** We were playing the 1921 season with pretty much a new team. Bibb Falk took over in left field. He was no Joe Jackson to be sure, but he was a decent player and a decent guy. He was up with us briefly in 1920, so he knew Joe a little, but all during his first full year, he kept asking me how Joe played this hitter or that. He wanted to be Joe.

In the middle of the season, I got a letter from the league saying I might have to testify at the trial. Some other players got the same letter. Ty Cobb told me before a game in Detroit that he got one, too, and asked how I felt about that. I felt uneasy I told him. He said he felt the same.

Then the league told us, if necessary we would have to miss games to testify. Here we go again, I thought, disrupting the game because of the actions of a few greedy men.

**GEORGE GORMAN** At our request, the state made public the 1919 salaries of the accused men.

Gandil made $4,000 for the season; Risberg, $3,250 plus $187.76 for the extra time required for the World Series; Weaver $7,250 for the season and $419.36 for the Series; McMullin, $3,000 for the season and $149.94 for the Series; Jackson, $6,000 for the season and $229.97 for the Series; Felsch, $4,287 for the season and $214.38 for the Series; Williams, $3,000 plus $875 in bonuses and $149.94 for the Series; and Cicotte, $5,712 plus $3,000 in bonuses and $285.75 for the Series.

Technically, the men were not under contract to the club during the Series, the contracts having expired at the end of the regular season. The men were paid at a pro rata for the time of the Series.

It certainly wasn't difficult to see who was making the money, and it wasn't the players. Each man was paid on a monthly basis for the six months of the season, and generally nothing during the offseason. So, a player like Gandil was paid $666.66 a month before taxes for six months. No wonder he was angry at Comiskey.

**HUGH FULLERTON** While the trial was in the jury selection phase, someone broke into Comiskey Park during the wee hours of the morning and blew the safe, making off with a nice handful of cash from stadium concessions. Rumor had it that papers pertaining to the players on trial were also taken. Comiskey denied that and we all know that Comiskey was an honorable man.

**GEORGE GORMAN** One sticky hot afternoon Kid Gleason, Dickie Kerr, Red Faber, and Eddie Collins were brought in to testify.

Risberg was the first to see them as they came into the room.

"Hello, Kid," he called out to Gleason. "How's the boy?"

"Pretty good, Swede," replied the manager as he shook hands with Risberg. "How's yourself?"

"And there's old Buck Weaver," added Gleason sighting his former third baseman. "Stacking up pretty good, Buck?"

"Sure," said Weaver.

The men talked of the present season for a few minutes.

"How's Falk doing?" asked Joe.

"He can't throw with you, Joe, nobody can," replied Collins. Joe smiled.

They exchanged chit-chat like this for a short time, but then as the players had been released because we were not yet ready for them, they had to leave.

"Hope you win the pennant, boys," Felsch called out.

"Thanks, Happy," several of them responded.

"Good luck to you boys in your trial," said Gleason.

It was truly one of the saddest exchanges I ever heard, but it did show how the players were wont to stick together.

The players heard the state's request. We were going for jail sentences of five years and $2,000 fines. They stopped horsing around when they heard that.

**B.J. SHORT** On the first day of testimony, the courtroom was, as usual, filled to capacity. The crowd was silent through most of the day, punctuating the affair occasionally with vocalized "Ah's," and "Oh's."

The spectators gave the room a bleacher-like appearance, as most sweltered in shirtsleeves. Scores of small boys jammed their way into seats, and as Mr. Gorman told of the alleged sellout, they repeatedly looked at each other in awe, remarking under their breaths the likes of:

"What do you think of that?" or "Well, I'll be darned."

It was clear from their reaction that they had a real favorite among the accused—Shoeless Joe.

Joe sat silently with the rest of the players, listening to the testimony, but showing little overt reaction, other than when their former boss, Charles Comiskey took the stand.

I asked Mr. Comiskey if he had not jumped from the National League to the rival Brotherhood some years earlier. He took exception to this and became very angry, a condition I was not unhappy to see.

At one point he became so exercised that he rose in the witness stand, shook his fist at me and shouted: "Don't you dare say I ever jumped a contract. I never did that in my life."

After numerous other such exchanges, he sank back in the witness chair seemingly greatly fatigued.

By the end of the tiring day the jousting got to the point of ridiculousness.

We won a point when the judge ruled that the state could make no mention in its opening statement of the grand jury confessions of Cicotte, Williams and Jackson.

"You won't get to first base with those confessions," shouted co-defense counsel, Michael Ahern.

"We'll make a home run with them," came back Mr. Gorman.

"You may get a long hit, but you'll be thrown out at the plate," responded Ahern.

At the end of the day Mr. Gorman commented, "We used our weakest lineup and shut them out. Wait till our real hitters get in."

Another one of the defense team replied. "We took everything they sent over and didn't even burn our hands. We'll fan their heavy hitters."

To which I heard a spectator reply, "This may be the only part of the trial the players actually understand."

**JOE JACKSON** My lawyer, he asked me to tell him the whole story in my own words which I done and then he said he thought he could get me off if I just trusted him and did exactly what he said I should do. And that's exactly what I done.

We joked around a little—the players, but mostly that was because we was all a little nervous and the joking made it seem like we wasn't so much.

It was the terribilist time of my life I can tell you that. I didn't like having to sit out there in front of all them people while they talked bad about me. I didn't like looking at the audience, even though Katie was there most of the time. I didn't tell her, but I really wished she wasn't there. Every night after the trial I went back to the apartment and she fixed dinner because we didn't dare go out in public. Sometimes we talked about something somebody said at the trial, but mostly we didn't talk about it.

The season was going on, too, so sometimes we talked a little about that. That season the Sox, without us dropped all the way down to seventh place. I didn't want them to do bad really, but I had to feel a little good that they missed us. That was the season, too, where Babe Ruth hit 59 home runs, because the ball was different or something. At least that's what they said. Anyway, I would loved to have hit that season. Maybe I wouldn't hit 59 home runs, but I would of hit a bunch.

Mostly though, I felt sad.

**GEORGE GORMAN** We decided to play our ace early—Sleepy Bill Burns. Burns had turned state's evidence in return for immunity. He was a skittery and nervous witness who had to constantly wipe the sweat from his brow as he answered questions in a voice barely above a whisper.

He sang the complete song, including names and dates. He even quoted Eddie Cicotte as saying: "I will throw the first game if I have to throw the ball clear out of Cincinnati."

I looked over at Cicotte for a reaction. He broke into a grin.

Burns named Rothstein, Attell and Maharg as co-conspirators, and went into a lengthy two-daylong, detailed account of the fix.

Here was a knowledgeable and credible witness who gave great credence to our charges. I knew he was going to be a difficult witness to ignore.

**B.J. SHORT** Burns was a damaging witness, make no mistake about it, but as I was representing Jackson, I was thrilled to note that he made no mention at all of Joe Jackson as being one of the conspirators. In fact, he never mentioned his name once in any context although he had no difficulty in remembering all manner of small details.

When Gorman asked him if he remembered the room number in which he met the players at the Sinton Hotel in Cincinnati, he responded without hesitating, "I think it was room 708."

"Who was there?" was Gorman's next question.

"There was Gandil, Fred McMullin, Lefty Williams, Happy Felsch, Eddie Cicotte, Swede Risberg and Buck Weaver," he answered.

"Was that all?"

"All I remember."

"How about Jackson?"

"I did not see him there."

**GEORGE GORMAN** Burns' long, convoluted tale of graft, bribery, and interlocking double crossing came out during tedious questioning and cross-questioning. He told of gamblers double crossing ballplayers and ballplayers double-crossing gamblers, of the gamblers making a fortune on the first two games and then losing it on the third when their cupidity led them to double cross the players and then refuse to pay them the bribe promised.

Near the end of his testimony I had him tell how he had fled to Mexico as soon as he found out he was under indictment. He explained how he talked to Ban Johnson in Del Rio, Texas, on the border, and how Johnson talked him into coming to Chicago. I wanted the jury to hear this from him before the defense got it out of him in a way that might look like he was hiding something.

**B.J. SHORT** I jumped all over the Burns testimony. I asked him if he got any money from Johnson to testify. He admitted Johnson sent him expense money for himself and for his wife while he was in Texas and Mexico.

Then he was asked: "You knew there was a bitter personal feud between Charles A. Comiskey and Ban Johnson, did you not? You knew at the time you told Johnson this story that it would hurt Comiskey, did you not?"

"No," answered Burns.

But the point was made.

**BUCK WEAVER** I wanted to tell my side of the story real bad. I thought that if I could just get in front of the jury and tell the truth, they would believe me precisely because it was the truth. But the lawyers—including mine—all got together and decided that none of the players would be allowed to testify. That seemed to me then, as it does now, to be a mistake, but there was nothing I could do about it.

Although nobody said it then, I have always assumed the reason was that they were afraid to put some of the players on the stand because they would get flustered and not say the right thing. Joe in particular. I think they didn't dare put him on the stand, and that hurt all of us.

**BAN JOHNSON** Although initially I thought Arnold Rothstein wasn't involved, information came to me that made me change my mind.

A few days into the trial, the issue arose about the legality of putting into evidence the actual confessions of Cicotte, Jackson and Williams, but since the original confessions had mysteriously disappeared, they were forced to rely on some imperfect and unclear carbon copies. The judge eventually ruled that they could be admitted, but while the arguments about this were flying around, I was told that A.R. had paid $10,000 to someone in the district attorney's office for the original copies. The tip came anonymously but contained such detail that I had every reason to believe in its fidelity.

I immediately demanded a grand jury investigation. Rothstein threatened to sue me over the allegation but didn't. I think he didn't because it was true.

**GEORGE GORMAN** We paraded out a long procession of witnesses for the state—Burns, Maharg, players, gamblers, assorted others. They all basically reiterated the same story of deceit, double crosses and duplicity—each with some variation, but the essence of the story remained constant. Players conspired to throw the Series. They had different levels of complicity, Gandil and Cicotte at the top of the list, Weaver and Jackson at the bottom, but nonetheless, they were all involved.

**JOE JACKSON** I got real tired of people asking me how the trial was going all the time. I didn't have no idea of how it was going. There was a lot of lawyering stuff going on, that's all I can tell you.

We all dragged down there every day and sat while one person after another told what they knew about everything. Let me tell you, most of it was pure malarkey, but we wasn't allowed to say nothing so that's exactly what we said.

**HUGH FULLERTON** To the hundred or so fans who packed themselves into the courtroom each day, the trial was grand drama, as stirring and emotional as the World Series itself. The crowd let the principals in the trial know exactly how they felt about them and the statements they made, the judge's warnings notwithstanding. They were rooters with rooters' interests, plain and simple. They seemed more interested in winners and losers than in guilt or innocence. Phrases like "who's coming to bat next?" and "that was a high hard one" could be heard as often as "do you swear to tell the truth?" I half expected a hot dog vendor to work the aisles.

If there was anyone who captured more interest than the rest, it was Joe. He had ascended to the level of myth, and myths on trial draw attention. They also draw hyperbole and exaggeration, both of which were flying around Joe's head with consistency and fervor.

**GEORGE GORMAN** The players were on trial for five separate conspiracies: to defraud the public; to defraud Ray Schalk; to engage in an illegal confidence game; to injure the business of the American League; to injure the business of Charles A. Comiskey.

After Burns' testimony we were extremely confident. Hell, we were ecstatic, particularly when Burns stated that it was Cicotte and Gandil who approached him with the plan to throw the Series, not the other way around.

**JOE JACKSON** That was something I didn't know nothing about—Eddie and Chick talking to the gamblers first. I mean I always thought that it was them who came to us with the plan. That's what Chick told me, so that's what I believed. But if Burns was right, then I was damn mad. I was mad at myself, too for going along with everything they told me. If only I could go back in time to those meetings in the hotel, I would walk out just like that, and I'd never talk to those players again. At the time it didn't seem like nothing more than the griping and complaining players always did. My mistake was talking to those guys about their plans that's all. I was a fool, not a cheat.

**B.J. SHORT** The witness who got my goat more than any of the others was Bill Burns. This opportunistic, little, two-timing hood turned on the players the minute it looked like there was an edge in it for him.

I asked him directly, "You told Gandil you would spill the beans if they didn't come through with your share, didn't you?"

"That's right he said," real cocky like.

"The players double-crossed you, didn't they?"

"Yes."

"Well, you double-crossed them, didn't you?"

"Not until they crossed me."

"Is that your reason for testifying?"

"One of them."

"Then it's not for the purity of baseball?"

"Well they double-crossed me and I would have been the fall guy for the whole outfit."

"If the players had really been crooked, you would have been satisfied! Do you think you are even with the boys now?"

"I am liable to be before I leave here!"

That brought a burst of laughter from the bleacherites.

"You don't like me much, do you, Bill?" I asked with utter disdain.

"Sure I do, Ben. You're a smart fellow, and I wish we had someone like you at the head of the deal; we'd all be rich now."

**JOE JACKSON** That Ben Short, he was one hell of a tough lawyer. He sounded good to me, but we couldn't none of us, tell if we was winning or if we was losing the trial. At least in baseball they have a big scoreboard so everybody knows who's ahead.

**B.J. SHORT** In the end we decided to put some of the defendants on the stand. This came about at the judge's request following a lengthy debate revolving around the issue of whether the players had or had not signed immunity waivers. The players were to be asked about only one issue—immunity. During the rest of the trial they were silent.

Joe was one of the players put on the stand. I specifically asked him if anyone had said anything at all to him about immunity. He looked more confused than usual. I don't think he understood the implications of the issue.

"Did they say anything to you about immunity?" I asked him bluntly after an initial less subtle approach yielded a look of bewilderment.

"They told me I could tell my story and then go anywhere I liked," Joe answered. "The judge suggested the Portuguese Islands."

"Did you talk to the judge the next morning after you talked to the grand jury?" I continued.

"I was supposed to but I went out and got drunk. I had the judge's two bailiffs with me."

"Now Mr. Jackson, were you drunk when you went before the grand jury?"

"About half drunk I guess. I'd been drinking."

"Did Mr. Replogle tell you that you would have to sign an immunity waiver and that you would later be held responsible for what you told the jurors?"

"He read a lot of stuff from a paper to me. I don't know what it was. He said it was a waiver or something."

"Didn't you read what you signed?" I asked him knowing darn well what the answer was.

"No. They gived me their promise. I'd have signed my death warrant if they would of asked me to," Joe said showing a welcome wit and earning scattered laughter.

"Did the judge give you any promise?"

"He told me that if I talked I would not be indicted-- I wouldn't have to go to jail, put up bonds or nothing. All they wanted, they said, was my address."

"Did you leave town immediately after you were through at the State Attorney's office?"

"No. I got polluted again."

**KATIE JACKSON** All during this, offers kept flooding in for Joe to play baseball someplace. For some reason, Wisconsin was a hotbed of Joe Jackson interest. I imagine we must have had something like a dozen inquiries from up there. Little towns, medium sized towns, they all wanted Joe to play for them. A couple of them offered as much as $200 a game plus expenses. That wasn't bad money after all. Now, if some small town could pay that much, why was Mr. Comiskey, who was making a ton in a big city like Chicago, unable to pay his players much more than that? That's what I want to know.

**KID GLEASON** I went over and testified at the trial, but it didn't amount to much. They asked me a handful of questions that everybody knew the answers to anyway, then got down to this one: "Do you have an opinion about whether the defendants played the game to the best of their abilities?"

Well, that was about the biggest waste of time I could imagine. I'd been answering that question for a year and everybody who wanted to, heard me give my answer a million times. But what happened here was that some other attorney jumped up and he yelled some legal objection about something or other and they wouldn't let me answer the question. Talk about a waste of effort!

Oh, they also called in Schalk, and Eddie Collins and Dickie Kerr, and maybe a couple of others, and from what I heard the same thing happened to all of them.

Kerr even said to me afterwards, "I came a hundred miles to tell this!"

The whole trial with all the missing evidence and all was a joke.

**B.J. SHORT** One of our best strategies was bringing Harry Grabiner to the stand. From his lips we heard the truth about the gate receipts of the White Sox for the last couple of years. According to Grabiner—and he wouldn't dare embroider the truth under oath with the amount of publicity this trial was receiving—the White Sox gate receipts in 1919 were $521,175.75. In 1920 the receipts were $910,206.59—almost double the previous year. So much for the prosecution argument that the defendants had destroyed the White Sox as a business.

This was a very strong point in our favor, so we decided to quit on a high note. We had concluded our calling of witnesses. Now all that was left were the summaries, and hopefully, the celebrations.

**JOE JACKSON** We sat there for more than a month watching the trial and we was all pretty happy, though when they said we was done with the witnesses and could get on with deciding what had to be decided.

**VAUGHN GLASER** I can't help thinking there was a deal cut from the very beginning. Let's face it, this whole imbroglio was prompted by the players' adverse reaction to Comiskey. They wanted revenge against what they thought was gross mistreatment at the hands of the owner. That's what made all of them at least think and talk about a plan for vengeance—Comiskey. So why didn't this come out in the trial? Why weren't the players allowed to say this on the stand? Why wasn't Comiskey vilified?

I can only think of one reason—it wasn't in the best interests of baseball. Attacking Comiskey publicly would have been akin to attacking the great national pastime, and that was a no-no.

Here's my best guess: baseball cut a deal. The players would remain silent about Comiskey in return for protection.

This wasn't a trial, it was a show. The conclusion was written long before it began. Why did it take so long to begin the trial? Why were there so many delays? It takes time to hammer out a deal like this.

The eloquent summaries of the distinguished counselors at law were beautifully scripted. The institution of baseball employed its highly-developed self-protective mechanism.

**HUGH FULLERTON** The prosecution team was at the top of its elocutionary form for its summation.

Gorman strutted around the room delivering carefully turned phrases like they were barbed arrows.

"The attorneys for the defense will ask for mercy," he began. "They point out that Lefty Williams got only five hundred dollars a month for his services. They charge that Charles Comiskey, the grand old man of baseball, is persecuting the players because he has tried to clean out rottenness in the national game. Gentlemen, Charles Comiskey wants to keep the game clean for the American public and I will tell you now that if the owners don't get busy when rottenness crops up, baseball won't last long."

Baseball, that's what he was talking about, the great national game.

"Comiskey gave these men a job," he declared in his best imitation of William Jennings Bryan. "And here we find the defendants deliberately conspiring to injure and destroy his business. They have dragged the game through the mire and in their blunders deliberately fouled their own nest."

Then it was Short's turn and he was not about to be out-elocuted.

"Ban Johnson was the directing genius of the prosecution. His hand runs like a scarlet thread through the whole prosecution. Johnson is boss. The czar of Russia never had more power over his subjects than Johnson has over the American League. He controlled the case. His money hired Burns and Maharg to dig up evidence. The state's attorneys have no more control over the prosecution than a bat boy over the direction of play in a World Series game."

**JOE JACKSON** I guess there was millions of words spoken at the trial and about as many people listening. It was almost like we was in jail already. We couldn't go no place without somebody bothering us. I think we was more famous for being on trial than we was as ballplayers.

The judge, he seemed like an OK guy. He really even seemed almost friendly like to us, and that made us feel better.

Our attorneys told us that what was really important was what the judge told to the jury after all the arguing was done with.

**B.J. SHORT** We couldn't have been happier after hearing the judge's instructions to the jury.

"The state must prove that it was the intent of the ballplayers and gamblers charged with conspiracy through the throwing of the World Series, to defraud the public and others, and not merely to throw ballgames."

What more could we ask for?

Now all we had to do was wait for the jury's decision.

**KATIE JACKSON** The night before the jury was to announce its decision, me and Joe went to this old ice cream parlor where the elderly man who owned the place and scooped ice cream seven days a week pretended to not know Joe. He had a booth in the back that you couldn't see into from the rest of the parlor.

We never once even mentioned the trial. The big topic of conversation was the price of ice cream. Apparently some commissioner in the city decided that all ice cream would be reduced to 10 cents a dish plus one cent war tax when served at the counter and all sodas would be 15 cents including the war tax. The owner informed us that it cost him only 7 1/2 cents to make an ice cream soda containing crushed fruits.

Joe always liked ice cream so we stayed late talking. We both knew Joe would be back in the courtroom within hours and would have to face his future. Found innocent, and he would be able to continue his career; guilty, it would be over. But at least for that night, his biggest concern was the price of ice cream.

**HUGH FULLERTON** When the jury came in, the hundreds of spectators who had crammed into every free inch of the courtroom went dead silent.

"Gentlemen of the jury, have you reached a verdict?" asked the judge.

"We have, your honor," answered the jury foreman according to the time-honored tradition.

The foreman then handed a slip of paper to the court clerk.

The clerk opened the paper and read. "We the jury find the defendant Claude Williams not guilty."

And so it went. A roll call of names, and a chorus of "not guilty."

The courtroom erupted into total bedlam. Scores of flash bulbs went off lighting the room like a lightning strike in an attempt to freeze the moment onto film forever. Hats, and almost everything else not nailed down flew into the air. It sounded like the final out in the bottom of the ninth of a tight and important game. Backs were slapped until they turned blue.

A momentary attempt to regain control of the room by the officials was quickly given up. The judge was smiling, I swear he was.

It was the most euphoric spontaneous eruption of joy I have ever witnessed.

Cicotte was delirious; Williams was running around in circles like a little kid.

Gandil screamed loud enough for everyone to hear, "I guess that'll learn Ban Johnson he can't frame an honest bunch of ballplayers!"

Weaver repeated his mantra, "I knew I'd be cleared because I didn't do anything wrong."

Felsch followed suit: "I never had anything to do with any so-called conspiracy and now everybody knows it, too."

Jackson was smiling, but of all the players, he was by far the most subdued.

**GEORGE GORMAN** All I can say is we did our best. Maybe the outcome was preordained.

**LEFTY WILLIAMS** We all went to a victory celebration that night. Joe was with us, too. I say that because he didn't always mix with the other players socially. But that night he was there as we all went to an Italian restaurant over on Hubbard Street. It was a place Cicotte recommended because it was close by and because it served the kind of food he loved.

It was one of those rare times in a person's life that was pure ecstasy.

We ate and drank, laughed and carried on like kids getting out of school for the summer.

We were there for maybe an hour or two before Eddie came in and said that the jurors were having their own party in a room upstairs. So we invited them all down to join us, and things really got hopping. We got so loud as the night wore on that Comiskey himself probably could have heard us in his mansion up by the lake. At least I hope he did.

The party didn't break up until the small hours of the morning, when we all drifted (or perhaps staggered would be a better description) to our homes, high on the alcohol and the intoxicated feeling of vindication.

**JOE JACKSON** When I finally fell asleep that morning the sun was already starting to come up. I remember dreaming about joining the pennant race. It was still August, so there was plenty of time left in the season. The Sox wasn't doing so hot, so in my dream, me and the boys got back on the team and played so good that we made it into the World Series against Brooklyn. In the final game I come up against Sherry Smith, Brooklyn's best pitcher, and win the game when I hit a ball into the outfield and then keep running all the way till I get home. I know that ain't really possible, but it was only a dream, a beautiful dream. But then I woke up.

# 52

## IT WASN'T RIGHT, WHAT LANDIS DONE

**KATIE JACKSON** Joe slept late the day after the jury decision. I didn't want to wake him. I didn't have it in me. The papers were filled with stories of the acquittal. They also carried a statement from Kenesaw Mountain Landis.

**KENESAW MOUNTAIN LANDIS** Regardless of the jury verdict, no player who threw a ballgame, or promised to throw a ballgame, or even consorted with crooked players and gamblers where the ways and means of throwing a game were discussed and not immediately reported to his club would ever play professional baseball again as long as I had any control over the matter.

I made this declaration public as soon as the trial ended: cheat, talk about cheating, associate with cheaters, and you are finished forever as a professional baseball player. There would be no exceptions, no modifications, no appeals. Justice would prevail.

**HUGH FULLERTON** Here was a case where the sheriff took the law into his own hands. He was willing to gun down not only the guilty, but anyone who so much as thought about being guilty. His hat was so white it could blind a gunslinger at 50 yards. No one was quicker on the draw or surer of his targets; no one shot straighter.

**CHARLES COMISKEY** I was, to put it mildly, shocked at the outcome of the trial. I would have bet my last cent on a guilty verdict and if they were tried again, I would still bet that way. Landis did the only thing he could have under the circumstance and the only thing that could have saved baseball.

**EDDIE CICOTTE** What Comiskey failed to mention in his pontificating was that Landis did the only thing he could have done to save the reputation of Comiskey. Believe me, the only thing he cared about in baseball was the money he could make from it. If he could have gotten his players back without losing face he would have done it in a heartbeat.

I don't mind saying it. Comiskey was the biggest phony in the history of the game. He was a hypocrite through and through, a liar and a user. He used players for his own gain, and when their usefulness to him was over, he threw them out with the garbage and suffered not a moment of conscience.

**KID GLEASON** If the boys had been allowed to play ball again, I would have quit on the spot. And you can quote me on that.

**BAN JOHNSON** The trial uncovered the greatest crime it was possible to commit in baseball. The fact that they were freed did not alter the conditions one iota or minimize the magnitude of the offense.

Sure, baseball would miss the appeal that someone like Joe brought, but I knew that ultimately the game would fare better without him than with him.

**JOE JACKSON** It wasn't right what Landis done. It wasn't fair. I thought this country was proud of the fact that it was a law-abiding place. Well, the law said we was innocent, didn't it? So how come we was thrown out anyway? What it looked to me like was that some people was more important than the law, and some people wasn't.

**HUGH FULLERTON** The banishment signaled the end of one era and the start of another. Gone were the players with the 19th-century mind-set.

Gone were the Hal Chase's with their reckless devil-may-care attitude toward gambling. Gone was the small town, rural idealization of the sport, replaced by an expanding urban consciousness. Gone were the gentleman owners, replaced by a corporate-demand-for-bottom-line-responsibility bias.

Gone was the dim-witted, slow-talking, Southern, illiterate, mill hand, replaced by a myth of Ruthian proportions.

**CONNIE MACK** I called Joe as soon as I heard. I had my fair share of troubles with him early in his career, but I never took him to be anything other than advertised. Joe always told you what he thought and did what he said. When he played, he played hard. He earned his salary.

I told him I had to agree with the decision, but that I believed him to be an honest man. He seemed to be sincerely appreciative of my call.

**VAUGHN GLASER** So Landis and the lords of baseball ultimately came out on top. The law was one thing, and the law said they were innocent, but baseball was quite another thing and baseball said they were guilty, so guilty they were.

To baseball, the issue was simple: the game was now clean and would be forever thus; the players were dirty and would be forever thus.

There is something of the truth in the adage about the higher you are the farther you have to fall. Joe was the biggest star and so had the farthest to fall, and fall he did. Nobody got hurt more than Joe. He was the blackest of the Black Sox, the one most remembered for his participation in the scandal. Think Black Sox and you think Shoeless Joe.

It's interesting to speculate what he might have gone on to accomplish had he not been banned. He was still in his early thirties—probably 33, although apparently there was some doubt about his exact age. He might easily have played another, say five, six years. Assuming no serious injuries in those years, he would have ranked among the best that the game has ever seen in a number of categories—certainly, hits and runs. As it was he ended up with a lifetime .356 batting average, behind only Ty Cobb and Rogers Hornsby. Even when his average is adjusted for the years in which he played relative to all the other players of that time, he comes in second only to Ty Cobb. There are no records for outfield arms, but according to many of us who saw Joe throw and have seen countless others over the years, he was certainly one of the greatest ever.

They may have taken away his ability to play through and past his prime. They may have taken away much of the recognition he was due. They may have taken away his good name. But they can't take away his accomplishments, and those are among the best the game has ever seen. Joe was a naturally gifted athlete who played with grace and dignity. The rest is not baseball.

# 53

## IF THEY PLAYED, I PLAYED

**JOE JACKSON** I never really wanted to live in the North, not in a city like Chicago anyway, so when they said I couldn't play no more, me and Katie, we packed up as fast as we could and made a bee-line out of there about as fast as a gangster getting away from a bank stick up. I mean, we still had some time left on our lease and all, but that didn't matter because there was nothing left to keep us there. I didn't feel I owed Chicago nothing.

We boarded the first fast train we could get for Savannah. I remember many trips back down South, but none like that one. As far as I was concerned, we was leaving the North for good. I don't recall we talked much on that train, but we knew what each other was thinking anyway. We was heading home.

**KATIE JACKSON** Back home in Savannah we settled into our quiet routine as quickly as we could. Folks there knew about Joe's troubles in Chicago, but on the whole, they seemed less judgmental, less likely to make an issue of it.

One thing was for certain, though: once a celebrity, always a celebrity. There was no such thing as walking away from your past if your past included great fame. Joe would always be known as a great baseball player. Whether he could shake the image of being involved in a scandal, well, that was another matter altogether. But as Joe must have said a million times along the streets of Savannah, "Remember, we were tried and found innocent."

**MYRON McCREERY** The Savannah Valet Service—I remember it well. It was a dry cleaning establishment, a little store front operation run by Joe and Katie Jackson after they returned. Joe wasn't afraid of hard work, I can tell you that. I used to go in there all the time, and sometimes I'd see Joe working away in the back just like he was a regular person. I'll admit I went in there because of Joe, and seeing as how I was a fan, it just seemed like a fun thing to do.

Once in a while Joe would come out and talk about hitting against Walter Johnson or something like that and we'd all listen to his stories until he got tired of talking and went back to work.

He was a nice guy really, and he was always polite to everybody in the shop as far as I noticed.

**JOE JACKSON** I played a lot of ball after I left the Sox. For a while I played in the South Georgia League which had teams in several Georgia cities. They was outside of organized baseball, so nothing Commissioner Landis said about me made any difference to them. Tons of players were blacklisted by the Commissioner, not just the eight of us. A lot of people don't realize that. They think that it was just us he threw out illegally.

I signed up to play for the Americus team and spent a whole season with them. Some people thought I was done, but I wasn't. They didn't always keep the best records down there but I think I hit close to .700 that season, with a lot of home runs. Then at the end of the season in the Georgia League championships I got 11 hits in 22 at bats. Just like the last championship series I played, I played good and I played to win, no matter how good the competition was. Oh, I know, a lot of people said that there was no good players in that league, but that's not true. Some of the boys in that league should of been playing in the majors. Some of them was better than some of the players I played with in Cleveland and Chicago, they just didn't get the breaks, that's all.

There was no gamblers hanging around to make problems for us. We didn't exactly travel in style, but we ate good southern food, and that counted for something.

**WILLIE SHAW** I played with Joe on the Americus team in the summer of 1922. Although he had put on a bit of weight now that he was eating southern cooking, he still could swing a mean bat.

To say that Joe was the star of the team is an incredible understatement. He was the star of the league. Hell, he was the biggest star in the state!

Sometimes we played doubleheaders. A couple of times we even played triple headers. I remember once he hit two grand slams in one day, and caught a ball in center field that I swear was uncatchable. He seemed never to tire of playing, and he never let up.

Once he barreled into a skinny kid catcher, knocking the kid almost into the next county and sending him to the hospital for a long row of stitches across his chin. I suggested to Joe that maybe he shouldn't have been so rough on the kid. He looked at me like I was crazy.

"I gave him a souvenir he'll never forget," he said, meaning the stitches.

A couple of times I felt bad for him because a father would come up to his kid talking to Joe and whisk him away like he was afraid the kid was going to catch something from Joe—like cheateritis or something..

Eventually, the team became known as "Shoeless Joe Jackson's Americus Bunch." Wherever we played huge crowds turned out, including thousands who never went to other baseball games. Towns held parades when we arrived, banners were strung out over the main streets announcing the arrival of the great Joe Jackson and his team. That was the way they said it, "his team," and it was his team for sure. City officials had their pictures taken with him, and keys to the cities were presented to him. Posters were placed in shop windows then quickly snapped up by kids who needed new decorations for their rooms.

Joe was a celebrity, maybe more in demand than he had ever been—at least in the South.

Of course, there was the other side, too. Some people, a lot of them good church goers, didn't think it was appropriate to go out and support his appearance. Some preachers spoke against him in their sermons as if he represented all that was evil in our society, but mostly folks were curious. They were curious to see a real live major leaguer play ball, because remember, there were no major league franchises in the South then. Joe was a novelty not to be missed. It was better than catching the circus when it came to town.

**HUGH FULLERTON** Joe was playing against talent so inferior to his own that the games became shams. He simply overpowered the pitchers, and completely dominated the games. Baseball is a game that demands reasonably equal opponents. I suppose that's probably true to some degree in all sport, but baseball is a particularly well balanced game. The shortstop stopping a grounder and throwing to first base will catch the runner by only a step or two. Even the smallest change in the dimensions of the field and the whole game is drastically altered. Joe altered all the games he played down there by dint of his sheer physical prowess. He didn't play in fair contests, he played in exhibitions.

As bad as that was, Joe began wandering outside the confines of organized league play, and began playing in impromptu games. He looked like a junkie in search of a baseball fix.

**COOPER ANDERSON** Joe had become a regular baseball gypsy, or maybe more accurately, a hired gun, a soldier of fortune. Offer to pay him, and he'd play in just about any level game. Need a celebrity player for your charity baseball game? Call Joe. Need to rekindle the baseball spirit in your community? Call Joe. Want to say you played against a baseball legend? Call Joe.

Joe was an equal opportunity player. Anybody with a buck could play with or against him and if you listen to some of the old-timers, it seems like almost everybody did. In time, Joe became a phenomenon. Have bat and glove; will travel. You pay, I play.

It didn't matter the level of the competition, Joe played like he actually wanted to win. Maybe he was trying to prove something to everyone—that he always played his best. At times it was ludicrous. Joe playing against kids 20 years younger. Joe playing against teams no better than rank beginners. But always, always, the fans loved to see him. They thronged to games. They bought tickets to see this curiosity, and they cheered for this good son of the South. It didn't matter that there was no real competition, for when he swung Black Betsy and hit a blue darter, they cheered. When he hit one over the fence, they were ecstatic.

"Joe once hit one over my head that must have gone at least 600 feet," bragged more than one father to his disbelieving son.

"I struck out Joe Jackson. You bet I did," became an account retold in countless bull sessions.

**CHARLIE LEBEAU** One afternoon in Montgomery, Alabama where I had gone to visit my sick sister, I ran into a pickup game in a field on the outskirts of town. I had no intention of watching, but as I passed by, the figure of the center fielder caught my eye. I knew that stance anywhere—Joe waiting to spring like a caged lion on the crack of the bat.

He wasn't wearing a uniform, and he must have been 20 or 30 pounds heavier than I remembered him, but it was Joe, no doubt about that.

It was long past the Brandon Mills days and I wondered if he would recognize me as easily as I recognized him. I went over, bought a ticket and sat in the stands. I've got to admit, I got teary-eyed watching him again, and thinking of the carefree days of summer when baseball was nothing but fun and promise. Joe was the best player on the field back then and he was this day, too. He was still graceful, if somewhat slower, but that natural swing of his, well it was still a one-of-a-kind and a thing of joy.

When the game was over I went down by the player's bench. Joe walked by. He didn't recognize me so I didn't say anything to him, but now I'm sorry I didn't. I should have said, "thanks."

**KATIE JACKSON** Sometimes I went with Joe when he barnstormed around from town to town, but mostly I didn't. I would have preferred it if he would have stayed home more, but I knew that wouldn't happen until Joe couldn't play anymore. I just prayed he'd recognize it when that day came. I didn't want him to make a fool of himself. I didn't ever want to see the day come when he fell down chasing a ball in the outfield because that magnificent God-given coordination had left him.

When he returned home after these trips he was usually so exhausted for days that all he would do was sleep and eat. He'd maybe work for a few days then he'd disappear again to play for some team we'd never heard of in some town I'd have to find on the map for him.

He had plenty of choices, I'll say that. Offers poured in for many years. "Name your price," many of them said, or some variation on that. If Joe could have split himself up, he could have played in scores of games every day,

At first, after he was let go by the White Sox, he was bitter about it and would say so to almost anyone who asked, but as time went on, he mentioned it less and less. Oh, I knew the hurt was still there, but it was sinking deeper into his soul, and I wasn't at all sure that was a healthy thing.

**J.C. HATCH** You would have thought that Joe, who was dragged kicking and screaming into the major leagues, who ran away at every given opportunity early in his career, would have relished the enforced banishment and enjoyed the anonymity that followed. But, not so.

The first I heard, he was playing up in the New York area for $200 bucks a game. He was playing on small fields with little or no press coverage, but he was playing.

**JOE JACKSON** It wasn't so bad, playing in them semi-pro leagues. The people in the stands, they got awful excited just like they did in places like Comiskey Park, but they didn't take it so serious that they had to arrest players and put them on trial because they didn't like the way they thought they was playing.

Katie was able to handle business when I was gone, and besides, I think she actually liked me playing ball again.

**BAN JOHNSON** When Joe and some of the other disgraced athletes began showing up in semi-pro games around the country, it immediately evoked the ire of many of us who had worked so hard to clean up the game. The jury's message that crookedness in sport was not a crime in Cook County Illinois in spite of confessions of guilt, was unacceptable. It was our feeling that the jury should have been put on trial for libeling the moral atmosphere of the people of Illinois. At the very least, we set out to see that they would not be permitted to join minor league clubs at any level of competition.

**JOHN F. KLUWIN** Not all of us would lower ourselves to let the Black Sox play in our leagues. Oh, I know they sold tickets, but there were higher ethical considerations to take into account.

I was president of the Fox River Valley Baseball League in 1922 when Jackson and a couple of the other banned players hooked up with our team in Appleton, Wisconsin. As soon as I heard this, I called a meeting of our Directors, and without much prompting, we reorganized the club so that the outlaws couldn't play.

Our league always stood for good American values, and that didn't include cheaters.

**VINCENT ALEXANDER** An incredible thing happened to me one day, when on the invitation of an old friend from high school days, I went with him to a baseball game in Hackensack, New Jersey. My friend seemed unusually anxious to get me to the game for reasons which were unclear until the game started.

The game, played at the Oritani Field Club grounds, was between a team apparently from a town called Westwood, because that is what it said in big red letters across the front of their jerseys, and a team known as the Hackensack-Bogota nine. As the game began, my friend sat in silence, offering no clue as to why he had spirited me there with such vigor. The game was already a couple of outs old before I noticed the center fielder for the Westwood team. His name was Josephs the program said—just Josephs. But I knew better. Joe Jackson under any other name was still the great shoeless one. My friend couldn't help breaking into the broadest grin you ever saw.

During the course of the afternoon, Joe rang up a single, a double and a home run, the latter being a terrific drive which sailed over the center field fence. He also threw a runner out at the plate.

There must have been in excess of 2,000 fans at the game. My initial response was that they had come out to see Joe, but my friend insisted that he acted on inside information when he invited me, and that the public had no idea that Joe was to make an appearance. The giveaway, apparently was that throw he made to home. Few players in the world could have made that throw. As soon as the throw was made, a buzz began circulating through the stands. Who was this guy?

I found out later that before the game the manager of the Westwood team was asked to reveal the identity of his new player, but he declared he did not know, adding that he hired the player through a New York semi-professional promoter. After the game, however, the manager, admitted that the strange player was, in fact, Joe Jackson, and that they had made efforts to obtain the services of Buck Weaver and Swede Risberg as well, but were unable to do so.

As a result of the disclosure, a storm of protest spewed forth from the players on the Hackensack-Bogota team and they declared they would not play the Westwood team again if Joe was in the lineup. Apparently some of them aspired to play minor or major league baseball someday, and they were afraid to have this desire thwarted because they played against a banned player.

**W.W. WILGUS** I was president of the Hackensack team, also called the Neighbors.

We had absolutely no knowledge that Jackson was to play with Westwood. We did hear that Westwood was to bring to Hackensack two or three new semi-pros, but we never gave the matter a thought, believing we would beat them no matter how many new men they played. It was barely possible that the Westwood manager knew nothing of the real identity of Jackson. I told Gildersleve, their manager, that he would have to make a public disclaimer or all future games would be canceled.

One thing I want to make clear, though. There was no betting on the game we did play. Any rumor that $12,000 was cleaned up by Westwood supporters is absolutely untrue. We allowed no betting on our grounds. Everything was conducted in big league style, and that meant no gamblers. We had a baseball team in which many of the business men of our town took pride. In fact, they were so enthusiastic that on numerous occasions, they made up deficits in the running expenses of the club. They even gave bonuses to players for their skill and loyalty.

Why I'm telling you all this is because I want to make it very clear that we were not at fault when we played against Jackson. In my mind there is no room for the Joe Jacksons in baseball and I don't want our town to be in any way associated with his name.

**EDDIE PHALEN** As promoter of the New York Association of Semi-Professional Baseball Clubs, one of my first tasks was to sign up Jackson and Weaver. As far as I was concerned, they were great drawing cards, whether guilty or innocent. I put out a lengthy press release insisting that I had looked into the matter of their guilt with great diligence and found that they were entirely guiltless of any wrongdoing. They claimed that they did not get a square deal and I loudly and consistently agreed with them. I called on anyone who believed in fairness to give them another chance to earn a decent livelihood.

This was exactly what was put to the fans in Poughkeepsie when Jackson played there. They were asked if they wanted to see Jackson play and they all shouted that nothing would suit them better. Joe played merely as any professional player would—for the legitimate money offered him. This I had to make clear to the public because of allegations to the contrary.

The public loved the controversy and the public was eager and willing to pay for the privilege of seeing these suddenly famous outlaws. As long as they were willing to do so, I was willing to assert their innocence. It hurt nobody and was damn good business sense.

**SWEDE RISBERG** Life as an outlaw ball player wasn't always the easiest. Like some of the other guys, I played on a lot of different teams in a lot of different little towns, and spent a lot of time traveling from one to the other. I'll tell you, it was pretty rough at times, pretty tiring, too. But we got paid—usually. Maybe we were a little like freaks in a circus show, but hey, more people seemed to want to see us after we were banned than before.

One Friday afternoon I was playing up in Milwaukee on a team with Cicotte and he started rubbing me the wrong way as only he could, and we ended up getting into one hellacious fight—I mean fisticuffs and all. Nobody was hurt, but he took off like a bat out of hell, leaving us a player short.

I managed to get a hold of Joe who was playing in the New York area and talked him into coming out and playing a couple of games with us.

That's kind of the way the whole deal went. Informal and casual, and a lot less hassles than working for Comiskey.

Little by little, though it became harder to get engagements. First one league then another jumped on the morality bandwagon and decided that banning us was a moral posture that somehow elevated the stature of the hypocrites running the leagues to a new level.

At one point me and Joe had offers to go down and play with some teams in the Philadelphia Baseball Association. Joe turned them down right away saying Philadelphia wasn't exactly his favorite town, but I had no such aversion to the place, so I accepted and took a Pullman down there. Only when I arrived I was told that the league voted to not let any of us play. I was out the train fare and any contract.

Another time I was in Eveleth, Minnesota with Joe and Lefty to play in the Mesabi Range League. That time the players went on strike and refused to play with us, so they found three real amateurs to replace us.

That's how it, though. Some people loved us, some hated us. Some showed up to cheer us; some to jeer.

**BAN JOHNSON** I got wind of a rumor that Jackson and Risberg were going to go down to Mexico to play in a league down there. To make matters worse, I read an announcement that Hal Chase had been engaged to manage the team in Nogales, Mexico. As it so happens, I had long been interested in promoting the game in the Southern Republic so I had no intention of permitting outlaw players from the United States getting a foothold there.

I extended the ban on the players to include Mexico, and even offered a valuable trophy intended to stimulate competition among the Mexican baseball teams.

The last thing I wanted was to export our crooks to a friendly foreign country.

**KATIE JACKSON** We were comfortable in Savannah. The cleaning business was pretty much taking care of itself, because Joe was on the road a lot. We were making as much money as we ever did, maybe more, but the traveling was something awful. It seems like Joe was living on trains and in strange hotels, but the alternative was worse—sitting around the house with nothing to do.

**JOE JACKSON** I didn't realize how good I had it in the major leagues until I didn't have it no more. We used to have people who made all the train reservations for us, and at the hotels, too. We had people who took care of our equipment, and told us when we had to be at the stadium. Playing semipro ball, we didn't have none of that, but in time I got used to it and got along pretty good.

Once or twice I had a little trouble getting paid on time, but most of the time that wasn't a problem because nobody wanted to get a reputation for not paying the players. Mostly there were no contracts. We just agreed how much I would be paid for each game, and then after the game the promoter would give me an envelope with my money in it. Then, if I was going to play another game for him, we made another arrangement.

When Katie came along, and she did a few times, that was different. Sometimes I even signed a contract, particularly if I was going to play a bunch of games for the same team.

Sometimes, too, I played with one of the guys—Lefty, or Swede or Buck mostly. Gandil, I don't think he played much after we left the Sox, and Eddie, he didn't play much either. Then one day I heard he quit altogether and became a game warden up in Michigan, somewhere outside of Detroit.

It's funny how when you're with some guys for so long you think you're going to know them the rest of your life, but then you don't.

**EDDIE PHALEN** The summer after their expulsion, I set up a big meeting in New York for Joe to come and talk to the public and tell his side of the story. I hired the Manhattan Casino for a mass meeting and invited Joe to come. He didn't show which was a real shame because I know he still had a lot of supporters and I know they would have liked to hear from him.

Since the meeting didn't work, I went to plan B. I hired 400 men to carry placards during rush hours in the subways and on elevated lines appealing for a "square deal" for Jackson and Weaver. I also appealed to those who had taken up the cudgels on behalf of Jackson and Weaver to have such placards shown outside the Polo Grounds and Ebbets Field.

As a banker I knew the value of the campaign. I was even willing to assume a financial burden in order that Jackson and Weaver—just those two—might get what I considered a square deal.

Until and unless these two were reinstated by Landis, I was willing to feature them on a semi-pro team in New York. And I was willing to do it under their correct names. I even arranged for that to happen up in South Norwalk, Connecticut where Joe was playing while we were making arrangements in New York.

I also informed the Westwood team in New Jersey that if the Hackensack-Bogota club canceled their next game against them because Joe was playing as they had threatened, then I would send one of our New York Semi-Professional Association teams to give the Westwoods a contest in order that the fans would not be deprived of seeing Jackson.

I offered Joe a contract calling for $1,000 a week, which was probably more than he was making with the White Sox. Several reporters questioned how I could afford to do that, but the answer was really simple. I was getting more offers for bookings than I could possibly handle. I began by arranging a series of seven games. The team would be known as Shoeless Joe Jackson's All-Stars. Once Weaver joined him, I would build another team around him, thereby setting the stage for a Jackson-Weaver showdown.

I want to make it perfectly clear that these were the only so-called Black Sox I was willing to handle, as I believed both of them to be innocent of any wrongdoing.

I arranged for a respectable team of players to support him. I even got

Marty Walsh, brother of Big Ed Walsh who pitched for years with the White Sox, to be our pitcher. Dutch Voltz signed on at shortstop. Our outfield was set to be Tom Gregory, Joe Jackson and Jack Hayes. Not exactly murderer's row, but good, solid semi-pro players who knew the game and played hard. I was set to catch.

Eventually we changed the name to Joe Jackson's Big League Martyrs.

I had also hoped to bring the Sons of David to New York to meet Jackson's team, and was about to announce a new baseball attraction in a team called the Scranton Miners who were going to play with the lights they use in the mines on their caps.

No miscarriage of justice was going to stop Joe and Buck from playing baseball.

**BAN JOHNSON** Eddie Phelps was a lying con artist extraordinaire. He pretended to care about Jackson and Weaver, but all he really cared about was making an easy buck. He wanted to put on a baseball sideshow with him as the barker. Baseball is too good of a game to put up with that kind of hucksterism.

**JOE JACKSON** People kept asking me if I was trying to get reinstated. What I told them was I wasn't trying to get reinstated, anyhow not like Buck was trying, but that if Commissioner Landis wanted to reinstate me, that would be fine, too. I told them that as long as I had strength, I was going to play the game, even if I had to do it by myself. Baseball was the only thing I knowed how to do.

Some of them, they acted real disappointed that I didn't say I was real sorry for what I done, but I didn't say that because I wasn't sorry, and the reason I wasn't sorry was that I didn't do nothing wrong so I didn't have nothing to be sorry about. The only thing I felt guilty about was hanging around the wrong guys and listening to the wrong people at the wrong time.

**MARTY WALSH** All that stuff Ed Phalen put out about me being associated with Joe Jackson was just that much bunk. At the time, I was pitching for the Highbridge Athletics and never had any connection with Jackson or Phalen.

I didn't associate with cheaters or liars, so that immediately ruled me out with both of them.

**NAT STRONG** I was President of the Metropolitan Baseball Association when Phelps and his troupe of trained monkeys tried to invade the city. What he forgot was we controlled all of the enclosed parks in and around Greater New York, and we simply would not tolerate Joe Jackson either on their teams or club playing against them.

**EDDIE PHALAN** I began a nationwide movement to restore Shoeless Joe Jackson in the good graces of organized baseball. The appeal to Landis for reinstatement was to be based on signed petitions asking that Joe Jackson get a "square deal." Once printed, these petitions were sent to every city in the country in which there was an organized baseball team. My intention was simple: get a million signatures and then send the petitions to Judge Landis. I believed that there was no way he could ignore such an outpouring of public sentiment.

I spent considerable time in wording the body of the petition: "We the undersigned baseball fans, devotees and law-abiding American citizens respectfully and earnestly petition those organized baseball interests represented by the Honorable Kenesaw M. Landis as their High Commissioner, to take immediately those measures and steps necessary to clear the professional reputation of Joe Jackson, formerly of the Chicago White Sox from odium or discredit before the American public in connection with any so-called baseball scandal. In view of his acquittal by jury in a duly constituted court of justice in Chicago, Illinois, and his well-known innocence of any wrongdoing, to cease to countenance the justice of truth of any rumor or publicity which refers to Joe Jackson as an "outlaw," and to lift all bans against Joe Jackson, and leaving Joe Jackson free to solicit without stigma and practice in peace, without hindrance, his honorable livelihood and calling before the world as a great artist in the game of baseball."

**KENESAW MOUNTAIN LANDIS** Oh, I got bushels of letters, and stacks of petitions. Some asking Joe and Buck to be exonerated, some asking that they be dammed in eternal hell. The latter was outside even my jurisdiction, but I never gave a moment's thought to reducing their penalties.

The petitions did, however, come in handy as scrap paper, and I do appreciate the contributions to keeping the overhead of the Commissioner's office to a minimum.

**BAN JOHNSON** It seems like every bleeding heart and his sister had some petition or other to collect signatures calling for reinstatement. The good people, though, knew better.

**JOE JACKSON** There was a lot of hubbub about me playing in all them semi-pro games, but mostly I didn't pay no attention. If they paid me I played, if they didn't I didn't. It was as simple as that.

I guess I stayed playing longer than most of the guys, but after a while I really didn't hear from them much anymore. Lefty I did, for a while I guess. He took over the pool room in Chicago which I opened. He ran that for a while, then gave that up and moved out to Laguna Beach, California. Somebody told me later that he ran some kind of garden-nursery out there. I never talked to him again after he moved out there. I don't know if he played ball in California or not, but my guess is that he probably didn't. Maybe he saw Chick, though, because Chick became a plumber in California. I never heard from him neither.

I'll tell you, there was some good players on some of them teams I played with. I saw a kid named Stanley make a play in the hole at second base once that would have made Eddie Collins and Nap Lajoie stand and applaud, and I saw dozens of kids playing for the fun of the game with all their heart.

# 54

# I DIDN'T LIKE THE IDEA ONE BIT

**JOE JACKSON** Lawyers kept coming after me and telling me I should let them sue the White Sox because the team let me go illegally and that they really owed me my salary for the rest of my contract. They said the team would have sued me if I didn't do what was in the contract and that they probably expected me to do the same to them.

"It's your money, Joe," they kept telling me. "If you don't want it, that's OK, but it's your money."

The lawyers said if we sued that there would be another trial that might take weeks, and that we would have to start with finding a new jury and all that stuff. I didn't want to do it, that's all, but everybody kept telling me that I was stupid if I didn't get the money that was owed to me. I also heard some of the other fellows like Buck was going to do the same thing, but I've got to tell you, I really didn't like the idea one bit.

**BUCK WEAVER** I guess I was the first player to file suit against the club, and I urged Joe to do the same.

My goal was simple: I wanted to be reinstated. I wanted to play major league ball again. I was only 30 when I got dumped, surely young enough to have some good years ahead of me if only I could get the chance again. I don't think Joe really thought about reinstatement. At least that's what he kept saying. I guess he had resigned himself to playing semi-pro ball. Either that, or he just didn't want to deal with the tension and anxiety which the process would inevitably entail.

I went ahead and filed my own suit, although I would like to have done so in conjunction with Joe. Technically what I did what was called filing a writ of attachment. (Unfortunately, I've become something of an expert in these matters.) The writ, filed in the municipal court in Chicago, was an attempt to collect the $20,000 back salary which both my lawyer and me believed was due me under my contract.

Remember, we were found not guilty by verdict of the jury. What I was really hoping was that the suit might force the hand of the league resulting in reinstatement. If that didn't work, I'd take the $20,000.

**KENESAW MOUNTAIN LANDIS** George Weaver continually applied for reinstatement, arguing every time that he was innocent. He was pushing Joseph Jackson in the same direction.

I reminded Mr. Weaver that indictments were returned against both of them, and at the trial which followed, a witness for the prosecution gave what he claimed was a detailed account of the meeting with the indicted men at which arrangements for the throwing of the World Series games were made.

The report showed that Mr. Weaver was present in court during the testimony of this witness, and yet the case went to the jury without any denial from Weaver.

If the incriminating evidence was false, the baseball public had a right to Weaver's denial under oath. It was also likewise true that the same jury returned the same verdict in favor of Mr. Jackson.

**HAPPY FELSCH** Trying to get money out of that liar Comiskey wasn't easy when we played for him, and it certainly didn't get any easier after we were out.

**HARRY GRABINER** On at least one occasion we tried to settle the dispute with Happy Felsch. I sent a check to Mr. Felsch. Six months later I received a letter from him stating that the check had never arrived. I mailed a second check. Mr. Felsch returned that one, and then complained to the press that we owed him money.

**RAYMOND CANNON** As Felsch's attorney I made every effort to settle the controversy without court action. I was referred by Comiskey by their attorney, Alfred Austrian, who in turn referred me back to Mr. Comiskey. After that we were referred to Mr. Landis, then back to Comiskey, then back to Austrian again.

This is a story similar to the one reported to me by Jackson's attorney. It appeared that the only channel we had to have our grievances heard, was the court ... again.

**HAPPY FELSCH** I had no choice but to file suit. Included in my suit was the story of the 1917 American League pennant race. If they wanted to dig up dirt so badly, I figured I might as well give them some.

I was on the Sox in 1917 when we raised a fund to reward Detroit battery men with money to induce extra effort for the Tigers to defeat our rivals for the pennant. I went public with the story to try to force Comiskey to pay attention to our grievances. It wasn't ever easy to get his attention. It wasn't even easy when I played for him.

**BAN JOHNSON** Felsch's story was nothing new, for we had all the evidence ready in the trial of the corrupt players, but it never was presented. I had unearthed the evidence in my own investigation and even told Landis about it.

It must be borne in mind that the money was not used to make any players throw games. It was simply a reward for a player to use extra effort against a pennant rival of the White Sox. Of course it was wrong and not permissible, yet it was not a criminal act like that of the Sox.

Felsch, and Weaver, and Jackson were merely seizing the straw to get money out of organized baseball, but we weren't about to give them a cent.

**FRANK J. NAVIN** Felsch was a discredited man, known to be dishonest, and in making the charge he was unquestionably actuated by ulterior motives. If he had anything to say about the Tigers throwing a pennant, he should have said it when he was on trial.

The fact is, we were all getting a little tired of the players' complaints. They were the ones who were constantly whining about being mistreated. They were the ones always suing somebody or at least threatening to sue somebody. We just wanted them to disappear into the California sunset like Gandil, and leave us alone to get on with the running of baseball.

**EDDIE COLLINS** Felsch was merely seeking to hurt organized baseball which had cast him out. If anyone needs any evidence of that, just look at Detroit's late-season successes against us in the 1917 season. If that doesn't show the fallacy of his claim, I don't know what does.

As for Joe, I hated to see him getting caught up in all these spurious charges and countercharges. He had taken enough of a beating as it was.

I didn't see Joe again for years after he left the team, but if I had, I would have strongly suggested he listen to counsel other than those who had his ear.

**RAYMOND CANNON** I first met Joe in a little diner outside of New York. I can't remember exactly where but Joe was playing in some outlaw league in the vicinity and he agreed to meet me.

I told him about my baseball playing experiences in the Wisconsin-Illinois League while I was pursuing a law degree. I was either a baseball-playing lawyer, or a lawyering baseball player, depending on one's perspective. At any rate, I thought I might be of some help to Joe, and I thought he might listen to me inasmuch as we shared at least a partial common vocabulary.

I had long felt that the business of baseball was all wrong, that the players were not getting a fair deal from owners, and that a professional baseball union was essential for the future of the game. Baseball was being run by the Comiskeys of the world with callous regard for the players' welfare. What chance did someone like a Joe Jackson have against the likes of an Alfred Austrian? About as much as I would have had against Joe Louis in the ring. Austrian was a graduate of Harvard Law School. Joe's only training was in a cotton mill. Austrian was a collector of fine prints and expensive works of art. He even owned a page from the original Gutenberg Bible. Joe was, let's say, considerably less sophisticated in his tastes.

Clearly, the organization of baseball was counter to the best interests of the players, and was a clear violation of their rights as defined by the Sherman Antitrust Law. That law, passed by Congress by an almost unanimous vote in 1890 declared "every contract, combination in the form of trust or otherwise, or conspiracy in restraint of trade or commerce" was illegal. It remains one of the most fundamental and important laws of the land.

Organized baseball violated both the letter and principle of the law, and there was no appeal process for the player. Do what the owner says for what the owner will pay, or you don't play. The only answer was a players' union, a union strong enough to stand up to the imperious acts of Comiskey and his buddies.

I had agreed to help Felsch, and I was willing to do the same for Joe. Partly this came out of a sense of truly wanting to help him in what was a lopsided battle, and partly as an attempt to gain visibility and favor with the players. I wanted their support in forming a union for them.

**JOE JACKSON** Ray Cannon was OK. He offered to help me against the Sox and he seemed to know what he was talking about seeing as how he was a baseball player himself once. I don't think he was all that good, though, as a player, but as a lawyer I liked him.

We had dinner one night and he explained to me just how he thought we could go after the White Sox for money they owed me. He said it in a way that didn't make it look cheesy. He also seemed like the first lawyer who really cared that I got what was due me.

The other thing that I liked about him was that he reminded me of a Ty Cobb-like fighter, like somebody who was going to do whatever it took to win the game in the bottom of the ninth, even with two outs.

**RAYMOND CANNON** Before we even got to the dessert, Joe had agreed to let me file suit on his behalf. The suit was for $9,000 a year for the two years remaining on Joe's contract.

The key to the argument was the deliberately underhanded ploy by Harry Grabiner in getting Joe to sign the contract without letting him have someone to read it to him. Everyone, including Mr. Grabiner, knew that Joe was illiterate, so any attempt to pressure him to sign something he couldn't read was patently misleading, and perhaps fraudulent. A section in the contract read that the White Sox could void the contract with a 10-day notice to the player.

According to Joe, he specifically asked Grabiner about this, and was assured there was no such clause in the contract. Joe said he asked about this a second time, and even said he would not sign a contract with this in it. Again Grabiner avowed there was no such clause in the contract.

Joe then signed the contract on the basis that it was an ironclad three-year contract at $9,000 per year. Forget that the salary itself was ludicrous, the very act of lying to Joe by misrepresenting the contract to an illiterate individual was enough to win the case.

I talked to Joe at some length about this. He was very definite in all of his answers and very sure of himself on all of the particulars.

**JOE JACKSON** Mr. Grabiner told me there was no 10-day out clause in the contract. Look, I may not be a lawyer or nothing but I was around enough baseball contracts in my life to know what that meant. I signed the contract on the hood of the car outside my house because I believed what he told me.

**HARRY GRABINER** I had explained the contract very carefully to Joe, and I did it in front of his wife while we were all seated in the living room of their house. Mrs. Jackson read the contract word-for-word, and then told Joe to sign it, which he did. There was nothing shady about the deal.

**RAYMOND CANNON** The owners were getting the best of it both ways. They could sign a young kid for say $4,000 for four years. While he develops into a star worth three times that, they have him signed at a bargain-basement price. But if the kid should break a leg going into second base trying to win a game so the owner can make more money, the owner can quickly give the player his 10-day notice and he's not liable for any more of the salary. That's why the players need a union! The deck was not only stacked in favor of the owners, they owned the deck as well.

**CHARLES COMISKEY** Ray Cannon talked Joe into the suit for one reason only—he wanted a platform for his own union organizing schemes. He was a publicity monger and a trouble maker, but we were not about to be black-jacked into meeting unreasonable demands by the players.

Here's the point though, isn't it? It was Jackson who failed to comply with his contract, not the White Sox. Cannon wanted it to look like I was the bad guy, but I didn't throw the World Series, now, did I? This is a typical trick of many attorneys—divert attention from the issues to some procedural matter.

**RAYMOND CANNON** Joe was less than enthusiastic about going back into the courtroom, but it was necessary. I assured him that I would be with him all the way, and that there wouldn't be anything similar to the circus-like atmosphere he had experienced in his trial.

There was, however, one giant surprise waiting for all of us. Fairly early on in the proceedings, I had Comiskey on the stand and he was saying that it was Joe, not him who broke the contract.

I came back quickly, "The law has tried my client and acquitted him! Where then is there any proof of guilt?"

One of Austrian's henchmen, working the trial for him, immediately referred the court to Joe's grand jury confession.

"What confession?" I demanded, knowing damn well that the so-called confessions were lost.

Well, surprise of surprises! The Austrian flunky reached into his expensive leather briefcase and out popped the missing documents.

"My, my!" I responded. "Look at that, a magic briefcase!"

The flunky looked completely nonplused. So did Comiskey for that matter.

"How is it that those restricted grand jury records are in your hands?" I demanded at full vocal power.

The flunky looked at Comiskey. Comiskey looked at the flunky. Obviously neither one of them was prepared to answer. They each fumbled around for a moment, obviously hoping the other would have some clever answer.

The best these two brilliant minds could come up with though was Comiskey's, "I don't know."

"You don't know!" I bellowed in my finest oratorical voice. I had visions of myself arguing the most important case in the country in front of the Supreme Court, and I was enjoying myself immensely.

"You don't know!" I repeated. Only this time I looked over at Joe and gave him a big wink. It wasn't often one could experience Comiskey at a loss for words and on the defensive.

"I'm sorry I don't know," he muttered shooting an arrow of disdain toward his hired hand who was doing nothing to come to his rescue.

Poor Comiskey, even he was having difficulty in hiring good help in those days.

It didn't take an Einstein to figure out the life story of the transcripts. Arnold Rothstein, our foremost gambler and fixer, had them purloined from the State's Attorney's office so as to maintain a respectable distance from anything quite so sordid as a Series fix. To help Comiskey out of an $18,000 jam he loaned Austrian the documents. Now Comiskey owed him, and in A.R.'s world, chits like this were the coin of the realm.

Plant a seed of doubt in the jury's mind. That was all I could do. I wasn't interested in guilt or innocence, leave that to St. Peter. No, I was interested in doubt. Get the jury to think, "well, maybe ...." Confusion and doubt were my allies. Every time a definitive statement was made I tried to obfuscate the issue; every time someone offered a fact, I added skepticism.

When a section of the grand jury records was read where Joe apparently answered yes to the question of whether he had done anything to fix the World Series, I countered with another section where he apparently answered no. When Comiskey offered that he believed Joe to be guilty, I extracted from him the statement that he could not come up with a single concrete example of Joe making one dishonest move to throw a game. When the defense attorney brought up Joe's confession, I brought up Joe's repudiation of the confession. No statement was left unchallenged; no seed of doubt left unsowed.

When the defense brought in an expert who testified that the contract was indeed signed on a flat, even surface, I found one who testified that it was definitely not signed on a flat, even surface. I love expert witnesses! You can find one to testify about almost anything.

I couldn't help but to paint a picture of Joe as a confused, not-too-sharp, gullible, athlete who was susceptible to the caprice of others. But after all, wasn't that the public image of him anyway? I have to admit to a certain degree of compassion and pity for the player sitting in the courtroom for the full three weeks of the trial, dressed in his Sunday best, trying to appear as if he was following everything that was going on while innuendoes and guile were flying above his head.

Knowing that a good offense is a good defense, I kept the pressure on Comiskey. Paint him as the villain in the proceedings and divert attention from Joe.

"Comiskey's investigation after the World Series was merely a subterfuge to fall back on in the event that the disloyalty of the ballplayers was later discovered!" I told the jury. "Comiskey accused Gandil of being a ringleader immediately after the Series was over, and not withstanding that fact, he sent him a contract for the following year."

Comiskey the hypocrite was a picture I painted as carefully as I could.

"If Comiskey intends to hold the confidence of the American public, he will have to refrain from highhanded methods of dealing with his players. The truth is, his Secretary, Harry Grabiner, tricked Jackson into signing his three-year contract, and slipped into it a 10-day clause. The contract itself, thusly forced on a ballplayer, is so grossly and obviously unfair that Comiskey himself must blush with shame at the signing of it."

Some of the press attacked me, saying I was making it look like Comiskey was the bad guy. All I can say to that is, I sure hope so.

By the time the jury retired to begin their deliberations, I was feeling pretty good about things. Joe asked me what was going to happen. I told him that I was cautiously optimistic.

The jury was out only a short time. When they returned, the question was put to them, "Did the plaintiff Jackson unlawfully conspire with Gandil, Williams and other members of the White Sox, or any of them, to lose or 'throw' any of the baseball games of the 1919 World Series to the Cincinnati Baseball Club?" The foreman of the jury answered loudly and decisively, "No." Joe was awarded $16,711.04.

As far as I was concerned, it was a victory so far reaching as to bring about Joe's ultimate return to organized baseball. Joe had endured two, long, separate trials at which time he was up against the mighty forces of organized baseball and the considerable resources they demanded. Both juries found him innocent; both juries agreed there was no evidence that said he threw any games. This was the American way, wasn't it? He was found twice innocent by a panel of his peers. Joe should have been able to resume his professional career.

The Judge in the case, Judge Gregory, however had his own ideas. He called Joe to the bench and berated him as if he were a small child.

"Mr. Jackson, you are guilty of perjury. You signed a sworn confession of your complicity before the grand jury. You have now testified under oath in my courtroom of your innocence. I therefore order you to be placed under arrest and fix your bail at five thousand dollars."

He then laced into the jury declaring the entire case was based on

Jackson's perjury, and then set aside the verdict, and dismissed the case.

Shock overtook everyone in the room. Joe was escorted out of court by two bailiffs. He stopped at the door, turned and looked at me. As long as I live, I will never forget the look on his face. It is one of the few images in my life that is permanently etched in my memory. Joe looked completely bewildered, like a puppy dog who was just spanked for something he didn't understand. His look said it all: "I thought we won. What did I do wrong now?"

I'm not absolutely sure about this, but at the time I thought I saw his eyes moist up. If they didn't they should have.

Once again, the system found him innocent, but he was punished anyway. That's not how it is supposed to go, is it?

Joe was carted off to jail. I don't think he was ever the same again.

# 55

## NO USE TELLING THE TRUTH

**JOE JACKSON** There I was in this little dark cell by myself, locked up like I was a criminal, only every time a jury got together, they said I wasn't a criminal. Something ain't right, I tell you. Something ain't right at all.

I came to a decision that night sitting in the jail. I realized it was no use telling the truth because every time I did I got into more hot water. I made up my mind that I wasn't going to talk about the 1919 Series no more. Let Chick and Eddie if they wanted to, but not me. Nobody wanted to hear the truth anyways. They only wanted to hear what they wanted to hear.

From the time of the jail on, I turned my back completely on the Chicago White Sox and the major leagues. I told myself that I would never make any request to be reinstated and would never make any campaign to have my name cleared in the baseball records.

I thought when my first trial was over that Judge Landis might have put me back to good standing. But he never did. And I have never gone before him or sent him any kind of written matter pleading my case.

I gave baseball my best and if the game didn't care enough to see me get a square deal, then I wasn't going to go out of my way to get back in.

Baseball failed to keep faith with me. When I got notice of my suspension it said that if I was found innocent of anything wrong, I would be reinstated. If I was found guilty I would be banned for life. I was found innocent and I was still banned for life. How do you suppose that made me feel about baseball?

It was never explained to me officially, but I was told that Judge Landis said I was banned because of the company I kept. I roomed with my friend Lefty Williams, one of the ringleaders they told me. But I am not going to say he wasn't my friend, because he was. He also wasn't no ringleader.

My brother, Jerry, was a pretty good minor league pitcher they tell me, only I didn't get to see him pitch because I was always away playing myself. Anyway, it's probably a good thing none of my brothers made it to the major leagues. Maybe they was better off playing where they did.

I never had no ax to grind, and I never asked nobody for anything. It's all water over the dam as far as I'm concerned. I can say that my conscience is clear and that I'll stand on my record. I'm not what you call a good Christian, but I have asked the Lord for guidance before, and I am sure He gave it to me. I'm willing to let the Lord be my judge.

# 56

# I KNOW WHAT THEY SAY

**CHICK GANDIL** I haven't spent the rest of my life trying to get back into baseball like Buck has. To me that would have been nothing more than an exercise in frustration. I've got a life to live outside the game, and I'm living it. Besides, I've never truthfully resented the banishment, because, even though the Series wasn't thrown, we were guilty of a serious offense, and we knew it.

I've come to accept responsibility for what I did, and that puts me at ease with myself. Not like some. Not like Joe, for instance. If you ask me, he's been fighting with himself. He's never been quite willing to acknowledge his role. Until and unless he does, he's never going to rest easy.

**HUGH FULLERTON** Some of the players went quietly into the night. Others railed on for some time screaming "injustice." What they failed to realize is that the supreme court of baseball is not governed by the same restrictions as a court of law.

I don't think Joe ever understood this. Say something enough times, even a lie, and eventually you begin to believe it. I'm convinced that Joe actually came to believe what he was saying—that he was innocent. Later in life he became intransigent. He lost touch with the reality of his actions. He became angry when challenged on his word. Joe simply couldn't tell the difference between the truth and what he wanted to be the truth.

**JOE JACKSON** The truth? I've said it over and over again, only some people don't want to hear it. Some people would rather have the lie that makes things right rather than the truth that makes things hard.

**RAYMOND CANNON** I talked to Joe about appealing, but he had no stomach left for courtroom brawls. He had fought twice but lost in the winning. I contacted Comiskey without Joe's knowledge, and upon lying to him about Joe's demand to appeal, he agreed to an out-of-court settlement. Joe ended up getting only a small part of the $18,000 owed him, but I thought it was the least I could do for him.

By the time I had collected the money, Joe and his wife had moved back to Greenville. I sent him a check and a nice letter telling him I wished it was for more. I never heard from him again.

**KATIE JACKSON** For a while, Joe's mother came to live with us. She had had a stroke and was paralyzed then, so I had to spend a lot of time looking after her, especially when Joe was off playing. It wasn't easy.

We liked Savannah all right, and we had some good friends there, but the time came when we both yearned to return home to Greenville.

One night I said to Joe right out of the blue, "Joe, why don't we go back to Greenville? Buy a little house on the edge of town. Be close to our families again."

"You know, I was thinking the same thing," he said.

And that was it. That was the whole discussion. We put the business and the house up for sale, got on a train and headed for home.

We took the money from the dry cleaning business and set up a bigger one in Greenville.

After we were there a while, we opened a barbecue place out on Augusta Road, a few blocks beyond the Greenville city limits. I got a good deal on it, and when Joe was in town, he hung around enough to attract extra customers. Folks, they liked to talk baseball to Joe, and he made each person feel like they were important. He took the time with little kids, and I guess he must have said at least 5 million times, "no, it ain't so."

Later, we bought a liquor store in West Greenville, which just happened to be the part of town where Brandon Village once was. Not much was left of the old village except memories, but I think Joe liked being there.

Many a night he talked of playing there as a kid. He talked about his brothers, and playing on a team with them. He talked a lot about how the game used to be played. About how the newer players were spoiled.

Despite what some of the writers wrote, we were happy back in

Greenville. Business went well, and Joe continued to play semi-pro and amateur ball in the summers. Joe insisted that as long as he was physically able, he was going to continue to play. Not every league or team would let him, but there were plenty who would.

Joe, of course, was a celebrity in town, and everywhere he went, he drew attention. Still, these were our folks and the attention was far less critical and more accepting than in the North. I venture to say that more people recognized Joe than recognized the mayor. He was maybe the most famous person in the history of Greenville.

Sometimes he teamed up with a couple of his brothers who were still in the area and they went hunting.

Joe sometimes even went to Harrison's and talked baseball with the boys.

Lots of times people would cut out articles from northern papers and send them to me. Most of them I put in a scrapbook but didn't dare read to Joe.

They claimed things like "Joe was starving down in South Carolina, eking out a bare and brutal living pressing pants." Or, "Joe Jackson is destitute and on the verge of total financial and psychological collapse."

I had to laugh. Our business was doing quite well, thank you. We employed almost 30 people in our two stores and our cleaning plant. We owned our own home outright, and a nice place it was, too. We owned not one, but two shiny automobiles.

There was even one cartoon in a Chicago paper which showed a picture of a very depressed Joe standing over an ironing board in a shabby room next to a large pile of pants which presumably he was about to iron. Oh, yes, he was in his bare feet. The caption read: "Shoeless Joe's Ironing Bored."

I assure you, Joe never pressed a pair of pants in his life. I pretty much ran the business. Joe helped out some, but not by ironing. We hired help to do that.

The fact of the matter is, we were making more money than when Joe was in the major leagues. Thank you, Mr. Comiskey!

One paper claimed he was getting all of \$5 a game, \$7.50 for a doubleheader. The fact of the matter is, he was often making \$150 a game or 40 percent of the receipts whichever was more. Joe could still draw a crowd, have no doubt about that.

Let's look at it this way: he was making more than double what Mr.

Comiskey paid him, and his expenses weren't nearly as high.

I guess Joe sold a lot of newspapers for writers who made up stories about him, but like so much written about him, much of it wasn't true.

We may not have been the richest folks in town, but we were doing right well.

**J.C. HATCH** Joe was something of a character around Harrison's. He started seeing himself as a regular raconteur. As time went on, I think he actually began believing some of the things he was saying.

I remember him telling people that Frazier Heath was better than Honus Wagner. Well, I'm here to tell you, that just wasn't anywhere near the truth. Oh, Frazier was a decent little player, all right—I saw him many times—and he could go into the hole pretty good. But better than Wagner? All Wagner could do in his career was to win eight National League Batting titles and finish with a career .327 average. Frazier couldn't have carried his jock strap!

**HUGH FULLERTON** It seems like every season some do-gooder began a campaign to get Joe reinstated, and with every campaign came the opposition. Westbrook Pegler, the syndicated columnist even began a counter campaign arguing that the banned players should have been sent directly to jail, if for nothing else, tax evasion. He waxed poetic on the evils of gambling and, "the wages of sin," and he wrote with a preacher's zeal on the morality of not pardoning Joe. There are times when not being able to read must have been a blessing to Joe.

If Pegler was adamant, Landis was even more so. Forgiveness seems not to have been a part of his constitution; vindictiveness was. While he never forgave any of the eight men out, he seems to have harbored a special distaste for Jackson.

**JOHN MAULDIN** I was mayor of Greenville when Joe and Katie returned, and I must say, we were pleased to have them back in our community. Most of the citizens accepted them into the life of Greenville, but it was clear from the outset that they would always be somewhat apart. It was almost as if when you met them you had to pass judgment, you had to take a position about the morality of interacting with them. Reactions varied from one extreme to the other. From Joe as a wronged hero, to Joe as a defiler of the American way of life. It seems that everybody, if they were of a mind to, could convince themselves that they were better than Joe—either smarter or more virtuous.

Shortly after they returned, the organizers of the semiprofessional leagues in the area expressed interest in having Joe join the league. They said lots of people who saw him play on his way up, were eager to see him play on his way down. And, it would be good for baseball in the area, went the refrain.

The only problem was that none of us wanted to see the young men who might play with or against him get punished. The idea of contamination was real. Judge Landis was a vengeful man.

So to appease everybody, I circulated a petition addressed to Landis asking permission for Joe to play in Greenville, and for anyone who played with or against him to be automatically cleared of any wrongdoing.

The boys over at Harrison's all signed it, and so did most of the good folks of our community. A few refused, and that was understandable, but in all, we collected about five thousand signatures and sent it off to the commissioner.

He turned us down cold with nary an explanation. Now, some of the folks in town were so nettled by Landis' callous actions that they supported Joe anyway, and made him player-manager of the local team.

I must say, in all the years they were with us, Joe and Katie were model citizens. They minded their business, paid their taxes and stayed out of trouble. Would that everybody were such good citizens.

**KENESAW MOUNTAIN LANDIS** There are not, and cannot be, two standards of eligibility, one for the major leagues, and one for the minors. Mr. Jackson's actions back in Greenville were in direct defiance of my decision that he should not engage in any professional baseball activity. He proved over and over again, that he was not a man of character.

**JOE JACKSON** Some people will tell you I ain't smart enough to manage, but I did. In fact, I managed a number of teams, including the Woodside Mill team in the King Cotton League, where we won a couple of championships.

**CHARIE LEBEAU** Maybe you wouldn't want him to do brain surgery on you, but if you had a baseball team, you could find a lot of worse managers.

One game I remember, Joe was playing center field and managing Woodside Mill when in the ninth the bases were loaded against him in a tie game and the batter hits a high fly down the left field line only foul by a couple of feet. Well, the left fielder takes off like a bat out of hell and is just about to catch up to the ball when Joe yells at him to let it fall which he does at the last minute. Now it looked to the crowd like Joe was crazy for giving up the out, but he knew that if the ball was caught, the runner from third would have scored easily after the catch. He figured the heart of his lineup was coming up in the bottom of the inning with him right in the middle, so he was willing to take the chance. As it turns out, he was spot on. On the next pitch, the batter with a second life, lined into an inning-ending double play, and Joe drove in the winning run with a long double.

There's intelligence, and there's intelligence. At least when it came to baseball, Joe was intelligent.

**JOE JACKSON** Two things I know about: baseball and pants pressing. Pants pressing paid better, but baseball was still a hell of a lot more fun.

I played for years down in the Greenville area. I played against kids half my age and more than held my own. I hit down here as good as I ever did. A fly ball looked just like it used to look—just as easy to catch. At running I wasn't so good. When I had to run I could do it I guess. But I just sort of trotted out my singles and doubles most of the time and walked out my home runs.

**EDDIE PLANK** By the time I caught up with Joe again playing for some team in South Carolina, I found a ruddy-faced, pot-bellied, slow-moving, middle-aged man. My goodness, he had put on a lot of weight! But the kids still followed him and he was still patient with everyone.

In this particular game Joe came up against a young, cocky pitcher, who figured the old man with the huge Santa Claus-like belly would be easy pickings. After all, the great man was no longer a kid, and the pitcher figured he would put a Joe Jackson notch in his belt. His first, and only, pitch to Joe was a low inside curve which he assumed would disappear from Joe's view under the weighty overhang of his stomach. Well, he threw the pitch he wanted where he wanted, and Joe unleashed his beautiful swing of old, sending the ball flying well over the center field fence. It was a prodigious blast of myth-making proportions. Joe lumbered around the bases enjoying his accomplishment, and when he got near third, he turned to the young pitcher and said, "Son, I always could hit them low inside curves."

It was truly a beautiful moment for me. I went over and congratulated Joe after the game. He seemed genuinely pleased to see me.

"Still playing, Eddie?" he asked.

"Haven't played for years, "I told him.

"A lot of good ball left in me," he insisted.

"So I see."

"My eyes are as good as ever, Eddie."

"You're a born hitter, Joe."

"If you see any of the boys, tell them I'm still playing."

"I'll do that."

"Because I can still hit."

"You can still hit."

It might be fair to assume that more men can say they played with or against Shoeless Joe Jackson than any other great star in the history of baseball.

**JOE JACKSON** Once, about 1932 I dropped into Yankee Stadium one day when I was up there visiting New York City. How I wished I could have stepped up to the plate that day. I know I could have banged one out of the park. My eyes was as good as ever.

**CHARLIE LEBEAU** Like so many great athletes before and after, Joe never knew when it was over for him—his athletic career. He played for years as a fat, ponderous legend. More sideshow than center ring. Then one day in Winnsboro, South Carolina, he stumbled over the first base bag and went sprawling face first in the dirt. As they say in the press, "He hung them up that day for good."

Other than at an occasional charity event, his playing days were over.

**JOE JACKSON** I could still hit the day I quit, but I was getting tired of all the travel, and the liquor store was needing more and more of my time. I could have played for a number of more years, you can believe that, because that's so.

# 57

## I DO THINK I BELONG

**SCOOP LATIMER** I saw Joe again one day in the late forties. He was slicing up a birthday cake on his 54th birthday. He had recently suffered a heart attack, so he was confined to bed. Around him was a cadre of little freckle-faced callers who had come bearing a gift. That gift which the young kids had saved up for, was a replica of "Black Betsy," the magic piece of hickory Joe wielded for 13 years.

Those kids were typical of the young boys who made almost daily pilgrimages to Joe's home once his mobility was limited by his health problems.

If ever a man wanted to live in a house by the side of the road and be a friend of all people, it was Shoeless Joe, who that day was calling on all the reserve energy in his massive frame and straining a weakened heart.

I distinctly remember Joe telling the boys, "I never pulled away from the plate as long as I was in baseball, and that goes from the time I played barefooted on the sand lots, on through my professional career and to the end of my active days as a volunteer manager of the Woodside Mills semi-pro team in 1937."

Joe's energy seemed to return the more he spoke to the kids.

"No sir, I never pulled away," he reiterated. "I gave the game all I had, and I'm now willing to share all I've got to make some poor soul smile."

**JOE JACKSON** The greatest sorrow of my life wasn't that I was thrown out of baseball, but that I never had any kids.

**KATIE JACKSON** Some people thought of Joe as nothing but a big kid. In a lot of ways that was right, but I think that's a good thing. As someone once said about the game, "You got to have a lot of kid in you to play baseball." Joe was a kid his whole life, and like a lot of kids, he was punished for something he never understood.

**LESTER IRWIN** I was one of Joe Jackson's nephews and I distinctly remember going over to Uncle Joe and Aunt Katie's house regularly when I was real small. I didn't know him as a famous man but as Uncle Joe who would sit out in the front yard and pitch to me. I remember him as a sweet-natured man, a man with a child's heart.

**KATIE JACKSON** The first time Joe had a heart attack he was working in the liquor store. He began breathing real hard and complaining of pains in his chest. Luckily I was there, so I called the ambulance which came and took him to the hospital. Like a lot of men I can think of, he didn't like being strapped to the stretcher and carried out of the store with people watching. Joe always could attract a crowd.

I followed him to the hospital and met with his doctor who said Joe was resting comfortably. They did a lot of tests but in a couple of days he was back home. The doctors told him to take it easy some because his heart was weakened by the attack. I think Joe thought he had beaten the problem and wouldn't have to worry about it again. But then, a few months later he had another attack. This time he was scared.

All at once, he was a patient. He started seeing the doctor regularly and trying to lose some of the weight he had put on. He was slowing down some, there was no doubt about that, but he still spent a fair amount of time talking baseball to almost anyone who would listen.

I know he regretted that we couldn't have kids, but after his retirement, he spent more and more time with them. Sometimes he played catch with them. That worried me a little, because of the heart problem, but I also knew that taking baseball away from him would have meant sure death. It was what Joe had to hang on to, and all he had to hang on to.

**JOE JACKSON** Thinking back on it, the one thing I regret more than anything was not staying with Mr. Mack. Mr. Mack did everything possible to make me see how foolish I was, but he finally lost patience and put me on the blacklist, where I would have stayed for the rest of my life if he hadn't been the kind of man he is.

He talked to me with tears in his eyes, but I wouldn't listen, so one fine day I found myself on the market. Even then he did a lot for me. He told me to pick out the club I'd prefer to go with and he'd see what could be done.

It wasn't until I was well on my way south that I began to realize what an opportunity I had lost. Mr. Mack was not the first manager whose friendship I had sacrificed by my foolish actions, but he was the one who brought me to my senses.

What I'm trying to say is, I made my share of stupid mistakes, but one mistake I never made was laying down in a game.

**KATIE JACKSON** After his first heart attack, we sold the liquor business because frankly we didn't need the money and thought it would be better if we didn't have to bother with it, but as soon as he was feeling better, Joe wanted to buy it back. Some people just aren't cut out for retirement.

We had a nice little brick home out on East Wilburn Street that even had a white picket fence around it. From the back porch Joe could sit eating breakfast and see Brandon Mills and the fields where he grew up playing ball.

We were comfortable, not wealthy, but by no means dirt poor as a lot of folks apparently thought.

**SCOOP LATIMER** Joe was hardly the first old ball player to relish the role of "grand old man of the game," but he did play it well. Joe had an advantage in that respect over other players in that he could add to his role the aspect of "the innocent, wronged victim."

As time went on, Joe became more and more comfortable in the part. Joe wasn't experienced in being the sage, but he took to it nicely. Ask him about the current players and he had an opinion. Ask him about what was wrong with the game, and he had an opinion about that, too. And, don't kid yourself, he loved to be asked.

Like many ex-players, Joe really had no other interest in life to fall back on when his playing days were over. Running barbecue stands or liquor stores, or pressing pants weren't professions, they were jobs.

To his dying day, Joe saw himself as a baseball player.

**JOE JACKSON** I couldn't play no more on account of my heart, but I could watch games, and I could still remember.

A lot of people asked me what my biggest thrill in baseball was. Well, I had many, but probably my biggest was the final game of the 1917 World Series when we played the New York Giants. That was the game when Heinie Zimmerman chased Eddie Collins across the plate with the tying run and, then, with me and Felsch on base, Gandil hit for two bases scoring us and we win the game.

I guess I told that story about a million times, but because people wanted to hear it, I kept telling it.

After I stopped playing because of my bum ticker, I became a director of the local

Textile League, and I went to see a lot of Sally League games.

**SCOOP LATIMER** There were Carolinians, you may be sure, who were vague as to the state topography, who were not quite certain of the extent of its fisheries or its mineral resources, but I never ran across a Carolinian, old or young, white or black, working or jobless who couldn't tell you Joe's batting averages. Taxi drivers, shopkeepers, soda jerkers, hotel bellmen—they all knew Joe Jackson.

Whatever Joe's cronies originally thought, they came to regard him as a baseball genius who got a tough break.

Whereas the North never did, the South forgot.

I can remember sitting around Harrison's with the old gang and I was once curious enough to ask him about the game in different eras.

"I had no experience with the so-called rabbit ball," he said, "and how are we to judge whether the present-day ball is livelier? Maybe there are more good hitters on each club now than in my time. That would account for a higher batting average in contrast to the old .250 team averages when a few of us managed to hit around .400. I imagine they've got great players as we had in our day, but I really would like to see Lajoie, Wagner, Speaker, and Cobb hitting up there today as in their prime."

Joe always believed in himself as a ball player. I mean he had the confidence in himself that all the great ones have. It's part of what makes them great. But Joe was a genuinely modest man who spent more time talking about the exploits of others than his own.

**NAPOLEON LAJOIE** One summer—maybe it was the late thirties—I was summering with my family in North Carolina mountain resort, when someone reminded me Joe was living nearby, so I dropped in to see him.

Other than being heavier, (weren't we all?) he looked like his old self. I told him what I guess he had heard thousands of times, that he was the greatest natural hitter the game ever saw. We recalled the 90-foot screen that was erected in right field in Cleveland to prevent Joe from knocking too many balls out of the park.

That was an era when the fans loved a great pitching duel. A slugfest was considered country fair. If he had been able to face the lively ball, he would have been the home run champion of all time, in my opinion.

When I said that to Joe he modestly dissented. "No, let Ruth have all the honors," he said. "The fact that Babe was quoted as saying he copied his batting stance and stride from me is enough praise for me, wouldn't you say?"

We never spoke about Joe's troubles with baseball. There hardly seemed a point in that

**TY COBB** One day many years after the World Series of 1919, I walked into Joe's liquor store in Greenville. I was passing through, and since I had worked up quite a thirst in the hot weather, I figured I might as well patronize my old rival.

When I walked in I thought Joe would be so surprised that he'd burst an artery laughing, but he didn't. In fact he acted like he didn't even know who I was which I found mighty strange since most people who ever met me, remembered me. I mean I wasn't exactly the wall flower type. We chatted about the weather for a bit and I was flabbergasted. Finally I said to him, "Don't you know me, Joe?"

"Sure," he said sadly. "But I didn't think you knew me after all these years. I didn't want to embarrass you or anything."

"Joe, I'll tell you how well I remember you," I said. "Whenever I got the idea I was a good hitter, I'd stop and take a good look at you. I don't think I ever saw a more perfect swing than yours."

**CHARLIE LEBEAU** I know for a fact that Joe followed the Cobb-Speaker affair from afar, and I also know that it bothered him, as well it should have. What this mess proved once and for all was that despite public pronouncements to the contrary, Landis had not cleansed the game of foul deeds. In fact, if anything, it proved the opposite. It also showed Landis to be the hypocrite many of us knew he was. Landis decided who he would punish and who he would not, and the decision was often based on capricious and frivolous criteria.

Following the 1926 season, both Tris Speaker and Ty Cobb abruptly resigned their managerial positions. Both resignations were baffling, Speaker's the more so because he had just led Cleveland to a second-place finish. It turns out that both resigned in the face of evidence implicating them in a scheme to rig a game involving Detroit and Cleveland near the end of the infamous 1919 season. Apparently Ban Johnson had recently come into possession of a damaging letter about the matter, supplied to him by Dutch Leonard, former Red Sox and Tiger pitcher, in which he charged that Cobb and Speaker knew of the fix and then, armed with that knowledge, bet on the game.

Exactly why Leonard waited six years to make the charges was never explained. Nevertheless, Johnson played his hand and bluffed the two accused players into resigning. Landis then, not wanting to let Johnson stake claim to the higher moral ground, made public Leonard's accusations and evidence.

Once out in the open, Cobb and Speaker were free to give voice to their positions, which they did loudly and frequently. They both denounced Leonard as a liar and a snake-in-the-grass, hired high-priced lawyers, and demanded apologies and complete exoneration. The case against Speaker relied almost entirely on the word of Leonard. Cobb's case was a little more complicated. It seems that there was a letter. A letter in which Cobb expresses his regrets about not having enough time to raise the cash in time to get the bet down.

The matter precipitated a shoot-out between Landis and Johnson. Johnson blatantly announced he had additional evidence in the matter, evidence Landis knew nothing about. So Landis called for the showdown. He summoned the American League owners to a meeting to hear Johnson's "new and incriminating evidence." Come the appointed hour, and Johnson delivered absolutely nothing. His humiliation was, to say the least, enjoyed by many, as was the enforced leave then mandated by the owners. Johnson had been, in one brief meeting, reduced to the status of figurehead.

Cobb, in a valiant attempt at self-defense, admitted to having written the letter, but insisted he was merely responding to Leonard's request to determine the amount of money bet on the game.

Landis "took the matter under advisement," which meant that he wasn't about to do a damn thing.

**KENESAW MOUNTAIN LANDIS** I looked into the Cobb-Speaker affair and found no proof of wrongdoing.

**HUGH FULLERTON** Privately, Landis was heard to complain: "Won't the goddamned things that happened before I came into baseball ever stop coming up?" It was apparently a rhetorical question. His next move was to announce a statute of limitations on anything that took place before he came to office.

What could Joe make of this other than to assume that Landis was mercurial at best and downright corrupt at worst? I wouldn't blame Joe, for Landis had singled him out for special treatment. I know I've always felt that way.

Life is filled with sweet ironies. Dickie Kerr was one of the clean Sox, the hero of the 1919 Series, one who upheld the honor of the game, one who played his heart out for Comiskey. So how did Comiskey reward him? By refusing to give him a raise. Kerr then quit the team and took off for Texas where he signed on to play semi-pro ball for more money than Comiskey offered. As fate would have it, his team played a game against a team which included some of his former teammates, all now branded outlaws. Comiskey found out about the game and showed his true colors by reporting the incident to Landis. Landis, true to form, suspended Kerr from organized baseball.

Kerr eventually got back into the game briefly, but boy was he ever bitter. I saw him a number of years later and he was still talking about it.

"I don't know, maybe Joe and the boys were right all along," he said. "It didn't pay to treat Comiskey right, at least not for me it didn't."

**B.J. SHORT** Oh, yeah, did I mention that a lot of Landis' court verdicts when he was still on the bench were later overturned in higher courts? The good judge just never could find it in him to pay much attention to the letter of the law he swore to uphold. Landis was a butcher, that's all. It's just too bad that Joe wasn't a sacred cow.

To his dying day, Landis went out of his way to make life miserable for Joe. His vindictiveness knew no limits. Years after Joe was thrown out of organized baseball, Landis made sure Joe didn't get a largely-token manergership of a team in the low minors. He even flew into rages when he saw positive articles about Joe in papers or magazines. He often called publishers to vent his anger.

Landis was obsessed with Joe. Not the other players, Joe. Landis' fame rested on his actions with Joe and he made damn sure everyone knew where he stood. Landis saw things in black and white. Joe was bad; he was good.

**CHARLIE LEBEAU** Talk of a real Hall of Fame had been around for years, but in 1936 the sportswriters finally got around to electing the first inductees—Babe Ruth, Ty Cobb, Honus Wagner, Walter Johnson and Christy Mathewson. Soon thereafter, Napoleon Lajoie, Eddie Collins, Cy Young and Tris Speaker went in. One name is obviously missing—Joseph Jackson. The sportswriters no sooner would have considered electing Joe to the Hall than they would have Adolf Hitler. They knew that even if they did, Landis would have overturned it somehow.

On his baseball record alone, Joe belongs with the elite in the Hall. There can be no argument about this. But if you factor in integrity, well, questions arise. The big problem with this, however, is that we don't really know about the foibles of the players who have been elected. We know about Joe's because they were so public. But what about some of the others? Surely there are some in the hall guilty of crimes far worse than Joe's. Should we require a lie detector test of all possible entrants? Even if we did, who would decide which sins were egregious enough to keep who out?

As I see it, the moral issue is impossible to police accurately, so why even try? If a player qualifies for the Hall, and his performance on the field is of the level to be elected, then, by all means, he should be.

Look at it this way. How many liars, cheaters, wife-beaters, tax-evaders, bad fathers, alcoholics, and worse are already in the Hall? I don't know the answer, but I'll bet you there's a bunch.

Oh, yes, let's get one thing straight right here. I know damn well Joe was guilty. The level of his guilt may be in some question, but only a fool argues that Joe did nothing wrong. Joe talked to cheaters about cheating. He took money from the cheaters for cheating. He didn't report or return the money, regardless of his excuse. But Joe's sentence does not fit the crime. Joe belongs in the Hall of Fame. It should be an open and shut case.

**JOE JACKSON** It didn't bother me much when that first group went into the Hall of Fame. They was all great players and they should have been the first group in. But a couple of years later when they let in Ban Johnson, and Charlie Comiskey, well, that got my dander up. When they let in Judge Landis, I got sick to my stomach.

I do think I belong in the Hall, I've got to say that, and maybe Eddie Cicotte does, too. He was a pretty good pitcher, you know. But I know I never will.

**KATIE JACKSON** Joe had another heart attack in the early hours of the morning, but once again, he got through it. I think we both knew that he couldn't keep having them without one being his last, but we never talked about it.

After Joe stopped playing, we pretty much stopped traveling. Oh, we took some drives in the car once in a while, and we occasionally went to visit family, but for the most part we stayed near home.

Then, when Joe was approaching his 60th birthday, the Greenville city fathers came up with this idea to have a big birthday party out at the old Brandon Mill ball field. They said they were going to call it "Joe Jackson Night," and make a big deal out of it. Joe wasn't sure but I figured it would do Joe some good having people applaud him again and we knew there were still a lot of people around who felt kindly to Joe. I had no idea, however, how many.

When the night came, it turned real drizzly and cold and it didn't seem to us like many people were likely to turn out in such conditions.

Joe put on his best suit and we walked on over to the field which looked a lot different than it did when Joe played there in the old Textile League. They had a big old cement grandstand out in what was once center field and home plate was where Joe used to run around in the outfield. When we got there for the celebration, there were thousands of people jammed in wherever they could find a place to sit or stand. The paper the next day said there were more than 2,500 of them and they were all there to show their appreciation for Joe. As soon as they saw us walking up, they began chanting, "Raw deal, raw deal!"

The mayor called Joe to home plate where they had a microphone set up. He gave a speech which was, of course, way too long, and a few of the people groaned a little, but they had come to expect that from his honor. The mayor recapped Joe's career and said lots of nice things about him. Then he embarrassed Joe some when he said, "Do you think Joe would have gotten the same bad breaks in the game if he had been able to read and write? Most certainly not."

He was undoubtedly right, but it was no fun for Joe to stand there in front of thousands of people and hear that being said out loud. When the mayor finally stopped, he asked Joe to come over and say a few words.

"Thank you Mr. Mayor," he said, "and thanks to all of you for coming out here on such a lousy night. I always said the folks of Greenville was the best, and you are. I played a lot of baseball here and they was probably the best times of my life. I've always played the game as best I could, and I think you good people know that. You are the best baseball fans I ever seen. Thank you for sticking by me all these years. Thank you very much."

He got lots of applause when he said that.

Then all sorts of people came up with presents. He got a new radio, a nice silk robe and slippers, a clock, and a big good luck horseshoe of flowers which came from the Greenville. At the end, someone came up with the idea of passing the hat around the stands just like years before when they did that for Joe's Saturday Specials.

I could see Joe didn't like this, though. He didn't like the idea of having to pass the hat for him, but he didn't want to hurt the feelings of the folks who were enjoying it, so he reluctantly accepted the money.

It was a fine, fine evening, and I know Joe was really touched.

**VINCENT ALEXANDER** Up in Philadelphia I read the stories of Joe's big birthday party which were picked up by the wire services.

They brought back a flood of memories. Memories of growing up in my father's restaurant and following Joe's career through the thousands of box scores I had collected over the years. His career was storybook stuff, and his feats became the defining moments of my life.

The next morning, I boarded a train for Greenville.

**JOE JACKSON** Sure I remember Mr. Alexander. He came down to Greenville once carrying big scrapbooks filled with nothing but the box scores of my games. He knew more about my career than I did. He must of been some kind of a genius because he remembered all sorts of figures and statistics about my career.

We sat out on the front porch and talked about some of the things I done, and he seemed to get a real kick out of that. When he left, he gave the scrapbooks to Katie and told her to keep them.

**VINCENT ALEXANDER** I hadn't seen pictures of Joe for some time, so it was something of a shock to see him looking his age. I'm not the first to recognize this obviously, but in many ways, our heroes never change. I still remember him as the lithe, graceful player of 22, the good-looking kid with cannon for an arm, and a natural swing the likes of which has never been equaled.

I talked to Joe for a while about the past and you know what? I should have been so thrilled at meeting Joe for the first time, but I wasn't quite that. I was a little sad. On the way back to Philadelphia I thought to myself that maybe it wasn't such a good idea to go down there after all.

Over the years there have been scores of attempts to get Joe reinstated, or at least to get his name cleared. One of the best organized occurred in 1951 when the South Carolina State Senate and House of Representatives passed a joint resolution requesting the Commissioner of Baseball to reinstate "Shoeless Joe Jackson as a member in good standing in professional baseball."

The resolution argued that Joe should be reinstated because it had been almost 32 years since the 1919 Series scandal and in that time reality and myth had become so intertwined that it was impossible any longer to know the truth. It further stated that there was a strong argument that he did nothing to actually throw any games, that he was twice acquitted in courts of law, that he had suffered lifelong ignominy as a result of his banishment while most persons actually convicted of crimes are not barred from the pursuit of their trades and professions upon their return to private life.

"Thirty-two years," the resolution read, "is too long for any man to be penalized for an act as to which strong evidence exists that it was never committed by him." It also praised Joe for his activities in the community, particularly with regard to his involvement in programs for the benefit of young boys.

The resolution was sent to Happy Chandler who had taken over as Commissioner upon Landis' death.

Chandler never responded.

I particularly remember one heated argument for his reinstatement surfaced after Alabama Pitts, a former convict was allowed to play professional ball. The argument was put forth, but nothing resulted.

Other attempts were equally futile. In more recent years it has been popular to write revisionist histories, many of which blatantly trumpet Joe's innocence. He was, of course, not innocent, but an innocent. He took the world at face value because that was the only way he knew. A naiveté and belief in the good intentions of others predestined his fall from the game.

**ED BANG** There was always a strong base of support for Joe among us committed Clevelanders. All he had done here was to play four full seasons never hitting less than .373, and parts of two others. He averaged 31 stolen bases a year and threw out about everything on 2 feet. He played hurt, he played hard, he played true. Cleveland didn't ban Joe, somebody else did.

I don't remember who started it, but the idea of creating a Cleveland Baseball Hall of Fame began gaining momentum in the early fifties. Let's celebrate our great accomplishments went the argument, and let's make a big deal of it. The Indians, as they were then known, got behind the idea, and voila, we had printed ballots and everything. The plan was to have the fans vote for the charter members, one at each position. These were to be ostensibly the greatest player at each position. Some of the choices were no-brainers. Who else but Larry Lajoie at second? How could you not include Cy Young on the mound and Tris Speaker in the outfield? Other positions were less clear, but that led to the fun. Arguments over "best evers" is the domain of the fan and part of what propels interest in the offseason. Cleveland fans jumped at the chance to give voice to their opinion with the hope that theirs would be immortalized on brass plaques in the new hall.

Ah, but there was one problem here. So as not to irritate the powers in professional ball, Joe's name was purposely left off the ballot. "Foul!" cried the fans. The uproar was loud and it was heard. New ballots with Joe's name on them were run off. For once the fans ruled.

After weeks of balloting, the votes were counted. Joe was in the Hall of Fame, Cleveland style, along with Cy and Larry and Tris.

**KATIE JACKSON** In the summer of 1951, Joe got a lovely letter from some people up in Cleveland saying that he had been elected as a charter member of the Cleveland Hall of Fame. Joe was pleased, real pleased. He asked me how I thought they got away with it.

"Got away with what?" I asked.

"Getting me in there," he said.

"Why? You deserve it, don't you?"

"I deserve to be in the other one, too, but I ain't"

"Take what you can get, Joe."

"I guess I will."

That's about the only time I ever remember him talking about the big Hall of Fame, the one in Cooperstown, the one that should be ashamed to call itself baseball's hall because it's not complete.

Anyway, Joe was happy to get the news and the invitation to go up there for the induction ceremonies in early September. He was looking forward to seeing some of his old playing buddies. Larry was 76 at the time and living down in Florida, Tris, 63 and back down in Texas. At least that's what a letter said that came from Ed Bang, a writer from up in Cleveland. He said that the folks who arranged for all of this hoped that they would be there for the festivities. He said he was pretty sure Cy Young was going to show up. Cy had to be well into his eighties, but was still living on his farm not far from Cleveland.

Joe didn't get invited to a lot of baseball functions, so this one promised to be a treat. I wrote back saying we would be there. But then as the particularly hot summer wore on, Joe began losing a lot of energy. His heart was giving out, and we knew it. The doctor said there was nothing he could do. Joe had just so many ticks left, so if he wanted to stick around for a while he was just going to have to take it real easy. The trip to Cleveland would be an exertion, no doubt about that. The question was, was it worth it? Joe thought it was. He wanted to go. He wanted to be honored once by baseball. But we both knew there would be opposition. The ever-present voice of indignity. There was a time Joe could have shrugged it off. He was almost immune from the pressure of it all, but was "almost" enough? At the last minute, in consultation with the doctor, we called it off. Joe stayed home, and once again missed out on honor that was his due.

**ED BANG** The ceremony was beautiful. Cleveland honored those who had honored it. The only real omission was Joe. We wanted him to be there, and he should have been. Several writers jumped on the "Joe the cheater" bandwagon and denounced the Hall for its selection, but on the whole, the sentiment was clearly in support of our selection.

Still, we wanted to do something for Joe. We wanted to find some way of acknowledging his greatness. Somebody on our board had an in to the old Ed Sullivan "Toast of the Town" television show. Sullivan was known to be a big sports fan. In those days that show was watched by just about everybody in America. It was about as big a Sunday institution as church. The guy with the "in" figured a special ceremony to honor Joe on national television would be appealing to the network. You either loved or loathed Shoeless Joe, but you wouldn't want to miss him went the logic.

Well Ed went for the idea. It was decided that if Joe was up to it, he would appear on the show of December 16th. Arrangements were made to make it as easy on Joe as possible. He would come up a day or two earlier, stay in a nice hotel, and relax. We arranged it with the hotel for him to be registered under a phony name so that he wouldn't be bothered, and we kept the publicity to a minimum.

The program was set up like this: right about in the middle of the show following a circus act, I would be called out by Sullivan and I would introduce Joe to the audience with some nice words written by one of the show's hacks. I was a writer for Pete's sake, and I had covered Joe for years, so I could have done it myself, but that's not the way television works. The speech was short but OK. Then Tris Speaker was to come out and present Joe with a gold clock which was the emblem of his membership in the Cleveland Hall of Fame. Joe would say something like "Thank you, Tris, this means a lot to me," and then we would go to a commercial. Simple but effective. I called Tris who was back in Texas and he said he'd be glad to come on up and take part.

I called Katie to tell her about the plans. She said she thought it would work well as long as we could guarantee there would be no hecklers. Although Joe was certainly used to such things by then, she felt he didn't need that on top of his heart condition. I spent a long time on the phone with her going over the arrangements. It was a good thing I wasn't paying for the long-distance call. Finally she seemed satisfied and said she'd wake up Joe who was taking a nap.

It took a couple of minutes, but Joe finally came to the phone, and I told him what we wanted to do.

"Thanks, Ed," he said. "I appreciate it and all, but I don't really care to go."

I told him it would be a great opportunity for him to receive some of the honor that was owed to him. I assured him Sullivan was on his side and that there wouldn't be any chance for him to be embarrassed or criticized.

"I don't think so, but thanks anyway," he said.

I asked him to talk with Katie and call me back if he changed his mind. He said he would.

I had to call the network and tell them that Joe declined but not to give up on the idea, that it just might take a little more time to convince Joe.

"Let us know," the man at the network said. "In the meantime, we'll extend the jugglers."

I called Tris and told him to hold onto his ticket.

**KATIE JACKSON** I thought it would be good for Joe to go on national television. The plan seemed sensible and not too taxing. I talked to Joe's brothers and sisters and they agreed.

**GERTRUDE TRAMMEL JACKSON** It seemed to us that Joe was feeling a little sorry for himself, which is something the Jackson family don't tolerate. So I told Joe it was no good just moping around the house and making poor Katie nuts, because that's exactly what he was doing. Go up and get your award I told him and we'll all watch you on television with old smiley Sullivan. I wasn't the only one that told him that, either.

**JOE JACKSON** It wasn't that I didn't want to go on the show, but it seems like every time I tried to say something in public, somebody decided I shouldn't. I learned to keep my mouth shut and let whatever happen, happen. But so many people like Katie and others, they kept saying I should go that after a while I said OK I guess I would. Like my sister, Gertrude said, "You ain't a crook, so why hide out like one."

**KATIE JACKSON** Since Joe was still feeling a bit tired from his last heart attack, his doctor agreed to go with us on the train up to New York. He said Joe should take it easy and not rush things too much but he didn't see that it would make a whole lot of difference where he was.

We made the arrangements to take the train up and meet Mr. Bang at the station and then go directly to the hotel so Joe could rest.

The Saturday before we were to leave Joe said he was feeling poorly, so he stayed in bed most of the day. Sunday morning he awoke and said he was feeling better. He ate breakfast then went over to the store and stayed there till late in the afternoon. That night he went to bed early but woke up about 9:30 complaining about a pain in his chest. We both knew what it was. I ran down and called the doctor. He said he was coming straight over. By the time I got back to Joe, he was feeling more pain. He looked up at me and said plainly, "this is it." Then he closed his eyes and he was gone.

# 58

## Yeah, He Used To Play Ball

**KATIE JACKSON** We had a nice ceremony over at Woodlawn Memorial Park on the other side of town. Lots of folks said nice words about Joe. I guess that's what funerals are for—saying all the things that were good about a person.

His brother, Davey, he took it real hard, but he stood up straight at the cemetery and thanked everybody for coming. The place was crowded. I didn't know everyone, but I know some were from the local teams in the area, and even a few of the old players from the major leagues were there. The funeral director said he never saw so many flowers at one funeral.

For weeks afterwards, I received hundreds of letters and cards from fans and friends. Tributes came in from everywhere.

**EDDIE COLLINS** I saw all the best players in my day and no one was better than Joe. I never tired of watching him bat. It was a pleasure to see him swing and when he hit the ball there was a ring to it that pleased the ear.

**"BIG" ED WALSH** I pitched against Joe many times while he was with Cleveland, and despite that, I still made it to the Hall of Fame. No thanks to Joe, though. He hit the ball harder than any man that ever played in the big leagues, and I don't except Babe Ruth.

**CHARLIE LEBEAU** I can still see Babe standing in there, carefully fashioning his swing after that of Jackson. Joe's swing, Babe always said, was 'the perfectest.'

**VINCENT ALEXANDER** As soon as Joe was gone, there were efforts to get him reinstated and into the Hall of Fame but all were too little too late, and ultimately ineffective. Joe died believing that a sizable portion of the people who knew who he was, thought he was a cheater who got what he deserved. He was right about that.

**COOPER ANDERSON** For many years, particularly when he was working in the liquor store or out at his barbecue stand, people would come by, many of them children, and ask for his autograph. Not wanting to refuse them, he asked them for a baseball or some other article that could be signed and then tell them that he didn't have time at the moment, but to come back the next day to pick it up. Then, at night, Katie would sign it for him, and Joe would deliver it as promised.

Now, who in their right mind in those days would have thought about the value of such things? Years later, some of those "Joe Jackson" signatures were selling for upward of $1,000 each—all of them fraudulent, of course. In fact, one Jackson autograph sold at auction for the record price of $23,100, a figure which supposedly rivaled that of a signer of the Declaration of Independence.

There are apparently a couple of "real" Jackson signatures still around. One is on a driver's license. It's a shaky "drawing" of a signature. There's big space between the 'J' and the 'a' and the rest is all scrunched together. It's nothing like the smooth signature his wife turned out.

So there are "real" Jacksons out there and fake ones. How fitting!

**J.C. HATCH** Katie stayed on in Greenville after Joe died and then after battling cancer for a few years, passed on herself in 1959. She left the bulk of her estate to the American Cancer Society and the American Heart Fund. There was apparently $60,000 in liquid assets which was split between the two organizations. She also requested that their remaining assets be liquidated and used for medical research.

A number of years later, a genuine Joe Jackson drawn signature which was ripped from a lease he had signed in 1936, was sold at Sotheby's auction house for over $23,000. The two charitable organizations attempted to obtain the actual will, which also had a valuable signature. They believed it was only one of six authentic signatures known to exist.

In a most unusual lawsuit, the two charities sued the judge of the Greenville County Probate Court and the county itself to get the will. Their argument was that it was Joe's personal property, which was left to Katie when he died, and therefore belonged to them.

Their intention was to take possession of the will, put it up for auction, and then use the proceeds for medical research as was requested by Mrs. Jackson.

The judge, however, refused to hand over the will claiming that the South Carolina Supreme Court, which oversees the operations of all state courts, mandated that the wills be kept for 75 years. He argued that the government kept the wills for a variety of reasons, including genealogical and sociological research, and land ownership disputes. "The whole ebb and flow of the country can be traced back," he said.

The charities countered that the will wasn't a government document and that the government had no right to keep it, and besides, they wanted the money for medical research, certainly a worthy cause.

The court kept the will.

The two charities then signed a deal with the Curtis Management Group, an Indianapolis company which represented the heirs of a number of former big leaguers like Babe Ruth and Lou Gehrig. The agreed to increase the value of the estate by marketing merchandise with a "Shoeless Joe" theme by releasing such items as posters, cards and replicas of "Black Betsy." Here, too, all the money went back to medical research.

**COOPER ANDERSON** Joe may have done a couple of stupid things in his life, but haven't we all? But as far as I know, he didn't cheat on his taxes, he didn't get involved with shady business deals like many players did, he never hurt anybody, he never took or asked for what wasn't his. He was just a simple guy who happened to be more physically coordinated than most and that pushed him into a spotlight for which he was unprepared.

He came along at a time when baseball needed to set a public example so as to cure the ills in the game which it had caused. Joe was the example largely because he couldn't fight back the way many others could have.

**J.C. HATCH** Back when me and Joe growed up, we lived for baseball, played three days a week and got paid on the side for it. They called us lintheads but we didn't really care as long as we got to play ball.

The other day I was down in Greenville at a lunch counter and I asked the kid working there if he remembered Joe Jackson. He said, "I've heard of him. Didn't he used to play ball."

Yeah, he used to play ball.

CPSIA information can be obtained at www.ICGtesting.com
Printed in the USA
BVOW08s0003100416

443197BV00003B/40/P

9 780692 557877